The Researcher's Guide to American Genealogy

Val D. Greenwood

2nd Edition

Genealogical Publishing Co., Inc.

Genealogical Publishing Co., Inc.
1001 N. Calvert St., Baltimore, Md. 21202

Library of Congress Catalogue Card Number 89-81464
International Standard Book Number 0-8063-1267-X
Made in the United States of America

Dedication

To my devoted parents,
David Hartley and Mary Thelma (Cox) Greenwood

Contents

Part 2
Records and Their Use

Part 3
Some New Ideas

Illustrations and Charts

Preface

Seventeen years ago, after seven years of preparation and writing, I completed *The Researcher's Guide to American Genealogy* in an attempt to provide an adequate textbook for the serious student of genealogy. As an instructor of genealogy I had been frustrated with the lack of a comprehensive textbook on American genealogical research. In the years since that first edition, many things have changed in the world of genealogy. Many sources are more readily available to us that were not available then, and technological enhancements have also made some sources easier to use. These things are exciting and great masses of people, previously indifferent, have become involved.

Some think that changing the name from genealogy to family history and creating massive computer data bases somehow make genealogy simpler and easier to do. They will tell you that genealogy has been simplified and demystified. But these things did not, in fact, change the realities. Yes, there is some evidence of simplification because of the creation of massive computer data bases of genealogical information and of lineage links. And though these are wonderful, exciting, and helpful—and certainly a blessing to the researcher—their value may be overstated. Many people have been led erroneously to put more trust in them than they deserve and thus lower the quality of their research results.

The beginning genealogist—and others who are not so new at the game—are being lulled into a false sense of security because they are led to believe that these tools are something that they are not. Yes, the indexes and data bases are a great blessing to us all, and the computer technology which has made them possible is thrilling, but we must never forget that these tools are just tools and that they are no better (or worse) than the research and the manual efforts which produced them. Certainly they should be used and they can expedite some aspects of the research, but we should never believe that we can be good genealogists without doing some basic pick-and-shovel work in original records.

Genealogy is still a matter of research, and though some sophisticated tools can help, knowledge of sources—what they contain, how to find them, and how to use them—is still critical. Use the fancy tools, take what they give you, but never trust them to give you the final answer. Too much is at stake.

I have added three new chapters to this edition and have made significant updates throughout the book. After all, much has happened since 1973. Chapter 4 deals with the subject of genealogical evidence, giving emphasis to proper research methods and proper use of the available sources. In spite of the new tools, this is just as important as ever. Chapter 25 deals with the selection of personal computers and computer programs to assist with record keeping, should you wish to use them. And chapter 26 is an effort to expand the view of the traditional genealogist to that of the sensitive family historian that he ought to become.

The chapter on Canadian research which I included in the first edition was deleted this time around because there are some excellent works on Canadian research now available, particularly the works of Eric Jonasson and Angus Baxter.

There are now other textbooks also available on American genealogy—some good and some not so good—but I feel strongly that *The Researcher's Guide to American Genealogy* (an updated edition) is still needed. The truth of the matter is that the essential elements of genealogical research have not changed, nor will they change. The records which are discussed in depth in this book, and which are the sources of essential genealogical evidence, have not changed and must still be used to provide proof of identity and family linkage. They must still be searched and they must still be appropriately analyzed and synthesized to achieve an adequate result in genealogical research. I believe that *The Researcher's Guide to American Genealogy* provides the basis for this to be accomplished.

PART 1

Background to Research

1

Understanding Genealogical Research

A song familiar a few years ago alleged that happiness is "different things to different people."[1] Sadly the same seems to be true of genealogy—not because it actually is different things, but because it is widely misunderstood. With this in mind, let me offer two basic definitions before proceeding further:

Genealogy: That branch of history which involves the determination of family relationships. This is not done by copying but rather by *research.*

Research: An investigation aimed at the discovery and the interpretation of facts and also the revision of accepted theories in light of new facts.

You should never approach a pedigree problem as a student in a history class would pursue knowledge of secular history. If the history student has an assignment to study the American Revolutionary War he will probably read an assigned text (or a chapter therein), perhaps check an encyclopedia, and, if he is especially diligent, read about the subject in other history books. But he takes someone else's word for everything—that is, *if* he believes what he reads.

If you have a genealogical problem you may well *begin* in the same place as did our history student—you can read printed genealogies and family

[1] Quoted with permission of Belwin-Mills Publishing Corp., Rockville Centre, NY 11571. All rights reserved.

histories, and well you should, but the prevalent notion that when you are copying someone else's records you are doing research is a gross misconception. This is also true when it comes to copying published and compiled works—they are *only* someone else's records.

Before you progress very far in genealogical research you ought to be on the same plane as the author of the textbook used by our history student—and perhaps even beyond that point. You will be engulfed in searching out and studying original documents and accounts, doing work to dig out the facts, to interpret those facts, and to compile them into a meaningful and usable format.

Though a branch of history, genealogy is not a subject which you can approach in the same way you would approach most other branches. In genealogy you cannot make a brief general summary of a historical period—but must consider the details of each ancestral problem individually and thoroughly.

One other significant difference between the study of history and the study of genealogy is that genealogy is a technical rather than an academic subject. It is a "how-to" subject in which you must learn and apply certain principles and facts relating to many academic disciplines. You must actually learn how to do the research. The traditional study of history, on the other hand, is mostly informational.

I. THE NATURE OF RESEARCH

As a genealogist you must work much like the research chemist (or anyone else who does research). Once a decision has been made on the focus of the research the steps are as follows:

1. Just as the chemist does, before you begin work on your actual problem, you must first make a study to see what others may have done already with the same problem. This is secondary research. In genealogy we often call it the "preliminary survey."

The chemist will carefully and systematically seek out everything on the problem that he can find. How foolish it would be for him to spend ten years (or even one year or one month) on a special project only to find, upon presenting his findings to his colleagues, that someone else had already accomplished the same work. It is no less foolish for you to do the same thing in genealogical research.

2. As the scientist completes this secondary research, he must analyze what he has found and make some judgment about its validity. He must

study the material and sift the information very carefully. If he accepts it he will begin his own research where it leaves off; but if he questions part of it or if he rejects it totally, his point of beginning will be quite different. But in any case his activities will be influenced by what has already been done. The same is true of the genealogist. It is not my feeling that the researcher should never repeat research that has been previously done. It *is* my feeling, however, that when he repeats research he should be aware that he is doing so and should know why.

3. The chemist's next step will be to determine his objectives, based upon his analysis, and to plan his primary research. He should know by now what his problems are and be able to decide how he will seek their solutions. The genealogist must do the same.

4. After this both the chemist and the genealogist will gather data from primary investigation and will record them systematically so they will have a complete record of all they have done. The approach will be logical and in complete agreement with the predetermined plan. The only difference is that the chemist's sources are his own research and experimentation while the genealogist's sources are records and documents.

5. Then, as they complete their gathering of relevant data, they will evaluate those data—analyze them to ascertain whether they have reached the objectives set earlier and then synthesize them into meaningful form. If the desired objectives have been reached, they will begin the entire cycle again with a new problem. If not, they will *also* complete the cycle again but will probably skip the secondary research step (unless sufficient additional evidence has been brought to light to make it profitable) and will continue the quest with a fresh analysis of the problem in light of the recent failure.

6. A sixth step, not a part of the actual research process yet very important to it, is to make the results of your research findings available to others (perhaps by publication).

These steps comprise the cycle of research. They are basic to the research process, though the explanation I have given of them is greatly oversimplified and the steps themselves are not clear-cut. I have divided them only for clarification and discussion. But the basic process is the same whether you are a research chemist or a research genealogist.

Also, by dividing the research process into its components we are able to observe some other interesting phenomena. Note that of the six steps listed, three (the second, third, and fifth) involve analytical activity of some type. Thus we see that in most research one of the chief requirements of the researcher is the ability to evaluate and analyze properly. Almost anyone can search records if he is told what to search, but to make an accurate evaluation of what is found is usually much more difficult, as is the setting of reasonable objectives and planning for their fruition—this requires both aptitude and training.

Another thing we can readily observe from this research cycle is that many would-be genealogists do not use all of the steps required for complete research. Too many spend their entire efforts on secondary research, thinking they are doing all that can be and needs to be done when they are copying the records of others and searching old family histories.

This is the approach to research used by a lady who once approached the reference desk at a large genealogical library with a printed family history open in each hand. She carefully laid the two books on the counter and then, apparently quite perturbed, queried the reference assistant as to which was correct. One book said that the father of a certain ancestor was one man while the other claimed it was someone else. The assistant examined the two sources and explained that he did not know the answer. He said it would be necessary for her to check some original source materials for her answer. Her reply: "I don't have time to do that!" And so she did not do it.

Others feel that non-original sources are generally so unreliable that they cannot bother with them at all, thus spending all of their research efforts in original records, not caring whether anything has been done before. To illustrate partially the extent and seriousness of this approach here are some impressive figures: In the first four months of 1968 there were 96,904 family group records submitted by patrons to the Genealogical Society of The Church of Jesus Christ of Latter-day Saints. Of these, 24,296 (25 per cent) were duplicates of records already on file with the Society—the research already completed.[2]

One of my most satisfying experiences in teaching genealogical research came one day when a student sat in class, scratched his head intuitively, and then philosophized: "Research in genealogy isn't really any different from research in any other field." This is a truth that many never learn, and he figured it out all by himself.

---

[2] The Church of Jesus Christ of Latter-day Saints, "Services to Help Avoid Duplication," *The Priesthood Bulletin* IV (November 1968), p. 12. Note that in 1987 the Genealogical Library of the LDS Church was renamed the Family History Library and will be referred to by that name hereafter.

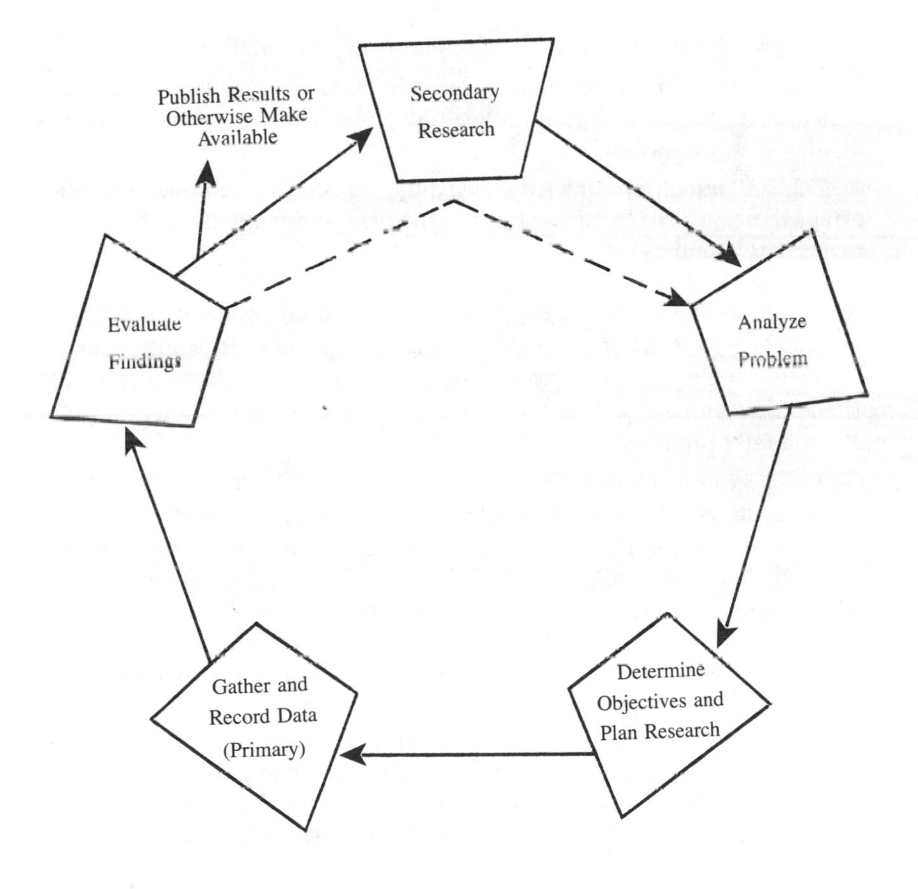

FIGURE 1—THE RESEARCH PROCESS

II. GENEALOGY AND SCIENCE

Thus far I have not come right out and said that genealogy is a science, though I have certainly hinted at this idea and hope you have gotten the message. It might be well, however, to pursue this idea a little further.

First let's define the word *science* and look at its etymology. It comes from the Latin term *scientia* which means "having knowledge," and Webster gives the following definitions:

> 1. Originally, the state or fact of knowing; knowledge.
>
> 2. Systematized knowledge derived from observation, study, and experimentation carried on in order to determine the nature or principles of what is being studied.
>
> 3. A branch of knowledge or study, especially one concerned with establishing and systematizing facts, principles, and methods, as by experiments and hypotheses.[3]

All of these definitions clearly apply to genealogy when it is properly practiced. However, as practiced by many it falls short in some respects. Genealogy should be a science—it deserves to be a science—but the methods of some tend to lower it to the level of a mere pastime, and that built upon false premises.

Genealogy will reach its proper place of respectability among the sciences only as we, its devotees, adopt sound scientific principles in our research. We must learn to consider all relevant evidence before we reach our conclusions. No scientist would do less. When tempted to do less than our best we should remember two things:

1. Those who come after us will eternally judge us by what we have actually produced and not by our ability.

2. An error on an ancestral line extended many generations can be far-reaching in its effect. One wrong ancestor on a line extended five short generations will have those who follow working on 32 wrong lines, and on 64 wrong lines in six generations, and so on, doubling each generation.

Thus, to the definition of genealogy given earlier, let me add the word *scientific* and say that GENEALOGY IS THAT BRANCH OF HISTORY WHICH

---

[3] From *Webster's New World Dictionary of the American Language,* Second College Edition. Copyright 1970 by the World Publishing Company, Cleveland. By permission. All rights reserved.

INVOLVES A *SCIENTIFIC* STUDY FOR THE DETERMINATION OF FAMILY RELATIONSHIPS.

III. COMPLETING THE GENEALOGICAL PICTURE

Perhaps the one thing that would improve the quality of genealogical research being done more than any other single factor would be a concern for complete families rather than just direct lines. Genealogy involves much more than just a pedigree with its names, dates, and places. Though such a pedigree is a basic essential, it can be very deceptive if that is all you have.

For example, if a man was born in 1845 and his father was born in 1780, such a connection may appear dubious until you know (because you have gathered data on the complete family) that the father was 20 years older than the mother (born 1800), that she was his second wife, and that the son in question was the last child in a large family, the eldest being born in 1820. Knowing all this you can put the problem into proper perspective and it does not seem unusual at all. But only by seeing the complete picture is this possible.

On the other side of the coin we often have pedigrees alleging to be true, that look quite logical and possible, that prove otherwise when we get information on the entire family. (One of the children may have been born when his alleged mother was 65 years old or perhaps when she was 10.) Yet, if we had dealt with only the direct line and not with complete families, these incorrect connections might have been accepted—as they so often are.

All good genealogists now agree on the importance of compiling complete families with complete data on the family members. The late Donald Lines Jacobus, writing on this matter, said:

> For many reasons it is advantageous in doing genealogical research to consider the family group, not to look upon each ancestor as an isolated individual, or as a mere link in a chain of descent. One of the most important reasons is, that it enables us to check the chronology. Very often, the relations of dates determine or negate the possibility of an alleged line of descent, or provide clues which might otherwise elude detection. It is a good idea to write out the full family history, or chart of relationships, while working, inclusive of "guessed" dates where positive dates are not known. It is an aid to the memory as well as to the imagination, if the eye can see the members of the family grouped together.[4]

[4] Donald Lines Jacobus, "Genealogy and Chronology," in *Genealogical Research: Methods and Sources*. Vol. 1 (rev. ed.), ed. by Milton Rubincam (Washington, DC: American Society of Genealogists, 1980), p. 28. By permission.

There is too great a tendency among ancestor hunters to see how far back they can go rather than how accurate and complete they can be. Somehow it seems to matter little whether a pedigree is accurate or not just so long as it goes back a long way. Maybe this is what the Apostle Paul was talking about in his epistles to Titus and Timothy when he instructed that they should not "give heed to . . . endless genealogies" (I Tim. 1:4 and Titus 3:9).

There are myriad sheets and forms available from suppliers of genealogical materials on which you can compile family groups. Some are designed as work sheets and others as complete and final record forms to be used only after research on a family is completed. These forms can make your job much easier.[5]

Another thing that will add to the quality of your genealogical research, as well as to your success, is your being concerned for every person of the surname of interest who was living in the localities where your ancestors lived at the time your ancestors lived there, rather than being concerned only for those whom you can already identify. This measure is closely allied to the compiling of complete families. It is impossible to compile complete families without first identifying the potential candidates. As you search the records of a geographical area where your ancestors are known to have lived, every record relating to every person with the same surname (in all of its spelling variations) should be read and carefully recorded in your research notes. You may not identify these persons with your ancestors immediately, but most of them will probably fit into place as you analyze your findings and put the complete families together. If the surname you seek is a common one, however, there are likely to be some exceptions. There may even be persons whom you will prove are definitely *not* related to your ancestors, but this is also useful.

As an example of this principle let's consider a hypothetical (though certainly not unusual) situation: You are searching for the records of your ancestor Charles Pebble in Mugwump County in an effort to identify his father. You find nothing. However, if you had extended your search in the Mugwump County records for everyone named Pebble (in all its variations) you would have found the will of one John Peppell, probated in 1805, wherein he named "my brother Charles" as executor and also bequeathed to his son James an old saddle which he had "bought from my father, Thomas Peppell."

---

[5] Since the first edition of this work, personal computers and a multitude of genealogical programs for tracking and charting families and family members have become available. See chapter 25, "Computers in Genealogy," for more information.

It may or may not be your Charles who is referred to by John Peppell as his brother. This information would have to be analyzed as it relates to other evidence, but the possibilities are obvious.

If families are related, the records of the area where they lived will usually tie them together, but you must exhaust the records for that surname. And you must not be too upset if you find the name spelled a variety of ways (Pebble, Peppell, Pebbel, Pepple, Pebell, Peble, Peple, Pebel, etc.). If your ancestor could not write (which is quite a common situation) his name was spelled the way it sounded to the person who happened to be spelling it at the time. More is said about spelling in chapter 2.

IV. GENEALOGY AND HISTORICAL BACKGROUND

Genealogy and history (religious, economic, social, and political) cannot be separated. Men cannot be dissociated from the times and places in which they lived and still be understood. It is impossible to recognize the full extent of research possibilities if you are not aware of the historical background from which your ancestors came.

History actually dictated the types of records kept, together with the format and content of those records. It also dictated those which were not kept and those which were lost or destroyed. History dictated social stratification, patterns of migration and settlements, and even occupations. Hostile Indians, wars, land policies, political figures and legislation, persecutions, disease, epidemics, droughts, fires—all of these factors and many more have had a profound effect on genealogy and genealogical records in America.

If you can understand the forces which shaped men's lives then you can better understand those men. If your ancestor was of age to fight in the Civil War you would miss a good bet if you did not investigate the records of that war. If you find that he did not serve then perhaps his religious affiliation should be examined more closely. He may have been a conscientious objector on religious grounds (as were the Quakers and others)—this too would be significant.

Success in genealogical research depends largely on an understanding of events—events in the lives of your ancestors. Thus to successfully research an ancestor is to determine the events in which he may have been involved, to determine whether those events would have been recorded and, if so, to determine where the records are located. To locate those records and to take from them, and use, the pertinent genealogical/historical data is the essence of success.

V. THE IMPORTANCE OF PLACES

As one considers the importance of events to genealogical research, he comes to realize that for him to find the record of an event he must usually know where the event occurred. Events do not happen in a vacuum or in the abstract; they happen in specific places. And it is in these places—within established record jurisdictions—that those events are chronicled. The more specifically you can identify the place, the better are your chances for research success. A detailed discussion of places is in chapter 3.

VI. NOTHING BUT THE FACTS

If you are afraid of skeletons then stay out of closets. And if you are ashamed to have ancestors who do not meet your own social standards then stay away from your genealogy. There are illegitimate children in the best of families—none of us is free from this. An outlaw or the proverbial horse thief may show up on any pedigree. You will also find the opposite—nobility and social status. But remember well the words of Sir Thomas Overbury, in his *Characters* (1614):

> The man who has not anything to boast of but his illustrious ancestors is like a potato—the only good belonging to him is underground.

It is also very true that often some of the most shameful carryings-on took place in the most illustrious families. Chaucer puts it very nicely in the "Wife of Bath's Tale":

> It is clear enough that true nobility
> Is not bequeathed along with property,
> For many a lord's son does a deed of shame
> And yet, God knows, enjoys his noble name.
> But though descended from a noble house
> And elders who were wise and virtuous,
> If he will not follow his elders, who are dead,
> But leads, himself, a shameful life instead,
> He is not noble be he duke or earl.
> It is the churlish deed that makes the churl.[6]

Regardless of what you find, your first responsibility is to the truth. A true report, unaffected by the nature of the facts, is the responsibility of the

[6] Theodore Morrison (trans. and ed.), "The Wife of Bath's Tale," *The Portable Chaucer* (New York: The Viking Press, 1940), pp. 250-251. By permission.

genealogist as it is the responsibility of any historian or scientist. Those who attempt to alter or color the truth are a liability to the science of genealogy—they are the millstone which tends to drag us all down. They are not genealogists and do not deserve the title. In your dedication to truth, however, remember that you also have a responsibility to present it objectively and in its proper perspective.

Never be ashamed of the truth or of your ancestors. After all, who knows how they might feel about you!

VII. WHAT IS EXPECTED?

Is it necessary to be a professional genealogist in order to be successful in locating your ancestors? Should this work be left to the professionals? The answer to both of these questions is the same—a resounding (yet qualified) *NO!*

With proper instruction and discipline many persons can and do become proficient genealogists and have the deeply satisfying experience of seeking—and finding—their ancestors. But whether you seek your ancestors out of pure curiosity, out of a desire to join a patriotic or hereditary society, out of the intrigue of the study, out of a sense of duty to your religion, or for any other reason, the requirement is the same—you must know what you are doing.

It can also be appropriately stated that no matter how good your tools may be and no matter how complete your collection, such tools are of little worth if you are not skilled in their use.

If you had a severe appendicitis attack in some remote place and could not get to a hospital, you would be grateful for the surgeon who came along with a tin can, a pocketknife, and a needle with thread (all of which he would surely boil) to take care of you. In fact you would probably much prefer this to being in the most modern hospital in the world, with the best available equipment, and the hospital janitor to act as surgeon. When it comes down to bare facts, tools are not the most important thing—knowledge is. However, after you have the knowledge there is much to recommend being properly tooled. Certainly you would much prefer to have both the skilled surgeon and the modern hospital. Can't this same principle apply to genealogical research?

We would not think of turning a man loose to do research (of even the most basic type) in a chemistry laboratory filled with equipment and chemicals without some instruction. We would instruct him carefully about both the equipment and the chemicals. It is true, is it not, that the more he knows about these things, the better his chances for success will be? Any lack of knowledge may not only result in failure but also produce some very destructive results. Yet how often does a person with a similar lack of genealogical experience and know-how undertake "research" in the historical and documentary laboratory?

Is it any wonder that some get discouraged and that the results are often unsatisfactory and even disastrous? Is it any wonder that so many compiled genealogical records lack credibility and so many published family histories and genealogies are pure tripe?

If you have an aptitude for history and the social sciences, are good at remembering details, and enjoy intellectual problem-solving, you have the basic aptitudes required by the genealogist. You should be able to learn quite easily the things you will need to know in order to use the available tools properly—you merely need a guide. Instruction and guidance, together with the empirical knowledge of actual practice, can prepare you to be a good genealogist, even though not a professional. You do not have to be an expert in all phases of genealogical research to do good genealogical research; you need only to become an expert on genealogical research in the specific geographical locality (the place) where your problem is centered —you can become an expert one step at a time.

VIII. THE PROFESSIONAL GENEALOGIST

If you desire to pursue genealogy as a vocation the requirements are no different. You must have good instruction and plenty of practical experience while you are learning, but beyond this you must be able to devote yourself whole-heartedly to the pursuit of information. You must be more than a scientist; you must be a detective as well. More than ever you must be able to remember and to categorize details. You must be especially painstaking in the recording of information and sources, and you must be able to do these things rapidly. These qualities, of course, are improved and intensified through greater use, but you should be aware of their necessity before you pursue genealogy as a profession. As the satisfaction is great, so are the demands.

What can the professional genealogist do? Can he find work? If so, where? These questions are legitimate and are often asked by those interested in the field. There are several possibilities:

A. Free-Lance Research

Anyone, living almost anywhere, can do research on a free-lance basis for those wishing to engage his services. It is usually to the free-lancer's advantage, however, to live near and have access to important record repositories or libraries and other genealogical research facilities. But if you are free to travel this is not necessary. Large cities, especially Washington, D.C., and Salt Lake City, have their advantages; but again, living in or near such places is not essential. Most free-lance researchers build up their clientele by their reputations for good work. If you do a good job the person you do it for will tell others. So, once you get started, you will have no problems if you are good. Many researchers have several months' work ahead of them all the time.

The Family History Library in Salt Lake City has a program for accrediting free-lance genealogists. Persons who pass tests showing their proficiency in doing genealogical research in specific geographical areas of the world are accredited to research in those areas, and their names are placed on a list of "recommended" researchers which the library distributes upon request. Most of these Accredited Genealogists live in or near Salt Lake City where they can take advantage of the facilities and records in the library. Generally these persons do not travel extensively but write letters to local officials and/or researchers and record searchers when the library does not have microfilms of the records they need.

Anyone who feels he can pass the tests (in a given geographical area) and has had extensive practical experience (a minimum of 1,000 hours) doing research in the records of the locality of his interest is welcome to take the tests.[7] For the U.S., different tests are given for New England, the middle-Atlantic states (Delaware, New Jersey, New York, and Pennsylvania), the South, the West, and the Mid-West. A person may take the tests in as many areas as he likes so long as he meets the requirements.

A national Board for Certification of Genealogists (BCG) was formed in Washington, D.C., in 1964, which is also good and which adds stature to the researcher's credentials. The board certifies, for a period of five years (renewable at the end of that time for another five-year period), persons found to be qualified as Genealogists, American Lineage Specialists, American Indian Lineage Specialists, Genealogical Record Searchers, Genealogical Lecturers, and Genealogical Instructors. The board has devised a Code of

---

[7] An exception to the 1,000-hour time requirement is offered to those who have satisfactorily completed the equivalent of this through genealogical research courses at Brigham Young University in Provo, Utah, and Ricks College in Rexburg, Idaho.

Ethics for professional workers in this field which has been accepted by leading genealogical organizations. For further information about certification you should write to the Executive Secretary, Board for Certification of Genealogists, P.O. Box 19165, Washington, DC 20036-0165.

B. Free-Lance Record Searching

A record searcher is a person who does nothing more than the mechanics of the research—finds records, searches them, and reports his findings. His function is extremely important because many persons need to have records searched to which they do not have personal access. Above all he must be able to follow instructions and do precisely what he is asked to do. He might make suggestions, but should never make a search that is not authorized and expect to get paid for it. The record searcher does not usually make as much money as the genealogist; but good record searchers, especially those who are free to travel, are in great demand. And if they are good, they can command a good price. Like researchers, these persons are also usually located near large genealogical collections or libraries. There is a great need for record searchers who will go into courthouses, churches, cemeteries, and other places where they might find working conditions cramped, uncomfortable, and dusty. As mentioned earlier, certification is available for Genealogical Record Searchers.

C. Library and Archives Work

More and more libraries, historical societies, patriotic and hereditary organizations, and archives are demanding that their employees be knowledgeable in genealogy. They seek employees who can take care of their collections, assist library patrons, and answer correspondence of a genealogical nature. If you are interested in this phase of genealogy you should consider the study of library science in connection with your study of genealogy. Library training is essential for those who would pursue this course.

D. Editorial Work or Writing

Hundreds of genealogical and historical periodicals are currently being published in the United States. These publications not only demand qualified editorial personnel but are an endless market for good, well-written material. Many persons in other areas of genealogy also do free-lance writing for such publications. But to do any kind of writing you need an above-average command of English. Generally those who write genealogical articles do so because they like to write, for there is very little monetary reward.

E. Teaching

The market for genealogy teachers is scant, but it is growing. If you desire to teach genealogy I recommend that, in addition to genealogical training and experience, you should pursue an advanced degree in some related field of the social sciences—perhaps history or library science—but above all you should qualify yourself as both a genealogist and a teacher.

Brigham Young University in Provo, Utah, offers degrees in family and local history. Both BYU and Ricks College, Rexburg, Idaho, have broad and diversified genealogical curricula. Some other institutions in the U.S. offering courses in genealogy are American University, Washington, D.C.; Samford University, Birmingham, Alabama; Western Illinois University, Macomb; and BYU-Hawaii, Laie. There are others overseas.

F. Computer Technology

With the movement of electronics into the fields of demography and genealogy there is a growing need for persons who have a background in computer science and mathematics as well as genealogy. If you are interested in this area you should plan your schooling accordingly. Future possibilities in this field seem good.

IX. CONCLUSION

Regardless of the impetus which inspires you to pursue the study of American genealogy, one point is clear: Success and competence are dependent on *both* adequate instructional guidance and practical experience. Remember that a book, no matter how good, can go only so far. A good cook book does not make a good cook, though it surely helps. Edwin Slosson summarized the matter appropriately:

> One cannot, of course, become a scientist by merely reading science, however diligently and long. For a scientist is one who makes science, not one who learns science. A novelist is one who writes novels, not one who reads them. A contortionist is one who makes contortions, not one who watches them. Every real scientist is expected to take part in the advancement of science, to go over the

> top . . . But of course the number of those who are in reserve or in training must always outnumber those at the front.[8]

The way is clear and the goal is attainable. You can be a good genealogist if you are willing to pay the price—not just here and now, but all along the way. If you are good, be you amateur or professional, the rewards and the satisfaction can be great.

For the benefit of those interested, it is worthwhile to mention the home study course offered in American genealogical research by the National Genealogical Society. This course, now in its second edition, is very good. It can, if you're willing and able, give you the foundation to help you become a pretty fair genealogist. The first edition of that course used the first edition of *The Researcher's Guide* as its text. There are also adult education classes available in many communities that provide useful instruction.

Good luck!

---

[8] Edwin E. Slosson, "Science from the Side-Lines," *Chats on Science* (New York: Appleton-Century-Crofts, 1924), p. 140. By permission.

2

Familiar Record Practices: Problems and Terminology

In order to be a good genealogist you must be familiar with the basics of genealogy. Every field of study—whether physics, chemistry, sociology, medicine, law, art, photography, or genealogy—has its own basic vocabulary or jargon and its own rules. To succeed in any field of study you must know those rules.

I have a friend who comes from Sweden, so when I encounter a term in my Swedish research that I do not understand, I call and ask him about it. Often the term is not familiar to him even though he was born and raised in that country. This is not a problem of his not understanding Swedish but rather of his not having the vocabulary needed by the genealogist. We can toss out certain English language terms to the man on the street here in America, too, with the same result. Thus the purpose of this chapter is to *help* bridge the gap across some of the more common problem terms and also to look carefully at other practices and problems inherent in American genealogical research. Other specific terms and problems are discussed in every chapter of this book.

I. HANDWRITING

Perhaps you wonder why handwriting is discussed in an American research text. Most American records are recent enough that the handwriting is not too different from your own. Or is it? Actually there are enough serious problems, especially in the colonial period, that a brief discussion should prove useful. Handwriting is always a problem. Even in our own time some of us write so that others of us cannot read it except with great difficulty. (Sometimes we can't even read our own handwriting after it gets cold.) But if your ancestors were in America in the 1600s, and even the 1700s, you will find enough carry-over of Middle English in the records that a study of the simpler Middle English alphabets would prove beneficial.[1]

Many records in early America were not written in English at all but in various European languages; however, that is another problem and I will not deal with it here. Your best action when you meet that situation is to seek the help of an expert.

Sometimes when we examine records from past generations we conclude that the most important qualification for a keeper of public records was that he was able to write so that no one else could read it. However, there is some early handwriting which is carefully written and very readable. In fact, most of the earlier scripts can be read (often quite easily) when we are aware of a few common record practices.

A. Abbreviations

One of the most commonly confused and unappreciated practices in earlier American documents is the practice of abbreviating—a carry-over from the practice of abbreviating in Latin (the official formal record language of early England). England passed an act in 1733 forbidding the use of Latin in parish registers, but some Latin and the extensive use of abbreviations persisted after that time. Many writers also used abbreviations just to shorten the amount of writing they had to do; the quill pen was not an instrument of great writing pleasure.

Most abbreviations are recognizable if you are aware that the writer was using them and you are watching for them. There were very few of what might be called "standard" abbreviations, and most words were abbreviated several ways. However, the following are typical:

accomptant – accompt^{t}
according – accord^{g}
account or accompt – acco^{t}, acc^{t}
administration – admin^{ion}, admon., admon:
administrator – admin^{r}
administratrix – admin^{x}

---

[1] Excellent helps in studying Middle English can be found in David E. Gardner and Frank Smith, *Genealogical Research in England and Wales,* Vol. III (Salt Lake City: Bookcraft, 1964).

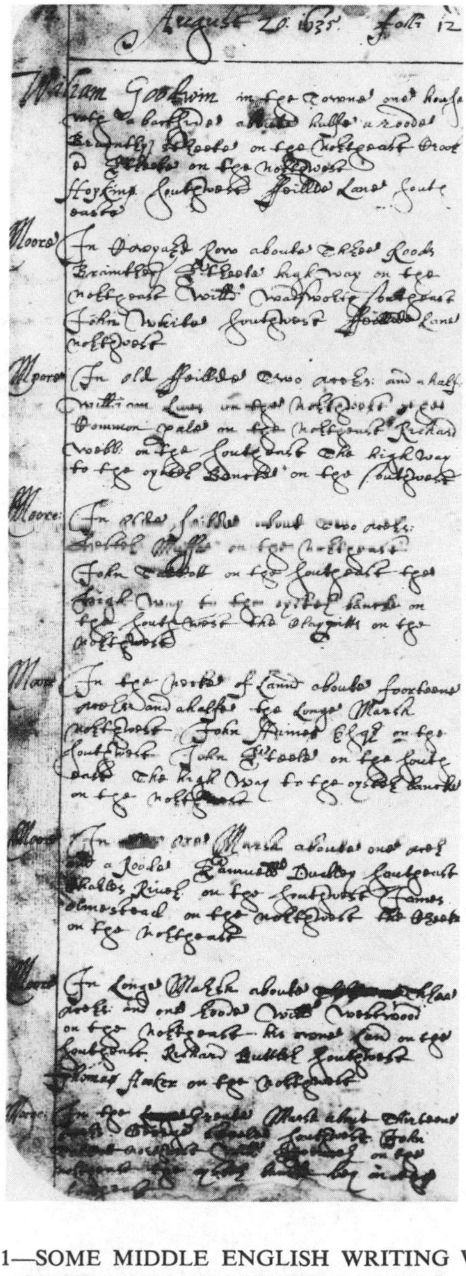

August 20: 1635: folio 12

William Goodwin in the towne one house [illegible] a barnyard about halfe a roode [illegible] on the northeast [illegible] on the northwest
[illegible] southwest [illegible] Lane south east

Moore: In [illegible] Row about three Roods [illegible] highway on the northeast Willm [illegible] southeast John White southwest [illegible] Lane northwest

Moore: In old feilde two acres: and a half William [illegible] on the northwest the Common [illegible] on the northeast Richard [illegible] on the southeast the highway to the [illegible] on the southwest

Moore: In [illegible] feilde about two acres: [illegible] on the northeast John [illegible] on the southeast the high way to the [illegible] on the southwest the [illegible] on the northwest

Moore: In the [illegible] of land about fourteene acres and a halfe the Longe Marsh northwest John [illegible] on the southwest John [illegible] on the south east the high way to the [illegible] on the northwest

Moore: In [illegible] Marsh aboute one acre and a roode Samuell Dudley southeast [illegible] on the southwest James [illegible] on the northwest the [illegible] on the northeast

Moore: In Longe Marsh aboute [illegible] three acres and one roode Willm Westwood on the northeast his owne land on the southeast Richard [illegible] southwest Thomas [illegible] on the northwest

Moore: In the [illegible] Marsh about thirteene acres [illegible] southwest John [illegible] on the [illegible] in [illegible]

FIGURE 1—SOME MIDDLE ENGLISH WRITING WITH ITS MANY UNFAMILIAR CHARACTERS

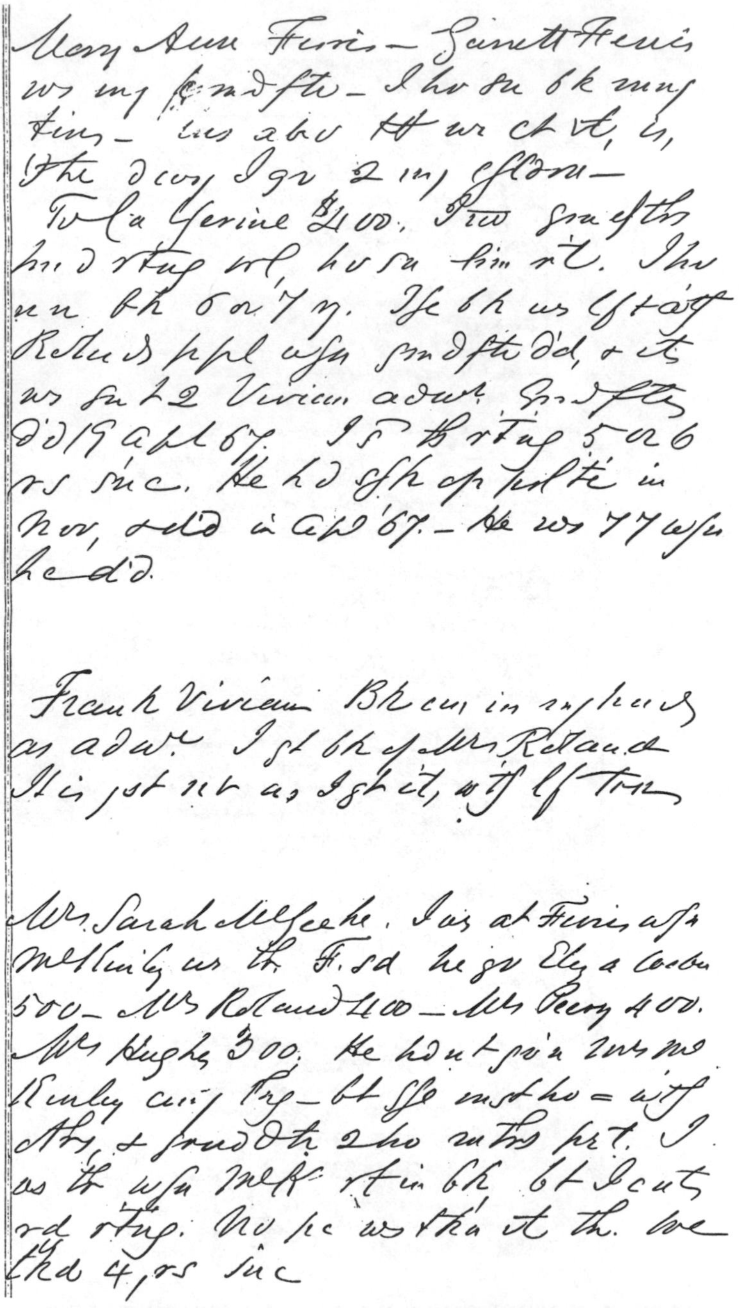

Mary Ann Ferris — Garrett Ferris
ws my grndfthr — I hv sn bk many
tims — ws abt tt wr ct vt, is,
the dcvs I gv 2 my gchdrn —
To Ca Yerine $400. Two grndfthr
hd rtng wl, hv sn him rt. I hv
sn bk 6 or 7 ys. The bk ws lft at
Rolands ppl wn grndfthr dd, & its
ws snt 2 Vivian adwt. Grndfthr
dd 19 Apl 67. Is [illegible] rtng 5 or 6
yrs snc. He hd [illegible] in
Nov, & dd in Apl '67. — He ws 77 wn
he dd.

Frank Vivian [illegible] in [illegible]
as adwt. I gt bk of Mrs Roland
It is jst nt as I gt it, [illegible] lf [illegible]

Mrs Sarah McGeehe. I ws at Ferris aftr
McKinly ws thr. F. sd he gv Ely a [illegible]
500 — Mrs Roland $400 — Mrs Perry 400.
Mrs Hughes 300. He hd nt gv a [illegible] Mc
Kinly [illegible] — bt [illegible] = [illegible]
[illegible], & grndchr 2 hv [illegible] prt. I
[illegible] wn McK [illegible] bk bt I cnt
rd rtng. No [illegible] ws thr at th. [illegible]
[illegible] 4 yrs snc

FIGURE 2—SOME SCRIBES DEVELOPED THEIR OWN BRANDS OF SHORTHAND

aforesaid – afors^{d}, fors^{d}, afors:, afsd.
and – &
and so forth – &c, etc. (*et cetera*)
captain – capt^{n}, capt:
church – chh
daughter – dau, dau^{r}
deceased – dec^{d}
ditto – do, d^{o}
Esquire – Esq:, Esqr, Esq.
executor – exec^{r}, ex^{r}, ex^{or}, exor:
executrix – exec^{x}, ex^{x}, ex^{ix}
Gentleman – Gentl^{n}, Gent:, Gent.
honorable – hon^{ble}, hon:
improvement – improvem^{t}, improv^{t}
inventory – invent^{y}, inv:
Junior – Junr, J^{r}, Jun:
Messieurs – Messrs, Messrs
namely – viz, viz:, vizt (*videlicet*)
paid – p^{d}
pair – p^{r}
per – p^{r}
personal – person^{l}, p'son^{l}
probate – prob^{t}
probate register – p. regist^{r}
received – rec^{d}, recv^{d}
receipt – rec^{t}
record – rec^{d}
register – reg^{r}, regist^{r}
said – s^{d}
Senior – Senr, S^{r}, Sen:
testament – testam^{t}, testa:
the – ye, y^{e} (This usage is a carry-over from the ancient Anglo-Saxon letter, *thorn,* which looked similar to a *Y* and had a *TH* sound. Other words beginning with the same sound were also thus written: y^{en}, y^{ere}, y^{is}, y^{at}, etc.)

A good example of what you might find is shown in the account of Elizabeth Hodsdon's administration of her deceased husband's estate in 1763, York County, Massachusetts (now Maine):

> The acco^{t} of Eliz^{a} Hodsdon of her admin^{ion} of the Estate of her late Husband John Hooper the third late of Berwick in ye County of York dec^{d} Intestate. The S^{d} accompt^{t} chargeth her self with the person^{l} Estate of S^{d} Dec^{d} as p^{r} Invent^{y} £21·13·-.

Let me point out a few important things from the above example.

Most of the abbreviations are formed by merely shortening the word, sometimes even as we might abbreviate it today, but then putting the last letter (sometimes even two or three letters) of that word above the line. This is called *superior letter* abbreviation. Another form is that of *termination*—that is, merely cutting short the word to be abbreviated and putting a period or a colon (:) after it, or by drawing a line (——) through it like this: ~~Tho~~ (for Thomas). In very early periods often only the first letter of the word was used.

Another common form of abbreviation was the contraction. A word like *parish* might be contracted to *p'ish,* or *present* might be contracted to *p'sent.* In these examples an apostrophe (') is used, but at other times contractions were also made by putting a curved line like a tilde (~) above the contracted word like this: *p̃sent*. You will also find occasions where a word with a double consonant was written with only one consonant and a line drawn over it to show that it should be doubled. For example, *common* might be written as *com̄on*. This was especially used in connection with the letters *m* and *n*, and the line was sometimes curved (*com̃on*).

In actual practice any word might be abbreviated in several different ways depending on the scribe. In many instances the abbreviation for two different words might even be the same, but most can be recognized within the context of the writing.

B. Name Abbreviations

Given names are often abbreviated as in Elizabeth (Eliz^{a}) in the example. Ordinarily names were abbreviated in the same way as other words; however, there are a few exceptions to this rule also. Here are just a few popular name abbreviations:

Aaron – Aar^{n}
Abraham – Abra^{m}
Andrew – Andr^{w}, And^{w}
Arthur – Art^{r}, Arth^{r}
Barbara – Barb^{a}
Benjamin – Benj^{a}, Benjn, Benj:
Charles – Chas, Char^{s}

29 To Edmd Angier One Acre a Quarter & twenty five Rods (being [illegible] of his Lott). Bounded Easterly wth ye Countrey Road, North Westerly wth high way & Southerly wth Peter Town's heirs . . . .
also three Acres a Quarter & three Rods. (being the Remainder of his Lott) Bounded Easterly wth Charlstown Line, Westerly wth ye Countrey Road, Northerly wth D. Hastings heirs & Southerly wth a gravil pitt & ye way to it . . . . .

30 To Dea. Hastings' heirs One Acre & twenty Seven Rods Bounded Easterly wth Charlstown Line, Westerly wth the Countrey Road, Northerly wth Jos. Crackbon & Southerly wth Edmd. Angier . . . .

31. To Joseph Crackbon three Acres & an half, & one Rod Bounded Easterly wth Charlstown Line, Westerly wth ye Countrey Road, Northerly wth Jona Nutting & Southerly wth Dea. Hastings heirs . . . .

32 To Jonathan Nutting Two Acres a Quarter & fourteen Rods, Bounded Easterly wth Charlstown line, Westerly wth ye Countrey Road, Northerly wth mr President Leverett & Southerly wth [illegible] Crackbon . . . .

33 To mr. President Leverett four Acres & an half & Twenty eight Rods Bounded Easterly wth Charlstown line Westerly wth ye Countrey Road, Northerly wth [illegible] Belcher Esqr & Southerly wth Jona Nutting, a highway to [illegible] Watson, house & Barn being included within [illegible] boundaries . .

34 To Jonathan Belcher Esqr four Acres & an half and Twenty eight Rods bounded Easterly & North Easterly wth Charlstown line & Saml Cook, Westerly wth ye Countrey Road, Northerly wth Jonathan Gove & Southerly with mr President Leverett . . . .

35 To Jonathan Gove Three Acres & an half & One Rod Bounded North Easterly wth Saml Cook, Westerly wth the Countrey Road, Northerly wth W. Pattin's heirs & Southerly Jonathan Belcher Esqr . . . .

36 To W. Pattin's heirs two Acres a Quarter & fourteen Rods Bounded North Easterly wth Saml Cook, Westerly wth ye Countrey Road, Northerly wth Widow Cooper & Southerly wth Jona: Gove. a high[way] to Saml Cook's house included in ye lott . . . . . .

37 To Widow Cooper Two Acres a Quarter & fourteen Rods Bounded Easterly wth Saml Cook, Westerly wth ye Countrey Road, Northerly wth Edmd Angier & Southerly wth W. Pattin's heirs

38 To Edmd Angier two Acres a Quarter & fourteen Rods, bounded Easterly wth Saml Cook, Westerly wth ye Countrey Road, Northerly wth Highway & Jason Russel & Southerly wth Wid: Cooper. a high way to ye [illegible] Running thro' his Lott . . . . . .

FIGURE 3—A DOCUMENT WITH EXTENSIVE ABBREVIATIONS

Christopher – X^{r}, Xopher, Xofer
Daniel – Danl
David – Dav^{d}
Ebenezer – Eben^{r}
Franklin – Frankl^{n}, Frank^{n}, Frank:
Frederick – Fred^{ck}, Fredr^{k}
George – Geo:, G^{o}
Gilbert – Gilb^{t}, Gil^{rt}
Hannah – Hañah
James – Ja^{s}, Jas:
Jeremiah – Jer^{a}, Jerem^{a}, Jer:
Jonathan – Jonath^{n}, Jon^{n}, Jon:
John – Jno:, Jno
Joseph – Jos, Jos:
Leonard – Leon^{d}
Margaret – Marg^{t}
Nathan – Nath^{n}
Nathaniel – Nathl, Nathan^{l}
Patrick – Patr^{k}
Richard – Rich^{d}, Rich:
Robert – Robt, Rob:
Samuel – Saml, Sam:
Stephen – Steph^{n}
Thomas – Thos, Tho:, ~~Tho~~
Vincent – Vinc^{t}, Vinc^{nt}
Virginia – Virg^{a}, Virg:
Wilford – Wilf^{d}, Wilf:
William – Willm, W^{m}, Will:
Zachariah – Zach^{a}, Zachar^{a}, Zach:

Many other names were also frequently abbreviated (and many of those shown were abbreviated in different ways), but most can be recognized quite easily. Nearly every given name of any length and often even surnames will be found abbreviated at one time or another. If you have trouble identifying an abbreviated name you may find it written out some other place in the same record, though this is not always the case.

C. Irrelevant Capitals

There was a tendency to capitalize words for no apparent reason, and capitalized words might be found anywhere within a sentence. There seems to have been a tendency to capitalize nouns, but it was not consistent. Some writers simply capitalized certain letters whenever they began a word with them, and there is some variation from scribe to scribe.

D. Punctuation

There is no punctuation in the Hodsdon example except the periods at the ends of the sentences. There are two main types of exceptions to this kind of punctuation in early records: (1) In some writing you will find an occasional comma, and (2) in other writing you will find no punctuation at all.

One practice followed by some scribes was to use dots (•) to indicate pauses. A dot on the line indicated a brief pause, a dot above the level of the writing indicated a full stop, and a dot between the words indicated a phrase separation. These dots, when used, took the place of all other punctuation.

E. Look-Alike Letters

Another problem, only partially observable in the sample documents shown in this chapter, is that some letters look almost exactly like other letters. The capital letters *I* and *J* are very difficult to distinguish, as are also *U* and *V*. (In the original Roman alphabet there was only one letter for each of these pairs.) *L* and *S* and even *T* and *F* are also easily confused. However, much depends on the scribe, and there are frequently other capital letters which are confusing. Study the handwriting very carefully in order to make a distinction whenever there is a problem. Initials in names are the chief villains and are especially troublesome in census returns (and these are in the nineteenth century) and other lists of names.

Small, or lower case, letters also cause many misunderstandings. Curlicues on the letter *d* above the line and on *y* and *g* below the line can be troublesome as they often run into other letters, even on other lines of writing. But they are not much trouble when you recognize them for what they are. Another troublesome character is the long *s* (ſ). To the inexperienced observer this may appear as either an *f* or a *p* or even as a double *f* or double *p* depending on how it was used. It was seldom used at the beginnings or endings of words but was almost always used as the first letter of the double *s* and frequently in other instances. This usage persisted into the middle 1800s.

In early writing (this is strictly from Middle English) the small *e* was made to resemble the modern-day *o*, and it can cause errors if undetected. Another difficult problem is the similarity between the *n* and the *u* and all other letters with up-and-down strokes (minims) in a series. We still have problems with these in our modern chirography. Some scribes in the 1600s put a crooked line (ʃ) above one of the letters when there was more than one letter with these up-and-down strokes in sequence. Thus *punish* might appear as *punish.*

F. Word Divisions

When a word was divided at the end of a line it was not usually divided with a hyphen (-) as in modern usage, but rather with either an equals sign (=) or a colon (:), often put at the *beginning* of the line where the last part of the divided word was being continued rather than at the end of the preceding line (and sometimes in both places). As mentioned earlier, colons were also used frequently in forming suspension abbreviations. These two usages should not be confused even though they may be confusing.

G. Number Problems

Numbers can also cause difficulties. Many of the numbers people wrote two or three hundred years ago are different from the same numbers as we write them. Numbers and dates written in the arabic form should be studied carefully to make sure they are being properly interpreted. Sometimes numbers may not look like numbers at all and you may erroneously try to make something else out of them. The *8*, for example, was often made to lie almost flat on its side, and most scribes would write a series of numbers (such as a year) without lifting the pen from the paper. Also, roman numerals are found with great frequency in older records and familiarity with them is essential.

H. Latin Terms

You may encounter some Latin terms or their abbreviations with which you may not be familiar. These are not generally extensive in American records but, as a carry-over from British and European practice, they are common enough that you ought to be aware of some of those most frequently used outside of legal and court records. Consider the following:

Anno Domini (A.D.) – in the year of our Lord
circa (c., ca., circ.) – about
died *sine prole (d.s.p.)* – died without issue
et alii (et al.) – and others
et cetera (etc., &c) – and so forth
item – also, likewise

liber or *libro* – book or volume
nepos – grandson
obit (ob) – he died, she died
obit sine prole (o.s.p.) – (he or she) died without issue
requiescat in pace (R.I.P.) – may he (or she) rest in peace
sic – so, thus (intentionally so written to show exact reproduction of original)
testes – witnesses
ultimo (ult.) – last
uxor (ux, vx) – wife
Verbi Dei Minister (V.D.M.) – minister of the word of God
videlicet (viz, viz[t]) – namely

If you come across other Latin terms (and you assuredly will), there are many reference books and dictionaries you can use. The likelihood of your encountering records written entirely in Latin in American research is quite remote; however, the possibility is not excluded and, should you find such records, you should never try to make a translation on your own (unless you have a good background in the language), even when the words appear familiar. In Latin the way a word ends determines the meaning, and the ending of one word can change the meaning of an entire sentence. Word endings have more significance than word sequence. Thus in such cases you should seek the help of someone who knows the language.

I. Not the Originals

If you use any records which are not originals—either manuscript or published—remember that they too are subject to the same errors of which we have been speaking. Many of the persons who make extracts and/or abstracts of original records are not completely qualified to do so, and many who are qualified make honest mistakes. In either case the effect is the same. Persons who make copies or indexes can also have the same problems. A name can be misread and thus be incorrectly indexed, or a document can be missed completely. These things can happen even in making the original index, so every index and every non-original source must be approached with due caution.

J. A General Rule

In any record the most important thing to do when you have difficulty in reading it is to study the handwriting very carefully and learn how to read that particular hand. (It's worth the time if the record has information you need.) You should study it solicitously, read and "translate" a small portion of it word-by-word and note how the various letters are formed. You will have to study the more difficult problems letter-by-letter, comparing similar characters in the same handwriting until you recognize the word in question. This is especially important when you are reading names, as in a census, since some names are easily confused with others at first glance. Some relief lies in the fact that documents of the same kind contain set phrases and words which seldom vary from one instrument to another. Be familiar with these words and phrases before you attempt to read them in any early script.

When you are working with vital records certificates it is sometimes difficult to apply these rules completely because the certificate of concern is usually the only example you have of the handwriting in question. In such situations, do your best with what you have, but be very, very careful.

For more help with handwriting problems refer to E. Kay Kirkham, *How to Read the Handwriting and Records of Early America,* 2nd ed. (Salt Lake City: Deseret Book Co., 1964). This book provides solutions to many of the handwriting problems you will encounter in American records.

K. Spelling

The lack of standardized spellings and the use of phonetic spellings can be very sticky problems. If you go back just 100 years you will find that a large percentage of the population could not read, more still could not write (and many people were able to write only their own names), and even more could not spell. Most persons who did write did not concern themselves particularly with so-called standard spellings, but rather spelled words just as they sounded—phonetically—with local accents. Also realize that the early settlers of America were emigrants from many foreign lands. There were many accents, and when records were made the scribe wrote what he heard, accent and all. (Note that the examples of various records given in this book have retained original spellings.)

What is the significance of these facts? It means that you will oftimes be called upon to decipher scripts in which you will puzzle over simple words just because they are misspelled and in an unfamiliar hand.

However, the main problem is in the spellings of names (especially surnames) and places. In the will which he made in 1754 in Pasquotank County, North Carolina, Jeremiah Willcox's surname is spelled two different ways—Willcox and Willcocks (see Figure 4). In other documents it is spelled still other ways—Wilcox, Wilcocks, Wellcox, Wellcocks, Welcocks,

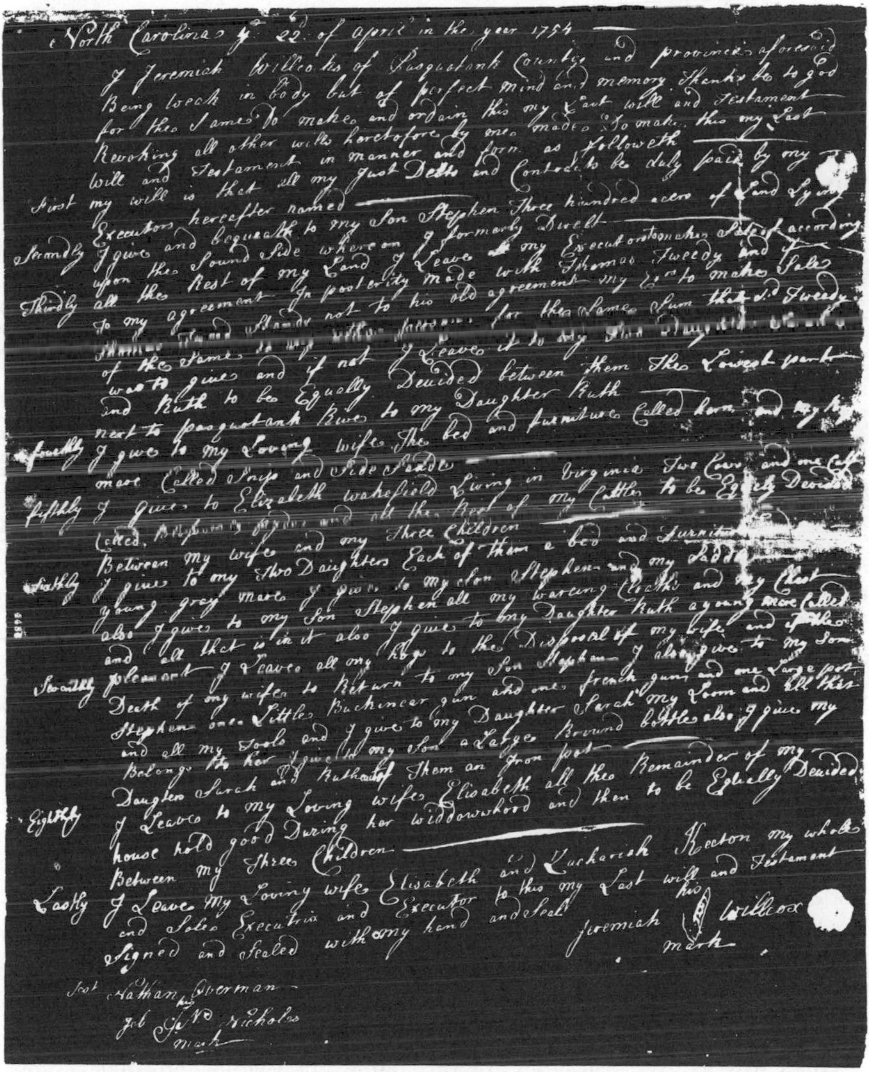

North Carolina ye 22d of April in the year 1754
I Jeremiah Willcocks of Pasquotank County and province aforesaid
Being weak in body but of perfect mind and memory thanks be to god
for the same do make and ordain this my Last will and Testament
Revoking all other wills heretofore by me made do make this my Last
will and Testament in manner and form as followeth
First my will is that all my just Debts and Contracts be duly paid by my
Executors hereafter named
Secondly I give and bequeath to my Son Stephen Three hundred acres of Land Lying
upon the Sound Side whereon I formerly Dwelt
Thirdly all the Rest of my Land I Leave my Executors to make Sale of according
to my agreement In posterity made with Thomas Tweedy and if
[illegible] not to his old agreement my Exrs to make Sale
[illegible] for the same Sum that sd Tweedy
[illegible] it to my [illegible]
of the same [illegible] and if not I Leave it to my [illegible]
was to give and if not I Leave it [illegible] between them The Lowest part
and Ruth to be Equally Devided between them The Lowest part
next to Pasquotank River to my Daughter Ruth
fourthly I give to my Loving wife The bed and furniture Called hers and my
mare Called [illegible] and Side Saddle
fifthly I give to Elizabeth wakefield Living in Virginia Two Cows and one Calf
Called [illegible] and all the Rest of my Cattle to be Equally Devided
Between my wife and my Three Children
Sixthly I give to my Two Daughters Each of them a bed and Furniture
young gray mare I give to my Son Stephen and my Saddle
also I give to my Son Stephen all my wareing Cloaths and my Chest
and all that is in it also I give to my Daughter Ruth a young mare Called
pleasant I Leave all my hogs to the Disposal of my wife and after the
Seventhly Death of my wife to Return to my Son Stephen I also give to my Son
Stephen one Little Buckineer gun and one french gun and one Large pot
and all my Tools and I give to my Daughter Sarah my Loom and all that
Belongs to her I give to my Son a Large Round bottle also I give my
Daughters Sarah and Ruth each of Them an Iron pot
Eighthly I Leave to my Loving wife Elisabeth all the Remainder of my
house hold good During her widdowwhood and then to be Equally Devided
Between my Three Children
Lastly I Leave my Loving wife Elisabeth and Zachariah Keeton my whole
and Sole Executrix and Executor to this my Last will and Testament
Signed and Sealed with my hand and Seal
his
Jeremiah [mark] Willcox
mark

Test Nathan Overman
his
Job JN Nicholes
mark

FIGURE 4—THE WILL OF JEREMIAH WILLCOX

etc.— but Jeremiah could not write himself (he made a mark for his signature) so he probably had no idea as to what the correct spelling was or if it was ever being spelled correctly. The name and its spelling were entirely at the mercy of the person who chanced to make the record.

This points up the fallacy of a practice common in many modern families —that of assuming that if the name is not spelled in a certain way it cannot belong to the same family. Persons with such ideas will pass over important genealogical records because the name happens to be spelled with an *a* rather than an *e*, with an *ie* rather than a *y*, or with one *n* rather than with two. Be especially careful of this when the two related spellings of a name are found in the same geographic area. The connection, of course, is not guaranteed, as it is not guaranteed even when the spellings are exactly the same, but it is worth investigating the possibility.

Also, because of this spelling problem, we must be extremely careful in our use of indexes. We must consider every possible spelling of the name sought. It is very easy to overlook some of the less logical (to us) possibilities and thus many valuable records. Local dialects and foreign accents often make a significant difference. The pronunciation of a name may be quite different in Massachusetts than it is in Georgia, and so might its spelling.

In law this is called the Rule of *"Idem Sonans."* This means that in order to establish legal proof of relationship from documentary evidence it is not necessary for the name to be spelled absolutely accurately if, as spelled, it conveys to the ear, when pronounced in the accepted ways, a sound practically identical to the correctly spelled name as properly pronounced.

A few years ago I worked for some time on a problem where the same surname was found spelled twenty-four different ways in the very same locality, some of them even beginning with a different letter of the alphabet. The correct spelling of the name (supposedly) was *Ingold,* but the following variations were found: Ingle, Ingell, Ingles, Ingells, Ingel, Ingels, Ingeld, Inkle, Inkles, Inkell, Ingolde, Engold, Engolde, Engle, Engell, Engles, Engells, Engel, Engels, Engeld, Angold, Angle, and Ankold. These several variations were all found in the same family at the same time. Would you have considered all of them, or would you have stopped with those that began with *I?*

Other less likely possibilities for this name are Jugold and Jugle. Such errors could easily occur in an index because of the similarities between the capital *I*'s and *J*'s and the small *n*'s and *u*'s.

Another family changed the spelling of its name from Beatty to Baitey when moving from one location to another. In still another instance the surname Kerr was found interchanged with Carr. Whether these spelling changes were intentional is unknown, but the intention makes little difference. In one family three brothers deliberately spelled their surname in different ways—Matlock, Matlack, and Matlick. In his history of the Zabriskie family,[2] George O. Zabriskie reports having dealt with 123 variations of that name, though certainly not all in the same locality or the same time period.

L. Marks and Signatures

Very often the records we use are not the original records but copies made in official registers by recorders and clerks, and the signatures on these registered copies are only copied signatures, so they have no value in identifying an ancestor. But even then you can get an important clue if the person concerned (the ancestor) could not write. That value lies in the mark with which he signed his name, because the clerk usually copied the exact mark (as best he could) into the register. If it was an *X* the value is minimal because so many persons used *X*'s, but if another type mark was used, it may be useful for identification. This is especially true if the ancestor had a common name, and often those with the most common names used the most distinctive signature marks in their striving for individuality and identity.

If you can definitely identify your ancestor in a deed (or some other type of record) where he used a distinctive mark, you can be quite sure you have your ancestor when you find the same mark in another contemporaneous document. Almost anything except an *X* can be helpful, and one should not even rule out the possibility that an *X* may also be helpful.

If original documents are available, signatures can be used in the same way, but only if the party concerned signed his own name or used a distinctive mark. However, both practices can be tricky and you must be extremely careful. People's signatures do change over time.

M. Poorly Preserved Records

Often you will find that the records you need have not survived the onslaught of nature and the ravages of time. In addition to acts of nature, some record custodians have been careless and some users of the records

---

[2] George Olin Zabriskie (comp.), *The Zabriskie Family* (Salt Lake City: Publishers Press, 1963).

have been inconsiderate. There is not a great deal you can do if the records you need are destroyed or badly damaged, but you can be more concerned about the records you use so that the same fate will not befall them. Careless use of records is one of the chief reasons why so many records are either damaged or non-existent.

If you are in a position to handle the old, original documents, please treat them gently and do not touch them. Regardless of how clean your hands are, skin oil is on your fingers and, in time, the paper will darken in every place it is touched. Turn pages with the eraser end of your pencil or with a rubber finger. Keep your pens and pencils off the records. There is no reason to leave any marks on them. Proper document care is an important responsibility of the record user.

II. EVOLUTION OF THE LANGUAGE

Whenever we deal with writing or language from a different period of time there are semantics problems. The history of linguistic development is a story of constant change. Meanings and usages are not static. They have changed in the past, they are changing today, and they will continue to change as long as men use language to communicate with one another.

Early American colonization was somewhat concurrent with the publishing of the King James Bible in 1611, so let's take a simple example from the Bible to illustrate the point. In the King James translation, Mark 10:13 reads: "Suffer the little children to come unto me." The same verse in a more recent translation says: "Let the children come to me."[3] This is the type of problem we are dealing with, and it truly can cause us suffering (in the modern definition of the word). Only when you realize that a word might have a different meaning than the one you personally ascribe to it do you really grasp the full impact of how easily you might be misled.

Let's discuss this problem and some of the more common usage variations as they affect American genealogical research.

A. Relationships

Relationships and terms connected with them can be sources of trouble for the uninitiated.

---

[3] From *The New English Bible, New Testament.* © The Delegates of the Oxford University Press and the Syndics of the Cambridge University Press, 1961. Reprinted by permission.

Junior and *Senior* are terms we usually think of as indicating a father-son relationship, but in early records this was not necessarily true. They were used merely to distinguish between two persons with the same name, usually of different generations, living in the same locality. They were often uncle and nephew rather than father and son. In some parts of the United States, particularly the South, it was as common, or even more so, for a man to name his sons for his brothers as for himself. And you should also watch for the changing of designations. A man once known as junior may be called senior after the death of the earlier senior, and then someone of a younger generation may be called junior.

Be very careful of this usage. I once checked a Daughters of the American Revolution lineage, based on a junior-senior, son-father assumption, where the junior was allegedly the son of the senior who had served from Virginia in the Continental Line. Research proved that this was actually an uncle-and-nephew situation—not father-and-son.

In-law relationships and *step relationships* can also cause confusion if you are not careful. In earlier times people often stated that an in-law connection existed when there was actually a step relationship. Any relationships created by legal means, including step relationships, were often identified simply as "in-law." The following excerpt from a release executed by the heirs of William Bryer, 1738/9, in York County, Massachusetts (now Maine), provides a good example:

> Know all men by these Presents that we William Bryer Shipwright Richard Bryer Weaver Andrew Haley husbandman and Mary his Wife Caleb Hutchins Caulker and Sarah his Wife Joseph Hutchins Weaver and Elizabeth his Wife William Willson Weaver and Eadah his Wife John Haley Husbandman & Hephzib^{a} his Wife all of Kittery in the County of York in the Province of the Massachusetts Bay in New England and William Tapley Taylor of New Hampshire & R [*sic*] his Wife Do forever acquit exonerate and discharge *our Father in Law Benjamin Hammond* of Kittery & Province afors^{d} and our Mother Sarah Hammond lately call'd Sarah Bryer from the Demands of us or our or either of our Heirs in and unto any part of the Cattle or Household Goods or moveable Estate of our hon^{d} Father William Bryer late of Kittery afores^{d} dec^{d} . . . this 31st Day of January Anno Domini 1738/9. [Emphasis added.]

Another example of this situation is found in the will of Francis Champernoun, dated November 16, 1686, in the same place. I quote in part:

> I give and bequeath & confirm unto my Son in Law Humphrey Elliot & Elizabeth his now wife and their heirs forever the other part of my s^{d} Island, which I have allredy given by Deed under my hand

> and Seal to the s^{d} Humphery & Elizabeth his wife— Item I give and bequeath unto my Son in Law Robert Cutt my daughter in Law Bridget Leriven my daughter in Law Mary Cutt and my daughter in Law Sarah Cutt and their heires forever all that part of three hundred acres of land belonging unto me lying between broken Neck and the land formerly belonging unto Hugh Punnison.

It is easy to see the confusion this usage can cause if you are not aware of the possibility. However, this type of problem cannot be predicted. Usually the records mean exactly what they say in this regard—they say "in-law" and mean just that. But you must be alert to possible exceptions.

The terms *cousin, brother,* and *sister* are also significant because of varied usage. However, they do not assume so great an importance in American research as the terms previously mentioned. Concerning these three, Donald Lines Jacobus said:

> The term "cousin" is perhaps the one which is most puzzling to the untrained searcher. It was applied loosely to almost any type of relationship outside the immediate family circle. It was most frequently used to denote a nephew or niece, but it could be applied to a first cousin or more distant cousin, or to the marital spouse of any of these relatives, and sometimes to other indirect connections who were not even related by blood. The first guess should be that a nephew or niece was meant; if this does not work out, then try to prove that cousin in our sense of the word was meant; if this also proves impossible, it may require long and profound study to determine just what the connection was. This applies, generally speaking, to the use of the term in the colonies prior to 1750. No definite and exact date can be fixed, for the terms nephew and niece gradually supplanted cousin to denote that form of relationship. . . .
>
> . . . Husband and wife were identified as one person. Hence, when a man writes in his will of "my brother Jones" and "my sister Jones," he may be referring to his own sister and her husband, to his wife's sister and her husband, or to his wife's brother and that brother's spouse.
>
> It is not always possible to decide, in the will of a puritan around 1650, whether the "Brother Peck" and "Brother Perkins" whom he appointed overseers of his estate were relatives by marriage or merely brothers in the church. The expression "*my* Brother Peck" makes it sound a little more like relationship, but is not conclusive. The same uncertainty attaches to the use of the term "Sister" in these early wills.[4]

---

[4] Donald Lines Jacobus, "Interpreting Genealogical Records," in *Genealogical Research: Methods and Sources,* ed. by Milton Rubincam (Washington, DC: American Society of Genealogists, 1960), pp. 22-23. By permission.

You will occasionally see the term *german* (or *germane*) used in connection with some types of relationships, especially brothers, sisters, and cousins. Brothers (or sisters) german are children of the same parents (as opposed to half-brothers or sisters), and cousins german are the children of brothers and sisters, i.e., first cousins.

The terms *niece* and *nephew* can cause confusion as used in early records. They did not always have the meanings we attach to them. Niece derives from the Latin term *neptis* and nephew from the Latin term *nepos,* which actually mean granddaughter and grandson, respectively. In early American records the usage of niece for granddaughter and nephew for grandson is rarely found but is certainly not unknown. In most cases these relationships, when stated, mean the same as they do today. During the evolution of meaning you may find niece and nephew used for either, but after 1690 I have found no use of them to mean grandchild, while finding frequent mention of grandson and granddaughter. However, if you find the Latin word *nepos,* you can almost count on it meaning grandson.

The term *my now wife* is very often misunderstood as it appears in various records. It is often misinterpreted to mean that the person making the statement or to whom it applies (as in the will of Francis Champernoun where he mentioned "my Son in Law Humphrey Elliot & Elizabeth *his now wife*") has been previously married. But this is not necessarily true and the person making the statement had something quite different in mind. Usually the term was used in wills when the testator (the person making the will) wanted to place a limitation on that will which the court would recognize when he wasn't around to explain. This was not an explanatory phrase but a phrase used to limit the inheritance rights of any *future* wife in case the "now wife" should die and he should remarry. The person making such a statement in a will *may* have been previously married, but the statement was not made to protect property from the claims of a previous spouse but from possible future spouses.

B. Titles

There were some other terms in quite common usage in earlier periods with which you should become familiar. British America during the colonial period was naturally caught up in many British traditions and usages. Hence the terms of British social rank were also used here though they commonly lacked the strict meanings and social implications of gentility which were attached to them in the mother country. In many records (some of them quite recent) we find persons referred to as *Esquire* (Esqr) or *Gentleman* (Gentl^{n}).

In Britain a person with "Esquire" tacked on the end of his name was able to bear arms and was next in social precedence to a knight. If he had "Gentleman" at the end of his name this signified gentle birth also, but one more step down the social ladder.

The use of these terms became quite loose in England, but especially so in America. Even here, the earlier the period, the more strict the usage. The terms were mainly used as titles of courtesy to designate the most influential (or most prosperous) persons in a community. They were used by the social elite—lawyers, physicians, notable political figures, clergy, large landowners, magistrates, and justices of the peace—but the meaning was not precise. You will occasionally find these terms used in America, even as late as the middle 1800s, by some public officials such as justices of the peace, magistrates, and church leaders. The most valuable thing about the use of these titles in America is that they often provide an additional means to identify the persons so designated as you search for them in the various records.

The title *Colonel* was also used frequently by many of the old southern planters, and though the title had nothing to do with military rank, it is useful for identification purposes.

Also among the early colonists, the terms *Mr.* and *Mrs.* followed the English precedent and were used only by the upper classes of society, those with "Esquire" and "Gentleman" after their names. In this connection Mrs. was not a term identifying a married woman but rather a title of courtesy for a woman of "gentle" birth, married or single. In this sense it was ordinarily used before both the given name and surname of the unmarried woman. However, it wasn't too long before our current usage of the terms became the common one.

You may also find the terms *goodman* and *goodwife* (frequently shortened to *goody*) used in the older records you search. They simply mean the head of a household and the mistress of a household, respectively.

III. NAMING PRACTICES

A. Given Names

As we have already discussed various problems of surnames, let us now discuss some familiar practices relating to given names. In both New England and the South, Bible names had great popularity. However, New Englanders used both common and uncommon Bible names while their southern cousins stuck with the more conventional. New Englanders are also known for the frequent bestowal of the names of qualities of the soul, or spiritual gifts, upon their children. This was perhaps partially due to their dislike of the old established English names. Faith, hope and charity were more than just words to live by—they were very common female given names. Other popular names for girls included Prudence, Sympathy, Mirth, Kindness, Mercy, Constance, Submit, Silence, and Deliverance. Popular male names included Remember, Comfort (also sometimes feminine), Ransome, Consider, etc.

Given names of the past also had more of a tendency to be carried on in a family from generation to generation than they do today, though we still have some tendencies in this direction. Even very unusual names were carried on—a practice which often provides circumstantial evidence for certain genealogical connections. You must be careful, however, and not accept a connection on this basis without proof that such a connection was indeed a fact.

A child very often was given the name of a grandparent. (This custom was more common in some other countries than in America, but it was also quite common here among certain ethnic groups.) Or, he may have been given his mother's maiden surname. A boy might have been given the name of one of his father's or mother's brothers, and a girl might have been given the name of one of her parents' sisters. This means that if a man and his brothers all had large families and they came from a large family themselves, you will find many contemporaneous cousins all bearing the same given names—and often very hard to separate one from the other as you read of them in the records.

It is not unusual for the researcher to find more than one child in the same family unit with the same given name. Usually when this happened it was because one child of that name died and the name was given to a later child. Occasionally there was more than one living child in the same family with the same given name, but this is rare and happened mostly in German or Dutch families or when there was a great age difference between the two children. In the latter case they were frequently the children of two different marriages of their father.

Several children in the same family were often given the same middle name (after middle names became popular), often their mother's or even their grandmothers' maiden surname. This practice, however, does not date back quite so far as some of the others.[5]

---

[5] For further discussion on names (especially in New England), see chapter 5 of Donald Lines Jacobus, *Genealogy as Pastime and Profession*, 2nd ed. rev. (Baltimore: Genealogical Publishing Co., 1968).

Names are usually indicative of sex and most names can usually be identified as belonging to persons of one sex or the other. However, there are some names that were given to persons of either sex. Consider names like Christian, Evelyn, Sharon, and Shirley. The names Francis and Marion are usually considered as masculine while Frances and Marian are usually considered feminine. But you cannot always count on that.

Even names we think clearly belong to one gender or the other are found borne by members of the opposite sex. Thus we must be careful about all conclusions of identity on the basis of names. A good rule, when names leave you confused, is to look for more evidence.

B. Nicknames and Pet Names

Nicknames are often descriptive names given to individuals, such as Shorty, Slim, and Red. However, they also include the familiar forms (and often diminutive forms) of proper names, such as Jim for James, Beth for Elizabeth, Sally for Sarah, and Bill for William. Pet names are given as an expression of endearment and include names like Muffy, Pinky, and Buddy.

Nicknames are often found in records, and some people can be identified more easily if you are aware of the possibilities. Consider that the following names and their diminutives were often interchanged:

Nancy – Ann
Agnes – Nancy
Margaret – Peggy, Maggie, Mitzi, and Meg
Martha – Patsy and Patty
Mary – Molly and Polly
Abigail – Abby
Melissa – Missy
Elizabeth – Betty, Beth, Lizzy, and Liz

IV. SOME SYMBOLS

It also seems wise to list a number of symbols widely used by those who compile genealogies. You will encounter these often as you use various published sources. Some of the main ones follow:

* – born
(*) – born illegitimate
X – baptized or christened
⊂⊃ – baptized or christened
∼ – baptized or christened

O – betrothed
OO – married
O/O – divorced
O-O – common-law marriage
✝ – died
⁄– – died
☐ – buried
▭ – buried
✝ ✝ – no further issue
(✝) – no further issue

V. THE CALENDAR

Calendar difficulties may come as a surprise to you unless you have either studied astronomy or have a good background in history. However, the calendar and its transition from the Julian to the Gregorian system and other changes involved therewith have considerable impact on many early American genealogical problems.

The main problem has to do with the changing of the calendars—when the switch was made from the Julian to the Gregorian. In Britain and her colonies (which included most colonies in America) this took place in 1752.[6] Remember that date; it is important. During the period while the Julian Calendar was used, the Christian church and the countries within which that church prospered used what we call an ecclesiastical calendar (dating back to the Nicean Council of 325 A.D.) which had New Year's Day falling on March 25. This was the day of the Feast of the Annunciation (commonly called Lady Day) which commemorates the visit of the Angel Gabriel to the Virgin Mary to inform her that she would be the mother of the Messiah.[7] Note that this date is exactly nine months before Christmas, when we celebrate that birth.

Let's take an example to show the effects of this situation. You have several documents (such as wills) recorded in chronological order. The dates on these might run something like this:

---

[6] The Dutch in New Netherland never used the Julian Calendar. The Dutch had accepted the Gregorian Calendar prior to their American colonization. These people even continued to use New Style dates in their private records after England had control of their colony. The Quakers did not accept the ecclesiastical calendar but began their year on January 1 even though they otherwise accepted the dates of the Julian Calendar. (Note that the examples in chapter 20 show an exception to this general rule.)

[7] Luke 1:26-28.

November 14, 1718
December 26, 1718
January 3, 1718
January 22, 1718
February 16, 1718
March 5, 1718
March 23, 1718
March 28, 1719
April 12, 1719

This is very simple, isn't it? The main difficulty here is that we are accustomed to beginning our years on January 1, so when we see a date like one of these (say February 16, 1718) we automatically put it in the wrong year —and we are automatically one year off.

One year off isn't bad, you say? That is true *unless* it leads you to make incorrect conclusions. If the record in question happens to be a church register and the christenings, etc., of your ancestor's children are recorded therein, you may have a problem. Let's say you find two christenings on the following dates for persons you suppose are your ancestor's children:

April 1, 1720
March 22, 1720

If you didn't know that the year 1721 began three days after the second of these two christenings, what would be your conclusion?

Or, what about the case of the man who draws his will in October of 1692 and that will is admitted to probate in February 1692? What would you think?

Because of this problem we use what we call *double-dating*. This means that whenever a date falls between January 1 and March 24, inclusive, *before 1752,* it should be recorded to reflect both the ecclesiastical and the historical calendars. You do this by writing the dates in the previous list as follows:

November 14, 1718
December 26, 1718
January 3, 1718/9
January 22, 1718/9
February 16, 1718/9
March 5, 1718/9
March 23, 1718/9
March 28, 1719
April 12, 1719

And the two christening dates given earlier should be written:

April 1, 1720
March 22, 1720/1

And the dates on the will would actually be October 1692 and February 1692/3.

This double-dating indicates that the year was actually (in the case of the christening) 1720, but that *if* the year had begun on January 1 as it now does, then it would have been 1721. Very simple, isn't it?

There was some pressure for the change to January 1 before it actually took place officially in 1752, and it is not uncommon to find double-dating used in many of the early records, especially after 1700. Some Christian countries were using the new system as early as 1582.

You may also find double-dating used incorrectly in these records on occasion, but do not let this alarm you. You can usually make the corrections. For example, you may find a date incorrectly written as "April 12, 1718/9." This is much the same problem that we have today when we keep writing the old year for a month or so after the new year has begun. It would be corrected to 1719. You might also see some double-dating after 1752. This is merely a case where the writer either had a habit of writing dates that way or was just opposed to change.

Also, since the year began in March, you will find March referred to as the first month, April as the second month, and so on. So when you see the months written as *7ber* and *8ber* (before 1752) they actually mean September and October and not July and August. In Latin, September and October mean seventh month and eighth month, respectively. The same applies to November and December—they mean ninth month and tenth month. But, regardless of name, the other months were also numbered differently. You may find it helpful to remember this—it makes quite a difference.

3

Analyzing the Pedigree and the Place

I. PEDIGREE ANALYSIS

It goes without saying that you can never arrive at your destination if you do not know where you are going. The person who does not know where he is going is like the proverbial ship that leaves port with no particular destination in mind and drifts aimlessly on the open seas. Unless you have goals you can never accomplish anything; and in genealogy an objective analysis of your pedigree is the thing which will help you visualize appropriate genealogical goals and channel your efforts correctly for their attainment. This does not actually make research any easier—the work is still there—but it can make it much more fruitful.

Before you can make a satisfactory analysis, however, you must first determine exactly where the research stands as of right now—you must find out what has already been done. This need not take forever as many suppose; it is quite a simple process if properly pursued. This secondary research, or preliminary survey as we sometimes call it, includes the use of home and family sources (both those in your own possession and those in the possession of relatives). It also includes three sources peculiar to the LDS Family History Library which are valuable to both Mormon and non-Mormon. These are the Temple Records Index Bureau, the Family Group Records Archives, and the International Genealogical Index (commonly referred to as the TIB, the Archives, and the IGI).

The TIB is a card index file which contains genealogical data cards on nearly 40,000,000 persons from many generations and many countries. The

Archives are a collection of records of entire families (more than 5,000,000 of them) arranged alphabetically by the name of the father in each family. There is a cross-reference system between these two collections so if there is information in both places it can be detected. The IGI is a computer index (output on microfiche) of more than one hundred million individuals, primarily referenced to births, christenings, and marriages. You can easily use these sources, if you desire, by submitting a special form. Copies of the form may be obtained by writing to the Family History Library, 35 North West Temple Street, Salt Lake City, Utah 84150. Local Family History Centers (formerly Branch Libraries) have copies of the IGI, many of them having it on compact disc. In the not-too-distant future, the IGI will be replaced by a more complete, more extensive index to a wider variety of records.

Various compiled sources are also essential to your survey, and chapter 9 discusses these in some detail. Printed genealogies are only a record of the research that someone else has done, and any research you do in them, as important as it may be, is only secondary research.

As you progress through your survey you should make a careful record of all the information you find. You should also remember that the survey is not your ultimate objective and the data found are subject to error. These data are no more reliable than the persons and the research methods which produced them, and this cannot be determined except by careful study. Your first objective, however, is to gather the data—then you can perform your analysis.

Some type of pedigree chart (see Figure 2) should be prepared from the information found so that you can get a true picture of what you actually have in relation to the information still required. Family group forms (see Figure 1) should also be completed as far as the information found will allow. If family group forms are used you can readily get a true perspective of the information you have and that which you still need to make the record complete for each family.

Once you have your pedigree and family group forms complete as far as you can go from your survey, you are in a position to analyze the data they contain and decide on your research objectives.

As you analyze your pedigree remember that you cannot do everything at once. It would be folly to try to work on every ancestral line simultaneously. Pick a line that needs work—even two or three lines if they are in the same geographical area during the same time period—and you are ready to begin working on a problem.

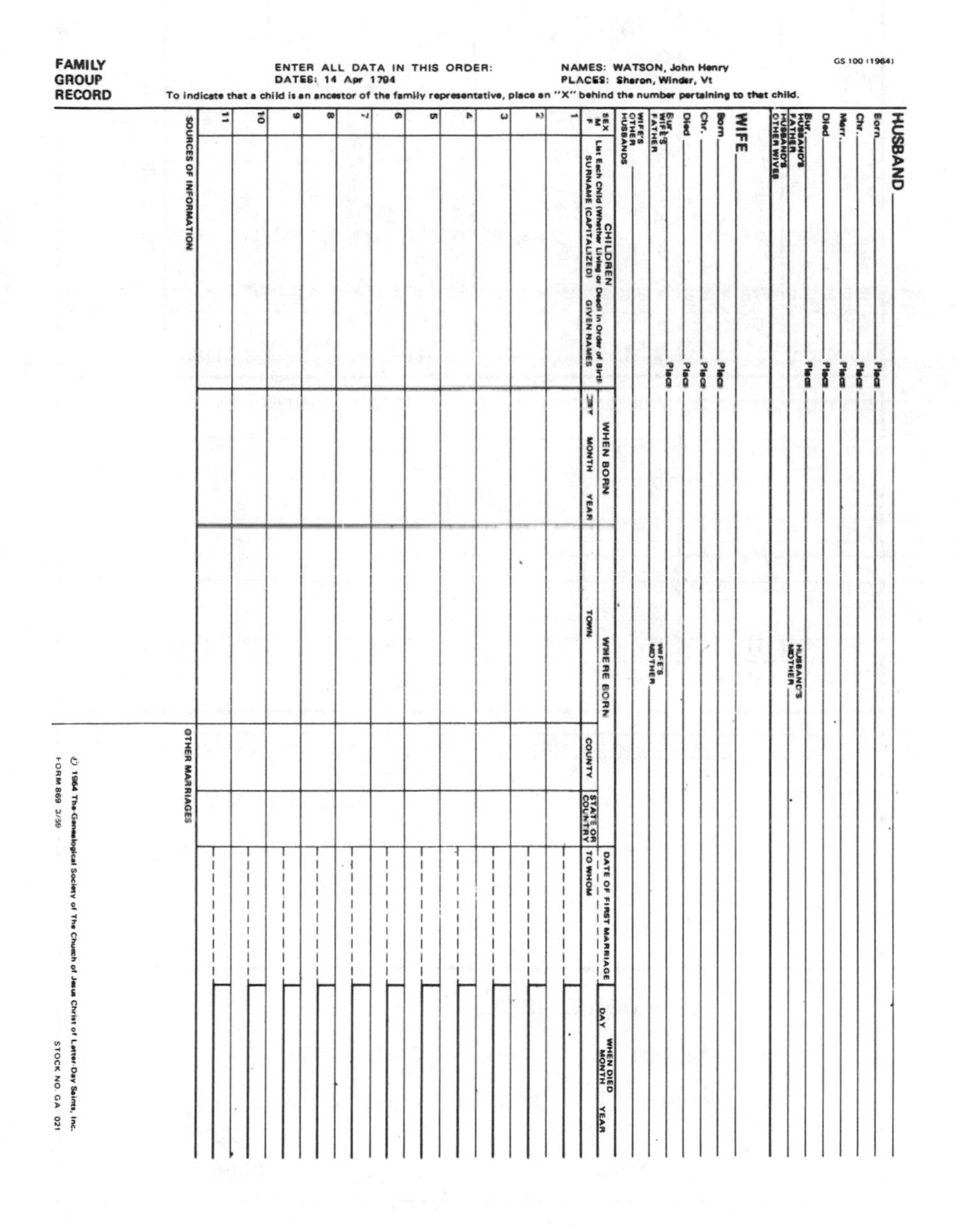

FAMILY GROUP RECORD

GS 100 (1964)

ENTER ALL DATA IN THIS ORDER: NAMES: WATSON, John Henry
DATES: 14 Apr 1794 PLACES: Sharon, Windsr, Vt

To indicate that a child is an ancestor of the family representative, place an "X" behind the number pertaining to that child.

HUSBAND
Born Place
Chr. Place
Marr. Place
Died Place
Bur. Place
HUSBAND'S FATHER HUSBAND'S MOTHER
HUSBAND'S OTHER WIVES

WIFE
Born Place
Chr. Place
Died Place
Bur. Place
WIFE'S FATHER WIFE'S MOTHER
WIFE'S OTHER HUSBANDS

SEX M F	CHILDREN List Each Child (Whether Living or Dead) in Order of Birth SURNAME (CAPITALIZED) GIVEN NAMES	WHEN BORN DAY	MONTH	YEAR	WHERE BORN TOWN	COUNTY	STATE OR COUNTRY	DATE OF FIRST MARRIAGE TO WHOM	WHEN DIED DAY	MONTH	YEAR
1											
2											
3											
4											
5											
6											
7											
8											
9											
10											
11											

SOURCES OF INFORMATION

OTHER MARRIAGES

FORM 869 3/59 STOCK NO. GA 021

FIGURE 1—A TYPICAL FAMILY GROUP FORM

8. MATHIUS KELLY of Va.
Brn
Chr
Die
Bur

Mar'd

9. BETSY BLACK
Brn
Chr
Die
Bur

10. MIDDLETON JAMENSON
Brn
Chr
Die
Bur

Mar'd

11. POLLY HARRIS
Brn
Chr
Die
Bur

12. SIMON GILBERT
Brn
Chr
Die
Bur

Mar'd

13. BETSY HUTSON
Brn
Chr
Die
Bur

14. CHARLES BAKER
Brn
Chr
Die
Bur

Mar'd

15. POLLY GIRE or McGUIRE
Brn
Chr
Die
Bur

4. JAHUE KELLY
Brn 1782 Of Virginia
Chr
Die c. 1820
Bur

Mar'd

5. RHODA JAMENSON
Brn c. 1791 Of Virginia
Chr
Die Feb 1881 Kentucky
Bur

6. QUILLER GILBERT
Brn 1791
Chr
Die
Bur

Mar'd

7. POLLY BAKER
Brn
Chr
Die
Bur

2. WILLIAM SAMUEL KELLY

Brn	1815	Of Virginia
Chr		
Die	20 Mar 1865	Kentucky
Bur		

Mar'd

3. NANCY JANE GILBERT

Brn	2 Dec 1825	Of Kentucky
Chr		
Die	9 Nov 1908	Kentucky
Bur		

1. JOHN SAMUEL KELLY

Brn	24 Aug 1851	Booneville, Owsley, Kentucky
Chr		
Die	8 Feb 1909	St. David, Cochise, Arizona
Bur		

Mar'd 16 Mar 1894 to MARY ELLEN SMYTH

FIGURE 2—PEDIGREE OF JOHN SAMUEL KELLY

II. THE BASIC APPROACH

The first rule to remember is that *you must work with the information which you already have.* Just as you do not build a house separately from its foundation, genealogical evidence also requires a foundation. This means that you must begin your research on ancestors about whom you already know something. To do effective research you must have a *name,* a *date* (at least a period of time), and a reasonably specific *place* or *locality.* You are wasting your time if all of these factors are not known. Too many so-called genealogists find a "desirable" person with the right surname then try to trace the line of descent down until they make a connection. If such methods work then the person who uses them is either a very successful gambler (because of his ability to beat the laws of probability) or else the connections he has accepted are erroneous.

Prepare for your analysis by making a "T" chart on a blank sheet of paper, like this:

On one side write the question,

What do I already know?	

On the other side write the question,

	What does this suggest?

So that you wind up with a "T" chart that looks like this:

What do I already know?	*What does this suggest?*

Next, analyze carefully to determine just what you do "already know" about the person (or persons) on whom you are doing research. Analyze his name, the places with which he was associated, the dates connected with those places, and his relationships to other persons. Usually your research will begin in the earliest place that you find this person, unless you wish to do research in some later places of residence to complete information on the family group form you are preparing.

Consider whether the dates associated with your ancestor are historically significant. Might this person have lived at the right time to have served in one of this country's many wars? Might he or his widow have applied for a pension for that service? Did he die when his children were young? Might you find guardianship records for them? Did he die several years before his wife died? Might she have remarried? Or vice versa? Was he several years older than his wife? Might she have been a second wife? These possibilities and any other which you observe as you study the pedigree should be carefully noted. You will want to check them out later; as yet they are only possibilities. Many things of significance have occurred which are lost to family tradition.

As an example, let's consider the pedigree of John Samuel Kelly. First, from what you see on the pedigree form in Figure 2, where should research begin? On Simion Gilbert? On Rhoda Jamenson? Or just where? Quite obviously neither of these persons should be a primary objective to begin with. You do not know enough about them. Though you know a little about Rhoda, you still do not have a definite locality in which research can be conducted. And there seems to be quite complete information on John Samuel Kelly himself. Thus he would not be your objective unless you lacked information on his complete family.

There are actually only two logical possibilities—William Samuel Kelly and his wife, Nancy Jane Gilbert—and they can be combined into a dual objective. Why? Because you need further information on both of them and it can likely be found in the same locality. More is said later about searching for all persons of the surname(s) of interest during your research.

Let's list a few things on the left side of our "T" chart that you already know about William Samuel and Nancy Jane (assuming, for the sake of this example, that all data stated are true):

What do I already know?	
1. He is ten years older than she.	
2. He died forty-three years before she did.	
3. He was about five years old when his father died.	
4. He died sixteen years before his mother did.	

5. His mother was about twenty-four years old when he was born, his father about thirty-three.

6. He came from Virginia and she came from Kentucky. (The use of the word "of" here merely indicates that we are not sure of birth places, and that these are the earliest known places of residence.)

7. They had a son born in 1851 and were apparently married before that year.

8. They resided in Booneville, Owsley County, Kentucky, in 1851. (Note that this is the earliest specific known place of residence we have and is thus quite significant.)

9. Both of them died in Kentucky.

10. We know the names (apparently) of both sets of parents.

Now we ask our *second question:* Do any of these facts suggest possibilities to be investigated? Let's list a few of them:

What does this suggest?

1. Because he was ten years older than she, he *may* have had a previous marriage.

2. Because she outlived him by forty-three years, she *may* have remarried after his death.

3. Because his mother outlived his father by so many years, she *may* have remarried also.

4. Their marriage (William Samuel and Nancy Jane's) *probably* took place in Kentucky since she was from that state and their son John Samuel was born there. (Under these circumstances it is much more likely that he came to Kentucky to marry her than that she went to Virginia to marry him.)

5. *If* he came to Kentucky before his marriage and *if* it was his first marriage, he *probably* came with his mother and her family, *possibly* a stepfather. (Note also that his mother did come to Kentucky. She died there.)

6. They *possibly* resided in Booneville and Owsley County for more than just the one year (1851) and *our research should begin there.*

7. His date of death suggests that he *may* have died in the Civil War. Though he was fifty years old this is still a *possibility*. (Being from Kentucky, a border state, there is no suggestion as to

whether this might be a Union or Confederate Army connection. You would need to learn more about local history.)

8. There is also a possibility of other children, both before and after John Samuel, because Nancy Jane was twenty-six years old when John Samuel was born. (There would be none later than 1865 when William Samuel died.)

As research is begun each of these possibilities must be investigated in the appropriate records.

This is the way that every pedigree should be analyzed, not necessarily on paper, though that may prove helpful to the beginner. This is the type of analysis that clearly enables us to put the individual, the locality, the records, and history in their true perspective with one another.

III. GET THEM ALL

During the research for your ancestor it will be to your advantage if you read and extract *all* information relating to all persons of the surname(s) of interest in the locality of interest. If you do not do it, someday you will be sorry and you will wind up going back through the same records again, and it will likely be sooner than you think. You may not be able to identify all of these persons as you find them, but when you begin to synthesize your findings and put them into families, most of the pieces will fall into place and the information you have found on those "unknown" persons will often provide clues to help extend your pedigree. Some argue that if the surname is common it takes too much time to follow this procedure. Actually the more common the name the more essential this procedure becomes so that proper identification can be ascertained.

An example of the value of this procedure is shown in the Charles Pebble example in chapter 1. The "easy way"— of picking out only "the important records"— falls short in actual practice.

Also, before research can commence, you must know what records are available in the locality of your problem and what you might find in those records that would be useful in solving your problem. This is an area of American research that is especially fascinating, and somewhat complicated, because you can never be sure what you are going to find in so many of the available records. Though you can usually get a pretty fair idea, you will often be surprised by the actual content of many records. Names or titles of records often mean little as the same types of records in different localities may bear different titles. Because of this no record should be sold short or overlooked until it has been put to the test. You can't afford to decide a case without considering all the evidence.

It is also essential that you know something about the location of records and the jurisdictions in which those records were originally kept.

IV. JURISDICTIONS

By "jurisdiction" I mean the *legal* or *traditional* authority to carry out certain activities. A *legal* jurisdiction is established by law and might have to do with a case in civil court, or vital records, land records, wills, censuses, etc. A *traditional* jurisdiction might include christenings (or baptisms), marriages, burials, and other activities carried on by a church. Also, activities carried on by private businesses, institutions, fraternal organizations, etc., in behalf of their membership or patrons would be in traditional jurisdictions.

To the genealogist it is important to know who had jurisdiction over certain activities if he wishes to locate and use any of the records which those activities produced.

The most logical approach to almost every American genealogical problem is the jurisdictional approach—that is, each locality and each jurisdiction of interest must be studied carefully as to its record keeping procedures before research begins therein. Once you know what records were kept, who kept them, and who is their present custodian you are ready to proceed. And let me emphasize here the necessity of searching all existing records produced by all jurisdictions or spheres of authority within which your ancestors lived—the home, the church, the county, the state, etc.

Closely related to jurisdictional knowledge is that most essential knowledge of records and their contents. When you search a record you should at least have a general idea of the kind of information usually found in that type of source. To help provide that knowledge is one purpose of this book. And this knowledge will obviously be enhanced by your own research experience.

A good example of what I am talking about is found in probate jurisdictions. In most states these records are kept in the county, but if you were tracing ancestors in Vermont it would be worthwhile to know that the records are kept in special probate districts which do not always correspond to the counties. In Rhode Island probate records are kept in the towns, and in Delaware all probate records for the state are kept in one central repository. See why it's important to understand jurisdictions as well as record content?

You should also be careful of jurisdictional changes. Records kept in one place at one time may have been kept somewhere else during another period. In New Hampshire, for example, probate and land records have traditionally been kept by the counties, but between 1671 and 1771 both types of records were kept by the province or colony. (This was prior to statehood.) You must know that in order to find those records.

V. LOCALITY ANALYSIS

Closely related to the jurisdictional analysis already discussed is an examination of other data relating directly to the locality of your research. You must know much more about that locality than who kept the records and when they kept them. You must consider the history and the geography in minutiae.

If you knew that your great-grandfather lived in Zanesville, Ohio, what would you do to learn more about him?—a very simple question with a not-so-simple answer. Do you have it figured out?

A. Some Basic Tools

The first thing you need to do (and this applies whether you are looking for Zanesville, Ohio; Picabo, Idaho; Punxsutawney, Pennsylvania; or Booneville, Kentucky) is to find out exactly where that place is located. A gazetteer, a postal directory, an encyclopedia, or a good map may provide this information.

The dictionary defines a gazetteer as "a geographical dictionary,"[1] but the term is actually used more broadly to include almost any work which lists geographical names in alphabetical order. There are several of these and also several postal directories that might be useful to you, but some are better than others because they include more places.

To begin with, we need to determine in which Ohio county Zanesville is located. Since, in America, most (but certainly not all) records are kept on a county basis, this is an essential piece of datum. You can do very little toward completing the research picture unless you know that Zanesville is in Muskingum County. At least one of four good sources of this information is available in most libraries:

1. United States Postal Service. *United States Directory of Post Offices*. Washington, DC: U.S. Postal Service (annual). The first section in this source lists towns alphabetically by state and tells in which

---

[1] By permission. From *Webster's Seventh New Collegiate Dictionary*. © 1969 by G. & C. Merriam Co., publishers of the Merriam-Webster Dictionaries.

county each one is located. This is not a complete source, however, as it is limited to only those towns with post offices.

2. *Bullinger's Postal and Shippers Guide for the United States and Canada.* Westwood, NJ: Bullinger's Guides, Inc., 1897—. This source provides the same information as the post office directory (item 1) except that all towns are listed in strict alphabetical order rather than by state. It is much more extensive also because it is not limited only to those towns with post offices. It is good for finding places that are very small. And, as the title indicates, Canada is also included.

3. *Columbia-Lippincott Gazetteer of the World.* Morningside Heights, NY: Columbia University Press and J. B. Lippincott Co., 1905 and 1952. This is a good source because of the information it gives about the places listed, but it is less than complete in its coverage. All entries are arranged in strict alphabetical sequence.

4. *Webster's Geographical Dictionary.* Springfield, MA: G. and C. Merriam Company, 1957. This volume, though it may not be comprehensive enough to meet your need on every occasion, does contain some 40,000 entries (worldwide) and can be a useful tool.

Of these sources, though recent editions are generally available, the older editions have the most value. The names of some places change; other places become ghost towns for one reason or another. Because of these facts our slogan might be: "The older the better." I have never seen the early edition of *Columbia-Lippincott,* but I am sure there are a few around. I found one catalogued in the Sugar House Branch of the Salt Lake City Public Library in 1964, but it was not on the library shelves. When I asked the librarian about it she merely assured me that it was "too old to be any good anyway." She was obviously not a genealogist.

Other gazetteers, especially of the individual states, can also be located and are usually of even greater value in solving locality problems. J. H. French's *Gazetteer of the State of New York* (1860), of which there are more recent reprints, is a good example.

Maps are also a "must" item for the genealogist. A good map can fill the same requirement that a gazetteer does; it too will tell you the name of the county in which a particular town is situated. Unless a map is quite detailed, though, it may not show small towns. Our motto about the older gazetteers also holds true with maps, and for basically the same reason—changes. If you can find a map of a locality made about the time your ancestors lived there, the boundary and jurisdiction changes will be reflected as the old map is compared with a more recent one. More is said later about the importance of understanding these changes.

Maps also help us understand the geographical and physical features which often affect a genealogical problem. They may suggest some patterns of settlement and migration and completely rule out others. A range of mountains is a barrier to migration while a river may aid migratory travel. It is much easier to travel on water than through dense forests and undergrowth; however, a river might also be an obstruction to travel. Crossing it could be difficult for those not properly equipped.

A map also shows the relationship of a town or county to other towns and counties in the same area. This may suggest other searches to you, especially if the place your ancestors lived happened to lie near a boundary line. Too often we tend to restrict our searches by boundaries when we cannot see relative locations on a map, but the persons who lived there were never thus restricted. They went where they pleased and records relating to them may be found in several different places.

For any locality, detailed local maps are the most valuable. This is an obvious conclusion since it naturally follows that the smaller the area covered the better will be the coverage. As has already been mentioned, old maps are the best *if* they can be found; however, if they cannot be found modern maps will suffice. Road maps are surprisingly good and usually serve quite well. They are generally available through chambers of commerce, magazine and book distributors, and state publicity and/or highway departments.

Most larger libraries, and some smaller ones, have the *Rand McNally Commercial Atlas and Marketing Guide* (New York: Rand McNally and Co., annual). This atlas contains excellent maps of the individual states. The maps are very detailed, showing nearly all of the towns, water courses, county boundaries and, in places where it is pertinent, township boundaries. These atlases are placed in libraries by subscription and each year the publisher replaces the old atlas with a new one in order to keep the marketing data current. Some small genealogical libraries not subscribing to this service have been able to obtain copies of older atlases through the influence of their U.S. Congressional Representatives.

The maps in this atlas are good for other countries also, but those for the United States are the strong feature of the book, at least from a genealogical point of view. The quality of the U.S. maps, in an atlas of this type, is unsurpassed. My major criticism is that they are too new.

If, after you have checked maps and gazetteers, you are still unable to locate a certain place, there are other approaches that should be used. Historical societies and local libraries can often provide information on defunct place names, as can books on local history. The reason that a place name cannot be found might be that the town is now a ghost town, the name has been changed, or the place is too small to be found in the regular sources. Regardless of the reason, meaningful research cannot be initiated until that problem is solved and the county has been identified.

If your ancestor lived in a large city and you can locate his address in some way (perhaps with an old city directory), a map of that city may help you limit your search. For example, if you can determine that your ancestor lived in Ward 14 of Philadelphia and you want to find him in the 1860 census with his family, you will find it much easier to search the census for just one ward than to search the entire city. You can accomplish in perhaps thirty minutes to an hour what might otherwise take several days.

B. Genealogy of Places

Because America is a relatively new country there are some special kinds of research problems caused by frequent boundary changes. Thus you may often need maps which show boundary lines only, especially state maps which show county boundaries. These not only help to locate counties in their relationships to each other generally but to specifically locate them in relation to their parent and child counties. Some of the better maps of this type are the individual state maps in the 200 Series, produced by the American Map Co. in New York City. There are also other good sources.

Almost every early American genealogical problem is affected by boundary changes of one kind or another. Even those families who lived in only one place had the boundaries changed around them, thus making it necessary to search the records of several counties or several towns. For example, if a family lived at Jefferson, North Carolina, for a 100-year period between 1700 and 1800 you might well find records of that family in seven different counties even though the family never moved even so far as across the street. You would first find them in Bath County (organized 1696), next in Bladen County (organized 1734), next in Anson County (organized 1750), next in Rowan County (1753), next in Wilkes County (1777), and finally in Ashe County (1799) where Jefferson is still located.

I could show several good examples of this type situation from many states, but let me mention just one more. In western New York, or what is called "up-state" New York, the area which now comprises forty-five entire counties and parts of two others was all in Albany County in 1683.

This "genealogy" of places is vital; you must know it or you will not find the records you need. When a county was divided the records concerning the area which was divided off remained in the original county and that is where they are usually found. It would be impossible to satisfactorily sepa-

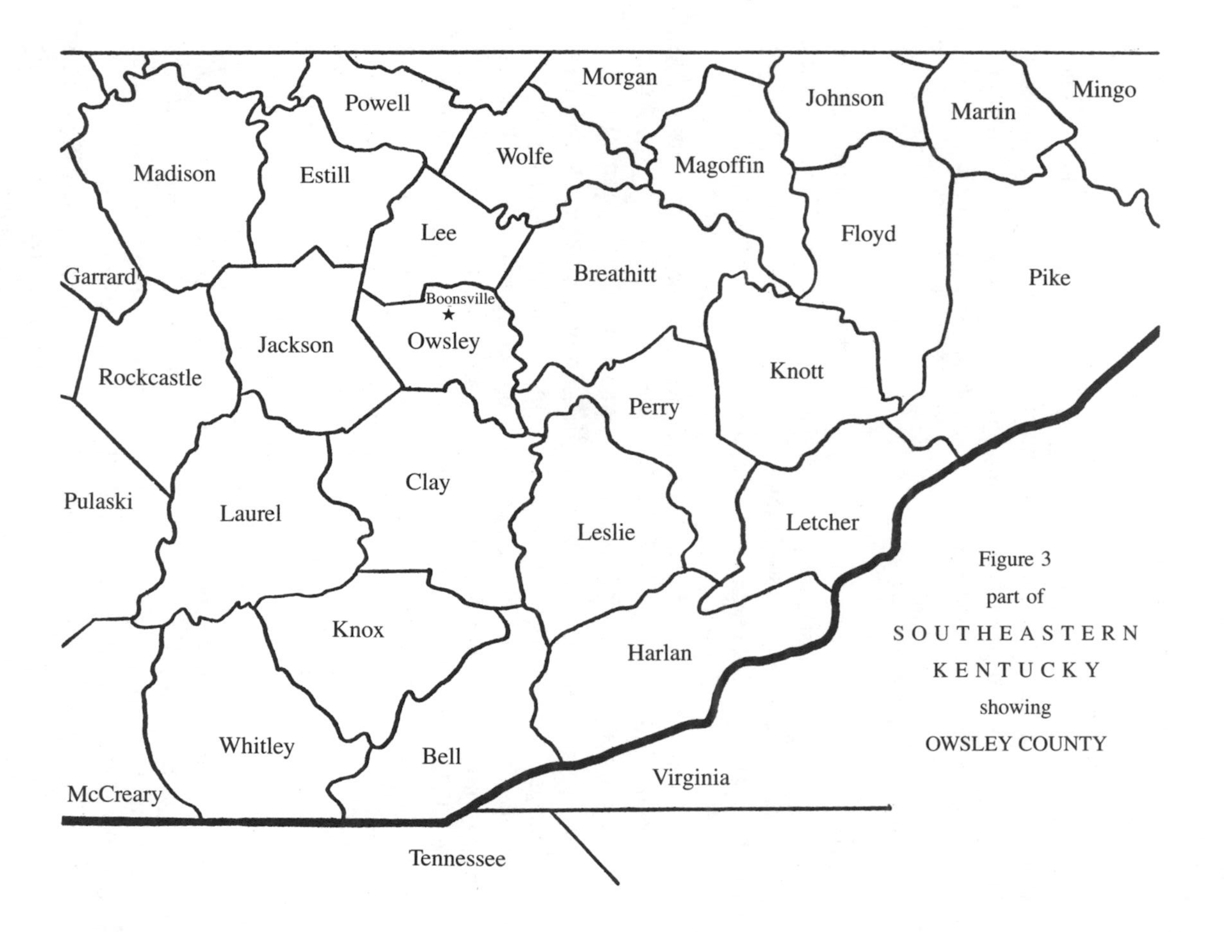

Figure 3
part of
S O U T H E A S T E R N
K E N T U C K Y
showing
OWSLEY COUNTY

rate them because they are kept in the same registers intermingled with other records of the parent county. There are a few situations where some records have been copied and the copies placed in the new county, but this is rare.

In our John Samuel Kelly problem discussed earlier, it would be important for the researcher to know that Owsley County, Kentucky, was formed in 1843 (just eight years before John Samuel's birth) from parts of Breathitt, Clay, and Estill counties. If the families (either the Kellys or the Gilberts) were in Kentucky before 1843 then records relating to them would likely be found in one of these parent counties. A map would show where Booneville is located and *might* suggest in which of the three parent counties it was located before Owsley County was created (see Figure 3).

Of course a map will not tell you the "genealogy" of a county, but it will help you picture the patterns of division and lend some understanding to the problems. "Genealogies" of counties can be found in several sources. Two are George B. Everton's *The Handy Book for Genealogists,* 7th rev. ed. (Logan, UT: Everton Publishers, 1981) and *Ancestry's Red Book,* ed. by Alice Eichholz (Salt Lake City: Ancestry Publishing Co., 1989). Both of these books contain information essential to American research. In addition to data on county origin, both also provide the name of the county seat for each county. Postal directories tell county seats, too, as do several other sources. This information is significant because records are usually housed at the county courthouse in the county seat. Another useful book, showing the evolution of American counties at ten-year intervals from 1790 to 1920, is William Thorndale and William Dollarhide's *Map Guide to the U.S. Federal Censuses, 1790-1920* (Baltimore: Genealogical Publishing Co., 1987).

Pedigree analysis is not complete without locality analysis, and the purpose of this discussion has been to illustrate the necessity for knowledge of the locality where your genealogical problem exists and to introduce a few basic tools which will provide some of that knowledge.

If you will make a good preliminary survey, analyze your pedigree carefully, and then learn all you can about the locality, you will have laid a good foundation on which to do productive and accurate research. Careful work should now produce some satisfying results.

VI. TRADITION, COMMON SENSE, AND HELPFUL CLUES

Do you know the religious affiliation of your ancestor? What was his position in the community? Was he prominent or obscure? Did he have land or money? These are also factors which would affect your approach to the research problem. If any or all of them can be determined it is that much more to your advantage. Maybe your ancestor was a Quaker or belonged to another religious group which refused to bear arms in time of war. This would certainly be significant. Maybe he was loyal to Britain during the Revolutionary War. You ought to know.

Family tradition also tells us much about family origins; however, such traditions, on the whole, are notoriously unreliable and no tradition should ever be accepted at face value. Dr. Ethel Williams says, "They have value but should be evaluated."[2] Surely we could add: They should be chewed and tasted but never swallowed. More often than not they contain threads (sometimes even cables) of truth that, when unraveled, provide useful clues and leads upon which to base research.

However, if family tradition says that you descend from the *Mayflower* Fullers, do not start in 1620 and try to trace the pedigree down to yourself. That could prove to be a very sad experience. Remember the rule we gave earlier: Work first with the information you already know—FROM THE KNOWN TO THE UNKNOWN. A genealogy, like a house, must be built from the foundation up and not from the roof down.

Common sense is practical judgment and ordinary good sense. Much of this is needed by the genealogist as he pursues his ancestors. It is best typified by looking at each problem individually, logically, and thoroughly and then proceeding one step at a time to do those things suggested by your analysis.

---

[2] Ethel W. Williams, *Know Your Ancestors* (Rutland, VT: Charles E. Tuttle Co., 1960), p. 23. By permission.

4

Evaluation of Evidence

In the first edition of this work I avoided including a chapter on evidence because I believed that the principles I considered critical to proper evaluation of "facts" were implicit in the discussion in other chapters. However, I have since changed my mind. I still believe that the desired message is implicit throughout the book, but I no longer believe that everyone who reads it gets the intended message.

The message of this chapter is not a new one, but it is an essential one if we wish to produce reliable genealogies. Since the first edition of *The Researcher's Guide* in 1973 the market has been flooded with genealogical "how-to" books—some good, some not so good. Some have survived (because of their merit, hopefully) while others have disappeared and have been long since forgotten (usually because of their lack of merit). One book that stands out in the former group is Noel C. Stevenson's excellent work, *Genealogical Evidence* (Laguna Hills, CA: Aegean Park Press, 1979). I highly recommend Mr. Stevenson's book to anyone who is serious about being a good genealogist. The author's primary interest in genealogy, and his main contributions to the field, have been in the area of evidence. That contribution is considerable.

I will not pretend, in the space available here, to give exhaustive coverage to the subject of genealogical evidence, but I feel that a few significant principles can be taught effectively enough to make a difference. Perhaps you can get some important insights into matters you have not previously considered.

I. GENERAL BACKGROUND

The best point to begin our discussion is with some basic definitions. Once this is taken care of we will be in a much better position to discuss principles and applications.

Evidence: Something that relates to or provides proof concerning a matter in question. We use evidence to prove facts. In law, evidence may be a weapon, an object, a photograph, a record, a document, the testimony of a witness, the opinion of an expert, the existence of a known fact, even circumstances. In genealogy we obtain evidence from these same sources, but if the fact or issue in question relates to remote ancestors beyond the recollection of living witnesses, then most evidence must come from records, documents, and circumstances.

Fact: The circumstance or event as it actually occurred. Fact relates to actuality, as distinguished from supposition or opinion.

Proof: The effect of evidence. We prove the facts with the evidence.

Presumption: An inference of a proposition or fact based on probable reasoning, in the absence of actual certainty. Though few things can be proved with absolute certainty, many things in both law and genealogy are presumed to be true and are accepted as fact in the absence of actual proof. For example, we always presume that a woman's husband is the father of her child—unless there is good evidence to the contrary. This is considered a rebuttable or disputable presumption. Presumptions have the same effect as evidence.

II. TYPES OF EVIDENCE

A. Primary and Secondary Evidence

Primary and secondary evidence are most easily discussed together. Primary evidence is sometimes also called "best evidence." It is the best evidence available to prove the fact in question, usually in an original document or record. The so-called "best evidence rule" says that the highest possible degree of proof must be produced. The rule is realistic in its approach to evidence inasmuch as it does not ask the impossible, but rather looks at each question individually, on its own merits and circumstances. For example, it does not require evidence from a birth certificate to establish genealogical fact if the birth in question took place before birth registration. If, however, the primary evidence is from a document or record, rather than from first-hand testimony of an eye-witness, then the person who created that record (or who provided the information for its creation) must have been an eye-witness to, or have had a special immediate interest in, the event recorded.

Secondary evidence is harder to define meaningfully. In essence it is all that evidence which is inferior in its origin to primary evidence (i.e., not the best evidence). That does not mean secondary evidence is always in error, but there is a greater chance of error. A copy of an original record provides secondary evidence, as does oral testimony of the record's contents. Published genealogies and family histories, as this definition should make clear, also provide secondary evidence.

Classifying evidence as either primary or secondary does not tell us anything about its accuracy or its ultimate value. This is especially true of secondary evidence. Thus it is always a good idea to ask the following questions:

1. How far removed from the original is it (when it is a copy)?
2. What was the reason for the creation of the source which contains this evidence?
3. Who was responsible for creating this secondary evidence and what interest did he have in its accuracy?

There are some situations where secondary evidence might be of even greater worth than primary evidence. These include those situations where the creator has carefully collected information from many sources (actually working with the primary evidence) into one place, such as a good family history. However, a useful example of what *can* happen, when those with little personal interest undertake projects to make the contents of certain records more available and usable for the genealogist, is found in chapter 14 where the will of George Blackburn, Sr., is discussed. A published abstract of that will omitted three of the Blackburn children named in the will and designated two other individuals mentioned in the will as children. (They were actually Negro slaves bequeathed by Mr. Blackburn to his wife Prudence.)

Another point I want to make relates to the distinction between records and evidence. For generations genealogical authors, myself included, have written about primary and secondary *sources*. But my feeling now is that it is much more feasible (and meaningful) to talk about evidence and to classify the evidence rather than the sources. Let me illustrate: Take a death certificate. It is confusing to classify it as a primary source, as is usually done, because this one document contains both primary and secondary evidence. It has primary evidence of the individual's death, but secondary evidence of other important things—such as his birth and parentage. In fact the "parentage" information could be either primary or secondary evidence, depending on the decedent's age and on the relationship between him and the informant. And the same principle applies to most sources of genealogical data.

As you can see, it is much easier, and much more reasonable, to classify evidence than to classify sources.

B. Direct and Circumstantial Evidence

Direct and circumstantial evidence are also best discussed together. Direct evidence is the very best evidence you can get. It is proof of facts resulting from the timely testimony of an eye-witness or a first-hand witness of an event. This evidence, standing alone, tends to show the existence of the fact in question without any further analysis of circumstances. It should also be stated, in this regard, that after the passage of time eye-witnesses can provide much better evidence of some things than they can of other things. Generally the evidence they provide on relationships is much better than the evidence they provide on dates.

Circumstantial (or indirect) evidence relates to the specific circumstances from which the existence of certain facts is inferred. It is significant and important evidence and is not less evidence than if it were direct. It is, however, important to recognize it for what it is and not accept these inferences as the ultimate answers without additional evidence to support them. A good example of this is found in the federal population censuses. Let's suppose that in the 1850 census you find the household of Walter Potelli. The record shows a woman about his age (who could be his wife), a group of seven children (of age to be his children), and an older woman named Potelli (of age to be his mother). Because no relationships are stated in the 1850 census you do not have direct evidence that these individuals are Mr. Potelli's wife, children, and widowed mother, but you can infer such from the circumstances. However, because of the absence of direct evidence of these connections, other records must be searched for the evidence necessary to verify their accuracy.

This is the area of greatest concern to seasoned genealogists as they consider the work of the inexperienced. Too often circumstantial evidence is given more weight than it deserves. Sometimes it looks so good—it is so convincing on its face, especially if it provides the answer you have been seeking—that it is accepted without question, as if it were direct evidence, and erroneous pedigree connections are innocently made. Say you are looking to identify the father of William Warner. In a county not far from where your William lived you discover the will of one Joseph Warner in which, among several children, he names his son William. Or what if you are researching John Randall and find the christening (baptism) in an early church record (in about the year of your John's birth) of a John Randall, giving the names of the parents? The locality is near where your John later lived. Consider these two examples carefully because it is with circumstantial evidence such as this that most of us get into trouble. We are too ready to accept the circumstance as absolute proof and call off the search.

As good as circumstantial evidence may be (or may appear to be) in some cases, it is not to be casually accepted as absolute proof of fact. Though there are times when you can establish proof through the use of circumstantial evidence, one piece of such evidence (or one isolated circumstance) will not do it. Often circumstantial evidence will lead you to other sources or suggest possibilities for further research. These should be pursued. Other sources of potential evidence must be searched. Then, after all available sources are exhausted, you can reconsider your circumstantial evidence in a new light, adding to it any other discovered circumstances. This may include the very fact that nothing else was found. Where circumstantial evidence is concerned, what you *don't* find in some cases is just as significant as what you do find.

C. Collateral Evidence

Collateral evidence is evidence found in a source that has nothing to do with that record itself and the purpose for which the record was created. Such evidence is usually unexpected but is always welcome. An example is Henry Hershey's will in which he mentioned his wife's father, Ralph Dayton, as the source of a particular tract of land in Henry's ownership. This is direct evidence of the identity of Mary Hershey's father and, if the will you have access to is the original, it also provides primary evidence of that relationship.

D. Hearsay Evidence

Hearsay evidence is widely misunderstood by genealogists (as well as others). It is evidence which is based not on the witness's personal knowledge but on information given to him by another source. I was once asked to review a manuscript for a genealogical text (which I do not believe was ever actually published) wherein I found the following erroneous statement near the beginning of a discussion on evidence:

> Care should be taken in genealogical research not to rely on hearsay evidence.

In actual fact, if I could not accept hearsay evidence, I could not be a genealogist. For every publication, record, and document which I would wish to rely upon contains only hearsay evidence. Only oral testimony from family members who *personally* know the specific genealogical facts is not hearsay.

The question is asked how the will prepared by John Hicks is hearsay evidence, or how the birth certificate of Sarah Bailey, prepared from information provided directly by her mother, can contain hearsay evidence. The answer is simply that John Hicks and Sarah Bailey's mother are not in fact the witnesses we are relying on. We are relying on the documents—documents which themselves know nothing except what somebody "told" them. They contain only second-hand information—hearsay evidence. A document cannot verify its own accuracy nor can it respond to questioning or cross-examination to verify that it is telling the truth.

The general rule of law (the "Hearsay Evidence Rule") is that hearsay evidence is not reliable because of the witness's lack of personal knowledge. It is thus considered inadmissible—unacceptable—for legal proof unless an exception to the rule applies.

In genealogy we pay little attention to the hearsay evidence rule. Hearsay evidence is essentially all we have—we must use it. The issue is not whether the data found constitutes hearsay evidence, but (1) whether it is relevant to the issue at hand and (2) how much weight it should be given (based on such factors as whether it is primary or secondary or whether it is direct or circumstantial, etc.).

Few of us will ever go to court to prove a pedigree and have to overcome the apparent obstacles of the hearsay evidence rule. But even if it were necessary to do so, we could come out quite satisfactorily. There are important exceptions to the hearsay evidence rule which the law has developed. It turns out, in fact, that in many instances the rule is observed in its exceptions more than in its applications. These exceptions have been developed in the law because, in the circumstances in which the evidence exists, (1) it is most likely to be accurate, (2) there is no other place to get the same information, and (3) it originated before the present question arose.

I shall not go into detail on these exceptions but will mention some that I feel are of most interest. As I observed earlier, I believe that the issue of whether or not the evidence presented is hearsay is of little import. It is more an academic question than a useful one.

Some notable exceptions to the hearsay evidence rule are:

1. *Ancient document exception:* Documents over thirty years old coming from a natural and reasonable official custody are considered reliable. Only the original copy of a deed or will can be an ancient document, not the recorded copy.

2. *Public records exception:* Records made by trusted public officials are considered trustworthy also. It is presumed that those who file or record documents about their personal and business affairs do not falsify them. There is also an issue here of necessity, as there may be no other source of this same evidence.

3. *Certified copy exception:* A document certified by proper authority to verify its origin and content is usually considered authentic and is thus admissible evidence, if other conditions are satisfied, especially in these days when most copies are made by the photoduplication process.

4. *Dying declarations exception:* Statements made by a person when on his deathbed are given special credence in many jurisdictions because of the belief that there is seldom reason to lie when one stands on the brink of eternity. In some states dying declarations are admissible only in criminal cases.

III. STANDARD OF PROOF

Many discussions of genealogical evidence become exercises in semantics and meanings of words. I hope that such is not the result of this discussion. Such is not the intent. After all, it is the final result which is the most important—not how we define certain words or describe certain principles. It doesn't really matter how the principles are described or defined if they are followed and the results are acceptable.

Many ask a question that is impossible to answer: "How many pieces of evidence are necessary to prove a genealogical fact?" That is a silly question because it does not take into account the differences either in the nature of problems, or in the nature and availability of evidence. If I have one piece of primary direct evidence on a particular issue, that may be sufficient, while if my direct evidence is secondary it must not be considered sufficient by itself. Corroborating evidence must be sought. Keep in mind also that secondary evidence from several sources (especially published sources), even though in agreement, may in many instances be inadequate for proof. You may have a case, such as we have all seen, where these published sources are merely relying on one another. Seek primary evidence to establish all proof.

There will be, however, as every genealogist knows, those situations where your case must be built on circumstantial evidence. In these cases it is important that your evidence be primarily primary.

You do the best you can, you search every available source, and you analyze your evidence with great care. You look for possible flaws in your theory and seek to remove all obstacles to your thesis. If those obstacles cannot be removed then you must consider their magnitude. Be realistic. Face the fact that insurmountable obstacles cannot be surmounted no matter how much you like your theory.

In the law there are two standards of proof used—one for civil cases and another for criminal cases. In civil cases the facts are proven based on "the preponderance of the evidence," while criminal cases require proof "beyond reasonable doubt." There is a great deal of difference between those two standards. You can have the preponderance of the evidence on your side but still have much room for doubt, even reasonable doubt. In fact the reasonable man might have serious doubts about the conclusion. We have already discussed the fact that *absolute proof* is not possible in genealogy or in many other things in life. But just how far should we go? Which of the two standards should be applied?

If a genealogical matter were being litigated in court, the civil standard (the preponderance of the evidence) would certainly apply. That is the same standard *required* of you in your research. But remember that the preponderance is based more on weight and power of evidence than on sheer numbers. You must consider the nature of the source. You can consider all relevant evidence, but you cannot give all of it the same weight.

If you wish to apply the higher standard (beyond reasonable doubt) that is your business. In many cases this will not be an issue. Your evidence, if you have done good research, will be clear and convincing. The time when you will have to deal with the issue is in the hard cases—after exhaustive research but less-than-satisfying results.

5

An Introduction to Research Tools: The Library

Just as carpenters have saws, hammers, and tri-squares and chemists have beakers, test tubes, and graduated cylinders, genealogists also have basic tools. One of the most important of these is the library (if I may be allowed to so classify a library).

I. THE PURPOSE OF LIBRARY RESEARCH

Most genealogical research is not done in libraries, and those who devote themselves solely to the printed word do not understand what genealogical research is all about.

Note first that there are libraries, such as the National Archives, the Family History Library of The Church of Jesus Christ of Latter-day Saints, and others, including archives and history departments (called also by other titles), and libraries of various states, that have vast collections of original records and microfilms of original records. (Such libraries might more appropriately be called archives.) If the record collections of the locality of your genealogical concern are available in a library or archival collection to which you have access, you are most fortunate and should feel no qualms about doing that type of library research. Often you will be able to do research there much more easily than you could in the actual record repository. However, if you cannot find the answers you need in these library and archival collections, a personal visit to the locality may still be necessary.

Though library collections have serious limitations, histories, periodical literature, etc., must be checked *before* you begin actual primary research and *also* as you proceed. Often much information and many important clues can be gleaned in a few well-spent hours in a public library. Consequently this chapter is devoted to libraries and their use.

There are several libraries in the United States with large, important collections of printed genealogical materials as well as archival materials. These include the following:

ALLEN COUNTY PUBLIC LIBRARY, 900 Webster St., Fort Wayne, IN 46802.

AMERICAN ANTIQUARIAN SOCIETY, 185 Salisbury St., Worcester, MA 01609.

BOSTON PUBLIC LIBRARY, Copley Square, Box 286, Boston, MA 02117.

CALIFORNIA STATE LIBRARY–SUTRO LIBRARY, 2495 Golden Gate Ave., San Francisco, CA 94118.

CONNECTICUT HISTORICAL SOCIETY, 1 Elizabeth St., Hartford, CT 06105.

CONNECTICUT STATE LIBRARY, 231 Capitol Ave., Hartford, CT 06115.

DALLAS PUBLIC LIBRARY, 1515 Young St., Dallas, TX 75201.

DAUGHTERS OF THE AMERICAN REVOLUTION LIBRARY —See National Society, Daughters of the American Revolution Library.

DENVER PUBLIC LIBRARY, Genealogy Division, 1357 Broadway, Denver, CO 80203.

DETROIT PUBLIC LIBRARY, BURTON HISTORICAL COLLECTION, 5201 Woodward Ave., Detroit, MI 48202.

THE FAMILY HISTORY LIBRARY (THE CHURCH OF JESUS CHRIST OF LATTER-DAY SAINTS), 35 N. West Temple St., Salt Lake City, UT 84150. (There are also branches throughout the country.) A useful guide to the library is *The Library: A Guide to the LDS Family History Library,* edited by Johni Cerny and Wendy Elliott (Salt Lake City: Ancestry Publishing, 1988).

FILSON CLUB LIBRARY, 118 W. Breckinridge St., Louisville, KY 40203.

GENEALOGICAL CENTER – LIBRARY FOR THE BLIND AND PHYSICALLY HANDICAPPED, Box 88534, Atlanta, GA 30356.

GENEALOGICAL SOCIETY OF NEW JERSEY, Manuscript Collections, Rutgers University Library, College Ave., New Brunswick, NJ 08903.

GENEALOGICAL SOCIETY OF PENNSYLVANIA, 1300 Locust St., Philadelphia, PA 19107.

GROSVENOR LIBRARY, 383 Franklin St., Buffalo, NY 14202.

HOLLAND SOCIETY OF NEW YORK, 122 E. 58th St., New York, NY 10022.

HOUSTON PUBLIC LIBRARY–CLAYTON LIBRARY, Center for Genealogical Research, 5300 Caroline St., Houston, TX 77004.

HUGUENOT HISTORICAL SOCIETY, 18 Broadhead Ave., Box 339, New Paltz, NY 12561.

INDIANA STATE LIBRARY, 140 N. Senate St., Indianapolis, IN 46204.

KANSAS CITY PUBLIC LIBRARY, 311 E. 12th St., Kansas City, MO 64106.

KANSAS STATE HISTORICAL SOCIETY, 120 W. 10th St., Topeka, KS 66612.

LIBRARY ASSOCIATION OF PORTLAND, 801 SW 10th Ave., Portland, OR 97205.

LIBRARY OF CONGRESS, Thomas Jefferson Bldg., Rm. 5010, Washington, DC 20540.

LONG ISLAND HISTORICAL SOCIETY, 128 Pierrepont St., Brooklyn, NY 11201.

LOS ANGELES PUBLIC LIBRARY, 630 W. 5th St., Los Angeles, CA 90017.

MARYLAND HISTORICAL SOCIETY, 201 W. Monument St., Baltimore, MD 21201.

MASSACHUSETTS HISTORICAL SOCIETY, 1154 Boylston St., Boston, MA 02215.

MID-CONTINENT PUBLIC LIBRARY, 15616 E. Hwy. 24, Independence, MO 64050.

MISSOURI HISTORICAL SOCIETY, Jefferson Memorial Bldg., Forest Park, St. Louis, MO 63112.

NATIONAL GENEALOGICAL SOCIETY LIBRARY, 4527 17th St. North, Arlington, VA 22207.

NATIONAL SOCIETY, DAUGHTERS OF THE AMERICAN REVOLUTION LIBRARY, 1776 D St., NW, Washington, DC 20006.

NEBRASKA STATE HISTORICAL SOCIETY, 1500 R St., Lincoln, NE 68508.

NEWBERRY LIBRARY, 60 W. Walton St., Chicago, IL 60610.

NEW ENGLAND HISTORIC GENEALOGICAL SOCIETY, 101 Newbury St., Boston, MA 02116.

NEW HAMPSHIRE HISTORICAL SOCIETY, 30 Park St., P.O. Box 478, Concord, NH 03301.

NEW HAMPSHIRE STATE LIBRARY, 20 Park St., Concord, NH 03301.

NEW JERSEY HISTORICAL SOCIETY, 230 Broadway, Newark, NJ 07104.

NEW ORLEANS PUBLIC LIBRARY, Louisiana Division, 219 Loyola Ave., New Orleans, LA 70140.

NEW YORK GENEALOGICAL AND BIOGRAPHICAL SOCIETY, 122-126 E. 58th St., New York, NY 10022.

NEW YORK PUBLIC LIBRARY, United States History, Local History, and Genealogy Division, 5th Ave. and 42nd St., Rm. 305 N, New York, NY 10018.

NEW YORK STATE LIBRARY, Manuscripts and Special Collection, Cultural Education Center, Empire State Plaza, Albany, NY 12230.

OHIO HISTORICAL SOCIETY, Archives and Library, I–71 and 17th Ave., Columbus, OH 43211.

ST. LOUIS PUBLIC LIBRARY, 1301 Olive St., St. Louis, MO 63103.

SAMFORD UNIVERSITY, HARWELL GOODWIN DAVIS LIBRARY, 800 Lakeshore Dr., Birmingham, AL 35229.

SEATTLE PUBLIC LIBRARY, 1000 Fourth Ave., Seattle, WA 98104.

SOUTH CAROLINA HISTORICAL SOCIETY, Fireproof Bldg., Meeting and Chalmers Sts., Charleston, SC 29401.

SOUTHERN CALIFORNIA AREA FAMILY HISTORY LIBRARY (LDS), 10741 Santa Monica Blvd., Los Angeles, CA 90025.

STATE HISTORICAL SOCIETY OF WISCONSIN, 816 State St., Madison, WI 53706.

U.S. LIBRARY OF CONGRESS—See Library of Congress.

VIRGINIA STATE HISTORICAL SOCIETY, 428 N. Blvd., Richmond, VA 23220.

VIRGINIA STATE LIBRARY, 12th and Capitol Sts., Richmond, VA 23219.

WESTERN RESERVE HISTORICAL SOCIETY, 10825 E. Blvd., Cleveland, OH 44106.

The above is not an exclusive list. There are many other libraries with significant genealogical collections, some of which you may already know about. Of special note are the libraries of some universities and colleges. If you are looking for libraries with genealogical collections you should be especially aware of the work by Brigitte T. Darnay (ed.), *Subject Directory of Special Libraries and Information Centers* (5 vols.), published by Gale Research Co., Detroit (most recent edition). Check the index to volume 4 *(Social Sciences and Humanities Libraries)* under "genealogy." There are libraries which have limited collections of a very specialized nature that may have just what you need.

II. THE CATALOG

When you use any library you must first understand how to use the library's catalog—the index to the library's holdings. Just like an index to a book, this catalog is in an alphabetical arrangement. It is much more than just a shelf-list; it is a complete index which should enable you to find the location of any book, manuscript, or serial within that library by looking in at least three different places in the catalog—under author, title, or subject and, in the case of many genealogical sources, locality. A shelf-list does not have this advantage; it is merely a list of holdings by only one category—title, locality, or perhaps author; but rarely, if ever, subject—unless the subject and title happen to be the same.

The catalog is usually on 3″ x 5″ index cards so that it can be up-dated as new books are added to the library collection. However, in recent years more and more libraries have installed automated (computer) catalog systems.

III. CLASSIFICATION

It is possible for a library to catalog its holdings because each book is classified and assigned a number. That number is written on the book (usually on the spine) and the books are shelved consecutively according to these numbers.

In the United States there are two popular classification systems in general use—the Library of Congress Classification System (L.C.) and the Dewey Decimal Classification System (named for Melvil Dewey, its originator). Some libraries, such as the LDS Family History Library in Salt Lake City, use a modification of one of these systems and there are, no doubt, some libraries that use other systems. However, it doesn't matter much which system is used if the catalog is complete.

Many libraries have "open stacks" where you are free to go into the areas where the books are shelved and serve yourself, but in those libraries where the stacks or shelves are closed to public access you must fill out a book order slip with the correct information and present it at the designated desk, counter, or window, and an attendant will bring you the book you want. You use the book and then return it to the desk. In some libraries many books can be checked out (or circulated, as they call it), but most libraries keep their genealogy collections for library use only.

A. Library of Congress

The Library of Congress Classification System, though not so widely used as the decimal system, is becoming more popular. It is sometimes considered the better of the two because it has more latitude for expansion as new areas of learning are developed, and it is especially helpful in classifying large collections in certain subject areas. It is considered a "must" in many large libraries, and even many smaller libraries that formerly used the Dewey system are switching.

L.C., like Dewey, classifies according to subject. The system utilizes the letters of the alphabet, but knowledge of this classification system will not substitute for your using the library catalog. Browsing is a very risky practice since significant materials will be classified throughout the system.

I will refrain from listing here the various areas of classification. Such a list would add nothing to your ability to use the library properly.

B. Dewey Classification

The Dewey Decimal Classification System is based on ten major subject divisions, each further subdivided through the use of arabic numbers and decimals. Every classification is based on a three-digit number; and, if the subject is a more minute subdivision of the main subject, additional digits are added after a decimal.

At the LDS Family History Library in Salt Lake City the use of the Dewey system has been modified so that research source materials are also assigned the class number for history (strictly by locality) instead of the usual subject heading. This modification facilitates browsing.

Knowledge of the classification numbers in either the L.C. or the Dewey systems should never excuse you from using the library catalog. Those numbers are used primarily to facilitate the shelving of the books and to aid library patrons in locating them *after* checking the catalog. Often important works would be completely overlooked if you checked only those shelves where you thought the material you wanted ought to be. Also, there may be such a divergence of material classified in one area that you could easily overlook important materials unless the specific catalog reference is used. Even though the books on one subject are not scattered throughout the library quite so much with the decimal system as they are inclined to be with L.C., there is still no excuse for not using the catalog.

C. Cutter Classification

Even when two books are written on exactly the same subject they do not have exactly the same classification numbers. This is because library materials are classified by author as well as by subject. This is accomplished by assigning a second number—a Cutter number—to each book. The system was named for its originator, Charles Cutter. In the call number as it is written on the book, the Cutter number is usually placed directly below the subject class number. In the Dewey system it consists of the first one or two letters (depending on the name) of the author's surname, followed by a number which is assigned to that particular author (determined by formula).[1]

When an author has written more than one book and it is classified under Dewey, the letter-number combination already described will be followed by another letter (sometimes more than one) which is the first letter(s) of the first word of the book title, not including the articles "the" and "a." For example, if the book title were "The Search for Your Ancestors" by John Doe, the Cutter number might be something like "D64s." The "D" stands for Doe, the "64" for the number assigned to this author, and the "s" for "Search," the first letter in the title of the book which is not an article. The article "the" is not considered. Some libraries follow this procedure just as a matter of course even when the author may have written only one book. This system allows for the shelving of books alphabetically by author within each subdivision of the subject and then alphabetically by title.

The L.C. system also frequently uses Cutter numbers to indicate things other than author, and often a book may have two Cutter numbers (seldom

[1] Note that the LDS Family History Library has also modified its use of Cutter numbers so that the number refers to record category rather than author. This works well because they have modified the Dewey number to indicate locality rather than subject.

more)—one for the author and one for something else (usually placed before the author number). For example, a Cutter number may indicate a locality, thus facilitating the arrangement of books in a certain class by their geographic area (if pertinent). Most often when there are double Cutter numbers the first is for the purpose of further subdividing the subject in some way.

It is not necessary here to discuss all of the intricacies of the system nor the many exceptions to the various rules. It is perhaps necessary only to stress again the importance of using the catalog. Your propensity to browse must be curbed sharply in any library where the L.C. classification system is used.

IV. THE NATIONAL ARCHIVES AND ITS BRANCHES

Though it is not a library in the sense described in this chapter, one of the most important repositories of records containing genealogical data is the National Archives in Washington, D.C. And because of the importance of the collections of that great institution, no book would be complete without some general introduction thereto.

There are many references throughout this work to records located in the National Archives. There are also extensive references and quotations from both the 1964 publication *Guide to Genealogical Records in the National Archives,* by Meredith B. Colket and Frank E. Bridgers (Washington, DC: The National Archives), and a more up-to-date guide published since, which is discussed in the next paragraph. Though the Colket and Bridgers work is outdated and no longer in print, those quotations from it which are included in this work are not redundant.

As noted, the 1964 *Guide* by Colket and Bridgers has been replaced by a more comprehensive and up-to-date work with a slightly different title: *Guide to Genealogical Research in the National Archives,* by the National Archives Trust Fund Board (Washington, DC, rev. ed., 1983). This newer guide is a "complete revision and enlargement, [and] . . . includes records not described in the earlier work, particularly records of genealogical value in the regional archives branches [recently called National Archives Field Branches, now known collectively as the Regional Archives System]. It also contains illustrations and photographs, citations to microfilm publications, and expanded and clarified descriptions of the records" (from the "Preface," p. xiii).

No serious genealogist will be without easy access to this important work. There are twenty chapters in four sections. I shall not take the space here to list the chapters, but the four sections are: (A) "Population and Immigration;" (B) "Military Records;" (C) "Records Relating to Particular Groups," including, among others, American Indians and black Americans; and (D) "Other Useful Records."

As you will learn, there are certain record inadequacies that face researchers at the National Archives. The "Introduction" to the *Guide* (1983) lists three important limitations:

> First, NARS [acronym of the former official title, National Archives and Records Service] keeps only federal records. Birth, marriage, and death—the milestones of life and the backbone of genealogy—have never been the first concern of the federal government, and the best evidence of these will be found, if it exists, in family, local, and state records.
>
> Second, the colonial period of American history is not documented in the National Archives; very few records predate the Revolutionary War. Most of the records . . . pertain to the nineteenth century, a time when the government did not touch the lives of most Americans to the extent it does today . . .
>
> The third limitation arises from the nature of archives: records are arranged to reflect their original purposes, usually just as they were kept by the agency that created them. They cannot be arranged in ways that might seem most helpful to genealogists, partly because family history is only one of many present-day uses of archives."[2]

As to the nature, extent, and arrangement of the records, I quote again from the *Guide:*

> The records of genealogical value . . . were created to satisfy legal requirements or to meet the administrative or other needs of the originating federal agencies. Every document in the National Archives has been assigned to a numbered *record group* on the basis of its origin. A record group commonly consists of the records of a bureau (e.g., Records of the U.S. Customs Service, Record Group 36), but some record groups may include the records of an entire agency, and a few include records collected from several sources. Record groups are sometimes very large, measured in cubic feet. There are more than 450 record groups for the 1,369,000 cubic feet of records in the National Archives. The holdings of the archives include billions of pages; millions of photographs, motion pictures, aerial photographs, and charts; thousands of sound recordings, video

[2] *Guide to Genealogical Research in the National Archives,* rev. ed. (Washington, DC: The National Archives, 1983), p. 3.

recordings, architectural and engineering drawings; and more than 1,000 machine-readable tapes.[3]

The record groups are divided into *series,* smaller bodies of records which are "filed together because they relate to the same subject, function, or activity, or because of some other relationship arising from their origin and use." [4]

The "Introduction" states further:

> The National Archives . . . publishes several different kinds of finding aids to assist researchers. . . . Some record groups are described in inventories or preliminary inventories (PI). Such finding aids contain a history of the organization and functions of the agency that created the records and descriptions of the series in the record group. . . .
>
> Other types of finding aids include guides, reference information papers, and special lists relating to particular subjects. . . .
>
> All finding aids are listed in General Information Leaflet 3, *Select List of Publications of the National Archives and Records Service* (Washington: National Archives and Records Service, 1982).[5]

Those finding aids of value to the genealogist are also listed in the *Guide,* being cited in the appropriate sections of the text.

Many important records in the National Archives have been microfilmed to provide better access for users. In addition to their use at the archives itself, many important filmed records are also available in other repositories, including the eleven National Archives Field Branches. As will be noted in more detail at various places later in this work, some National Archives microfilm publications (especially military and census records) are now available on interlibrary loan or direct through the National Archives Microfilm Rental Program.

The eleven National Archives Field Branches are:

1. **Boston:** 380 Trapelo Road, Waltham, MA 01254 (serving Connecticut, Maine, Massachusetts, New Hampshire, Rhode Island, and Vermont).

---

[3] *Ibid.,* p. 4.

[4] *Ibid.,* p. 4.

[5] *Ibid.,* pp. 4-5.

2. **New York:** Building 22-MOT Bayonne, Bayonne, NJ 07002 (serving New Jersey, New York, Puerto Rico, and the Virgin Islands).

3. **Philadelphia:** 9th and Market Streets, Philadelphia, PA 19144 (serving Delaware, Maryland, Pennsylvania, Virginia, and West Virginia).

4. **Atlanta:** 1557 St. Joseph Avenue, East Point, GA 30344 (serving Alabama, Florida, Georgia, Kentucky, Mississippi, North Carolina, South Carolina, and Tennessee).

5. **Chicago:** 7358 South Pulaski Road, Chicago, IL 60629 (serving Illinois, Indiana, Michigan, Minnesota, Ohio, and Wisconsin).

6. **Kansas City:** 2312 East Bannister Road, Kansas City, MO 64131 (serving Iowa, Kansas, Missouri, and Nebraska).

7. **Fort Worth:** 501 West Felix Street (P.O. Box 6216), Fort Worth, TX 76115 (serving Arkansas, Louisiana, New Mexico, Oklahoma, and Texas).

8. **Denver:** Building 48, Denver Federal Center, Denver, CO 80225 (serving Colorado, Montana, North Dakota, South Dakota, Utah, and Wyoming).

9. **Los Angeles:** 24000 Avila Road, Laguna Niguel, CA 92677 (serving Arizona; California counties of Imperial, Inyo, Kern, Los Angeles, Orange, Riverside, San Bernardino, San Diego, San Luis Obispo, Santa Barbara, and Ventura; and Clark County, Nevada).

10. **San Francisco:** 1000 Commodore Drive, San Bruno, CA 94066 (serving American Samoa, California [except counties served by the Los Angeles branch], Hawaii, and Nevada [except Clark County]).

11. **Seattle:** 6125 Sand Point Way NE, Seattle, WA 98115 (serving Alaska, Idaho, Oregon, and Washington).

A brief booklet entitled *Regional Branches of the National Archives* (General Information Leaflet 22) gives more details.

You might note that although I refer to the regional branches of the National Archives throughout this book as "Field Branches," their official name was changed in 1988 and they are now known collectively as the Regional Archives System. The individual name changes are as follows:

Boston Branch—National Archives/New England Region
New York Branch—National Archives/Northeast Region
Philadelphia Branch—National Archives/Mid-Atlantic Region
Atlanta Branch—National Archives/Southeast Region
Chicago Branch—National Archives/Great Lakes Region

Kansas City Branch—National Archives/Central Plains Region
Fort Worth Branch—National Archives/Southwest Region
Denver Branch—National Archives/Rocky Mountain Region
Los Angeles Branch—National Archives/Pacific Southwest Region
San Francisco Branch—National Archives/Pacific Sierra Region
Seattle Branch—National Archives/Pacific Northwest Region

The National Archives Field Branches are unable to provide research assistance, but they do have many records of importance to the genealogist, including many microfilm publications. The National Archives does provide some research assistance and can, for a fee, provide some photocopies of records by mail when exact identifying information is provided. It cannot, however, do complete census searches in response to mail requests. Of some interest to those who will use the National Archives Field Branches is the book by Loretto Dennis Szucs and Sandra Hargreaves Luebking, *The Archives: A Guide to the National Archives Field Branches* (Salt Lake City: Ancestry Publishing, 1988).

V. CONCLUSION

This chapter should contain sufficient information to enable you to use the library catalog to its fullest advantage in locating the materials you seek within almost any library. However, I should stress one more thing: If you have any difficulties, do not hesitate to ask the librarian for help. He is there to help those who need it, so you need not be afraid of showing your ignorance. Also, if you are interested in U.S. Government Documents such as maps, gazetteers, etc., and the library you are using happens to be a repository for Government Documents, remember that they present additional problems in locating. The librarian can save you a lot of time and effort with these if given a chance.

Let's look now at some of the materials found in most libraries that can help make your research easier.

6

An Introduction to Research Tools: Reference Materials

The real purpose behind the use of reference sources is to help locate various records and/or to facilitate use of those records. There are many problems that the beginning genealogist struggles to solve which could be solved in a few minutes by using some common and readily available reference source. One of the main differences, then, between a good researcher and a poor one is his knowledge of, and his ability to correctly use, critical reference works. For our purposes these reference works can be divided into three categories:

I. Guides to locality data.
II. Guides to non-original sources.
III. Guides to original sources.

I. GUIDES TO LOCALITY DATA

Chapter 3 discussed the value of maps, gazetteers, and postal directories as reference tools, but there are also other useful sources that can help us find out about places. There are five types of sources which give data on American localities. They are:

A. Atlases and maps.
B. Gazetteers.
C. Postal directories.
D. Specialized locality sources.
E. Local histories.

The following bibliography lists examples of works available in the first four categories. Some of the sources already mentioned in chapter 3 are repeated here. This is not intended to be a complete bibliography of reference tools on American localities; there are many other sources of great value, especially those which relate to specific geographical areas.

A. Atlases and Maps

Adams, James Truslow (ed.). *Atlas of American History*. New York: Charles Scribner's Sons, 1943.

Andriot, John L. (comp. and ed.). *Township Atlas of the United States*. McLean, VA: Androit Associates, 1979.

Bartholemew, John (ed.). *The Times Atlas of the World*. 5 vols. Mid-Century ed. London: The Times Publishing Co., Ltd., 1955-59.

Daly, John and Allen Weinberg. *Genealogy of Philadelphia County Subdivisions*. 2nd ed. Philadelphia: City Department of Records, 1966.

Everton, George B., Jr. *Genealogical Atlas of the United States of America*. Logan, UT: Everton Publishers, 1966.

Fox, Dixon Ryan (ed.). *Harper's Atlas of American History*. New York: Harper and Brothers, 1920.

Kagan, Hilde Heun (ed.). *The American Heritage Pictorial Atlas of United States History*. New York: American Heritage Publishing Co., 1966.

The Official State Atlas of Kansas. (1887). Topeka, KS: Walsworth Publishing Co., 1982 (reprint).

Rand-McNally Commercial Atlas and Marketing Guide. New York: Rand-McNally and Co. (annual).

Rand-McNally's Pioneer Atlas of the American West. New York: Rand-McNally and Co., 1956.

Thorndale, William and William Dollarhide. *Map Guide to the U.S. Federal Censuses, 1790-1920*. Baltimore: Genealogical Publishing Co., 1987.

One of the best collections of American period maps is located in the Library of Congress in Washington, D.C. This collection includes a vast, though incomplete, inventory of land-ownership maps for U.S. counties during the 1800s. They show who owned what land in the various counties when the maps were prepared. The Library of Congress has published an excellent inventory of these maps which is available from the Superintendent of Documents, U.S. Government Printing Office, Washington, DC 20402.[1]

B. Gazetteers

The Columbia-Lippincott Gazetteer of the World. Ed. by Leon E. Seltzer. Morningside Heights, NY: Columbia University Press by arrangement with J. B. Lippincott Co., 1952.

DeColange, L. *The National Gazetteer: A Geographical Dictionary of the United States.* London: Hamilton, Adams & Co., 1884.

French, John H. *Gazetteer of the State of New York.* (1860). Port Washington, NY: Ira J. Friedman, Inc., 1969 (reprint). (This work was also reprinted in 1980 by Heart of Lakes Publishing, Interlaken, NY.)

Gordon, Thomas F. *A Gazetteer of the State of Pennsylvania.* Philadelphia, 1832.

Hayward, John. *A Gazetteer of the United States of America.* Hartford, CT: Tiffany and Company, 1853.

Nason, Elias. *A Gazetteer of the State of Massachusetts.* 2 vols. Boston, 1874.

Pease, John C. and J. M. Niles. *Gazetteer of the States of Connecticut and Rhode Island.* Hartford, CT, 1819.

Powell, William Stevens. *The North Carolina Gazetteer.* Chapel Hill, NC: University of North Carolina Press, 1968.

Sherwood, Adiel. *A Gazetteer of the State of Georgia . . .* (1827, 1939). Athens, GA: University of Georgia Press, 1969 (reprint).

United States, Geological Survey. *The National Gazetteer of the United States of America—[individual states].* Washington, DC: U.S. Government Printing Office for U.S. Geological Survey, 1982——.

Webster's Geographical Dictionary. Springfield, MA: G. and C. Merriam Co., 1957.

C. Postal Directories

Bullinger's Postal and Shippers Guide for the United States and Canada. Westwood, NJ: Bullinger's Guides, Inc. (annually since 1897).

United States, Postal Service. *United States Directory of Post Offices.* Washington, DC: U.S. Postal Service (annual).

---

[1] Richard W. Stephenson (comp.), *Land Ownership Maps—A Checklist of 19th Century U.S. County Maps in the Library of Congress* (Washington: The Library of Congress, 1967).

D. Specialized Locality Sources

Ancestry's Red Book. Ed. by Alice Eichholz. Salt Lake City: Ancestry Publishing, 1989

Chadbourne, Ava H. *Maine Place Names and the Peopling of Its Towns.* Bangor, ME: Furbush-Roberts Printing Co., 1955.

City Directories of the United States, 1860-1901: Guide to the Microfilm Collection. Woodbridge, CT: Research Publications, 1983.

Corbitt, David Leroy. *The Formation of North Carolina Counties, 1663-1943*. Raleigh, NC: State Department of Archives and History, 1950.

Espenshade, Abraham Howry. *Pennsylvania Place Names.* (1925). Baltimore: Genealogical Publishing Co., 1970 (reprint).

Everton, George B., Sr. *The Handy Book for Genealogists*. 7th rev. ed. Logan, UT: Everton Publishers, 1981.

Field, Thomas P. *A Guide to Kentucky Place Names* . . . Kentucky Genealogical Survey. Ser. X, Special Publ. 5. Lexington, KY: College of Arts and Sciences, University of Kentucky, 1961.

Filby, P. William (comp.). *A Bibliography of American County Histories*. Baltimore: Genealogical Publishing Co., 1985.

Gannett, Henry. *Boundaries of the United States and of the Several States and Territories*. 3rd ed. Washington, DC, 1906.

Hummel, Ray O., Jr. *A List of Places Included in Nineteenth Century Virginia Directories*. Virginia State Library Publ. 11. Richmond: Virginia State Library, 1960.

Kaminkow, Marion J. (ed.). *United States Local Histories in the Library of Congress: A Bibliography*. 5 vols. Baltimore: Magna Carta Book Co., 1975.

Kane, Joseph Nathan. *The American Counties.* New York: The Scarecrow Press, 1960.

Kirkham, E. Kay. *The Counties of the United States and Their Genealogical Value*. 3rd ed. Salt Lake City: Deseret Book Co., 1965.

Shelley, Michael H. (comp.). *Ward Maps of United States Cities: A Selective Checklist of Pre-1900 Maps in the Library of Congress.* Washington, DC: Library of Congress, 1975.

These are some of the sources which you will find essential to your research as you seek to learn about the localities of your problems. I will not list local histories in bibliographic form here because of their great multiplicity. However, you should be aware of their existence (on town, county, and regional levels) because they contain invaluable information about places which is seldom found in other sources. Chapter 9 discusses them in more detail.

II. GUIDES TO NON-ORIGINAL SOURCES

Also useful as reference tools are those sources which help us locate and use non-original source materials pertinent to our genealogical problems. More is said about the value and use of these in later chapters, but they can be conveniently divided into four major categories:

A. Directories.
   1. of newspapers and periodicals.
   2. of libraries and societies.
   3. telephone and city directories.

B. Bibliographies.

C. Indexes.
   1. to periodicals.
   2. to published genealogies and pedigrees.
   3. to multiple source types.

D. Texts and specialized reference sources.

Let's look now at a few reference tools in each of these categories.

A. Directories

1. Of newspapers and periodicals.

Ayer Directory of Newspapers and Periodicals. Philadelphia: N. W. Ayer and Sons, Inc. (annual).

Conrad, John (ed.). *Directory of Family One-name Periodicals.* Munroe Falls, OH: Summit Publications (biennial, odd years).

————. *Directory of Genealogical Periodicals.* Munroe Falls, OH: Summit Publications (biennial, odd years).

National Directory of Weekly Newspapers. New York: American Newspaper Representatives (annual).

2. Of libraries and societies.

American Library Directory. New York: R. R. Bowker Co. (annual).

Darnay, Brigitte T. (ed.). *Subject Directory of Special Libraries and Information Centers.* 5 vols. Detroit: Gale Research Co. (regular intervals since 1974). Of special note is volume 4, *Social Sciences and Humanities Libraries.*

Directory—Historical Societies and Agencies in the United States and Canada. Nashville: American Association of State and Local History (biennial).

International Library Directory. Ed. by A. P. Wales. London: The A. P. Wales Organization (biennial).

Meyer, Mary Keysor (comp.). *Directory of Genealogical Societies in the U.S.A. and Canada*. Mt. Airy, MD: the compiler (biennial, even years).

3. **Telephone and city directories.**

These give addresses of living persons, including possible relatives, so that they can be readily contacted. Any large telephone office or large library will have a good collection of them. Chambers of commerce can also help you locate directories. Old phone books and city directories can help you find the specific place where your ancestor lived and thus add a special insight to your family history in applicable situations.

B. Bibliographies

The American Genealogist, Being a Catalogue of Family Histories Published in America From 1771 to Date. 5th ed. Albany, NY: Joel Munsell's Sons, 1900. Reprinted Detroit: Gale Research Co., 1967; Baltimore: Genealogical Publishing Co., 1967.

Brigham, Clarence Saunders. *History and Bibliography of American Newspapers, 1690-1820*. 2 vols. (incl. additions and corrections). Hamden, CT: Shoe String Press, 1962.

Brown, Stuart E., Jr. (comp.). *Virginia Genealogies—A Trial List of Printed Books and Pamphlets*. Berryville, VA: Virginia Book Co., 1967.

Cappon, Lester Jesse. *American Genealogical Periodicals: A Bibliography with a Chronological Finding-list*. 2nd printing with additions. New York: New York Public Library, 1964.

Catalogue of American Genealogies in the Library of the Long Island Historical Society. Ed. by Emma Toedteberg (1935). Baltimore: Genealogical Publishing Co., 1969 (reprint).

Daughters of the American Revolution. *Library Catalogue. Volume One: Family Histories and Genealogies*. Washington, DC: D.A.R., 1982; suppl. 1983.

Filby, P. William (comp.). *American & British Genealogy & Heraldry: A Selected List of Books*. 3rd ed. Boston: New England Historic Genealogical Society, 1983; *1982-1985 Supplement* (1987).

————. *Passenger and Immigration Lists Bibliography 1538-1900.* 2nd ed. Detroit: Gale Research Co., 1988.

Genealogy and Local History: An Archival and Bibliographic Guide. 2nd ed. rev. Evanston, IL: The Associates, 1959.

Gregory, Winifred (ed.). *American Newspapers, 1821-1936: A Union List of Files Available in the United States and Canada.* New York: H. W. Wilson Co., 1937.

Hamer, Philip May (ed.). *Guide to Archives and Manuscripts in the United States.* New Haven, CT: Yale University Press, 1961.

Jarboe, Betty M. *Obituaries: A Guide to Sources.* Boston: G. K. Hall & Co., 1982.

Johnson, Arta F. (ed.). *Bibliography and Source Materials for German-American Research. Vol. 1: U.S.A.* Columbus, OH: the editor, 1982.

Kaminkow, Marion J. (ed.). *Genealogies in the Library of Congress: A Bibliography.* 2 vols. Baltimore: Magna Carta Book Co., 1972. Suppl. for 1972-76 publ. 1977; 2nd Suppl., 1976-86, publ. 1986.

————. *A Complement to Genealogies in the Library of Congress: A Bibliography.* Baltimore: Magna Carta Book Co., 1981.

Lancour, Harold (comp.). *A Bibliography of Ship Passenger Lists, 1538-1825.* 3rd ed. Rev. and enl. by Richard J. Wolfe. New York: New York Public Library, 1963.

Meynen, Emil (comp. and ed.). *Bibliography on German Settlements in Colonial North America.* Detroit: Gale Research Co., 1966 (reprint).

Milden, James Wallace. *The Family in Past Time: A Guide to the Literature.* New York: Garland Publishing, Inc., 1977.

Schreiner-Yantis, Netti (comp.). *Genealogical & Local History Books in Print.* Springfield, VA: Genealogical Books in Print (periodically updated, latest ed. [4th ed.] 1985).

Schweitzer, George K. *Genealogical Source Handbook: A Compendium of Genealogical Sources with Precise Instructions for Obtaining Information From Them.* Knoxville, TN: the author, 1980.

Slocum, Robert B. *Biographical Dictionaries and Related Works.* Detroit: Gale Research Co., 1967, with suppls. in 1972 and 1978.

Sperry, Kip. *A Survey of American Genealogical Periodicals and Periodical Indexes.* Vol. 3 in Gale Genealogy and Local History Series. Detroit: Gale Research Co., 1978.

Virkus, Frederick A. *The Handbook of American Genealogy.* 4 vols. Chicago: Institute of Genealogy, 1932-43.

United States, Library of Congress. *American and English Genealogies in the Library of Congress.* 2nd ed., 1919. Baltimore: Genealogical Publishing Co., 1967 (reprint).

————. *American and English Genealogies in the Library of Congress* (microcards). Comp. by Dr. and Mrs. C. K. Jones. Middletown, CT: Godfrey Memorial Library, 1954.

————. *The National Union Catalog of Manuscript Collections, 1959-61; Based on Reports From American Repositories of Manuscripts.* Ann Arbor, MI: J. W. Edwards Publisher, 1962.

————. *The National Union Catalog of Manuscript Collections, 1962; Based on Reports from American Repositories of Manuscripts.* Hamden, CT: Shoe String Press, 1964.

————. *The National Union Catalog of Manuscript Collections, 1959-62: Index.* Hamden, CT: Shoe String Press, 1964.

————. *The National Union Catalog of Manuscript Collections, 1963——* (with indexes). Washington, DC: Library of Congress (various dates).

C. Indexes

1. To periodicals.

Genealogical Periodical Annual Index. Ed. by Ellen Stanley Rogers, George Ely Russell *et al.* Bladensburg and Bowie, MD: Heritage Books (annually, since 1962).

Jacobus, Donald Lines. *Index to Genealogical Periodicals.* 3 vols. Baltimore: Genealogical Publishing Co., 1963-65 (reprint). (The three volumes were reprinted in one volume by this publisher in 1978.)

New England Historical and Genealogical Register: Consolidated Index, Vols. 1-50. 4 vols. Boston: New England Historic Genealogical Society (1906-11). Baltimore: Genealogical Publishing Co., 1972 (reprint).

————. *Index (Abridged) to Volumes 51 Through 112 (1897-1958).* Comp. by Margaret W. Parsons. Privately published, 1959.

Periodical Subject Index (PERSI). Fort Wayne, IN: Allen County Public Library, 1986—. (A retrospective index covering 1847-1985 is planned for release.)

Sperry, Kip. *Index to Genealogical Periodical Literature, 1960-1977.* Vol. 9 in Gale Genealogy and Local History Series. Detroit: Gale Research Co., 1979.

Swem, Earl G. *Virginia Historical Index.* 2 vols. in 4. Gloucester, MA: Peter Smith, 1965 (reprint).

Topical Index to the National Genealogical Society Quarterly, Volumes 1-50, 1912-1962. Comp. by Carleton E. Fisher. Washington, DC: National Genealogical Society, 1964.

2. **To published genealogies and pedigrees.**

Crowther, George Rodney, III. *Surname Index to Sixty-five Volumes of Colonial and Revolutionary Pedigrees.* Washington, DC: National Genealogical Society, 1964.

McAuslan, William A. (comp.). *Mayflower Index.* 2 vols. Rev. by Lewis E. Neff. Boston: General Society of Mayflower Descendants, 1960.

3. **To multiple source types.**

Biography Index; A Cumulative Index to Biographical Material in Books and Magazines, 1946—. New York: H. W. Wilson Co., 1964.

Filby, P. William and Mary K. Meyer (eds.). *Passenger and Immigration Lists Index.* 3 vols. Detroit: Gale Research Co., 1981 and annual suppls. (A four-volume cumulation for 1982-85 was published in 1985.)

The Greenlaw Index of the New England Historic Genealogical Society. 2 vols. Comp. under the direction of W. P. Greenlaw. Boston: New England Historic Genealogical Society, 1979.

Herbert, Miranda C. and Barbara McNeil (eds.). *Biography and Genealogy Master Index.* 2nd ed. 8 vols. Detroit: Gale Research Co., 1980. (A *1981-85 Cumulation,* in five volumes, was published in 1985.)

Index to American Genealogies and to Genealogical Material Contained in All Works As Town Histories, County Histories, Local Histories, Historical Society Publications, Biographies, Historical Periodicals, and Kindred Works. 5th ed., 1900, and Suppl. of 1908. Comp. and originally publ. by Joel Munsell's Sons. Baltimore: Genealogical Publishing Co., 1967 (reprint).

LeBeau, Dennis and Gary C. Tarbert (eds.). *Biographical Dictionaries Master Index.* 3 vols. Detroit: Gale Research Co., 1975.

Newberry Library (Chicago). *The Genealogical Index.* 4 vols. Boston: G. K. Hall, 1960.

Passano, Eleanor Phillips. *An Index of the Source Records of Maryland—Genealogical, Geographical, Historical.* (1940). Baltimore: Genealogical Publishing Co., 1967 (reprint).

Rider, Fremont (ed.). *American Genealogical Index.* 48 vols. Middletown, CT: Godfrey Memorial Library, 1942-52.

————. *American Genealogical-Biographical Index.* Middletown, CT: Godfrey Memorial Library, 1952—. (In 1986 this monumental work had progressed into the R's and to more than 140 volumes.)

Stewart, Robert Armistead. *Index to Printed Virginia Genealogies; Including Key and Bibliography.* (1930). Baltimore: Genealogical Publishing Co., 1965 (reprint).

United States, Library of Congress. *The Library of Congress Index to Biographies in State and Local Histories.* Baltimore: Magna Carta Book Co., 1979, microfilm publ.

D. Texts and Specialized Reference Sources

I give you no list here, but rather refer you to the list of texts and specialized reference sources under "Guides to Original Sources." Virtually every source listed in that section, as well as many others, gives extensive guidance to the use of both original and non-original sources of genealogical evidence. Those who seek background on a particular ethnic group to assist in research and understanding should refer to the *Harvard Encyclopedia of Ethnic Groups,* ed. by Stephan Thernstrom (Cambridge, MA: The Belknap Press of Harvard University Press, 1980). It contains useful information on virtually every ethnic group and minority from Acadians to Zoroastrians.

III. GUIDES TO ORIGINAL SOURCES

In the area of original source materials there are also some good guides to assist you in finding and using the records you need. These fall into five main categories, and some of them duplicate those listed as guides to non-original sources in the previous section because they are guides to both. My note under "Texts and Specialized Reference Sources" in that section has already suggested as much. The five categories are:

A. Government publications.
   1. National.
   2. State and regional.

B. Non-government local research aids.

C. Texts and specialized reference sources.

D. Special publications.

E. Indexes.

Let's look at some of these.

A. Government Publications

1. National.

Davidson, Katherine H. and Charlotte M. Ashby (comps.). *Preliminary Inventory of the Records of the Bureau of the Census.* Washington, DC: The National Archives, 1964.

Military Service Records in the National Archives of the United States (General Information Leaflet 7). Rev. ed. Washington, DC: The National Archives and Records Administration, 1985.

United States, Department of Health and Human Services. *Where to Write for Vital Records.* Hyattsville, MD, 1987. (Available from the Superintendent of Documents, Government Printing Office, Washington, DC; DHHS Publ. No. (PHS) 87-1142. It supersedes four *Where to Write . . .* pamphlets.)

United States, National Archives and Records Service. *Guide to Genealogical Research in the National Archives.* Rev. ed. Washington, DC: The National Archives, 1983. (This volume supersedes the 1964 publication, *Guide to Genealogical Records in the National Archives,* by Meredith B. Colket, Jr., and Frank E. Bridgers. Quotations from Colket and Bridgers are included in this work and are still up-to-date and relevant.)

2. State and regional.

Georgia: "Genealogical Research in Georgia." Atlanta: Georgia Department of Archives and History, 1966.

New Jersey: *Genealogical Research: A Guide to Source Materials in the Archives and History Bureau of the New Jersey State Library and Other State Agencies.* Trenton, NJ: New Jersey State Library, 1966.

South Carolina: "Ancestor Hunting in South Carolina." Columbia, SC: South Carolina Department of Archives and History, 1969.

Utah: *Guide to Official Records of Genealogical Value in the State of Utah.* Salt Lake City: Department of Finance, Utah State Archives and Records Service, 1980.

B. Non-Government Local Research Aids

Arizona and Nevada: Spiros, Joyce V. Hawley. *Genealogical Guide to Arizona and Nevada.* Gallup, NM: Verlene Publishing, 1983.

California: Sanders, Patricia. *Searching in California: A Reference Guide to Public and Private Records.* Costa Mesa, CA: ISC Publications, 1982.

Connecticut: Kemp, Thomas Jay. *Connecticut Researcher's Handbook.* Vol. 12 in Gale Genealogy and Local History Series. Detroit: Gale Research Co., 1981.

Connecticut: Sperry, Kip. *Connecticut Sources for Family Historians and Genealogists.* Logan, UT: Everton Publishers, 1980.

Florida: Robie, Diane C. *Searching in Florida: A Reference Guide to Public and Private Records.* Costa Mesa, CA: ISC Publications, 1982.

Georgia: Davis, Robert Scott, Jr. (comp.). *Research in Georgia.* Easley, SC: Southern Historical Press, 1981.

Georgia: Dorsey, James E. *Georgia Genealogy and Local History.* Spartanburg, SC: The Reprint Co., 1983.

Illinois: Beckstead, Gayle and Mary Lou Kozub. *Searching in Illinois: A Reference Guide to Public and Private Records.* Costa Mesa, CA: ISC Publications, 1984.

Illinois (Chicago): Meyer, Virginia M. *et al.* (comps.). *Genealogical Sources in Chicago, Illinois,* 1835-1900. Chicago: Chicago Genealogical Society, 1982.

Illinois (Chicago): O'Hara, Margaret. *Finding Your Chicago Ancestor.* N.p.: the author, 1981.

Indiana: Carty, Mickey Dimon. *Searching in Indiana: A Reference Guide to Public and Private Records.* Costa Mesa, CA: ISC Publications, 1985.

Indiana: Newhard, Malinda E. E. *A Guide to Genealogical Records in Indiana.* Harland, IN: the author, 1979.

Kentucky: Hathaway, Beverly West. *Kentucky Genealogical Research Sources.* West Jordan, UT: Allstates Research Co., 1974.

Michigan: McGinnis, Carol. *Michigan Genealogy: Sources & Resources.* Baltimore: Genealogical Publishing Co., 1987.

Missouri: Parkin, Robert E. *Parkin's Guide to Tracing Your Family Tree in Missouri.* St. Louis: Genealogical Research and Publications, 1979.

Nevada: See Arizona.

New England: Crandall, Ralph (ed.). *Genealogical Research in New England.* Baltimore: Genealogical Publishing Co., 1984.

New England: Sperry, Kip. *New England Genealogical Research: A Guide to Sources.* Bowie, MD: Heritage Books, 1988.

New Hampshire: Towle, Laird C. and Ann N. Brown. *New Hampshire Genealogical Research Guide*. 2nd ed. Bowie, MD: Heritage Books, 1983.

New Mexico: Spiros, Joyce V. Hawley. *Handy Genealogical Guide to New Mexico*. Gallup, NM: Verlene Publishing, 1981.

North Carolina: Draughon, Wallace R. and William P. Johnson. *North Carolina Genealogical Reference—A Research Guide*. New ed. Durham, NC: The authors, 1966.

North Carolina: Leary, Helen F. M. and Maurice Stirewalt (eds.). *North Carolina Research: Genealogy and Local History*. Raleigh, NC: The North Carolina Genealogical Society, 1980.

Ohio: Bell, Carol Willsey. *Ohio Guide to Genealogical Sources*. Baltimore: Genealogical Publishing Co., 1988.

Oklahoma: Blessings, Patrick J. *Oklahoma: Records and Archives*. Tulsa: University of Tulsa, 1978.

Pennsylvania: *The Pennsylvania Line: A Research Guide to Pennsylvania Genealogy and Local History*. 3rd ed. Laughlintown, PA: Southwest Pennsylvania Genealogical Services, 1983.

South Carolina: Côté, Richard N. *Local and Family History in South Carolina: A Bibliography*. Easley, SC: Southern Historical Press, 1981.

South Carolina: Holcomb, Brent H. *A Brief Guide to South Carolina Genealogical Research and Records*. Columbia, SC: the author, c. 1979.

South Carolina: Schweitzer, George K. *South Carolina Genealogical Research*. Knoxville, TN: the author, 1985.

Tennessee: Fulcher, Richard C. *Guide to County Records and Genealogical Resources in Tennessee*. Baltimore: Genealogical Publishing Co., 1987.

Tennessee: Schweitzer, George K. *Tennessee Genealogical Research*. Knoxville, TN: the author, 1981.

Texas: Kennedy, Imogene and Leon Kennedy. *Genealogical Records in Texas*. Baltimore: Genealogical Publishing Co., 1987.

Virginia: "Genealogical Research at the Virginia State Library." An information pamphlet. Richmond: The Virginia State Library, no date.

West Virginia: McGinnis, Carol. *West Virginia Genealogy: Sources & Resources*. Baltimore: Genealogical Publishing Co., 1988.

West Virginia: Stinson, Helen S. *A Handbook for Genealogical Research in West Virginia*. South Charleston, WV: Kanawha Valley Genealogical Society, 1981.

Wyoming: Spiros, Joyce V. Hawley. *Genealogical Guide to Wyoming.* Gallup, NM: Verlene Publishing, 1982.

C. Texts and Specialized Reference Sources

Babbel, June Andrew (comp.). *Lest We Forget: A Guide to Genealogical Research in the Nation's Capital.* 4th ed. rev. Annandale, VA: Annandale and Oakton Virginia Stakes of The Church of Jesus Christ of Latter-day Saints, 1976.

Beard, Timothy Field and Denise Demong. *How to Find Your Family Roots.* New York: McGraw-Hill, 1977.

Eakle, Arlene and Johni Cerny (eds.). *The Source: A Guidebook of American Genealogy.* Salt Lake City: Ancestry Publishing Co., 1984.

Johnson, Arta F. (ed.). *Bibliography and Source Materials for German-American Research. Vol. 1: U.S.A.* Columbus, OH: the editor, 1982.

Kurzweil, Arthur. *From Generation to Generation: How to Trace Your Jewish Genealogy and Family History.* New York: William Morrow, 1980.

Lichtman, Allan J. *Your Family History: How to Use Oral History, Personal Family Archives, and Public Documents to Discover Your Heritage.* New York: Vintage Books, 1978.

Rottenberg, Dan. *Finding Our Fathers.* New York: Random House, 1977.

Rubincam, Milton (ed.). *Genealogical Research: Methods and Sources.* Rev. ed. Vol. 1. Washington, DC: The American Society of Genealogists, 1980.

Smith, Jessie Carney (ed.). *Ethnic Genealogy: A Research Guide.* Westport, CT: Greenwood Press, 1983.

Stevenson, Noel C. *Genealogical Evidence: A Guide to the Standard of Proof Relating to Pedigrees, Ancestry, Heirship and Family History.* Laguna Hills, CA: Aegean Park Press, 1979.

Stratton, Eugene A. *Applied Genealogy.* Salt Lake City: Ancestry Publishing Co., 1988.

Stryker-Rodda, Kenn (ed.). *Genealogical Research: Methods and Sources.* Rev. ed. Vol. 2. Washington, DC: The American Society of Genealogists, 1983.

Wright, Norman E. *Preserving Your American Heritage.* Provo, UT: Brigham Young University Press, 1980. (Originally published in 1974 with the title *Building an American Pedigree.*)

D. Special Publications

Neagles, James C. and Lila Lee Neagles. *Locating Your Immigrant Ancestor: A Guide to Naturalization Records.* Logan, UT: Everton Publishers, 1975.

Research papers of the Family History Department of The Church of Jesus Christ of Latter-day Saints, including "Records of Genealogical Value for the United States" and "County Formations and Minor Civil Divisions of the State of New York," both published in 1978. (Available from the Family History Library, 35 N. West Temple Street, Salt Lake City, UT 84150, for a reasonable fee. A complete list of available papers is available without charge from the library. Enclose a stamped, addressed envelope.)

Scherer, D. J. (ed.). *Birth, Marriage, Divorce, Death—On the Record.* Boca Raton, FL: Reymont Associates, 1977 (update planned).

Stemmons, John D. (ed.). *The Cemetery Record Compendium: Comprising a Directory of Cemetery Records and Where They May Be Located.* Logan, UT: Everton Publishers, 1979.

————. *United States Census Compendium: A Directory of Census Records, Tax Lists, Poll Lists, Petitions, Directories, Etc., Which Can Be Used As a Census.* Logan, UT: Everton Publishers, 1973.

———— and Diane Stemmons (comps.). *Vital Records Compendium: A Directory of Local Records and Where They May Be Located.* Salt Lake City: the compilers, 1979.

United States, Library of Congress. *The National Union Catalog of Manuscript Collections.* (See listings under "Guides to Non-original Sources: Bibliographies"— section II B of this chapter.

United States, National Historical Publications and Records Commission. *Directory of Archives and Manuscript Repositories in the United States.* Washington, DC: The Commission, 1978. (Available from the Publications Sales Branch (NEPS), National Archives and Records Service, Washington, DC 20408.)

World Conference on Records, seminar papers. Salt Lake City: The Family History Department of The Church of Jesus Christ of Latter-day Saints, 1969 and 1980. (In 1969 the primary emphasis was on records preservation and genealogy. In 1980 the emphasis was on family history.)

E. Indexes

It has not been my intention to be exhaustive in any of the bibliographic listings in this chapter. However, that is more particularly true in this section than in any other. What you see here are a few items listed as examples only.

Bowman, Alan P. *Index to the 1850 Census of the State of California.* Baltimore: Genealogical Publishing Co., 1972.

Houston, Martha Lou (comp.). *Indexes to the County Wills of South Carolina* (1939). Baltimore: Genealogical Publishing Co., 1964 (reprint).

Index of Revolutionary War Pension Applications. Rev. ed. Comp. by Frank Johnson Metcalf, Max Ellsworth Hoyt, Agatha Bouson Hoyt, Sadye Giller, William H. Dumont, and Louise Dumont. Washington, DC: National Genealogical Society, 1976.

Johnson, William Perry. *Index to North Carolina Wills, 1663-1900.* 3 vols. Raleigh, NC: the author, 1963-68.

McLane, Mrs. Bobby Jones and Inez H. Cline. *An Index to the Fifth United States Census of Arkansas.* Fort Worth: Arrow Printing Co., 1963.

Magruder, James Mosby. *Index of Maryland Colonial Wills, 1634-1777, in the Hall of Records, Annapolis, Maryland.* 3 vols. (1933). Baltimore: Genealogical Publishing Co., 1967 (reprinted in one volume).

New Jersey Index to Wills. 3 vols. (1901). Baltimore: Genealogical Publishing Co., 1969 (reprint).

This list, of course, could be endless. Those few works listed here were arbitrarily chosen only for the purpose of illustration.

IV. CONCLUSION

Any source to which you refer for information can properly be called a reference tool. And since genealogy is so closely related to so many different subjects, these are myriad. You will use reference sources dealing with handwriting (calligraphy, chirography, and orthography), with history and geography, with biography, with bibliography itself, with law, with origins of words and names (etymology), with dates and calendar problems (chronology), with heraldry and, of course, with genealogical methodology. Some bibliographies dealing with these various subjects and with others are found in two older works: Norman E. Wright and David H. Pratt's *Genealogical Research Essentials* (Salt Lake City: Bookcraft, 1967) and Ethel W. Williams's *Know Your Ancestors* (Rutland, VT: Charles E. Tuttle Co., 1960).

Let me also make note of the excellent bibliographical sections in more recent works: Timothy Field Beard and Denise Demong's *How to Find Your Family Roots* (New York: McGraw-Hill, 1977); Arlene Eakle and

Johni Cerny's *The Source: A Guidebook of American Genealogy* (Salt Lake City: Ancestry Publishing Co., 1984); and Norman E. Wright's *Preserving Your American Heritage* (Provo, UT: Brigham Young University Press, 1980).

The most accurate and complete genealogical bibliography that exists is P. William Filby's *American & British Genealogy & Heraldry,* 3rd ed. (Boston: New England Historic Genealogical Society, 1983); with *1982-1985 Supplement* (1987). It is an essential source for every genealogist. Watch for future editions.

Another major category of reference sources—those which actually provide secondary genealogical evidence—is discussed in some detail in chapter 9. This category includes various kinds of biographical works—dictionaries, directories, lists, registers, etc.—which, though reference sources in the usual sense, do not fit the definition of genealogical reference tools found in the first paragraph of this chapter. They do not usually provide direct assistance in locating records nor do they facilitate our use of records. However, they can provide some useful data—some better than others—depending on the origin of their information.

If you can familiarize yourself with the reference tools listed in this chapter and become aware of the existence of other similar works, and know their value and use, you will have acquired one of the major requisites of the competent genealogist.

7

Organizing and Evaluating Research Findings

I. PURPOSE OF RECORD KEEPING

The basic purpose of genealogical research is to gather the details about possible ancestors from the various records created as a result of the events of their lives, to compile those details into meaningful form, and to evaluate them to determine genealogical connections. You cannot do this properly without keeping a record of your research.

In chapter 1 we discussed the importance of organizing your research findings into complete families on some type of family group form. In this chapter we will attempt to show how this can be done effectively—how the information found can be taken through every step, from original source to final family group form, without something being lost along the way—and still allow you to easily retrace your steps at any time.

Too many of us learn neither the purposes nor the processes of keeping good research notes until too late. And some, much to the consternation of those who wish to check their work or to take over where they have left off, never learn. Others are well convinced of the value of good notes but are never quite willing to make the effort required to keep them. They feel that other people should keep good notes but that they are personally justified with something less—that their situation is somehow different.

There is probably no other area where your ability as a genealogist will be judged more critically than in the notes and records you keep during your research and the documentation of your completed records. Regardless of how thorough you are in research and how good you are at correct analyses, if your notes are poorly kept and your records poorly documented the work you do will never be appreciated by any competent genealogist who views it or reviews it. He will probably repeat the same searches because he is not sure what you have done. Then, if he finds your work was good, he will condemn you the more for not keeping a good record. It will cost time and money to duplicate your work if you do only half the job.

When a student writes a library research paper he carefully notes each source checked and what he finds therein. As the paper appears in its final form it is well documented; the information from the various sources is carefully footnoted. Genealogical research should require no less than this. Data in the records you compile are acceptable only if their origin is known. Undocumented "facts" have no weight of authority.

In the most practical terms the purpose of good research notes is two-fold:

1. To keep you, the researcher, constantly and completely in touch with the problem in all its aspects. You must know exactly what has been done, why it was done, when it was done, and the results of it. You should also be able to tell readily what still needs to be done and why—all this after any length of time.

2. To aid those who follow you so that they can check quickly for completeness and accuracy and/or continue research where you left off. No one should ever have to re-do your work because he is not sure whether you did it correctly.

Not only must you keep and organize your research notes, together with the records and documents which you accumulate, but those notes must indicate the purpose of every search. If you do not know why you are searching a particular source perhaps you should re-evaluate. No search should be made without a purpose. Your goals should be outlined carefully and each step should be directed toward reaching those goals.

The purpose of each search should be recorded somewhere in your notes so that anyone looking at those notes will know why you did what you did. Your purposes must be clearly indicated.

Just as it is true with the preliminary survey, so it is true with good research notes and thorough documentation: *Everything possible must be done to prevent needless duplication of effort.* There is too much to be done and the expense is too great for us to spend time needlessly repeating ourselves and each other.

II. METHOD

There are many different systems of keeping research notes in current use, which is just as well, because what pleases me may be distasteful to you. We each have our own ideas about what is best. Any system is good which gets the job done with a proper balance between completeness and simplicity. An imbalance in either direction is serious. It is as bad to spend too much time and effort on over-elaborate notes as it is to be too brief. No system is good if the note keeping takes more time than the research.

Some persons become so involved with keeping notes and setting up filing systems that they forget their real purpose—the proper determination of family relationships. Make your notes as complete as necessary, but no more complete than your purpose demands. If shortcuts will work use them, but be careful that your shortcuts are not actually booby traps.

Here are two simple housekeeping rules that will help prevent your notes from taking too much time and will ensure the quality of those notes for years to come:

1. Keep all of your notes on the same size paper, preferably on standard 8½" x 11" paper. Steer clear of paper scraps, backs of old envelopes, and odd size papers of all kinds. Actual size is not important if everything is essentially the same size and can be conveniently filed. There are two things you can't control—the size of papers on which other people write letters and the size of photocopied documents—so it is important that you control what you can.

   Also, use a good quality paper so that it will not crumble or become brittle after a few years. Newsprint paper is unsatisfactory. A good acid-free bond paper will usually serve best, and paper of not too light a weight will be easier to maintain in good condition.

2. Do not recopy your notes. Make your first copy good enough to be your final copy. Some persons diligently type all of their longhand notes so they will look nice when completed. These do look nice but they are hardly worth the time they take. If you are careful your original notes will be completely adequate.

   You do not have time to recopy your notes; it is only busy work. And every time something is copied there is a chance of error. Surely we make enough errors without this.

   When you take notes you should use a good pencil. (Many libraries and record depositories request that pens not be used.) Your pencil should be sharp (take more than one with you) and the lead should not be so hard that the writing is too light to read. Neither should it be so soft that the writing smears. (A #3 or HB lead is usually best.) When possible use ink; it will make a better record. Lined paper may also help you make a better record.

III. RESEARCH CALENDARS AND NOTES

Though style and form may vary from one person to another, each set of research notes will have certain things in common with every other set. One thing that each system requires is a list of the sources searched. For our discussion we shall call this a RESEARCH CALENDAR, though different persons call it by different names (such as calendar of search, source book, research organizer, research index, research log, etc.).

This "calendar" is more than a list of sources, but the amount and arrangement of other information varies from person to person. It must, however, be a list of properly identified sources. Too many researchers make lists of library call numbers (or microfilm numbers) or of book titles only. Proper note keeping requires more than this.

The list of sources you make on your calendar may include library classification numbers if you wish, but they are the least significant items you will record there because they are often different from one library to another. If you list them it will be for your own convenience only. If you record all other essential data about the source, it can be located, if available, in any library. If you include classification numbers you might somehow indicate the library from which each number comes. Initials of the library could suffice, such as "FHL" for the LDS Family History Library, "LC" for the Library of Congress, "DAR" for the National Society, Daughters of the American Revolution library, "NBL" for the Newberry Library of Chicago, "NYP" for the New York Public Library, and "PC" for the Podunk City Library. Develop your own designations based on the libraries to which you have access. Unless you have access to extensive microfilm collections of original records, such as those at a state archives or at the LDS Family History Library, most of your sources will not have classification numbers anyway. They will be the original records found in their original repositories.

Source descriptions on your calendar are best written in footnote form if the source is a book or a periodical. Such a description should include:

1. Author, compiler, or editor.
2. Title and edition.
3. Place of publication.
4. Publisher.
5. Date of publication.
6. Page number(s) where applicable.

Sidney Orbeck – 138 N. Westside Ave, Haysbury, Ga.

Surname(s) of interest: Black, Creer, / Jackson /

Locality of interest: Henrico Co, Va.

Library Call No.	Description of source	Purpose of search	Comments	Date of search	Ms. page
7560 (GS)	Colonial records	Blacks and Creers	Found mention of	13 Sep 1967	1
(film)	pt 1 - Bks 1-2 (1677-1693)	were in Henrico Co. before	William & Samuel		
	pt 2 - Bks 3-5 (1677-1739)	1700 til abt 1795. Looking	Black, Hyrum Creer.		
	pt 3 - Index, Bks 1-5	for any mention.			
7559 (GS)	Court records (deeds, wills, etc.)	Same	found a few —	13 Sep 1967	1-9
(film)	pt 1 - 1677-1697 (indexed)		(see notes)	↓	
	pt 2 - 1697-1714 (")			↓	
	pt 3 - 1714-1737 (")			↓	
	pt 4 - 1748-1750 (")			↓	
	pt 5 - 1750 - 1767 (")			↓	
	pt 6 - 1767 - 1787 (")			↓	
VaHc (GS)	Marriage bonds, 1780-1861	Same	found nothing	19 Sep 1967	Nil
	(typescript)				
VaHca (GS)	Beverly Fleet (comp.), Virginia	Same	found entry relating	19 Sep 1967	9
(mimeo)	Colonial Abstracts, Vol 21, Henrico		to Samuel Black (see		
	County, Southside (Richmond, 1956)		notes)		
———	Records of Creer Family in	For possible Creer	Some good information,	2 Oct 1967	See Creer
	poss. of Mrs. Nellie C.	connection.	but doesn't fit in		corresp.,
	Reynolds, 321 Western Drive		yet. (corresp.)		Extr. 5
(more)	Chaffee, N.D., 58014				

FIGURE 1—A RESEARCH CALENDAR

If your source is an original record you will modify this but must always list sufficient information to identify the source completely, leaving no question as to what or where it is. If you use personal interviews, unpublished manuscripts, or family records in private hands, names and addresses are essential. (See Figure 1.)

Perfect footnote form (if there really is any) is not the most important thing, but your form should be consistent from entry to entry and sufficiently detailed that anyone, even those who know nothing about genealogy, can use your references and readily find the sources listed. Any good book on English fundamentals or on the use of libraries will give you guidance on procedure and form in footnotes. Many genealogists use Richard S. Lackey's *Cite Your Sources* (New Orleans: Polyanthos, Inc., 1980) as their guide.

Another item which many persons include on a research calendar is a brief notation of the significant findings within each source. This is optional but it does have some merit.

Often the sources on the calendar will not be searched in the order listed since there is really no one correct order of search. The order in which sources are used depends entirely upon the problem at hand and your analysis thereof. This is one reason why the date each source is used should be noted on the research calendar; it will help you recall your order of search at a future date and may suggest the need for repeating a particular search.

Every source searched should be listed on your research calendar without regard to whether anything was found. For *this* record the important thing is that a source was searched. If negative sources (those in which nothing is found) were not listed, after the passage of time you would probably find yourself searching them again, and again finding nothing. Or those who follow you may search those sources again. The purpose here is to prevent duplication of research effort.

In addition to being a list of sources searched and the dates of those searches, there is another purpose which a research calendar must serve: It must provide a direct reference to the notes of your research and serve as their table of contents.

As you search a particular record, say an 1860 census, and make notes of its contents on pages five through eight of your manuscript notes, you will indicate pages "5-8" on your research calendar adjacent to the entry for that census. Next to those sources which prove negative, a notation to that effect should also be made. "Negative," or "nothing," or "nil," or anything else which conveys the idea, may be used. (See again Figure 1.)

The question always arises as to whether the research calendar should be limited in some way. Should you make a separate calendar for each objective, for a group of related objectives, for each locality, or should you make just one all-inclusive calendar for everything? You will likely be happier with a system which provides for some kind of limitation. I use a system (and this is quite common) wherein a separate research calendar is kept for each pertinent locality (usually for each county, but this varies with the situation). As I do research in the records of that locality, the pages of my manuscript notes, including documents and photocopies—numbered consecutively—are filed in sequence behind the proper calendar. These research calendars thus serve as tables of contents for the notes of all research in the separate localities. When research in a given locality is completed I have, filed together, my research calendar (as a table of contents) and all notes from the research done there. The research calendar and manuscript notes are kept together in either a manila file folder or a looseleaf binder. Avoid using a spiral or solid-bound notebook for keeping notes. They lack versatility—they cannot be added to conveniently and they cannot be spread out during analysis. They are too limiting.

As you keep notes make sure that your name, your address, and the date are written on every page. This helps prevent possible loss. A typical heading might read something like this:

> DATE: 22 June 1972
> RESEARCHER: Sidney Orbeck, 138 N. Westside Ave., Haysbury, GA.
> LOCALITY OF SEARCH: Henrico County, Virginia
> SURNAME(S) OF INTEREST: Black, Creer, Jackson

One research calendar (it can be more than one page) is all you need if your research is limited to one locality. But as your research expands into other localities, your filing system must also expand. To avoid confusion as your files grow, you will find it helpful to use some type of systematic arrangement. Some researchers use a system wherein they arrange localities alphabetically, but I prefer to alphabetize surnames. This could create a problem, but it is not serious.

The problem is this: if you arrange surnames alphabetically and you have three surnames (as Black, Creer and Jackson) on one calendar, or in one locality, obviously the calendar can be filed in only one place. What about the two surnames under which it cannot be filed? One answer is to make three identical research calendars for the locality—one for each of the surnames. However, this leads to lots of extra work. The best alternative is cross-referencing.

File your main calendar under the surname Black, then begin a calendar for the surname Creer (and another for Jackson) in Henrico County with the usual heading; and then, instead of re-listing the sources already recorded on the first calendar, write in large letters across the front of the new calendar: "SEE BLACK, HENRICO COUNTY, VA." Next, file these cross-referenced calendars in their correct alphabetical sequence and the problem is solved.

Another filing problem arises when research on one surname is performed in several localities. Some researchers prefer to arrange localities alphabetically under the surname. This works well, but I prefer to arrange the localities under each surname in the sequential order in which the surnames are identified with those localities, from the most recent to the most remote (so that I am generally adding on new notes at the end rather than in the middle). For example, if you do research on the Black family beginning in Maricopa County, Arizona, and trace the family from there to Gunnison County, Colorado, then to Osage County, Missouri; Pulaski County, Kentucky; Henrico County, Virginia; and James City County, Virginia, your research notes under that surname would be arranged in just that order, with a separate calendar and a separate set of notes for each of those places. This system follows the family as it is followed on the pedigree chart. In your file, at the beginning of each surname, keep a copy of the appropriate portion of the pedigree.

In your manuscript notes you should always make an adequate reference to the specific source and its location. This will be more detailed in most cases than the reference on the research calendar because you must indicate volume and page numbers for specific entries. For example, on the calendar you indicate only that the source was the 1860 census of the locality, while in your manuscript notes you give the exact references for its specific entries where your surnames were found in that census.

Your notes should also indicate the purpose for which each search is made. Some persons make this notation in their manuscript files while others have a special column for it on their research calendar as illustrated in Figure 1. Your notation may be something quite specific like: "For the death of Charles Black." Or it may be quite general like: "For all families of above surnames in the county." The latter example may be typical for most census searches, and similar references are often appropriate for other records too. However, be cautious about becoming too general; you must tell why a specific source is being searched. In the case of the census search you might state: "Family in area, 1836 to abt. 1875." Do not be afraid to give as much detail as necessary.

It is also essential that your notes include pertinent descriptions of the source materials. If the record was not legible, if the microfilm was unreadable because of focus or light, or if there is another problem which would affect your research, some type of notation should be made. Missing pages (or parts thereof), smeared ink, non-intelligible shorthands, etc., are all significant problems. If you say nothing, those who follow must assume that the record was perfect.

All research may not be in a specific locality. Often, because of incomplete information and lack of success with the various "finding tools," you may find yourself making an "area search" in an effort to locate an ancestor. For example, you may make a search of the deed indexes in every county in southwest Virginia for a surname or for a specific individual when more definite clues of origin have not been forthcoming. You may find that a search of the 1830 census of every county in Alabama is necessary for the same reason. Such searches are not to be made impulsively because they can be very time-consuming, but there are times when they cannot be avoided if further progress is to be made. Usually these searches can be centralized around what appears to be the most probable location and then expanded as necessary until the required information or clue is found.

Your research calendar, in such a case, must be able to meet your demands. Usually all you need to do is write, under the "Locality" heading, something like: "Deeds, southwest Virginia counties." The surname heading is filled in as usual, then as the deed indexes of each county are checked, the proper listings can be made on both the calendar and the manuscript notes. The same procedure would be followed with the Alabama census search or any other area search.

If you are making a preliminary survey or searching in various compiled genealogical sources such as family histories, periodicals, or biographical works, it is entirely appropriate to write "preliminary survey" or "compiled sources" in the "Locality" blank on your calendar.

These calendars and their related notes fit into your filing system quite readily. An area search can easily be filed chronologically in relation to the various localities, and the survey-type search can usually be filed at the beginning of the file of the appropriate surname, before the locality notes. This can all be worked out to your liking.

IV. EVALUATING YOUR NOTES

Once you have exhausted all records pertinent to your problems in a given locality you are ready to evaluate your findings in depth. Since you have been collecting every bit of information on every person of the surname of your interest, and not just on those who are your primary objectives, you will often accumulate a great bulk of material and some quite extensive notes. You will have already made some superficial analyses, but to get all pertinent data from those notes will require very careful study. For the novice this can be especially difficult, and even those with more experience must use great care.

One way to find out just how much information you have is to take the information in your notes, item by item, and record it on family group forms. (These should be inexpensive work sheet forms.) Most data must be recorded on more than one work sheet since they pertain to the person both as a child and as a parent, or the data from one source may refer to several persons. Always make sure that each item of information is recorded in *every possible place*. This is essential to a proper evaluation. There are other ways to tabulate data, but this method is especially useful for the beginner.

Some researchers use family group forms as a note-keeping device, taking notes directly from the records onto the family group forms. I strongly oppose such a system for two reasons:

1. Complete information on record content is not as easily recorded. The group sheet does not reflect exactly what the record said—only your interpretation of it.

2. The nature of such a system tends to produce an excessive bulk of work sheets, many of which are completely without meaning or value in the final analysis.

As you work, keep your work sheets in alphabetical sequence (by name of husband) so that you can refer back to any sheet instantly. When there are two husbands with the same name (and this will happen often when you are dealing with all persons of a single surname in a given locality), arrange them chronologically, eldest first insofar as this can be determined.

Some researchers make a separate work sheet from the information found in every document or record entry. I also oppose this because, just as with taking notes directly onto the work sheets, it is too bulky and many of the sheets have absolutely no value. Every time you can make a *positive* identification, record the information on the same family group record with all other information on that same family. However, be cautious about two things:

1. Before putting data on a sheet with other data, be *absolutely certain* that they refer to the same family. Just because you *think* the family is the same is not enough. If there is any doubt, make two work sheets. The work sheets can be combined later if you conclusively establish that they are the same family.

2. Footnote the information from each source carefully so that there will be no doubt as to which information came from which source. This makes it easy to re-check your work should you desire. It also makes it easier to solve discrepancies in record information. If you know the sources of conflicting evidence you can usually decide which is more likely to be correct, especially when considered in light of other evidence. One means of identifying the sources of your evidence is to record the information from each source with a different color of ink and/or pencil on your work sheet and then make your footnote or source reference note in the same color. Another, and perhaps better, system is to merely use numbers.

After your research findings have been thus tabulated you can easily see what has been accomplished on your primary objectives and what still remains to be done. In all of this your chief concern should be for the families of your lineal ancestors, with collateral families having significance primarily because they are essential to complete research.

Insofar as possible, complete and finished records should be compiled from the data tabulated, and then, depending on which sheets still indicate a need for work, research continues. The process is continual just as explained in chapter 1. You must analyze the problem, decide on a proper course of action, search the appropriate records and record the results, tabulate your findings, evaluate again, and then start over.

Remember in all your research that without proper analysis there is no sense of direction and it is easy to get lost in mechanics. There must be a good reason for everything you do.

V. ONE MORE STEP

To help you keep your sense of direction and make meaningful evaluations, one more thing is necessary: periodic research reports. If you were doing professional research you would make reports to your patrons as a matter of course. You would carefully explain the nature of your searches, the results therefrom, and the reasons you have done what you have. Too often, however, those who work on their own genealogy do not give themselves the same courtesy.

Every qualified professional can vouch for the value of the reports he writes to his patrons. (He always keeps a copy.) After a break of several months, or even years, in working on a problem, he can know, by merely reading the report, exactly where the research stands and what steps are necessary to continue. Hence the professional strives to make his reports meaningful to both himself and his clients. When you work on your own pedigree, do you not deserve the same advantage?

As research progresses, you will find it worthwhile to sit down periodically and outline in some detail what you have done and what the results have been since your last such report. A report should be made while both the problem and the research are still clear in your mind. Six things belong in this report:

1. An explanation of the problem.
2. A notation of the records you have searched.
3. A statement of your reasons for searching those records.
4. Your findings therein.
5. Your interpretation and evaluation of these findings as they relate to the problem (in whatever detail is required).
6. An outline of the problem as it now stands and suggestions for future research.

It is not essential (or even advisable) that the points in this list be numbered and kept separate, but merely that each be covered.

If you have proved a difficult connection, the evidence which verified that connection should be laid out with great care, step by step, so that it can be easily reviewed. When a line or a connection long accepted by the family is disproved, it is doubly important to make a written report of the details and the evidence. Sources and their contents must be listed with particularity—not just in a general way. Others in the family will question your conclusions, as well they should, and if a careful report has not been prepared, you will in time forget the details of your proof. You will find that it is difficult for some persons to accept new conclusions even when supported by impeccable evidence, so you had better be well prepared. Though all the sources from which your proof was derived are in your notes, that is not the same as having the details of your proof and analysis summarized systematically in a report. Your reports become an important part of your permanent research file, and no requirement of record keeping is more important.

It is also useful to accompany your reports with visual aids such as small maps, hand-drawn if necessary. Your ancestors can "come alive" in pictures of tombstones, houses, churches, etc.

VI. REMINDER NOTES

As research progresses from day to day, or from one research trip to the next, it is easy to forget the specific details of your problem and your research. When you leave the library or the courthouse you can think of many possibilities that need to be investigated. But when you return a week (or a month) later, most of those ideas have been forgotten and are only recalled as you spend time reviewing the problem. Because of this difficulty with the human memory it is a good idea to drop a note into your research file as you conclude your day's work. This note can say anything you want it to say or need it to say, but its design is to put you back on the track as quickly as possible. It may be a list of sources that need checking or just a note of "things to do next," with reasons. As research is resumed all you need do is read your reminder and proceed from where you left off.

These reminder notes should *not* become a permanent part of your research file as they would cause confusion in later years when your files are used by your successor. They should be retained only until they have served their purpose and should then be discarded.

VII. ABSTRACTS AND FORMS

Though chapter 18 discusses extracts and abstracts in some detail, I think it appropriate to introduce you to the subject here during our discussion of research notes. You will find that it is sometimes unwise to copy source materials verbatim. This is especially true when you are working with court records, including both land records and probate records, since there is much verbiage which does not contain genealogical evidence and it is only time-consuming to hand copy it. Even photocopies are impractical if the records are extensive. It is therefore a requirement of efficient research to be able to read records and pick out the important details. However, you must always be careful to copy *all* that is important. When there is a question as to value, include the information in question. It is better to make your abstracts (as we call them) too detailed than too brief. Even by eliminating unnecessary modifiers and parenthetical phrases you can dispose of much excess without harm to meaning.

Abbreviations may be used, but be wary lest you are unable to interpret them when they are cold. If you use good judgment, abbreviations can be used to great advantage. Names, however, should always be copied *exactly* as they appear in the records. This allows for more accurate analysis.

Some persons have special forms which they use for abstracting various types of records. If you like to use them they are good. They can serve as a useful guide for the beginner, but they are not mandatory and most experienced researchers prefer to limit their use. However, forms for extracting census information are a necessity because they save so much time. (This is true of any source with a tabular format.) The use of abstracting forms must be left to individual preference.

VIII. CARD FILES

In addition to the foregoing, some researchers keep card indexes of the ancestors they identify in their research. You may want to consider making such a file, especially if you plan to publish a family history, but it does involve a lot of extra work. If you use it you must list sources on the cards or the file will be worthless. I also recommend that you limit it pretty much to your lineal ancestors or the project will become much too unwieldy. (See the next section.)

IX. COMPUTER INDEXES

In fact, card files are rapidly becoming relics of the past. Computers and computer genealogy programs have essentially eliminated, for the serious genealogist, the need for *manual* control of data of the kind that a card file can provide. Only those who refuse to learn computers, or whose work is limited, can afford to turn their backs on computer technology in genealogy. With the equipment and programs now available, you can create, in just a matter of minutes, virtually any kind of genealogical list you desire from the data you have entered. More is said about the selection of computers and computer genealogy programs in chapter 25.

X. CONCLUSION

Much more could be said about keeping research notes, but I think enough has been said to help you set up a system that will work. The only thing I will add here is that you should never destroy any of your notes. If it is a question of space, store those files not in current use in boxes under your bed; but somehow preserve them.

Notes should also be made of the research you accomplish through correspondence, but this aspect of record keeping is discussed in the next chapter, along with other facets of research through the mail.

The following list outlines the essentials of a workable record-keeping system as they have been discussed in this chapter:

1. Research notes must be simple enough so that anyone can understand them.

2. Your notes must also be complete enough to reflect adequately the research done.

3. Your notes should not be so time-consuming that they detract from your research.

4. Your notes must be neat and orderly on uniform-size good quality paper.

5. Your notes should be done well enough the first time that it is unnecessary to recopy them.

6. You should keep a research calendar that gives a list of all the sources searched, in footnote form.

7. The research calendar will list sources in which nothing is found as well as those that contain useful information.

8. Your notes should include the date of every search.

9. References to sources must be sufficiently complete that anyone who is so inclined can use them to locate those sources.

10. Your notes must indicate the purpose of every search made.

11. Limit your research calendars in some way. Do not use one calendar for everything. A division by locality (or jurisdiction) is recommended.

12. Your research calendar should make direct reference to the notes you take, serving as a table of contents to those notes.

13. Your notes should ordinarily be kept in either file folders or looseleaf binders, in preference to spiral or solid-bound notebooks.

14. Your name and address should be on every page of your notes.

15. File your notes systematically. A good system is to file them alphabetically by surname and, under each surname, chronologically by locality.

16. Cross-reference your research calendars to each other when you have more than one surname in a locality rather than making identical calendars for each surname.

17. Keep a copy of the appropriate portion of your pedigree in every research file.

18. Your notes must indicate the condition of the records being searched and the conditions of the search itself.

19. Your notes, including research calendars, must be suited for the handling and filing of all materials and documents searched in a survey, in an "area search," or in your regular routine.

20. Your notes should be tabulated in some form suitable to you and evaluated periodically to determine if your objectives are being reached.

21. Your notes should be as easy to analyze and evaluate as possible.

22. Make detailed periodic reports of the searches you make and the results of those searches.

23. Use reminder slips during your research, but do not make them a permanent part of your research files.

24. Never throw away any of your research notes.

8

Successful Correspondence

Correspondence is essential to genealogical research. Complete research cannot be accomplished without it unless you have unlimited funds for travel. Certainly there is no doubt that personal research in the appropriate archives is the best way to obtain information but, since this is often financially impossible, you must write letters.

Writing good letters is not easy and many people expend a great deal of time and effort in genealogical correspondence with very little to show for it. Before discussing the actual problems of correspondence, however, let's talk about a system for filing correspondence and the materials accumulated as a result thereof.

I. THE CORRESPONDENCE CALENDAR

Just as it is necessary to organize, file, and index the information acquired through your personal research, the same requirement exists for data arising from your correspondence. This can be best accomplished by keeping some type of correspondence calendar (or index). This is just as essential to a well-planned, functional record-keeping system as is a research calendar.

There are different forms that a correspondence calendar can take. It is really a matter of personal preference. Some like a simple three-column form—one column for the date of your outgoing letter, a second for your addressee's name and the purpose of the letter, and a third for the date you

Sidney Orbeck – 138 N. Westside Ave., Haysbury, Ga.

Surname: Gregg

Date sent / Money	Follow-up	Date of answer / Refund	Correspondent and address	Subject	Results	Extract number
18 Apr 1969 $1.50	29 May 1969	5 June 1969 —	County Clerk Yolo County, Calif.	Probate of Charles Gregg (d. abt 1908)	Found will (1908), Received copy – good!	1
10 June 1969 $2.00	—	21 June 1969 —	Bur. of Vital Statistics, Sacramento, Calif	Death certif. of Charles Gregg	Received copy – b. Gresham, Nebr. died 4 July, 1908	2
16 July 1969 $1.50	—	1 Aug 1969	Gresham Gazette, Gresham, Nebr.	Newspaper ad for possible relatives	Ad in news columns 29 July – got copy	3
		3 Aug 1969	Wendell Shedd Gresham, Nebr.	Shedd is relative (3C1R) – info. on Charles Gregg's brothers and sisters	He saw ad – Gave info. on Charles Gregg's brothers and sisters	4
4 Aug 1969	—	19 Aug 1969	"	Thank you note for info. Asked abt. Wm. Gregg and about Wilders	Has no more info – sugg. contact Harry Gregg, Seward, Nebraska.	5
3 Sep 1969	—	27 Sep 1969	Harry Gregg, Seward, Nebr.	Info on Gregg and Wilder in Nebr. (feeler)	Sent info on bros and sisters of Wm. Gregg – told parents of Jno. C. Wilder – has more	6.
3 Sep 1969 $2.50	—	1 Oct 1969 $2.50	Register of Deeds York County, Nebr.	Gregg & Wilder deeds (index check) – 1840-1870	Found 3 deeds for Wm. Gregg, 4 for J. C. Wilder – few others for both surnames	7
5 Oct 1969 $18.00	—	26 Oct 1969	"	Copies of 12 deeds on Gregg & Wilder	Got deeds – good info! Wm Gregg from Berkeley Co, W. Va.	8
13 Nov 1969 $2.00	26 Dec 1969	6 Jan 1970	County Court, Berkeley Co, W. Va.	Gregg wills (index check) 1772-1850	Found 5 wills	9
7 Jan 1970 $10.00			"	Copies of wills (5)		10
9 Jan 1970 $3.00			Nat'l Archives Wash, D.C.	3 Gregg Revolutionary pension files – Va & Pa		11

FIGURE 1—A CORRESPONDENCE CALENDAR

receive a reply. A more complex correspondence calendar is shown in Figure 1. You will note that this form is much like the research calendar discussed in chapter 7 in that it serves as a table of contents and direct reference guide. With the type of system which this calendar represents, a file of letters and documents is usually maintained separately from the manuscript file you keep in conjunction with your personal research, but this is not mandatory if you can work it out otherwise to your satisfaction. The only requirement is that your basic filing divisions are the same for both.

Let's look now at each of the columns on this sample calendar and discuss its value and content.

The first three columns—one for the date the original letter is sent, one for the date(s) of any follow-up correspondence that may prove necessary, and one for the date on which the answer is received—provide a quick picture of the status of all correspondence. If there are several queries out at the same time, it can be easily seen which ones have been answered and which require follow-up action. Columns one and three also provide a place to keep track of money sent and refunded in connection with any individual situation.

Note that in column four the complete address of the correspondent is not given. It is unnecessary to include the complete address here since it is on the copy of the letter in your files. (More is said about copies later.) However, if you want to list a complete address, you may do so.

The "Subject" and "Results" columns are for a few brief and appropriate words to help you remember something about your letters and their answers without going completely through the file. These brief notations should enable you to determine whether you have already written a letter about a particular matter, perhaps several years past, and already received a negative reply.

The "Extract number" column is for reference convenience. This column makes the calendar a table of contents for your correspondence. There are various ways that correspondence might be numbered. The system used in the example is quite simple. It merely requires that the copy of your original letter (and any follow-up letters), the letter of reply from your correspondent, and all documents and copies enclosed with the reply all be given the same extract number. The number is conveniently placed in the upper right corner, and each item bearing that number is filed according to date so that you can follow the developments of a correspondence request with relative ease. Manila file folders and looseleaf binders are best for filing.

A. Filing Documents

In filing those documents received by correspondence there are several possibilities. I feel, however, that there is a need to somehow correlate all documents with the letters to which they relate. The reason this question arises is because documents are of so many varied sizes and shapes that it is often difficult to keep them neatly in the same file with your letters. One way to file them is to fold them individually and place them in envelopes which are glued to appropriately-numbered and titled sheets of file-size paper. They can then be filed in their proper places among the letters.

Another way is to make a separate file for documents received through correspondence. Documents are given the same numbers as the letters to which they are related and are filed accordingly. This provides a direct-reference system between the two files. One apparent disadvantage of this system is that it creates an additional file. This is not serious but may detract from the simplicity of your filing system.

A third system, widely used, is a combination file. With this system you interfile all the fruits of your research, whether from your personal searches or from correspondence. To use this system you must maintain your manuscript file separate from both your research calendar and correspondence calendar. You must also develop a numbering system that relates to both. This is not difficult if your filing divisions are the same. This can be accomplished by making a separate correspondence calendar for each locality or jurisdiction as suggested for your research calendars. (See chapter 7.)

You must always cross-reference between the two calendars. This requires that you list searches made through correspondence on your research calendar (as well as on your correspondence calendar) with a notation to the effect that the results are under a certain extract number in a specific correspondence file.

Just as you can use the same research calendar for more than one surname if in the same locality, you can do the same with your correspondence calendar, but you must cross-reference them. There is no problem in writing about more than one surname in the same letter.

B. Tabulating Results

You must tabulate and evaluate the results of your correspondence just as carefully as you do the findings of your personal research. The best time to do this is immediately upon receipt of the reply. Get any important family data recorded on your work sheets and analyzed as soon as possible. Such immediate analysis is important because the next step in your research may be influenced by it. Research, especially by correspondence, often is a one-step-at-a-time process with the next step being dependent on the results of the previous one. Use the same work sheets to tabulate the results of your correspondence as to tabulate the results of your personal searches.

If you follow with circumspection the basic principles outlined here, your correspondence file will be not just a stack of letters but a versatile and accessible record of your research by mail.

II. REVIEW OF RESEARCH NOTE REQUIREMENTS

At this point it may be useful to point out, in review, the requirements of good research and correspondence notes. Wright and Pratt list five essentials of a good record-keeping system: [1]

> 1. Initiate a *work pedigree chart* showing a selected line or two of interest, and include all known genealogical facts. . . .
>
> 2. Initiate *work family group sheets* on those families of special concern, and show all genealogical . . . facts pertaining to them. . . .
>
> 3. Initiate a *calendar of correspondence* and index letters sent or received which apply to the lines of interest. . . .
>
> 4. Initiate *calendars of search* for each jurisdiction of interest, and list on them bibliographic information for sources searched or to be searched. . . .
>
> 5. Maintain a *manuscript note file* of searches and findings. [Emphasis added.]

To the five requirements listed by Messrs. Wright and Pratt I would add a sixth—your *periodic research reports*. These, too, are essential to good note keeping.

This chapter and the preceding one outline in some detail how these requirements can be met satisfactorily. Any rule can be altered to fit your personal preference or circumstance if none of the six essentials listed is neglected. However, so far as American research is concerned, the steps as outlined have proved very workable.

---

[1] Norman E. Wright and David H. Pratt, *Genealogical Research Essentials* (Salt Lake City: Bookcraft, 1967), pp. 139-144.

III. LET'S WRITE A LETTER

A. The "Letter" Formula

There is much to be said about letter writing in general, but there are a few rules which apply more specifically to genealogical correspondence. Let's talk first about six such rules. The initial letters of the key words in these rules spell the world *LETTER* and provide a simple formula for better genealogical correspondence.

1. **LIMIT your requests.** Do not ask for too much. There is no more sure way to destroy the good will of someone whose assistance you need than to make an unreasonable request of him. If you know something about the records held by a certain public official, you are in a better position to judge what a "reasonable request" would be, thus the importance of studying and understanding records. If you need additional information, you can always write another letter (or several) once you have secured the good will of your correspondent. You should never write a relative and ask for "everything you have." The late Archibald F. Bennett told the story of his sister who had never been interested in the genealogical research he was doing until late in life. Not realizing the extent of the records he had compiled, she unthinkingly wrote to him: "Dear Archie, please send me all you have." This was not a reasonable request.

2. **Make your requests EASY TO ANSWER.** There are several suggestions you can follow to help make your requests easy to answer:

(a) If you want answers, ask specific questions. Do not be vague or beat around the bush.

(b) Do not lose your questions in the body of a long letter. Very often the best procedure is to write your questions on a separate sheet of paper in questionnaire form, leaving space for answers.

(c) Be careful of sending forms such as pedigree charts and family group record forms. Sometimes these forms can be used to advantage in your correspondence, but they are confusing to the average person. If the person to whom you are writing knows little or nothing about genealogy you will likely get a more satisfactory response if you copy any family data you wish to send him in tabular form on a plain sheet of paper. You might then say something like this: "The above information is all I have on this family. Can you make any additions or corrections?" I am not saying that you should never use forms in your correspondence; I am merely saying that you should use them wisely and with caution. And never send them to public officials.

3. **Make TWO COPIES of each letter you write.** You do not have a complete record of your research unless you have a copy in your files of every letter you write. There are several reasons why this is necessary. Let's consider some of them:

(a) If a follow-up letter becomes necessary it will be much easier to write if you know the specific requests and wording of the original.

(b) As research progresses and you desire information on a specific matter, you can tell from your letters if previous attempts have been made to locate the same information. Often we make ourselves offensive by asking for the same non-existent information over and over again because we did not keep a copy of a letter. In the same light we may have located additional data in the interim which would make it possible now to locate the required information, but it is impossible to know unless a copy of the original request is preserved.

(c) A third and very obvious motive is the necessity for such copies in a complete research file.

4. **Express THANKS to those who help you.** Most of those who assist you through the mail have no legal obligation to do so. Their help is a favor for which you should show your gratitude. On the other hand, however, it is not necessary to apologize for the requests you make.

5. **Fair EXCHANGE will work to your advantage.** Never expect to get something for nothing; in our time it is often difficult to get something for something. To a public official of whom you have asked a favor, a small sum (with an offer to pay any reasonable additional charges) is a must. Usually if you send an amount somewhere between $3.00 and $5.00, depending on what you ask, this is sufficient. If you feel that $5.00 is not enough you are probably asking for too much and need to limit your request. If you request copies of specific documents more money may be required, depending on the cost of those copies. This same principle applies when you write seeking favors of newspapers, libraries, historical societies, church officials, or other private organizations, except when there are established fees for such services.

When you write to a private individual or a relative, your "fair exchange" is not necessarily monetary unless that person happens to have services for hire as a genealogist or record searcher. You should always offer to pay the cost of copying important materials, but more important is your offer to share information and to make the final results of your research available to those interested.

Many public officials, as well as private organizations, may return the money you send, but they appreciate your willingness to pay and will feel more inclined to help if they do not think you are trying to get something for nothing.

6. **Provide for RETURN POSTAGE.** Ethel W. Williams tells the story of the lady who wrote Abraham Lincoln asking for a bit of advice and his signature for a keepsake. He replied: "When asking strangers for a favor, it is customary to send postage. There's your advice and here's my signature. A. Lincoln."[2] This is excellent advice.

It is not necessary to offend close relatives with this practice (though that will seldom happen), but all others will appreciate your thoughtfulness and will often feel a greater obligation to answer your queries.

When you write to a federal or state agency it is not necessary to provide for postage, but letters addressed to officials of counties or towns, or to newspapers, historical societies, church officials, etc., within the U.S. should include a stamped envelope addressed back to you. The only exception to this would be when you allow money for postage in your remittance or when you are paying a set fee for a service.

B. The "4S Formula"

In addition to the above rules, which relate especially to genealogical letters, there are other rules which will add to your effectiveness whether your letters are of a genealogical nature or not. Among the most important of these is a formula for clarity promulgated by the U.S. Government. It is called "The 4S Formula."[3] The four *S*'s stand for *shortness, simplicity, strength,* and *sincerity*. The formula goes like this:

1. Shortness.

(a) Don't unnecessarily repeat inquiry.
(b) Avoid needless words, information.
(c) Shorten prepositional phrases.
(d) Watch "verbal" nouns, adjectives.
(e) Limit qualifying statements.

I recall an old maxim which says, "Good things, if short, are twice as good." Most things written can be improved much more by deletions than by additions. A stone is polished by breaking off and wearing down the rough edges, not by filling in around them. Busy public officials, especially, do not have time to read lengthy letters; so if you can say something in one or two words, don't use three or four. A good rule of thumb is that when asking

---

[2] Ethel W. Williams, *Know Your Ancestors* (Rutland, VT: Charles E. Tuttle Co., 1960), p. 271. By permission.

[3] G.S.A., Washington 58-7468.

favors your letters should never be more than one page long, with adequate (even generous) margins on all four edges. A friend of mine says he never writes a letter that he cannot get on half a sheet of 8½″ x 11″ paper. He has the right idea on brevity but the wrong idea in halving the paper.

2. Simplicity.

(a) Know your subject.
(b) Use short words, sentences, paragraphs.
(c) Be compact.
(d) Tie thoughts together.

Your letters should be written in a friendly, conversational style. Write as you would talk. Try to write from the other person's point of view, keeping his interests dominant. Also remember that nothing adds to simplicity more than knowing something about the subject on which you are writing.

3. Strength.

(a) Use specific words.
(b) Use active verbs.
(c) Give answer, then explain.
(d) Don't hedge.

Don't beat around the bush; avoid clichés, stilted language, and word crutches.

4. Sincerity.

(a) Be human.
(b) Admit mistakes.
(c) Limit intensives and emphatics.
(d) Don't be servile or arrogant.

Try to be yourself and to "put yourself on paper." As was stated under "simplicity," you should try to write as you speak (your very best speech).

C. Objectivity

If I can take all four of the "S" principles and draw from them one important idea perhaps it would be the need for objectivity—the ability, in this situation, to look at your own letters and see them for what they really are. If you could do this, a good many problems would be solved.

You have undoubtedly experienced writing something that you thought was pretty good at the time, but upon re-reading it later you received quite a different impression. The difference in your reaction on those two occasions is the result of objectivity. It is much easier to be objective about something after it has grown cold and you have removed yourself from it. I was much more excited about the rough draft for this book right after completion than I was later when I went back to re-work and polish it.

It is not practical to let your letters sit for six months before you send them, but if you can be aware of your usual lack of objectivity when something is first written, you can achieve a bit of the objectivity you need. Perhaps a better idea, if your ego can stand it, is to have someone else read and criticize your letters. See if he can understand clearly what you are trying to say and if you are saying it inoffensively. He will be in a better position to judge this. Also, have him check spelling, grammar, and punctuation; you may have overlooked something.

Plan your letters. Make rough drafts of them, have them checked and corrected, and then write them in their final form. (Make either carbon copies or photocopies.) After you have done this re-read them carefully before signing. Be prepared to redo any letter which you would not like to receive personally. Word processing software in your personal computer can greatly facilitate corrections.

If you cannot endure criticism at least let your letters sit overnight before you finalize them. That much time will seldom hurt you, and you can gain a little objectivity even overnight if you try.

IV. HOW DOES THE LETTER LOOK?

This is not a text on business communications, but a brief summary of some items which make a letter look inviting to its recipient is in order:

1. Leave adequate margins on all four edges. Nothing gives a letter a worse appearance than crowding it to the edge of the paper. No matter how neatly you write or type or how well you spell, the letter will look sloppy. If you have to crowd your margins to keep the "one-page" rule, then break the rule.

2. Use short paragraphs and double-space between them. This additional white space on the page breaks up the letter, making it more attractive and easier to read.

3. Keep your left margin straight. Do not wander all over the page.

4. Use proper letter form. Any good English text will give you information on the acceptable forms. Your letters must be business-like or people will think you don't know what you are doing.

5. Type your letters if possible. If you cannot type, write neatly, legibly, and evenly.

V. TO WHOM DO I WRITE?

One of the genealogist's biggest problems is knowing who has custody of the records and information he needs. This is especially perplexing to the beginner. First make every possible effort to obtain information from relatives. If you are attempting to locate unknown relatives, a newspaper advertisement in the locality where your ancestors lived might be helpful in locating them. The *Ayer Directory* (see chapter 6) lists addresses of newspapers and thus provides a partial answer to this problem.

For information which relatives do not have (and most genealogical information falls into this category) you must determine who has jurisdiction over the required records. Record custodians can usually be identified by using proper reference tools. When these fail you can always write to a probable record custodian and ask him about the actual location of the records you need. Later chapters provide information on the location and custody of several kinds of genealogical research sources.

VI. CONCLUSION AND CHECKLIST

In 1964 I picked up a checklist designed to help letter writers pin-point trouble-spots in their letters. This list was distributed in a class taught at the LDS Family History Library and its actual origin is unknown. I have taken the liberty to modify that list slightly to fit my needs and am passing it along to you. Questions are worded so that a "no" answer may indicate a problem area. Go through it and see how you fare.

	YES	NO
1. Are most of your letters less than one page long?	____	____
2. Is your average sentence less than 22 words long?	____	____
3. Are your paragraphs short—always less than ten lines?	____	____

4. Do you avoid beginning a letter with: "I am doing genealogical research . . ."? ____ ____

5. Do you know some good ways to begin letters in a natural and conversational manner? ____ ____

6. Can you think of four different words that will take the place of "however"? ____ ____

7. Do you know what is wrong with phrases like: "held a meeting," "are in receipt of," "gave consideration to," etc.? ____ ____

8. Do you use personal pronouns freely, particularly "you"? ____ ____

9. Do you use active verbs ("I read your letter" rather than "Your letter has been read")? ____ ____

10. When you have a choice, do you use little words (pay, help, error) rather than big ones (remuneration, assistance, inadvertency)? ____ ____

11. Whenever possible, do you refer to people by name and title (Dr. Brown, Mr. Adams) rather than categorically (our researcher, the patron, etc.)? ____ ____

12. Compare your letters with your speech. Do you write the way you talk (your most careful talk, of course)? ____ ____

13. Do you answer questions before you explain your answers? ____ ____

14. Do you resist the use of phrases like: "Attention will be called to the fact," "It is to be noted," "It will be apparent"? ____ ____

15. Do you organize your ideas and data before you write your letters? ____ ____

16. Have you tried setting off lists of various types into easily-read tables? ____ ____

17. Do you number and/or indent important points, explanations, etc., and attach explanations to the data they explain? ____ ____

18. Do you highlight important facts by underlining or by separate paragraphs? ____ ____

19. Do you re-read your letters before you send them to see if you actually said what you intended to say?[4] ____ ____

---

[4] "The Letter Writer's Checklist," instructional hand out, The Genealogical Society of The Church of Jesus Christ of Latter-day Saints (Salt Lake City: unpublished, 1964). Modified and used by permission.

Experience is a good teaching tool, especially when combined with proper instruction and guidelines. If you will carefully follow the guidelines given in this chapter you should obtain good results from your research experience. And though I have no panacea that will guarantee success every time you write a letter, I do guarantee that if you follow good procedures your chances for success will be vastly improved.

PART 2

Records and Their Use

9

Compiled Sources and Newspapers

I. THE NATURE OF COMPILED SOURCES

The term "compiled sources" encompasses a great variety of materials. The thing which distinguishes them is that they bring together (compile), in one place, information from more than one root. I have classified them into seven categories:

A. Family histories and genealogies.

B. Local histories.

C. Compiled lists (dictionaries, directories, lists, registers, etc.).

D. Biographical works.

E. Genealogical and historical periodicals.

F. Compendium genealogies.

G. Special manuscript collections.

Compiled sources are of relatively recent origin. They have grown almost simultaneously with genealogical interest, for only as people do research are they able to compile the results thereof.

Compiled sources are often referred to as "printed secondary sources" because they contain secondary evidence. The term "secondary" is not necessarily a mark of inferiority or unreliability; it merely indicates a greater potential for error because the information is compiled or copied from other sources. Errors are certainly not mandatory in these sources, but they are easily made.

Some compiled sources represent extensive research and bring together valuable data of many different origins. If such sources are well documented their value is inestimable—provided the material put forth is based on sound research and evaluation.

The discussion in this chapter excludes all publications of single-source materials such as censuses, church records, military records, etc. The exclusion is intentional because of the vast area covered by such publications. However, you will find a discussion of several of these types of publications in the chapters relating to the records themselves. I have also omitted indexes, bibliographies, and reference tools of all kinds because I have already discussed them in chapter 6.

Let's look now at each of the categories of compiled sources listed above.

A. Family Histories and Genealogies

One of the largest and fastest-growing categories of compiled sources is family histories and genealogies. These are the chief objects of our earlier reference to sources that bring together, in one place, valuable data from many different sources. Because of this "bringing together" they are very useful, but you cannot rely on their accuracy until it has been proven. Too many compilers do not follow proper scientific procedures and many of the connections therein are nothing more than guesses—many of them quite uneducated guesses—and wishful thinking. The late Donald Lines Jacobus discussed four reasons why the compilers of these records have not adhered more prudently to proper research methods:

> There are several reasons why scientific methods have been unpopular with many genealogical students and writers. First in responsibility is that all-too-human trait of *laziness*. It is much easier to make a "likely guess" than to collect data with infinite labor and attention to detail. Second, comes the factor of sheer *ignorance*. Many compilers of family histories quite evidently have no knowledge of the existence of documentary archives, and assume that the only way the early generations of their family can be put together is by accepting what little is to be found in print and guessing at connections.
>
> A third and very important factor is that of *expense*. Many amateur genealogists and compilers cannot afford the cost of thorough research in documentary sources. With this factor, the present writer has an understanding sympathy. Yet it is an old maxim that "whatever is worth doing at all is worth doing well," and one may be entitled to ask whether it never occurs to the perpetrators of the worst genealogical atrocities to give consideration to this maxim. And it may be observed that, despite the lack of funds to compile a

worthwhile genealogy, the compilers nearly always seem able to raise the funds to publish their productions.

For the professional genealogist, as for the amateur, there are valid excuses for failure to take advantage of the opportunities for original research. The professional, dependent upon his work for a livelihood, is restricted by the limitations of cost set by his client, and these limitations frequently do not permit as thorough a search as should be made. Errors made by professionals very often are due to the fact that, to keep within authorized limits of expense, they were forced to rely to a greater extent than they desired on printed sources of information. No one is responsible for this situation, for a large number of those who employ the services of genealogists are not people of large wealth.

A final reason for the unpopularity of scientific methods in genealogy is *the romantic temperament of some of those who pursue genealogy as an avocation or hobby*. To people of that type, scientific methods are a bore. It irritates them to be told that a line of descent, innocently accepted from an unmeritorious printed source, is incorrect. They like that ancestral line, and intend to keep it. Denial or question of its accuracy seems to them purely destructive and negative. With people of this temperament, genealogy is not a serious study; it is a mere diversion, and they derive more pleasure from the exercise of their imaginative talent than they could from grubbing for facts. They believe what they want to believe, regardless of facts and scornful of evidence. Let us concede, without argument, that "genealogists" of this type are entitled to their opinions; just as those who believe that the earth is flat are entitled to that opinion. It is entirely natural that these temperamental enthusiasts should oppose scientific methods, and that with the uninformed their opinions may have weight. [Emphasis added.] [1]

It is difficult to evaluate genealogies and family histories, but you can make a fairly good evaluation by answering the following questions as they relate to a specific source:

1. Are the materials which the source presents well documented? Some sources merely state "facts" with no indication of their sources.

2. What kinds of sources are represented in the documentation? Are they original records (or photocopies of such) or are they other non-original materials? It could make quite a difference.

3. Are the research and analyses of difficult problems and connections explained in detail so that the bases for their acceptance can be completely understood and even re-examined?

---

[1] Donald Lines Jacobus, "Is Genealogy an Exact Science?" *The American Genealogist,* Vol. X, No. 4 (October 1933), pp. 68-69. By permission.

There are some good things written that are poorly documented, but they are the exception and not the rule. And the sad thing about such works is that those using them have no idea of either the completeness of the research or the accuracy of the analysis. Though the percentage of *good* family histories and genealogies is low, those of inferior quality can still be useful in providing clues for research. Any information which you have to work with is better than no information at all and can be a great time saver in research. But remember that just because something is "in the book" does not make it true. Far too many genealogical authors fall into the categories described by Mr. Jacobus for you to indiscriminately believe everything you read.

A useful guide to the available published family histories has been compiled. It is Marion J. Kaminkow (ed.), *Genealogies in the Library of Congress: A Bibliography,* 2 vols. (Baltimore: Magna Carta Book Co., 1972). Later supplements of this work have also been published.

Better-informed, better-trained genealogists are producing a product of higher quality today than was produced in Mr. Jacobus's day, but we still have a long way to go.

B. Local Histories

You will find town, county, and regional histories among those in this category. Many have been written, mostly in the 1800s and early 1900s, and many are still being written. In the eastern states and in some of the middle-western states the writing of such histories has been very popular. And there has been great variation in the quality and reliability of the resulting works. In several states there are published histories of every county (as in New York and Iowa), and in some of the states the number of town histories which have been written is unbelievable.

Regional histories are those which cover more than one county within the scope of the same work. A good example is John Thomas Scharf, *History of Western Maryland,* 2 vols., 1882. (Baltimore: Regional Publishing Co., 1968 reprint).

An important feature of many local histories is a biographical section (sometimes in a separate volume) with short biographical sketches of prominent citizens and early settlers in the locality. Some of these are quite authentic because the families provided the information, and others contain many errors for the same reason. Those books which specialized in biographical sketches accompanied with pictures of the persons named therein are often referred to by book dealers and genealogists as "mug books" because anyone could get his "mug" in one if he paid the fee, and no one could if he didn't.

Though your ancestors may not have been eulogized in such books as these, you can often find information about them in sketches of their in-laws. For example, there is no biographical sketch of William Jasper Kerr in the published history of Jefferson County, Iowa, but there is a sketch of one of his sons-in-law, John Workman. This sketch says that John's wife, Amanda J. Kerr, was born in White County, Tennessee, October 14, 1825. This is very useful information when you consider that we knew only that William Jasper Kerr came from Tennessee, but did not know the specific county.

These histories, exclusive of any biographical materials—whether they be for town, county, or region—provide useful information on the settlement patterns of the locality and on the origins of the settlers. They tell of religion, economics, education, and social conditions which might affect research procedures and direction. They tell of geography and terrain, water courses, and their effects upon settlement and population. Events molded the lives of the people and were controlled by those people. And even the records that were kept were dictated by the lips of history. No genealogist knows all he should about research in any given area until he knows something of that area's history.

A helpful guide to county histories is P. William Filby (comp.), *A Bibliography of American County Histories* (Baltimore: Genealogical Publishing Co., 1985). Access to these books can usually be had through local libraries.

C. Compiled Lists (dictionaries, directories, lists, registers, etc.)

Many different, though related, types of materials are included under this heading. Any lists—pioneers, early settlers, soldiers, patriots, immigrants, petitioners, etc., etc.—compiled from several (usually original) sources with some data or information on the persons listed would be included here. Some are quite comprehensive in their general coverage, others are comprehensive in their coverage of specifics, and others are not comprehensive in any way. The purposes for which they were compiled may have been quite different. A few of the important works of this type will give you an idea of the nature of these very useful tools:

Bancroft, Hubert H. *California Pioneer Register and Index, 1542-1848. Including Inhabitants of California, 1769-1800, and List of Pioneers*. Extracted from *The History of California* 1884-1890. Baltimore: Regional Publishing Co., 1964.

Coulter, Ellis M. and A. B. Saye. *A List of the Early Settlers of Georgia*. (1949). Baltimore: Genealogical Publishing Co., 1983 (reprint).

Farmer, John. *A Genealogical Register of the First Settlers of New England* (with additions and corrections by Samuel G. Drake). (1829). Baltimore: Genealogical Publishing Co., 1964 (reprint).

Heitman, Francis B. *Historical Register and Dictionary of the United States Army, from Its Organization, September 29, 1789, to March 2, 1903.* 2 vols. (1903). Urbana, IL: University of Illinois Press, 1965 (reprint).

Hinman, Royal R. *A Catalogue of the Names of the First Puritan Settlers of the Colony of Connecticut.* (1846). Baltimore: Genealogical Publishing Co., 1968 (reprint).

Holmes, Frank R. (comp.). *Directory of the Ancestral Heads of New England Families, 1620-1700.* (1923). Baltimore: Genealogical Publishing Co., 1964 (reprint).

Kaminkow, Jack and Marion Kaminkow. *A List of Emigrants from England to America, 1718-1759.* Baltimore: Magna Carta Book Co., 1964.

Noyes, Sybil, Charles T. Libby and Walter G. Davis. *Genealogical Dictionary of Maine and New Hampshire.* 5 parts. (1928-39). Baltimore: Genealogical Publishing Co., 1972 (reprinted five parts in one).

Pope, Charles Henry. *The Pioneers of Massachusetts, A Descriptive List, Drawn from Records of the Colonies, Towns and Churches, and Other Contemporaneous Documents.* (1900). Baltimore: Genealogical Publishing Co., 1965 (reprint).

————. *The Pioneers of Maine and New Hampshire, 1623-1660; A Descriptive List Drawn from the Records of the Colonies, Towns, Churches, Courts and Other Contemporary Sources.* (1908). Baltimore: Genealogical Publishing Co., 1965 (reprint).

Savage, James. *A Genealogical Dictionary of the First Settlers of New England, Showing Three Generations of Those Who Came Before 1692 on the Basis of Farmer's Register.* 4 vols. (1860-62). Baltimore: Genealogical Publishing Co., 1965 (reprint).

Skordas, Gust. *The Early Settlers of Maryland: An Index to Names of Immigrants, Compiled from Records of Land Patents, 1633-1680, in the Hall of Records, Annapolis, Maryland.* Baltimore: Genealogical Publishing Co., 1968.

These sources are usually quite reliable (though not always complete) because they are based on data found in original records but, due to the secondary nature of the evidence they contain, they do have errors in them just as family histories and genealogies do. Generally, however, accuracy is somewhat greater because of the nature of the sources and the experience of their compilers. There is usually little information in them that will prove a genealogical connection, but they are helpful in finding families.

D. Biographical Works

Almost every library contains several useful biographical works. You ought to investigate the ones in your local library for information on your American ancestral lines. Of course most of these deal with persons who have achieved some degree of prominence in one field or another. Even those which deal with specific geographic areas have information on only the prominent citizens. Because of this, the average genealogist will often pass them by. He will say: "My ancestors were just common folks," and this is a point well taken if the assumption is true. However, there is a "multiplier factor" in this type of source which makes it much more useful than it might ordinarily be. Though your direct ancestors may not be included, sometimes descendants of these ancestors on lines other than your own have achieved prominence and are included. Since the ancestry of these persons is the same as yours, the value is practically the same. This is illustrated in the case of Robert Lowe.[2]

Robert was known to be the son of William Lowe who had been killed by some outlaws when he first came into Kentucky. It was not known where William Lowe was born or where he came from. Neither Robert nor any of his descendants achieved any prominence that would put their names in any biographical work, but Robert Andrew Lowe, a son of Robert's brother James, did achieve sufficient prominence that he was listed in *Who's Who in America*. In the short biographical sketch of him it told that his father, James, was born in Laurens County, South Carolina—a breakthrough on the problem.

The possibility that your ancestors had prominent descendants on lines other than your own should not be overlooked. And biographical works often provide the needed clues, just as in the Lowe example. Don't overlook in-laws either. You can get the same kind of good data out of these sources as we got from the Iowa county history in the Kerr problem discussed earlier in the chapter.

A good bibliography of some important American biographical sources is Robert C. Slocum's *Biographical Dictionaries and Related Works* (Detroit: Gale Research Co., 1967, with supplements in 1972 and 1978). A few of the early American sources listed in Slocum include:

---

[2] The names used in this example are not the actual names.

Allen, William. *The American Biographical Dictionary: Containing An Account of the Lives, Characters and Writing of the Most Eminent Persons Deceased in America From Its First Settlement.* 3rd ed. Boston: J. P. Jewett, 1857. (Originally published in 1809 as *An American Biographical and Historical Dictionary.*)

American Biography, a New Cyclopedia. New York: The American Historical Society, Inc., 1916—.

Appleton's Cyclopaedia of American Biography. 7 vols. New York: D. Appleton, various editions, 1887-1900. (New, enlarged ed. was published from 1915 to 1931 as *The Cyclopaedia of American Biography* by Press Association Compilers.)

Biographical Dictionary of Early Virginia, 1607-1660. Ed. by Ransom B. True. Richmond: Association for the Preservation of Virginia Antiquities, 1980.

The Cyclopaedia of American Biographies. 7 vols. Ed. by John H. Brown. Boston: Cyclopaedia Publishing Co., 1903. (Also published in 1904 in ten vols. under the title *The Twentieth Century Biographical Dictionary of Notable Americans.*)

Drake, Samuel F. *Dictionary of American Biography, Including Men of the Time; Containing Nearly Ten Thousand Notices of Persons* . . . Boston: Houghton and Osgood, 1879.

Hall, Henry. *America's Successful Men of Affairs. An Encyclopedia of Contemporaneous Biography.* 2 vols. New York: New York Tribune, 1895-96.

Herringshaw, Thomas W. (ed. and comp.). *Herringshaw's National Library of American Biography.* 5 vols. Chicago: American Publishers' Association, 1904-14.

Men and Women of America; A Biographical Dictionary of Contemporaries. Ed. by John W. Leonard. New York: L. R. Hamersly, 1908.

The National Cyclopaedia of American Biography. New York: James T. White Co., 1893-19—.

Officers of the Army and Navy (Regular and Volunteer) Who Served in the Civil War. Philadelphia: L. R. Hamersly, 1894.

Rosenbloom, Joseph R. *A Biographical Dictionary of Early American Jews: Colonial Times Through 1800.* Lexington, KY: University of Kentucky Press, c. 1960.

Sketches of Representative Men, North and South. Ed. by Augustus C. Rogers. New York: Atlantic Publishing Co., 1872.

United States Congress. *Biographical Dictionary of the American Congress, 1774-1961* . . . Rev. ed. Washington, DC: U.S. Government Printing Office, 1961.

Wakelyn, Jon L. *Biographical Dictionary of the Confederacy*. Westport, CT: Greenwood Press, c. 1977.

Who Was Who in America. Historical Volume, 1607-1896. Chicago: A. N. Marquis Co., 1963.

Who's Who in America. A Biographical Dictionary of Notable Living Men and Women. Chicago: A. N. Marquis Co., 1899-*1900*—. (Indexes are available.)

The salient differences between this type of source and the compiled lists discussed earlier are that most of these are usually current or semi-current biography at the time they are published and their purpose is always biographical rather than either historical or genealogical. Some well-known sources of more recent American biography are:

The American Catholic Who's Who.
American Men of Science.
Celebrity Register.
Contemporary Authors.
Current Biography.
Dictionary of American Biography.
Dictionary of American Scholars.
Leaders in Education.
Who's Who in American Art.
Who's Who in American Jewry.
Who's Who in American Junior Colleges.
Who's Who in Colored America.
Who's Who in Commerce and Industry.
Who's Who in Genealogy.
Who's Who in Labor.
Who's Who in Our American Government.
Who's Who in the Central States.
Who's Who in the East.
Who's Who in the Northwest.
Who's Who in the South.
Who's Who in the West.
Who's Who of American Women.

And there are many, many more—some of them for specific states, regions, counties, and even cities.

Most of the data in these sources are provided by the subjects and are usually quite reliable.

E. Genealogical and Historical Periodicals

This too is an area which is much larger and more comprehensive in scope than is usually suspected by the beginning genealogist. It runs the gamut all the way from the scholarly journal to the mimeographed, one-man, low-budget publication of a specific family. There are literally hundreds of publications—monthlies, bi-monthlies, quarterlies, semi-annuals, and annuals—each making its own contribution to the science of genealogy. Governmental units, libraries, historical societies, genealogical societies, patriotic and hereditary societies, families, and private individuals all play an important role. Some are excellent, some are good, and some are pretty bad.

Many of these periodicals are published on a very restricted basis and copies are almost impossible for the average person to obtain—in fact, something which may be of interest to you might well be published without your ever knowing of it unless someone makes a specific effort to inform you or you come across it accidentally. Very few libraries, if any, have all such publications, though several subscribe to all of the most reputable publications. Many have extensive holdings. The New York Public Library receives some 600 genealogical periodicals annually and the LDS Family History Library in Salt Lake City subscribes to most of the same ones. Every library subscribes to at least a few periodicals—usually some of the most important ones. (Bearing in mind the inaccessibility of genealogical periodicals, you should note that the Genealogical Publishing Company of Baltimore has reprinted articles from many of the key journals. To date they have published some seventy-five volumes of compiled excerpts, comprising several thousand articles, most of them selected and introduced by Gary Boyd Roberts.)

Following is a list of some of the current, available genealogical periodicals published in the United States:

A.P.G. Quarterly, Association of Professional Genealogists, P.O. Box 11601, Salt Lake City, UT 84147.

The American Genealogist, 128 Massasoit Dr., Warwick, RI 02888.

Avotaynu, The International Review of Jewish Genealogy, P.O. Box 1134, Teaneck, NJ 07666.

Branches and Twiggs, Genealogical Society of Vermont, RFD #3, Box 986, Putney, VT 05346.

Car-Del Scribe, Box 73, Ludlow, MA 10156.

Central Illinois Genealogical Quarterly, Decatur Genealogical Society, P.O. Box 2205, Decatur, IL 62526.

The Colonial Genealogist, The Augustin Society, P.O. Box P, Torrence, CA 90507-7766.

The Connecticut Nutmegger, The Connecticut Society of Genealogists, P.O. Box 435, 2906 Main Street, Glastonbury, CT 06033.

Deep South Genealogical Quarterly, Mobile Genealogical Society, P.O. Box 6224, Mobile, AL 36606.

The Detroit Society for Genealogical Research Magazine, Detroit Public Library, 5201 Woodward Avenue, Detroit, MI 48202.

Family Puzzlers, Heritage Papers, Danielsville, GA 30633-9611.

Federation of Genealogical Societies Newsletter, P.O. Box 220, Davenport, IA 52805.

The Genealogical Helper, 526 N. Main Street, Logan, UT 84321.

The Genealogical Journal, Utah Genealogical Association, P.O. Box 1144, Salt Lake City, UT 84110.

The Genealogical Magazine of New Jersey, P.O. Box 1291, New Brunswick, NJ 08903.

The Genealogist, Association for the Promotion of Scholarship in Genealogy, Ltd., P.O. Box 1058, Rochester Center Station, New York, NY 10185.

Genealogy, Indiana Historical Society, 315 W. Ohio Street, Indianapolis, IN 46202.

Georgia Genealogical Magazine, Georgia Genealogical Reprints, P.O. Box 738, Easley, SC 29641-0738.

Hawkeye Heritage, Iowa Genealogical Society, P.O. Box 7735, Des Moines, IA 50322.

Idaho Genealogical Society Quarterly, 325 W. State Street, Boise, ID 83702.

Illinois State Genealogical Society Quarterly, P.O. Box 157, Lincoln, IL 62656.

Journal of the Afro-American Historical and Genealogical Society, Box 13086, T Street Station, Washington, DC 20009.

The Kansas City Genealogist, Heart of America Genealogical Society, 311 E. 12th Street, Kansas City, MO 64106.

The Kentucky Genealogist, 3621 Brownsboro Road, 201B, Louisville, KY 40207.

Maryland and Delaware Genealogist, Box 352, St. Michaels, MD 21663.

The Mayflower Descendant, 101 Newbury Street, Boston, MA 02116. (Publication resumed in 1985 with volume 35 after hiatus of 47 years.)

National Genealogical Society Quarterly, 4527 17th Street North, Arlington, VA 22207.

New England Historical and Genealogical Register, New England Historic Genealogical Society, 101 Newbury Street, Boston, MA 02116.

The New York Genealogical and Biographical Record, 122 E. 58th Street, New York, NY 10022.

The North Carolina Genealogical Society Journal, P.O. Box 1492, Raleigh, NC 27602.

Ohio Records and Pioneer Families, Ohio Genealogical Society, 419 W. 3rd Avenue, P.O. Box 2625, Mansfield, OH 44906.

Oregon Genealogical Society Bulletin, P.O. Box 10306, Eugene, OR 97440-2306.

Pennsylvania Genealogical Magazine, Genealogical Society of Pennsylvania, 1300 Locust Street, Philadelphia, PA 19107.

St. Louis Genealogical Society Quarterly, 1695 S. Brentwood, Suite 203, St. Louis, MO 63144.

Search: International Quarterly of Jewish Research, P.O. Box 481022, Niles, IL 60648.

Southern Genealogist's Exchange Quarterly, P.O. Drawer 50610, Jacksonville Beach, FL 32250.

Stirpes (Texas State Genealogical Society Quarterly), 2507 Tannehill, Houston, TX 77008-3052.

The Tree Searcher, Kansas Genealogical Society, Box 103, Dodge City, KS 67801.

Tree Talks, Box 104, Colvin Station, Syracuse, NY 13205.

The Virginia Genealogist, Box 4883, Washington, DC 20008-0083.

A few of the most widely-circulated of these periodicals are listed in the *Ayer Directory of Newspapers and Periodicals,* and it is often useful to refer thereto, under the place in which the periodical is published, to determine when the periodical started. However, the *Standard Periodical Directory* (Lexington, NY: Oxbridge Publishing Co.) and *Ulrich's International Periodicals Directory* (New York: R. R. Bowker) have easier-to-use, more complete lists of genealogical periodicals and give the same information. Mary K. Meyer's *Directory of Genealogical Societies in the U.S.A. and Canada* (updated biennially) has the most current listing of genealogical periodicals. Since the first edition of *The Researcher's Guide* was published in 1973, an excellent work on genealogical periodicals and periodical indexes has become available. This work, *A Survey of American Genealogical Periodicals and Periodical Indexes,* by Kip Sperry, has excellent information on both periodicals and indexes, but is now becoming somewhat dated itself.[3]

Contained between the covers of these many periodicals is a wealth of genealogical and historical information. All types of information are included—genealogies, family histories, family sketches, biographical sketches, indexes to otherwise unindexed records, locality histories, information from valuable private record collections, copies of lost records, genealogical queries with useful data, procedural instructions on the use of various record types, guides to record use and research standards, etc., etc. —and most of this information lies hidden and undetected because of limited circulation and lack of indexes (and lack of knowledge of existing indexes).

There are some useful periodical indexes. (Some of the general ones are listed in chapter 6 under "Guides to Non-original Sources.") Among them are Jacobus's *Index to Genealogical Periodicals,* the *Genealogical Periodical Annual (GPA) Index,* Swem's *Virginia Historical Index,* and Munsell's *Index to American Genealogies.* Some periodicals have special indexes of their own which are excellent. These include the *Pennsylvania Magazine of History and Biography,* the *National Genealogical Society Quarterly,* and the *New England Historical and Genealogical Register.* There are many others. Indexes to state publications are also frequently found in state libraries and historical societies. For example, the *Maryland Historical Magazine* is card-indexed at the Maryland Historical Society.

Certainly periodicals should be used when their use is feasible, but even a good thing can be overdone. It would be unwise to spend hours searching haphazardly through periodical literature for information on your ancestors if you didn't know what you were looking for or where to look for it. Also, notwithstanding the great genealogical value of periodicals, remember that the evidence they contain is secondary and the possibility of error must be considered.

It might be well to note that sometimes there are valuable genealogical and local history data in general circulation magazines that are not primarily or ordinarily of a genealogical or historical nature. I have in my files an informative article on probate records from a leading "Sunday supplement" and another on the history of the Moravian Church in America from a well-known women's magazine.

---

[3] Kip Sperry, *A Survey of American Genealogical Periodicals and Periodical Indexes* (Detroit: Gale Research Co., 1978. This is volume 3 in the Gale Genealogy and Local History Series.)

F. Compendium Genealogies

A compendium is a work which treats a broad subject in brief form. These are usually comprehensive treatises with only abstracts of information. One compiler of a compendium genealogy said it was his objective "to compress the lineages contained in thousands of individual family genealogies into a single volume."[4] Genealogical compendia are notoriously inaccurate because the data presented therein are generally from sources other than original records—usually from family histories or even family members. They are useful but should be used with great care. Some of the most widely known compendia in American genealogy are:

d'Angerville, Count Howard H. *Living Descendants of Blood Royal in America.* 5 vols. London, 1959-80.

Hardy, Stella Pickett. *Colonial Families of the Southern States of America.* 2nd ed. Baltimore: Southern Book Co. (now Genealogical Publishing Co.), 1958 (reprint).

Mackenzie, George Norbury (ed.). *Colonial Families of the United States of America.* 7 vols. (1907-20). Baltimore: Genealogical Publishing Co., 1966 (reprint).

Munsell, Joel *et al. American Ancestry: Giving the Name and Descent, in the Male Line, of Americans Whose Ancestors Settled in the United States Previous to the Declaration of Independence, A.D. 1776.* 12 vols. Comp. and originally published by Joel Munsell's Sons, 1887-99. Baltimore: Genealogical Publishing Co., 1968 (reprint).

Pittman, Hannah D. *Americans of Gentle Birth and Their Ancestors: A Genealogical Encyclopedia.* 2 vols. (1903-7). Baltimore: Genealogical Publishing Co., 1970 (reprint).

Virkus, Frederick A. (ed.). *The Compendium of American Genealogy. The Standard Genealogical Encyclopedia of the First Families of America.* 7 vols. (1925-42). Baltimore: Genealogical Publishing Co., 1968 (reprint).

G. Special Manuscript Collections

Some persons go to great time and expense gathering data and materials for publication (or just for the joy of gathering) which are never published for one reason or another. Many of these collections have found their way into libraries, historical societies, and archives, but many more still lie hidden

---

[4] Frederick A. Virkus (ed.), *Compendium of American Genealogy,* Vol. 1 (Baltimore: Genealogical Publishing Co., 1968 reprint), p. 5.

away in private collections and family records. The obvious disadvantage of this type of record, even those in libraries and archives, is that it is hard to locate even when you know it exists. Some of them have been microfilmed and this helps, but it does not completely solve the problem. The best guides to such materials—these records hidden away in unexpected places—are the continuing series of the *National Union Catalog of Manuscript Collections (NUCMC)* being prepared by the Library of Congress with assistance from the Council on Library Resources.[5]

Many family and personal records fall into this manuscript category, but mainly it comprises compilations and collections of original documents of various kinds. If you are using *NUCMC* to seek genealogical data, there are a number of approaches that can be rewarding. Always search the indexes of these volumes under the heading "genealogy" as well as under your surnames of interest and under the specific localities where the family lived. One approach to the locality angle that sometimes is fruitful is to look at lawyers' papers—especially in burned counties. If your ancestor was in the military, and you know the service regiment, look for the papers of commanding officers.

Of special interest to the user of *NUCMC* is the geographical guide published in the 1981 volume. This guide shows which repositories have reported and when they did so. There is an index to repositories every few years and a cumulative index every four or five years, in addition to the regular yearly indexes.

II. NEWSPAPERS

Another very useful, though far from trustworthy, printed (but not actually compiled) genealogical source is the local newspaper of the geographical area where your ancestor lived. Obituaries, marriage and engagement stories and announcements, birth announcements, probate court proceedings (legal notices), notes of thanks (statements by families of deceased persons expressing appreciation for sympathies extended), news items, etc., can all be sources of important family data. I have known of several situations where the only information that could be found relative to a person's

[5] United States, Library of Congress, *National Union Catalog of Manuscript Collections (1959-61; 1962; 1959-62 Index; 1963-64; 1965, Index 1963-65; 1966, Index 1963-66; 1967, Index 1967;* ——). First volume publ. Ann Arbor, MI: J. W. Edwards (1962); vols. 2-3 publ. Hamden, CT: Shoe String Press (1964). Remaining vols. publ. Washington, DC: Library of Congress (1965-69——).

birthplace was in his obituary. Generally weekly newspapers are your better source because they usually contain more detailed information than do the larger dailies, though there are exceptions.

When you use newspapers, especially older ones, remember that journalism has not always had the "objective reporting of facts" as an avowed goal.

Following are some examples of marriage notices and obituaries from early newspapers.

A. Marriages

Raleigh Register and North Carolina Gazette–Tuesday, June 10, 1834:

— Marriages —

In this City, on Thursday evening last, by the Rev. Mr. Dowd, Mr. Thomas J. Johnson to Miss Ann Maria Walton.

In this county, on the 29th ultimo, Mr. John M'Cullars to Miss Aley Ann Warren, eldest daughter of Nathaniel Warren, Esq.

In Orange county, on the 8th ultimo, Col. Jehu Ward to Miss Martha M'Callian, daughter of John M'Callian, Esq.

In Person county, on the 14th ultimo Mr. Irby Sanders to Miss Sarah Briggs. Also on the 15th Mr. John H. Jones to Miss Rebecca Winstead.

In Franklin county, on the 14th ultimo, Mr. Thomas Debnam to Miss Priscilla Macon, daughter of Nathaniel Macon, Esq.

At Oxford, on the 27th ultimo, Capt. Samuel B. Meacham to Miss Martha Curran.

In Chowan county, by Rev. John Avery. Mr. Robert T. Paine to Miss Lavinia Benbury.

B. Obituaries

Virginia Argus (Richmond)–Wednesday, August 6, 1806:

— Deaths —

DIED—On Friday evening Mrs. AMBLEM of this city of the most elevated standing in the city, and beloved by all who knew her.

On Sunday morning, Mrs. FRANCES GAUTIER an old and respectable inhabitant of this city.

On the 28th of July last in Goochland county, at their dwelling house, Mr. WILLIAM POWERS and his wife JUDITH, within a few hours of each other; he lay sick 19 days with a dysentery which he bore with christian fortitude; she was taken with a shock of the dead Palsy which carried her off in about twenty-six hours; in her

> health before she was taken ill, she often declared there would not be two days difference in their deaths. They lived 57 years together in a well spent life of conjugal affection, and by their care and industry had raised a plentiful fortune, together with a numerous family; and like Theodocius and Constance, were both buried in one grave, and as they were lovely and pleasant in their lives, in their deaths they were not divided.

You will note from the examples that have been given that very often the details in early newspapers are sketchy, even for persons of "the most elevated standing." Sometimes, however, these newspaper accounts provide useful data for identifying ancestors and especially for distinguishing them from other persons of the same name. One of the greatest identity problems in research is that of contemporaneous men with the same names. Any information which helps distinguish one from the other is invaluable.

There is often some difficulty in locating old newspapers which might be of value to your research. If you find this to be true, the best helps are Clarence Saunders Brigham, *History and Bibliography of American Newspapers, 1690-1820,* 2 vols., incl. additions and corrections (Hamden, CT: Shoe String Press, 1962); Winifred Gregory (ed.), *American Newspapers 1821-1936: A Union List of Files Available in the United States and Canada* (New York: H. W. Wilson Co., 1937); and Anita Milner, *Newspaper Indexes: A Location and Subject Guide for Researchers,* 3 vols. (Metuchen, NJ: Scarecrow Press, 1977-82). These cover extant newspapers published after 1690 in the United States and tell the location (specific library, historical society, newspaper office, etc.) of the extant numbers. They tell how often each paper was published (weekly, daily, etc.) and the time period covered by publication. Many libraries have copies of these works.

If the newspaper you seek is still in publication the *Ayer Directory*[6] is a useful guide to its location. The date the paper began publication and whether it has weekly or daily circulation is indicated. If you are unaware of any specific newspaper in the locality from which your ancestor came and you do not have access to Brigham, Gregory, or Milner, you should certainly consult Ayer for possibilities. If there are no newspapers being published (or none were published during the proper time period) in the town where your ancestor lived, get the names of nearby towns from a map (there are maps in Ayer) and see if any of those towns had newspapers that might interest you.

---

[6] The *Ayer Directory of Newspapers and Periodicals* (Philadelphia: N. W. Ayer and Sons, annual).

A good use for current newspapers, and again weeklies seem to yield the most success, is in locating unknown relatives. You may still have relatives living in places where your ancestors lived many years ago. Though your direct ancestors moved away, some of their brothers and sisters may have remained and there may be a sizable branch of the family still living in the area. An advertisement in a local paper, with sufficient identifying information, can often produce surprising results. Frequently a kind letter and a small remittance to the editor of the local weekly will put your query in his news columns rather than with the ads. This can be even more effective.

III. LIMITATIONS OF COMPILED SOURCES

This chapter has already discussed limitations as they relate to the various categories of compiled sources, but it seems appropriate now to summarize briefly some of the major problems of these materials so that you can establish them more clearly in your mind. It is important that you understand these problem areas, but at the same time you ought not to become so obsessed with negatives that you overlook the good points.

Consider the following.

A. Accessibility and Availability

Because of limited publication and lack of indexes we cannot always take full advantage of many compiled sources. Of many items which could be useful, we are often never cognizant—others, of which we are aware, we cannot find.

B. Reliability

When it comes to credibility gaps most compiled sources are hard to compete with. The gap is wide and the main reason for it is that fact that scientific research methods were seldom used by many of the authors. All printed sources should be approached with due caution for in them we frequently find that the families are inaccurate and the pedigree connections lack verification. Hence they do not often contain even good circumstantial evidence. Clerical errors are also possible whenever anything is copied, and in research the effect of these can be serious.

C. Completeness

The most incomplete compiled sources are no doubt family histories and compendium genealogies. Other sources are generally limited in nature and scope and are not expected to be complete in quite the same way. We often find that family histories have been compiled without thorough research and by persons not qualified. They are frequently full of information gaps which might have been filled if the research had been better. There are not only incomplete families but also incomplete information on many family members.

D. Documentation

If stated "facts" lack documentation they mean nothing. Too many printed sources indicate that something or other is true but give no indication of the source of the information. Footnotes and/or complete source references are essential in credible compiled sources, and if these do not exist there is no way of determining authenticity. Also, even when complete and detailed source references are given, if the information comes from other compiled sources they cannot be accepted as facts unless substantiated by data from original sources. Merely finding something stated in two or three different family histories does not make it true. These books often go on and on quoting each other, accepting something as fact merely because "it's in the book." Well, to borrow an old bromide, "It ain't necessarily so."

I have seen books which had some (usually not extensive) documentation and, upon careful checking of the sources listed, I have found no resemblance between those sources and their alleged product. This is nothing more than sloppiness and can usually be traced directly to poor methods of record keeping, but it all adds up to poor research. Most writers do not do this; they usually just omit all documentation.

E. Our Dilemma

No doubt there are other problems which you will encounter in the use of compiled sources, but the above are the main ones. William Bradford Brown made a sobering summary of the situation when he wrote the following in the *Pilgrim News Letter:*

> When I enter a genealogical room and see the many workers industriously copying from the printed records, I have a feeling almost of dismay, realizing that each one is perhaps adding to the already hopeless tangle of twisted pedigrees.[7]

---

[7] As quoted by Donald L. Jacobus in *Genealogy as Pastime and Profession,* 2nd ed. rev. (Baltimore: Genealogical Publishing Co., 1968), p. 61. By permission.

This is the dilemma into which compiled sources are leading us, and the thing which makes it so serious is the fact that so many uninformed pseudo-genealogists never progress beyond the compiled sources in that "genealogical room" of which Mr. Brown wrote. Their research begins and ends in a library. Jacobus explained the problem further when he said that most family histories are written

> in blissful ignorance of record sources, only scratching the surface of the research, full of erroneous deductions and inconsistencies, bearing evidence of rank amateurishness. . . . Too often . . . [the authors] are satisfied to follow what is found in print on the early generations, in total ignorance of its trustworthiness, and to reconcile all difficulties they encounter by assumptions and guesses. In view of this situation, it is remarkable that so many good family histories have been written, and that the average one is even as good as it is.[8]

My sentiments exactly!

IV. FINAL OBSERVATION

This discussion on compiled sources was the source of some criticism in the first edition of this work. It has been duly pointed out to me that what I have written is an attack on the work of good genealogists. It was noted that while "Mr. [Milton] Rubincam and Mr. [John] Coddington [*et al.*] are continually producing valuable works, *The Researcher's Guide* . . . belittles their efforts and is an insult to their work"!

If I have insulted good genealogists, I apologize. However, I seriously doubt that the good genealogists—the Rubincams and the Coddingtons *et al.*—have taken offense. Mr. Rubincam, who so kindly reviewed my original manuscript and wrote the introduction, offered no criticism of this discussion and indicated no need for softening the blow. These men indeed share my concerns and follow these same rules—weighing the merits of each compiled source they use and accepting each according to its merits.

I am pleased to observe that many good works are being compiled. We should utilize them and recognize their value. But we should also be aware that much of what is currently being written is still of questionable value. That is a truth which I cannot ignore. I must stick to my guns.

---

[8] *Ibid.*, pp. 64-65.

10

Vital Records

Vital records, as considered here, are primarily civil (or non-church) records of births, marriages, and deaths and can be an important source of genealogical evidence. They do not have a place in every American pedigree problem because they are a relatively recent source in most areas of the country, but where they apply their use is essential and research is not complete without them.

I. BEGINNING AND BACKGROUND

A. The Colonial Period

The American system of keeping vital records is found to be, in many ways, unique when compared with the systems used by other countries, even though the roots of at least part of the system began on foreign soil. The main roots of American vital records, however, lie in America herself.

Since the early settlers in most of the colonies which later became the United States of America were predominantly British, they followed British customs. Beginning in 1538, shortly after the separation of the English church from the church in Rome, it was required that ministers keep a record of christenings (baptisms), marriages, and burials in the registers of their individual parish churches. This was nearly seventy years before the first permanent British colony was established on American soil, and the practice was continued in the early colonies, being implemented and facilitated by statute.

The first known law in the colonies to this effect was passed by the Grand Assembly of Virginia in 1632. This law required the minister or warden from each parish to appear in court once a year on the first of June and present a record of christenings, marriages, and burials for the preceding year.[1] These were the traditional events recorded by the church, but, in effect, they provided a record of births, marriages, and deaths.

A statute passed by the General Court of the Massachusetts Bay Colony in 1639 required town clerks in that colony to make a record of the actual births and deaths rather than christenings and burials. This act was also different in that it placed the burden for keeping such records upon governmental rather than church officials. Connecticut, Old Colony (New Plymouth), and other colonies soon followed this same pattern.

B. The System Grows—Slowly

As time went by, legal machinery was effected to help collect and preserve the records. The early laws were repeatedly strengthened to better meet this obligation. Again the Massachusetts Bay Colony provides a good example of this strengthening procedure. In 1644 that colony added a penalty to its registration laws for those who failed to report vital events and in 1692 went so far as to establish registration fees. This act of 1692, the most comprehensive vital registration law of the period, empowered town clerks to collect three pence for each birth or death registered and to assess fines upon those failing to report. The act also allowed for the issuance of certificates by the clerks.[2]

None of these early laws was ever very effective. Even much later than the colonial period already discussed, problems plagued those responsible for keeping the records. For one thing, coverage was incomplete. Many towns and cities had legislation but there was not one state which had anything close to complete registration coverage before the mid-nineteenth century.

The most significant problem affecting the existing laws was the lack of concern for property rights (the only reason given for the existence of such laws) by a population swelled with immigrants who settled only temporarily, waiting for a chance to move west. The population was so unsettled that enforcement of these laws was next to impossible.

---

[1] United States. National Office of Vital Statistics, *Vital Statistics of the United States 1950* (Washington, DC: U.S. Public Health Service, 1954), Vol. I, p. 3.

[2] *Ibid.*, Vol. I, p. 3.

C. The Turning Point

A better reason than the protection of property rights was needed to induce compliance. And a better reason was finally provided by a group of medical men and statisticians who saw the importance of knowing about births and deaths—especially deaths, by cause—in order to fight disease and control epidemics. This held true in both Britain and America. Speaking of the situation in Britain, Sir Arthur Newsholme wrote:

> Panic was a large factor in securing repentance and good works when cholera threatened; as it, likewise, was in an earlier century when plaque became epidemic; and in both instances the desire for complete and accurate information as to the extent of the invasion led England to the call for accurate vital statistics. It may truly be said that the early adoption of accurate registers of births and deaths was hastened by fears of cholera, and by the intelligent realisation that one must know the localisation as well as the number of the enemy to be fought.[3]

The English-speaking peoples were considerably slower to develop vital registration than were many other peoples of the world, and the entire world was relatively slow. By 1833 only one-tenth of the world's population lived in the areas covered by regular vital registration. This included Austria, Bavaria, Belgium, Denmark, Finland, France, Norway, Prussia, Saxony, Sweden (some of which had vital registration systems operated by their churches), and five U.S. cities (6 per cent of the U.S. population)—Baltimore, Boston, New Orleans, New York, and Philadelphia.[4]

Though these five cities were the forerunners in the development of American vital registration, and though some of them had health departments and kept statistics of death by cause, complete records are not available for them from this early period because the laws were essentially ineffective. In Baltimore, for example, it was not until 1875 that death certificates were *required* by statute.

England and Wales had no vital registration until July 1837 (Act of 1836) when a central registry office was established with responsibility for recording all births, marriages, and deaths. This was probably in response to the cholera epidemic which took 42,000 lives in Great Britain and Ireland during 1831 and 1832. The Act of 1836 is regarded by many as the turning point in the development of vital registration in both England and

---

[3] Sir Arthur Newsholme, *Evolution of Preventive Medicine* (Baltimore: Williams and Wilkins, 1927), p. 113. By permission.

[4] United States. National Office of Vital Statistics, Vol. I, p. 4.

the United States. Vital records began to improve consistently from that time. Part of the impetus behind these improved records was security of property rights, but the chief motivation was the gathering of facts that would facilitate war against disease and poor sanitary conditions.

In the U.S., vital records have never been kept on a national level as they are in Britain, but rather their keeping is largely a state responsibility. When our nation's founders framed the Constitution in 1787 they created a republic in which all rights and duties not expressly given to the federal government automatically belonged to the individual states. And practically no one saw the need for vital registration in 1787. Hence each state has developed its own system of vital registration, but not without the prodding and direction of federal agencies and other interested organizations.

The one man with perhaps the greatest influence on the early development of American vital records was Lemuel Shattuck of Massachusetts. Shattuck was inspired by England's Act of 1836 and made it the model for the statute adopted by Massachusetts in 1842 and strengthened in 1844. This legislation (1844) was the first in America to require centralized state filing of records and to provide for standard forms. The American Statistical Association, which Shattuck founded, was the pressure group which worked to secure this legislation.[5] New Jersey was not far behind, making registration of births, marriages, and deaths mandatory on a state-wide basis in 1848.

D. Vital Registration and the Census

Shattuck's accomplishments in Massachusetts vital registration were by no means the end of his influence upon vital records. Because of his work in designing the 1845 census of Boston, he was called to Washington in 1849 to help draw up plans for the 1850 federal census. This census bore the marks of his genius and foresight and also of his interest in vital records. That census inaugurated the most important innovations in the history of the federal census.

It is not my purpose here to discuss the census in detail—that is done in chapters 11 and 12—but some of Shattuck's census innovations do relate to vital records. The 1850 census included an attempt to collect vital data by enumeration. He apparently was not convinced that such a system would work, but felt that if it produced any information at all it would be of more value than what was being done otherwise at the time—the old idea that anything is better than nothing.

[5] *Ibid,* Vol. I, p. 5.

To the population schedules of the census was added an additional column asking: "Married within the year?" Also added was a mortality schedule to gather data on persons dying within the census year. In 1860 a column was added to the population schedules to tell the month of birth for each child born within the census year. The birth and death statistics published by the federal government up through 1900 were collected by the decennial censuses.[6]

Shattuck's fears for the effectiveness of the system were confirmed, but, for lack of something better, the program was continued. The method was quite unsatisfactory. For one thing these enumerations in each case covered only the twelve months immediately preceding the date of the census—only one year out of ten. A second problem was getting people to report events accurately, especially deaths. Apparently memories were very short. The 1850, 1860, and 1870 counts of deaths, it is estimated, fell short of the actual number by 40 per cent.[7] With the census of 1880, the census law was amended to withdraw mortality schedules from the enumerators in those cities and states with official registration of deaths and to secure the needed information from the actual death records.[8]

The census as a tool for collecting vital records was not abandoned until the 1910 census when registration within the several states had developed sufficiently to provide better national statistics than enumeration could produce.[9] However, nothing is known of the location of any 1900 mortality schedules except that they were probably destroyed prior to World War I, and those for 1890 were destroyed by fire on March 22, 1896.[10]

In defense of these vital records by enumeration (if indeed they need defense) it must be said that the only other choice was to have practically no vital records at all.[11]

E. Organization and Standardization

Registration was working well in a handful of large U.S. cities as early as the mid-1800s, but in the rest of the country the records were very poor. It

---

[6] *Ibid.*, Vol. I, p. 5.

[7] *Ibid.*, Vol. I, p. 7.

[8] Katherine H. Davidson and Charlotte M. Ashby (comps.), *Preliminary Inventory of the Records of the Bureau of the Census* (Washington, DC: The National Archives, 1964), p. 110.

[9] United States. National Office of Vital Statistics, Vol. I, p. 7.

[10] Information provided by National Archives in letter of February 1970.

[11] Mortality schedules are discussed in more detail in chapter 11.

was this condition which prompted the American Medical Association, in 1855, to adopt a resolution calling for all members to petition their state legislatures to establish vital statistics offices. In 1879 an act of Congress created the National Board of Health which began almost immediately to publish health statistics for cities that could provide them. That their main emphasis was directed toward uniformity of registration is not difficult to appreciate when you realize that from the twenty-four cities which participated in the program at its outset, fourteen separate forms were used. The differences among these forms were so vast that any comparison of data was next to impossible.[12]

The effect of this new national board was almost unbelievable. By March of 1880, in only its second year, weekly information was being received from about ninety cities. Also in 1880 the board called a meeting of all state and local registration officials (which proved to be the beginning of an annual convention) and, among other things, this conclave discussed collection procedures, standard forms, and uniform legislation from state to state.[13]

As mentioned earlier, the 1880 census on mortality was operated quite differently from those of 1850, 1860, and 1870. The legislative adjustment which effected this change also put the National Board of Health's Committee on Vital Statistics in charge of the mortality schedules of that census.

Prior to the taking of the mortality census of 1900 the Census Office carried on extensive correspondence with each of the states and with those cities with populations over 5,000. It collected extensive data on registration procedures and then published its findings for the benefit of all registration personnel. It recommended a death certificate form and suggested that all areas adopt it before January 1, 1900. Eighteen states and the District of Columbia adopted the form either wholly or with slight modifications, and seventy-one major cities in the remaining states followed suit. On this basis it is believed that the 1900 mortality census was 90 per cent complete.[14]

Various interested organizations continued to have tremendous effect on the local registration of births and deaths even though they had no direct control. By 1910 registration was considered complete enough that it was no longer necessary to attempt to collect vital information as part of the census. These organizations and their progeny under the Census Office (later the Bureau of the Census; then the Federal Security Administration;

---

[12] United States. National Office of Vital Statistics, Vol. I, p. 7.

[13] *Ibid.*, Vol. I, p. 7.

[14] *Ibid.*, Vol. I, p. 7.

still later the Department of Health, Education and Welfare; and today the Department of Health and Human Resources) have continued their efforts, and since 1933 every state in the Union has had a model (uniform) law, or modification thereof, and is in a national registration area which assures sameness from one state to another, both in procedures and in forms used. The last states to actually adopt state-wide birth and death registration (Georgia and New Mexico) did so in 1919, but they were close on the heels of a half-dozen other states.

Useful death records generally developed slightly earlier than good birth records, understandably enough considering the motivation behind the registration movement—the war against disease. And, of the three kinds of vital records being considered here, marriage records have been the slowest to develop. Though in most localities marriage records are often found for periods earlier than either birth or death records, their rate of development has not kept pace. Marriages still have not reached the point of state-wide registration in all states, nor has a standard form been accepted by all states. However, all states do keep good marriage records at some level of jurisdiction.

II. THE USE OF VITAL RECORDS

The utility of American vital records as a source of genealogical evidence is questioned by many in light of the foregoing historical data. These records, in most states, are considered too modern. In some respects this is true, but there is sufficient value in them that they should not be passed over lightly. Death records, especially, contain information of exceptional genealogical value even though most of the records are of relatively recent vintage.

The death certificate form calls not only for information on the death but also on the birth (date and place) and on the parentage of the deceased. As an example, if an elderly person, say eighty-two years old, died in 1915, his death certificate might well provide valuable information about the family (time and place) for an event which transpired in 1833. Of course some certificates lack some of this information because of a lack of knowledge on the part of the informant. Also, for the same reason (and others) some information on a death certificate might be in error. This is not uncommon. I have a death certificate for one of my ancestors which gives a fictitious name for her father because the informant, a son-in-law, apparently did not want to disclose that the decedent's birth was out of wedlock. Those who have willfully given erroneous information create some serious problems for the genealogist.

FIGURE 1—IMPORTANT DATES IN THE HISTORY OF BIRTH AND DEATH REGISTRATION: UNITED STATES

AREA	RECORDS ON FILE FOR ENTIRE AREA		ADMITTED TO REGISTRATION AREA*		AREA	RECORDS ON FILE FOR ENTIRE AREA		ADMITTED TO REGISTRATION AREA*	
	DEATHS	BIRTHS	DEATHS	BIRTHS		DEATHS	BIRTHS	DEATHS	BIRTHS
Alabama	1908	1908	1925	1927	Nevada	1911	1911	1929	1929
Arizona	1909	1909	1926	1926	New Hampshire	1850	1850	1890	1915
Arkansas	1914	1914	1927	1927	New Jersey	1848	1848	1880	1921
California	1905	1905	1906	1919	New Mexico	1919	1919	1929	1929
Colorado	1907	1907	1906	1928	New York	1880	1880	1890	1915
Connecticut	1897	1897	1890	1915	North Carolina	1913	1913	1910	1917
Delaware	1881	1881	1890	1921	North Dakota	1908	1908	1924	1924
District of Columbia	1855	1871	1880	1915	Ohio	1909	1909	1909	1917
Florida	1899	1899	1919	1924	Oklahoma	1908	1908	1928	1928
Georgia	1919	1919	1922	1928	Oregon	1903	1903	1918	1919
Idaho	1911	1911	1922	1926	Pennsylvania	1906	1906	1906	1915
Illinois	1916	1916	1918	1922	Rhode Island	1852	1852	1890	1915
Indiana	1900	1907	1900	1917	South Carolina	1915	1915	1916	1919
Iowa	1880	1880	1923	1924	South Dakota	1905	1905	1906	1932
Kansas	1911	1911	1914	1917	Tennessee	1914	1914	1917	1927
Kentucky	1911	1911	1911	1917	Texas	1903	1903	1933	1933
Louisiana	1914	1914	1918	1927	Utah	1905	1905	1910	1917
Maine	1892	1892	1900	1915	Vermont	1857	1857	1890	1915
Maryland	1898	1898	1906	1916	Virginia	1912	1912	1913	1917
Massachusetts	1841	1841	1880	1915	Washington	1907	1907	1908	1917
Michigan	1867	1867	1900	1915	West Virginia	1917	1917	1925	1925
Minnesota	1900	1900	1910	1915	Wisconsin	1907	1907	1908	1917
Mississippi	1912	1912	1919	1921	Wyoming	1909	1909	1922	1922
Missouri	1910	1910	1911	1927	Alaska	1913	1913	1950	1950
Montana	1907	1907	1910	1922	Hawaii	1896	1896	1917	1929
Nebraska	1905	1905	1920	1920	Puerto Rico	1931	1931	1932	1943
					Virgin Islands	1919	1919	1924	1924

[Courtesy of Department of Health, Education and Welfare, U.S. Public Health Service, National Center for Vital Statistics. From *Vital Statistics of the United States 1950* (1954), Vol. 1, p. 13.]

*A state was admitted to the registration area when it was felt that its level of registration had reached 90 per cent.

The information on a death certificate can help you verify information from family sources too. I recently worked on a problem where the female ancestor had never been positively identified even though her name, approximate age, and place of birth were all apparently known. The problem was during the census period, but a search of the appropriate census schedules failed to show a person of this identity even though there were several families of the correct surname in the area. A death certificate for this woman's son was secured which showed the maiden surname of his mother (the person for whom we had been searching) as something entirely different from what the present family records had stated. Further investigation proved the death certificate to be correct; the ancestor was properly identified and the pedigree was extended.

Dates and places can also be verified through vital records. Whenever there are vital records available in connection with the persons on your pedigree beyond the immediate generation, they should be secured and analyzed for any value they might have in preparing an accurate genealogical record. These records must not be overlooked even when you think you already have the needed information on the person. Dates and places passed down in the family are often the victims of copying errors and poor memories.

III. SECURING THE RECORDS

A. Since State-Wide Registration

It is a relatively easy matter to locate and secure copies of those vital records kept since the instigation of state-wide registration in the several states. Much has been written about this and many books have been published with lists of essential data. Such a list could be given here, too, but data in lists of this kind tends to become outdated rather quickly (especially the prices), so I shall forbear. Rather, I refer you to the booklet (already mentioned in chapter 6) published by the Department of Health and Human Services, *Where to Write for Vital Records.*

This booklet is periodically revised in an effort to keep the information current and is obtainable from the Superintendent of Documents, U.S. Government Printing Office, Washington, DC 20402, for a small fee, order no. S/N 017-022-00794-1.

The booklet includes information on registration areas (usually the states, but also some large cities), the cost of certified copies of certificates, the

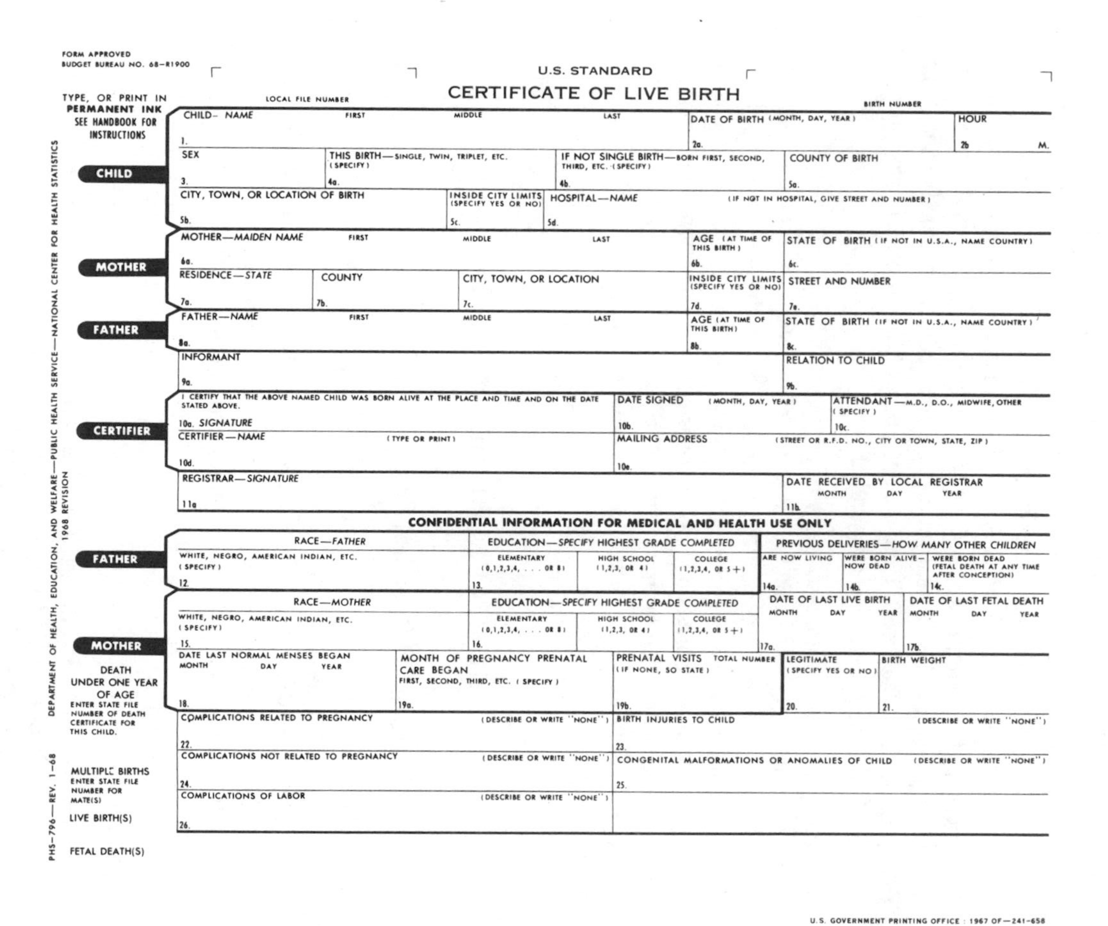

FORM APPROVED
BUDGET BUREAU NO. 68–R1900

U.S. STANDARD
CERTIFICATE OF LIVE BIRTH

TYPE, OR PRINT IN **PERMANENT INK** SEE HANDBOOK FOR INSTRUCTIONS

LOCAL FILE NUMBER — BIRTH NUMBER

CHILD
1. CHILD— *NAME* FIRST MIDDLE LAST
2a. DATE OF BIRTH (MONTH, DAY, YEAR)
2b. HOUR M.
3. SEX
4a. THIS BIRTH—SINGLE, TWIN, TRIPLET, ETC. (SPECIFY)
4b. IF NOT SINGLE BIRTH—BORN FIRST, SECOND, THIRD, ETC. (SPECIFY)
5a. COUNTY OF BIRTH
5b. CITY, TOWN, OR LOCATION OF BIRTH
5c. INSIDE CITY LIMITS (SPECIFY YES OR NO)
5d. HOSPITAL—*NAME* (IF NOT IN HOSPITAL, GIVE STREET AND NUMBER)

MOTHER
6a. MOTHER—*MAIDEN NAME* FIRST MIDDLE LAST
6b. AGE (AT TIME OF THIS BIRTH)
6c. STATE OF BIRTH (IF NOT IN U.S.A., NAME COUNTRY)
7a. RESIDENCE—*STATE*
7b. COUNTY
7c. CITY, TOWN, OR LOCATION
7d. INSIDE CITY LIMITS (SPECIFY YES OR NO)
7e. STREET AND NUMBER

FATHER
8a. FATHER—*NAME* FIRST MIDDLE LAST
8b. AGE (AT TIME OF THIS BIRTH)
8c. STATE OF BIRTH (IF NOT IN U.S.A., NAME COUNTRY)
9a. INFORMANT
9b. RELATION TO CHILD

CERTIFIER
I CERTIFY THAT THE ABOVE NAMED CHILD WAS BORN ALIVE AT THE PLACE AND TIME AND ON THE DATE STATED ABOVE.
10a. *SIGNATURE*
10b. DATE SIGNED (MONTH, DAY, YEAR)
10c. ATTENDANT—M.D., D.O., MIDWIFE, OTHER (SPECIFY)
10d. CERTIFIER—*NAME* (TYPE OR PRINT)
10e. MAILING ADDRESS (STREET OR R.F.D. NO., CITY OR TOWN, STATE, ZIP)
11a. REGISTRAR—*SIGNATURE*
11b. DATE RECEIVED BY LOCAL REGISTRAR MONTH DAY YEAR

CONFIDENTIAL INFORMATION FOR MEDICAL AND HEALTH USE ONLY

FATHER
12. RACE—*FATHER* WHITE, NEGRO, AMERICAN INDIAN, ETC. (SPECIFY)
13. EDUCATION—*SPECIFY* HIGHEST GRADE *COMPLETED* ELEMENTARY (0,1,2,3,4, . . . OR 8) HIGH SCHOOL (1,2,3, OR 4) COLLEGE (1,2,3,4, OR 5+)
PREVIOUS DELIVERIES—*HOW MANY OTHER CHILDREN*
14a. ARE NOW LIVING
14b. WERE BORN ALIVE—NOW DEAD
14c. WERE BORN DEAD (FETAL DEATH AT ANY TIME AFTER CONCEPTION)

MOTHER
15. RACE—*MOTHER* WHITE, NEGRO, AMERICAN INDIAN, ETC. (SPECIFY)
16. EDUCATION—*SPECIFY* HIGHEST GRADE *COMPLETED* ELEMENTARY (0,1,2,3,4, . . . OR 8) HIGH SCHOOL (1,2,3, OR 4) COLLEGE (1,2,3,4, OR 5+)
17a. DATE OF LAST LIVE BIRTH MONTH DAY YEAR
17b. DATE OF LAST FETAL DEATH MONTH DAY YEAR
18. DATE LAST NORMAL MENSES BEGAN MONTH DAY YEAR
19a. MONTH OF PREGNANCY PRENATAL CARE BEGAN FIRST, SECOND, THIRD, ETC. (SPECIFY)
19b. PRENATAL VISITS TOTAL NUMBER (IF NONE, SO STATE)
20. LEGITIMATE (SPECIFY YES OR NO)
21. BIRTH WEIGHT

DEATH UNDER ONE YEAR OF AGE
ENTER STATE FILE NUMBER OF DEATH CERTIFICATE FOR THIS CHILD.

22. COMPLICATIONS RELATED TO PREGNANCY (DESCRIBE OR WRITE "NONE")
23. BIRTH INJURIES TO CHILD (DESCRIBE OR WRITE "NONE")
24. COMPLICATIONS NOT RELATED TO PREGNANCY (DESCRIBE OR WRITE "NONE")
25. CONGENITAL MALFORMATIONS OR ANOMALIES OF CHILD (DESCRIBE OR WRITE "NONE")
26. COMPLICATIONS OF LABOR (DESCRIBE OR WRITE "NONE")

MULTIPLE BIRTHS
ENTER STATE FILE NUMBER FOR MATE(S)
LIVE BIRTH(S)
FETAL DEATH(S)

DEPARTMENT OF HEALTH, EDUCATION, AND WELFARE—PUBLIC HEALTH SERVICE—NATIONAL CENTER FOR HEALTH STATISTICS
1968 REVISION
PHS–796—REV. 1–68

U.S. GOVERNMENT PRINTING OFFICE : 1967 OF—241-658

FIGURE 2—STANDARD CERTIFICATE OF BIRTH
(Certificates with this format are in use in many states.)

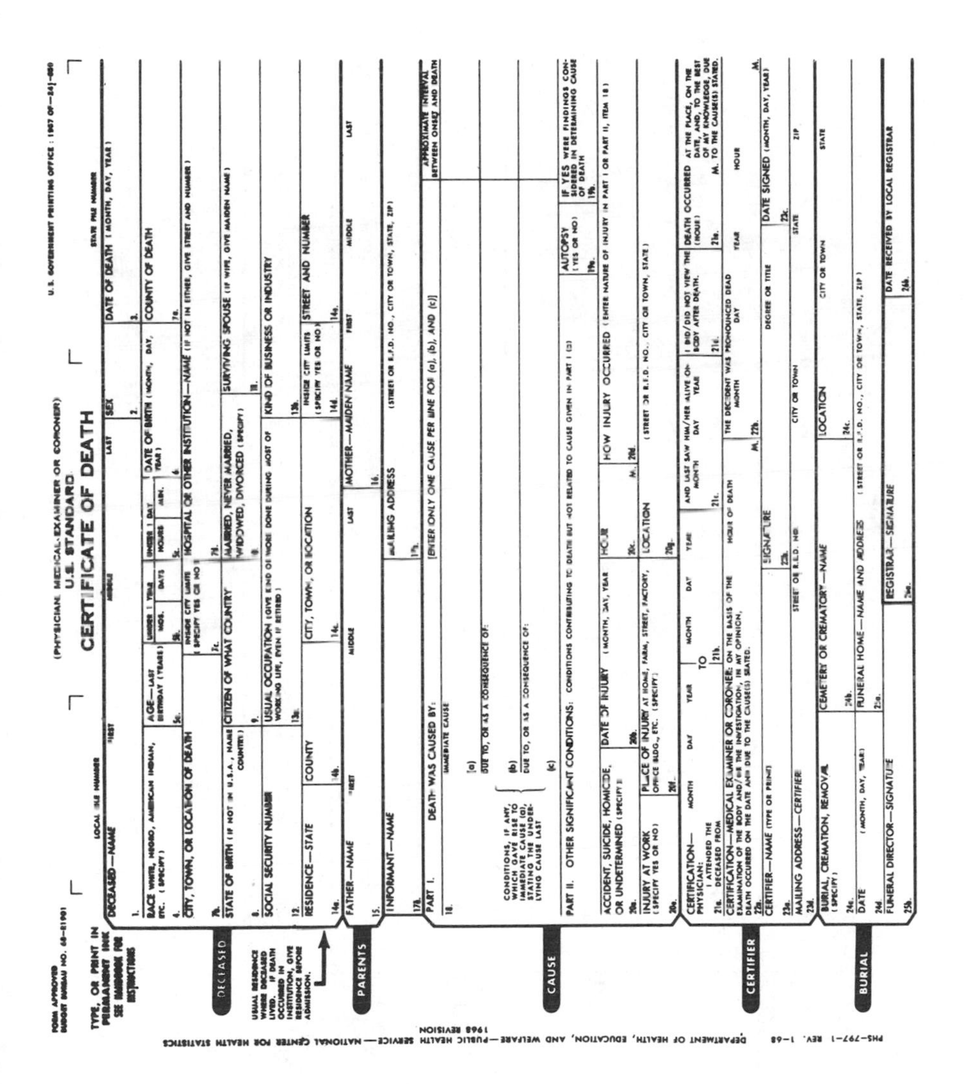

FORM APPROVED
BUDGET BUREAU NO. 68–R1901

(PHYSICIAN, MEDICAL EXAMINER OR CORONER)
U.S. STANDARD
CERTIFICATE OF DEATH

U.S. GOVERNMENT PRINTING OFFICE : 1967 OF—241—050

TYPE, OR PRINT IN PERMANENT INK
SEE HANDBOOK FOR INSTRUCTIONS

LOCAL FILE NUMBER
STATE FILE NUMBER

DECEASED

DECEASED—NAME FIRST MIDDLE LAST 1. | SEX 2. | DATE OF DEATH (MONTH, DAY, YEAR) 3.

RACE WHITE, NEGRO, AMERICAN INDIAN, ETC. (SPECIFY) 4. | AGE—LAST BIRTHDAY (YEARS) 5a. | UNDER 1 YEAR MOS. DAYS 5b. | UNDER 1 DAY HOURS MIN. 5c. | DATE OF BIRTH (MONTH, DAY, YEAR) 6. | COUNTY OF DEATH 7a.

CITY, TOWN, OR LOCATION OF DEATH 7b. | INSIDE CITY LIMITS (SPECIFY YES OR NO) 7c. | HOSPITAL OR OTHER INSTITUTION—NAME (IF NOT IN EITHER, GIVE STREET AND NUMBER) 7d.

STATE OF BIRTH (IF NOT IN U.S.A., NAME COUNTRY) 8. | CITIZEN OF WHAT COUNTRY 9. | MARRIED, NEVER MARRIED, WIDOWED, DIVORCED (SPECIFY) 10. | SURVIVING SPOUSE (IF WIFE, GIVE MAIDEN NAME) 11.

SOCIAL SECURITY NUMBER 12. | USUAL OCCUPATION (GIVE KIND OF WORK DONE DURING MOST OF WORKING LIFE, EVEN IF RETIRED) 13a. | KIND OF BUSINESS OR INDUSTRY 13b.

USUAL RESIDENCE WHERE DECEASED LIVED. IF DEATH OCCURRED IN INSTITUTION, GIVE RESIDENCE BEFORE ADMISSION.

RESIDENCE—STATE 14a. | COUNTY 14b. | CITY, TOWN, OR LOCATION 14c. | INSIDE CITY LIMITS (SPECIFY YES OR NO) 14d. | STREET AND NUMBER 14e.

PARENTS

FATHER—NAME FIRST MIDDLE LAST 15. | MOTHER—MAIDEN NAME FIRST MIDDLE LAST 16.

INFORMANT—NAME 17a. | MAILING ADDRESS (STREET OR R.F.D. NO., CITY OR TOWN, STATE, ZIP) 17b.

CAUSE

PART I. DEATH WAS CAUSED BY: [ENTER ONLY ONE CAUSE PER LINE FOR (a), (b), AND (c)] | APPROXIMATE INTERVAL BETWEEN ONSET AND DEATH

18. IMMEDIATE CAUSE (a)

DUE TO, OR AS A CONSEQUENCE OF: (b)

DUE TO, OR AS A CONSEQUENCE OF: (c)

CONDITIONS, IF ANY, WHICH GAVE RISE TO IMMEDIATE CAUSE (a), STATING THE UNDERLYING CAUSE LAST

PART II. OTHER SIGNIFICANT CONDITIONS: CONDITIONS CONTRIBUTING TO DEATH BUT NOT RELATED TO CAUSE GIVEN IN PART I (a) | AUTOPSY (YES OR NO) 19a. | IF YES WERE FINDINGS CONSIDERED IN DETERMINING CAUSE OF DEATH 19b.

ACCIDENT, SUICIDE, HOMICIDE, OR UNDETERMINED (SPECIFY) 20a. | DATE OF INJURY (MONTH, DAY, YEAR) 20b. | HOUR 20c. M. | HOW INJURY OCCURRED (ENTER NATURE OF INJURY IN PART I OR PART II, ITEM 18) 20d.

INJURY AT WORK (SPECIFY YES OR NO) 20e. | PLACE OF INJURY AT HOME, FARM, STREET, FACTORY, OFFICE BLDG., ETC. (SPECIFY) 20f. | LOCATION (STREET OR R.F.D. NO., CITY OR TOWN, STATE) 20g.

CERTIFIER

CERTIFICATION—PHYSICIAN: I ATTENDED THE DECEASED FROM 21a. MONTH DAY YEAR TO 21b. MONTH DAY YEAR | AND LAST SAW HIM/HER ALIVE ON MONTH DAY YEAR 21c. | I DID/DID NOT VIEW THE BODY AFTER DEATH. 21d. | DEATH OCCURRED (HOUR) 21e. M. AT THE PLACE, ON THE DATE, AND, TO THE BEST OF MY KNOWLEDGE, DUE TO THE CAUSE(S) STATED.

CERTIFICATION—MEDICAL EXAMINER OR CORONER: ON THE BASIS OF THE EXAMINATION OF THE BODY AND/OR THE INVESTIGATION, IN MY OPINION, DEATH OCCURRED ON THE DATE AND DUE TO THE CAUSE(S) STATED. 22a. HOUR OF DEATH M. | THE DECEDENT WAS PRONOUNCED DEAD MONTH DAY YEAR HOUR 22b. M.

CERTIFIER—NAME (TYPE OR PRINT) 23a. | SIGNATURE 23b. DEGREE OR TITLE | DATE SIGNED (MONTH, DAY, YEAR) 23c.

MAILING ADDRESS—CERTIFIER STREET OR R.F.D. NO. CITY OR TOWN STATE ZIP 23d.

BURIAL

BURIAL, CREMATION, REMOVAL (SPECIFY) 24a. | CEMETERY OR CREMATORY—NAME 24b. | LOCATION CITY OR TOWN STATE 24c.

DATE (MONTH, DAY, YEAR) 24d. | FUNERAL HOME—NAME AND ADDRESS (STREET OR R.F.D. NO., CITY OR TOWN, STATE, ZIP) 25a.

FUNERAL DIRECTOR—SIGNATURE 25b. | REGISTRAR—SIGNATURE 26a. | DATE RECEIVED BY LOCAL REGISTRAR 26b.

PHS–797–1 REV. 1–68 DEPARTMENT OF HEALTH, EDUCATION, AND WELFARE—PUBLIC HEALTH SERVICE—NATIONAL CENTER FOR HEALTH STATISTICS
1968 REVISION

FIGURE 3—STANDARD CERTIFICATE OF DEATH

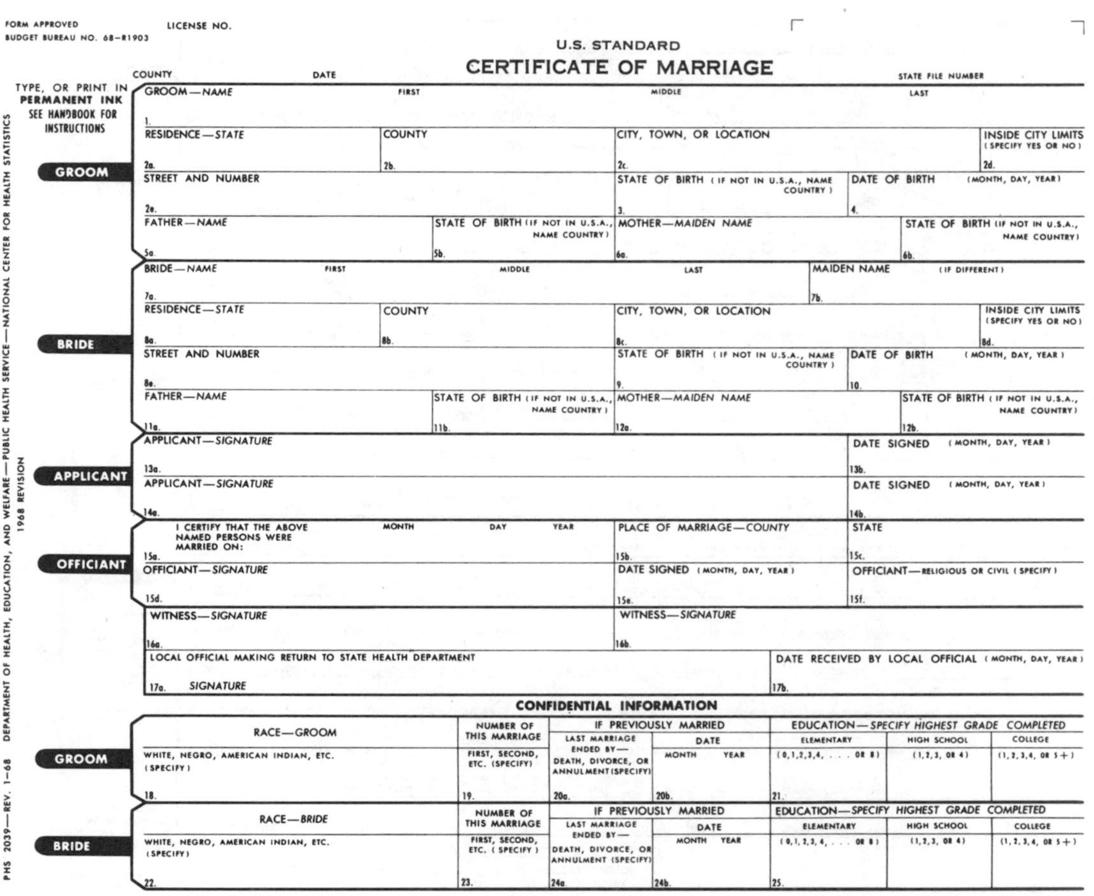

FORM APPROVED
BUDGET BUREAU NO. 68–R1903
LICENSE NO.

U.S. STANDARD
CERTIFICATE OF MARRIAGE

COUNTY | DATE | STATE FILE NUMBER

TYPE, OR PRINT IN **PERMANENT INK** SEE HANDBOOK FOR INSTRUCTIONS

GROOM

GROOM—NAME: FIRST, MIDDLE, LAST (1.)
RESIDENCE—STATE (2a.) | COUNTY (2b.) | CITY, TOWN, OR LOCATION (2c.) | INSIDE CITY LIMITS (SPECIFY YES OR NO) (2d.)
STREET AND NUMBER (2e.) | STATE OF BIRTH (IF NOT IN U.S.A., NAME COUNTRY) (3.) | DATE OF BIRTH (MONTH, DAY, YEAR) (4.)
FATHER—NAME (5a.) | STATE OF BIRTH (IF NOT IN U.S.A., NAME COUNTRY) (5b.) | MOTHER—MAIDEN NAME (6a.) | STATE OF BIRTH (IF NOT IN U.S.A., NAME COUNTRY) (6b.)

BRIDE

BRIDE—NAME: FIRST, MIDDLE, LAST (7a.) | MAIDEN NAME (IF DIFFERENT) (7b.)
RESIDENCE—STATE (8a.) | COUNTY (8b.) | CITY, TOWN, OR LOCATION (8c.) | INSIDE CITY LIMITS (SPECIFY YES OR NO) (8d.)
STREET AND NUMBER (8e.) | STATE OF BIRTH (IF NOT IN U.S.A., NAME COUNTRY) (9.) | DATE OF BIRTH (MONTH, DAY, YEAR) (10.)
FATHER—NAME (11a.) | STATE OF BIRTH (IF NOT IN U.S.A., NAME COUNTRY) (11b.) | MOTHER—MAIDEN NAME (12a.) | STATE OF BIRTH (IF NOT IN U.S.A., NAME COUNTRY) (12b.)

APPLICANT

APPLICANT—SIGNATURE (13a.) | DATE SIGNED (MONTH, DAY, YEAR) (13b.)
APPLICANT—SIGNATURE (14a.) | DATE SIGNED (MONTH, DAY, YEAR) (14b.)

OFFICIANT

I CERTIFY THAT THE ABOVE NAMED PERSONS WERE MARRIED ON: MONTH DAY YEAR (15a.) | PLACE OF MARRIAGE—COUNTY (15b.) | STATE (15c.)
OFFICIANT—SIGNATURE (15d.) | DATE SIGNED (MONTH, DAY, YEAR) (15e.) | OFFICIANT—RELIGIOUS OR CIVIL (SPECIFY) (15f.)

WITNESS—SIGNATURE (16a.) | WITNESS—SIGNATURE (16b.)
LOCAL OFFICIAL MAKING RETURN TO STATE HEALTH DEPARTMENT (17a.) SIGNATURE | DATE RECEIVED BY LOCAL OFFICIAL (MONTH, DAY, YEAR) (17b.)

CONFIDENTIAL INFORMATION

GROOM

RACE—GROOM	NUMBER OF THIS MARRIAGE	IF PREVIOUSLY MARRIED		EDUCATION—SPECIFY HIGHEST GRADE COMPLETED		
		LAST MARRIAGE ENDED BY—	DATE	ELEMENTARY	HIGH SCHOOL	COLLEGE
WHITE, NEGRO, AMERICAN INDIAN, ETC. (SPECIFY) 18.	FIRST, SECOND, ETC. (SPECIFY) 19.	DEATH, DIVORCE, OR ANNULMENT (SPECIFY) 20a.	MONTH YEAR 20b.	(0,1,2,3,4, . . . OR 8) 21.	(1,2,3, OR 4)	(1,2,3,4, OR 5+)

BRIDE

RACE—BRIDE	NUMBER OF THIS MARRIAGE	IF PREVIOUSLY MARRIED		EDUCATION—SPECIFY HIGHEST GRADE COMPLETED		
		LAST MARRIAGE ENDED BY—	DATE	ELEMENTARY	HIGH SCHOOL	COLLEGE
WHITE, NEGRO, AMERICAN INDIAN, ETC. (SPECIFY) 22.	FIRST, SECOND, ETC. (SPECIFY) 23.	DEATH, DIVORCE, OR ANNULMENT (SPECIFY) 24a.	MONTH YEAR 24b.	(0,1,2,3,4, . . . OR 8) 25.	(1,2,3, OR 4)	(1,2,3,4, OR 5+)

PHS 2039—REV. 1–68 DEPARTMENT OF HEALTH, EDUCATION, AND WELFARE—PUBLIC HEALTH SERVICE—NATIONAL CENTER FOR HEALTH STATISTICS
1968 REVISION

U.S. GOVERNMENT PRINTING OFFICE : 1967 O—241-663

FIGURE 4—STANDARD CERTIFICATE OF MARRIAGE

addresses of the record custodians, and some brief remarks relating mainly to the completeness and time period of the records. Everyone doing American research would do well to secure this valuable tool and use it. Another book I would recommend is Thomas Jay Kemp's *Vital Records Handbook* (Baltimore: Genealogical Publishing Co., 1988). This provides addresses of vital records offices, starting dates of the records, fees, and *copies of application forms.*

B. Before State-Wide Registration

Locating extant vital records in any state or registration area prior to the adoption of state-wide registration laws is usually a more difficult task. There were many differences in custom and practice even within the same state. Some places kept records very early; others kept no records at all until required to do so by state statute.

The most exhaustive attempt to compile a list of available vital records in the U.S. was made by the federal government's Works Projects Administration (WPA) as part of the Historical Records Survey projects in the late 1930s and early 1940s. Forty states participated in this program. The participants included all states *except* Alaska (not then a state), Connecticut, Delaware, Hawaii (not then a state), Maine, Maryland, Ohio, Pennsylvania, South Carolina, and Vermont. Each participating state published, as a result of the project, inventories or guides to the vital statistics records available for various counties, cities, and towns within its boundaries and told where and how they were filed. A "WPA List of Vital Statistical Records" issued in 1943 shows the publications for each of the participating states.

Copies of these inventories are available at various larger libraries and historical societies, especially in the states concerned. A list of the several inventories, including guides to inventories of church records (see chapter 20), follows:

ALABAMA:
- "Guide to Public Vital Statistics Records in Alabama: Preliminary Edition." March 1942.
- "Guide to Vital Statistics Records in Alabama: Church Archives." May 1942.

ARIZONA:
- "Guide to Public Vital Statistics Records in Arizona." August 1941.

ARKANSAS:	"Guide to Vital Statistical Records in Arkansas." Vol. I, Public Archives. c. 1942. Vol. II, Church Archives. c. 1942.
CALIFORNIA:	"Guide to Church Vital Records in California: Alameda and San Francisco Counties; Six Denominations." May 1942. "Guide to Public Vital Statistics Records in California." Vol. I, Birth Records. June 1941. Vol. II, Death Records. July 1941.
COLORADO:	"Guide to Vital Statistics Records in Colorado." Vol. I, Public Archives. 1942. Vol. II, Church Archives. 1942.
FLORIDA:	"Guide to Public Vital Statistics Records in Florida." February 1941. "Guide to Supplementary Vital Statistics from Church Records in Florida: Preliminary Edition." Vol. I, Aluchu. June 1942 Vol. II, Gilchrist. June 1942. Vol. III, Orange. June 1942.
GEORGIA:	"Guide to Public Vital Statistics Records in Georgia." June 1941.
IDAHO:	"Guide to Public Vital Statistics Records in Idaho: State and County." March 1942.
ILLINOIS:	"Guide to Public Vital Statistics Records in Illinois." May 1941.
INDIANA:	"Guide to Public Vital Statistics Records in Indiana." July 1941.
IOWA:	"Guide to Public Vital Statistics Records in Iowa." October 1941.
KANSAS:	"Guide to Public Vital Statistics Records in Kansas." March 1942.
KENTUCKY:	"Guide to Public Vital Statistics Records in Kentucky." February 1942.
LOUISIANA:	"Guide to Public Vital Statistics Records in Louisiana." December 1942. "Guide to Vital Statistics Records in Church Archives in Louisiana." Vol. I, Protestant and Jewish Church. December 1942.

Vol. II, Roman Catholic Church. December 1942.

MASSACHUSETTS: "Guide to Public Vital Statistics Records in Massachusetts." 1942.

MICHIGAN: "Vital Statistics Holdings by Government Agencies in Michigan."
Birth Records. 1941.
Marriage Records. 1941.
Death Records. July 1942.
Divorce Records. May 1942.
"Guide to Church Vital Statistics Records in Michigan: Wayne County." April 1942.

MINNESOTA: "Guide to Public Vital Statistics Records in Minnesota." 1941.
"Guide to Church Vital Statistics Records in Minnesota." April 1942.

MISSISSIPPI: "Guide to Vital Statistics Records in Mississippi."
Vol. I, Public Archives. April 1942.
Vol. II, Church Archives. July 1942.

MISSOURI: "Guide to Public Vital Statistics Records in Missouri." July 1941.
"Guide to Vital Statistics: Church Records in Missouri." April 1942.

MONTANA: "Guide to Public Vital Statistics Records in Montana." March 1941.
"Inventory of the Vital Statistics Records of Churches and Religious Organizations in Montana. Preliminary Edition." July 1942.

NEBRASKA: "Guide to Public Vital Statistics Records in Nebraska." September 1941.

NEVADA: "Guide to Public Vital Statistics Records in Nevada." December 1941.

NEW HAMPSHIRE: "Guide to Church Vital Statistics Records in New Hampshire. Preliminary Edition." May 1942.
"Guide to Public Vital Statistics Records in New Hampshire." 1942.

NEW JERSEY: "Guide to Vital Statistics Records in New Jersey."
Vol. I, Public Archives. 1942.
Vol. II, Church Archives. 1942.

"Guide to Naturalization Records in New Jersey." December 1941.

NEW MEXICO: "Guide to Public Vital Statistics Records in New Mexico." March 1942.

NEW YORK: "Guide to Public Vital Statistics Records in New York State (Inclusive of New York City)."
Vol. I, Birth Records. January 1942.
Vol. II, Marriage Records. August 1942.
Vol. III, Death Records. 1942.
"Guide to Vital Statistics Records in Churches in New York State (Exclusive of New York City)."
Vol. I. May 1942.
Vol. II. June 1942.
"Guide to Vital Statistics Records in the City of New York: Churches."
Borough of Bronx. April 1942.
Borough of Brooklyn. 1942.
Borough of Manhattan. 1942.
Borough of Queens. May 1942.
Borough of Richmond. 1942.

NORTH CAROLINA: "Guide to Vital Statistics Records in North Carolina."
Vol. I, Public Vital Statistics. June 1942.

NORTH DAKOTA: "Guide to Public Vital Statistics Records of North Dakota." August 1941.
"Guide to Church Vital Statistics Records in North Dakota." March 1942.

OKLAHOMA: "Guide to Public Vital Statistics Records in Oklahoma." June 1941.

OREGON: "Guide to Public Vital Statistics Records in Oregon." April 1942.

RHODE ISLAND: "Summary of Legislation Concerning Vital Statistics in Rhode Island." July 1937.
"Guide to Public Vital Statistics Records: Births, Marriages, Deaths in the State of Rhode Island and Providence Plantations." June 1941.

SOUTH DAKOTA: "Guide to Public Vital Statistics Records in South Dakota." January 1942.

TENNESSEE: "Guide to Public Vital Statistics Records in Tennessee." June 1941.

"Guide to Church Vital Statistics Records in Tennessee." August 1942.

TEXAS: "Guide to Public Vital Statistics Records in Texas." June 1941.

UTAH: "Census of Weber County (Exclusive of Green River Precinct), Provisional State of Deseret, 1850." October 1937.

"Guide to Public Vital Statistics Records in Utah." November 1941.

VIRGINIA: "Index to Marriage Notices in the *Southern Churchman,* 1835-1941."
Vol. A-K. May 1942.
Vol. L-Z. May 1942.

"Guide to the Manuscript Collections of the Virginia Baptist Historical Society. Supplement No. 1, Index to the Obituary Notices in the *Religious Herald,* Richmond, Virginia, 1828-1938."
Vol. I, A-L. August 1941.
Vol. II, M-Z. September 1941.

WASHINGTON: "Guide to Public Vital Statistics Records in Washington." June 1941.

"Guide to Church Vital Statistics Records in Washington. Preliminary Edition." February 1942.

WEST VIRGINIA: "Inventory of Public Vital Statistics Records in West Virginia: Births, Deaths, and Marriages." March 1941.

"Guide to Church Vital Statistics Records in West Virginia." February 1942.

WISCONSIN: "Guide to Public Vital Statistics Records in Wisconsin." September 1941.

"Guide to Church Vital Statistics Records in Wisconsin." September 1941.

"Outline of Vital Statistics Laws in Wisconsin." September 1941.

WYOMING: "Guide to Public Vital Statistics Records in Wyoming." June 1941.

"Guide to Vital Statistics Records in Wyoming: Church Archives. Preliminary Edition." March 1942.

As I do not know where all of these guides are available, I suggest that a letter to the county clerk or other appropriate jurisdictional authority in the locality of your interest will usually provide a quick answer as to whether any vital records are available for any time period prior to state-wide registration. The booklet *Where to Write for Vital Records* offers some very brief information on this subject, as does Kemp's *Vital Records Handbook.*

It might also be appropriate to mention that, though these inventories were up-to-date in 1942, etc., many changes in the interim have outdated much of what they say.

C. Other Helps

In the foregoing historical discussion, I mentioned that registration of births and deaths in large cities usually antedated state-wide registration by several years. In New Orleans, for example, there are birth records from 1790 and death records from 1803, while there was not state-wide registration in Louisiana until July 1914. Four large cities which had vital registration before the states in which they are located are still self-contained registration districts. They are:

Baltimore, Maryland—records from 1875.

Boston, Massachusetts—records from 1639.

New Orleans, Louisiana—birth records from 1790, death records from 1803.

New York, New York:

- Bronx Borough—records from 1898. (Records from 1866 to 1897 are in Manhattan Borough at the Municipal Archives, 31 Chambers St., New York, NY 10007.)
- Brooklyn Borough—death records from 1847; others from 1866 (at Municipal Archives, Manhattan).
- Manhattan Borough—records from 1847 at Municipal Archives, also some death records from 1795.
- Queens Borough—became a separate district after the beginning of state-wide registration.
- Richmond Borough—became a separate district after the beginning of state-wide registration.

Several other cities which originally fell into this category have since ceased to function as separate entities and are now within the state registration areas. In most cases, however, the records from those early periods are still on file in the cities concerned. Of special note here are Philadelphia, from 1860, and Pittsburgh, from 1870 (including Allegheny City—now a part of Pittsburgh—from 1882 to 1905). There was state registration in

Pennsylvania from 1885, but records in the present Bureau of Vital Statistics date from 1906. Albany, Buffalo, and Yonkers, New York, also had their own registration offices prior to 1914 when they joined the state system.

In many states you may secure copies of vital certificates from either the state vital records office or from some local official; in other states you can get them only from the state office.

There are also a few states which have had their early vital records (from various sources) collected and indexed in their state libraries and/or archives and (sometimes) even published. If you happen to have ancestry in one of these you may get some real help from those records. The following states have such collections:

CONNECTICUT: "The Barbour Collection" (vital records compiled from church, cemetery, and town records before 1850).
"The Hale Collection" (marriages, deaths, and burials from cemetery inscriptions and newspapers (pre-Civil War).

DELAWARE: Birth records, 1861-1913 (with a card index for the same period); death records, 1855-1910 (with a card index to records from very early to 1888); index cards of baptisms, 1759-1890; and index cards of marriages, 1730-1850, are at the Hall of Records, Dover. These were mostly collected by the Clerks of the Peace in the counties.

MAINE: Vital records index, early to 1892. (The records are for only eighty towns, and only seventeen of these have been published under authority of the Maine Historical Society.)
Brides' Index to Maine Marriages, 1895-1953.

MARYLAND: Indexes are in the Hall of Records, Annapolis, for births, 1801-1877, and deaths, 1865-1880, for Anne Arundel County and some during the 1600s in Charles, Kent, Somerset, and Talbot counties. There are also card indexes to pre-Revolutionary marriages in Charles, Kent, and Somerset counties; to later marriages in Anne Arundel, Caroline, Cecil, Dorchester, Frederick, and Prince George's counties; and a separate index for Baltimore County marriages.

MASSACHUSETTS: From early to 1850. (Church, cemetery, and town meeting records for more than 200 towns have been collected and published, mostly by the New England Historic Genealogical Society, Franklin P. Rice, and the Essex Institute. Many more are still in the towns themselves. Also, the Massachusetts State Archives, State House, Boston, MA 02133, has all available vital records for the state from 1841 to 1890.

NEW HAMPSHIRE: Town records, many extending to the 1850s, 1860s, and later, have been transcribed and indexed in a special collection at the State House in Concord. (There is a complete card index to surnames.)

RHODE ISLAND: "The Arnold Collection of Vital Records" (1636-1850) is published (in 21 volumes) and is available in many libraries.

VERMONT: There is an index to vital records from early to 1870 and also an index to vital records from 1871 to 1908 at the Secretary of State's Office, Montpelier.

VIRGINIA: Birth and death records, 1853-1896, were kept in the towns and cities, within which they are arranged chronologically. They are on non-circulating microfilms at the Archives Branch of the Virginia State Library, Richmond, where there is also a state-wide index to births. Inquiries concerning photocopying or certifying these records should be addressed to the Bureau of Vital Records and Health Statistics, James Madison Building, P.O. Box 1000, Richmond, VA 23208. All available marriage records prior to 1853 are also on microfilm in the Archives Branch. A guide to these is John Vogt and T. William Kethley, *Marriage Records in the Virginia State Library: A Researcher's Guide* (Athens, GA: Iberian Press, 1984). Marriage registers, 1853-1935 (with indexes 1853-1899), are also in the Archives Branch. Photocopies, however, are available only from the Bureau of Vital Records and Health Statistics.[15]

It is interesting to note that, of the states in the above list, all except Delaware, Maryland, and Virginia are in New England. New England, as a whole, was a leader in the keeping of vital records; but, as good as these collections are, none of them is complete. The South and the middle-Atlantic states, however, were generally much less record-conscious. As you leave New England and go south, the further you go, as a general rule, the more deficient are the vital records.

D. Marriage and Divorce Records

Marriage records are most often found in the county where the licenses were issued, usually in the jurisdiction of the county clerk or county recorder. However, in New York and New England they were kept in the town. The early records consist mostly of records of licenses and bonds. Many of these early records have been published in books and periodicals, but the quality often leaves much to be desired. One such publication of importance to those with early New England ancestry is Clarence Almon Torrey's *New England Marriages Prior to 1700* (a manuscript index in twelve handwritten volumes of some 37,000 marriages from about 100,000 references in about 2,000 sources). This alphabetical listing is available on microfilm and on photocopy at the New England Historic Genealogical Society Library in Boston. The listing includes many marriages in England for people who later came to New England. The Barbour Collection (Connecticut) was apparently not used as an input source. Listings are alphabetical according to husbands' names. A published version of the Torrey work was produced by the Genealogical Publishing Company, Baltimore, in 1985.

Marriage records are, for the most part, available quite early in many areas of the U.S., with such well-known exceptions as South Carolina, which did not have official marriage records until 1911. Most early marriage records do not contain detailed genealogical data; however, there are exceptions to this.

Some substitutes for original marriage records that are of interest to the genealogist are newspaper notices and announcements, as well as the vital records lists of marriage licenses which most newspapers have carried. The former, especially, can provide interesting details.

---

[15] Letter to author from Donley L. Edwards, Head Public Services Section, Archives Branch, Virginia State Library, dated January 21, 1988.

There are often errors in marriage records, and you should always be alert to that possibility. The parties themselves sometimes falsified the data they gave to the record keeper. Also, some county clerks followed the questionable practice (in order to be more efficient) of recording the date of the marriage at the time the license was issued instead of waiting for the certificate to be returned. There are also spelling errors in these records, as in all other records you will use.

In addition to possible errors, the researcher should be aware that some marriage records will be wholly or partially unreadable for one reason or another. Some of those on microfilm have been poorly filmed. In others the record keepers had poor handwriting. Some records have been damaged and/or faded by time and the elements.

Though they are not actually vital records, there are other possible sources of marriage information. These include widows' pension applications, family Bibles, and census records. These sources are all discussed elsewhere in this book.

While on the subject of marriages, I would also like to make a few brief comments on common-law marriages. They are widely misunderstood and many relationships which people call common-law marriages are not marriages at all but only unlawful cohabitations. A common-law marriage *is* a legal marriage. Its existence is largely a matter of legality, eligibility, and intent.

On the issue of *legality,* note that, in order for a legal common-law marriage to exist, such a relationship must be recognized as a legal marriage in the state where the relationship existed. In the United States many states (as well as the District of Columbia) now recognize common-law marriages, and many others have recognized them at some time in the past. The states which currently recognize common-law marriages are Alabama, Georgia, Idaho, Iowa, Kansas, North Dakota, Ohio, Oklahoma, Pennsylvania, Rhode Island, South Carolina, and Texas. Some states which have recently recognized and permitted common-law marriages are Colorado (before 1973), Florida (before 1968), Indiana (before 1958), Michigan (before 1957), Minnesota (before 1941), Mississippi (before 1956), Montana (before 1978), Nevada (before 1943), and South Dakota (before 1959). For a thorough state-by-state analysis see Noel C. Stevenson, *Genealogical Evidence* (Laguna Hills, CA: Aegean Park Press, 1979), pages 93-102.

Eligibility is another matter. In order for a legal common-law marriage (or any other legal marriage) to come into existence, both parties must be eligible for marriage. There can be no marriage if either has a legal, undivorced spouse or if there are other impediments, such as a relationship between the man and woman too close to permit marriage.

Lastly, there must be *intent* of the parties to be husband and wife to each other. Some indications of this intent which must be present include consummation, cohabitation, and a reputation in the community that they are husband and wife.

When a common-law marriage exists it is the same as any other marriage in the eyes of the law, and such a marriage is usually given full faith and credit even in the states which do not permit or recognize creation of such within their own boundaries. And a common-law marriage can be dissolved only by a legal divorce or by the death of one or both parties. There is no common-law divorce.

A few states today (such as Utah) are statutorily recognizing presumptive marriages. That is, the state presumes that a couple are married to each other if they have lived together as if they were married for a specified period of time. Such presumptions, of course, can be rebutted through presentation of evidence on such grounds as lack of eligibility. The real target of these statutes is prevention of welfare abuse, and they have nothing to do with the common law. They essentially say "we will presume you are married if you live together, regardless of your intent." Such statutes will certainly be tested in the courts and will no doubt create some bigamists.

Divorce records follow much the same pattern as marriage records but are not generally as early. Most of the records are in the counties where the divorces were granted, but many states now have central filing of official divorce records. More is said about divorce records, their location, and their use in chapter 19.

E. Writing for the Records

When writing for copies of certificates, be as brief as you can. This is not a matter of winning good will; it is just a matter of practicality. In the first place, busy public officials do not have time to read long letters; in the second place, your specific requests and desires may be overlooked in the body of a long letter; and in the third place, time is too precious to spend it writing verbiage that may only be confusing.

It is a good idea to tell your relationship to the person about whom you are inquiring, as some vital statistics offices will supply records only to relatives. Insofar as possible the correct amount of money should be sent with your request. Personal checks should be avoided in favor of cashier's checks and money orders; some offices will not accept personal checks. You may also send cash if you like, but it is not recommended as a standard practice. It is impossible to prove that cash was sent and it is also more difficult to keep a good record of it.

When you request a copy of a certificate you should state all you know about the event, or the record may not be found; but it is not necessary to give information about a person's *death* when you are requesting his *birth* certificate as I have seen some persons do. If you desire a death certificate the date of death is needed. (Note that there are a few exceptions to this rule depending upon the filing systems used in the state. Most states file their records chronologically, but some have special indexes.)

The specific place of death is not always important, but it may help registration officials determine if they are sending you the correct certificate. Correct names are important. You will appreciate this when you write for the death certificate of someone you know died on a certain date in a certain place, and the certificate cannot be found. The certificate is there, all right, but you sent the wrong name. This often happens with women. A remarriage you have forgotten, or about which you may not have known, can cause many difficulties. And efforts to secure the dcath certificate of a married woman under her maiden surname will be disappointing.

A request for a birth certificate must include the names of parents, but parents' names are not quite so important in securing a copy of the death record or marriage record. However, they can be helpful if some other important data are unknown. Ages on death certificates fall into this same "helpful" category. If you do not have all pertinent names and dates it is still worthwhile to try to obtain a copy of the record. If it is found it will have even greater value for you. Vital records officials must have some information with which to work—and the more the better, so long as it is relevant to the request.

The following letter is a typical request for a death certificate, but remember that this example is given only by way of suggestion and will not fit every situation:

138 N. Westside Ave.
Haysbury, GA
September 30, 1989

Section of Vital Statistics
State Department of Health
350 State Office Building
St. Paul, MN 55101

Gentlemen:

Please send me a copy of the death certificate of my great-grandmother, Martha Black, who died June 7, 1928, in Cloverton, Pine County, at about age 59. Her father was Mendon Marshall and her husband was Braxton Black.

Three dollars ($3) are enclosed to cover your fee.

Thank you for your help.

Sincerely yours,

(signed) Sidney Orbeck

The dates in which the several states began registration of vital records are shown in Figure 1, earlier in this chapter.

IV. TOWN MEETING RECORDS

In most of New England vital information was recorded in the town meeting records. Typical of these are the ones of Chester, Vermont. Note from the following extracts that births and marriages were generally recorded much more faithfully than were deaths. You will also note that it was quite common to record the births of all the children in a family at one time, often several years after the actual dates of some of those births:

> Jacob Chase of Chesterfield and Olive Wilson of Chester were Joined in Marriage Feb^{ry} 1st, 1792 by Daniel Heald Jus^{t} Peace

> October ye 3: 1792 then personally came before me the subscriber at my dwelling house in Chester John Chandler and Anna Tarlick Both of Chester and Said John Chandler Did then and there Say the following words /viz/ I take this wooman to be my weded wife and then Said Ann Tarlick Said Likewise I take this man to be my weded husband but nither of them took eatch other by the hand.
>
> Daniel Heald Just. Peace

> Polly Ston Dafter of John Ston June by Lucy his wife born September ye 30 1773

Rhoda Ston Dafter of John Ston Juner by Lucy his wife born October 8th 1774

Sally Ston Dafter of John Ston Juner by Lucy his wife born Jany 4th 1777

Lucy Ston Dafter of John Ston June by Lucy his wife born Jany 4th 1779

John and Betsy Ston Son and Dafter of John Ston Juner by Lucy his wife born Sept 4th 1783

John Ston Son of John Ston June by Lucy his wife born July 28th 1784

Earl and Betsy Ston Son and Dafter of John Ston Juner by Lucy his wife born April 13th 1786

Ivanna Ston Dafter of John Ston Junr by Lucy his wife born June 2th 1788

Ivanna Ston Dafter of John Ston Juner by Lucy his wife born June 2th 1790[16]

Calvon Here and Abner Here Sons of William Here by Merean his wife May 22 1788

Abner Here Departed this Life May 23 1788

Calven Here Departed this Life August 6 1788

Thomas Riggs Here Son of William Here by Merean his wife born July 13 1789

Aber^{n} Here Son of William Here by Merean his wife born June 29 1791

Stephen Here Son of William Here by Merean his wife born March 22 - 1796

Though some town meeting records have been published and others have been microfilmed, most must still be searched at the town hall.

V. RECORD PROBLEMS

The main problems and limitations in the use of vital records by the genealogist are as follows.

A. Limitation of Time

The greatest weakness, of course, is the time limitation. Certainly vital records are of no value for the periods not covered, but too often we imagine

---

[16] This family was recorded in the Chester town meeting records in 1798.

greater limitations than actually exist. As already discussed, many gaps *can* be bridged through efficient use of even relatively recent records.

B. Lack of Needed Information

Another limitation is that it is frequently necessary to have quite detailed information in order to secure the needed records. Too often the vital records office, because of the filing system employed, will request the very information from you that you are trying to obtain. Some data always necessary, regardless of filing system, are:

1. Name at the time of the event.

2. Place of the event (at least the state). Many persons, when they get older, go to live with their children, and it is sometimes difficult to find this information.

3. Date of the event. (In all states it is necessary to have at least an approximate time; some require the exact date.)

4. For a birth record you must have the names of the parents. For a marriage or death certificate those names are also helpful. (In any case the name of one parent is better than the name of neither.)

Without this information on names, places, and dates you really have nothing with which to work, and the need for complete identifying data is even more acute if the surname happens to be a common one.

C. The Reliability Question

There is always a reliability question on vital records which must be considered. On a marriage record an age or the name of a parent may be deliberately falsified for one reason or another. These same items of information might also be unintentionally mis-stated with just as serious an effect. With a death certificate you are at the mercy of the informant. If his connection to the deceased was close the data may be accurate, but often even those close to a person really know little about him. The date and place of birth and the names of parents as given on the death certificate of an elderly person are strictly secondary evidence. Also consider that even members of the immediate family who would otherwise furnish reliable data do not think as clearly as they should when confronted with the shock of the death and the pressure of the situation, and the record suffers. (Note that this is also one reason why obituary notices are often inaccurate or incomplete.)

D. Early Forms

Some of the early forms used by the states before they entered the national registration areas left much to be desired (especially death records). Many of them called for only limited information of a genealogical nature. Texas is one such state. The early Texas death certificates asked only for the country of birth (and "U.S.A." doesn't really give much assistance in research). This was the case as late as 1927.

E. Handwriting

Handwriting is sometimes a problem. If you have trouble reading a prescription written by your family doctor you should have no difficulty imagining that a birth or death certificate filled in, at least partially, by that same physician might also be hard to read. Today these certificates are usually typewritten and death certificates are generally the responsibility of the funeral director, but these practices are both of relatively recent adoption. Thus some old handwritten certificates hold many secrets, undecipherable by even the most adept. One advantage you have is that most registration offices make photocopies of their records when you request copies and do not attempt to interpret them for you. This gives you the opportunity to puzzle over the actual handwriting and study it to your heart's content in an effort to discover the correct interpretation. You do not have to accept anyone else's say-so; and you may have clues in what you already know about the person that will lead you to a correct interpretation of the writing.

F. Other Legibility Problems

Other things are often responsible for illegibility also. Acts of God such as floods and fires take their toll. Mildew, insects, poor ink, and inferior grades of paper can render a record (or portions thereof) unreadable after a time and thus limit its genealogical value. Those record collections which have most often become the victims of improper care are the ones kept on the local (town or county) level. Elected public officials too often have no idea or feeling about the value of the records left in their custody; and among vital records, marriage records and those birth and death records kept before state-wide registration have suffered most. Overheated attics and musty basements have too long been used as repositories for the oldest and most valuable records.

Some states are passing legislation to bring old records into a place where they can be properly cared for and preserved. This is a step forward and should be encouraged by every genealogist and genealogical organization.

G. Restrictive Legislation

Another, more recent, problem is that some states are enacting laws designed to restrict access to their vital records. Missouri is a good example of this. The law in that state provides that:

> The state registrar shall not permit inspection of the records or issue a certified copy of a certificate or part thereof unless he is satisfied that the applicant therefore has an interest in the matter recorded and that the information therein contained is for a research project, study, newspaper, radio, television, or other news media reports or reporting, or it is necessary for the determination of personal or property rights. The registrar may require an applicant to sign an affidavit reciting the grounds on which he seeks to acquire the information requested. His decision shall be subject, however, to review by the division or a court.[17]

This is the law. It is quite restrictive on its face, but the Director of Vital Records for the state advises that:

> If a person is interested in the record of a member of his family and will indicate his relationship to the person and . . . [will] furnish all available information such as the name of the person at the time of the event, the approximate address, and approximate year in which the event occurred . . . [the request will be given serious consideration].[18]

Being aware of laws like this one can assist you immeasurably as you seek to secure copies of records pertaining to your ancestors. An interesting law was adopted by Connecticut requiring a person who is not an attorney to be a member of the state genealogical society to obtain access to public records.

It is plain that vital records are not without fault as a genealogical source, but the perfect source does not exist. If you overlook vital records when they are available you are not doing the best research you can do. In the interest of complete and accurate records, your research must also be complete and accurate.

---

[17] Revised Statutes of Missouri, Chapter 193.240.

[18] Letter from Charles L. Bell, Director of Vital Records, Missouri Division of Health, dated May 7, 1969. Mr. Bell also advised in his letter that the term "research project" as used in the statute has been held to refer to a matter concerning the Public Health.

11

Census Returns

There is probably no other single group of records in existence which contain more information about persons and families who lived during the 1800s than do the population schedules of the U.S. federal censuses. Though these population censuses are still largely unindexed, and only on *rare* occasions are families arranged alphabetically (in just a few counties in some of the earlier years), their value is great. A census search can be laborious and very time-consuming as you must read name-by-name and page-by-page. But no research on an American genealogical problem after the beginning of the census is complete until all pertinent census schedules have been searched.

I. WHAT IS THE CENSUS?

The first United States census was taken in 1790 as a result of a Constitutional provision that:

> Representatives and direct Taxes shall be apportioned among the several states which may be included with this Union, according to their respective Numbers . . . The actual Enumeration shall be made within three Years after the first Meeting of the Congress of the United States, and within every subsequent Term of ten Years, in such Manner as they shall by Law direct.[1]

---

[1] United States Constitution, Article 1, Section 2.

It is indeed a unique historical phenomenon for a government to set out in the document which formed it the means and method of taking a census, but, due to the very nature of this new government, it was a political necessity.

The first census did just what it was designed to do—it counted the population, but within limited age categories by sex. However, it did go one step beyond this—it also listed the names of the heads of families—and through several decades the same basic pattern remained unchanged except that the age groupings became more specific. Since 1790 the federal census has been taken every ten years (as the Constitution provided). As already mentioned, many of the early censuses contained a minimal amount of genealogical data; but, notwithstanding this fact, they have proven to be invaluable aids in painting a complete genealogical picture as well as useful tools to help locate and identify specific persons and families.

If you will carefully study Charts 1, 2, and 3 and the reproductions of the various census schedule forms in this chapter you can gain an excellent knowledge of the various censuses and their contents. The time you spend studying these will be well spent. In connection with the censuses you should note that there were no printed schedule forms for any of the censuses prior to 1830, though the form to be followed was prescribed in the various census acts. Because of this there is little uniformity in the early schedules. Presumably the persons taking the census, the marshals' assistants, provided their own paper, except for the 1790 census of Massachusetts where printed forms were used. The remaining 1790 enumerations were taken on paper ranging in length from four inches to three feet, and some were taken "in merchants' account books, journals, or ledgers; and others were bound with old newspapers, wrapping paper, or wallpaper." [2]

The greatest, and surely the most significant, changes in the census schedule forms (see glossary at the end of this chapter) came in 1850. The entire format of that census was altered from that used in previous years. Lemuel Shattuck of Massachusetts, probably America's greatest crusader in the vital registration and public health movement (see chapter 10), was the man chiefly responsible for the innovations of this and later censuses.

Shattuck prepared a census for Boston in 1845 which so impressed federal officials that they invited him to Washington in 1849 to help with plans for the 1850 U.S. census. Apparently he was almost solely responsible for the great improvements which were made. The most important change

---

[2] Katherine H. Davidson and Charlotte M. Ashby (comps.), *Preliminary Inventory of the Records of the Bureau of the Census* (Washington, DC: The National Archives, 1964), p. 99.

CHART 1–CENSUS CONTENT (1790-1840)

CONTENT	1790	1800	1810	1820	1830	1840
Names of heads of families only.	X	X	X	X	X	X
Number of free white males under 16 in family.	X					
Number of free white males 16 and over in family.	X					
Number of free white females in family (no age breakdown).	X					
Number of free white males and females (separately) in family, in age groups: under 10, 10-15, 16-25, 26-44, 45 and over.		X	X	X		
Number of free white males and females (separately) in family, in 5-year age groups under 20 years of age.					X	X
Number of free white males and females (separately) in family, in 10-year age groups, ages 20-99.					X	X
Number of free white males and females (separately) in family, 100 years of age and over.					X	X
Number of free white males in family, ages 16-18.				X		
Number of all other free persons (including colored).	X	X(a)	X(a)	(a) X(b)	X(c)	X(c)
Number of slaves.	X	X	X	X(d)	X(e)	X(e)
Number of foreigners not naturalized.				X	X	
Number of deaf and dumb (white and colored enumerated separately).					X(f)	X
Number of blind (white and colored enumerated separately).					X	X
Number of insane or idiotic (white and colored enumerated separately).						X(g)
Civil division of place of residence.	X	X	X	X	X	X
Number of persons engaged in agriculture.				X		X
Number of persons engaged in commerce.				X		X
Number of persons engaged in manufacture.				X		X(h)
Number of persons employed in mining.						X
Number of persons employed in navigation of canals, lakes, and rivers.						X
Number of persons employed in navigation of the ocean.						X
Number of persons employed in the learned professions and engineers.						X
Names and ages of pensioners for Revolutionary or military service.						X
Number of white males over 21 years of age who cannot read and write.						X
Number of scholars (of various types)						X
Total number of persons in household.					X	X

General note: All of the above categories which refer to "number of persons" have to do with each household individually.

(a) Except Indians, not taxed.

(b) Free colored persons in age groups (under 14, 14-25, 26-44, 45 and over) by sex.

(c) Free colored persons in age groups (under 10, 10-23, 24-35, 36-54, 55-99, 100 and over) by sex.

(d) In age groups (under 14, 14-25, 26-44, 45 and over) by sex.

(e) In age groups (under 10, 10-23, 24-35, 36-54, 55-99, 100 and over) by sex.

(f) In age groups (under 14, 14-24, 25 and over). Slaves and free colored are grouped together.

(g) Those in public charge and those in private charge are separately listed.

(h) And the trades.

CHART 2—CENSUS CONTENT (1850-1910)

CONTENT	1850	1860	1870	1880	1900	1910
Name of every person whose usual place of abode on the census date was in this household. (1)	X	X	X	X	X	X
Dwelling houses are numbered in order of enumerator's visit.	X	X	X	X	X	X
Families are numbered in order of enumerator's visit.	X	X	X	X	X	X
Enumeration districts listed at top of pages.	X			X	X	X
Post office addresses at top of pages.		X	X	X	X	X
Street addresses given in cities.				X	X	X
Age of every person at last birthday prior to census date. (1)	X	X	X	X	X(9)	X
Sex of every person.	X	X	X	X	X	X
Color or race of every person. (2)	X	X	X	X	X	X
Profession, occupation, or trade of every person. (3)	X	X	X	X	X	X
Value of real estate owned by person.	X	X	X			
Value of personal property owned by person.		X	X			
Place of birth (state, territory, or country) of each person.	X	X	X	X	X	X
Place of birth (state, territory, or country) of each person's father and mother. (7)				X	X	X
If person was married within the census year. (1)	X	X	X(8)	X		
If person attended school within the census year. (1)	X	X	X	X	X(12)	X
If person could not read or write. (4)	X	X	X	X	X	X
If person was deaf and dumb, blind, insane, idiotic. (5)	X	X	X	X		X
If person was a pauper or a convict. (6)	X	X				
Month of birth if born within year prior to census date. (1)			X	X		
If person's father/mother were of foreign birth. (7)			X			
If person was a male citizen of the U.S. age 21 or over.			X			
If person was a male citizen, age 21 or over, whose right to vote was denied or abridged on grounds other than rebellion or other crime.			X			
Relationship of each person to head of family.				X	X	X
Civil (marital) condition.				X	X	X
Time unemployed within census year. (10)				X	X	X
Sickness or disability, if person was sick or temporarily disabled (on date of enumerator's visit).				X		

CHART 2 (continued)

CONTENT	1850	1860	1870	1880	1900	1910
If person was maimed, crippled, bedridden, or otherwise disabled.				X		
Length of time in U.S. (for immigrant) and whether naturalized.					X	X
If a farm or a home was owned or rented and whether owned property was mortgage free.					X	X
Number of years of person's present marriage.					X	X
If person spoke English.					X	X(11)
How many children a mother had had and how many were still living.					X	X
If person was a Civil War veteran or widow.						X

(1) Census date was June 1 for 1850-1900; April 15 for 1910.

(2) In 1850 and 1860 this included white, black, and mulatto. In 1870 and 1880 it added Chinese and Indian. In 1900 and 1910 there was only a blank space to record "color or race."

(3) In 1850 this included only males over 15; in 1860 it included all persons over 15; in 1870 and 1880 it included all persons; in 1900 it included all 10 and older, and in 1910 it included all persons and indicated the type of business in which employed and whether "employer, employee, or working on own account."

(4) In 1850 and 1860 this specifically related to only persons over 20. In 1870 and later there were two separate columns. Also in 1880 and later it identified those who "can," not those who "cannot."

(5) In 1850, 1860, and 1870 the correct word was to be written in the column; in 1880 and 1910 there were separate columns, but 1910 included only "deaf and dumb" and "blind in both eyes."

(6) The correct word was to be written in the column.

(7) There are separate columns.

(8) Gives the specific month.

(9) Gives month and year of each person's birth.

(10) In 1880 and 1900 this figure is stated in number of months; in 1910 it is in number of weeks.

(11) Identifies language spoken.

(12) Asked for number of months attended, while all others only inquired as to whether the person attended school during the year.

CHART 3–IMPORTANT CENSUS DATA

STATE	BECAME A TERRITORY	BECAME A STATE	FIRST AVAILABLE CENSUS	PERTINENT COMMENTS	MISSING CENSUSES								
					1790	1800	1810	1820	1830	1840	1850	1860	1870
Alabama	1817	1819	1830	Before creation of the State of Miss. in 1817 Ala. formed the E. half of the Miss. Terr. It had been a part of Ga. until 1802. That part of the state S. of the 31st parallel was in Spanish W. Fla. until 1812.			All (as part of the Miss. Terr.)	All. (Census of some counties is in *Alabama Historical Quarterly* [Fall 1944, Vol. 6].)					
Alaska	1912	1959	1900	Those censuses before territorial status were taken while Alaska was still a district.									
Arizona	1863	1912	1870 (1850 and 1860 are in N.M. Terr.)	Ariz. was in N.M. Terr. 1850-63. A portion in the S. was added by the Gadsden Prchs. in 1852 while still in N.M. Terr.									
Arkansas	1819	1836	1830	Ark. was in the La. Prchs. of 1803 and was part of the Mo. Terr. 1812-19 when Mo. first applied for statehood. The Ark. Terr. included the Indian lands in Okla.				All				Little River County	
California		1850	1850	Spain controlled Calif. before 1822. From 1822 to 1848 it was owned by Mexico.							San Francisco, Santa Clara, and Contra Costa cos.		
Colorado	1861	1876	1870 (1860 Census of Arapahoe Co. in Kan. Terr.)	The area now comprising Colo. included about 50 million acres previously assigned to Utah and Kan., about 10 million from the N.M. Terr. The Terr. of Jefferson was voted by the residents in 1859 but was never recognized by Congress.									

CHART 3—(continued)

STATE	BECAME A TERRITORY	BECAME A STATE	FIRST AVAILABLE CENSUS	PERTINENT COMMENTS	MISSING CENSUSES								
					1790	1800	1810	1820	1830	1840	1850	1860	1870
Connecticut		1788	1790	One of the original 13 states. Fifth to ratify the Constitution.									
Delaware		1787	1800	One of the original 13 states. First to ratify the Constitution.	All (reconstructed)								
District of Columbia	1790	Became seat of govt. in 1800.	1800 (Part of 1790 is in Montgomery and Prince George's counties, Maryland.)	Land area was taken from both Va. and Md. to form the district.		Incomplete	All (including Alexandria Co., now in Va.)						
Florida	1822	1845	1830	Fla., which early included parts of S. Miss. and Ala., had at various times belonged to Spain and Britain, was ceded to U.S. by Spain in 1819.								Hernando County	
Georgia		1788	1820	One of the original 13 states. Fourth to ratify the Constitution.	All (reconstructed)	All except Oglethorpe County	All	Franklin, Rabun, and Twiggs cos.					
Hawaii	1900	1959	1900	Ruled by native monarchs until 1893, was then a republic until 1898, then ceded itself to U.S.									
Idaho	1863	1890	1870 (Part is in Utah census.)	Originally a part of the Oregon Terr., 1848-53; Wash. Terr., 1853-63; became Idaho Terr. in 1863 including small parts of Mont. and Wyo. W. of the divide.									Kootenai County

CHART 3—(continued)

STATE	BECAME A TERRITORY	BECAME A STATE	FIRST AVAILABLE CENSUS	PERTINENT COMMENTS	MISSING CENSUSES								
					1790	1800	1810	1820	1830	1840	1850	1860	1870
Illinois	1809	1818	1820	Ill. was part of the N.W. Terr. (1787), became part of Ind. Terr. (1800), thus remained until 1809. Original Ill. Terr. included area of present Wisc. and E. part of Minn.		All (as part of the Ind. Terr.)	All except Randolph County						
Indiana	1800	1816	1820	Became part of the N.W. Terr. (1787). The Ind. Terr. as set up in 1800 incuded Ill., Wisc., W. Mich., E. Minn., with E. Mich. being added in 1803.		All	All	Daviess County	*				
Iowa	1838	1846	1840	Iowa was part of the La. Prchs. (1803). Was in Mo. Terr. 1812-21, unorganized territory 1821-34, Mich. Terr. 1834-36, Wisc. Terr. 1836-38.									
Kansas	1854	1861	1860	Kan. was part of the La. Prchs. (1803). Was in Mo. Terr. 1812-21, unorganized territory (Indian) 1821-54.									Arapahoe County
Kentucky		1792	1810	Very early the Ky. area was considered part of Augusta Co., Va. Later (1584) part of Virginia Co. Pre-settlement Ky. called Fincastle Co., Va. During time of early settlement it was called Kentucky Co., Va. (c. 1775-76). In 1776 it was divided into 3 counties—Fayette, Jefferson and Lincoln. Further divided into 9 counties in 1790. The early settlers called it Transylvania.	All. (Tax lists have been substituted.)	All. (Tax lists have been substituted.)							

*Wabash County, Indiana, for 1830 was originally reported missing. However, the county was not created until 1832 (from Cass and Grant counties).

CHART 3—(continued)

STATE	BECAME A TERRITORY	BECAME A STATE	FIRST AVAILABLE CENSUS	PERTINENT COMMENTS	MISSING CENSUSES								
					1790	1800	1810	1820	1830	1840	1850	1860	1870
Louisiana	1805	1812	1810	Part of the La. Prchs. (1803). S. part of prchs. lands became Orleans Terr. in 1804. La. was the major portion of this territory.			St. Landry and W. Baton Rouge p'sh. and some areas no longer in state.					Bienville Parish	
Maine		1820	1790 (in Mass.)	This territory was annexed by Mass. in 1693 as York(shire) Co. and remained part of Mass. until 1820. In 1760 the one county was divided to form three.		Part of York Co.							
Maryland		1788	1790	One of the original 13 states. Seventh to ratify the Constitution.	Allegany, Calvert, and Somerset counties	All of Baltimore Co. except the City of Baltimore			Montgomery, Prince George's, St. Mary's, Queen Anne's, and Somerset counties				
Massachusetts		1788	1790	One of the original 13 states. Sixth to ratify the Constitution. Included Maine until 1820.		Part of Suffolk County							
Michigan	1805	1837	1820	Part of the N.W. Terr. (1787). In 1800 the W. part of lower Mich. and E. part of upper Mich. became part of Ind. Terr. In 1802 all of state was in Ind. Terr. and thus remained until 1805 when			All						

CHART 3—(continued)

STATE	BECAME A TERRITORY	BECAME A STATE	FIRST AVAILABLE CENSUS	PERTINENT COMMENTS	MISSING CENSUSES								
					1790	1800	1810	1820	1830	1840	1850	1860	1870
Michigan (continued)				Mich. Terr. was created. Jurisdiction extended W. to the Miss. River, including Wisc. and E. Minn. (1818-36).									
Minnesota	1849	1858	1850 (There was also a special enumeration in 1857.)	In 1787 E. part of area became part of N.W. Terr. W. part was in La. Prchs. of 1803. In 1800 E. part was in Ind. Terr.; 1818 in Mich. Terr.; 1836 in Wisc. Terr. Thus remained until 1849. Wisc. Terr. also included the W. part of the state. The Minn. Terr. (1849) extended W. to the Mo. River including much of what later became the Dakota Territory.									All originals missing except the counties alphabetically from Stearns to Wright. (State Hist. Soc. and Nat'l Archives have copies of missing schedules.)
Mississippi	1798	1817	1820	Originally claimed by Ga. Remained loyal to the Crown during Revolutionary War, but was taken over by Spain 1789-91. Held by Spain until 1798. All of the state S. of 31st parallel was in Spanish W. Fla. until 1812. In 1817 Ala. was separated from the Miss. Territory.		All	All (including Alabama)		Pike County			Hancock, Sunflower, and Washington counties	
Missouri	1812	1821	1830	N. part of the La. Prchs. was made Mo. Terr. in 1812. Originally this territory included Ark., Iowa, Kan., Neb., and Okla.			All (in La. Terr.)	All					
Montana	1864	1889	1860 (in Neb. Terr. and Wash. Terr.)	Extreme N.W. part of state was in Ore. Terr. 1846-53, Wash. Terr. 1853-63, Idaho Terr. 1863-64. Most of state part of La. Prchs. (1803).									

CHART 3—(continued)

STATE	BECAME A TERRITORY	BECAME A STATE	FIRST AVAILABLE CENSUS	PERTINENT COMMENTS	MISSING CENSUSES								
					1790	1800	1810	1820	1830	1840	1850	1860	1870
Montana (continued)				In La. Terr. 1805-12, Mo. Terr. 1812-54, Neb. Terr. 1854-61, Dakota Terr. 1861-64.									
Nebraska	1854	1864	1860	Originally part of La. Prchs. (1803). Part of Mo. Terr. 1812-20 (no settlers until 1823), unorganized territory 1820-34. In 1834 part of area was placed under jurisdiction of Ark., part under Mich., and part under Mo. When Neb. Terr. was created it included parts of Colo., Mont., Wyo., and N. and S. Dakota (N. from the 40th parallel to Canada and W. from Mo. River to continental divide). Area was reduced to present size of state in 1861 with creation of Colo. and Dakota Terr.									
Nevada	1861	1864	1860 (in Utah Terr.)	Land ceded to U.S. by Mexico 1848. From 1850 to 1861 it was part of Utah Terr., except S. tip of state which was in N.M. Terr. 1850-63, before Ariz. Terr. was organized.									
New Hampshire		1788	1790	One of the original 13 states. Ninth to ratify the Constitution.		Parts of Rockingham and Strafford counties		Grafton Co.; parts of Rockingham and Strafford counties					
New Jersey		1787	1830	One of the original 13 states. Third to ratify the Constitution.	All	All	All	All					

CHART 3—(continued)

STATE	BECAME A TERRITORY	BECAME A STATE	FIRST AVAILABLE CENSUS	PERTINENT COMMENTS	MISSING CENSUSES								
					1790	1800	1810	1820	1830	1840	1850	1860	1870
New Mexico	1850	1912	1850	Land ceded to U.S. by Mexico in 1848, except for strip of land which Texas had claimed E. of the Rio Grande. When territory was created in 1850 it included Ariz. and part of Colo. (A small area in S.W. corner and a larger area now in Ariz. were added by Gadsden Prchs., 1852.)									
New York		1788	1790	One of the original 13 states. Eleventh to ratify the Constitution.			Courtland County						
North Carolina		1789	1790	One of the original 13 states. Twelfth to ratify the Constitution. Included Tennessee until 1796.	Caswell, Granville, and Orange counties		Craven, Green, New Hanover and Wake counties	Currituck, Franklin, Martin, Montgomery, Randolph, and Wake counties					
North Dakota	1861	1889	1860 (as the Dakota Terr.)	Area was originally part of the La. Prchs. (1803). Later when Minn. Terr. formed in 1849 it included all of the area of N.D. as far W. as the Mo. River, but was left in unorganized territory in 1859 when Minn. was cut to its present boundaries. As Dakota Terr. was organized in 1861 it included both Dakotas									

CHART 3—(continued)

STATE	BECAME A TERRITORY	BECAME A STATE	FIRST AVAILABLE CENSUS	PERTINENT COMMENTS	MISSING CENSUSES								
					1790	1800	1810	1820	1830	1840	1850	1860	1870
North Dakota (continued)				and most of Wyo. and Mont. In 1864 Wyo. and Mont. separated to form Mont. Terr. A movement to divide the Dakotas began in early 1870s but was not legislated until 1889 when both became states.									
Ohio	1799	1803	1820	Ohio was originally part of the N.W. Terr. (1787) and was the first state carved out of this area. It began to function as a state in 1802.		All	All	Franklin and Wood counties					
Oklahoma	1890	1907	1890 (partial)	Okla. became part of the Ark. Terr. in 1819 but the relevant history dates from 1866 when the Indian tribes ceded the W. portion of their domain to the U.S. Land was not opened for white settlement until 1889. The Indian Terr. (about the E. ⅓ of the present state) was not officially organized but remained under the jurisdiction of Ark. until statehood.									
Oregon	1848	1859	1850	Original Oregon Terr. embraced all of Wash. and Idaho, British Columbia to 54°40′, and Mont. and Wyo. W. of the continental divide until cut to present size to become a state.									

CHART 3—(continued)

STATE	BECAME A TERRITORY	BECAME A STATE	FIRST AVAILABLE CENSUS	PERTINENT COMMENTS	MISSING CENSUSES								
					1790	1800	1810	1820	1830	1840	1850	1860	1870
Pennsylvania		1787	1790	One of the original 13 states. Second to ratify the Constitution.		Part of Westmoreland County	Parts of Bedford, Cumberland and Philadelphia counties						
Rhode Island		1790	1790	One of the original 13 states. Thirteenth to ratify the Constitution.									
*South Carolina		1788	1790	One of the original 13 states. Eighth to ratify the Constitution.		Richland County							
South Dakota	1861	1889	1860 (as the Dakota Terr.)	Originally part of the La. Prchs. (1803). When Minn. Terr. was formed (1849) it included all of the area of S. Dak. E. of the Mo. River, but this area was later left unorganized (1859) when Minn. was cut back to its present size. When the Dak. Terr. was created in 1861 it included both Dakotas and most of Mont. and Wyo. In 1864 Mont. and Wyo. separated to form the Mont. Terr. and in the early 1870s a movement to form two Dakotas began, but no legislation to this effect was passed until 1889 when both were									

*It was previously reported that the censuses for Clarendon County, South Carolina, for 1820-1850 were missing. However, the present-day Clarendon County was not created until 1855 (from Sumter District). The old Clarendon County (created in 1785 from Camden) became defunct in 1800.

CHART 3—(continued)

STATE	BECAME A TER-RITORY	BECAME A STATE	FIRST AVAIL-ABLE CENSUS	PERTINENT COMMENTS	MISSING CENSUSES								
					1790	1800	1810	1820	1830	1840	1850	1860	1870
South Dakota (continued)				made states. Before the area E. of Mo. River was in Minn. Terr. it had been in the Wisc. Terr. (1836-49).									
Tennessee		1796	1820 (one county in 1810)	Tenn. was originally a part of N.C. In the early settlement period it was called Washington Co., N.C. The State of Franklin was formed in an effort to separate from N.C. but it was never recognized.		All. (Part reconstructed from tax lists.)	All missing except Rutherford County. Grainger County published.	Anderson, Bledsoe, Blount, Campbell, Carter, Claiborne, Cocke, Grainger, Greene, Hamilton, Hawkins, Jefferson, Knox, McMinn, Marion, Monroe, Morgan, Rhea, Roane, Sevier, Sullivan, and Washington counties					

CHART 3—(continued)

STATE	BECAME A TERRITORY	BECAME A STATE	FIRST AVAILABLE CENSUS	PERTINENT COMMENTS	MISSING CENSUSES								
					1790	1800	1810	1820	1830	1840	1850	1860	1870
Texas		1845	1850	Texas belonged to Spain before 1822. In 1822 Mexico became sovereign. It belonged to Mexico until an independent republic was set up in 1836 by the settlers.								Blanco, Coleman, Concho, Duval, Edwards, Hardeman, Kimble, Knox, LaSalle, McCullock, McMullen, Tarrant, Taylor, Wichita, Wilbarger, and Wilson cos.	Archer, Baylor, Concho, Edwards, Hardeman, Knox, Taylor, Wichita, and Wilbarger counties
Utah	1850	1896	1850	Original territory included all of Nevada except S. tip. It also included W. Colo. and S.W. Wyo. (as far N. as the present Utah-Idaho border).									
Vermont		1791	1790	Prevented from being one of the original states by claims made on her territory by N.H. and N.Y. Fourteenth state.									
Virginia		1788	1810	One of the original 13 states. Tenth to ratify the Constitution. Included W.Va. until 1863; Ky. until 1792. Alexandria Co. was in the Dist. of Col. in the censuses of 1820, 1830 and 1840. The 1810 of Alexandria Co. is missing.	All. (Tax lists have beeen substituted.)	All	Cabell, Grayson, Greenbrier, Halifax, Hardy, Henry, James City, King Wm., Lee, Louisa, Mecklenburg, Nansemond, Northampton, Orange, Patrick, Pittsylvania, Russell, and Tazewell cos.						

CHART 3—(continued)

STATE	BECAME A TERRITORY	BECAME A STATE	FIRST AVAILABLE CENSUS	PERTINENT COMMENTS	MISSING CENSUSES								
					1790	1800	1810	1820	1830	1840	1850	1860	1870
Washington	1853	1889	1860	In Ore. Terr. 1848-53. What later became Idaho Terr., with small sections of Mont. and Wyo., was included in Wash. Terr. from 1853-63.									
West Virginia		1863	1810 (in Va.)	Separated itself from Va. and was admitted to the Union during the Civil War.	All (part of Va.)	All (part of Va.)	Cabell, Greenbrier, and Hardy counties (in Va.)						
Wisconsin	1836	1848	1820 (in Mich. Terr.)	Was part of the N.W. Terr. (1787). In Ind. Terr. 1800-09, in Ill. Terr. 1809-18, in Mich. Terr. 1818-36. In the beginning the Wisc. Terr. extended W. as far as Mo. River and included what later became the Minn. Terr. and much of the Dakota Terr.		All (as part of Indiana Terr.)	All (as part of Illinois Terr.)						
Wyoming	1868	1890	1860 (in Neb. Terr.)	The area was mainly in the La. Prchs. (1803). Later it was in Neb. Terr. 1854-61, Dakota Terr. 1861-64, Mont. Terr. 1864-68. The extreme W. part was in the Ore. Terr. 1848-53, Wash. Terr. 1853-63, Idaho Terr. 1863-68; and the S.W. corner was in Utah Terr. 1850-68.									

FIRST CENSUS OF THE UNITED STATES 1790

HEADS OF FAMILIES ______________________
(STATE)

____
(COUNTY)

NAME OF HEAD OF FAMILY	Free white males of 16 years and upward, including heads of families.	Free white males under 16 years.	Free white females including heads of families.	All other free persons.	Slaves.
______ Town, City					

FIGURE 1 — THE 1790 FEDERAL CENSUS

CENSUS OF 1800

SCHEDULE OF THE WHOLE NUMBER OF PERSONS WITHIN THE DIVISION ALLOTTED TO. . . . .

Name of county, parish, township, town or city, where the family resides. Names of heads of families.	Free white males: Under 10 years of age; Of 10 and under 16; Of 16 and under 26, including heads of families; Of 26 and under 45, including heads of families; Of 45 and upwards, including heads of families	Free white females: Under 10 years of age; Of 10 and under 16; Of 16 and under 26, including heads of families; Of 26 and under 45, including heads of families; Of 45 and upwards, including heads of families	All other free persons, except Indians not taxed	Slaves

FIGURE 2 — THE 1800 FEDERAL CENSUS
(Note that the same schedule form was also used for the 1810 census.)

CENSUS OF 1820

SCHEDULE OF THE WHOLE NUMBER OF PERSONS WITHIN THE DIVISION ALLOTTED TO. . . . .

<table>
<tr><td>Name of county, parish, township, town or city, where the family resides.</td><td rowspan="2">Free white males:
Under 10 years of age
Of 10 and under 16
Between 16 and 18
Of 16 and under 26, including heads of families
Of 26 and under 45, including heads of families
Of 45 and upwards, including heads of families</td><td rowspan="2">Free white females:
Under 10 years of age
Of 10 and under 16
Of 16 and under 26, including heads of families
Of 26 and under 45, including heads of families
Of 45 and upwards, including heads of families</td><td rowspan="2">Foreigners not naturalized</td><td rowspan="2">Number of persons engaged in:
Agriculture
Commerce
Manufacture</td><td rowspan="2">Slaves:
Males:
Under 14 years
Of 14 and under 26
Of 26 and under 45
Of 45 and upwards
Females:
Under 14 years
Of 14 and under 26
Of 26 and under 45
Of 45 and upwards</td><td rowspan="2">Free colored persons:
Males:
Under 14 years
Of 14 and under 26
Of 26 and under 45
Of 45 and upwards
Females:
Under 14 years
Of 14 and under 26
Of 26 and under 45
Of 45 and upwards</td><td rowspan="2">All other persons, except Indians not taxed</td></tr>
<tr><td>Names of heads of families.</td></tr>
<tr><td></td><td></td><td></td><td></td><td></td><td></td><td></td><td></td></tr>
</table>

NOTE: In addition to the columns shown on this reproduction of the 1820 census form provided by the Census Bureau, there was also a column which showed, for those engaged in manufacturing, the "nature of manufacturing."

FIGURE 3 — THE 1820 FEDERAL CENSUS

Department of Commerce
Bureau of the Census
CENSUS OF 1830.
SCHEDULE of the whole number of persons within the Division allotted to .... by the Marshal of the District (or Territory) of ....

Name of county, city, ward, town, township, parish, precinct, hundred, or district	Names of heads of families	Free white persons, including heads of families																										Slaves												Total	White persons included in the foregoing				
		Males:													Females:													Males:						Females:											
		Under 5 years of age	Of 5 and under 10	Of 10 and under 15	Of 15 and under 20	Of 20 and under 30	Of 30 and under 40	Of 40 and under 50	Of 50 and under 60	Of 60 and under 70	Of 70 and under 80	Of 80 and under 90	Of 90 and under 100	Of 100 and upwards	Under 5 years of age	Of 5 and under 10	Of 10 and under 15	Of 15 and under 20	Of 20 and under 30	Of 30 and under 40	Of 40 and under 50	Of 50 and under 60	Of 60 and under 70	Of 70 and under 80	Of 80 and under 90	Of 90 and under 100	Of 100 and upwards	Under 10 years of age	Of 10 and under 24	Of 24 and under 36	Of 36 and under 55	Of 55 and under 100	Of 100 and upwards	Under 10 years of age	Of 10 and under 24	Of 24 and under 36	Of 36 and under 55	Of 55 and under 100	Of 100 and upwards		Who are deaf and dumb, under 14 years of age	Who are deaf and dumb, of 14 and under 25	Who are deaf and dumb, of 25 and upwards	Who are blind	Aliens—foreigners not Naturalized

FIGURE 4 — THE 1830 FEDERAL CENSUS

NOTE: This reproduction of the 1830 census form provided by the Census Bureau fails to show that this census also enumerated in each household "free colored persons" within the same sex and age categories as it did slaves. This census also gives the same information as for "white persons included in the foregoing" on slaves and free colored persons who were deaf and dumb and blind. On this part of the form slaves and free colored persons were counted together.

Department of Commerce
Bureau of the Census
CENSUS OF 1840.

SCHEDULE of the whole number of persons within the Division allotted to .... by the Marshal of the ....
District (or Territory) of ....

Name of county, city, ward, town, township, parish, precinct, hundred, or district	Names of heads of families	Free white persons, including heads of families																										Slaves												Total	Number of persons in each family engaged in	Pensioners for Revolutionary or military services, included in the foregoing	
		Males:													Females:													Males:						Females:								Name	Age
		Under 5 years of age	Of 5 and under 10	Of 10 and under 15	Of 15 and under 20	Of 20 and under 30	Of 30 and under 40	Of 40 and under 50	Of 50 and under 60	Of 60 and under 70	Of 70 and under 80	Of 80 and under 90	Of 90 and under 100	Of 100 and upwards	Under 5 years of age	Of 5 and under 10	Of 10 and under 15	Of 15 and under 20	Of 20 and under 30	Of 30 and under 40	Of 40 and under 50	Of 50 and under 60	Of 60 and under 70	Of 70 and under 80	Of 80 and under 90	Of 90 and under 100	Of 100 and upwards	Under 10 years of age	Of 10 and under 24	Of 24 and under 36	Of 36 and under 55	Of 55 and under 100	Of 100 and upwards	Under 10 years of age	Of 10 and under 24	Of 24 and under 36	Of 36 and under 55	Of 55 and under 100	Of 100 and upwards				

FIGURE 5 — THE 1840 FEDERAL CENSUS

NOTE: The 1840 census contains extensive information not included on this reproduction of the form provided by the Census Bureau. The same information, by sex and age, is included for free colored persons as for slaves. The unnamed "number of persons engaged in . . ." columns included mining; agriculture; commerce; manufacturing and trades; navigation of the ocean; navigation of canals, lakes, and rivers; and learned professions and engineers. There are also columns giving the number (among those already enumerated) of deaf and dumb, blind, and insane and idiots, for both white and black—and whether the insane and idiots were at public or private charge. With regard to education, it enumerated the number of scholars in universities and colleges, academies and grammar schools, and primary and common schools. The number of scholars at public charge was also stated, as was the number of white males over 21 in each household who could not read and write.

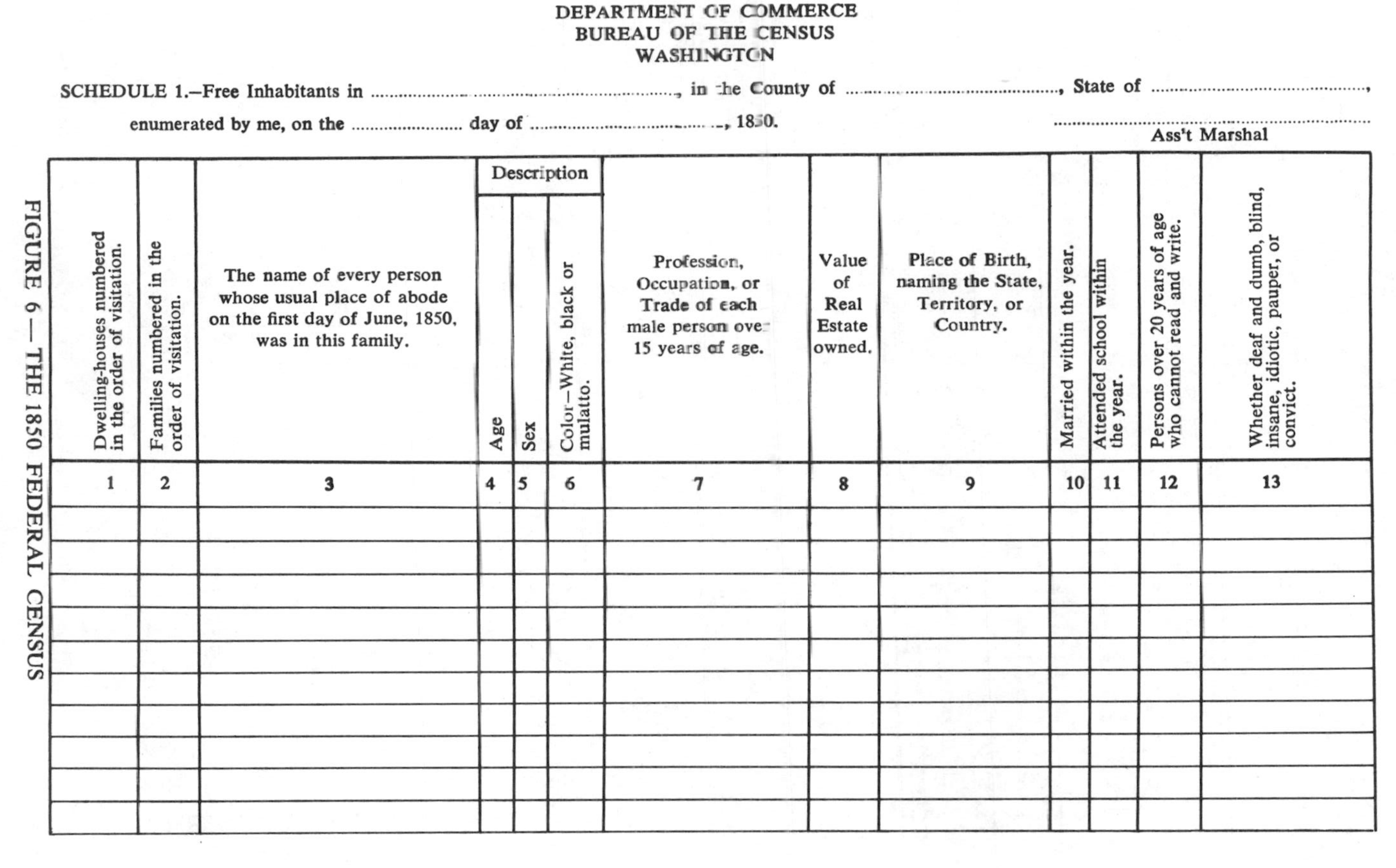

DEPARTMENT OF COMMERCE
BUREAU OF THE CENSUS
WASHINGTON

SCHEDULE 1.—Free Inhabitants in ...., in the County of ...., State of ....,
enumerated by me, on the .... day of ...., 1850.

....
Ass't Marshal

Dwelling-houses numbered in the order of visitation.	Families numbered in the order of visitation.	The name of every person whose usual place of abode on the first day of June, 1850, was in this family.	Description: Age	Description: Sex	Description: Color—White, black or mulatto.	Profession, Occupation, or Trade of each male person over 15 years of age.	Value of Real Estate owned.	Place of Birth, naming the State, Territory, or Country.	Married within the year.	Attended school within the year.	Persons over 20 years of age who cannot read and write.	Whether deaf and dumb, blind, insane, idiotic, pauper, or convict.
1	2	3	4	5	6	7	8	9	10	11	12	13

FIGURE 6 — THE 1850 FEDERAL CENSUS

Page No. ______

SCHEDULE 1.—Free Inhabitants in ____________ in the County of ____________

State of ________ enumerated by me, on the ______ day of ______, 1860.

Post Office ____________ ____________, Ass't Marshal.

	Dwelling Houses—numbered in the order of visitation.	Families numbered in the order of visitation.	The name of every person whose usual place of abode on the first day of June, 1860, was in this family.	DESCRIPTION. Age.	Sex.	Color, White, Black, or Mulatto.	Profession, Occupation, or Trade of each person, male and female, over 15 years of age.	VALUE OF ESTATE OWNED. Value of Real Estate.	Value of Personal Estate.	Place of Birth, Naming the State, Territory, or Country.	Married within the year.	Attended School within the year.	Persons over 20 years of age who can not read and write.	Whether deaf and dumb, blind, insane, idiotic, pauper, or convict.	
	1	2	3	4	5	6	7	8	9	10	11	12	13	14	
1															1
2															2
3															3
4															4
5															5
6															6
7															7
8															8
9															9
10															10
11															11
12															12
13															13
14															14
15															15
16															16

FIGURE 7—THE 1860

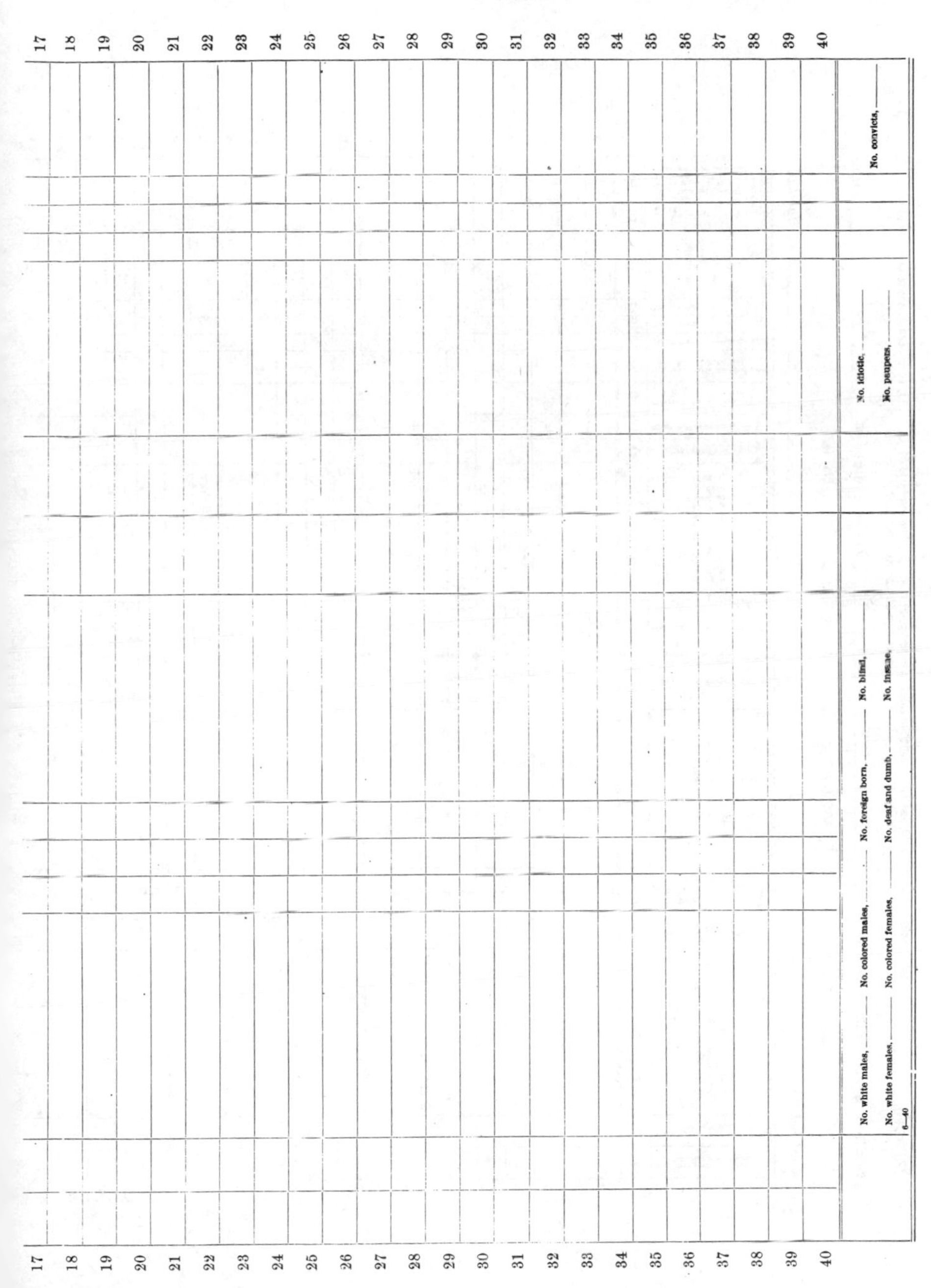

FEDERAL CENSUS

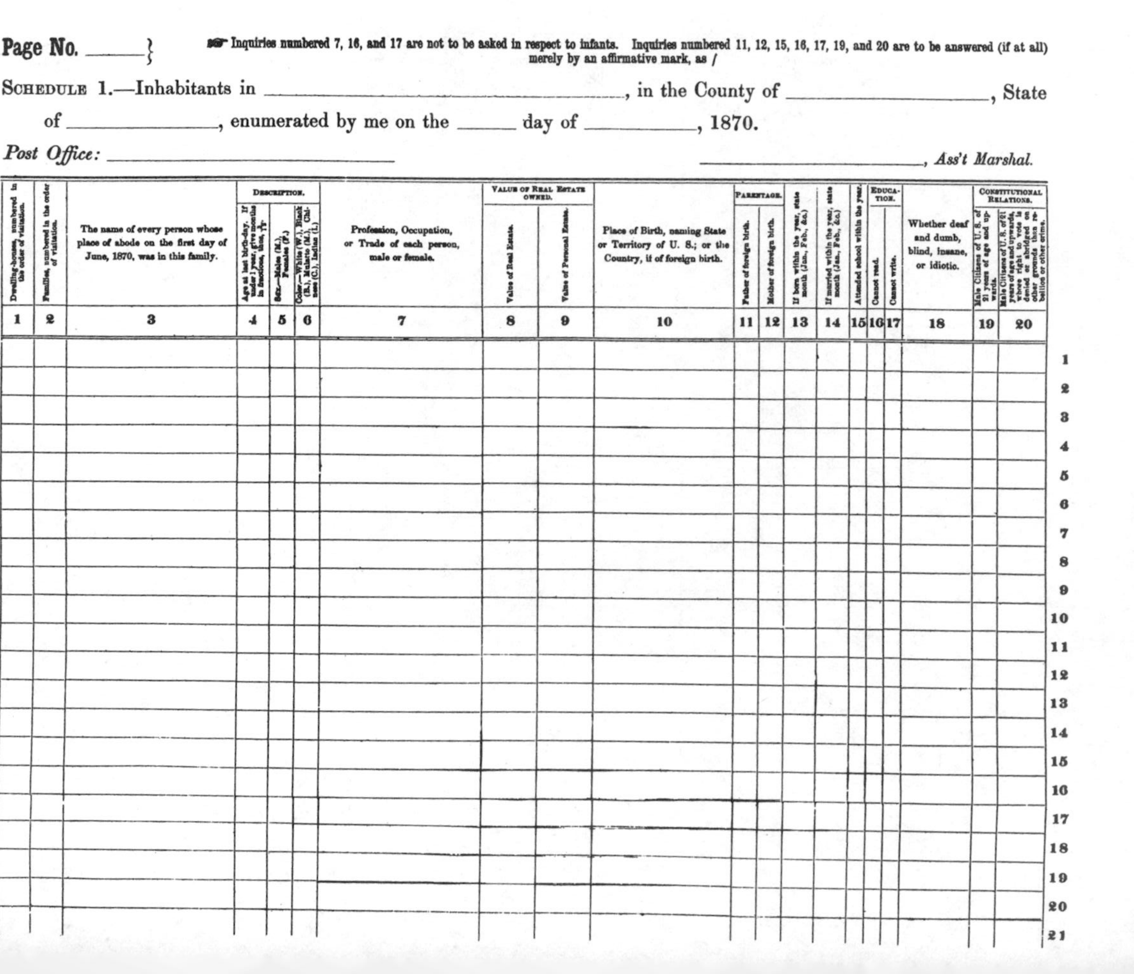

Page No. ______}

☞ Inquiries numbered 7, 16, and 17 are not to be asked in respect to infants. Inquiries numbered 11, 12, 15, 16, 17, 19, and 20 are to be answered (if at all) merely by an affirmative mark, as /

SCHEDULE 1.—Inhabitants in ____________________, in the County of ______________, State of ____________, enumerated by me on the _____ day of __________, 1870.

Post Office: ____________________ ____________________, *Ass't Marshal.*

				Description.				Value of Real Estate owned.			Parentage.					Education.			Constitutional Relations.	
	Dwelling-houses, numbered in the order of visitation.	Families, numbered in the order of visitation.	The name of every person whose place of abode on the first day of June, 1870, was in this family.	Age at last birth-day. If under 1 year, give months in fractions, thus, 3/12.	Sex.—Males (M.), Females (F.)	Color.—White (W.), Black (B.), Mulatto (M.), Chinese (C.), Indian (I.)	Profession, Occupation, or Trade of each person, male or female.	Value of Real Estate.	Value of Personal Estate.	Place of Birth, naming State or Territory of U. S.; or the Country, if of foreign birth.	Father of foreign birth.	Mother of foreign birth.	If born within the year, state month (Jan., Feb., &c.)	If married within the year, state month (Jan., Feb., &c.)	Attended school within the year.	Cannot read.	Cannot write.	Whether deaf and dumb, blind, insane, or idiotic.	Male Citizens of U. S. of 21 years of age and upwards.	Male Citizens of U. S. of 21 years of age and upwards, whose right to vote is denied or abridged on other grounds than rebellion or other crime.
	1	2	3	4	5	6	7	8	9	10	11	12	13	14	15	16	17	18	19	20
1																				
2																				
3																				
4																				
5																				
6																				
7																				
8																				
9																				
10																				
11																				
12																				
13																				
14																				
15																				
16																				
17																				
18																				
19																				
20																				
21																				

FIGURE 8—THE 1870 FEDERAL CENSUS

[7-296]

Page No.............................
Supervisor's Dist. No..................
Enumeration Dist. No. ....

Note A.—The Census Year begins June 1, 1879, and ends May 31, 1880.
Note B.—All persons will be included in the Enumeration who were living on the 1st day of June, 1880. No others will. Children BORN SINCE June 1, 1880 will be OMITTED. Members of Families who have DIED SINCE June 1, 1880, will be INCLUDED.
Note C.—Questions Nos. 13, 14, 22 and 23 are not to be asked in respect to persons under 10 years of age.

SCHEDULE 1.—Inhabitants in ...., in the County of ...., State of ....

enumerated by me on the .... day of June, 1880.

....
Enumerator.

	In Cities.					Personal Description.					Civil Condition.				Occupation.		Health.						Education.			Nativity.		
	Name of Street.	House Number.	Dwelling houses numbered in order of visitation.	Families numbered in order of visitation.	The Name of each Person whose place of abode, on 1st day of June, 1880, was in this family.	Color.—White, W; Black, B; Mulatto, Mu; Chinese, C; Indian, I.	Sex.—Male, M; Female, F.	Age at last birthday prior to June 1, 1880. If under 1 year, give months in fractions, thus: 3/12.	If born within the Census year, give the month.	Relationship of each person to the head of this family—whether wife, son, daughter, servant, boarder, or other.	Single, /.	Married, /.	Widowed, /. Divorced, D.	Married during Census year, /.	Profession, Occupation or Trade of each person, male or female.	Number of months this person has been unemployed during the Census year.	Is the person [on the day of the Enumerator's visit] sick or temporarily disabled, so as to be unable to attend to ordinary business or duties? If so, what is the sickness or disability?	Blind, /.	Deaf and Dumb, /.	Idiotic, /.	Insane, /.	Maimed, Crippled, Bedridden, or otherwise disabled, /.	Attended school within the Census year, /.	Cannot read, /.	Cannot write, /.	Place of Birth of this person, naming State or Territory of United States, or the Country, if of foreign birth.	Place of Birth of the Father of this person, naming the State or Territory of United States, or the Country, if of foreign birth.	Place of Birth of the Mother of this person, naming the State or Territory of United States, or the Country, if of foreign birth.
			1	2	3	4	5	6	7	8	9	10	11	12	13	14	15	16	17	18	19	20	21	22	23	24	25	26
1																												
2																												
3																												
4																												
5																												
6																												
7																												
8																												
9																												
10																												
11																												
12																												
13																												
14																												
15																												
16																												
17																												
18																												
19																												
20																												
21																												
22																												
23																												
24																												
25																												
26																												
27																												
28																												
29																												
30																												
31																												
32																												
33																												
34																												
35																												
36																												
37																												
38																												
39																												
40																												
41																												
42																												
43																												
44																												
45																												
46																												
47																												
48																												
49																												
50																												

NOTE D.—In making entries in columns 9, 10, 11, 12, 16 to 23, an affirmative mark only will be used—thus /, except in the case of divorced persons, column 11, when the letter "D" is to be used.
NOTE E.—Question No. 12 will only be asked in cases where an affirmative answer has been given either to question 10 or to question 11.
NOTE F.—Question No. 14 will only be asked in cases when a gainful occupation has been reported in column 13.
NOTE G.—In column 7 an abbreviation in the name of the month may be used, as Jan., Apr., Dec.

© U.S. GOVERNMENT PRINTING OFFICE : 19[illegible]

FIGURE 9—THE 1880 FEDERAL CENSUS

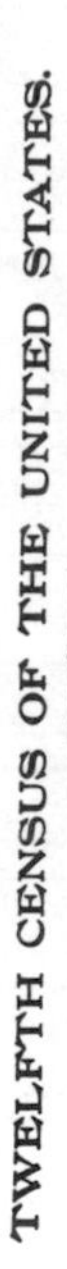

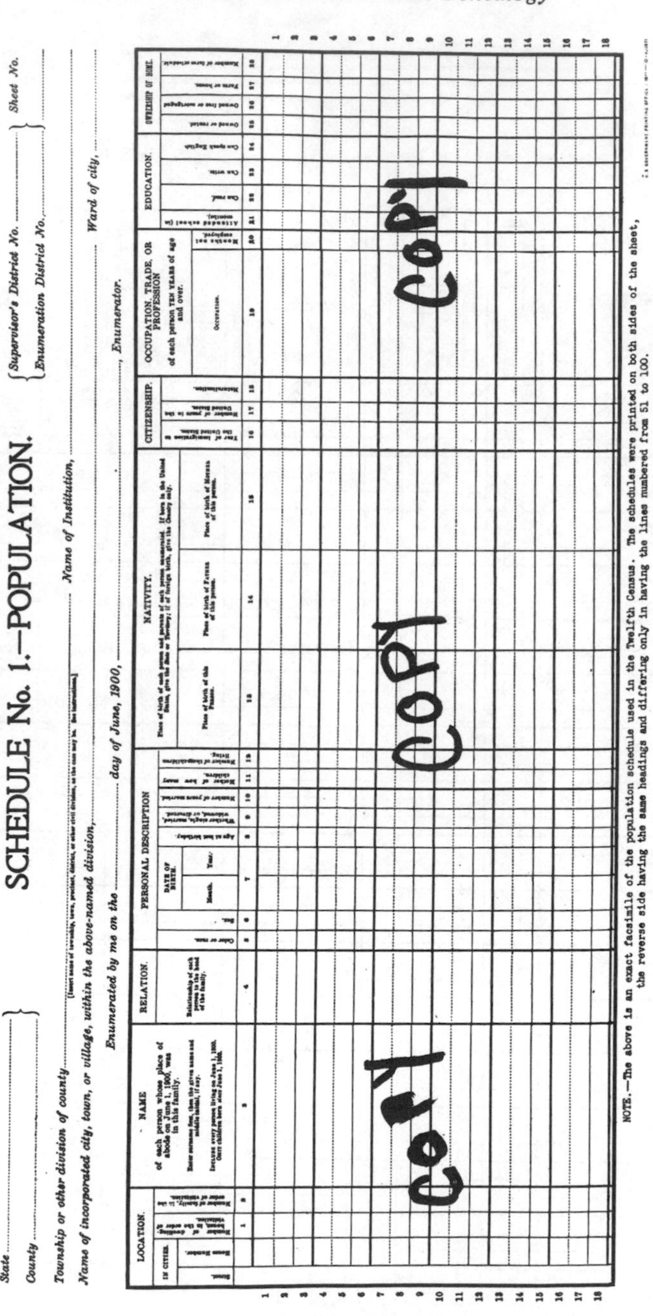

7—224

TWELFTH CENSUS OF THE UNITED STATES.

SCHEDULE No. 1.—POPULATION.

State .... } *Supervisor's District No.* .... } *Sheet No.* ....

County .... } *Enumeration District No.* .... }

Township or other division of county .... [Insert name of township, town, precinct, district, or other civil division, as the case may be. See instructions.] *Name of Institution,* ....

Name of incorporated city, town, or village, within the above-named division, ... *Ward of city,* ....

Enumerated by me on the .... *day of June, 1900,* ...., *Enumerator.*

	LOCATION.				NAME	RELATION.	PERSONAL DESCRIPTION									NATIVITY. Place of birth of each person and parents of each person enumerated. If born in the United States, give the State or Territory; if of foreign birth, give the Country only.			CITIZENSHIP.			OCCUPATION, TRADE, OR PROFESSION of each person TEN YEARS of age and over.		EDUCATION.				OWNERSHIP OF HOME.			
	IN CITIES.								DATE OF BIRTH.																						
	Street.	House Number.	Number of dwelling-house, in the order of visitation.	Number of family, in the order of visitation.	of each person whose place of abode on June 1, 1900, was in this family. Enter surname first, then the given name and middle initial, if any. INCLUDE every person living on June 1, 1900. OMIT children born since June 1, 1900.	Relationship of each person to the head of the family.	Color or race.	Sex.	Month.	Year.	Age at last birthday.	Whether single, married, widowed, or divorced.	Number of years married.	Mother of how many children.	Number of these children living.	Place of birth of this PERSON.	Place of birth of FATHER of this person.	Place of birth of MOTHER of this person.	Year of immigration to the United States.	Number of years in the United States.	Naturalization.	Occupation.	Months not employed.	Attended school (in months).	Can read.	Can write.	Can speak English.	Owned or rented.	Owned free or mortgaged.	Farm or house.	Number of farm schedule.
			1	2	3	4	5	6	7		8	9	10	11	12	13	14	15	16	17	18	19	20	21	22	23	24	25	26	27	28
1																															
2																															
3																															
4																															
5																															
6																															
7																															
8																															
9																															
10																															
11																															
12																															
13																															
14																															
15																															
16																															
17																															
18																															

NOTE.—The above is an exact facsimile of the population schedule used in the Twelfth Census. The schedules were printed on both sides of the sheet, the reverse side having the same headings and differing only in having the lines numbered from 51 to 100.

FIGURE 10—THE 1900 FEDERAL CENSUS

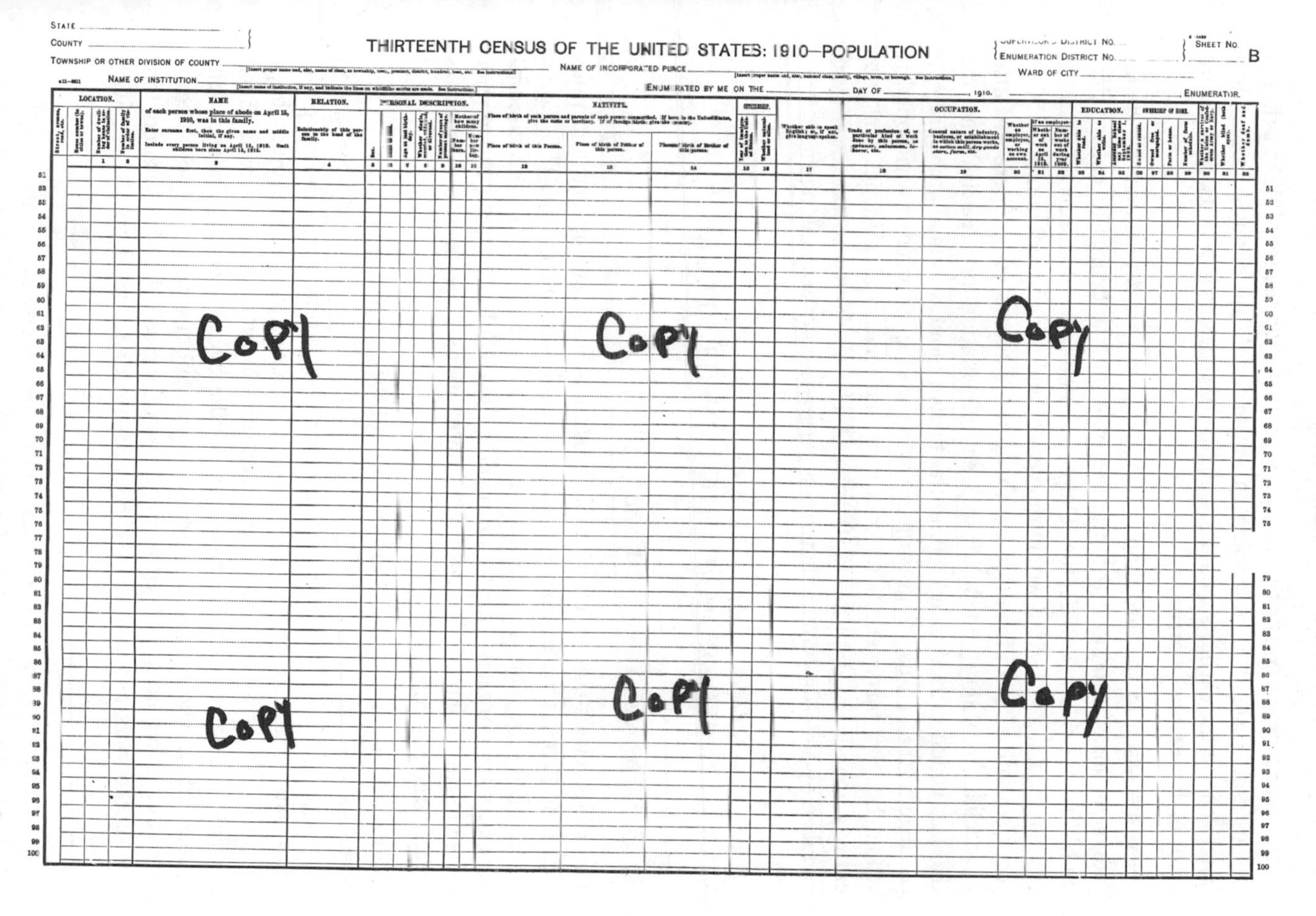
THIRTEENTH CENSUS OF THE UNITED STATES: 1910—POPULATION

STATE ______ COUNTY ______ TOWNSHIP OR OTHER DIVISION OF COUNTY ______ NAME OF INSTITUTION ______

NAME OF INCORPORATED PLACE ______ WARD OF CITY ______

ENUMERATED BY ME ON THE ______ DAY OF ______, 1910. ______ ENUMERATOR.

SUPERVISOR'S DISTRICT NO. ______ ENUMERATION DISTRICT NO. ______ SHEET NO. ______ B

LOCATION. | NAME. | RELATION. | PERSONAL DESCRIPTION. | NATIVITY. | CITIZENSHIP. | OCCUPATION. | EDUCATION. | OWNERSHIP OF HOME.

FIGURE 11—THE 1910 FEDERAL CENSUS

in this census was to make the individual, rather than the family, the primary census unit. Instead of describing an entire family on a single line as had been done in the earlier schedules, one line of the census was used to record information on each person.

As discussed in the last chapter, Shattuck, apparently against his better judgment, also introduced the practice of using the census to collect data on births, marriages, and deaths. The population schedule forms allowed for a column asking "Married within the year?" and added a column in 1870 to record month of birth for those born within the census year. There was also a special "mortality schedule" seeking information on deaths (and the diseases which caused them) within the twelve months immediately prior to the date of the census.[3] This program was never quite what it was hoped it would be, yet this method of collecting national vital statistics was not entirely abandoned until the 1910 census.[4] The 1910 census was the first to be taken by a census bureau that was a permanent government agency.

II. WHERE ARE THE CENSUS RECORDS?

A. 1790 Through 1880, 1900, and 1910

The 1790 census—as much of it as is extant—has been indexed and published, and copies are available in many libraries throughout the U.S. Some of the 1790 schedules were destroyed and are not available. In this circumstance contemporaneous tax lists provide quite useful substitutes, though not so complete. Some of these tax list compilations have been published as "reconstructed" censuses.

Some other censuses have also been published in part by interested individuals and organizations. In 1966 the National Genealogical Society in Washington, D.C., undertook a project of transcribing and indexing the 1850 census. The society began by using Tennessee as a pilot project, hoping eventually to cover all states and territories included in that census. Each schedule was to be transcribed from microfilm by two persons, independent of each other. The results of these two transcriptions were then to be compared and differences rectified through use of the schedules in Washington. The project was abandoned in 1968 because of its great cost (even with

---

[3] For more information on vital statistics by enumeration see chapter 10.

[4] United States. National Office of Vital Statistics, *Vital Statistics of the United States 1950* (Washington, DC: U.S. Public Health Service, 1954), Vol. 1, p. 6.

volunteer labor), before the state of Tennessee was completed. (That state has since been completed.) More is said later about indexes.

All of the census schedules, from 1800 through 1880, and 1900 and 1910, except those no longer in existence, are available for personal searching at the National Archives in Washington, D.C. However, constant use had a wearing effect on the original schedules and by the beginning of the present century the pre-1890 schedules had shown excessive damage. The older ones had also deteriorated with age. Though efforts were made to keep the old volumes repaired, it finally became necessary to withdraw the original schedules from public use and replace them with copies. The 1790 schedules were then published, as I have already mentioned, in the several volumes of *Heads of Families at the First Census of the United States Taken in the Year 1790* (Washington, 1907-8, and since reprinted by both the Reprint Company, Spartanburg, South Carolina, and the Genealogical Publishing Company, Baltimore, Maryland). The 1800 through 1830 schedules were photostated and the photostatic copies were bound for use. This work began as a Civil Works Administration project in 1934 and was completed by the Census Bureau in 1939. Thus the original pre-1840 schedules were retired from active public service.

Between 1936 and 1940 the Census Bureau microfilmed the schedules of 1840-80 and retired the originals. The 1900-40 schedules have also been filmed but neither the originals nor the films of those taken within the last seventy-two years (the current official restriction period) are open to public use. For the most part these microfilm copies were made from the original schedules, but some of the original schedules of 1860 and 1880 were damaged and pages in others were torn and faded. The damaged pages were removed and replaced in the bound volumes by photocopies.[5]

All nonrestricted decennial population censuses are available on microfilm at the LDS Family History Library, and some parts are in various libraries, genealogical societies, historical societies, and agencies throughout the country. All available census schedules from 1790 through 1910 are available on interlibrary loan or direct through the National Archives Microfilm Rental Program. Some military record films from the Revolutionary War are also available. (See chapter 22.)

Many libraries have the census schedules for their own states. One library that has all available U.S. census microfilms is that of Washington State University at Pullman. There are no doubt many more such libraries.

---

[5] Davidson and Ashby, pp. 93-101.

During various sessions of Congress in the 1920s and 1930s, legislation was introduced in the House of Representatives to provide for the copying and publishing by the Bureau of the Census of the names of heads of families in the 1800 through 1840 enumerations, but none of these bills passed Congress.[6]

B. Missing Census Schedules

As I have said, parts of the early schedules are missing for various reasons. The most extensive losses are among the early censuses. It has been reported by some that the loss of the missing 1790, 1800, and 1810 schedules was the result of the fire in Washington set by the British during their siege of that city in the War of 1812, but this assumption is unfounded. The actual reasons are unknown. In fact, under the provisions of the Census Acts from 1790 through 1820, the population schedules were deposited in the U.S. District Courts where they were to be preserved by the clerks. It was by a resolution of May 28, 1830, that the District Court clerks were finally requested to forward the schedules for the first four censuses, then in their possession, to the U.S. Secretary of State.[7]

In 1849 the responsibility for the census was shifted from the State Department to the Interior Department with the creation of the latter, and all records were transferred to the new department. No inventories of the materials transferred have been found.

The earliest inventories of census holdings that have been located were made in 1865 and 1870, and comparison of these with later inventories suggests that many of the missing schedules, including seventeen volumes of 1790-1820 censuses, were lost before 1895. Extensive efforts were made to locate the missing schedules, but most such efforts have been futile. One of the few records to be turned up was the 1830 schedules for the Western District of Missouri.

Apparently it was customary in the early times for both the State and Interior departments to lend census schedules to agency officials and con-

---

[6] Typical of this legislation was H.R. 5626 (70th Congress, First Session, 1927-28) introduced by Representative Andrew Jackson Montague (D) of Virginia. Montague introduced essentially the same bill in the First Session of the 73d Congress (1933, H.R. 4343) and in the First Session of the 74th Congress (1935, H.R. 1408). Also, Representative George Huddleston (D) of Alabama introduced a bill in the House during the First Session of the 70th Congress (1927-28, H.R. Res. 127) calling for the names of heads of families in the second, third and fourth (1800, 1810, and 1820) censuses to be published, but this bill failed too.

[7] Davidson and Ashby, p. 94.

gressmen upon request, and it may be that some of the schedules were thus lost.

The inventory of 1895 cannot now be found, but a comparison has more recently been made between the 1870 inventory and that of 1903 which revealed many discrepancies—some apparently due to the binding and rebinding of the schedules. It is really impossible to say how or when those missing early schedules were actually lost,[8] except that they were *not* casualties of the War of 1812.

Congress prescribed the process for getting census schedules into the hands of the federal government after they were taken. As mentioned, the 1790-1820 schedules were sent to Washington pursuant to the Congressional resolution of 1830. In 1830 and 1840 the marshals who took the censuses were required to make two copies. One of these was to be sent to the clerk of the District Court and the other sent to Washington. In 1850-70 the assistants were to turn over their original enumerations to the clerks of the County Courts plus two copies "duly compared and corrected" to the marshals of the District Courts. The marshals were then to send one of these copies to the Secretary of the Interior in Washington and the other to the secretary of the state or territory of which that District was a part.

Those census schedules which are missing from the National Archives collection, up through 1870, are identified on Chart 3. In a *few* instances, because Congress required that duplicate copies be made, those which are not in the National Archives are in the states. There are no missing schedules in any of the censuses after 1870, according to a 1968 letter from Milton D. Swenson, chief of the Personal Census Service Branch of the Census Bureau, with one major exception—the 1890 census.[9]

C. The 1890 Census

Most of the 1890 schedules do not exist. A fire in the Commerce Department (note another new department) building on January 21, 1921, is to blame for this destruction. Though not all of the schedules were consumed in the blaze, most were so badly damaged that Congress authorized their disposal. Those persons who would blame Congress for the destruction of a large portion of this census are in error. After all, what can you do with a pile of ashes? Inasmuch as those ashes were once a census they could not be thrown away unless Congress gave its approval. This it did.

---

[8] *Ibid.*, pp. 94-95.

[9] Letter from Mr. Swenson, dated March 11, 1968.

Fragmentary schedules for some of the states do exist, and a card index to the names on those schedules has been prepared by the National Archives. This index, available on microfilm (National Archives microcopy No. M496, two rolls), relates to schedules, arranged by state, for Alabama, the District of Columbia, Georgia, Illinois, Minnesota, New Jersey, New York, North Carolina, Ohio, South Dakota, and Texas. The schedules themselves are also available on microfilm but comprise only three rolls of 35mm film.[10] The National Archives microcopy number for these is N407.

The contents of these schedules include:

ALABAMA:	Perry County (Perryville Beat No. 11 and Severe Beat No. 8).
D.C.:	Q, R, S, 13th, 14th, 15th, Corcoran and Riggs Streets, and Johnson Avenue.
GEORGIA:	Muscogee County (Columbus).
ILLINOIS:	McDonough County (Mound Township).
MINNESOTA:	Wright County (Rockford).
NEW JERSEY:	Hudson County (Jersey City).
NEW YORK:	Westchester County (Eastchester) and Suffolk County (Brookhaven Township).
NORTH CAROLINA:	Gaston County (South Point and River Bend Townships) and Cleveland County (Township No. 2).
OHIO:	Hamilton County (Cincinnati) and Clinton County (Wayne Township).
SOUTH DAKOTA:	Union County (Jefferson Township).
TEXAS:	Ellis County (J.P. No. 6, Mountain Peak and Ovilla Precinct), Hood County (Precinct No. 5), Rusk County (No. 6 and J.P. No. 7), Trinity County (Trinity Town and Precinct No. 2), and Kaufman County (Kaufman).[11]

The 1890 census was the only one (until 1970) to use a "family schedule"—a separate schedule for each family enumerated. (See Figure 12.) On the two sides of the schedule there was room to enumerate ten family members. If the family was larger than that, two schedules were used.

---

[10] Davidson and Ashby, p. 102.

[11] United States. National Archives, *Federal Population Censuses, 1790-1890* (Washington, DC: National Archives, 1966), p. 145.

FAMILY SCHEDULE—1 TO 10 PERSONS.

[7—556 *b*.]

Supervisor's District No.________

Enumeration District No.________

Eleventh Census of the United States.

SCHEDULE No. 1.

POPULATION AND SOCIAL STATISTICS.

Name of city, town, township, precinct, district, beat, or other minor civil division.________; County:________; State:________;

Street and No.:________; Ward:________; Name of Institution:________.

Enumerated by me on the ______ day of June, 1890.

________, Enumerator.

A.—Number of Dwelling-house in the order of visitation.		B.—Number of families in this dwelling-house.		C.—Number of persons in this dwelling-house.		D.—Number of Family in the order of visitation.		E.—No. of Persons in this family.	

	INQUIRIES.	1	2	3	4	5
1	Christian name in full, and initial of middle name.					
	Surname.					
2	Whether a soldier, sailor, or marine during the civil war (U. S. or Conf.), or widow of such person.					
3	Relationship to head of family.					
4	Whether white, black, mulatto, quadroon, octoroon, Chinese, Japanese, or Indian.					
5	Sex.					
6	Age at nearest birthday. If under one year, give age in months.					
7	Whether single, married, widowed, or divorced.					
8	Whether married during the census year (June 1, 1889, to May 31, 1890).					
9	Mother of how many children, and number of these children living					
10	Place of birth.					
11	Place of birth of Father.					
12	Place of birth of Mother.					
13	Number of years in the United States.					
14	Whether naturalized.					
15	Whether naturalization papers have been taken out.					
16	Profession, trade, or occupation.					
17	Months unemployed during the census year (June 1, 1889, to May 31, 1890).					
18	Attendance at school (in months) during the census year (June 1, 1889, to May 31, 1890).					
19	Able to Read.					
20	Able to Write.					
21	Able to speak English. If not, the language or dialect spoken.					
22	Whether suffering from acute or chronic disease, with name of disease and length of time afflicted.					
23	Whether defective in mind, sight, hearing, or speech, or whether crippled, maimed, or deformed, with name of defect.					
24	Whether a prisoner, convict, homeless child, or pauper.					
25	Supplemental schedule and page.					

TO ENUMERATORS.—See inquiries numbered 26 to 30, inclusive, on the second page of this schedule. These inquiries must be made concerning each family and each farm visited.

(19278—1,780,000.) 1 b 34

FIGURE 12—THE 1890 FEDERAL CENSUS

There were also some Civil War Union Army Veterans' Schedules, prepared in connection with this census, which are still available. They are discussed later in this chapter.

D. Later Censuses—Confidential

Recent census schedules (less than seventy-two years old) are restricted to protect the privacy of the living. However, the personal information from the restricted population schedules can be furnished by the Bureau of the Census under special circumstances. The Bureau can furnish census information to the person to whom that information relates, and in some instances to the legal representative of that person upon presentation of a certified copy of the court order which appointed him. If the record sought relates to a deceased person the application must be accompanied by a certified copy of the death certificate or other evidence of death and can be filed by any of the following:

1. A blood relative in the immediate family—i.e., parent, child, brother, or sister.
2. The surviving spouse.
3. A direct bloodline descendant.
4. A beneficiary with legal proof of such beneficiary relationship.

The requester must be at least eighteen years of age.

In all except the 1920 schedules, the exact address of the person's residence at the time of the census must be given.[12] The name of the head of the household is also essential. If possible, the names of other family members should be given in order to remove all questions of identity. Search application forms (the forms required for such a search—form BC-600) and details for a search of restricted censuses are available from the Personal Census Service Branch, Bureau of the Census, Pittsburg, KS 66762. (See Figures 13 and 14.) Fees for the search are subject to change but are currently $15 (1988). For an additional $4 per individual family member the Bureau will provide a full schedule of the family if requirements for the release of each individual's census data are satisfied.

As for the reasons behind these recent censuses being confidential (and hence so inaccessible), a letter of explanation was sent to the LDS Genea-

---

[12] It is necessary to know only the name of the state to locate families in the 1920 census because it is indexed. However, the more specific your information, the better are your chances for success.

logical Society, dated January 12, 1960, by the Personal Census Service Branch which explains the government's position quite clearly. Following is a portion of that letter:

> The present official viewpoint of the Bureau is that at least an interval of seventy-five years or longer must elapse before consideration could be given to removing the confidential restrictions on the 1900 Census.[13]
>
> On the occasion of each decennial census enumeration, assurances have been given that the information collected regarding any individual will not be disclosed and that it will be combined with similar information for other individuals to provide statistical totals. Presidential Proclamations have been issued prior to decennial censuses assuring the American people that the information given to the census enumerator would be confidential. Repudiation of this pledge would seriously reduce public confidence and would lead to doubts as to whether future legislation might make personal information available within a short period of time.
>
> The insurance of confidentiality of the information is an important element in securing reliable information from the public. We regularly receive information which the respondent would be unwilling to give to other agencies. If the confidence which people have in Census operations were to be shaken, the problems of getting reliable information and the cost of the censuses would be substantially increased. At the present time there are approximately thirty million persons who were living at the time of the Census of 1900. Most of these people were living in the United States at that time and, presumably, were included in that census. Some of them no doubt were living in institutions at the time of the census; others were living in unusual family arrangements which they may prefer not to be disclosed. The possibility that such facts would be revealed, even after a substantial period of years, might be a source of embarrassment to some families. In future enumerations, knowledge that this might occur could result in the withholding of correct information.

A provision in the Census Acts (Sect. 32 of 1909 Act; Sect. 33 of 1919 Act; and Sect. 18 of 1929 Act) authorized the Census Director, "in his discretion, to furnish to individuals such data from the population schedules as may be desired for genealogical or other proper purposes." Thus the Census Bureau will furnish information from a person's own enumeration as proof of age. A person's making a personal application for information relating to

---

[13] As previously stated, the current restriction is seventy-two years rather than seventy-five, and the 1900 and 1910 schedules are now (1989) unrestricted.

FORM **BC-600**
(6-6-85)

U.S. DEPARTMENT OF COMMERCE
BUREAU OF THE CENSUS

O.M.B. No. 0607-0117:
Approval Expires 5-31-87

APPLICATION FOR SEARCH OF CENSUS RECORDS

DO NOT USE THIS SPACE

$ ________ **(Fee)**

☐ **Money Order**
☐ **Check**
☐ **Other**

CASE NO.

PURPOSE FOR WHICH RECORD IS TO BE USED (MUST BE STATED HERE) *(See Instruction 1)*

RETURN TO: Bureau of the Census, 1600 North Walnut Street, **PITTSBURG, KANSAS 66762**

FULL NAME OF PERSON WHOSE CENSUS RECORD IS REQUESTED *(Print or type)*

FIRST NAME	MIDDLE NAME	MAIDEN NAME *(If any)*	PRESENT LAST NAME	NICKNAMES

DATE OF BIRTH *(If unknown, estimate)*	PLACE OF BIRTH *(City, county, State)*	RACE	SEX

FULL NAME OF FATHER *(Stepfather, guardian, etc.)*

FULL MAIDEN NAME OF MOTHER *(Stepmother, etc.)*

Please give FULL name of husband or wife of person whose record is requested.

FIRST MARRIAGE *(Name of husband or wife)* — YEAR MARRIED *(Approximate)*

SECOND MARRIAGE *(Name of husband or wife)* — YEAR MARRIED *(Approximate)*

GIVE PLACE OF RESIDENCE AT EACH DATE LISTED BELOW

CENSUS DATE	NUMBER AND STREET *(Very important)*	CITY, TOWN, TOWNSHIP *(Precinct, beat, etc.)*	COUNTY AND STATE	NAME OF PERSON WITH WHOM LIVING *(Head of household)*	RELATIONSHIP
JUNE 1, 1900 *(See instruction 2)*					
APRIL 15, 1910 *(See instruction 3)*					
JAN. 1, 1920 *(See instruction 2)*					
APRIL 1, 1930 *(See instruction 3)*					
APRIL 1, 1940 *(See instruction 3)*					
APRIL 1, 1950 *(See instruction 3)*					
APRIL 1, 1960 *(See instruction 3 and 9)*					
APRIL 1, 1970 *(See instruction 3 and 9)*					
APRIL 1, 1980 *(See instruction 3 and 9)*					

Names of brother and sisters

I certify that information furnished about anyone other than the applicant will not be used to the detriment of such person or persons by me or by anyone else with my permission.

- If the census information is **to be sent to someone other than the person whose record is requested,** give the name and address, including ZIP code, of the other person or agency.
- This authorizes the Bureau of the Census to send the record to: *(See Instruction 4)*

FEE REQUIRED: *See Instructions 5, 6, and 7 on the reverse side.*

A check or money order **(DO NOT SEND CASH)** payable to "Commerce—Census," must be sent with the application. This fee covers the cost of a search of not more than two census years about one person only.

Fee required . . . . **$ 15.00**

_____ **extra copies @ $2.00 each** $_____

_____ **full schedules @ $4.00 each** $_____

TOTAL amount enclosed _____ $_____

SIGNATURE — ***Do not print*** *(Read instruction 8 carefully before signing)*

PRESENT ADDRESS

NUMBER AND STREET		
CITY	STATE	ZIP CODE

PHONE NUMBER *(Include area code)*

IF SIGNED ABOVE BY MARK (X), TWO WITNESSES MUST SIGN HERE

SIGNATURE	SIGNATURE

NOTICE — Intentionally falsifying this application may result in a fine of $10,000 or five years imprisonment, or both (title 18, U.S. Code, section 1001).

FIGURE 13—THE FORM USED TO REQUEST SEARCH OF MODERN CENSUS SCHEDULES

GENERAL INFORMATION

The Application on the reverse side of this sheet is for use in requesting a search of the census records and an official copy of the personal information found which includes age, place of birth, and citizenship. This application should be filled in and mailed to BUREAU OF THE CENSUS, 1600 N. Walnut Street, PITTSBURG, KANSAS 66762, together with a money order or check payable to "Commerce – Census."

Birth certificates, including delayed birth certificates, are not issued by the Bureau of the Census but by the Health Department or similar agency of the State in which the birth occurred. In most Federal Censuses, the census takers obtained the age and place of birth of individuals. Copies of these census records often are accepted as evidence of age, citizenship, and place of birth for employment, social security benefits, insurance, and other purposes. *Since the place of birth and citizenship were obtained only on a sample basis during the 1960, 1970, and 1980 Censuses, this information will not be shown on transcripts for those years.*

Census records for 1910 and prior years have been transferred to the National Archives and Records Service, Washington, D.C. 20408, and are considered public records. Requests for information from these Censuses should be addressed to that agency.

If you authorize the Bureau of the Census to send your record to someone other than yourself, attention is called to the possibility that the information shown in the census record may not agree with that given in your application. The record must be copied exactly as it appears and will be sent as you direct regardless of what it shows.

INSTRUCTIONS FOR COMPLETING THIS FORM

► 1. Purpose

The purpose for which the information is desired must be shown so that a determination may be made under 13 U.S.C. 8(a) that the record is required for a proper use. The statement of purpose also provides a basis for determining which census records would best serve such purpose and thereby, save the expense of additional searches.

► 2. Censuses 1900 – 1920

A system for filing names by sound is available for these census years. Information can be furnished in many instances when only the following information is given:

The name of the person about whom the information is desired.

The name of the city or county and State where the person resided.

The name of the head of the household with whom this person was living on the various dates of these censuses.

Additional information such as the names of brothers and sisters is helpful if it can be furnished.

► 3. Censuses – years 1910–1930–1940 – 1950–1960–1970 – 1980

If residing in a city at the time these censuses were taken, it is necessary to furnish the house number, the name of the street, city, county, and State and the name of the parent or other head of household with whom residing at the time of the census. If residing in a small town or a rural area, give all available information as to cross-streets, road names, township, district, precinct, or beat, etc. If the district or township is unknown, give the distance from the nearest town and the direction, also the rural route number.

► 4. Confidential information given to other than person to whom it relates

(a) Census information for the years 1900 and on is confidential and ordinarily will not be furnished to another person unless the person to whom it relates authorizes this in the space provided or there is other proper authorization as indicated in 4(b), 4(c), and 4(d) hereof.

(b) Minor children

Information regarding a child who has not reached legal age may be obtained upon the written request of either parent or the legal guardian.

(c) Mentally incompetent persons

Information regarding persons who are mentally incompetent may be obtained upon the written request of the legal representative supported by a certified copy of the court order naming such legal representative.

(d) Deceased persons

If the record requested relates to a deceased person, the application must be signed by (1) a blood relative in the immediate family (parent, brother, sister, or child), (2) the surviving wife or husband, (3) the administrator or executor of the estate, or (4) a beneficiary by will, or insurance. In all cases involving deceased persons, a certified copy of the death certificate must be furnished, and the relationship to the deceased must be stated on the application. Legal representatives must also furnish a certified copy of the court order naming such legal representatives, and beneficiaries must furnish legal evidence of such beneficiary interest.

► 5. Fee required

The $15.00 fee is for a search in regular turn, based on the date the request is received, of not more than two suggested censuses about one person only. The time required to complete a search depends upon the number of cases on hand at the particular time and the difficulty encountered in searching a particular case. The normal processing time would require from two to six weeks. Since the fee covers return postage, do not send stamped self-addressed envelope with the application.

Not more than two censuses will be searched and the results furnished for one fee. Should it be necessary to search more than two censuses to find the record, you will be notified to send another fee before further searches are made. Tax monies are not available for the furnishing of the information. Accordingly, even though the information is not found, if a search has been made, the fee cannot be returned.

► 6. Additional copies of Census information

Additional copies of this information furnished will be prepared at a cost of $2.00 for each additional copy. Fill in the amount of money enclosed and the number of extra copies desired in the spaces provided.

► 7. Full schedules (For Genealogy)

Upon request, a full schedule will be furnished. There is an additional charge of $4.00 for each full schedule requested. The full schedule is the complete one-line entry of personal data recorded for the individual. The name of the head of household may also be shown, but the names of other persons will not be listed.

► 8. Signature

In general, the signature should be the same as that shown on the line captioned "full name of person whose census record is requested." When the application is for the census record concerning another person, the authority of the requester must be furnished as set forth in instruction 4 above.

► 9. 1960–1970–1980 Censuses

Since the place of birth and citizenship were obtained only on a sample basis during the 1960, 1970, and 1980 Censuses, this information will not be shown on transcripts.

FORM BC-600 (6-6-85)

FIGURE 14—INSTRUCTIONS FOR COMPLETING CENSUS SEARCH FORM

himself does not constitute publication, and it has also been ruled that personal application releases the Census Bureau from the confidential restrictions of the law.[14]

III. SPECIAL INDEXES

During the 1930s, under the auspices of the Works Projects Administration (WPA) as part of a Federal Works Project, names and other pertinent data on persons enumerated in the censuses of 1880, 1900, 1920, and part of 1910 were copied onto file cards. The cards for each of these censuses were alphabetically coded and filed by state under a system where all names sounding alike, regardless of spelling differences or errors (if they began with the same letter of the alphabet), would be interfiled. (This is called "Soundex indexing.") The cards contain complete family listings and greatly facilitate the location of families in the census.

The 1880 index is not a complete index. It includes only those households with children ten years of age or below. When such a child was in a home where he was not a child of the head of the household a separate index card was made for him as well as the card for the household. This was true even when the child had the same surname as the family with whom he resided. The index is located in the National Archives, where it has been since 1964, and searches will be made in it by archives workers without charge, provided the required information is furnished on the state of residence and the family. (It is best to furnish as much information as possible for identification purposes.) If you desire a photocopy of the page of the census on which your ancestral entry is found, this will be made for a reasonable fee.

The LDS Family History Library and other libraries have copies of the 1880, 1900, and 1910 indexes on microfilm, and they can be used in conjunction with the census films. Personal use of the indexes is helpful because it enables you to "look around" for your family and also to pick up other families of the same surname that may have been in the same locality or anywhere in the same state.

To use the Soundex indexes you must encode the surname you wish to find and then look for the code number under the proper state, because all cards are filed by their Soundex codes under the separate states.

Should you have opportunity personally to use these indexes you will find that detailed instructions on how to use the Soundex system are included

---

[14] Davidson and Ashby, pp. 96-99.

therewith. The system is based on the principle of assigning a numerical value to each consonant letter, letters having similar sounds being assigned the same code numbers. Each surname is then filed under the letter of the alphabet with which it begins and a three-digit number representing its consonant sounds. If there are not three codable letters in the name then zeros are added at the end. If there are more than three, only the first three are considered. The initial letter of the surname is not coded and is used for filing only. As an example of how the system works consider the surname *Greenwood,* which has a code of G653. The "G" comes from the initial letter, the "6" is the code number assigned to *r,* "5" is the code for *n,* and "3" is the code for *d.* (*E*'s, *w*'s and *o*'s are not codable.) Hence the number *G653.* Any variation of spelling or misspelling should, in theory, produce the same code number and be properly filed. However, one minor problem is that surnames like Garnett, Gerrand, Grant, Grende, Grund, Grimaud, and Grimmett are also coded as G653.

The Soundex code numbers are:

1 = b, p, f, v.
2 = c, s, k, g, j, q, x, z.
3 = d, t.
4 = l.
5 = m, n.
6 = r.

No code is assigned to the letters *a, e, i, o, u, y, w,* or *h.* And whenever any two letters with the same code number are in immediate consecutive sequence the two are coded as if they are one letter.

The index to the 1910 census is called a Miracode index. The Miracode index uses the Soundex codes, but the index lists the visitation number assigned by the enumerator rather than the page and line number as on the indexes for 1800, 1900, and 1920. In addition to using the same coding system, the Miracode index also uses a separate index card for each household and gives the volume number and enumeration district number. There is also a useful index card for each individual who either is not a member of the immediate family where he resided or who has a surname different from the family head.

The 1910 Miracode index covers only twenty-one states: Alabama, Arkansas, California, Florida, Georgia, Illinois, Kansas, Kentucky, Louisiana, Michigan, Mississippi, Missouri, North Carolina, Ohio, Oklahoma, Pennsylvania, South Carolina, Tennessee, Texas, Virginia, and West Virginia. Rolls 28-40 of Microfilm Publication T1224, *Census Enumeration*

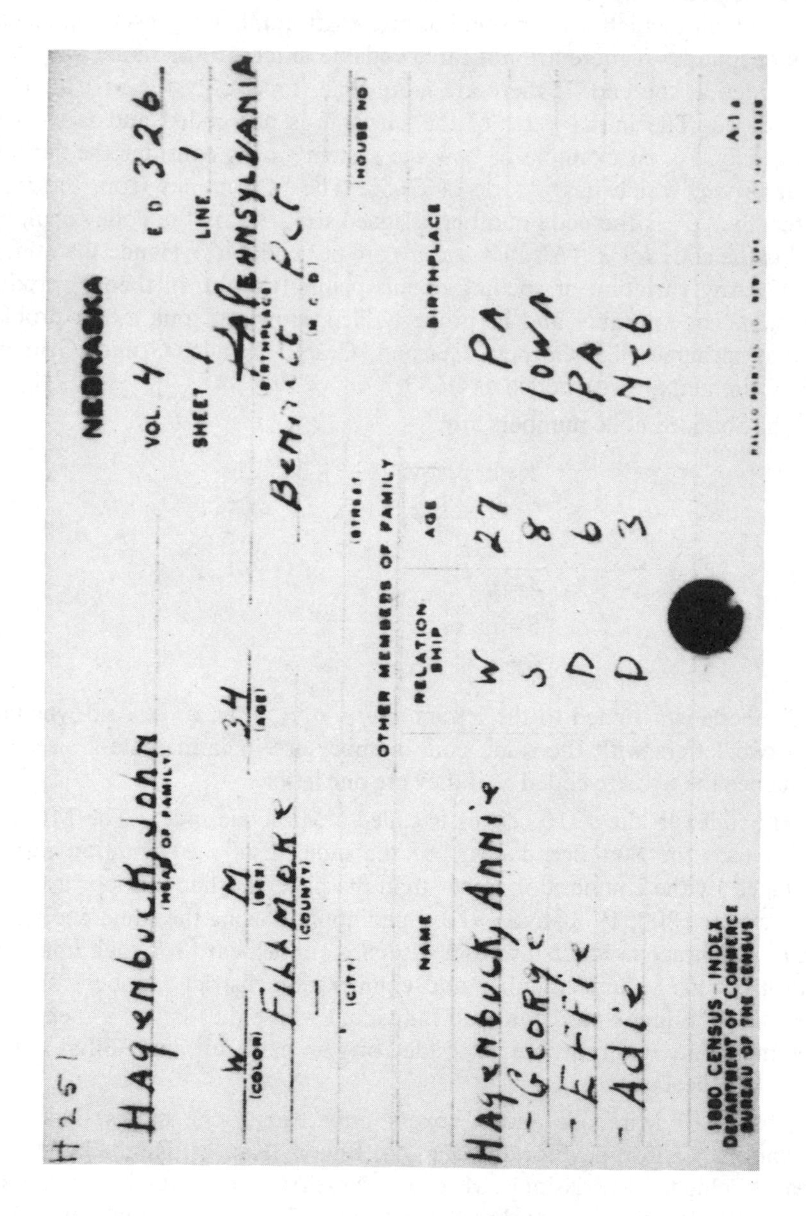

H 251

NEBRASKA

Hagenbuck, John (HEAD OF FAMILY) VOL. 4 E D 326

W (COLOR) M (SEX) 34 (AGE) SHEET 1 LINE 1

Fillmore (COUNTY) Ben[illegible] Pct (M C D) Pennsylvania (BIRTHPLACE)

— (CITY) (STREET) (HOUSE NO)

OTHER MEMBERS OF FAMILY

NAME	RELATIONSHIP	AGE	BIRTHPLACE
Hagenbuck, Annie	W	27	PA
- George	S	8	Iowa
- Effie	D	6	PA
- Adie	D	3	Neb

1880 CENSUS—INDEX
DEPARTMENT OF COMMERCE
BUREAU OF THE CENSUS

FIGURE 15—A CARD FROM THE 1880 CENSUS INDEX

District Descriptions, contain the enumeration district numbers and facilitate the location of specific places on the census films.

There was an error made when the 1880 Soundex for Illinois was microfilmed. Some of the Soundex cards for the letter "O" were inadvertently skipped—specifically the Soundex codes O-200 to O-240. The information from these omitted cards has been photocopied and published in a book entitled *The 1880 Illinois Census Index: Soundex Code O-200–O-240, the Code That Was Not Filmed,* compiled by Nancy Gubb Franklin (Evanston, IL: the compiler, 1981).

In recent years there have been many other projects to index and/or publish census schedules by individuals and commercial establishments, as well as special-interest groups and organizations. There has been a virtual explosion of census indexes since the first edition of *The Researcher's Guide* in 1973. And it is certain that there will be many more. Computer technology is largely responsible. Check with your library and with your local genealogical organizations about their holdings. Use these indexes with caution and with some skepticism, but by all means use them. The National Archives is attempting to secure copies of all such indexes.

IV. 1910 STREET INDEX

In connection with the 1910 population census there is a street index to thirty-nine of the nation's largest cities. The index was created by the Bureau of the Census to assist in finding personal data which was needed by government agencies and which individuals requested on themselves. This index, which was recently filmed and made available on microfiche through a special Archives Gift Fund from the Federation of Genealogical Societies, is on fifty microfiche as part of Record Group 29 of the records of the Bureau of the Census (Microfilm Publication M1283). It enables the user to determine the enumeration district and the corresponding bound volume in which a specific address is located.

The cities, the fiche numbers, and the streets (as applicable) are shown in the following table prepared by the Federation of Genealogical Societies and published in their May/June 1984 *Newsletter:*[15]

[15] Used by permission.

FICHE	CITY	STREETS
1	Akron, Ohio	
	Atlanta, Georgia	
2	Baltimore	A St. through Haubert St.
3	Baltimore	Haw St. through Sycamore Ave.
4	Baltimore	T Alley through 42d St. North
5	Canton, Ohio	
	Charlotte, North Carolina	
6	Chicago	A St. through Curtis St.
7	Chicago	Curtis St. through Ingraham Ave.
8	Chicago	Institute Pl. through Ogden Ave.
9	Chicago	Ogden Ave. through Wabash Ave.
10	Chicago	Wabash Ave. through 38th Pl. East
11	Chicago	38th Pl. East through 87th St. West
12	Chicago	87th St. West through 138th St. East
13	Cleveland, Ohio	Abbey Ave. through Woodbridge St. West
14	Cleveland, Ohio	Woodbridge Ct. SW through West 125th St.
15	Dayton, Ohio	
16	Denver, Colorado	
17	Detroit, Michigan	
18	District of Columbia	
19	Elizabeth, New Jersey	
	Erie, Pennsylvania	
	Ft. Wayne, Indiana	
	Gary, Indiana	
20	Grand Rapids, Michigan	
21	Indianapolis, Indiana	
22	Kansas City, Kansas	
	Long Beach, California	
23	Los Angeles (and county), California	A St. through Oxford Ave. South
24	Los Angeles (and county), California	Oxford Way through 134th St.
25	Newark, New Jersey	
26	New York City (Brooklyn)	A St. through Ivy St.
27	New York City (Brooklyn)	J St. through Westminster Rd.
28	New York City (Brooklyn)	Westminster Rd. through East 109th St.
29	New York City (Manhattan & Bronx)	Abbott St. through Patterson Ave.
30	New York City (Manhattan & Bronx)	Paul Ave. through West 38th St.
31	New York City (Manhattan & Bronx)	West 39th St. through 13th Ave.
32	New York City (Richmond)	Abbotsford Ave. through Elwood Pl.

33	New York City (Richmond)	Ely St. through Mystic Ct.
34	New York City (Richmond)	Nahant St. through Willowbrook Park
35	New York City (Richmond)	Willowbrook Rd. through 18th St.
	NOTE: There is no index for the Queens Borough of New York City.	
36	Oklahoma City Omaha, Nebraska Paterson, New Jersey	
37	Peoria, Illinois	
38	Philadelphia	A St. through Dingler's Ct.
39	Philadelphia	Discount Pl. through Landsdowne St.
40	Philadelphia	Larch St. through Pennsgrove St.
41	Philadelphia	Pennsylvania Ave. through Walnut Ln.
42	Philadelphia	Walnut Ln. East through 95th St. South
43	Phoenix, Arizona Reading, Pennsylvania Richmond, Virginia	
44	San Antonio, Texas San Diego, California	
45	San Francisco, California	A St. through Washburn St.
46	San Francisco, California	Washington St. through 49th Ave. South
47	Seattle, Washington	A St. through 73d East St.
48	Seattle, Washington	73d North St. through 89th St. North
49	South Bend, Indiana Tampa, Florida Tulsa, Oklahoma	
50	Wichita, Kansas Youngstown, Ohio	

You should also note that there is an outline of the 1910 boundaries of each of the 329 enumeration districts in the United States on rolls 28 through 40 of Microfilm Publication T1224, *Census Enumeration District Descriptions.*

V. MILITARY SERVICE INFORMATION IN THE CENSUS

Two censuses—the 1840 and the 1890—included valuable information about persons who performed military service. The 1840 census included an enumeration of Revolutionary War pensioners of the federal government, and the 1890 census, as mentioned earlier, included a special enumeration of Union Army veterans of the Civil War and widows of deceased veterans.

In the 1840 census of pensioners there seem to be some omissions as well as some men listed as pensioners who were not. The LDS Family History Library has prepared an index to the government publication of this pensioner census, *A Census of Pensioners for Revolutionary or Military Services* (Washington, DC, 1841). Both this list and the index[16] have been published by the Genealogical Publishing Company in Baltimore.

The 1890 special enumeration is incomplete. Those fourteen states and territories alphabetically from *A* through Kansas (and part of Kentucky) have been lost. These schedules include the veteran's name (also the widow's name if the veteran was deceased); his rank; company; regiment (or vessel); enlistment and discharge dates; length of service in days, months, and years; post office address; nature of any disability, and other remarks.[17]

Both of these military service enumerations are useful tools which can lead you to other genealogical records, but the 1890 veterans' schedules have more useful features than their early cousin.

There are also some special veterans' schedules for the Dakota Territory taken in 1885.

VI. SPECIAL ENUMERATIONS, STATE CENSUSES, AND OTHER CENSUS SCHEDULES

In addition to the federal decennial censuses which we have discussed, a few limited censuses were taken during the colonial period, and several states have taken their own censuses for various reasons. Also, the federal government has taken a few special censuses in some of the states between the regular enumerations. The exact nature and extent of the various colonial and state censuses is itself a complete study and will not be dealt with in this volume. For the present you should be aware of a little U.S. government pamphlet, *State Censuses; an Annotated Bibliography of Censuses of Population Taken After the Year 1790 by States and Territories in the United States,* by Henry J. Dubester (Washington, DC, 1948). This booklet is out of print but can be found in some libraries and government document depositories. A more recent and up-to-date listing is a little catalog entitled *U.S. and Special Censuses* (Salt Lake City: Ancestry Publishing, 1985). Most colonial censuses have been published.

---

[16] *Census of Pensioners, A General Index for Revolutionary or Military Service (1840),* prep. by The Genealogical Society of The Church of Jesus Christ of Latter-day Saints (Baltimore: Genealogical Publishing Co., 1965).

[17] Meredith B. Colket, Jr., and Frank E. Bridgers, *Guide to Genealogical Records in the National Archives* (Washington, DC: The National Archives, 1964), pp. 8-9.

Special enumerations taken by the federal government are as follows:

1857: MINNESOTA TERRITORY. (This is in the National Archives in five printed volumes.)

1864: ARIZONA TERRITORY. (The Secretary of State in Phoenix has the originals. The National Archives has copies.)

1866: ARIZONA TERRITORY. (Photostats are in the National Archives.)

1867: ARIZONA TERRITORY (Mohave, Pima and Yuma counties). (Photostats are in the National Archives.)

1869: ARIZONA TERRITORY (Yavapai County). (Photostats are in the National Archives.)

1880: SPECIAL CENSUS OF INDIANS NOT TAXED, within the jurisdiction of the United States. The schedules show the name of the tribe, the Indian Reservation, the Agency, the nearest post office; the number in each household and a description of the dwelling; the Indian name, with its English translation, of every person in the family; his relationship to the head of the family; his marital and tribal status; his description; his occupation; health; education; ownership of property, and means of subsistence. (There are only four volumes in the National Archives:

Vols. I and II: Indians near Fort Simcoe and at Tulalip, Washington Territory.

Vol. III: Indians near Fort Yates, Dakota Territory.

Vol. IV: Indians in California.)

1885: COLORADO, DAKOTA TERRITORY, FLORIDA, NEBRASKA, and NEW MEXICO TERRITORY. (This census was taken by the states and territories on a federal option and promise of partial reimbursement. The schedules are similar in form to those of 1880, and photostats of all except Dakota are in the National Archives. They are also available there on microfilm. The Dakota census, with several counties missing, is located at various sites in North and South Dakota. Filmed copies of the South Dakota schedules are in the National Archives and the schedules for areas now in North Dakota have been published in a volume called *Collections of the State Historical Society of North Dakota,* Vol. 4 [1913], pp. 338-448. There is a general index.)[18]

1907: OKLAHOMA (Seminole County).

[18] *Guide to Genealogical Research in the National Archives,* rev. ed. (Washington, DC: The National Archives, 1983), p. 35.

In addition to the federal population schedules, the mortality schedules, and the military veterans' schedules, there are some other census schedules also of interest. All censuses from 1840 on include agricultural schedules. These included every farm with an annual produce worth $100 or more (in 1850 and 1860) and gave the owner or tenant, the kind and value of the acreage, machinery, livestock, and produce.

For the years 1820 and 1850 through 1880 there are manufacturing/industrial schedules which included every business that had more than $500 in gross profits. The 1880 schedules for cities of 8,000 and over are missing.

The 1880 census included a supplementary schedule providing additional information on "dependent classes" enumerated in the population schedules. This included blind, deaf-mute, idiotic, insane, and permanently disabled persons. Note that the population schedules prior to 1870 included schedules of slaves as well as of free persons. Also be aware that some of the aforementioned census schedules were prepared in connection with other decennial censuses but have not survived. Those listed here are the ones that are substantially complete.

VII. MORTALITY SCHEDULES

Beginning with the 1850 census—the first attempting to enumerate every person in every household—the persons in charge conceived the idea that a certain amount of useful vital (birth, marriage, death) information could be collected through the census medium. (See chapter 10.) This was the beginning of mortality schedules. A separate schedule was thus devised in compliance with an act of Congress. This schedule was for the purpose of collecting data about persons who died during the census year. (See glossary of terms at the end of this chapter.) These mortality censuses still exist for the years 1850, 1860, 1870, 1880, and the limited census of 1885.

In 1918 and 1919 (before the creation of the National Archives) these schedules, with the exception of those for 1885, were removed from federal custody and each state was given the option to secure the ones relating to itself. This is explained by Davidson and Ashby:

> The 1850-80 nonpopulation schedules [including schedules of mortality, industry, manufacturing, agriculture, business, and social statistics], which were seldom used by the Census Bureau, were authorized for disposal (65th Cong., 2d sess., H. Doc. 921). When the Daughters of the American Revolution and other organizations objected to the destruction of these records, the 1,349 volumes of these schedules were transferred in 1918-19 by the Census Bureau to

state libraries and historical societies or, in cases where state officials declined to receive them, to the DAR Library in Washington.[19]

The original schedules claimed by the DAR were for the states of Arizona, Colorado, Georgia, Kentucky, Louisiana, Tennessee, and the District of Columbia. Most, but not all, of these have been indexed by the DAR and some have been transcribed. In 1980 those original schedules still in custody of the DAR were sent to the National Archives.

Chart 4 shows the locations of the various mortality schedules, with the exception of those connected with the limited census of 1885 (Colorado Territory, Florida, Nebraska, and New Mexico Territory). All of the 1885 schedules are in the National Archives except those for Dakota which are in the library of the North Dakota State Historical Society in Bismarck. These 1885 schedules have been filmed with the population schedules for the individual states.

The first edition of this work had two additional columns in Chart 4. One showed the locations of typescript copies and the other showed the locations of indexes. These two columns are no longer necessary inasmuch as the census mortality schedules are so widely published and because of the services of the National Archives Microfilm Rental Program which provides copies of census films either direct or through interlibrary loan. The National Archives, the DAR, and the LDS Family History Library all have extensive holdings, and other libraries have holdings relating to their areas.

The mortality schedules comprise a valuable source and should not be overlooked. However, there are problems of which you should be aware. In the first place they represent the deaths for only one year out of every ten. There were four mortality schedules to cover deaths over a thirty-one-year period (1849-80). That would have given roughly 13 per cent of the deaths, but the Public Health Service reports that the actual count fell far short of this. It is estimated that in the mortality schedules for 1850, 1860, and 1870 only 60 per cent of the actual deaths within those twelve-month periods were reported.[20] If my math is correct that means that less than 8 per cent of the actual deaths for this thirty-one-year period are in the mortality schedules. (These figures are probably slightly off because the 1880 schedules had a somewhat higher percentage of completeness.)

The form and format of the mortality schedules were changed from one census to the next, but basically:

---

[19] Davidson and Ashby, p. 96.

[20] United States. National Office of Vital Statistics, Vol. I, p. 7.

CHART 4—AVAILABILITY OF CENSUS MORTALITY SCHEDULES

STATE	YEARS	LOCATION OF ORIGINALS	LOCATION OF MICROFILM COPIES	NATIONAL ARCHIVES FILM NUMBERS
Alabama	1850-1860-1870-1880	Department of Archives and History, Montgomery, Alabama		
Arizona	1870 (Mohave Co. through Yuma Co.)	National Archives	NSDAR Library National Archives	NARS—T655
	1880	National Archives	NSDAR Library National Archives	NARS–T655
Arkansas	1850-1860-1870-1880	University of Arkansas, Fayetteville, Arkansas	Secretary of State Little Rock, Arkansas National Archives	
California	1850-1860-1870-1880	California State Library, Sacramento, California		
Colorado	1870-1880	National Archives	NSDAR Library National Archives LDS FHL*	NARS—T655
Connecticut	1850-1860-1870-1880	Connecticut State Library, Hartford, Connecticut	National Archives LDS FHL	NARS—A1165
Delaware	1850-1860-1870-1880	Public Archives Commission, Hall of Records, Dover, Delaware	National Archives	NARS—A1155
District of Columbia	1850-1860-1870-1880	National Archives	NSDAR Library National Archives	NARS—T655
Florida	1850-1860-1870-1880	Department of Agriculture, Tallahassee, Florida (?)	National Archives	NARS–T1168
Georgia	1850-1860-1870-1880	National Archives	NSDAR Library LDS FHL National Archives	NARS—T655 and NARS—T1137
Idaho	1870-1880	Idaho State Library, Boise, Idaho		
Illinois	1850-1860-1870-1880	Illinois State Archives, Springfield, Illinois	National Archives	NARS—T1133
Indiana	1850-1860-1870-1880	Indiana State Library, Indianapolis, Indiana		

*LDS Family History Library, Salt Lake City, Utah.

CHART 4—(continued)

STATE	YEARS	LOCATION OF ORIGINALS	LOCATION OF MICROFILM COPIES	NATIONAL ARCHIVES FILM NUMBERS
Iowa	1850-1860-1870-1880	Iowa State Historical Society, Iowa City, Iowa	National Archives	NARS—T1156
Kansas	1860	Kansas State Historical Society, Topeka, Kansas	National Archives	NARS–T1130
	1870-1880	Kansas State Historical Society, Topeka, Kansas	NSDAR Library National Archives	NARS—T1130
Kentucky	1850	National Archives (Pendleton through Woodford counties)	NSDAR Library National Archives	NARS—T655
	1860-1870-1880	National Archives	NSDAR Library National Archives	NARS–T655
Louisiana	1850-1860-1870-1880	National Archives	NSDAR Library National Archives	NARS—T655 and NARS—T1136
Maine	1850-1860-1870	Office of Vital Statistics, Department of Health and Welfare, Augusta, Maine	LDS FHL	
	1880	Office of Vital Statistics, Department of Health and Welfare, Augusta, Maine		
Maryland	1850-1860-1870-1880	Maryland State Library, Annapolis, Maryland (?)		
Massachusetts	1850-1860-1870-1880	State Archives, Boston, Massachusetts	National Archives	NARS—T1204
Michigan	1850	Michigan Historical Commission, Lansing, Michigan	National Archives	NARS—T1164
	1860-1870-1880	Michigan Historical Commission, Lansing, Michigan	NSDAR Library National Archives	NARS–T1164
Minnesota	1850	Minnesota State Library, St. Paul, Minnesota		
	1860-1870-1880	Minnesota State Library, St. Paul, Minnesota (?)	National Archives (1870 only) LDS FHL	
Mississippi	1850-1860-1870-1880	Department of Archives and History, Jackson, Mississippi		

CHART 4—(continued)

STATE	YEARS	LOCATION OF ORIGINALS	LOCATION OF MICROFILM COPIES	NATIONAL ARCHIVES FILM NUMBERS
Missouri	1850-1860-1870-1880	Missouri State Historical Society, St. Louis, Missouri		
Montana	1870-1880	Montana State Historical Society, Helena, Montana	National Archives	NARS—GR6
Nebraska	1860-1870-1880	Nebraska State Historical Society, Lincoln, Nebraska	National Archives LDS FHL	NARS—T1128
*Nevada	1880	Nevada State Historical Society, Reno, Nevada		
New Hampshire	1850-1860-1870-1880	New Hampshire State Library, Concord, New Hampshire	LDS FHL	
New Jersey	1850-1860-1870-1880	New Jersey State Library, Archives and History Bureau, Trenton, N.J.	NSDAR Library National Archives	NARS—GR21
New Mexico	1880	National Archives	National Archives	
New York	1850-1860-1870-1880	New York State Library, Albany, New York		
North Carolina	1850-1860-1870-1880	North Carolina State Department of Archives and History, Raleigh, N.C.	National Archives	NARS—GR1
North Dakota	1870-1880	North Dakota State Historical Society, Bismarck, North Dakota (?)	National Archives	
Ohio	1850-1860 1880	Ohio Library of State, Columbus, Ohio	National Archives LDS FHL	NARS—T1159 NARS—T1163
Oregon	1850-1860-1870-1880	Oregon State Archives, Salem, Oregon		
Pennsylvania	1850-1860-1870-1880	Pennsylvania State Library, Harrisburg, Pennsylvania	National Archives LDS FHL	NARS—T956
Rhode Island	1850-1860-1870-1880	Rhode Island State Library, Providence, Rhode Island		
South Carolina	1850-1860-1870-1880	South Carolina Department of Archives and History, Columbia, S.C.	NSDAR Library National Archives	NARS—GR22

*The 1850, 1860, and 1870 enumerations of Nevada are supposedly with California.

CHART 4—(continued)

STATE	YEARS	LOCATION OF ORIGINALS	LOCATION OF MICROFILM COPIES	NATIONAL ARCHIVES FILM NUMBERS
South Dakota	1860-1870	South Dakota State Historical Society, Pierre, South Dakota (?)	National Archives	NARS—GR27
	1880	South Dakota State Historical Society, Pierre, South Dakota (?)		
Tennessee	1850-1860 1880	National Archives	NSDAR Library National Archives	NARS—T655 and NARS—T1135
Texas	1850-1860-1870-1880	Archives Division, Texas State Library, Austin, Texas	National Archives	NARS—T1134
Utah	1850-1860 1880	(?)		
	1870	Utah State Archives, Salt Lake City, Utah	National Archives LDS FHL	NARS—GR7
Vermont	1850-1860	Vermont State Library, Montpelier, Vermont		
	1870	Texas State Library, Austin, Texas	Vermont State Library National Archives	NARS—GR7
	1880	Vermont State Library, Montpelier, Vermont		
Virginia	1850 1880	Virginia State Library, Richmond, Virginia (?)	National Archives LDS FHL	NARS—T1132
	1860	Duke University, Durham, North Carolina	National Archives LDS FHL	NARS—T1132
	1870	Virginia State Library, Richmond, Virginia (?)	National Archives	NARS—T1132
Washington	1860-1870-1880	Washington State Library, Olympia, Washington	National Archives	NARS—A1154
*West Virginia	1870-1880	State Department of Archives and History, Charleston, West Virginia	National Archives	
Wisconsin	1850-1860-1870-1880	Wisconsin State Historical Society, Madison, Wisconsin		
Wyoming	1870-1880	State Law Library, Cheyenne, Wyoming (?)		

*1850 and 1860 are part of Virginia.

187

SCHEDULE 3.—Persons who Died during the Year ending 1st June, 1850, in the Towns of Castine and Penobscot **in the County of** Hancock, **State of** Maine, **enumerated by me,** S. K. Devereux **Ass't Marshal.**

NAME OF EVERY PERSON WHO DIED during the Year ending 1st June, 1850, whose usual Place of Abode at the Time of his Death was in this Family.	DESCRIPTION. Age.	Sex.	Colour White, black, or mulatto.	Free or Slave.	Married or widowed.	PLACE OF BIRTH. Naming the State, Territory, or Country.	The Month in which the Person died.	PROFESSION, OCCUPATION, OR TRADE.	DISEASE, OR CAUSE OF DEATH.	Number of DAYS ILL.	
1	2	3	4	5	6	7	8	9	10	11	
Wilber M. Vearie	1	M				Maine	October		Dysentery	3 months	1
Rufus F. Parker	42	M			M	Maine	October	Sea Captain	Unknown	Sudden	2
Thomas Cobb	77	M				Massachusetts	October	Lawyer	Consumption	7 yrs	3
Everett Eaton	8	M				Maine	April		[illegible]	–	4
Samuel A. Avery	26	M			M	Maine	August	Sea Captain	Fever	9	5
John H. Jarvis	63	M			M	Massachusetts	January	Merchant	Apoplexy	4	6
Frank Moore	3/12	M				Maine	August		Dropsy	7	7
John C. Dunlap	4	M				Maine	March		Fever	6 weeks	8
Alanson S. Glazier	5	M				Maine	May		Accident	Sudden	9
Daniel Sullivan	54	M			M	Ireland	January	Mariner	Dysentery	1 month	10
Caroline Sullivan	19	F				Maine	April		Consumption	6 weeks	11
Deborah Steele	55	F			M	Maine	February		Old age	2 months	12
Elias Conner	7	M				Maine	March		Fever	2 weeks	13
Temperance Hutchings	67	F				Maine	April		Consumption	1 year	14
Nancy Perkins	29	F				Maine	September		Consumption	1 year	15
Granville B. Leighton	3	M				Maine	September		Lung Fever	3 days	16
Edwin W. Leighton	1	M				Maine	March		Dropsy	14 days	17
Phebe A. Snow	16	F				Maine	February		Fever	14 days	18
Polly Carper	56	F				Maine	July		Consumption	3 months	19
Phebe Marks	21	F				Maine	January		Fever	3 days	20
Frances A. Wardwell	24	M				Maine	June		Drowned		21
David Montgomery	2/12	M				Maine	January		Fever	4 days	22
Martha Bowden	29	F				Maine	June		Consumption	2 months	23
Josiah Clement	38	F				Maine	March		Consumption	3 years	24
											25
											26
											27
											28
											29
											30
											31
											32
											33
											34
											35

Remarks.

FIGURE 16—A PAGE FROM THE 1850 MORTALITY SCHEDULE, STATE OF MAINE

> [t]he information usually shown in the schedules includes the name of the person, his age, sex, state of birth, month of death and cause of death. The 1880 [and 1885] Mortality Schedules include also the state of birth of each parent of the deceased person, but the names of the parents are not given. The schedules are set up by county, but, where indexed, are indexed by the state as a whole.[21]

For most people the best and most convenient access to the census mortality schedules is through the Census Microfilm Rental Program. If you desire to use the records in the DAR Library, you should know that library personnel do not do genealogical research for patrons.

Mortality schedules have special significance for blacks in 1850 and 1860 because of the absence of family and personal data in the slave schedules for those years. However, if a slave died during the census year, the same critical vital data were given on the mortality schedule as for any other person who died.

VIII. GLOSSARY OF CENSUS TERMS

The next chapter is devoted exclusively to helping you use the census; so, before embarking on that adventure, let's take a minute to become familiar with some common census terms. The following list is adapted from a list published in the previously cited inventory of the records of the Census Bureau. I think it will add to your understanding of census records. Some of these terms have already been used.[22]

ABSTRACT: The summary or aggregate of census results submitted by the assistant to the marshal or by the marshal to Washington.

ASSISTANT: The local census taker, 1790-1870.

CENSUS BUREAU: The Census Office, established 1902.

CENSUS DAY: The day set by law for the decennial enumeration to begin and the day for which certain census statistics were supposed to be taken. The census days were as follows:

1st-4th Censuses, 1790-1820	First Monday in August
5th-12th Censuses, 1830-1900	June 1
13th Census, 1910	April 15
14th Census, 1920	January 1
15th-20th Censuses, 1930-1980	April 1

[21] "Federal Mortality Schedules in the NSDAR Library, Washington, DC" (unpublished instruction sheet from NSDAR, 1967).

[22] Davidson and Ashby, pp. 139-141.

In researching the census it is always important to note and compare the actual date of enumeration with the census day. That can explain many inconsistencies.

CENSUS OFFICE: The temporary office set up for each decennial census before the permanent office, the Census Bureau, was established in 1902.

CENSUS YEAR: The twelve-month period immediately preceding the census day for which certain census inquiries are made. This term was first used in the seventh census act (1850).

CIVIL DIVISION: An area over which a state or local government has jurisdiction and which, beginning with the tenth census (1880), was one of the bases for establishing enumerators' subdivisions.

DECENNIAL CENSUS: The population enumeration required by the Constitution to be taken every ten years beginning in 1790.

DISTRICT: The enumeration area, often coterminous with a state or territory, over which a U.S. Marshal had jurisdiction, 1790-1870; also the smaller area assigned to a supervisor of the census beginning in 1880.

DIVISION: That portion of a district that was assigned to an assistant for taking the censuses, 1790-1840.

ENUMERATION: The population census required by the Constitution.

FAMILY SCHEDULE: The population schedules used only in 1890.

INTERDECENNIAL PERIOD: The time between decennial censuses.

MARSHAL: The judicial official who supervised the taking of the census in his judicial district, 1790-1870.

RECORDS: The term often used by the Census Office and the Census Bureau for all the census documentation except original schedules and published reports.

REGISTRATION AREA: A city in which an official registration of deaths or other vital statistics is maintained. Beginning with the tenth (1880) census, the Superintendent of the Census was authorized to obtain from such official records the statistics so maintained.

REPORTS: The term used for published census results.

RETURNS: A term often used interchangeably with schedules or completed questionnaires. Apparently the word *returns,* as used in the first census act, was interpreted by some assistants to mean abstracts or totals obtained from the schedules and by other assistants to mean the individual schedules themselves.

SCHEDULE: A completed census questionnaire.

SCHEDULE FORM: A blank census questionnaire.

SUBDIVISION: An enumeration area, the boundaries of which either are the limits of known civil divisions or are natural boundaries. The term was first used in the seventh (1850) census act.

12

Using Census Returns

Experience has taught that a student can memorize all of the essential data about a genealogical source but still not know how to use it. It is with that thought in mind that this chapter has been prepared. My sole purpose here is to help bridge the gap between theory and practice. In seeking this objective I will discuss the various benefits of census records as a genealogical source, as well as the limitations. I will also provide examples of how the census schedules are used to solve some specific types of problems.

I. BENEFITS AND USES

A. 1790

The greatest benefit to the user of the 1790 census schedules is the fact that they are published and completely indexed. Suppose you know that your ancestor lived somewhere in Pennsylvania and was in the proper age range to be the head of a family at the time of this census. By checking the index to the Pennsylvania census you might discover his county of residence. Even if your ancestor's name proved to be common and you find eight or ten people with the same name in various counties, the census is still useful because it at least limits the search to these few counties. Otherwise the entire twenty-one counties of 1790 Pennsylvania might need to be considered.

If your surname is at all common (at least 100 persons of that surname in the entire 1790 census) the geographic distribution of all persons of that surname, by state, is given in a special publication.[1]

The 1790 census has proven to be an excellent "finding tool." Even those published tax lists which have replaced the lost schedules in Delaware, Virginia, Kentucky (then part of Virginia), Georgia, and the three missing counties of North Carolina (Caswell, Granville, and Orange) are most useful in this function.

B. 1800-40

As the census schedules after 1790 are not so uniformly indexed, they do not serve quite the same function—they cannot ordinarily be considered finding tools. It is possible to read all the census schedules within a state as a means of locating a family, but such an action is usually taken only as a last resort because of the mammoth size of the task, especially in the more populous states. You must usually know the county of your ancestor's residence in order to locate him.

Many persons feel that there is little value in using the schedules before complete families were enumerated beginning in 1850. "Even after I find my family," they ask, "what do I have?" The truth is that if you can trace a family through these early censuses you can learn quite a bit. You will find some useful intelligence of any movements in and out of an area, of deaths, of younger members of the family coming of age and becoming themselves heads of families. Nevertheless, you can get this information from the censuses only if you search *all pertinent available schedules* and if you search for *all persons in the area with the surname of interest*. Information thus secured can also be a guide to the existence of other useful records relating to your family such as wills, marriage records, deeds, etc.

Note that many of the schedule forms for censuses before 1830 were hand-drawn by the enumerators (and not always on the same size paper). During this process some of the columns (especially those relating to slaves and "free persons of color") were not always included.

C. 1850-70

The great value of these schedules lies in the fact that they enumerate complete households. The relationships implied between the members of a

---

[1] United States. Census Bureau, *A Century of Population Growth From the First Census of the United States to the Twelfth, 1790-1900*, 1909. (Baltimore: Genealogical Publishing Co., 1967 reprint).

household provide some of the best circumstantial evidence available for the eventual proving of family connections. You cannot always safely assume what the relationship is between two persons in the same house, but you at least have some basic information with which to work. An elderly person living with a family may prove to be a parent of either the husband or the wife. (The person's surname will *often* indicate which.)

Just as with the earlier censuses, if you search all the schedules pertinent to your problem and extract information for all persons of your surname(s) you can better understand the family, its movements, marriages, deaths, etc. You can also find clues to suggest the use of other records. It is essential that you copy all information relating to everyone of the surname into your research notes. This includes, also, the complete household even when there is only one person of your surname living there. Though you may not see the necessity for this at the time, I promise that it is important. Nearly every genealogist has seen cases where important clues and even family connections have been passed over unnoticed when this has been neglected.

The movement of a family from one area to another and the length of time the family lived in a certain locality can often be told from studying census enumerations. The states of birth as given for the children in the household are most helpful in this regard. Whether you can expect to find land deeds for a family can often be told by whether the census lists the person as an owner of real estate. (The censuses tell the value of real estate owned.) The value of real estate (and also of personal property in the 1860 and 1870 schedules) can be an indication of the social prestige and economic status of the family. Also, those who had extensive possessions were more likely to leave wills behind at their deaths and to be written of in local histories. And you can also tell whether children attended school and whether members of the family could read and write.

Because most of these censuses are not indexed they are usually not finding tools, but the fact that they are family-oriented—just as is genealogy—makes them invaluable. And as more indexes are created there is more potential use of them as finding tools too.

D. 1880

The 1880 census is listed in a category by itself because it has some rather distinct differences from, and advantages over, its older brothers. However, everything we have said about using the earlier schedules also applies to the use of this one. The advantages (or differences) are as follows:

1. The partial index to this census, as discussed in chapter 11, makes it a useful finding tool.

2. The fact that the relationship of every person to the head of the household in which he lives is told makes family information much more authoritative than the circumstantial evidence on relationships found in the households of the 1850, 1860, and 1870 schedules.

3. Alleged states (or countries) of birth for each person's father and mother are stated in this census.

And though these advantages are significant, to each we add a word of caution: They can be deceptive and work to your disadvantage if not properly understood. Consider:

1. The index is only a partial one, including only households with children ten years of age and younger.

2. The relationships given are to the head of the household only and not to other members of the household. There is no indication as to whether the head of the house has been married more than once and whether his children are also his wife's children.

3. The states of birth listed for fathers and mothers are not necessarily correct. Some persons didn't even manage to get their own states of birth recorded correctly.

Sometimes the states of birth given for the parents of a child in the household can help you see if his father has been married more than once and which of his children belong to which marriage. For example, if the state of birth of the child's mother is different than the state of birth listed for the wife on that census, you have an obvious clue to the possibility of another marriage. But, of course, this certainly is not a fool-proof formula. If a man had more than one wife and they were both (or all) born in the same state there would be no clue.

E. 1900 and 1910

These census schedules are a great boon to the genealogist with more recent ancestral problems. In many ways they are not unlike the 1880 census—most differences being quite insignificant. By way of similarities, I should note that there are Soundex indexes to both (though the 1910 indexes cover only twenty-one states). Both give the relationship of each person to the family head. And both give the states or countries of birth for the parents of each person enumerated.

Similarities and differences between each other and the 1880 census include:

1. The 1880 census gives the month of birth if born within the year. The 1900 census gives the month and year of birth for everyone. The 1910 census gives the month and year of birth for no one.

2. Both 1900 and 1910 tell how long an immigrant has been in the U.S. and whether naturalized. The 1880 census does not.

3. Both 1900 and 1910 tell whether a home or farm is owned or rented and whether the owned property is owned free of mortgage. The 1880 census does not.

4. The 1880 census tells whether the person was married within the census year. The 1900 and 1910 do not—though both tell the number of years of the present marriage (which the 1880 does not).

5. The 1880 tells whether a person is temporarily or permanently disabled; the 1900 and 1910 do not—and the same with "crippled, maimed, or deformed."

6. The 1910 tells whether a person is "deaf and dumb" and "blind." The 1880 includes these as well as "idiot" and "insane." The 1900 has no such information.

7. The 1900 and 1910 both tell whether the person speaks English. The 1880 does not. The 1910 also identifies the language spoken.

8. The 1900 and 1910 both tell how many children a mother has had and how many of them are living. The 1880 does not.

9. The 1900 and 1910 both tell if the person is a Civil War veteran (Union or Confederate) or the widow of such. The 1880 does not.

As with the earlier censuses, the reliability of the stated information on any particular issue is dependent on many unknown and uncontrollable variables.

II. LIMITATIONS OF THE CENSUS AS A GENEALOGICAL SOURCE

As with most records, many weaknesses in the census as a source of genealogical evidence are self-evident. We have already discussed some of these, but a listing and some further categorizing may prove useful.

A. Limitation of Time

The fact that there was no general census taken of the families in America until 1790 is a limiting factor. Other records must be used for the colonial periods. Also, in connection with this problem, I might mention the nature of census development—the earlier schedules do not contain nearly as much genealogical data or personal data as do the later schedules.

B. Incompleteness

At the taking of every American census there have been families missed due to a built-in "error factor"—the length of time allowed for the taking thereof. The act providing for the 1790 census allowed nine months for the marshals to complete their enumeration. This same length of time was allowed for all censuses until 1850 when the time was cut to five months. In 1870 it was reduced to one month. When an enumeration went on over a period of time—even if it was only two or three days—some families were missed completely and others were enumerated more than once.

Also, the U.S. has never made use of "prior schedules," that is, schedules to be left at the residence in advance of the enumeration to be completed by the head of the family. Such schedules are used in nearly every European country and may or may not add to the validity of the census results, but they make it possible to take the entire census in a very short period of time (even one day). In 1970 and later enumerations the U.S. census utilized a form which was mailed to families, but this was the first move in that direction.

Another problem was that some families, especially in low-class, multiple-dwelling units (those made from large, old single-family units), were inadvertently bypassed because the enumerator (or the assistant) was not aware of their existence. And there were others missed also. Every genealogist has searched and searched for a family that "should have been there"—it was there in both earlier and later enumerations—but it was not to be found.

Under *incompleteness* I ought also to include those censuses for entire counties and even entire states which have been lost or destroyed.

C. Indifferent Enumerator (or Assistant)

In some instances incompleteness can be explained under this heading, but a census can be incomplete in spite of a conscientious census taker, so you should give him the benefit of the doubt. However, there have been census takers who took the job only for what they could get out of it or because it was assigned to them by legislative act. Many of these persons were not well qualified and did not fulfill their obligations satisfactorily. Many census schedules reflect this because the instructions which the census takers received (or should have received) were not followed.

Some schedules list the members of a household by initials only. A few schedules list no places of birth. Sometimes families were not home when the census taker made his visit and neighbors were asked to give the information, or, if he was personally acquainted with the family, the assistant would complete the schedules to the best of his own knowledge. There were also times when young children in the family provided the "facts" for the census enumeration if no one else was at home. I have observed that even the racial designation of a person or a family can be in error.

Some census takers padded the population. Apparently reimbursed according to the number of families enumerated, they listed some families twice in different parts of their schedules, sometimes varying the information slightly. Every genealogist has seen this type of double enumeration.

Before going on, however, let me say that most of the persons commissioned to take the census did a good job and the censuses they took represent their best and most conscientious efforts. Some were even over zealous, going well beyond the requirements made of them. A good case in point is provided by those census takers who listed counties of birth for all persons and not just states and countries.

D. Incorrect Information Given by Family Members

Often incorrect data, which resulted in inconsistencies in the records, were given to the assistants and enumerators by members of the family. Anyone who has read many censuses is aware of this problem. It manifests itself in almost any family that is traced through all available censuses. Inconsistent ages illustrate the problem best but names and places of birth also have some tendency to change from one census to the next. This is another reason why you should never stop after searching just one census, even though you think the family is complete. With this kind of problem the effect is the same whether or not the error was intentional.

E. Legibility

Too often the census schedules are difficult to read, and there are many reasons for this. Careless handwriting, unfamiliar abbreviations, the workings of time on poor quality inks—these are all familiar problems. The 1880 census, taken on such poor quality paper that it has not been able to withstand the ravages of time at all, was one of the first withdrawn from public use. (The originals are now in various non-federal repositories throughout the country as indicated on pages 130 and 131 of Katherine H. Davidson and Charlotte M. Ashby, *Preliminary Inventory of the Records of the Bureau of the Census* [Washington, DC: The National Archives, 1964].)

There are additional problems in reading microfilmed copies of the census schedules. On some the photography was poor—under-exposure, over-exposure, etc. Others present special photography problems, such as writing that has faded and simply does not photograph well. Another problem was found in the photographing of double pages on single frames—since one page often stood higher than the other it was impossible to get both into proper focus except near the center of the large bound volumes. This latter problem has now been solved, however, in the refilming of the 1850, 1860, and 1870 censuses on single-page frames by the National Archives. The difference is unbelievable! They are much more readable, not alone because everything is in focus, but also because the image is larger and the photography is generally better. The later censuses were initially microfilmed on single-page frames. Though most are quite readable, there are—unfortunately—some films of inferior quality.

Another problem with microfilms is that the filmer could inadvertently turn two pages at once. As this has been known to happen, you should be alert to the possibility.

F. You Must Know the Place of Residence

In the absence of indexes it is generally necessary to know at least the county in which a family lived in order to find it in the census. This problem is especially acute in large cities where a census may include many volumes. In this case it is almost essential that you know the ward (or other geographic division) in which your family lived in order to complete a satisfactory search. Without this information a simple census search may take many days.

If you know the street address in 1910 and if your ancestor(s) lived in one of the thirty-nine cities with street indexes, the index can be used to expedite your search. (See discussion and listing in chapter 11.)

III. WHEN SHOULD THE CENSUS BE SEARCHED?

As previously stated, there is no immutable rule about sequence of searches. It all depends on the nature of the individual problem and your analysis thereof. The census schedules must always be searched in those problems which fall into the proper time periods, whether early or late.

By its very nature a census search will usually be one of the first searches on a pedigree problem. And because of this it may frequently be necessary for you to read the same census again at a later date when further research has revealed other clues, such as the maiden surnames on female lines, etc. You should never hesitate to re-read a census if the need is indicated, but, on the other hand, you should be absolutely certain you are getting all you can on your first time through. Not to do so is a very serious (and common) error.

A good example of what not to do is provided by the man who reads a census for one surname on his pedigree and then looks closely at his pedigree only to discover that he had two more lines in that same locality at the same time for which he ought to have been searching. There is little excuse for this kind of double-reading. You can look for two or three surnames in a census as easily as you can look for one. (However, if you make this mistake, do not hesitate to do what needs to be done—go ahead and read the census again. You probably will not make that same error again for a while.)

IV. EXAMPLES OF CENSUS USE

A. Example No. 1

(Note that this is not an actual case but is presented here only for purposes of illustration.)

Frank James Shears was, according to family records, born in Missouri about 1857. This is all we know of him until his marriage. He died in Arkansas in 1920. We do not know the names of his parents or anything else about them, and we know nothing of any brothers and sisters.

SOLUTION: This is a problem where the census cannot be searched first. It is not a finding tool, and unless we can determine a specific place in Missouri there is little that can be done there. In this case, however, we would write to the State Bureau of Vital Statistics, State Health Department, in Little Rock, Arkansas, for the death certificate of Frank James Shears. This certificate should tell the date and place of his birth and the names of his parents. (This information would be secondary evidence because of the time element.)

The death certificate (giving his death as December 2, 1920, at Rumly, Searcy County, Arkansas) is secured. It states as follow:

Date of birth:	April 15, 1856
State of birth:	Missouri
Father's full name:	Findley Shears
Mother's maiden name:	Unknown

This information helps but is not sufficient yet. An obituary printed in the local newspaper, however, states that Frank J. Shears was born in Fulton, Missouri.

We now have sufficient data so that we can search the 1860 census schedule as soon as we learn from our gazetteer that Fulton, Missouri, is in

Callaway County (founded in 1820). Even if the death certificate had not given his father's name, this census search could still be made. In the search we would look for all families named Shears (or Sheers, or Shares, etc.), but we do this anyway. It does help, however, to know his father's name in case we find more than one child named Frank.

There are a number of places where we could find the 1860 census of Callaway County. In addition to some mentioned in the last chapter there are probably several libraries in the state of Missouri that have copies of Missouri censuses.

The 1860 census of Callaway County, Missouri, is searched and, among the various families found, is the following:

Findlay Sheers		28	Wagon maker	born Ky
Hulda	"	29	housewife	" Mo
William	"	6		" "
Frank	"	4		" "
Alice A.	"	2		" "
Jno. F.	"	8/12		" "

These results, of course, suggest the need for other censuses to be searched. Undoubtedly this couple were young enough to have more children, which indicates the necessity for searching both the 1870 and 1880 schedules if the family did not move away in the intervening years. If it did move it is important that its destination be determined and those censuses be searched also.

A search of the 1850 census is also indicated by the results of our 1860 search. Inasmuch as the eldest child of this couple is only six years old it is quite likely that Findlay and Hulda were not married until after 1850 and should hence be in the households of their parents in the 1850 census. However, we do not know Hulda's maiden surname, so the search for her will have to wait. This is one of those situations where a later, second search of the census will be necessary after we have gathered more information.

The 1850 census of Callaway County, Missouri, revealed the following family:

Francis Sheers		48	farmer	born Ky
Sarah	"	41		" "
Findlay	"	17	farm hand	" "
Sarah	"	14		" "
William	"	12		" Mo
Martha	"	7		" "
Frank	"	5		" "
Bethiah	"	3		" "

(This family was also found in the 1860 census, but we didn't know who they were then as Findlay was not in the household. It's a good thing we extracted all families of the surname.)

This 1850 census was very useful. It told a great deal about the "Sheers" family, including the approximate time of their migration from Kentucky to Missouri. As a result, the 1840 census of Callaway County was searched and also showed the Francis Shears family:

Francis Shears	1 male 30-40	1 female 30-40
	1 male 5-10	1 female 5-10
	2 males under 5	1 female under 5

Comparing these two censuses (the 1840 and the 1850) we see that there may be things that the 1850 census does not reveal about this family:

1. Where is the female in the 1850 census who was between five and ten in the 1840 census? Did she die? Did she marry? Or wasn't she a member of the family? We cannot say at this point.

2. Where is the other male in the 1850 census who was under five in 1840? William is the only one in 1850 who would have been in that age group.

3. We might also ask about the large gap between the ages of William (12) and Martha (7) in 1850. Such a gap suggests three possibilities:

a. One or more children born during this period may have died, perhaps the one unaccounted-for male from the 1840 census.

b. Francis Shears's wife may have died during this period and he may not have remarried for three or four years, and hence had no children then. (She would have to have died following the 1840 census.) If this were the case, Sarah (in the 1850 census) would not be the mother of our Findlay Shears.

c. There may have been no children born to the couple during this period. That wouldn't be too strange.

There is nothing to prove any of these possibilities now so we see that, though the census is invaluable in supplying evidence to help us solve our problems, it does not provide all of the evidence we need. We must have further evidence from other sources.

B. Example No. 2

Family tradition indicates that the ancestor sought—the father of William Jasper Kerr—is named Joseph Kerr. William Jasper (born 1781) died on

January 10, 1846, in Jefferson County, Iowa. His wife, Jemima, died there in 1842. William Jasper Kerr was supposedly born in North Carolina but tradition has it that he lived in Tennessee before coming to Iowa.

In a history of Jefferson County, Iowa, we read of one John Workman (born 1819 in Kentucky), an early resident of Jefferson County, who married in 1840 an Amanda J. Kerr, *born in White County, Tennessee,* on October 14, 1825. According to family records this Amanda J. was a daughter of William Jasper Kerr. This gave us a place to look in Tennessee.

The first step was to search and compare censuses in Jefferson County, Iowa, with those of White County, Tennessee, to see if we could find any correlation. The results of that search were as follows:

WHITE COUNTY, TENNESSEE—1820

Joseph Carr	3 males under 10 1 male 26-45	2 females 16-26
William Kerr	2 males under 10 1 male 26-45	1 female 26-45

(William Jasper would have been thirty-nine.)

WHITE COUNTY, TENNESSEE—1830

Joseph Kerr, Jr.	2 males 10-15 1 male 20-30 2 males 30-40 1 male 50-60	1 female 5-10 1 female 15-20 1 female 30-40
William Kerr	1 male 5-10 1 male 30-40 1 male 50-60	3 females under 5 1 female 20-30
William Kerr, Sr.	2 males under 5 1 male 5-10 1 male 10-15 1 male 15-20 1 male 40-50 1 male 60-70	1 female under 5 1 female 10-15 1 female 15-20 1 female 40-50

(William Jasper would have been forty-nine. William Kerr, Sr., is the only one with a male that age in his household. The older man living in this household might be either a father or father-in-law.)

WHITE COUNTY, TENNESSEE—1840

Levi J. Kerr	2 males under 5 1 male 15-20 1 male 20-30	1 female 15-20

William Kerr	3 males under 5	No females
	1 male 5-10	
	1 male 15-20	
	1 male 40-50	
	1 male 60-70	

(William Jasper would have been fifty-nine. The William who fiits seems to be gone.)

JEFFERSON COUNTY, IOWA—1840 (This is the first census of the county as the county was created in 1839 from Indian lands.)

Henry Kuerr (?)	2 males 5-10	2 females under 5
	2 males 20-30	2 females 20-30
William Kerr	1 male 5-10	1 female 5-10
	2 males 10-15	1 female 10-15
	1 male 15-20	1 female 20-30
	1 male 20-30	1 female 40-50
	1 male 50-60	

(William Jasper would have been fifty-nine, and if you carefully compare this family with the family of William Kerr, Sr., in the 1830 census of White County, Tennessee, you will note a close correlation.)

Archibald Kerr	1 male 20-30	1 female under 5
		1 female 20-30

(William Jasper had a son Archibald whom this fits.)

On the basis of these censuses the move seems likely and this could be the family we seek; however, nothing can be proven by these censuses alone; additional evidence is needed.

Further evidence needed to help solve the original problem was found in a Revolutionary War pension file for a veteran (a spy) named Joseph Kerr who applied for and received a pension while living in *White County, Tennessee,* in 1833. He was born in 1760 in Chester County, Pennsylvania (according to his application), and came to North Carolina with his parents as a child. It was in North Carolina that he served in the war. This might well be the man sought, but more evidence is needed to prove it. Perhaps he is the older man in William Kerr, Sr.'s, household in the 1830 census of White County.

These early censuses, even though they do not list the names of individual family members, have provided valuable evidence. This evidence should be considered carefully, along with the other evidence, but it cannot stand alone. It is insufficient to establish proof by itself.

C. Example No. 3

George Andrew Crossman and his wife, Lucy, came to the little mining town of Park City, Utah, in the 1880s. Here they resided as faithful members of the Roman Catholic Church, prospered, saw children grow up and marry, and then they died. They came from somewhere in New York State—just where was not certain, though in more recent years the children consistently said it was "Haminville" (or "Hammondville," etc.). Though this seemed like good information, a definite problem arose when such a place in New York State could not be identified though the best available gazetteers of that state were used, even those published during the proper period of time. This made it impossible to trace the family in earlier periods because New York is quite a big place.

Since the Crossman family migrated to Utah in the 1880s and the children were quite young at the time, the answer to locating them in New York obviously lay in the use of the partial index to the 1880 census. The surname Crossman was encoded according to the Soundex formula (see chapter 11) as C625 and was easily located in the New York index—not at any place the name of which even remotely resembled "Haminville"—but *at Crown Point in Essex County* (on lower Lake Champlain). The family was enumerated as follows:

Crossman,	George A.	27	Miner	born N.Y.
"	Lucy E. (wife)	21	Keeping house	" "
"	Emma E. (dau.)	4		" "
"	Cora A. (dau.)	3		" "
"	Henry G. (son)	1		" "
Bennett,	Newell R. (boarder)	21	Laborer	" "

(The family was located on p. 4, Supervisor's District 7, Enumeration District 44. I have omitted the information on the birth places of parents.)

Isn't this an easy way to solve an otherwise difficult problem?

V. CONCLUSION

Census schedules can help solve many genealogical problems, but they can also present problems if they are not properly used and properly interpreted. They must be read scrupulously—if you overlook or misread important data the results may be disastrous and far-reaching because everyone will assume that you did a good job. No one ever really checks you out. Perhaps we should all be checked on more often than we are—and this ought especially to include checking on ourselves. I like the motto of the Royal Society of London: "*Nullus in verba:* we take no man's word for anything."

A guide to help minimize the human-error factor and to mine the census for all its potential is found in the following eleven rules:

1. Note the heading on each column in each census schedule you use, and know what information you can expect to find in that column and the value of that information to your research. Extract all information from every column for every person in every household in which the surname of your ancestor is found.

2. Study the handwriting of the enumerator to minimize the possibility of misinterpretations. It is important that you do not miss the names you seek and that you do not misinterpret the given names of family members. Always watch for unusual spellings. If the census is hard to read, it is often wise to decipher every surname, at least to the extent that you are sure it is not the one you seek. There are some cases where you may need to search for specific given names rather than a surname.

3. Always consider the possibility that the enumeration of a family may be split between two pages, and may even begin with the listing of the head of the family on the bottom line of a page—and perhaps with no repetition of the surname at the top of the next page. Be sure to look at every line.

4. Look for and extract every family (the complete household) with the surname of your ancestor, as well as every household (regardless of the family head's surname) if a person of your ancestor's surname is found living there. (Use wisdom if the county is large and the surname is common, but be prepared to do what you need to do.)

5. In hard cases you should extract several families before and several families after your ancestor. Check these families for similar migration patterns, occupations, and naming patterns. Remember that relatives often lived near each other. If your ancestor owned no land you will be able to identify the area of the county where your ancestor lived through the land records of his neighbors—helping you to also locate nearby cemeteries and churches.

6. Find your ancestor and the members of his family in every census during their lives, always considering the rules stated above.

7. If you find it necessary to limit your searches to specific townships, towns, or cities because of the large population, remember that parts of a township may be separated in the census schedules and that a city or town may be enumerated separately from the township where it is situated. County histories and maps can help you make the proper research decisions. And inasmuch as place names change, histories and contemporaneous maps are of much value in your pre-search analysis.

8. Your census research can be greatly enhanced by the use of maps. Detailed maps of the area of interest can give you a perspective on your problems that you can get in no other way.

9. If your ancestor lived near a county or state boundary, extend your searches into the neighboring jurisdiction. Close neighbors are often separated by these arbitrary divisions.

10. Don't limit your research to the population schedules only. Utilize every available census schedule for the year and the area where your ancestor lived.

11. Don't be afraid to repeat a census search of a particular locality if you uncover new evidence which indicates the potential value of such a project. This is especially true when other research identifies additional ancestral families of which you were not previously aware in the area—such as the family of your ancestor's wife whose surname you have just learned.

As a final note may I also make some observations about the use of census indexes. Though they are an important tool if wisely used, in actual fact indexes may be more of a bane than a boon to the genealogist. Things you would almost certainly pick up reading through the census entry-by-entry are overlooked when you rely solely on the indexes. Thus, if you fail to find the family you seek in the index, yet there is some evidence that they should be there, don't hesitate to search the record. Before you do this, however, there are some suggestions I offer to help you get more mileage from those indexes. Essentially all of these suggestions should be prefaced with the reminder that you not be afraid to *use your imagination* when entries you seek do not appear. Also, do not be in too big a hurry; take your time and do it right.

1. Consider all possible spelling variations.

2. Consider that the indexer may have misread the name and mistaken one letter for another. Capital *T*'s, *L*'s, and *S*'s could be interchanged easily, as could small *n*'s and *u*'s, or *a*'s, *u*'s, and *o*'s, etc. Even whole names can be misread. I have seen James mistaken for Francis.

3. Consider possible phonetic spellings and silent letters, either dropped or added. *H*'s and *E*'s, in particular, are commonly dropped and added. Letters may be doubled or letters normally doubled may appear singly.

4. Consider that the sound of a vowel could have been misunderstood by the census taker, both at the beginning of the name and in the middle. Remember, for example, the Angle/Engle/Ingle and the Matlick/Matlock/Matlack cases.

5. Consider the possibility of typographical errors in indexing as well, such as transpositions of letters and adjacent keys on the typewriter being struck. Could you possibly find Ranold instead of Arnold or perhaps Amith or Smirh instead of Smith?

It is very important to your research success that you use the census records and that you use them correctly and thoroughly.

13

Understanding Probate Records and Basic Legal Terminology

I. DEFINITION AND BACKGROUND OF PROBATE RECORDS

All records which relate to the disposition of an estate after its owner's death are referred to as probate records. These are many and varied in both content and value but, basically, they fall into two main classes:

TESTATE
INTESTATE

If a person died leaving a valid will we say he died *testate,* if not he died *intestate*. In most localities in America these records comprise, as a group, one of the most useful genealogical resources available.

Historically, since the first permanent settlement, there has never been a time in America when men did not make wills or when the estates of those who failed to do so were not handled by a court, appointed for that purpose, to see that the legal heirs became the heirs in fact. In those colonies set up by British grant or dominion, English law and custom were meticulously followed. Thus the right of probate was never challenged.

Statutory probate law in America has developed as a state, rather than a federal, function; and laws do differ somewhat from one state to another. In general, however, especially insofar as wills are concerned, anyone was free to make a will if he was of sound mind, of legal age, and free from restraint. And, of course, anyone was free not to make a will and thus die intestate if he chose to do so. It can also be correctly stated that persons *not* of legal age, *not* of sound mind, and under the force of restraint (any or all of the above) could also make wills—but not legal ones. If a will was successfully challenged on any of these points, it was not acceptable as a valid will and its provisions could not be carried out.

II. CONTENT AND GENEALOGICAL VALUE

Some persons have died leaving no property of value and hence no record of probate. If you seek these persons in your research then probate records will have no *direct* value for you. Most persons in America, however, who have lived to adulthood, have left some type of estate to be administered, and in the resulting records your searches can achieve varying degrees of success. In fact, you cannot completely write off the value of probate records even for those who died without property. They are often mentioned in probate records, especially wills, of others—sometimes as witnesses, sometimes as beneficiaries, sometimes as executors or trustees, and sometimes just as innocent third parties (such as the persons from whom something being bequeathed was acquired or as owners of adjacent property). I estimate that roughly half of the people in America, historically, have either left wills or have been mentioned in them.

The very nature of probate records recommends them as an invaluable genealogical source. They exist because of relationships, both family and social, between various persons. When a man makes a will it is because he wants those whom he loves—generally his family—to have the substance and benefits of his worldly estate after his death. The laws set up to govern intestate estates are based on the same premise—members of the deceased's family are his rightful beneficiaries. Thus the great value of probate records lies in their content, and those direct statements of relationship between persons who made wills and those named therein stand as powerful evidence in the genealogical "court."

Because more persons are involved than just those who made wills (testators) and those who died without so doing (intestates), the true value of probates is multiplied far beyond what one might ordinarily expect. Every person named therein and every relationship stated increases the value of the records. Probates are a family-oriented source, and families—complete families—after all, are the very essence of genealogical research. They are what genealogy is all about.

In colonial and frontier America the proportionate number of persons who left wills was greater than we often imagine. This is because our American forebears were a land-and-property-minded people. Land was inexpensive and even those of humble circumstances could be land owners. Thus the proportionate number of wills is likely to be higher in rural and agrarian communities than in the larger cities and industrial areas where large numbers of persons owned nothing of sufficient value to warrant the making of a will. Due to this factor, in those earlier periods of time when the population was nearly all rural and practically everyone owned land, and especially in those localities where few other records were being kept, the genealogist must depend heavily on probate records. And, incidentally, they meet the challenge very well.

III. THE LIMITATIONS OF PROBATE RECORDS

I will say more about record problems later, particularly as they concern individual record types; however, at this point let me mention a few problems of a general nature. Though probate records are good, they are not a perfect source, and the following points illustrate where and why they fall short of that mark:

1. It is obvious that not everyone left a will and, as I have already said, for some persons it is impossible to find any kind of probate record. And there would undoubtedly be many more wills if everyone who intended to make one had gotten around to it.

2. All next-of-kin are not named in probate records, nor are spouses named in every case. In a will a person *usually* names his spouse and his *living* children, as these are the natural objects of his benevolence and the ones who normally have a legal claim on his estate. If some of his children died leaving children of their own, he *may* name them (his grandchildren) as they too are his issue and appropriate objects of his bounty. If he died intestate they would have been legal heirs. Please note, however, the use of the words *usually* and *may* in the above statements; for what is *usual* is not sure, and what *may* be is even less certain. In fact there are many wills wherein no one is named directly but only by relationship—"my wife," "all my children," etc. And sometimes persons are named, but no relationships are stated.

In an intestacy your problem is usually even more difficult because in so many cases, until quite recent years, there are no statements in surviving probate documents as to the names and relationships of beneficiaries.

3. To find places of residence of next-of-kin stated either in a will or in the proceedings of the court is rare in early probate cases. However, in the state of New York, when a petition for probate or administration was filed with the court, that petition required a list of all possible heirs,

regardless of whether they were named in any extant will, plus their addresses. This practice dates back to about 1790. Petitions of this type are also common in other states but not generally so early.

4. To find maiden surnames of female spouses of next-of-kin in probate records is almost unheard of, but very often you will find the names of sons-in-law and brothers-in-law.

5. Only occasionally in the records of the probate court can dates of death be found. However, any lack of these is usually not serious because the dates relating to the granting of probate, etc., establish an approximate time of death, *usually* sufficient for identification.

6. Not knowing a person's place of residence at the time of his death will often be a barrier to your finding probate records for him. A person may live in a locality most of his life and then disappear about the time you expect him to die. Because you can find no record of probate you erroneously assume that there was no such record—that he died without one. It is more likely that he moved to another place, to live with one of his children, in his old age. He would die there, his estate would be administered, and the whole matter would be recorded in that jurisdiction. Since there are few master indexes on a state level it is usually necessary that you know the county of residence at death in order to find that probate record.

7. Probates are usually indexed within each jurisdiction (mainly county), but most of these indexes are only to testators (the persons who made the wills) and intestates and not to beneficiaries or heirs. There are few exceptions.

Remember that probate records were not designed as a genealogical source but rather as a legal vehicle for settling estates in the most equitable manner and for legally transferring the deceased's property rights. No original record was ever kept with genealogy as its prime objective. However, we must make the most of what we have available, and some of these records are very good—probate records being among the best.

IV. LEGAL TERMINOLOGY

Though it may appear otherwise, my purpose here is not to write a legal dictionary. However, if I can help you gain an understanding of a certain amount of legal jargon you will be better equipped to understand probate records as a source of genealogical evidence. And, for that matter, you will also be better able to understand other court records. The various types of probate records are not included here but are discussed in chapters 14 and 15. Consider the following:

ABUTTALS: The lands, roads, streams, etc., to which a piece of land is abutted. (Also called buttals.) Sometimes the term is used to designate the end boundaries as opposed to the side boundaries, which are called *sidings*.

ACCOUCHMENT: Childbirth.

ADMINISTRATION: Administration is a process, not a record. It involves the method of setting legal machinery to work in a particular probate case and the modes of operation until the estate is settled. This is necessary because the laws of descent and distribution are not self-executing. They must be carried out by the established judicial machinery. The term applies to both testate cases and intestacies since the term *execution* (q.v.) is not in common use. Administration normally involves the collection, management, and distribution of an estate (q.v.) by the proper legal processes. (On the basis of this definition, I could have more accurately entitled this chapter "Understanding records relating to the administration of estates.")

ADMINISTRATION *CUM TESTAMENTO ANNEXO* (C.T.A.): (Administration with will annexed)—This is an administration granted by the proper court when the decedent (q.v.) has left a valid will and (1) has failed to name an executor (q.v.), (2) has named an incapable person as executor, or (3) the executor refuses to act. Such an administration is carried out according to the terms of the will, as if by the executor.

ADMINISTRATION *DE BONIS NON* (D.B.N.): (Administration of the goods not administered)—Administration of any goods (q.v.) of a deceased person not already administered by a former administrator (q.v.). It relates to the administration started by one administrator but finished by another.

ADMINISTRATION *DE BONIS NON CUM TESTAMENTO ANNEXO:* Administration granted by the court when the executor of a will has died leaving a portion of the estate (q.v.) still unadministered.

ADMINISTRATION WITH WILL ANNEXED: See ADMINISTRATION *CUM TESTAMENTO ANNEXO*.

ADMINISTRATOR: A person appointed by the proper court to administer a deceased person's estate. He resembles an executor (q.v.), but is appointed by the court rather than by the deceased. He is bound to settle the estate strictly according to statute unless he is appointed with the will annexed. He must give security by entering into a bond with sureties. See SURETY.

ADMINISTRATRIX: A woman who administers an estate (q.v.).

AFFINITY: A relationship (or rather a connection) through marriage rather than by blood. See CONSANGUINITY.

AGNATION: Kinship or relationship on the father's side, or by male descent.

ANCILLARY ADMINISTRATION: An administration of property located in a state other than the state of domicile (q.v.) at death. It is a subordinate administration and is an indication that the main administration has been granted in another state (the record will usually state where).

APPURTENANCE: Something which belongs to something else. In land deeds the term might refer to rights of way (q.v.) or other easements (q.v.), houses, barns, outbuildings, gardens, orchards, fences, or anything else which belongs to the land.

ASSIGNMENT: The transfer of the interest one has in property to another party; the document by which this is done. The parties are known as the *assignor* (the one who makes the assignment) and the *assignee* (the one to whom it is made).

ATTEST: To bear witness to something, as the execution (q.v.) of a will, and to affirm formally with your own signature that the document is genuine.

ATTORNEY: An agent or substitute, or anyone authorized to act in the stead of another. An *attorney in fact* is anyone appointed to act for another in a particular situation or transaction not of a legal nature. The bestowal of such authority is by a document called a *power of attorney* or *letter of attorney* (see chapter 17). An *attorney at law* acts for another person in legal matters.

BENEFICIARY: A person for whose benefit a trust (q.v.) is created or who receives benefit from property. Those receiving by will are often called beneficiaries. See also HEIR.

BEQUEATH: To give personal property (q.v.) by will. Distinguishable from devise (q.v.) which relates to real property (q.v.).

BEQUEST: A gift of personal property (q.v.) by will.

BODILY HEIRS: See HEIRS OF THE BODY.

BY THESE PRESENTS: See PRESENTS.

CHATTEL: A broad term for personal property (q.v.) which can include both animate and inanimate properties. All interests in real property (q.v.) which are *less than a freehold estate* (q.v.)—such as a lease—are also considered chattel. In early times chattel was also used as a synonym for *slaves*.

CHILD OF TENDER YEARS or OF TENDER AGE: A child under fourteen years of age. Such a child is generally not considered capable of making choices involving his own custody or guardianship.

COMMON LAW: That system of law which originated in England and was carried to her colonies and provinces. The common-law system is based on the authority of usage, custom, and court decrees rather than on statutory enactments. In the United States it may also include parliamentary English law inherited and perpetuated in the colonies, unless specifically repugnant to the Constitution or overruled by statutory rule or court action.

COMMUNITY PROPERTY: Property owned in common by the marital community of husband and wife as a kind of marital partnership. (This applies only in states where Spanish property law prevails. All property procured by either spouse during the marriage is community property.) Only Arizona, California, Idaho, Louisiana, Nevada, New Mexico, Texas, and Washington are community property states.

CONSANGUINITY: Blood relationship, either lineal or collateral. See AFFINITY.

CONSIDERATION: The price or motive, etc., in any contract.

CONVEYANCE: A deed, the document by which title to real property (q.v.) is transferred.

CORPOREAL PROPERTY: Any property which can be seen and handled, as opposed to INCORPOREAL PROPERTY which cannot, but exists only in contemplation. For example, a house is corporeal but the contemplated annual rents are incorporeal. Some incorporeal property such as easements (q.v.) can be inherited and are an appurtenance (q.v.) to the land.

COTENANCY: There are basically four types of joint ownership of land. One of these—community property—has already been discussed. The other three are associated with ownership under the English common law (q.v.). They are:

1. *Tenancy by the entirety.* This is joint ownership of land by husband and wife with rights of survivorship. It is usually considered that the joint acts of both parties during their lives are essential to terminate the cotenancy. Most states do not recognize this type of estate today and most others no longer allow it unless created by specific language. This type of estate probably had its origin in the premise of the old common law (q.v.) notion that a man and his wife were one person (and that one was the man).

2. *Joint tenancy.* Joint tenancy is much like tenancy by the entirety but is not limited to husbands and wives or to two owners, and it can be terminated by the individual acts (partition or sale) of any party. Each owner has exactly the same interest arising out of the same instrument, and the most important feature is the right of survivorship.

3. *Tenancy in common.* This is merely concurrent ownership by separate titles of undivided portions of the same real estate. There is no right of survivorship and each portion being held in fee simple (q.v.) by its owner is completely alienable. Any party may make moves to

terminate the cotenancy. The share of the property owned by each tenant need not be equal.

COURT OF PROBATE: Any court having jurisdiction over the probate (q.v.) of wills, the grant of administration, and the supervision of the administration (q.v.) and settlement of estates (q.v.) of decedents (q.v.). In some states these courts have other names such as Court of the Ordinary, Surrogate Court, Orphans' Court, Circuit Court, Superior Court, District Court, County Court, etc.

CURTESY: The life estate to which a man is entitled under the common law (q.v.), upon the death of his wife, in all lands she possessed in fee simple (q.v.), provided they had children born alive. Curtesy has been greatly modified in most American jurisdictions where it is still recognized, and is more like dower (q.v.).

CURTILAGE: The enclosed space of ground and buildings immediately surrounding a dwelling house (q.v.) or that land habitually used for family and domestic purposes.

DECEDENT: A deceased person, especially one who has recently died, testate or intestate.

DEGREE OF RELATIONSHIP: It has been erroneously assumed by some that *relationship* and *degree of relationship* mean the same thing. They are sometimes used interchangeably but *degree of relationship* is actually a legal term and does not state a specific relationship (i.e., cousin, brother, second cousin once removed, etc.) of one person to another. Degree simply means step and represents the distance between two persons who are related by blood. Under canon law (used in most states) two persons who descend from a common ancestor, but not one from the other (brothers, cousins, etc.), have collateral consanguinity (q.v.) and a degree of relationship of the same number as the number of generations the furthest is removed from the closest common progenitor. For example, an uncle and nephew are related in the second degree because the nephew is two generations from the common ancestor (his grandfather and his uncle's father). Two brothers are related in the first degree and first cousins are related to each other in the second degree, and so on. In lineal relationships (direct line) each generation is a degree. This means that both a man's parents and his children are related to him in the first degree. (Figure 1 shows degrees of relationship under both civil law and canon law. Those for the *civil law are in italics.)* Utah law prohibits marriage of persons within the fifth degree of consanguinity (civil law). Using the chart, can you identify what marriages are prohibited?

DEVISE: A gift of real property (q.v.) by will. See BEQUEATH.

DEVISEE: The person to whom real property is devised by will.

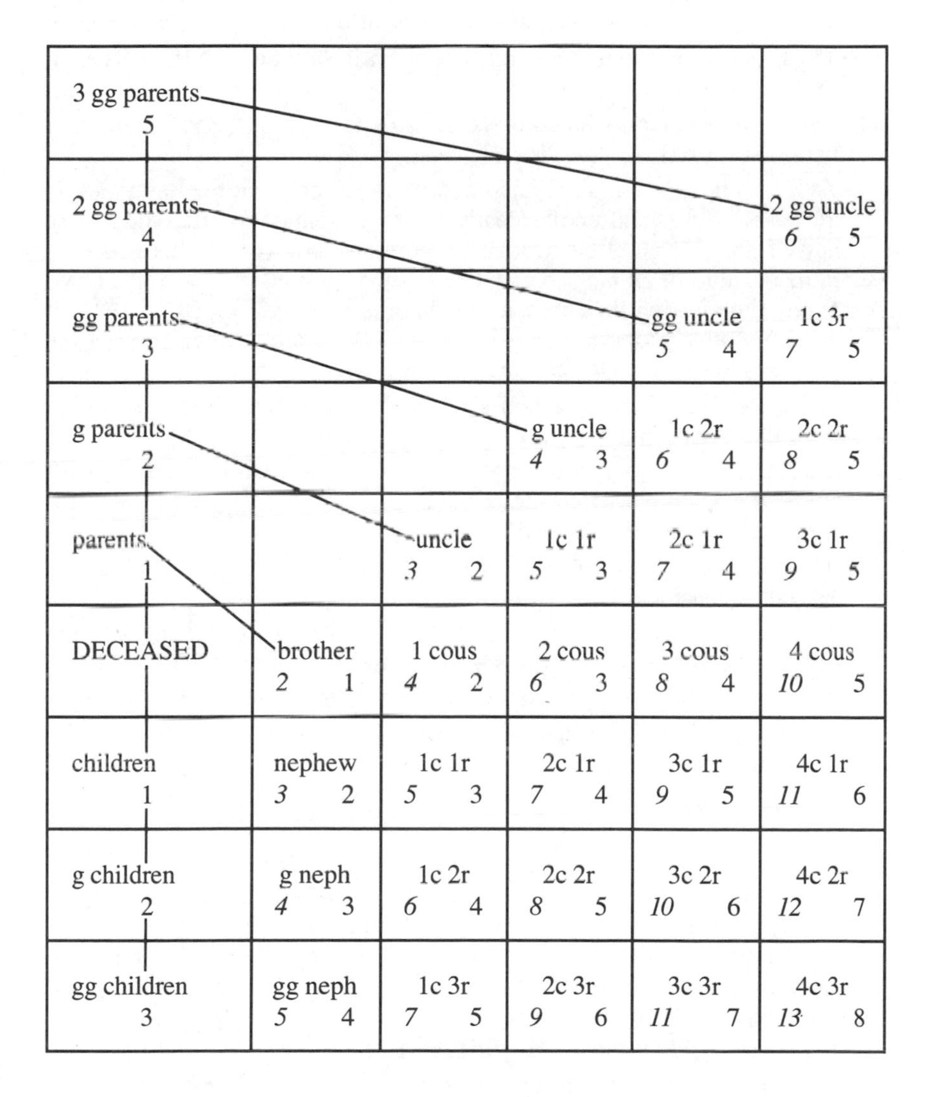

3 gg parents 5					
2 gg parents 4					2 gg uncle *6* 5
gg parents 3				gg uncle *5* 4	1c 3r *7* 5
g parents 2			g uncle *4* 3	1c 2r *6* 4	2c 2r *8* 5
parents 1		uncle *3* 2	1c 1r *5* 3	2c 1r *7* 4	3c 1r *9* 5
DECEASED	brother *2* 1	1 cous *4* 2	2 cous *6* 3	3 cous *8* 4	4 cous *10* 5
children 1	nephew *3* 2	1c 1r *5* 3	2c 1r *7* 4	3c 1r *9* 5	4c 1r *11* 6
g children 2	g neph *4* 3	1c 2r *6* 4	2c 2r *8* 5	3c 2r *10* 6	4c 2r *12* 7
gg children 3	gg neph *5* 4	1c 3r *7* 5	2c 3r *9* 6	3c 3r *11* 7	4c 3r *13* 8

FIGURE 1—RELATIONSHIPS AND DEGREES OF RELATIONSHIP ACCORDING TO *CIVIL LAW* AND CANON LAW

DEVISOR: A testator (q.v.) who disposes of real property by his will. Broadly interpreted to mean anyone who makes a will.

DOMICILE: The place of one's permanent home, and to which, if he is absent, he intends to return. The place of one's domicile at the time of his death is the place where his estate (q.v.) will be administered, though there may be ancillary administrations (q.v.) in other places.

DONEE: A person to whom lands are given in tail. See TAIL, ESTATE IN.

DONOR: The person who conveys lands or tenements (q.v.) to another in tail. See TAIL, ESTATE IN.

DOWER: The lands and tenements (q.v.) to which a widow has claim, in life estate (q.v.), after the death of her husband, for the support of herself and her children. Under the common law (q.v.) this was one-third in value of all lands which her husband owned in fee simple (q.v.) at any time during their marriage. There is no dower or curtesy (q.v.) in community property states, and statutes in most other states have provided other ways to look after the widow.

DWELLING HOUSE: The house where a person lives with his family, including the curtilage (q.v.).

EASEMENT: A non-possessory right which a real property (q.v.) owner has (without profit) to the use of adjacent land, such as a water course or a way over the land.

EFFECTS: Personal property (q.v.) of any kind. Sometimes context will make this include real property (q.v.) also.

ENDOWMENT: Assigning (see ASSIGNMENT) or setting off the widow's dower (q.v.) by the administrator (q.v.) or executor (q.v.).

ENFEOFF: To bestow a fee simple (q.v.) title in real property (q.v.).

ENTAIL: To limit succession of title in real property (q.v.) by creating an estate in tail. See TAIL, ESTATE IN.

ESCHEAT: The reversion of property to the state when there are no qualified heirs (q.v.) to claim it.

ESTATE: The sum total or aggregate of a person's property. An estate is not a legal entity so it cannot sue or be sued though the term may be found in court records for the sake of convenience. A person might also be referred to as having an estate in certain lands; this refers to the nature and duration of this title (e.g., fee simple [q.v.] estate, life estate [q.v.] etc.).

ESTATE IN TAIL: See TAIL, ESTATE IN.

ET UXOR: And his wife; a Latin term used in indexing and abstracting, often written simply as *et ux.*

EXECUTION: This usually means making or completing (the testator [q.v.] executes the will); however, it can also mean performing or carrying out (in which case the executor [q.v.] would execute the will —but the term usually preferred is *administer* [see ADMINISTRATION]). Legally a document is executed when it is sealed and delivered (q.v.).

EXECUTOR: A person named by the testator (q.v.) in his will to see that the provisions of that will are carried out after his (the testator's) death. The term *custodian and administrator* may be used. If there is more than one person so named they are called *coexecutors* or *joint executors*. In modern practice a preferred term is *personal representative*.

EXECUTRESS: See EXECUTRIX.

EXECUTRIX: A woman named in a will to administer it; also *executress*.

FAST ESTATE: See REALTY.

FEE: See FEE SIMPLE.

FEE SIMPLE: In American law, this is an estate in land which has the potential of lasting forever. The owner is entitled to the property to do with it as he wishes. He can convey it, devise (q.v.) it, or let it descend to his heirs after he dies. It is total ownership though it can be subject to easements and restrictions. It is often designated by only the word *fee* or by *fee simple absolute*. (There are also defeasable fees but these are less common. Such estates are terminated by the happening of a specified precedent condition. The failure of the specified condition of defeasance leaves the fee absolute.)

FEE TAIL: See TAIL, ESTATE IN.

FEUDAL SYSTEM: Under a feudal system the sovereign owns all the land. He subsequently grants his rights in the land to other persons whom we might call tenants-in-chief. These men in turn grant the right to the land to others, and this chain of subordination (subinfeudation) might go on and on. Feudalism means that the land is not owned by the person who appears to be its owner but is held by him from someone else. Those who hold the land have tenure (q.v.) in it and the types and forms of tenure vary, but most involve some type of service to the lord. Military service was important in early centuries. It often included payments of money which we have called quit rents (q.v.)

The colonial grants in America were indeed feudal grants, and land tenure existed in America in a watered-down form throughout the colonial period, but it was done away with by the various states once independence was gained. (Its existence makes little difference to land records, however, because subinfeudation was not allowed once the property was in private hands.)

FIDUCIARY: A person who has taken upon himself a position of trust or confidence in another's behalf. An attorney (q.v.), an executor (q.v.), a guardian (q.v.), and a trustee (q.v.) are examples.

FIEF: Something over which one has rights or executes (see EXECUTION) control. The term *fief* is seen only occasionally in early American (especially colonial) records and never in more recent records. Originally the term related to land (called the feud) held under feudal law on condition of rendering service to the proprietor.

FIXTURE: A chattel (q.v.) attached to the land and usually becoming part of the realty (q.v.). A house is an appurtenance (q.v.), but the cupboards built into that house are fixtures.

FOLIO: A leaf. In old records it was customary to number leaves rather than pages; hence a folio would be both sides of a leaf, or two pages. Occasionally you will find several pages numbered together as one folio.

FREEHOLD ESTATE: An estate in land held for uncertain duration and for free tenure (q.v.). There are four types: (1) fee simple absolute (see FEE SIMPLE), (2) defeasable fee (see FEE SIMPLE), (3) fee tail (see TAIL, ESTATE IN), and (4) life estate (q.v.).

GOODS: A term used to describe personal property (q.v.) but with varying definitions from place to place. Normally it would not include a leasehold (q.v.) title to real property (q.v.) or living animals.

GOODS AND CHATTELS: The most comprehensive description of personal property (q.v.).

GUARDIAN: A person who is invested with the right and the responsibility to manage the rights and property of another person, as of a minor child or a person incapable of managing his own affairs for some reason (an idiot, lunatic, spendthrift, habitual drunkard, etc.). A *testamentary guardian* is named in a deed or will of the child's parent. Otherwise the guardian is chosen by the *election* of the child (if over fourteen) or by *appointment* of the court (if the child is under fourteen). See CHILD OF TENDER YEARS or OF TENDER AGE.

GUARDIAN *AD LITEM:* (for the suit)—A guardian appointed by the court to represent a minor or incompetent person in a particular law suit only. This usually has little genealogical significance.

HEIR: A person who inherits or succeeds to the possession of property, through legal means, after the death of another, usually his ancestor. The term generally refers to cases of intestacy but is frequently used in a popular sense to designate any successor to a decedent's (q.v.) property either by will or by law.

HEIRS AND ASSIGNS: Under common law (q.v.) these "magic" words were essential to any conveyance (q.v.) which granted a fee simple (q.v.) title. Though they are no longer necessary for that purpose in a deed or will they are still often used.

HEIRS OF THE BODY: The term generally includes all lineal descendants of a decedent (q.v.) and excludes any surviving spouse, adopted children, and collateral relatives. The use of the term has nothing to do with whether a child is legitimate or born out of wedlock. The term "bodily heirs" is an equivalent.

HEREDITAMENT: Anything capable of being inherited—real (q.v.), personal (q.v.), corporeal (q.v.), or incorporeal. See LANDS, TENEMENTS, AND HEREDITAMENTS.

INCORPOREAL PROPERTY: See CORPOREAL PROPERTY.

INDENTURE: An agreement in which two or more parties are bound by reciprocal obligations toward each other and signed by both. Most deeds are not of this nature (though they may use that language) but are *deeds poll,* signed by only one of the parties, the grantor.

INFANT: Any person not of full legal age; a minor. Don't be confused by this term into thinking of only babes in arms. The person so designated may be six feet tall and weigh 200 pounds.

INSTRUMENT: Any formal legal document.

INTERMARRIAGE: A term used to indicate that the marriage contract was a reciprocal and mutual engagement by which each of the parties was "married" to the other. It has nothing to do with the parties being related to each other.

INTESTATE: The opposite to testate (q.v.). A person who dies without making a valid will. In an intestacy, statutes provide for the distribution and disposition of the estate to the lawful heirs. A person who makes a will also dies intestate if for some reason that will is not valid. A person with a valid will can also die intestate as to part of his property.

ISSUE: All lineal descendants of a common ancestor are his issue—not his children only.

ITEM: Also; likewise. The word was formerly used to mark the beginning of a new paragraph or division as in a will.

JOINT TENANCY: See COTENANCY.

LANDS, TENEMENTS, AND HEREDITAMENTS: The most comprehensive description of realty (q.v.).

LATE: Defunct; existing recently but now dead.

LEASEHOLD: An estate (q.v.) in realty (q.v.) held under a lease. It is usually considered a chattel (q.v.).

LEGACY: *Legacy* and *bequest* (q.v.) are equivalent terms. A legacy amounts to a gift of personal property (q.v.) by will.

LEGATEE: A person to whom a legacy is bequeathed. However, the term is often used to describe anyone receiving property by will, whether real (q.v.) or personal (q.v.).

LEGATOR: A person who makes a will and leaves legacies (q.v.).

LIFE ESTATE: An estate (q.v.) that lasts only during the life of the person holding it, or for the duration of someone else's life. (This latter type is called a life estate *per autre vie.*) Often in a will a life estate is devised to the widow. A dower (q.v.) estate and a curtesy (q.v.) estate are also life estates.

LITIGATION: A judicial contest or law suit.

MESSUAGE: A dwelling house (q.v.).

METES AND BOUNDS: Metes and bounds refer specifically to the boundary lines and limits of a piece of land. They are defined by reference to natural or artificial monuments such as trees, roads, ditches, rivers, etc. This method of describing land boundaries was used exclusively before the passage of the Land Act of 1785 and the introduction of the Rectangular Survey system (q.v.). In states not affected by that law this method of describing land continues in use. It is also used in connection with the Rectangular Survey system to describe a tract of land once a starting point is located within the system, but compass directions are used in the descriptions more often than geographical features.

MINOR: See INFANT.

MOIETY: Half (of anything).

MONEY: Money during the colonial period of America was mainly English or based on the English system of pounds (£), shillings (s), and pence (d). There are 20 shillings in a pound and 12 pennies in a shilling. Sometimes dollars are mentioned, but any similarity of these to our present dollar is purely coincidental. For a period in Virginia tobacco was used as legal currency because of the scarcity of precious metals, and the Dutch in New Netherland used beaver pelts (called simply "beavers") and wampum as media of exchange. See also PROCLAMATION MONEY.

MOVABLE ESTATE: Personal estate (q.v.) or personalty (q.v.).

MOVABLES: Not quite equivalent to movable estate (q.v.). These are personal property items which are attendant upon the owner and can be carried about from place to place. They include inanimate objects, vegetable products, and animals which are in the possession, power, and use of the owner.

NATURAL AFFECTION: Affection which exists naturally between near relatives and usually regarded as good and legal consideration (q.v.) in a conveyance (q.v.).

NATURAL HEIRS: Heirs (q.v.) by blood as distinguished from heirs by adoption.

NEXT-OF-KIN: A term used in the law of descent and distribution to identify the closest blood relatives of the deceased, and often used exclusively to identify those who shared in the estate (q.v.) under the relevant statutes.

ORDINARY: In some states (Georgia and formerly South Carolina and Texas) this judicial officer has power invested by statute in regard to wills and other probate (q.v.) matters.

ORPHAN: A minor or infant (q.v.) who has lost both (or one) of his parents.

PARTITION: The dividing of real property (q.v.) among all cotenants (see COTENANCY) according to their respective rights.

PER STIRPES: By roots or stocks; a Latin term used in the law of descent and distribution of estates (q.v.). It indicates a method of dividing an intestate estate so that a group of children take only the share to which their deceased ancestor would have been entitled had he been living—acting as a group and not as individuals. Today the term "by representation" is in more common usage. As you can see, a *per stirpes* distribution is quite different from a *per capita* distribution where each takes an equal share.

PERSONAL PROPERTY: See PERSONALTY.

PERSONALTY: Any personal or movable property; goods and chattels (q.v.).

PLEADINGS: The written statements of the parties to a legal suit or action in which each presents, alternately, either his allegations or claims for relief or his defense against the claims of the other. The most common pleadings are the declaration, complaint, bill, or information of the plaintiff and the answer of the defendant.

PRESENTS: This means literally "this document or instrument." In legal writing the term "by these presents" is used to designate the instrument in which the phrase itself occurs.

PROBATE: This term originally meant *prove,* especially proving that a will produced before the proper court as the "last will and testament" of a certain deceased person was, in reality, what it purported to be. In American law, however, you will find the term used as an inclusive term to describe all matters over which a court of probate (q.v.) has jurisdiction.

PROBATE COURT: See COURT OF PROBATE.

PROCLAMATION MONEY: Where reference is made in early deeds or other conveyances (q.v.) to consideration being in "proclamation money" (or "proc. money"), that refers to uniform coin values which were established in the American colonies by royal proclamation in 1704. Foreign coins were rated on the basis of their bullion content. The proclamation was not enforced and was effectively ignored.

PROGENY: Descendants of a common ancestor; issue (q.v.).

PROTHONOTARY: The chief or principal clerk who officiates in some courts.

PROVE: See PROBATE.

QUIT RENT: A rent paid by the tenant of a freehold estate (q.v.) which discharges him from any other obligation or rents, usually just a token payment. Under the feudal system (q.v.) this was a payment to one's feudal superior in lieu of services.

REAL PROPERTY: See REALTY.

REALTY: Relating to land, as distinguished from personalty (q.v.). The term applies to lands, tenements, and hereditaments (q.v.). It encompasses both appurtenances (q.v.) and fixtures (q.v.). Sometimes called *fast estate.*

RECTANGULAR SURVEY SYSTEM: A system of land survey adopted with the Northwest Ordinance of 1785 which provided that public lands be surveyed and described in terms of subdivision, section, township, and range before settlement. See METES AND BOUNDS.

REGISTER OF WILLS: In some states this is an officer in the county who records and preserves all wills admitted to probate (q.v.), issues letters of administration or letters testamentary, receives and files all accounts of executors (q.v.) and administrators (q.v.), and acts generally as clerk of the court of probate (q.v.). (See chapter 15 for a discussion of the various records.)

RELATIONSHIP: See DEGREE OF RELATIONSHIP.

RELICT: The surviving spouse when one has died, husband or wife. The term relates to the relict of the united pair and not the relict of the deceased person.

RIGHT OF WAY: Basically it is the right of one, either by law or by contract, for passage over the real property (q.v.) of another.

SEALED AND DELIVERED: These words, followed by the signatures of witnesses, are the usual formula for attesting a conveyance. They indicate that the document is authenticated by the affixing of a seal and that the transaction is complete. Sometimes written: *signed, sealed, and delivered.* (Most states today have abolished use of seals.)

SEISED: Used to express the seisin (q.v.) or owner's actual possession of a freehold (q.v.) or of fee simple (q.v.) title to property. (Often spelled *seized.*)

SEISIN: The possession of a freehold (q.v.) or of a fee simple (q.v.) estate in land by having a proper legal title thereto. (Often spelled *seizin.*)

SEPARATE EXAMINATIONS: The questioning of a married woman by a court official to acknowledge a deed or other instrument. This questioning is conducted out of the husband's hearing to determine if the wife has acted of her own free will and not under the husband's compulsion in making the instrument.

SIDINGS: See ABUTTALS.

SIGNED, SEALED, AND DELIVERED: See SEALED AND DELIVERED.

STIRPES: The person from whom a family is descended. See *PER STIRPES.*

SURETY: A person who gives security to make himself liable for another person's debts or obligations should the first default.

SURROGATE: In some states a judicial officer who has jurisdiction over probate matters, guardianships, etc. (New York and New Jersey).

TAIL, ESTATE IN: An estate (q.v.) which does not descend to heirs (q.v.) generally but rather to the heirs of the donee's (q.v.) body (his lawful issue [q.v.]) in a direct line as long as the posterity continues in regular order. Upon the death of the first owner without issue the estate is terminated. (For further explanation see chapter 17.)

TENANCY BY THE ENTIRETY: See COTENANCY.

TENANCY IN COMMON: See COTENANCY.

TENANT: A person who possesses lands or tenements (q.v.) by any right or title, either in fee simple (q.v.), freehold (q.v.), for life, for years, at will, or otherwise. Usually the use of the term is more restrictive in connotation and includes only those who hold the lands and tenements of other persons (called landlords), the term of tenancy usually being fixed by lease.

TENEMENTS: The word refers literally to anything held by a tenant (q.v.) in tenure (q.v.), but the term is often applied only to houses and other buildings. See LANDS, TENEMENTS, AND HEREDITAMENTS.

TENURE: Occupancy or tenancy.

TESTABLE: Capable of making a will.

TESTAMENTARY: Pertaining to a will.

TESTAMENTARY GUARDIAN: See GUARDIAN.

TESTATE: A person who dies leaving a valid will; the opposite of intestate (q.v.). To die leaving a valid will is to die testate.

TESTATOR: A person who leaves a will in force at his death.

TESTATRIX: A woman who dies leaving a valid will.

THESE PRESENTS: See PRESENTS.

TO WIT: Namely; *videlicet* (*viz.*).

TRACT: A lot, piece, or parcel of land of any size.

TRUST: The legal right or title to property held by one person for the benefit of another who has an equitable title thereto.

TRUSTEE: The person who holds and administers a trust (q.v.) estate. He holds legal title to property for the benefit of someone else.

UXOR: A wife. See *ET UXOR*.

VALID: Legally binding.

VIDELICET: Abbreviated *viz.*; namely, to wit.

VOID: Having no legally binding effect; invalid.

WILL CONTEST: Any kind of litigated controversy (see LITIGATION) concerning the eligibility of a document for probate (q.v.). It is not related to the validity of the will's contents (see chapter 14).

YOUNGER CHILDREN: A term used in English conveyances and somewhat applicable in colonial America with reference to settlements of land. It signifies all children not entitled to the rights of the eldest son, who held the right to succeed to the estate (q.v.) of his ancestor under laws of primogeniture. In its strict sense it included daughters who may be older than that son.

V. THE PROBATE PROCESS

Under the assumption that the more you know about the legal processes which bring a probate record into existence (within limits of course) the more value they will have for you, let me explain a few details about probate law.

A. The Philosophy of Probate

The general rule is that all rights and property which a person owns or is entitled to when he dies may be disposed of by a will, subject to the payment of debts and other legitimate obligations. A competent testator, subject to certain restrictions, can dispose of his property in any way he desires.[1] He can leave it to his widow, to his children, to other relatives; or he can leave it to strangers. Any restrictions are prescribed by state statute since the power to make a will is statutory and not a natural (or absolute) right.

Historically, under common law, a married woman was considered incompetent to make a will of real estate (even with her husband's consent) unless they had previously entered into an antenuptial contract or agreement (see chapter 15) to preserve that right. A woman could, however, make a will (or testament) of personal property with her husband's consent. A widow or unmarried woman could do as she pleased.

---

[1] Under the old common law, when a man died, one-third of his estate went to his wife (dower), one-third to his issue and one-third he could dispose of as he wished.

In more recent years, with the adoption of Married Women's Property Statutes, women generally have had the same probate rights as men.

The above are basic rules; however, there are a few exceptions to them, including:

1. Under common law the widow's dower was usually preserved for her and took precedence over any devise of realty in her husband's will unless she elected to accept the provisions of the will in lieu of dower or unless she had already forfeited dower claims by antenuptial agreement. There are a few states where the widow gets both dower and devised property.

2. There are some states (Arizona, California, Idaho, Louisiana, Nevada, New Mexico, Texas, Washington) where property acquired by either husband or wife during their marriage is regarded as community property and is the equal property of both, as a marital community, so that neither can devise the interest of the other. (Community property law comes from Spanish property law and not from English common law. There are variations of the law from one state to another also.)

3. Posthumous children (those born after the death of their father) who are not provided for in the will usually take of the estate as though the parent died intestate. In some states, if the parent had no children at the time the will was drawn and children were later born to him, the will is deemed revoked unless it makes provisions for such children.

4. Living children who are not provided for in the will are *usually* allowed to take of the estate as heirs, unless it appears that their omission from the will was intentional.

5. Several states will invalidate a will when the testator leaves his property for charitable purposes at the exclusion of his wife and children unless the will is made at least a specified time (often more than one year) before the testator's death.

6. There are also states which do not allow a will made in favor of a mistress and illegitimate children at the exclusion of the testator's wife and legal children. In Louisiana the law reserves certain portions of the deceased's estate, called legitime, to the descendants. These descendants are called "forced heirs." If there is one child, three-fourths of the estate may be willed to others; if there are two or more children, one-half is disposable. The issue of deceased children take by representation.

B. Legal Requirements

It was mentioned earlier that a will could generally be made by any person of sound mind and legal age who was free from restraint. Let's look briefly at each of these requirements:

1. Of sound mind: There is really no immutable rule as to what "of sound mind" means, but in general it does not require perfect mental sanity. Often a person may not be completely sane on all subjects yet have the capacity to make a will. The following quotation, though old, provides a good definition.

> If the testator is able, without prompting, to summon before his mind, on the same occasion, and hold there for a reasonable time the nature of the business about which he is engaged, the persons who might naturally be the objects of his bounty and his relations to them, the kind and extent of the property to be disposed of, and the scope and effect of the disposition which he is about to make, he will be considered to have sufficient mental capacity to make a valid will. . . .
>
> It is not necessary that the testator know the number and the condition of his relatives, or that he should be able to give an intelligent reason for giving or witholding from any of them; nor that he should remember the names of absent relatives; nor that he should know the precise legal effect of the provisions which he makes in the will.[2]

The claim that a would-be testator was not of sound mind is one of the most common reasons for challenging the validity of a will.

2. Of legal age: Legal age is somewhat easier to define than mental soundness. The age when a person becomes legally competent to make a will varies considerably from state to state. In more than half of the states it is now legal to make a will by age eighteen (some earlier), but historically this has not been so. The most common "legal age" for making a will has been twenty-one, though a few states have allowed persons younger than this to make wills (actually testaments) of personal property.

3. Free from restraint: In order for a will to become void because of restraint or undue influence, such restraint must destroy the free agency of the testator.

> Mere solicitations, however importunate, do not of themselves constitute undue influence, neither does honest persuasion, appeals to affection or gratitude, or to the ties of kindred, or for pity for future destitution; neither do fair and flattery speeches when not accompanied by fraud. To be sufficient the influence must amount to coercion or fraud, and must have overcome the free agency, or free will, of the testator.[3]

---

[2] Charles E. Chadman (ed.), *Chadman's Cyclopedia of Law* (Chicago: American Correspondence School of Law, 1912), Vol. VII, pp. 34-35. (I have chosen an old source because genealogy generally deals with old records. In this matter, however, time has wrought few changes.)

[3] *Ibid.*, pp. 50-51.

The acts which constitute undue influence or restraint may vary with each case. Often undue influence constitutes fraud, as has been suggested. This is a little easier to define and deal with. A will becomes invalid if:

1. The testator was fraudulently induced to sign a will which he believed to be another.
2. The testator was deceived as to the content of the will he signed.
3. A legacy was given to a person who fraudulently assumed a character not his real one.
4. There have been any fraudulent impositions on the testator. (Only fraud by a beneficiary gives grounds for contest.)[4]

However, in cases where fraud is claimed, it must be proven.

There is judicial machinery provided for the settlement of probate matters (whether there is a will or not). And because of legal requirements, probate matters cannot be settled apart from that machinery. When the researcher knows more about the nature and function of that machinery then the records created by that process become a more valuable tool for locating and identifying ancestors. In most states probate law is of English origin, with some modification by statute, but a few states settled by the French and Spanish—notably in the South and West—have statutes somewhat colored by French and Spanish law. In Louisiana the probate law is of French-Roman origin and has only gradually yielded to influences from outside. Anytime you use probate records you will find it helpful to understand the basics of probate custom and law in the state where your problem is centered. Thorough research may depend on that understanding.

---

[4] *Ibid.*, pp. 46-47.

14

What About Wills?

A will is just a wish or a desire, but in legal terminology it is specifically that declaration of a person's wishes or desires concerning the final disposition of his property which, if properly executed, becomes mandatory after he is dead. The form of a will is not significant legally so long as it is properly executed and it does not become effective until after the death of its maker.

A will, when it operates upon personal property, is sometimes called a *testament,* and sometimes, when it operates on real property, is called a *devise,* but historically the more popular appellative of an instrument embracing both real and personal property is *last will and testament.* For the sake of this discussion all such documents shall simply be referred to as *wills.*

You will encounter many different kinds of things in wills. Some wills are even humorous (though they may not have seemed so to the frustrated families of those who made them). One that seems to be a favorite of lawyers was made by a banker. It reads, in part:

> To my wife, I leave her lover, and the knowledge that I wasn't the fool she thought I was. To my son I leave the pleasure of earning a living. For twenty-five years, he thought that pleasure was mine. He was mistaken. To my daughter, I leave one hundred thousand dollars. She will need it. The only good piece of business her husband ever did was to marry her. To my valet, I leave the clothes he has been stealing from me. To my partner, I leave the suggestion that he take

some other clever man in with him at once if he expects to do any more business.[1]

Some wills are very long—others very short. The longest will on record was made in America by a Mrs. Frederica Cook in the early part of this century. It contained 95,940 words and comprised four bound volumes. The shortest known valid will merely says, "vse zene" (the Czech for "All to wife"). It was dated January 19, 1967, in Langen, Hesse, Germany. A will reading only "All for mother" was probated in England in 1906.[2]

I. KINDS OF WILLS

Though a will is a specific kind of document there are different kinds of wills, in addition to the regular everyday will, which you will see in your quest for forebears. Let's look at some of the more common ones quickly, in alphabetical order:

CONJOINT WILL: See JOINT WILL.

HOLOGRAPHIC WILL: A will written, dated, and signed in the testator's own handwriting. There are some differences in the statutes from one state to another, but such wills do not generally require witnesses. They are sometimes called *olographic* wills.

JOINT WILL: A will made by two or more persons together and signed by both. Such wills are usually executed to make testamentary disposition of joint property or of separately owned property to be treated as a common fund. Joint wills are sometimes called *conjoint wills*. They were especially popular with the Dutch in New Netherland because they protected their children from the orphan masters.

NUNCUPATIVE WILL: A will declared or dictated orally by the testator. Such wills can usually dispose only of personal property (in limited amount) and are valid only for persons in their last sickness, persons overtaken with sudden illness, or soldiers and sailors in actual combat. They are valid only if given before sufficient witnesses (numbers vary—usually two or three) and if they are reduced to writing within a limited time period (usually six to twelve days). No special form is required in a nuncupative will, but it must appear that the testator intended his words to amount to his will and that he desired

---

[1] Joe McCarthy, "To My Wife, I Leave Her Lover," *This Week Magazine* (September 26, 1965), p. 12. By permission.

[2] From *The Guinness Book of World Records,* by Norris and Ross McWhirter. © 1968 by Sterling Publishing Co., Inc., New York 10016. By permission.

the persons present to bear witness that what he said was said with the intent that it be his will. They are not allowed in some states.

The nuncupative will of Joseph Killgore was recorded in court as follows:

Memorandum. That on the Thirtieth Day of April last past, we the Declarants being at the House of Joseph Killgore late of York dec^{d}. when the Said Joseph was Sick on his Bed, when he had with him M^{r}. John Frost writing his Will, and to our best discerning the Said Joseph was of Sound and disposing Mind and gave express Directions to the Said Frost with respect to the Disposition of his real Estate, but as to his personal, he then Said that it was his Will that (it being so Small) It was not worth while to put it into his Will, But that John Should have his moveable Estate except a Coat and Jacket to a grandson and Son of his Daughter, and the Said Joseph then and there declared that the above was his Will relating to his personal Estate, and desired the Declarants to bear Witness to it accordingly, or Words to that Effect.

In Witness whereof we have hereunto Set our Hands this fifteenth Day of May Anno Domini 1764.

John Frost
Gilbert Warren
her
Jane X Hasty
mark

York ss. York May 15, 1764.

Messrs. John Frost Gilbert Warren and M^{rs}. Jane Hasty the above Declarants personnally appearinge Severally made Oath the Truth of the above to which they have Subscribed,

Before. Danl. Moulton, Jus. Peac

York ss. At a Court of Probate held at New York May 15, 1764

The above Instrument being presented to me under Oath as the nuncupative Will of Joseph Killgore above named dec^{d}. I do hereby approve and allow the Same, and do commit the administration of the personal Estate of the Said Dec^{d}. above mentioned to his Son John Killgore to be administered according to the Direction of the Said Will.

Jer. Moulton. Judge

OLOGRAPHIC WILL: See HOLOGRAPHIC WILL.

UNOFFICIOUS WILL: A will made in disregard to natural obligations of inheritance.

UNSOLEMN WILL: A will in which no executor is named. It will require that an administrator *cum testamento annexo* be appointed by the court.

While we are talking about wills let's also talk about codicils. A CODICIL is not a special kind of will, yet it deserves mention here because it is a supplement or an addition to a will that may explain or modify, add to or subtract from, qualify or alter, restrain or revoke the provisions of the will itself. It is a document which actually becomes a part of the will, as it is made with the same solemnity, and it supersedes the will wherever it differs therefrom. There is no limit to the number of codicils that can be added to a will so long as they are properly executed. The late P. T. Barnum died leaving a fifty-three-page will with eight codicils.[3]

Zachariah Gilson added the following codicil to his will. It is quite typical:

> I Zachariah Gilson of Westminster in the County of Windham & State of Vermont do this 19th day of June in the year of our Lord Christ [*sic*] make and publish this codicil to my last Will and Testament in manner following that is to say, I give to my beloved Annah Gilson, the whole of her wearing apparel of every description for her to dispose of at her own election. I also give unto my daughter Uceba Bewster the sum of ten dollars to be paid in one year after my decease and furthermore I give unto my youngest daughter Lois Gilson – the sum of twenty four dollars to be paid within two years after my decease. And it is my desire that this my present Codicil be annexed to and made a part of my last Will and Testament to all intents and purposes. In Witness where of I have hereunto set my hand and seal the day and year above written.
>
> Signed, sealed published and declared by the above named Zachariah Gilson as a codicil to be annexed to his last Will and Testament in presence of
>
> John Sessions
Hannah Foster
Sally White   (signed) Zachariah Gilson

II. PROVING THE WILL

Let's move along now and take a simplified look at the steps taken by a typical will as it goes through the processes of administration—from the time it is made until the estate is completely settled.

---

[3] McCarthy, p. 12.

1. The first step is the making and proper execution of the will. When a person decides that he wants his estate divided in a different manner from that provided for by statutes of descent and distribution in his state of residence then he must make a will. Stepchildren for whom the testator may wish to provide ordinarily have no rights as heirs in an intestacy. Or, some children may have already received their portions. Or, the testator may not wish to leave equal inheritances to all of his children but rather to show favoritism to one or more for some reason. Or, a specific piece of real estate or specific items of personalty may be earmarked for a certain child. There are innumerable situations which might bring a will into existence

When the will is made all formalities which the law requires must be followed. Generally this means that the will must be in writing, it must be signed, it must be acknowledged before competent and qualified witnesses who must so attest with their signatures, and in a few states it must be sealed. (The seal, which was such a commonplace thing in earlier years, has now been largely abolished.)

A typical, modest, and relatively short will was made by Skinner Stone in 1764:

> In the Name of God Amen.
>
> I Skinner Stone of Berwick in the County of York & Province of the Massachusetts Bay in New England yeoman, being of sound mind and Memory tho weak in Body, expecting shortly to put off this Body, do commit the Same to the Earth to be buried with decent Burial at the Discretion of my Execut^{x} hoping for a glorious Resurrection to Immortality, and my Soul into the Hands of God who gave it. Begging ye Pardon of all my Sins and the Salvation of my Soul thro the Merits and Mediation of the Lord Jesus Christ and with Respect to what worldly Estate God hath been pleas'd to bless me with I dispose of it in manner and Form following Viz^{t}
>
> Imp^{r} I give and bequeath unto my beloved Wife Judith Item. the whole of my Estate real and personal for her Use & Improvem^{t} and for her to dispose of by Sale if She see Cause therefor, Provided she take Care for and be at the Charge of the Education & Support of Such of my Children as are here named vizt William Gabriel Jude Abigail & Patience till they come of age, or Shall be otherwise So disposed of at the Discretion of my Said Wife as not to Stand in Need of any assistance from her, excepting what of my Estate is otherwise disposed of as hereafter mentioned.
>
> Item. I give to my beloved Son Jonathan Stone five Shillings lawful money to be paid by my Executrix.
>
> Item. Such part of my Estate as may remain undisposed of at the Decease of my Said Wife Jude, I give and bequeath to my five chil-

dren above named vizt William Gabriel Jude Abigail and Patience to be equally divided amongst them.

And I do hereby constitute and appoint my Said Wife Jude Stone the Sole Executrix of this my last Will & Testament And do hereby revoke and disannul all former Wills and Testaments whatsoever, and do confirm and declare this & this only to be my last Will and Testament.

In Witness whereof I have hereunto Set my Hand & Seal this 20th Day of March in the Year of our Lord One thousand Sevene Hundred and Sixty four.

Signed Sealed & delivered by ye Said Skinner Stone to be his last Will & Testam^{t} in presence of John Morse, Paul Stone	his Skinner X Stone mark

After a will is properly made, a codicil may be added at any time before the testator's death if correctly executed, or a new will can be drawn if this is desired. Any new will automatically voids its predecessor; so, quite strictly speaking, the *last* will and testament (properly executed) is the only one of legal effect. No special language is required in a will to void an earlier will.

2. The second step is the death of the testator. If there is any action which can be taken prior to his death then the instrument is not actually a will, regardless of how it is worded or what its maker may have called it. The only exceptions to this would be: (a) A document which was a combination will-something else or (b) a conditional will, the effectiveness of which depends upon the occurrence of some uncertain event or condition.

It is understood that the rights of devisees and beneficiaries under a valid will become vested property rights immediately upon the death of the testator but not one minute before.

3. However, before those vested rights become possessory, certain other steps are essential. The next step is that the will must be presented for probate before the proper judicial authority to show that it is what it claims to be—i.e., the *last* will and testament of the decedent. The executor or some other interested person must present the will upon his own oath before the proper court. (In each state there are special courts for the probating of wills, but these courts are not all called by the same name in every state. More is said about these courts, their names, and their jurisdictions later in this chapter.)

The will is ordinarily brought before the court of proper jurisdiction to be probated by the filing of a written application or petition for probate. In more recent years these applications have proven to be invaluable genealogical documents as they must include names of all next-of-kin of the testator, relationship or degree of relationship to him (with ages of minors), and post office addresses.

4. The next step is for the court to admit the will to probate. Usually a time for a hearing is set and notice of this fact is published (sometimes directly to all interested parties and sometimes in a newspaper, or both, depending on state statute.) If no one comes forward to contest the will at the hearing then it is considered that there is no contest and it is ordinarily admitted to probate on the testimony of one of the witnesses whose signature attested its validity. Even in the case of contest the testimony of only one witness is sufficient if he can show due execution.

Should all subscribing witnesses be dead or incompetent or beyond reach of the court, the will can still be proven by other witnesses with only slightly more difficulty. (In more recent years, probate laws have provided the means for wills to be "self-proving." In such case the witness's appearance at this point is unnecessary.)

Having passed all of the necessary requirements, the will is admitted to probate and letters testamentary (legal authorization to proceed with the administration) are granted to the executor by the court.

5. Upon admission to probate and upon payment of a small fee the will is recorded or registered by the court. In the modern probate court this usually takes place by a photographic process, but historically wills have been recorded by a clerk copying them verbatim in longhand into a "Register" kept by the court. It has not always been a legal requirement in most states that a will be thus recorded, but the advantages have generally been great enough so that most wills were recorded. In most states, before photographic registration, a copy of every will submitted for probate (an original) was also filed with the court in a special file (or dossier or probate packet) together with all other papers relating to the probate case in question. This is in addition to the recorded copy. Even those wills that were not recorded and those not admitted to probate can usually be found in the probate packet or estate file.

In addition to the recording (or registering), the recorded will is usually indexed at the same time so that it can be found later, if necessary. In most states today all documents filed with the court during the probate process are registered and indexed. Most courts make a *direct index*—that is, an index to testators only—but occasionally you will also find a *reverse index* which has been kept. A reverse index is an index to the beneficiaries of the wills. This, when available, is a most useful research tool.

6. Next the executor, with court authorization, proceeds to pay the just obligations of the deceased and to have this approved by the court. There is usually a "notice to creditors" published, and creditors must file their claims against the estate. Unless the will specified to the contrary, the executor's proper performance must be guaranteed by sureties posting a fiduciary bond; and he must adhere to the will's directions implicitly. Once probate has been granted by the court the only variations allowed from the will's provisions are in the settlement of all just debts and obligations and in setting off the widow's dower (where applicable).

During the process of the administration of the estate an inventory must be taken and an appraisal made of the property. The appraisal is usually accomplished by the executor petitioning the court to appoint appraisers. There may also be a sale (by public auction) as part of the administration to provide cash to settle obligations to creditors. As creditors are paid they sign releases or receipts.

7. After the obligations of the estate have been discharged and the court has approved, the specific provisions of the will are carried out as stipulated by the will.

Many states also require that a *decree of distribution* (or similarly titled document) be completed by the executor, through the court's authority, to show how the distribution to beneficiaries has been completed. This document is issued and recorded by the court as the final document in the probate proceedings and is often (again depending upon state statute) recorded both in the probate court and (when land is involved) with local land records. In the probate court it signifies that the executor has completed his job; and in the recorder's office (land records), in those states which require it, it stands as proof to the world that title to real property has passed. These documents generally do not go back a long way historically, but they are valuable as far as they go. The beneficiaries may also sign receipts.

If the executor happened to die before his responsibility was discharged (and this may have been either before or after the death of the testator), or if he renounced his right, the court would appoint another in his place to carry out the provisions of the will as if he (the replacement) had been named executor himself. This person is called the administrator *(de bonis non) cum testamento annexo* (or with will annexed). Such an appointment is made by a special court order and is also registered in the court along with the petition requesting the appointment.

Other records which could have been created as the administration or probate process was carried out include petitions for dower or curtesy, petitions and accounts relating to the support of orphans and the appointment of guardians (discussed in the next chapter), powers of attorney, etc.

III. THE CONTESTED WILL

One genealogical benefit of probate records is the fact that the average man tries to get everything he thinks he has coming, and often a little bit more if he thinks he can. If the will doesn't give him what he feels is justly due him, or if he is omitted completely, he will probably look for grounds upon which the will can be contested—usually that the testator was not of sound mind, that the will was made under restraint or undue influence, that it was not properly executed, or that some essential statutory requirement was not met by the will's provisions. The following news story illustrates a typical case:

KANSAS COURT HEARS UTAHN'S 'WILL' CASE

Phillipsburg, Kan.—The case of a Salt Lake City man who is contesting his uncle's will was continuing Thursday before District Judge William B. Ryan.

George T. Hansen Jr., president of the Hyland Oil Corp. of Salt Lake City, is seeking to have the will of the late Dane G. Hansen, who left a fortune estimated at $9 million, declared invalid.

The Salt Lake City man was left $10,000 under terms of the will. The elder Hansen left $1 million for a family trust fund and the remainder of his estate to a foundation for charitable, educational and scientific purposes.

The younger Hansen alleges his uncle was not competent when the will was signed. Hansen died Jan. 6, 1965, and his will was admitted to probate Feb. 12, 1965. He was 82 when he died of cancer.

Hansen was a bachelor and accumulated his wealth as an oil producer and a highway and bridge contractor.

Two witnesses to the will signing testified Tuesday that Hansen was mentally competent when he signed the document Nov. 2, 1964. A third witness, Dr. A. E. Cooper of the Norton County Hospital staff, was expected to testify Wednesday.[4]

Not everyone has the legal right to contest a will: only those who have an interest in the estate, and only then if they would receive more through laws of intestate succession than through administration of the will.

When a will is contested a law suit ensues with the executor as the defendant. (He is, of course, the natural defender of the will.) Some states

[4] *The Deseret News* (March 25, 1966), p. 12C. By permission.

require that all interested parties must be parties in the suit, plaintiff or defendant, and this includes husbands of female heirs. Thus the names of all these persons will be in the complaint. (They are called indispensable parties.)

The proceedings and documents resulting from such a suit can be virtual gold mines of genealogical evidence. When Philip Ryon died in Clark County, Kentucky, in the 1850s, his will was contested by some of his children. Philip had been twice married, leaving families by both wives. However, when he died at a good old age his will left all of his worldly goods to his second wife and the children of that marriage. The descendants of the first wife contested the will, presented their evidence, and thus provided a skeletal record of the descendants of Philip Ryon. The contention was that Philip, in his old age, was not of sound mind and that he acted under undue influence from family members. (And, incidentally, the contestants won the case.)

Though few wills are ever contested, when that has happened to a will of your ancestor it is important for you to know of it. Learning of the contest poses no special difficulties, however, and the existence of the contest and the records arising therefrom are usually quite easy to ascertain. The procedure differs from one state to another. In some states the will will be registered as if there had been no contest, and a notation of the contest will be made. In the book of registered wills this notation might be made following the recording of the will itself where information about probate is usually given. Here you may find a direct reference to the location of the record of the contest. Other states do not record a contested will unless the contest *does not* succeed and the will is probated.

The foregoing approach is pretty typical of most old records which the genealogist will be searching, but there are other procedures, especially in more recent times. There may be a notation in an index or a special register kept by the court clerk. In almost every state the clerk of the court keeps a special book or register, usually called a probate docket, in which there is a separate page for each action. On that page each instrument pertaining to the matter that has been filed with the court is listed. Thus by looking at the page in the docket book for any particular probate action you can tell immediately if the will was contested and be guided to the proper documents. The clerk (or his deputy) maintains an index to this probate docket, so the whole procedure is very simple.

This is only one example of the way such records are sometimes maintained, but the use of this principle, with slight variations, is common. The whole process is controlled by state statute.

A will is *always* contested in the court of original probate jurisdiction, but the final judgment of that court is appealable through regular appellate channels. Such appeals are rare, but they do happen. Ordinarily, however, you won't get any more information from the appellate court record than you got from the trial court because no new facts can be added to a case on appeal. The record is sent up on appeal just as it developed in the trial court, and becomes a part of the records of that court as well as being a record of the probate court. There will also be an opinion written by the appellate court which might interest you, but it will give no more genealogical data than the record of the trial court.

Sometimes other records (such as land records) offer clues that there may have been a probate contest. Deeds often state that the grantor received the land he is selling as a result of such and such suit. Never pass up a clue like that. Even family tradition may tell you of conditions which would make a law suit probable; do not overlook them. A man who has married more than once and who died leaving families by all of his wives could easily create such a condition if there were any hard feelings between the various families or apparent inequities in his will. (More is said about courts and their records in chapter 19.)

IV. THE VALUE OF WILLS

Much has been said about the legal details involved in probating a will. Let's look now at the fruits of these legal details and what they mean—in specifics—to you as a genealogist.

A. Relationships

As mentioned earlier, perhaps the most significant quality of a will is the fact that it usually states some pretty specific relationships—direct statements of relationship by a person who ought to know. Nothing is more critical in genealogical research than information on how people are related to each other. Names, dates, and places mean little unless relationships are established. Other records do not always give this type of direct evidence.

B. Time Period

I have also mentioned this before, but again let me stress that you can often find wills and other probate records for persons in America in periods and places when there are few other records. And most of these are reasonably accessible for research.

C. Values That Are Not So Obvious

The above are the more obvious values of wills; now let's look at some which might be less apparent:

1. A will often gives clues to former places of residence. For example, the will of Samuel Wheelwright (Vol. I, p. 69, York County, Massachusetts) tells where he previously owned some land:

> Item I do give and bequeath unto Hester my beloved Wife . . . all the rent which was dew to me from my land at Crofts in the County of Lincoln in England until the time it was sold by Mr. Ed^{w} Loyde.

2. When a name is common, legacies mentioned in a will can sometimes be traced to prove actual connections. If you find three contemporaries named Samuel Black living in the same locality, wills can often help prove (or disprove) parentage. You may find a William Black giving 200 acres of a certain description to his son Samuel. Once this information is known you need to locate the conveyance whereby one of the three Samuels disposed of that identical 200 acres. If you can positively identify the seller you have your answer, one way or the other.

3. A will may also give you an idea about the existence of other records. A man may mention his religious affiliation in his will, which could lead you to church records—often the specific parish or congregation. His profession is usually indicated in his will, either directly or indirectly. If he owned land this is a clue to search land records. If he has extensive property, financial means, or social status (usually quite obvious in the will), published sources may be available that tell something about him. Sometimes previous military or naval service is also mentioned in a will.

4. Wills and other probate records also provide information on when the death occurred—sometimes the exact date. In some cases this is essential for identification.

5. Often the persons who are named as executors, who sign as subscribing witnesses, or who bind themselves as sureties are relatives; and a careful study of records relating to these persons may lead to more information on your ancestors. Note, however, that a person who receives by a will cannot legally sign as a witness to it.

V. RECORD PROBLEMS

The last chapter discussed some rather general weaknesses of probate records as a genealogical source; now let's look at some specific problems of wills and consider a few examples without too much rehashing of what has already been said.

Of course every will does not have problems, and all problems are not manifested in the same way from one will to the next. Some of the more common difficulties are as follows.

A. Incomplete Lists of Family Members

A man may omit the names of one or all of his children from his will and neglect to tell his wife's name since "everybody knows." If children are previously deceased, especially if they died as children rather than adults, there is no good reason why they should be mentioned in the will. If a child dies as an adult he may be named in his parent's will because he left a spouse and children to receive his portion. If a person died intestate the children of a deceased child would have been legal heirs to their parent's portion.

Children who have already received their inheritances are sometimes left unmentioned by the wills of their parents, and children who may have been disowned may also be unnamed, but these two circumstances did not always cause an omission of the child's name. Statutes differ, but most states have laws which deal with this problem in some way. Many states allow a child to be omitted only if the intent of the parent to do so is clearly expressed in the will, unless there is evidence that the child was provided for outside the will or that substantially all of the estate was left to the child's other parent. The purpose of all such statutes is to protect the child from being negligently overlooked, and statutes to protect the rights of children born after the will has been executed are especially common. Laws to protect the rights of children mistakenly believed to be dead are also common. Most statutes protecting these pretermitted children, as they are called, provide that the child is to take of the estate as if the parent had died intestate.

B. Inconclusive Relationships

This problem is better illustrated than described, so let's take as an example the will of Francis Champernoun (York County, Massachusetts, Vol. I, p. 55), probated December 25, 1687, which was also used as an example in chapter 2.

> I give and bequeath & confirm unto my Son in Law Humphrey Elliot & Elizabeth his now wife . . . the other part of my sd Island . . . Item I give and bequeath unto my Son in Law Robert Cutt my daughter in Law Bridget Leriven my daughter in Law Mary Cutt and

> my daughter in Law Sarah Cutt . . . all that part of three hundred acres of land belonging unto me lying between broken Neck and the land formerly belonging unto . . .

Is it clear how all of these persons are related? If it is then you see something here that I do not. We are thus left to speculation as it seems quite unlikely that they are all children-in-law of the testator, especially in view of the surnames of the females. Could some (or all) be stepchildren?

C. No Relationships

Again let's go to an example to illustrate the problem. This one is from the will of Jeremiah Willcox (Pasquotank County, North Carolina, Vol. 34, p. 44, probated in July Court 1754):

> I give and bequeath to my son Stephen Three hundred acres of land, . . .
>
> . . . [Some other land to be sold to a certain party] and if not I leave it to my Two Daughters Sarah and Ruth . . .
>
> I give to *Elizabeth Wakefield Living in Virginia* Two Cows and one calf Called Blossom & Pyde and all the Rest of my Cattle to be Equally Devided Between my wife and my Three Children . . .
>
> I Leave my Loving wife Elizabeth all the Remainder of my house hold goods. . . . [Emphasis added; see Figure 4, chapter 2.]

Who is this "Elizabeth Wakefield Living in Virginia" that Jeremiah makes a beneficiary of his estate? We certainly cannot tell from his will—he seems to have had only three children, Stephen, Sarah, and Ruth. Perhaps other evidence will help.

D. Wife and Children Not Related

If a man has married more than once, that fact is seldom mentioned in his will. This means that the wife named in his will may or may not be the mother of the children named, and you have no way of telling. Also, if you know she is the mother of only some of the children, it is hard to tell which ones. In a situation like this it is often impossible, just on the basis of evidence found in the will, to even determine if a problem exists.

E. Other Problems

There are other common difficulties which you will encounter as you use wills in your research. These will include spelling, nicknames, handwriting, and legal jargon; but most of these can be solved by the conscientious genealogist. There are no general solutions other than those already given. Each problem must be studied and solved (if possible) on its own merits. Evidence from other sources is essential.

VI. FINDING AND USING WILLS

A. Original and Registered Wills

Most wills in the United States are registered and filed in the counties where they were probated (at the testator's place of domicile), though a few states have non-county jurisdictions. The courts may be called by different names but their responsibilities are the same, as those duties relate to probate matters and the administration of estates.

The present names of the courts and the limits of their jurisdiction in the several states are as follows:

ALABAMA: County Probate Court.

ALASKA: Superior Court of the judicial district.

ARIZONA: Superior Court in the county.

ARKANSAS: County Probate Court.

CALIFORNIA: County Superior Court.

COLORADO: District Court in the county (except in Denver City and County which have a Probate Court). There are twenty-two judicial districts.

CONNECTICUT: Probate Court in the district. (The state is divided into more than 100 probate districts with most large towns, and many smaller ones, having their own probate districts.) When the original counties were formed in 1666 probate was a responsibility of the County Court. (All extant original county and early district probate files are at the State Library where a complete index from 1641 has been made. There is a microfilm copy of both the files and the index at the LDS Family History Library.)

DELAWARE: County Registers' Court. (Though this court has probate jurisdiction, all probate records, and card indexes to them, are in the Hall of Records, Dover.)

D.C.: Probate Division of the District of Columbia Superior Court. (There are some transcripts in the National Archives, 1801-88, but originals are obtainable by addressing the Register of Wills, Superior Court, 500 Indiana Ave., N.W., Washington, DC 20001.)

FLORIDA: Circuit Court in the county.

GEORGIA: Probate Court in the county.

HAWAII: Circuit Court of the Island.

IDAHO: District Court in the county. (On January 11, 1971, county Probate Courts were absorbed by the District Courts.) There are seven judicial districts.

ILLINOIS: Circuit Court in the county. (There are twenty-one judicial circuits.)

INDIANA: County Probate Court has exclusive jurisdiction in Marion, St. Joseph, and Vandenburgh counties. In Allen, Madison, and Hendricks counties the Superior Court has exclusive jurisdiction. In all other counties the Circuit Court in the county has jurisdiction. However, in Bartholomew, Elkhart, Grant, Lake, LaPorte, and Porter counties the Superior Court and the Circuit Court have concurrent jurisdiction.

IOWA: District Court in the county. (There are eight judicial districts.)

KANSAS: District Court in the county.

KENTUCKY: District Court in the county.

LOUISIANA: District Court in the parish (county equivalent), and in Orleans Parish the Civil District Court. (There are thirty-nine judicial districts outside of Orleans Parish.)

MAINE: County Probate Court.

MARYLAND: Orphans' Court in Baltimore City and every county except Harford and Montgomery. In these two the Circuit Court sits as an Orphans' Court. (All Maryland probates—in fact all official records—prior to 1788 are at the Hall of Records, Annapolis, as per state statute. Many other records since that time are also filed there for safe keeping at the discretion of county officials.)

MASSACHUSETTS: Probate Court in the county.

MICHIGAN: Probate Court in the county or district.

MINNESOTA: Probate Court in the county (which is a division of the County Court in all but Hennepin and Ramsey counties, where Probate Court is a division of the District Court).

MISSISSIPPI: Chancery Court in the county. (There are twenty Chancery Court districts.)

MISSOURI: Probate Division of Circuit Court in the county.

MONTANA: District Court in the county. (There are twenty judicial districts.)

NEBRASKA: County Court.

NEVADA: District Court in the county. (There are nine judicial districts.)

NEW HAMPSHIRE: County Probate Court. (All probate records before 1771 were kept in the provincial capital; those between 1735 and 1771 have been published. Transcripts of these early records are in the State Archives Room in the Library of the New Hampshire Historical Society, Concord.)

NEW JERSEY: Chancery Division of Superior Court and Surrogate Court have concurrent jurisdiction. All New Jersey wills proved before 1901 have been filed in the State Library, Bureau of Archives and History, Trenton, since 1964. (Thirteen volumes of will abstracts, 1670-1817, have been published and are completely indexed.) All original probate records since 1901 are filed with the Clerk of the Superior Court, Probate Section, State House Annex, Trenton.

NEW MEXICO: County Probate Court has jurisdiction of informal probate; District Court in the county has jurisdiction of formal probate and of supervised probate. (There are thirteen judicial districts.)

NEW YORK: County Surrogates' Court. (Historically the County Clerk had custody of probate records, except in counties with more than 40,000 population, which have had a Surrogates' Court since about 1846. Today every county has a Surrogates' Court.)

NORTH CAROLINA: County Superior Court. (All prior to 1760 were kept on a colony-wide basis, and some were recorded by the Secretary of the Province as late as 1780.)

NORTH DAKOTA: County Court.

OHIO: Probate Division of Court of Common Pleas in county.

OKLAHOMA: District Court in county.

OREGON: County Court in Gilliam, Grant, Harney, Malheur, Sherman, and Wheeler counties; Circuit Court in all other counties. In Benton, Clatsop, Coos, Curry, Deschutes, Hood River, Lincoln, Wasco, and Washington counties the judge of the District Court exercises the authority of judge of Circuit Court in probate matters.

PENNSYLVANIA: County Register of Wills.

RHODE ISLAND: City or Town Court of Probate, except Town Council in town of New Shoreham.

SOUTH CAROLINA: County Probate Court. (Until 1785 all were probated at Charleston.)

SOUTH DAKOTA: Circuit Court in the county. (There are eight circuits.)

TENNESSEE: Probate Court in Shelby and Davidson counties; Law and Equity Court in Dyer County; Chancery Court in all other counties.

TEXAS: Generally in County Court, but some larger counties have Probate Courts.

UTAH: District Court in the county. (There are eight judicial districts.)

VERMONT: District Probate Court. (The districts in the North are the same as the counties, but in the five southern counties of Bennington, Orange, Rutland, Windham, and Windsor there are two districts per county.) A copy of each will is also recorded in the town clerk's office in every town where real property devised in the will is situated.

VIRGINIA:	Circuit Court in the counties and the independent cities (see chapter 19). (The Corporation Courts in the independent cities have been abolished.)
WASHINGTON:	County Superior Court.
WEST VIRGINIA:	County Commission.
WISCONSIN:	Circuit Court of county.
WYOMING:	District Court in the county. (There are nine judicial districts.)[5]

Except where indicated otherwise (with very few exceptions), the courts listed above have custody of the probate records. The main exceptions are states like Delaware, New Jersey, North Carolina, South Carolina, etc., where older records are being transferred from the courthouses to state archives and libraries for safekeeping.

As mentioned earlier, in addition to the recording of probate records in the courts of probate, some states also require that certified copies of decrees of distribution, affidavits of heirship, probate decrees, and even wills be registered with the custodians of land records and recorded by them as proof of title when land is devised.

Some archives and genealogical libraries, such as the LDS Family History Library, are also interested in these records and are taking steps to see that they are preserved. The above-named library has energetic microfilming programs going on in counties of several states, and recorded probate records (with their indexes) are a "must" source to its microfilm operators. That library also cooperates with many of the states' archives and other agencies in their microfilming projects. It also buys copies of many records which have already been filmed. The library does not claim to have all, or even most, of the available probate records, but its holdings are significant and growing. They should be checked by those who have access to them.

B. Published Wills and Abstracted Wills

I indicated earlier that some probate records have been published and are available in book form in various places. The quality of these publications varies considerably and is hard to explain in a general statement. However, it is recommended that if the originals (or films thereof) are available, they should be used. In the absence of originals, registered copies are the next best choice.

[5] *Martindale-Hubbell Law Dictionary,* 120th ed. (Summit, NJ: Martindale-Hubbell, Inc., 1988), Vol. VIII (by permission) and correspondence with various court officials.

Some parties have also undertaken to make abstracts (abbreviated extracts with only "essential" data) of wills and to publish them. These should be used with extreme caution though some are quite accurate.

A few years ago while doing research on a problem in Woodford County, Kentucky, I had occasion to use some typescript will abstracts which proved quite interesting. With this particular problem I also had access to microfilms of the registered wills. In the abstract of the will of one George Blackburn, Sr., in 1817, were listed the following beneficiaries:

1. Wife Prudence
2. Son-in-law William White
3. Daughter Mildred White
4. Son Churchill J.
5. Son Jonathan
6. Daughter Harrett
7. Daughter Margaret Kinkade
8. Daughter Maria
9. Son Edward
10. M. B. George
11. Daughter Nancy Bartlett

The microfilm copy of the registered will lists the following beneficiaries. (Compare the two lists.)

1. Wife Prudence
2. Son-in-law William White
3. Daughter Mildred White
4. Son Jonathan
5. Son Churchwill J.
6. Son George Blackburn, Jr.
7. Daughter Margaret Kinkiad
8. Son Edward M.
9. Daughter Nancy Bartlett
10. Son William B.
11. Daughter Elizabeth Peart
12. Daughter Mary Holloway

Do you see any differences? Well, that is why it is best to use the originals or the registered copies (when originals are unavailable). We humans are too prone to err. It was especially interesting in this case to note that the two persons which the abstracter listed as "Daughter Harrett" and "Daughter Maria" were actually named as Negro slaves in the will and were being bequeathed to George's wife Prudence. You need abstracts like this one as much as Custer needed more Indians at the Little Bighorn.

C. To Find the Will—Indexes

If you want to secure a copy of a will by correspondence or from a microfilm (or in any other way) it is essential that you know the jurisdiction that originally produced and recorded that will. Once you determine the proper jurisdiction, you will find that most wills are indexed and can be searched quite easily. As already said, the direct indexes (to testators) are usually the only ones you will find. The approaches that various jurisdictions use to make these indexes vary, but you can understand most of them quite easily because their basis is usually alphabetical.

Though such are not common, reverse indexes (to beneficiaries) will occasionally be found. (Most of those I have seen are in North Carolina.) These should never be overlooked. Consider an example of a reverse index and how it can be used to help solve a pedigree problem:

You know that the wife of Simon Hendricks is named Mahala, and that's about all you know concerning her identity. A reverse probate index, during the proper time period and in the locality where the family lived, shows that a Mahala Hendricks was named in the will of Shadrack Plant. Upon finding the will you discover that Plant named "my daughter Mahala Hendricks, wife of Simon." This may or may not be your Mahala, but the possibilities are obvious. Much depends on how many Simon Hendrickses there are with wives named Mahala.

Following is an extract of a portion of a page from the reverse index to wills in the Superior Court of Guilford County, North Carolina:

Name of Devisees	from	Name of Devisors	Date when Probated		Record of Wills	
					Book No.	Page
Cobb Susan		Cobb John	Aug	1846	C	252
John		"				
Christian		"				
Clapp Delilath		Hoffman Cathrine	Aug	1846	C	253
Clapp John R.		Clapp George	Aug	1846	C	254
Barbara H.		"				
Jacob		"				
Clapp Eve		Clapp Jacob	Nov	1846	C	256
Joshua		"				
Cobble Mary		Coble Abraham	Feb	1847	C	263
Roddy		"				
Louisa		"				
Cathrine		"				
Letitia		"				
Adaline		"				
Caulk Elizabeth		Caulk Hannah	Feb	1847	C	265
Hannah		"				
Clendenin Jenny		Donnell Robert	May	1847	C	274
Betsy Ann		"				
Cox Isaac		Mendenhall Moses	Aug	1847	C	277
Rachel		"				
Cain Andrew		"				
Sarah		"				

VII. THE IMPOSSIBLE DREAM

All agree that one of the most difficult problems in American genealogy is to find the specific place of your ancestor's origin in the Old World. Sometimes this can be accomplished through probate records. An example will illustrate what I mean:

Your immigrant ancestor dies and leaves a will in America. In that will he says something like Francis Champernoun did in his will, proved in 1687 in York County, Massachusetts (now Maine):

> To my grandson Champernoun Elliot, son of Humphrey Elliot all ye lands of Right belonging unto me or that may belong unto me either in Old England or in New England not by me already disposed of.

The fact of significance is that a man died in America leaving land in England. That property could not pass through probate in American courts but had to be probated by an ancillary proceeding in England. But where was the property? The will doesn't say and English probate jurisdictions are pretty complicated before 1858. Still, it might not be too difficult since the Prerogative Court of Canterbury (PCC) in London claimed probate jurisdiction over the estates of most persons who died outside of the country, regardless of where in England their property may have been, and the record of this probate may be located in that court. Since the probate records of the PCC are all available it might not be too difficult to find out where that land was and perhaps Francis's place of origin. The LDS Family History Library has these English probate records on microfilm along with calendars (indexes) and act books (minute books). Note also that abstracts of all PCC records with American references have been published in *American Wills & Administrations in the Prerogative Court of Canterbury, 1610-1857,* comp. by Peter Wilson Coldham (Baltimore: Genealogical Publishing Co., 1989).

15

The Intestate — Miscellaneous Probate Records — Guardianships

I. THE INTESTATE AND THE PROBATE PROCESS

The process of settling an estate is somewhat different when the decedent left no valid will behind at his death from the process when there is a will. In effect, when the intestate dies, the state makes his will for him; statute dictates completely the formula for settling his estate and distributing his property among the heirs.

Too often we think that the record of settlement of an intestate estate has little value (and sometimes this may be true), but there are frequently occasions when the intestacy creates records of equal or greater value than the probate and administration of a will. Especially when the estate is large, people claiming to be relatives seem to materialize from out of nowhere. People never heard of before claim inheritance rights in the estate. But before any of them can collect a cent they must first prove the validity of their claims, and such proof must be recorded in probate court. A case came into court a few years ago in Pennsylvania when a woman died intestate leaving an estate worth more than $17,000,000. Before final settlement was reached 26,000 persons claimed to be relatives and more than 2,000 hearings were held in probate court over a sixteen-year period, resulting in 115,000 pages of testimony.[1] True, this case is extreme, but the principle applies in estates of even much smaller size.

---

[1] Joe McCarthy, "To My Wife, I Leave Her Lover," *This Week Magazine* (September 26, 1965), p. 14.

Petition for Administration. Republican Job Printing House, Columbus, Wis

State of Wisconsin, Columbia County.

In the Matter of the Estate of Samuel Stahl deceased.

To the County Court of Said County:

The petition of Mary E. Grover, Wm E. Stahl and Winfield S. Stahl of the Residences as hereinafter stated, ~~in the County of~~ ~~and State of~~ respectfully represents:

That Samuel Stahl died at the village of Lodi in the County of Columbia and State of Wisconsin on the 7th day of February, 1904, intestate as petitioners believe, and being at that time an inhabitant of said County of Columbia residing at the Village of Lodi aforesaid.

That said deceased left personal estate to be administered within this State, the value of which does not exceed Thirty five hundred dollars, and real estate within this State, ~~exclusive of~~ consisting of his homestead, worth about Fifteen hundred dollars, the annual rents and profits of which do not exceed One hundred dollars, as petitioners believe; and that said deceased left no debts known to your petitioners ~~amounting to about~~.

That said deceased left surviving him next of kin and heirs at law as follows, viz.: No widow, Children as follows: Benjamin F. Stahl of Portland Oregon; Harriet Jane Tallman of Bancroft, Iowa; Mary E. Grover of Portland Iowa, P.O. Burt Iowa; Joseph C. Stahl, of Marysville, Washington; Almira A. Davidson of Marysville, Washington; William E. Stahl, of Burt, Iowa; Winfield S. Stahl of Bancroft, Iowa; and Grandchildren as follow: Guy F. Streeter of West Brook, Minn; John Burt Streeter of Lake Arthur, La; Lou Streeter of Pocahontas, Iowa; Winfield S. Streeter of Lake Arthur, La.; Wesley Streeter of Winnebago City, Minn.; George Streeter of Lake Arthur, La. Eugenie Streeter of Pocahontas, Iowa; Leo Streeter of Winnebago City, Iowa. Claire Streeter of Pocahontas, Iowa; the last three named are minors, and are children of Catherine Streeter deceased, and Samuel Barnett of Wausau, Wis son of David Barnett and Louise A. Barnett deceased.

That your petitioners are children of said deceased. Wherefore, your petitioners pray that administration of the estate of said deceased be granted unto Winfield S. Stahl of Bancroft Iowa or some other suitable person.

Dated, February 10th 1904.

Mary E. Grover
Wm E. Stahl
Winfield S. Stahl

STATE OF WISCONSIN, COLUMBIA COUNTY, } ss. Mary E. Grover, Wm E. Stahl and Winfield S. Stahl being duly sworn, on oath say that they are the petitioners above named; that they have heard read the above and foregoing petition, and know the contents thereof, and that the same is true to their own knowledge, excepting as to matters therein stated on information and belief, and as to those matters they believe it to be true.

Subscribed and sworn to before me this 10th day of February 1904.

S. D. Waters
Notary Public

Mary E. Grover
Wm E. Stahl
Winfield S. Stahl

FIGURE 1—A PETITION FOR PROBATE

(This is a very informative document. Compare it with the Assignment illustrated in Figure 2. They relate to the same estate.)

Assignment of Real Estate

FEIL'S PRACTICAL PRINTING, PORTAGE, WIS.

At a .... term of the County Court in and for the County of Columbia in the State of Wisconsin, held at the Probate Office in the City of Portage, on the 3rd Tuesday of November A. D. 1919, being the 18th day of said month, and on the 4th day of said term, to wit, on Nov. 21st 1919.

Present, Hon A. F. Kellogg *County Judge.*

IN THE MATTER OF THE ESTATE OF Samuel Stahl Deceased.

Whereas Samuel Stahl of Lodi in said County, died intestate on the 7th day of Feby 1914, and his estate has been fully and finally settled by and under proper proceedings in this Court, all his debts and the expenses of administration paid, and his personal estate fully accounted for and assigned to the persons entitled thereto: whereby the real estate owned by said deceased at the time of his death can now be assigned in accordance with law.

And Whereas, It has been established to the satisfaction of this Court, that said deceased left him surviving no widow and seven and only seven children viz: Benjamin F. Stahl, Harriet Jane Tallman, Mary E. Grover, Joseph E. Stahl, Alminar A. Davidson, William E. Stahl and Winfield S. Stahl; nine grandchildren, children of a deceased daughter Catharine Streator, to wit, Guy F. Streator, John Burt Streator, Lewis S. Streator, Winfield S. Streator, Wesley Streator, Geo. S. Streator, M. Jean Streator, Leo Streator and Ralph C. Streator; one grand child, child of a deceased daughter Louise A. Burnett, to wit: David Burnett; that said Benjamin F. Stahl died during the administration of said estate and before settlement of the account of administrator, leaving him surviving as heirs at law his widow Mary E. Stahl, and seven children to wit: Janette Louise Roberts, Lizzie Hay Roberts, John F. Stahl, Royal C. Stahl, Mary B. Robinson, Lilian A. Roberts and Benjamin F. Stahl. who ~~are the~~ heirs and only heirs at law and entitled to said real estate.

It is Therefore Ordered, Adjudged and Decreed, That all the real estate owned by said deceased at the time of his death be and the same is assigned to said Harriet Jane Tallman, Mary E. Grover, Joseph E. Stahl, Alminar A. Davidson, William E. Stahl and Winfield S. Stahl children, to each the undivided one ninth thereof; To Guy F. Streator, John Burt Streator, Lewis S. Streator, Winfield S. Streator, Wesley Streator, Geo. S. Streator, M. Jean Streator, Leo Streator and Ralph C. Streator, to each the undivided one eighty first thereof; To David Burnett the undivided one ninth thereof; To Janette Louise Roberts, Lizzie Hay Roberts, John F. Stahl, Royal C. Stahl, Mary B. Robinson, Lilian A. Roberts, and Benjamin F. Stahl, the undivided one sixty third thereof, subject to dower of Mary E. Stahl, widow of Benj. F. Stahl, ~~in common and undivided, share and share alike~~, to have and to hold the same to them and their heirs and assigns forever, ~~but subject to the dower and homestead rights therein of ...... widow of said deceased.~~

By the Court A. F. Kellogg
County Judge.

Dated Nov. 24 1919.

FIGURE 2—DECREE OF DISTRIBUTION (ASSIGNMENT OF REAL ESTATE)

(This document relates to the same estate as the Petition in Figure 1. Note that circumstances have changed somewhat in the years between the two documents.)

In some courts, records of intestate administrations are separated from the wills, while in other courts all probate records are recorded in the same books. It is not uncommon to find master probate indexes listing all documents on file for each probate case. Where they exist these indexes can save you much time and energy, and their existence signals the fact that all probate records are recorded in the same registers of the probate court. But whether or not recordings of such documents exist, the original documents (if still extant) will be found in the probate (or estate) files. These files (or packets) also contain unrecorded wills, such as those declared void and not probated.

Just as we surveyed the steps involved in the process of probating a will, let us also take a simplified look at the process, from beginning to end, for administering an intestate estate:

1. There is, of course, no case until after the person dies, and for the case to be intestate the person who dies must leave no valid will. No court can acquire jurisdiction unless there is proof of death.

2. Probate proceedings are usually set in motion by a petition from some person interested in the estate, showing the fact and nature of his interest, being filed in the proper court. This petition, usually called a petition (or application) for letters of administration, also tells that the death has taken place, that the decedent died intestate, and that property within that court's jurisdiction (and sometimes additional property) was left to administer. The approximate value of the property must be stated, and in more recent years, the names and relationships of those who may be entitled to share in that property must be given. Jurisdiction lies in the state where the decedent was domiciled at the time of death.

Persons most often claiming the right of administrator are the surviving spouse and next-of-kin. In the case of a wife surviving her husband, she often claims her right to administration (as a co-administratrix) in connection with another next-of-kin. When there are several next-of-kin in the same degree of relationship claiming rights to administer the estate, the court has power to select the most suitable. In appointing an administrator, the court usually follows certain guidelines; that is, a sole administration is preferred to a joint one, males are preferred to females (at least historically), residents are preferred to non-residents, unmarried women are preferred to married women, whole-blood relatives to those of half blood, those more interested in the estate to those less interested, etc. Those with no interest in the estate cannot petition to be appointed as administrators. If there are no relatives claiming the right of administration, creditors usually will have claim.

3. When the court receives a petition, a hearing is set and notice is given to all interested parties, either by direct notice or by publication, or both, depending upon state statute. The purpose of the hearing is to establish proof of the claims of the petition. This done, administration is granted and letters of administration (see the list of terms later in this chapter) are issued. The administrator now has authorization to proceed.

In some states the minimum size of an estate which requires administration is set by statute, and in other states there is no such statutory limitation, though there must usually be assets sufficient to justify an administration grant. This may be why we find no trace of probate records for some of our ancestors.

The administrator, once named, must give bond, with sureties, for the faithful performance of his administration[2] as required by statute, before the actual letters of administration can be issued.

4. Once the above details have been taken care of, the administrator can begin his task. After publishing the required notices to creditors and paying the decedent's just debts and obligations, the administrator must distribute the assets and real property and disburse the monies of the estate according to statute. One important duty which he must perform as part of his administration is to make a complete inventory of the assets of the estate and file it with the court. In most states the court will appoint appraisers to ascertain the true value of the estate. Failure to make an inventory is generally considered a breach of the administrator's bond.

5. The administrator keeps an accurate record of everything he does as part of his administration, as he must make an account thereof periodically, usually on a yearly basis (if his job takes that long). At the termination of his trust he must make a final account in any event. The final account (or settlement) must be accepted by those interested in the estate and may be disputed by them for appropriate reasons.

6. In some states, and especially in more recent years (so don't expect to find these in very many old records), a decree of distribution is issued by the court at the completion of the administration, as with the testate estate, to give proof of title. This document finally and officially vests the title to the decedent's property in his heirs. It is often (again depending upon state law) recorded in the local land records when real estate is administered, as well as being filed in the probate court. The document is called by various names in different places. Such terms as *decree of heirship, probate decree, assignment of real estate, order of distribution, probate assignment, decree*

---

[2] See definitions of terms in chapter 13.

of distribution, certificate of devise, as well as others, are used in different states. The creditors and the heirs will sign releases or receipts that are also filed with the court.

The great value of these records lies in the fact that they show how the estate was divided and who got what. Often these can be better sources of genealogical evidence than wills because they always name names and they cannot omit any living legal heirs. Law requires that *all* documents created during the process of administration be filed with the court.

7. Should the administrator be relieved of his duties before they are completed, either by death or for any other reason (perhaps even at his own request), the court will choose a successor. This person is called an administrator *de bonis non.* His job is to complete the work of the first administrator in the administration of the estate.

Other records which might have arisen as part of the administration process include petitions for (and assignments of) dower or curtesy; petitions, accounts, and other documents relating to orphans and guardianship (discussed later in this chapter); powers of attorney; etc.

II. MISCELLANEOUS PROBATE RECORDS

There are many other kinds of probate documents besides wills, as our discussion has already indicated. Some deal with testate estates, some with intestate estates, and some with both. We want to look now at some of the more important records in a little more detail. Before doing so, however, it should be said that many of these records are of inestimable worth. The originals of these records for each case—as well as the original will—are usually found in the estate files and are listed in the probate docket in the court. Estate files are seldom microfilmed because (1) they are so voluminous and (2) they consist of folded loose papers that are time-consuming to handle. However, they are generally easy to locate and can be very rewarding. Keep in mind that these are also the original records—while recorded wills are not.

ACCOUNT (or ACCOMPT): The administrator of an estate or a guardian is sometimes required by statute to make a periodic (often once a year) report of his administration or guardianship. And at the end of his trust he must make a final account. (See also SETTLEMENT.) These accounts are a record of the activities associated with his specific fiduciary duty. The following is a typical account of an administration from mid-eighteenth century New England:

The account of Elizabeth Hodsdon of her admin^{ion} of the Estate of her late Husband John Hooper the third late of Berwick in the County of York dec^{d} Intestate. The Said Accomptant chargeth herself with ye person^{l} Estate of S^{d} as p^{r} Invent^{y} £21"13"—And prayeth an Allowance of the following Articles of Charge vizt

To paid for Letters of Admin^{ion} Inventory & c	£—"12"—
To a Tourney to exhibit ye Inventory and give Bond for Admin^{ion}	—"10"—
To so much due to ye appriz^{rs} for their services	—" 9"—
To p^{d} for Swearing Apprizers	—" 1" 2
To so much for 3 Bondsmen to ye Admin^{x} 1 Day themselves & Horses and Expense each 4/	—"12"—
To p^{d} Doct^{or} Parsons for Visits & Medicins p^{r} Rec^{t}	—"12"—
To p^{d} Hall Jackson £ 17,17. N. Hampsh^{r} old Ten^{r}	—"17"10
To Eben^{er} Thomson to get a War^{t} of Apprizem^{t}	—" 3"—
To D^{o} to a Scribe for drawing this acco^{t}	" 1" 4
To Sundries allowed ye Widow as necessarye for Life	14"08"10
To Admin^{x} time attending the Apprizers 1 Day	—" 2"—
Probate Fees on this acco^{t}	—" 6"—
Due to Marg^{t} Norson for nursing ye Admin^{x} in ye lifetime of the Said Intestate	3"—"—
	£ 21"15" 2

Errors excepted   Eliz^{a} (her mark) Hodsdon

York Ss. At a Court of Probate held at York July 12, 1763.

Elizabeth Hodsdon above named made Oath that the above account is just and true. Ordered that She be allowed twenty one pounds fifteen Shillings and two pence out of the Said Estate in full discharge thereof.

Jer^{a} Moulton, Judge

ADMINISTRATION BOND: A bond (q.v.) posted by the person selected as administrator of an estate to ensure that his administration will be satisfactorily accomplished. Such a bond requires sureties. See also TESTAMENTARY BOND.

ANTENUPTIAL CONTRACT: Though an antenuptial contract or agreement is not a probate document, it does have substantial effect on the probate proceedings whenever it exists. It is a contract made between a man and the woman he is about to marry wherein certain property rights of one or both are secured and delineated. Such contracts have usually been made by persons who have been previously married and who want to preserve their properties and wealth for the issue of their previous unions in case of their own deaths, rather than to each other. Such contracts, in probate court, have precedence over laws of descent and distribution. They have been quite common, especially in states with community property laws and with the Dutch in New Netherland.[3] Another name is *marriage settlement*. If the contract is made after the marriage it is called a postnuptial contract (q.v.).

ASSIGNMENT OF DOWER: This is the document by which a widow's dower is assigned to her as part of the administration. There are many different terms used to describe this document in various states but they all boil down to the same thing. Often it is called a *dower division,* the *setting off of the dower,* and sometimes merely the *widow's dower*. Ordinarily there is not a lot of genealogical data in this kind of record, but occasionally you will find an accompanying *petition* or a *plat* (a map of the land) showing the division of the estate among the heirs. The assignment of Mercy Cloutman's dower provides a typical example:

York Ss. Lebanon June 20, 1763.

We the Subscribers being appointed by the hon^{ble} Jeremiah Moulton Esqr Judge of Probate for Said County to divide and set-off to Mercy Cloutman Widow of John Cloutman late of Said Lebanon dec^{d} Intestate one third part of the real Estate of the Dec^{d} We have attended that Service, and have Set off to the Said Mercy one third part of the Said Estate on the following Manner, Eight Acres of Land in the Lot originally granted to John Cartice, jun^{r} in Said Township. N. Seven in the first Range of the Home Lots which Lot ye Said Cloutman purchased of one Samuel Rounds beginning at the highway leading between the first and Second Range of Lots and extending Eastwardly the wedth of the Lot thirty two Rods which contains Eight Acres and is bounded Northerly by a Lot granted to Richd Cutt Esqr and Southerly by a Lot granted to Crisp. Bradbury and is Forty Rods in Breadth. As Witness our Hands.

Joseph Farnam
Philip Doe (his mark)
Paul Farnam

York Ss. At a Court of Probate held at York July 11, 1763

The within Instrument being presented to me under Oath for my Approbation. I do hereby approve and allow of the Same as the Division of the Widow's Dower in the Estate of John Cloutman Dec^{d} And do order that ye Same be assigned to her accordingly—

Jer^{a} Moulton Judge

[3] There is an example of an antenuptial contract in chapter 17.

BOND: This is an instrument with a sum of money affixed as a penalty, binding the parties to pay that sum if certain acts are not performed. If the obligation is properly discharged, the penalty is void. In probate matters the administrator whom the court appoints to settle the intestate estate and the executor of the testate estate (unless expressly excused from the bonding obligation by the testator in the will) must both be bonded. Often the bondsmen (sureties) for a bond of this type are relatives of the administrator or the executor, thus providing another research clue when the going gets tough.

CAVEAT: The Latin for "Let him beware", it gives formal notice to the court by an interested party to suspend a proceeding until he can be heard. This power is often used to temporarily prevent a will from being probated or letters of administration from being granted. In such a case the caveat is usually an attack on the validity of the will or administration. This is the document required by many states for contesting a will.

DECREE OF DISTRIBUTION: As mentioned earlier, the decree of distribution is the final instrument issued in the administration of an estate. By it the heirs receive actual title to the property of the deceased. In earlier periods in some localities this was sometimes called a *division*. Other names have also been applied, as previously mentioned. The following decree of distribution was made in Nevada County, California, in 1904:

In the Matter of the Estate of William D. Woods, deceased.

Decree of Distribution of Estate.

W.J. Woods, the Executor of the will of Wm. D. Woods, deceased having on the 21st day of July 1904 filed in this Court his final a/c and petition, setting forth among other matters that his accounts are ready to be finally settled, and said estate is in a condition to be closed, and that a portion of said estate remains to be divided among the devisees of said deceased, said matter coming on regularly to be heard this 1st day of August 1904 at 10 o'clock AM the said executor appearing by his counsel, Chas. W. Kitts, Esq. this Court proceeded to hear said final account and said petition for distribution; and it appearing that said executor has collected the sum of $50 and has expended the sum of $431.50 as such; that he has paid the legacies provided in said will to M.B. Townsend, E.M. Shaw and the heirs of J.A. Holman, deceased; that he waives his commissions as executor; waives repayment of the sums he has paid exceeding the amount collected by him and has settled on his own account with Chas. W. Kitts, as his attorney, and that said account is in all respects just and true. It is hereby ordered that the same be and the same is hereby settled, allowed and confirmed.

This court proceeded to the hearing of the petition, and it appearing to the satisfaction of this court that the residue of said estate, consisting of the property hereinafter particularly described, is now ready for distribution, and that said estate is now in a condition to be closed. That the whole of said estate is separate property. [California is a community-property state.] That the said William D. Woods, died testate, in the county of Nevada, Cala., on the 22nd day of Feby 1904 leaving him surviving, his son, W.J. Woods, a resident of Grass Valley, Cala., his daughter Matilda B. Townsend of said City of Grass Valley, his Daughter E.M. Shaw a resident of Bakersfield all of the age of majority and S.A. Holman, Jr., A.J. Holman, L.E. Holman, M.W. Holman and W.H. Holman, children of his deceased daughter, Julia A. Holman deceased. That since the rendition of his said final account nothing has come into the hands of said executor, and nothing has been expended by said executor as necessary expenses of administration; and that the estimated expenses of closing said estate will amount to the sum of nothing. That the said W.J. Woods is entitled to the whole of the residue after paying to said Matilda B. Townsend, E.M. Shaw legacies of $100 each, and to the heirs of said Julia A. Holman a legacy of $100, all of which have been paid.

Now on this, the 1st day of Aug 1904, on motion of Chas. W. Kitts Esq., counsel for said executor it is hereby ordered, adjudged and decreed, that the residue of said estate of William D. Woods, deceased, hereinafter particularly described, and now remaining in the hands of said executor and any other property not now known or discovered, which may belong to the said estate, or in which the said estate may have an interest, be the same is hereby distributed as follows, to wit: The "Woods Ranch" consisting of the W ½ of N.W. ¼ of Section 27 and the south east quarter of the north east quarter of Section 28 Tp 16 N.R. 8 E.M.D.M. containing 89 ac and being the whole of said legal sub divisions, save such portions as have been conveyed by said testator.

All that portion of lot 3 in Blk 15 in the City of Grass Valley, Nevada Co., Cala., as per map of said City of Grass Valley, made by Saml Bethell in 1872, fronting 50 ft on Carpenter Street, bounded south by Perdue's lot and thence extending back easterly 100 ft.

That part of lot 3 in block 15 aforesaid, bounded north by Main Street; east by west lines of lots of Pattison, Clemo & Wesley and Carpenter St.; on south by Grass Valley Townsite.

Lot 6 in Sec 27 Tp 16 NR 8 EMDM.

Done in open Court, this 1st day of Aug 1904.

F.T. Nilon, Judge

Filed August 1st 1904
F.L. Arbogast, Clerk
By A.J. Hosking, Deputy Clerk.
State of California,
ss.
County of Nevada.

DEED OF PARTITION: See chapter 17.

DEPOSITION: A deposition is not strictly a type of probate record but belongs to all types of court proceedings. It is a statement of a witness, under oath, on certain questions, not taken in open court but reduced to writing and intended for use in a court action. In a case where a will is being contested, the depositions of friends, neighbors, family, etc., on the mental soundness of the testator (or whatever) may be taken and presented to the court (and are sometimes admissible as evidence). Depositions are made in response to questions posed by the opposition.

DISCHARGE: See RELEASE.

DISTRIBUTION: The payment or division to those entitled to benefit from the decedent's estate, after payment of the debts and liabilities. It follows the settlement (q.v.) and is sometimes called a *final distribution.*

DIVISION: See DECREE OF DISTRIBUTION.

DOWER: See ASSIGNMENT OF DOWER.

FINAL DISTRIBUTON: See DISTRIBUTION.

FINAL SETTLEMENT: See SETTLEMENT.

INVENTORY: An inventory is a detailed list of all the goods and chattels of the decedent, made usually by the administrator, the executor of the estate, or by others appointed. The inventory gives a glimpse into the personal life of the decedent—his occupation, his wealth or lack of it, and the nature of the times in which he lived. In the absence of other probate records the inventory can also give some indication of the approximate time of death—a must in many problems. The inventory of William Gowen's estate in 1763 tells his occupation and also indicates that he was not a man of affluence:

A true Inventory of the Estate of William Gowen late of Kittery in ye County of York Mariner dec^d^ taken by us the Subscribers October 8th 1763. Shown to Abigail Gowen Widow and Admin^x^ of Said dec^ds^ Estate vizt.

To 1 feather Bed & Furniture	£6"10"—
One Ditto and Furniture	6"10"—
To 1 Desk 40/. a Trunk 10/. a Chest 6/.	2"16"—
A round Table 13/. two Small Ditto 6/.	—"19"—
2 Small old Chests 2/. a Spinning Wheel & Real 4/.	—" 6"—

12 old Chairs 10/. 2 old Bibles & Sunday Small Books 10/.	1"—"—
2 old Tramells grate from Toaster and Spit	—"12"—
a Small p[r] old handjrons fireslice & Tongs	—" 9"—
Ironing Box & Heaters 6/. old narrow ax 1/6.	—" 7" 6
a Coffee Mill 5/. three old pewter Dishes 6/.	—"11"—
12 old pewter Plates 6/. 2 old Basons 2/6.	—" 8" 6
4 pewter Porringes 3/6. old earthen Ware 6/.	—" 9" 6
Some old glass Bottles and Caps	—" 5"—
2 Small looking Glasses 5/. 1 D[o] 3/. 5 old Candlesticks 2/.	—"10"—
a marking Iron & Hammer 1/6.	—" 1" 6
a warming pan 12/. Six old maps 3/.	—"15"—
4 old casks 4/. Some old Knives & Forks 1/.	—" 5"—
2 old Razors 1/. old Cutlash 8[d]	—" 1" 8
two potts and Ten Kettle and frying pan 14/.	—"14"—
old Skimmer and flesh Forks 1/. 3 old Tubbs 2/4.	—" 3" 4
	£23"14"—

James Gowen
Japhet Emery
Joseph Goold

York Ss. Dec[r] 31, 1763.

Abigail Gowen within named made Oath that y[e] Sever[l] articles mentioned in the within Inventory are all y[e] Estate belonging to y[e] Said Dec[d] that has come to her hands, and that if any thing more here after appear, She will give it into y[e] Reg[er] office. The apprizers being Sworn.

Jer: Moulton Judge

LETTERS OF ADMINISTRATION: This is the document (singular) issued by the probate court appointing the administrator of an intestate estate and authorizing him to function in that assignment. The following example is a document commonly referred to as an "administration" but is actually a combination letters of administration and inventory. It also mentions a bond for £80 but is not itself a bond:

Letters of Administration granted to Elizabeth Littlefield on the Estate of Nathan Littlefield deceased she produceing in Court An Inventory of the said Estate and John Barrett was bound in Eighty pounds bond To our soveraigne Lord the King his Heires and successors that she the Said Elizabeth Littlefield shall administer according to Law.

	£	S	d
Imprimis[4] Wearing cloaths	3	00	00
Ip. Bed and bedding	04	00	00
Ip. Some household goods	01	00	00
Ip. 2 guns 2 pistols: 1 sword and amunition	03	00	00
Ip. 2 oxen and Two Steeres	12	00	00
Ip. 1 Cow and Calfe	03	00	00
Ip. 2 yearling	02	00	00
Ip. 1 Heyfor 2 year old	01	10	00
Ip. 1 Horse	02	00	00
Ip. 1 sow and 9 pigs	03	00	00
Ip. 3 yds Searge	01	10	00
Ip. Board and Shingle nayles	01	10	00
Ip. Sheeps Wool	00	10	00
Ip. to one quart pt of a p^{r} of Logging wheels	00	10	00
Ip. to Steel traps	01	00	00
	40	10	00

The prmisses abovesd were apprized th 13th of March 1688 by us here subscribed

Jonath Hamonds
Sam^{ll} Wheelwright

LETTERS TESTAMENTARY: An executor named in a will has no legal authority, even though the will names him and the testator is dead, until authorized by the probate court. The court authorization—letters testamentary—is equivalent to the letters of administration issued by the court to the administrator of an intestate estate.

MARRIAGE SETTLEMENT: See ANTENUPTIAL CONTRACT.

PETITION: An application, in writing, to the court for an exercise of judicial power in a matter which is not the subject of a suit. The would-be administrator or executor petitions the probate court to grant him letters of administration or letters testamentary.

POSTNUPTIAL CONTRACT: A written agreement made by a couple *after* their marriage concerning the inheritance of property of one or both. It takes precedence over statutes of descent and distribution. See also ANTENUPTIAL CONTRACT.

RECEIPT: A receipt is merely a written acknowledgement that goods or property have been received. In some states it is not uncommon to find them recorded in the probate court. Such receipts give the acknowledgement of creditors, heirs, or beneficiaries that they have received payment or property and discharge the executor or administrator from further responsibility in their behalf. An example, from the records of York County, Massachusetts (now Maine), follows:

---

[4] A Latin term meaning *first* or *in the first place.*

Know all men by these presents that we Samuel Whitmore and Mary his Wife of Gorham in the County of Cumberland do acknowledge to have rec[d] in full of Joel Whitney of Gorham in the County aforesaid Three pounds twelve Shillings in full for our Part & Portion in the Estate of Abel Whitney late of Gorham deceas'd We do hereby acquit exonerate and discharge the Said Joel his Executors and admin[rs] from every part and parcel thereof. In Witness whereof we have hereunto Set our Hands and Seals y[e] 28th Day of January Anno Domini 1765.

Ammos Whitney	Sam[ll] Whitmore
Zebulon Whitney	Mary Whitmore

RELEASE: There are many kinds of releases but two are significant here. The first is accomplished when an heir releases his expectancy interest to the source of that interest. The second conveys one person's rights or interest to someone else who has an interest in the same estate. As an example of the first, children might release certain rights in their deceased father's estate to their widowed mother. This document is sometimes called a *discharge*. It may be recorded in the land records since it acts more as a conveyance than a devise. Both types of release require fair consideration. An example used in chapter 2, and repeated here, illustrates the second type:

Know all men by these Presents that we William Bryer Shipwright Richard Bryer Weaver Andrew Haley husbandman and Mary his Wife Caleb Hutchins Caulker and Sarah his Wife Joseph Hutchins Weaver and Elizabeth his Wife William Wilson Weaver and Eadah his Wife John Haley Husbandman & Hephzib[a] his Wife all of Kittery in the County of York in the Province of the Massachusetts Bay in New England and William Tapley Taylor of New Hampshire & R [*sic*] his Wife Do forever acquit exonerate and discharge our Father in Law Benjamin Hammond of Kittery & Province afors[d] and our Mother Sarah Hammond lately call'd Sarah Bryer from the Demands of us or our or either of our Heirs in and unto any part of the Cattle or Household Goods or moveable Estate of our hon[d] Father William Bryer late of Kittery afores[d] dec[d] and We the Subscribers that have receiv'd of our Mother Sarah Hammond any part of the moveable Estate above mentioned We do hereby promise to return the Same to our Mother Sarah Hammond on her Demand. Furthermore we the Subscribers Do by these Presents promise and engage to let our Mother above named have and improve one third part according as the Law directs of the Land or Lands that was the Estate of our Father William Bryer as aforesaid during her natural Life.

In Witness whereof we have hereunto Set our Hands and Seals this 31st Day of January Anno Domini 1738/9.

Sam[l]. Haley
her
Elizabeth X Dill
mark

Andrew Haly
Caleb Hutchins
Joseph X Hutchins
William Willson
John Haley his
William Bryer X
mark

Witnesses for W[m]. Tapley
Andrew Haley
Caleb Hutchins.

his
William X Tapley
mark

RENUNCIATION: A renunciation, sometimes called a *disclaimer,* is a refusal to accept a testamentary transfer or a transfer by will. Under the common law an heir (one who took property by inheritance from an intestate) could not renounce.

SALE BILL: A sale bill is a record made of the goods and properties sold at public sale by the executor or administrator of the estate. The record is usually quite complete, listing items sold, buyers, and prices. Relatives often buy many of the articles offered at such sales and a thorough study of the record may provide useful clues to identities. However, you cannot expect to find conclusive genealogical proof in a sale bill by itself. One might also gain insight into an ancestor's lifestyle and material circumstances. Following is a sale bill for the estate of Newton Brent in 1795 from the records of Lancaster County, Virginia:

November 3[d] 1795. Memo[dum] of goods sold belonging to the estate of Newton Brent decd.

1 tenant Saw	To Wm Gibson	£0 . 12 . 0
7 walnut chairs	William Kirk	0 . 9 . 0
1 gun	James Pollard	1 . 5 . 0
1 do	John Thrall	0 . 3 . 0
1 sword	Thomas James	0 . 3 . 0
1 whip saw	Capt. Gibson	1 . 3 . 6
3 planes	Thomas Lawson	0 . 4 . 0
1 small box of tools	Thomas Short	0 . 4 . 0
parcel planes	Tarpley George	0 . 4 . 3
1 bead plane	John Flowers	0 . 1 . 0
1 red bull	Wm Eustace	2 . 10 . 0
1 pied cow & calf	Wm Eustace	1 . 14 . 0
1 cow & calf w horns	Capt Gibson	1 . 15 . 0
1 cow & calf	John Hunt	1 . 15 . 0
1 cow	Wm Eustace	2 . 0 . 0
1 Heifer	Vincent Brent	1 . 8 . 6
1 small bull	Wm Eustace	1 . 3 . 0
1 do do	John Thrall	1 . 8 . 6

254
July
1767

perfect Inventory of the Estate of his Testator so far as has come to his Hands Possession or Knowledge, and that if any thing hereafter appear he will give an Additional Inventory thereof into this Court the appraisers were likewise Sworn at the same Time Before me John Hill Judge of Probate

Recorded according to the Original
By David Sewall Reg.

Admin. acct. on the Estate of the Hon. Jer. Moulton Esq.

The Estate of the Hon.ble Jeremiah Moulton Esq. deceased
To Jeremiah Moulton Ex. to said Estate Dr.

To paid Daniel Moulton Esq. County Treasurer the Ballance due to the County from my Hon. Father as he was County Treasurer for the Year 1764	20..19.7½
To paid Grand Jurymens Wages which was due to them from my Hon. Father as he was County Treasurer	40..7..7
To paid for Funeral Charges	7..13..0
To p. Doctr Job Lyman p his account	24..6..10
To Edward Emerson p his account	3..1..4½
To Caleb Prebble p his account	0..11..3
To p. Martha Banks for nursing my Father	0..6..0
Due to me as p. my account	41..4..8¾
Due to me on a Note of Hand	11..2..0
To p. Joseph Simpson Jun. p his account	1..11..9
To Cash paid for proving the Deceased Will Recording the same and Letter Testamentary	1..15..0
To Probate Fee for examining this Account	6..8
	147..5..9¾

The Estate of the Hon. Jer. Moulton Esq. Cr. Credit

By so much Recieved of the several Constables in the County of York	32..18..6½
By so much ree. of his Personal Estate as appraised by Messrs. Jo. Simpson Jun. and Jo. Parsons which is as follows	
Three Cows & one Heifer £10..13..4 11 old Sheep & 4 Lambs £6..8/	£17..1..4
2 Swine 30/ one Silver Tankard £10..8/ 1 Silver Porringer 8/	13..6..0
one Silver Pepper box 10/ 1 pr. Silver Tea Tongs 12/ one pr. Silver Shoe & Knee buckles 18/	1..10..0
one China Bowl 12/ a Clock and Case 80/	4..12..0
an Iron Crow 9/4 a pr. Steelyards 8/ 1 Fire lock 12/ 3 old D.o 8/	1..19..4
7 old Cutlashes 3/6 one old Chain 5/7 12lb Leaden Bullets 4/8	0..13..9
an Flints 1/ Sundry Books and Pamphlets 40/	2..4..0
one Cane 2/ Rec. of Jos. Hall Jun. for a Calf 12/	0..14..0
Due to Ballance this Acc. to the Exe.	68..18..9½
	147..5..9¾

York, June 15th 1767
Errors Excepted p Jeremiah Moulton

York ss. At a Court of Probate held at York the 5th day of July 1767 The foregoing account being Examined, duly Vouched and Sworn to by the accountant, It is Considered that the same be

FIGURE 3—SETTLEMENT (FINAL ACCOUNT)

1 do do	Henry Palmer	1 . 6 . 0
5 first choice sheep	Thos Jaines	1 . 16 . 0
5 2nd do do	do do	1 . 3 . 6
5 3rd do do	Vinson Brent	0 . 16 . 6
		£24 . 4 . 9

At a court held for Lancaster county on the 21st day of February 1797 This account of the sale of part of the estate of Newton Brent decd was returned and ordered to be recorded—

Teste. Henry Towles cl. curia

SETTLEMENT: The settlement (or *final settlement*) is the instrument which itemizes payment of the expenses of the estate, showing how the monies were disbursed to settle the decedent's financial obligations. It also indicates the total assets and the individual shares of those left to benefit. All that remains is the final distribution to the heirs or beneficiaries. This is frequently called the *final account.*

TESTAMENTARY BOND: This is a bond (q.v.) posted with the court by the executor of a will guaranteeing a proper administration of the estate. Such a bond requires sureties. See also ADMINISTRATION BOND.

WARRANT: A warrant is a court order. In probate cases some state statutes require a warrant to precede nearly every action of the probate court. A warrant may be issued prior to the assignment of the widow's dower, prior to the taking of the inventory, prior to the settlement, prior to the distribution, or prior to almost any other action in which the court has interest. Genealogically the warrant seldom gives more (and often less) information than the record of the proceeding which it fathered.

III. GUARDIANSHIPS

A. Court Jurisdiction

Guardianships are very closely related to probate records and the probate or administration process. The reason for this, as you know, is that when the decedent is survived by minor children, such children are not considered capable by law of managing their own persons or properties. Hence a guardian must be appointed. In some courts the records arising out of guardianship matters are kept in the probate files, while in other courts these records are kept elsewhere. But, regardless of this, they are handled by the same courts in most states.

The following list shows the courts where guardianship matters are controlled in the several states. As you use it be aware that in most states the jurisdiction is in the county of the child's residence rather than the guardian's. This generally makes the records easier to locate and use as a genealogical source.

ALABAMA:	County Probate Court (but administration of guardianships may be removed to the County Chancery Court).
ALASKA:	State Superior Court.
ARIZONA:	Superior Court in the county.
ARKANSAS:	County Probate Court.
CALIFORNIA:	Superior Court in the county.
COLORADO:	District Court in the county. (The Juvenile Court has jurisdiction in Denver.)
CONNECTICUT:	Probate Court in the district (see chapter 14).
DELAWARE:	County Orphans' Court (for minors); County Chancery Court (for all others).
D.C.:	Probate Division of District Court.
FLORIDA:	County Judge's Court.
GEORGIA:	County Court of Chancery.
HAWAII:	Circuit Court of the Island.
IDAHO:	District Court in the county (see chapter 14).
ILLINOIS:	Circuit Court in the county.
INDIANA:	Court that has probate jurisdiction in the county (see chapter 14).
IOWA:	County Probate Court.
KANSAS:	County Probate Court.
KENTUCKY:	County Court.
LOUISIANA:	District Court in the parish (county equivalent) and, in Orleans Parish, the Civil District Court. (Guardianship is called *tutorship*.)
MAINE:	County Probate Court.
MARYLAND:	County Equity Court. (The County Orphans' Court may also appoint the guardian for a minor entitled to property in an estate.)
MASSACHUSETTS:	County Probate Court.
MICHIGAN:	County Probate Court.
MINNESOTA:	County Probate Court.
MISSISSIPPI:	County Chancery Court.
MISSOURI:	County Probate Court.

MONTANA:	District Court in the county.
NEBRASKA:	County Court.
NEVADA:	District Court in the county.
NEW HAMPSHIRE:	County Probate Court.
NEW JERSEY:	County Surrogate's Court. (In cases of dispute the County Court must order the Surrogate to act, and in cases of incompetency the County Court and the Superior Court have jurisdiction.)
NEW MEXICO:	Either in County Probate Court or in District Court in the county.
NEW YORK:	County Surrogate's Court.
NORTH CAROLINA:	County Superior Court.
NORTH DAKOTA:	County Court.
OHIO:	County Probate Court.
OKLAHOMA:	County Court.
OREGON:	Court having probate jurisdiction in the county (see chapter 14).
PENNSYLVANIA:	County Orphans' Court.
RHODE ISLAND:	Probate Court of the town (with right of appeal to Superior and Supreme Courts).
SOUTH CAROLINA:	County Probate Court.
SOUTH DAKOTA:	District Court in the county.
TENNESSEE:	Both County Court and County Chancery Court.
TEXAS:	County Court and County Probate Court (with right of appeal to the District Court).
UTAH:	District Court in the county.
VERMONT:	Probate Court in the district (see chapter 14).
VIRGINIA:	Courts of Equity (see chapter 19).
WASHINGTON:	County Superior Court.
WEST VIRGINIA:	County Circuit Court (in Chancery) has authority with some concurrent jurisdiction in the appointment of guardians lying in the County Court.
WISCONSIN:	County Court.
WYOMING:	District Court in the county.[5]

[5] *Martindale-Hubbell Law Directory*, 120th ed. (Summit, NJ: Martindale-Hubbell, Inc., 1988), Vol. 5 (by permission) and correspondence with various court officials.

Guardianship records which are kept under the jurisdiction of the court of probate are more likely to be indexed and easier to use, but this is not always the case. You will find in the availability of these records vast differences which apparently have nothing to do with the nature of the jurisdictions in which they are kept.

B. The Value of Guardianship Records

There are various kinds of situations in which guardianship records may have been kept. First, be aware that it is not always necessary for the parents to be deceased for guardianship records to exist. There are many instances where children are left legacies (often by a grandparent or other relative) and their own natural parents are appointed as special guardians of the property and rights which such a legacy may involve. In some states, however, statutes prohibit natural parents from acting as guardians in such situations; other states allow them to be co-guardians.

You may find a guardian *ad litem* being appointed to represent the minor child or the incompetent person in a specific law suit, but seldom is there great genealogical value in such an appointment in and of itself. The records of suit may provide useful information, however.

Another type of situation which you may encounter in your research that would suggest the necessity of investigating guardianship records is where you find a young person coming of age, marrying, and securing property in a locality, and there is no indication of a connection of that young person to persons of an earlier generation. Often the reason for this lack of connection is that his parents died when he was young. Never hesitate to check guardianship records when you find a situation like this. They may hold the answer to your problem.

There are several kinds of records and varying kinds and amounts of information which these records can give you if you are alert to them. These records include petitions, appointments, bonds, inventories, and accounts. Once the guardian is appointed, he must be bonded, and then must make an inventory. Throughout the term of the guardianship he must make periodic accounts to the court showing all his activities in relation to his charge. Then, as the guardianship terminates, either by the child coming of age or by the death or marriage of the child, a final account (or settlement) must be filed with the court.

The information found in these records will vary, but there are a number of things that are quite consistent. For one thing, there is usually a difference in how the guardian is chosen depending upon the age of the child. The general rule is that if the infant is under fourteen the court has full authority to name his guardian (usually giving preference to relatives), but if he is fourteen or older he can nominate his own guardian subject to court approval. Sometimes just this small detail can give you a general idea of the age of the child. If the guardian was named by the parent in the parent's will (a testamentary guardian) then the matter is settled, but it will be noted in the record of the appointment. The final account filed at the termination of the guardianship is sometimes even more useful in determining the child's age because this usually took place when the child arrived at legal age. The necessity for the bonding of the guardian is often waived by the testator when he names his child(ren)'s guardian by will.

Very often you will also find apprenticeship records for orphan children, especially in the earlier periods of time.

Other information often found in guardianship records will include the names of the natural parent(s), the name of the guardian, and the name(s) of the child(ren). Sometimes descriptions of real property are also given in these records and can be useful identification aids.

Following is a document wherein the court named Samuel Jefferds as guardian of Bartholomew Jefferds, the son of yet another Samuel:

> Jeremiah Moulton Esqr Judge of the Probate of Wills & c. for and within the County of York within the Province of the Massachusetts Bay.
>
> To Samuel Jefferds of Wells in Said County yeoman Greeting. Trusting in your love and Fidelity I do by these presents, pursuant to the Power & authority to me granted in and by an Act of the General Assembly of the Said Province nominate & appoint you *to be Guardian unto Bartholomew Jefferds a Minor and Son of Samuel Jefferds late of Wells afores^d Clerk dec^d who has chosen you to the Said Trust,* with full Power & authority to ask demand Sue for recover receive & take into your Custody all & Singular Such part & portion of Estate as recrues to him in Right of his S^d Father or which by any other way or Means whatsoever doth of Right appertain or belong to him; and to manage employ & improve the Same for his best profit & advantage; and to render a plain & true Acco^t of your Guardianship upon Oath, so far as the Law will charge you therewith when you Shall be lawfully required, and pay & deliver Such & so much of the Said Estate as shall be remaining upon your Acco^t the Same being first examined & allowed by the Judge of Probates for the time being unto the Said Minor when he Shall arrive at full age or otherwise as the Said Judge or Judges by his or their Decree or Sentence pursuant to Law Shall limit & appoint.

In Testimony whereof I have hereunto Set my Hand & Seal of the Said Court of Probate. Dated at York the fifth Day of April Anno Domini 1763.

Jer: Moulton

[Emphasis added.]

This is an interesting document because it is not clear whether this appointment is based on a testamentary designation by the boy's father. It all depends on what is the antecedent of "who has chosen you . . ." If this clause referred back to "Samuel Jefferds late of Wells afores[d] Clerk dec[d]" then Samuel the guardian is a testamentary guardian. But if it refers back to "Bartholomew Jefferds" then it would tell us that Bartholomew was fourteen or older and thus nominated his own guardian subject to court approval. Very confusing, isn't it?

The LDS Family History Library has some guardianship records for some localities on microfilm, but holdings there are not extensive. Never assume that because such records are not in that library that they do not exist, even in areas for which the library has extensive microfilm collections of other records.

IV. CONCLUSION

In concluding this discussion of probate records let me re-emphasize that in most localities in America these records comprise one of our most important sources (as a group) of genealogical data and evidence. They deal with families and family relationships—the very meat of genealogy. And they exist in places and for time periods for which few other records are available.

As a genealogist you would do well to gain a thorough understanding of records which relate to the probate and administration of estates and then to use those records knowledgeably.

16

Government Land: Colonial and American

I. BACKGROUND

To begin this discussion of land records let me say at the outset that it is rare to find complete basic genealogical data in them. Land records are not the type of source which you will find filled with names, birth dates, birth places, names of parents, etc., that identify and set apart one person from all others. Certainly some of this information can be found in some land records, but it is most uncommon to find all essential genealogical evidence in land records by themselves. Land records are not a perfect genealogical source; however, as a whole they comprise one of the most important sources for research in American genealogy.

There are three factors which make land records important to the American genealogist:

1. As was said in the discussion of probate records, the early American was land-minded. Land was inexpensive and readily available, so most people owned some. Hence, in early America and, in fact, until well into the nineteenth century, the great majority of males who lived to maturity can be found in the land records. Nowhere in the modern world has this been true to the extent that it has in North America. And any record type which includes a large part of the population has to be considered important.

2. Land records exist from the very beginning of the first permanent settlements in America and are frequently one of the few sources of identifying evidence in existence for early settlement periods. Their very existence in periods when there were few other records makes them valuable far beyond what their ordinary content might suggest.

3. The third factor is unique to those land records which result from private land transactions. This is discussed in greater detail in chapter 17 but, basically, it is that the older the records the more genealogical data (especially concerning relationships) they contain. How different this is from the pattern followed by most genealogical sources!

There are many different kinds of land records arising out of many different kinds of situations. The main situations which produce useful land records are:

When a government conveys land to an individual.

When individuals deal in land, conveying it from one to another.

Land transfers in America have gone through five important phases (overlapping somewhat in time period):

1. In the beginning all land was claimed by the British Crown. Because of this the first phase was for the Crown to make grants to the colonies. Such grants (or charters) were made between 1606 (Virginia) and 1732 (Georgia).

2. The second phase was for the colonies to transfer the land to the individual colonists or settlers. This phase, of course, lasted only through the colonial period, so the time period was from about 1607 until the Revolutionary War. The various methods involved in transferring the land are discussed in some detail later.

3. The third phase began when the United States became a sovereign power after winning independence from Mother England. It involved the transfer of land from various foreign powers and from the individual states to the federal government. This began in 1780, when New York and Connecticut ceded certain lands to which they held claim to the federal government, ar ended in 1867 with the purchase of Alaska from Russia. This phase made the federal government (we the people) a land owner, thus creating *public land* (or *public domain*). The entire nation was not a part of this public domain, however. The thirteen original states plus Kentucky, Maine, Tennessee, Texas, Vermont, and, later, West Virginia retained state ownership and control of the ungranted public lands within their boundaries and are called *state-land states.*

4. The transfer of the land from the federal government to private individuals was the fourth phase. This was accomplished by various means, as discussed later in this chapter. It began with the Land Ordinance of 1785—also known as the Northwest Ordinance—and ended, for all practical purposes, with the Taylor Grazing Act of 1934.

5. The fifth phase is probably the most significant to the genealogist. It involves all land transactions between individual parties and is under the

jurisdiction of the county (most common) or some other local government entity. This phase began as soon as individuals were able to hold land (see phase two) and has continued uninterrupted to the present.

Let's look now at the details of phases two and four and see what value lies within the records when a government transfers land to private parties. We will look at phase five in chapter 17.

II. LAND FROM THE COLONIAL GOVERNMENT

A. The Land-Grant Process

When a government, under English common law, gives land to an individual it is called a land grant, and a record is made of the transaction. Title to the land so granted is transferred by the issuance of a patent or letters patent. In the colonial period of American history the individual colonies, either by authority from the Crown or by the authority which they held under their charters, could make such grants to their settlers. Such a transfer was actually a state deed of real estate from the government to the individual and was for a specified tract of land rather than for land in general. A small consideration was usually involved, sometimes in cash or commodity in the form of a *quit rent*.[1] Quit rents were not imposed in New England (except in *early* Maine and New Hampshire) nor in Dutch New York, and were completely eliminated during the Revolutionary War.

Several records resulted from early colonial land grants. Let's look now at the grant process and at those records:

1. The first step in the land-grant process was the filing of an ENTRY (sometimes called a *petition* or *application*) by the person seeking the grant. The entry was filed with the colonial governor. Though you will find some of these colonial land entries recorded, many of them were probably never considered of enough importance to make a permanent record since they had nothing to do with the actual land title.

2. Upon approval of the entry a WARRANT was issued for the land. A warrant is an order, and in this case it was a directive for the "laying-out" of the lands to be granted. It was sometimes issued directly to the applicant

---

[1] The *quit rent* was a small fee paid as a rent for a special purpose. In its true usage under feudal law it was paid on property by a freeholder in lieu of feudal services. In America some colonies set up a quit rent system as a means of buying tenure on proprietary grants. Having such rents due did not prevent one from having freehold title—as good a title as anyone else had.

by authority of the governor or the Crown, to be surrendered by him (the applicant) at the office of local land jurisdiction where the warrant was to be carried out. This procedure was not followed in all colonies but, in those where it was followed, most of the warrants were recorded and preserved at the office where they were surrendered. The applicant was ordinarily given the right to specify the land he wanted "laid out."

3. Next the land was surveyed and measured to meet the requirements of the entry and warrant, and then a PLAT (sometimes called a *survey*) of the land was made. A plat is a map of the tract, often showing its location in relation to land held by others and having an accompanying written description with metes and bounds. Many plat (or survey) books and other records of these have been preserved, but again all colonies did not follow this same procedure.

The descriptions were very specific, but quite different from the Rectangular Survey system descriptions used later in the public domain. The following description is from a plat for fifty acres made in behalf of William Smith in Giles County, Virginia, and is typical:

> 50 acres . . . assigned to him . . . in the county of Giles on the South side of East River and bounded as followeth, To wit, Beginning at a beech on the bank of the River running thence 54° W 54 poles[2] to 4 Spanish oaks on the top of a hill S 66° E 34 poles to two white oaks on the side of a hill S. 31° E 28 poles to two white oaks East 20 poles to two white oaks N 31° E 36 poles to a Sugar tree and Spruce Pine on a cleft of rocks N. 14° W 39 poles to down the clefts and crossing the River to a large Sedar tree thence up the River with the meanders thereof and binding thereon 129 poles to the beginning variation three degrees East.

4. Some colonies also issued LICENSES to land-grant applicants. A license, in this sense, was a document which granted permission to the applicant to take up certain lands—usually a specifically described and surveyed tract. The colonies that used land licenses often preserved lists of the licensees with descriptions of the lands involved.

5. Now the grantee was ready to take possession of his land and the PATENT could be issued and recorded. Through the patent, title was secured. Everything done previously had fulfillment in the issuance and recording of the patent. The patent itself was sometimes nothing more than a brief statement of confirmation; it was documentary evidence of title to land and is probably the land-grant document most often preserved.

---

[2] A pole is equivalent to a rod (16½ feet or 5½ yards).

Technically, there is no one document type which can be called a land grant. The grant was not a document but a process and often involved several documents, as already pointed out. However, it is not unusual to find documents entitled "grants." Typical of these is the "grant," in 1643, to Francis Littlefield from Sir Ferdinando Gorges, Lord Proprietor of Maine, long before the entire colony was annexed by the Massachusetts Bay Colony. You will note that in form this is little more than a deed to Littlefield from Gorges's agent and deputy governor. The document is actually a patent:

> To all to whome theise presents shall come greeting know yee that I Thomas Gorges Deputy Governor of the province of Mayne by vertue of Authority from Sr fferdinando Gorges Knight Lord Proprietor of the said province for divers good causes & considerations me thereunto moveing have In the behalfe of the said fferdinando Gorges given granted & confirmed & by theise pnts do give grant & confirme unto ffrancis Littlefield of Wells in the county of Somersett the elder ffifty Acres of Land scituate Lying & being in Wells aforesaid adioning the land of Edmond Littlefield on the Easter side thereof containing twenty poles in breadth towards the sea & soe up into the Mayne Land till ffifty acres be compleated wth all the Marsh twenty pole likewise in breadth and eight acres or thereabouts to be ground lyeing betweene the said land & the Sea wall to contayne taken in Egunquick Marsh to have & to hould the aforesaid land & all & singular the primises wth the appurtenances unto the said ffrancis Littlefield his heirs & assignes for ever to the only use & behoofe of the said ffrancis Littlefield his heires & assignes for ever more, yeilding & paying for the prmises yearely unto the said Sir fferdinando Gorges his heires & assignes two shillings & six pence on the Nine & twentieth day of September And I the said Thomas Gorges doe hereby depute Edmund Littlefield to be my lawful attorney in the behalf of the Said Sr fferdinando Gorges to enter into the prmises or into pte thereof in name of the whole & to take possesion therof & after seisin & possesion so taken to deliver possesion & seisin of the prmises unto the said ffrancis Littlefield in witness whereof I the said Thomas Gorges have hereunto sett my hand & seale the ffoureteenth Day of July Anno Dmi 1643.
>
> Tho Gorges Deputi Govrnor
>
> Sealed Signed & Delivered
> in the presence of
> Roger Guarde
> George Puddinton
>
> Veareable & quyet possession taken & given to ffrancis Littlefield of all pts & prtlls of land & marshs with the apurtenances mentioned in the Deed
>
> By me Edmund Littlefield

B. Headright Grants

One special type of grant was known as a HEADRIGHT GRANT. This was not unlike other grants except in the consideration involved. Some of the colonies, in order to attract settlers, granted land to those who paid the passage fare for those settlers to come to the colony from the Old World. One man could pay the passage for several persons (often as his indentured servants) and would thus be granted so much land (initially fifty acres) "per head"— hence the term *headright* grant. Some of the records of these grants have been published in various forms. The best known example is Mrs. Nell M. Nugent's abstracts of the Virginia headright grants between 1623 and 1732 under the title *Cavaliers and Pioneers,* 3 vols. (Vol. 1: *1623-1666,* 1934 [Baltimore: Genealogical Publishing Co., 1963 reprint]; vol. 2: *1666-1695* [Richmond: Virginia State Library, 1977]; vol. 3: *1695-1732* [Richmond: Virginia State Library, 1979].)

C. Non-Grant Transfers

All of the lands which passed from the colonies to the individual owners were not as a result of grants. Another means of transfer was by cash sale. Such sales became increasingly popular during the eighteenth century. Often persons and companies with considerable capital bought huge tracts at bargain prices. Many of these owners never personally set foot in the colonies but were content to sit back in England and collect the rents from their tenants. Also, in those colonies which were established under proprietary grants (Delaware, Maryland, Pennsylvania, the Carolinas, and early Maine and New Hampshire) the Lord Proprietors collected rents annually (through their agents or deputies), and RENT ROLLS were religiously maintained—one copy in the county and a duplicate copy for the Lord Proprietor.

During the Revolutionary War most states seized the proprietary and Crown lands and sold them along with confiscated Loyalist properties.

D. Value of Grants and Associated Records

There is a great deal of genealogical value in the records discussed here—other than just historical interest. All of them contain valuable data on names, dates, and places which can help us put wandering ancestors in specific places at specific times and can provide other useful clues essential to genealogical investigation—even clues to connections between individuals and families. Do you think there might be any connection between Francis Littlefield and Edmund Littlefield in the land grant (patent) we looked at a few moments ago?

III. AFTER THE REVOLUTION

A. Initial Legislation

After the War of Independence the state-land states continued to grant their previously ungranted lands just as in their parent colonies. There is little difference in the land-grant records of these states before and after the war.

The main difference in records after the war was more apparent elsewhere. It was due to the creation of the public domain. Making the federal government a land owner fostered a completely different brand of land record—records of transfer from the federal government (all of us) to the private individual (one of us).

As stated earlier, the enactment of the Northwest Ordinance of 1785 signaled the start of these new records. The objective of the ordinance was to get the land settled quickly and to form new states. It provided:

1. That the land should be purchased from the Indians prior to settlement.
2. That land should be surveyed and laid out in townships and sections (Rectangular Survey system, based on meridians and base lines) before settlement.
3. That the first tracts surveyed would be drawn by lot for military bounties which had been promised earlier.
4. That remaining tracts should then be offered for sale at public auction in township and section-size units.
5. That certain lands would be set aside for educational purposes.
6. That absolute (or fee simple) title would be transferred with all lands.

A second Northwest Ordinance in 1787 specifically provided that if a land holder died intestate his widow would receive one-third of the land (in fee simple) and the remainder would descend to his children in equal portions. It also provided that wills and deeds had to be duly proved and recorded within one year or would be invalid. This ordinance also made both resident and non-resident land owners subject to taxation, but exempted all government land from taxes.

Prior to 1800 the size of land tracts available for purchase put the cost of land so high that it was mostly too expensive for those without military warrants to obtain. The Harrison Land Act of 1800 reduced tract sizes and allowed purchases on credit, thus providing procedures by which individual settlers could get title to their Western holdings.

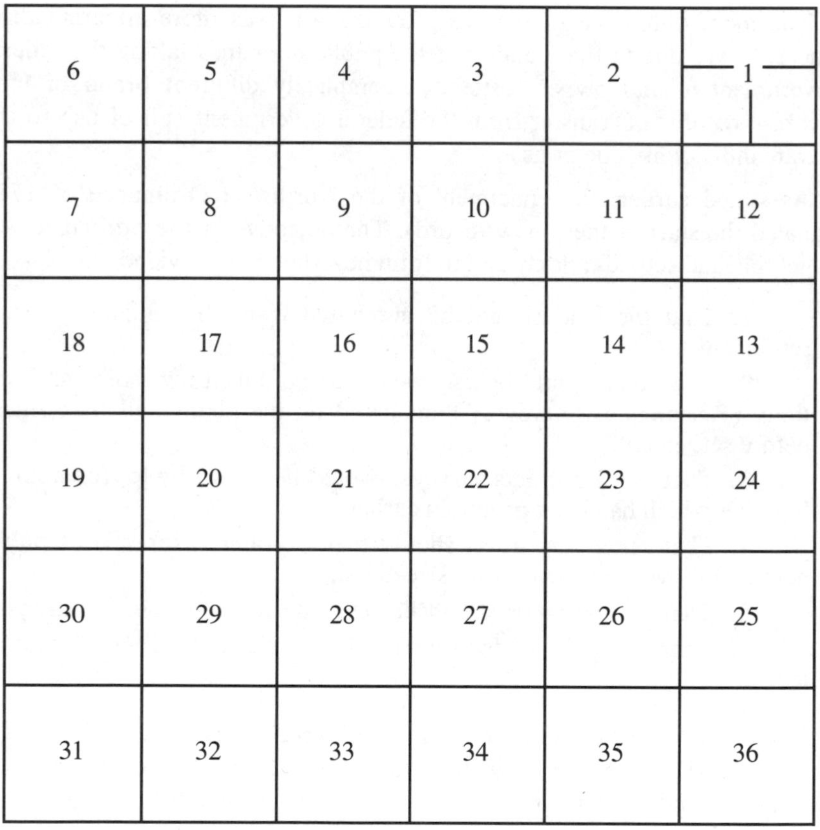

6	5	4	3	2	1
7	8	9	10	11	12
18	17	16	15	14	13
19	20	21	22	23	24
30	29	28	27	26	25
31	32	33	34	35	36

FIGURE 1—NUMBERING AND DIVIDING THE SECTIONS OF A TOWNSHIP

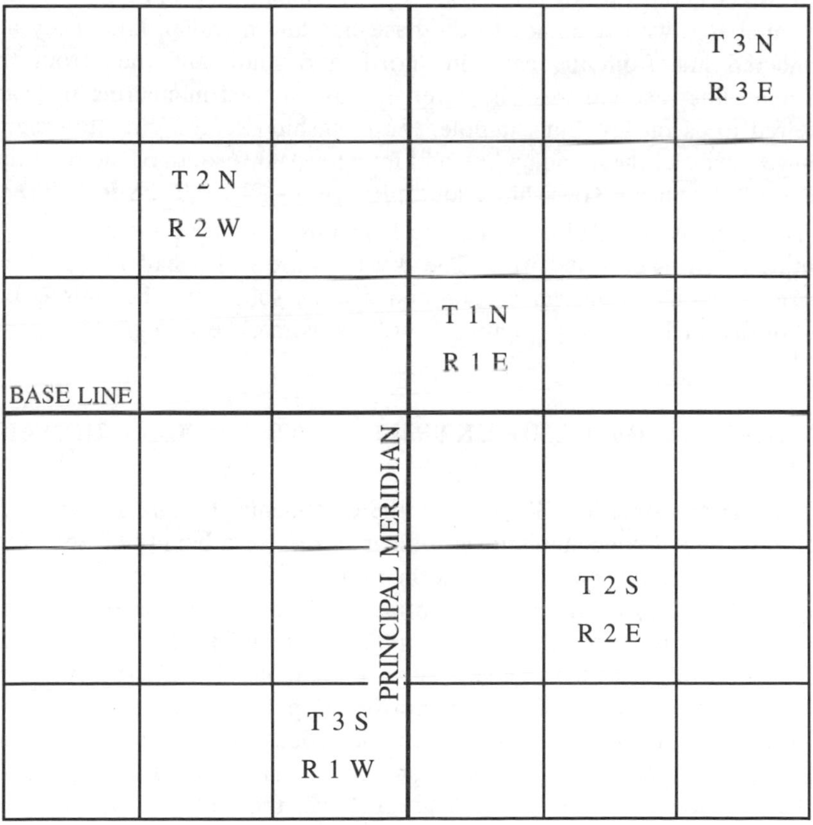

T 3 N
R 3 E

T 2 N
R 2 W

T 1 N
R 1 E

BASE LINE

PRINCIPAL MERIDIAN

T 2 S
R 2 E

T 3 S
R 1 W

FIGURE 2—NUMBERING TOWNSHIPS AND RANGES FROM THE BASE LINE AND PRINCIPAL MERIDIAN

B. Rectangular Survey System

Many have asked what the Rectangular Survey system involves, so let me explain it as simply as I can. First of all, when the public land system was adopted by Congress it was specified that two lines should be run through the territory to be surveyed—a *base line* running east and west and a *meridian line* running north and south—to intersect each other at right angles. Townships were surveyed from the point of this intersection. Each township is six miles square (thirty-six square miles) and is subdivided into thirty-six sections of 640 acres (one square mile) each, and all townships are numbered with reference to the base line and meridian line. They are numbered first from the base line north and south and then from the meridian line east and west; however, in east or west numbering they are referred to as ranges. For example, the township situated three townships (ranges) west of the meridian line and four townships south of the base line is described as being Township 4 south, Range 3 west (or T 4 S R 3 W).

The sections are divided by running lines through their centers north and south as well as east and west. The divisions are called half sections and quarter sections. A quarter section can also be subdivided but this is not part of the original survey. Figures 1 and 2 illustrate the system.

IV. HISTORY OF LAND ENTRIES IN THE PUBLIC DOMAIN

Early in the American Revolution the Continental Congress authorized each private and noncommissioned officer to receive a bounty of $50, fifty acres of land, and a new suit of clothes for his service. Various states, in addition to the promises of the Continental Congress, authorized bounty land for Revolutionary veterans and preserved tracts in their western territories to make good their pledges. A good example of this is the Western Reserve, a section of land now in northeastern Ohio, which Connecticut reserved to grant to her veterans when she ceded her western lands to the federal government in 1786. Later on, bounty land was also granted to soldiers for their service in the War of 1812, the Indian wars, and the Mexican War.

The first act passed by the U.S. government for military bounty land in the public domain was in 1812. These bounties were situated in special districts in Arkansas, Illinois, and Missouri and were non-transferrable. Four very important acts were passed between 1847 and 1856. The Act of 1847 provided for soldiers who served for at least one year in the Mexican War. The Act of 1850 extended this bounty to all War of 1812 veterans and

Indian wars veterans. The Act of 1852 extended benefits to officers as well as enlisted men and made all benefits assignable. And the Act of 1855 (amended in 1856) included every soldier (or his heirs) who had served at least fourteen days in any war since (and including) the Revolution. These acts of 1847 and later were unique because they offered bounty as a reward to soldiers who had already served, rather than as an inducement for enlistment as had been done by all previous legislation.

All of these acts provided that a warrant for a quarter section (160 acres) of land, *located on any part of the surveyed public domain,* would be granted to those who qualified. Scrip was issued which could be exchanged for title at any public land office or could be (and usually was) sold.[3]

As a result of the Northwest Ordinance of 1785 the federal government sold land in thirty-six-section townships (23,040 acres) and in sections (640 acres) for a minimum of $1 per acre payable within one year. A new ordinance in 1796 raised the minimum price to $2 per acre, and another in 1800 (the Harrison Land Act) reduced the minimum size of a sale tract to 320 acres (a half section). The 1800 ordinance also allowed for four payments over a five-year period, but this extension of credit encouraged speculation and the system proved unsuccessful.

A new ordinance in 1820 (passed because of the collapse the year before of the Western land boom) did away with credit sales, reduced the minimum size of a sale tract to eighty acres (one-eighth section), and lowered the minimum price to $1.25 per acre. Land was sold under this act until 1908.

In 1830 the first preemption act was passed by Congress, in an alliance between South and West, which allowed any settler (or squatter) on the public land who had cultivated a tract in 1829 to buy it (up to 160 acres) for $1.25 per acre. This was merely a pardon to those who had illegally settled. Once such a step had been taken it was difficult to reject demands for similar action later on, so for a time the act was renewed nearly every time Congress convened.

Following the financial panic of 1837, after much debate by government officials, a new act was passed in 1838 allowing any settler on the public domain, who was either over twenty-one or the head of a family, and who was living on the land when the act was passed and had been there for four months preceding the act, to have all the benefits granted in the Act of 1830. Preemption became a major issue in the Presidential campaign of 1840 (Harrison over Van Buren) and the act was again renewed by Congress.

---

[3] Roy M. Robbins, *Our Landed Heritage: The Public Domain 1776-1936* (Lincoln, NE: University of Nebraska Press, 1962), pp. 156-157.

In 1841 a permanent preemption act was passed which allowed anyone who was the head of a family (including widows) or over twenty-one, and who was a U.S. citizen or had declared intention to become one,[4] to stake a claim on any tract up to 160 acres and then buy it from the government for $1.25 per acre. Certain lands, including reservations, school lands, specific Indian lands, land already sectioned for town sites, mineral and saline lands, land within incorporated towns, and lands already granted for various reasons, were not open to preemption.

In 1854 another act made public land available for 12½ cents per acre if it had been on the market for thirty years, and in some remote areas other measures were taken to lure settlers. In the territories of Florida, New Mexico, Oregon, and Washington *donation land grants* were given by the federal government to those who would settle there. East Florida was extended this privilege in 1842 to attract men to protect the territory, and any man over eighteen or the head of a family who took up permanent residence was entitled to 160 acres of free land.

The next donation land act passed Congress in 1850 for the Oregon Territory. This act granted a "donation" of free land—320 acres to each single man and 640 acres to each married man—to anyone who had settled on the land before December 1 of that year. This act required four years of continued residence on the land and cultivation thereof in order to gain title, but in 1853 the residence requirement was cut in half. In 1854 another act extended the same donation land benefits to the Washington Territory which had been divided off the year previous. Both acts expired in December 1855.

On July 22, 1854, just three days after passage of the Washington Donation Land Act, donation privileges were extended to the New Mexico Territory. This act (10 Stat. 208) provided that donation claims could be changed to cash purchases for $1.25 per acre. The New Mexico act did not expire until 1883.

In essence, these donation land experiments were a limited trial of the principle of homesteading before the latter became a national policy.[5]

After the secession of the Southern states, which had opposed the homestead principle, cash sales and preemptions were largely replaced by *homesteads*. Under the Homestead Act of 1862 a settler could gain title to public lands without monetary consideration (except for a small filing fee) by meeting a five-year residency requirement and cultivating and improving the land. Any person who met the age and citizenship requirements of the

---

[4] Aliens could make claims under all earlier preemption acts.

[5] Robbins, pp. 153-154.

Preemption Act of 1841 could homestead up to 160 acres (quarter section) of public land. However, this law did not completely eliminate either direct cash sales or preemptions.

A provision in the Homestead Act allowed the homesteader to commute his homestead entry to a cash entry for $1.25 per acre after six months' residence and improvement of the land, if he desired. Union Army and Navy veterans (those who had served fourteen or more days during war time) were considered automatically to meet the age requirement. Those who had borne arms against the government or had given aid to its enemies were excluded, but only until January 1, 1867.

Many changes were made by various bills in Congress, and an act which passed in 1872 made it possible for all Civil War veterans with at least ninety days' service to apply that service, up to four years, toward the five-year homestead residency requirement.

Acts passed in 1879 and 1880 made it possible to commute a preemption claim to a homestead claim and vice versa, should the claimant so desire. The privileges and guarantees were the same. Preemption was finally repealed by Congress in 1891 with the provision that claims initiated before passage of the repeal could be completed.

Later bills provided for larger homesteads (320 acres) in the West on certain non-irrigable lands (Act of 1909) and for three-year homesteads (Act of 1912). Stock raising—primarily grazing—homesteads of 640 acres were specified in the Act of 1916.

Another type of grant was the *Private Land Claim.* This was merely an acknowledgement of title by the federal government to those who owned land or had been granted land by a foreign government before the U.S. became sovereign in the area concerned. These claims covered a broad period of time and extensive portions of the public domain—from Missouri to California to Wisconsin to Alabama. Portions of fifteen states were involved.

The Taylor Grazing Act of 1934, as amended, closed most of the public domain to entry, and grazing lands were left to be held by public ownership under control of the Interior Department; and in 1935, by Presidential order, all public lands were essentially closed to individual entry.

V. LAND ENTRY RECORDS FROM THE PUBLIC DOMAIN

As might be expected, most records of the land entries described here have been preserved. They were housed in the General Land Office and, when that office was discontinued, the records were sent to the National Archives. Most land entry records for the public domain are in this collection, but a few are still in land offices in the individual states.

The records in the National Archives are as follows:

A. Credit Entry Files

As indicated earlier, most of the land sold by the federal government between the passage of the Harrison Land Act of 1800 and the Act of 1820 was on five years' credit for a minimum of $2 per acre. The Credit Entry Final Certificates which were issued on all completed purchases are the most important records in this file, but you will also find an occasional Assignment filed with the certificates, along with other records.

All final certificates filed before the Act of 1820 are called "Credit Prior Certificates," and those filed after that date (under relief legislation) by those who had begun payment before the act was passed, but had not finished, are called "Credit Under Certificates."

Both types of final certificates normally show:

> the name of the entryman; the place of his residence as given at the time of purchase; the date of the purchase; the number of acres in the tract; the description of the tract in terms of subdivision, section, township and range; a summary of the payments made; and a citation to the record copy of the patent in the Bureau of Land Management.[6]

In addition to the records in the National Archives, the Bureau of Land Management in Washington, D.C., has five volumes of indexes for tract books from the Ohio land offices at Canton (Wooster), Chillicothe, Cincinnati, Marietta and Zanesville, and Steubenville.[7]

B. Cash Entry Files

Beginning with the Act of 1820 most land sold by the government was for cash at a minimum of $1.25 per acre. The Cash Entry Files are arranged at the National Archives under the names of the individual land offices, but there is a master card index to the cash entries for Alabama, Alaska, Arizona, Florida, Louisiana, Nevada, and Utah.

---

[6] Meredith B. Colket, Jr., and Frank E. Bridgers, *Guide to Genealogical Records in the National Archives* (Washington, DC: The National Archives, 1964), p. 106.

[7] *Ibid.*, p. 106.

An individual file contains an application for a tract, a receipt for money, and a Final Certificate which authorized the claimant to secure a patent. In cases where the land was claimed by preemption, the preemption proof may also be in the file. If the tract was entered as a homestead but commuted to a cash entry, the Homestead Entry File is included.

Ordinarily the most valuable document in a Cash Entry File is the Final Certificate. It:

> shows the name of the entryman; the place of his residence given at the time of the purchase; the description of the tract in terms of subdivision, section, township, and range; the number of acres in the tract, the date of the patent; and the volume and page of the record copy of the patent in the Bureau of Land Management . . . The testimony of claimant in a preemption proof shows the name of the claimant, his age, his citizenship, the date of his entry on the tract, the number and relationship of members of his household, and the nature of the improvements on the tract.[8]

All preemption entries were for cash and are therefore in these files. Cash Entry Files cover the period from 1820 to 1908, but the records of all land offices do not cover the entire period as many were opened at much later dates.

The Illinois State Archives in Springfield has a computerized index to over 550,000 public land sales in the state. The index makes possible easy location of the land on a state map. And for the price of the photocopies the Archives will provide copies of the printout and the map. The index includes the following information:

> Name of purchaser and record ID number, type of sale, description of land purchased, number of acres, price per acre, total price, male or female purchaser, date of purchase, county or state of residence of purchaser, and volume and page of original land record.[9]

C. Donation Entry Files

The Florida Donation files are mainly for 1842 through 1850 and are of varying degrees of completeness, depending on the extent to which title was perfected in the land. If the claimant completed the five-year residency requirement, his file—a complete one—contains a Permit to Settle, an Application for a patent, a Report by the land agent, and a Final Certificate

[8] *Ibid.*, p. 106.

[9] *Newsletter,* Chicago Genealogical Society, July/August 1982.

authorizing him to obtain a patent. All files that include Final Certificates are indexed in a master card index.

Regarding the information in these records, Colket and Bridgers state:

> A permit to settle shows the name of the applicant, his marital status, the month and year he became a resident of Florida, and a description of the land in terms of subdivision, section, township, and range. An application for a patent shows the name of the applicant, a description of the land, the date of the patent, and the volume and page number of the recorded copy of the patent in the Bureau of Land Management.[10]

The Donation Entry Files for Oregon and Washington are filed separately in the National Archives, and those for each state are divided into two series —one for completed entries and one for those not completed. Both the Oregon and Washington files are indexed. An alphabetical list of the Oregon claims has also been published serially in the *Genealogical Forum of Portland, Oregon* under the title of "Index to Oregon Donation Land Claims."

All completed files contain a Notification on the Settlement of Public Land and a Donation Certificate:

> [A] notification on the settlement of public land shows the description of the land in terms of subdivision, section, township, and range; the name of the entryman; the place of his residence at the time of notification; his citizenship; the date and place of his birth; and, if married, the given name of his wife and their date and place of marriage. A donation certificate shows the name of the entryman, the place of his residence, the description of the land, the date of the patent, and the volume and page number of the recorded copy in the Bureau of Land Management.[11]

Registers of the donation notifications and entries between 1855 and 1871 for New Mexico are at the National Archives Field Branch in Denver, from the land offices in Clayton, Folsom, Fort Sumner, LaMesilla, Las Cruces, Roswell, Santa Fe, and Tucumcari.[12]

D. Military Bounty Land Entries

Also in the National Archives are records of both the Virginia and the U.S. bounty land warrants surrendered at the various land offices for acreage in

---

[10] Colket and Bridgers, p. 107.

[11] *Ibid.*, p. 108.

[12] *Guide to Genealogical Research in the National Archives,* rev. ed. (Washington, DC: The National Archives, 1983), p. 225.

the public domain or for scrip certificates which could be used to purchase land. All except the War of 1812 warrants (which limited the location to military reservations in Illinois, Arkansas, and Missouri) were assignable, and most were assigned (i.e., sold) by the veterans who received them. The warrants could be exchanged for land (by scrip) virtually anywhere in the public domain.

The Virginia military bounty land warrants are indexed in one manuscript volume at the National Archives, entitled "Virginia Military Warrants, Continental Line, Alphabetical Index to Warrantees (vol. 30)." The names of these warrantees have also been copied onto cards which have been filed in a consolidated bounty land warrant index. The names are also in Gaius M. Brumbaugh, *Revolutionary War Records,* Vol. I (the only one published), 1936 (Baltimore: Genealogical Publishing Co., 1967 reprint), pp. 323-525.

These Virginia bounty land warrant records themselves show:

> such information as the name of the warrantee; the name of the patentee; the location of the land in terms of lot, quarter section, township and range; and the date of the patent. Some files show the dates and places of death of the warrantees, the names of their heirs and the places of their residence.[13]

Because of sales (or assignments) the warrantee and the patentee were often different persons, and there is an index to patentees in a manuscript volume at the National Archives entitled "Virginia Military Land Patent Index (vol. 34)." This index also tells the name of the warrantee and the location of the entry file, in addition to the name of the patentee.

As you know, much of Kentucky was settled as a result of Revolutionary War bounty land warrants from the Virginia Line, and Willard R. Jillson, *Old Kentucky Entries and Deeds,* 1926 (Baltimore: Genealogical Publishing Co., 1969 reprint), pp. 313-392, is a record of these warrants.

With regard to grants in the Virginia Military District of Ohio I would also mention two important works:

> Smith, Clifford Neal. *The Federal Land Series,* Vol. IV, Parts I and II. Chicago: American Library Association, 1982—.
>
> Smith, Alma Aicholtz. *The Virginia Military Surveys of Clermont and Hamilton Counties, Ohio, 1787-1849.* Cincinnati: The author, 1985.

The latter is superior to the first because it contains much more complete information, including the names of those who ultimately obtained the

[13] Colket and Bridgers, pp. 110-111.

patents or grants to that land from the federal government. While C. N. Smith's work lists the surveys, Mrs. A. A. Smith gives both surveys and patents/grants, plus numerous excellent maps and other useful data. The absence of the grant information in Mr. Smith's work is significant because many of those for whom the surveys were made never actually went west and took up the land.

While Virginia did give grants in her Kentucky Military District, she did not do so in the Virginia Military District of Ohio. Why not? Because she had ceded all of her land holdings in the Northwest Territory (north and west of the Ohio River) to the United States in 1784. Only the President of the United States gave patents/grants to this land.

Bounty land entries (other than the Virginia warrants) are filed and indexed in various series at the National Archives. They are discussed in some detail in chapters 22 and 23. Let it suffice here to mention briefly those warrants issued for unspecified public land as a result of the various Congressional acts between 1847 and 1855. (These acts, as mentioned earlier, were different from all prior legislative acts in that they were passed to reward those who had already served rather than to induce enlistment.) Nearly all of these warrants were sold by their recipients.

Most of the files contain no genealogical data about the warrantee except in the unlikely case that he died while still in possession of the warrant. In such an instance the file would contain the names and places of residence of his heirs. All patentees are identified and the location of the land is shown. The files are arranged by year of the basic Congressional act, thereunder by the number of acres awarded, and then chronologically by warrant number. *Applications* for these bounty land warrants are arranged alphabetically in two series at the National Archives—one series for those with Revolutionary War service and one for those with later service. Locating the application enables you to locate the applicant's file.[14]

No bounty land warrants were issued after passage of the Homestead Act in 1862. Veterans were instead given special consideration under the various homestead acts. Additional detail about bounty land warrant records is found in chapter 8 of *Guide to Genealogical Research in the National Archives,* published in 1983 (rev. ed.) by the National Archives Trust Fund Board.

E. Homestead Entry Files

The Homestead Entry papers are filed in the National Archives and the National Archives Field Branches under the names of the individual land

[14]*Ibid.*, pp. 90, 115.

offices, usually in two separate series—one series for those who completed their entries and the other for those who did not. These files cover 1863 to 1908. Chapter 15 of *Guide to Genealogical Research in the National Archives* (pages 222 and 225) tells which homestead records—as well as other land records—are in the National Archives Field Branches. A completed file includes:

> the homestead application, the certificate of publication of intention to make a claim, the homestead proof consisting of two witnesses and the testimony of the claimant, and the final certificate authorizing the claimant to obtain a patent; and also, when appropriate, a copy of naturalization proceedings or a copy of a Union veteran's discharge certificate.[15]

Regarding the information contained in these records, Colket and Bridgers further explain:

> A homestead application shows the name of the entryman, the place of his residence at the time of application, the description of the tract, and number of acres in the tract. The testimony of claimant on a homestead proof shows a description of the tract; the name, age, and post office address of the claimant; the date the patent was issued, and the volume and page number of the recorded copy of the patent in the Bureau of Land Management . . . A copy of naturalization proceedings relating to a naturalized citizen or an alien who had declared his intention of becoming a citizen shows such information as the name of the immigrant, the date and port of his arrival, and the place of his birth.[16]

Homestead entries which were commuted to cash entries are in the Cash Entry Files and include all previously completed homestead papers.

F. Private Land Claim Entries

The National Archives has records of private land claims relating to parts of fifteen states: Illinois, Indiana, Michigan, and Wisconsin (all originally in the Northwest Territory); Alabama and Mississippi (both originally in the Mississippi Territory); Louisiana and the Missouri Territory states of Arkansas, Iowa, and Missouri (all originally part of the Louisiana Purchase); Florida (originally the Florida Cession from Spain); and Arizona,

---

[15] *Ibid.*, p. 108.
[16] *Ibid.*, p. 108.

California, Colorado, and New Mexico (states in and adjacent to the southwestern territory ceded to the U.S. by Mexico).[17]

The records arising out of various private land claims vary with both time period and territory. Some of the available records include certificates of survey, surveyors' reports, Congressional reports, board of commissioners' reports, journals, claims papers, certificates of confirmation, and maps. Many of these records are indexed.

> Genealogical information in the claims varies. Some claims mention only the name of the claimant and the location of the land; others show such additional information about the claimant as place of residence at the time the claim was made and the names of relatives, both living and dead. Often there is more information about heirs than about the original claimant.[18]

G. Land Entries 1908-73

Land entry records between July 1, 1908 and May 16, 1973 are filed in the National Archives in one numerical series, according to patent number, regardless of the entry type. There are two card indexes: One is an alphabetical index to applicants which tells land office and serial application number. The other, by land office, is to the serial application numbers. It gives the patent numbers assigned to perfected patents. Concerning the content of the individual files, the following information is given in the *Guide to Genealogical Research in the National Archives:*

> Each file shows the name of the patentee, place of residence, a description of the tract (subdivision, section, township, and range), date of the patent, and number of the file, which is also the number of the record copy of the patent in the Bureau of Land Management. The type of land entry determines the nature of additional information in the file.
>
> Files relating to land entries that were canceled, relinquished, or rejected during this period have been retained in the legal custody of the Bureau of Land Management and are stored in the record center sections of the various Federal Archives and Records Centers [the National Archives Field Branches].[19]

---

[17] *Ibid.*, pp. 116-117.

[18] *Guide to Genealogical Research in the National Archives*, rev. ed., p. 222.

[19] *Ibid.*, p. 217.

VI. LAND PATENTS FROM THE BLM

In 1989 the Bureau of Land Management, with some project funding from the Department of Energy, began a project to computerize on compact disks, by means of optical scanning, all of the land patents in the BLM for the states east of the Mississippi River. The project began with the patents for the public lands in Arkansas, that part of the project being completed in January of 1990. The records are indexed in various ways and enhanced copies of the patents themselves can be retrieved and printed almost instantly.

The BLM is anxious to build a genealogical index into its system in order to facilitate greater use by genealogists. They are working with the LDS Family History Library to provide space in each record (if the library is willing) to insert the library's Ancestral File number. The numbers could be inserted later by library volunteers or other genealogists as the identities of the patentees are verified.

If adequate support for the project from Congressional leaders is forthcoming, the BLM anticipates that the records for the Western States can also be included, as well as local land records. The project has some exciting possibilities, and genealogists should watch it with interest.

VII. TEXAS

Earlier in this chapter I mentioned that Texas is not in the public domain even though it has no connection with the original states. At the time Texas was annexed in 1845 Texans considered themselves independent, though Mexico did not agree. (After the battle of San Jacinto in April 1836, Mexico had no actual control over Texas though such was never admitted.) Because of the unique situation of annexing an independent republic, special agreements were made in regard to the control of public land and the state's responsibility for her own debts.

Prior to the time when Texas entered the Union she proposed that the U.S. pay her $10,000,000 public debt in return for title to her public lands. The Congress rejected this arrangement on two occasions. The third time annexation came before Congress, Texas agreed to assume responsibility for her own public debt if she could retain title to her public land. This proposal was accepted as the condition of annexation.[20]

[20] Letter from Jerry Sadler, Commissioner of Texas General Land Office, Austin, February 18, 1969.

To help you appreciate the situation of Texas land, let's look at her land history. In 1820 Moses Austin left Missouri for Texas where he made an agreement with the Texas governor that he could bring 300 families into the republic. He died shortly after arriving back in the U.S. and left his son, Stephen F. Austin, to fulfill the agreement.

Young Austin brought the first settlers into the Brazos Valley in December 1821 only to learn that his father's agreement with the governor needed also to be ratified by the Mexican Congress. This was not finally achieved until 1823. Under the agreement Austin allowed each of the 300 families one *labor* (177 acres) for farming and seventy-four labors (13,098 acres) for stock raising. This made one *sitio* or one *square league* (13,275 acres) for each settler. He charged only 12½ cents per acre to cover expenses of administration and settlement.

By September 1824 there were 272 families who had received grants from Austin, and at about the same time he was given permission to bring another 300 families from the United States.

In March 1825 Mexico passed a Colonization Act under which it contracted *empresarios* to bring in families who, upon coming, would receive a *league* of land (4,428 acres) by paying $30 in three installments. If an *empresario* brought in 100 families he would be entitled to five leagues of grazing land and five labors of farming land for himself. However, Austin's colonies still proved the more popular; the *empresarios* were really no competition.

Most of the pioneers coming into Texas were Americans, chiefly from Missouri, Tennessee, and Kentucky. By 1830 there were some 20,000 Americans in Texas.

Later, after the battle of San Jacinto, when America was recovering from the financial crash of 1837, the Republic of Texas offered every family that would settle in her boundaries 1,280 acres of free land. This gift proved very popular despite unsettled conditions and threats from Mexico. Hence Texas grew rapidly in population as she continued to grant her land under this liberal policy, a policy which continued even after annexation.

All of these Texas land grant records are filed at the State Land Office in Austin.

VIII. THE *AMERICAN STATE PAPERS*

This may be a good place to make some observations concerning the *American State Papers*. These consist of nine classes, comprising thirty-eight volumes, of public documents from the legislative and executive branches of the United States government. Among them are eight volumes (in class eight) relating to the public lands and containing references to approximately 50,000 persons who obtained land from the federal government through one means or another between 1789 and 1887. And not only are individuals' land claims included, but claims of the heirs. Each volume is indexed in the back, but the indexes are not to be trusted.

The *American State Papers* are rare because of limited publication, but many large libraries have copies in microform. A computerized index to these eight public land volumes and an additional ninth volume on claims (class nine) was published in 1972 in a work entitled *Grassroots of America.*[21]

IX. OTHER STATE-LAND STATES

Just because the land in the thirteen original states, and a few others closely allied thereto, was not placed in the public domain is no indication that all available land in those states had already been granted. Many of these states—especially the newer ones—had considerable ungranted lands. The individual states, however, rather than the federal government, were in exclusive control of those lands.

There were many land grants issued by these states. In fact the process was not essentially different from what it had been in the colonies. So far as records are concerned the procedure varied from one colony to another (or from one state to another). Some, both before and after the Revolution, preserved land-grant records with the deeds and other local land records. Others—such as Georgia, Maryland, Massachusetts, Pennsylvania, Tennessee, and Virginia—kept their land-grant records in state land offices.

---

[21] Phillip W. McMullen (comp.), *Grassroots of America* (Salt Lake City: Gendex Corp., 1972).

17

Local Land Records

Local land records are those which result from the fifth phase of American land transfer as defined in the last chapter. They are the records of land transactions between individual parties under the jurisdiction of a local governmental unit, most often the county. As you use the records of such transactions the first two basic terms you will need to know are GRANTOR and GRANTEE. In a land conveyance the seller is called the grantor and the buyer is called the grantee.

I. LAND TITLES

Let's briefly examine the nature of land titles as a basis for better understanding land records. Earlier chapters mentioned many of the terms related to land titles, but we need to look at them again purely in the context of land records.

Land, together with whatever is erected on it or affixed to it, is called REAL PROPERTY, and the best title a person can hold in real property is called FEE SIMPLE. In America fee simple has always meant that the estate would potentially last forever and descend to one's heirs if he died intestate, or could be devised by will, or that the owner could sell it (or any part of it) any time he chose to do so and could find an interested buyer. The chief obstacles preventing fee simple title from being absolute ownership are:

1. The provisions in our land law which say that an estate will escheat (see chapter 13) to the state when there are no heirs. This is a carry-over from feudal law.

2. The right of eminent domain, which gives the government the right to take private lands for public purposes upon payment of just compensation.

There are many kinds of estates less absolute than fee simple, and most of these, with some limitations, can also be sold by the title holder and sometimes be left to his heirs or devisees. These include LIFE ESTATES, ESTATES IN TAIL (or FEE TAIL), ESTATES UPON CONDITION, ESTATES FOR YEARS, and ESTATES FROM YEAR TO YEAR (or ESTATES AT WILL), plus a few others. All of these types of estates represent ownership which is less than absolute. Though some give greater portions of the complete title than others, none is fee simple except certain estates upon condition.

A LIFE ESTATE merely entitles the holder to possess title to the property during the period of his own life or the life of some other specified person (life estate *per autre vie*). A dower estate is a life estate, but I will say more about this later. We also find some persons selling their lands in their old age, usually to their children or other relatives, and preserving a life estate for themselves. Thus they dispose of the fee simple estate before their deaths without being uprooted from the "old homestead." After the death which terminates a life estate, the future interest which has been created becomes a present possessory interest in fee simple.

In ESTATE IN TAIL the ownership is not absolute because of the limitation on the holder that he cannot convey more than a life estate (his own life) in the property and, upon his death, it will descend to some particular class of heir only, usually the heirs of his body (forever). Most estates in tail are created by wills, but not all of them. Should the line and the posterity entitled to tail cease, the estate terminates and the property title reverts (in fee simple) to the estate from which it was created. Tails can be either general, special, male, or female. Today they are not legal in most states because they make land inalienable (it cannot be bought and sold). If the language of an instrument created an estate in tail, different jurisdictions would react in different ways.

An ESTATE UPON CONDITION is based upon the happening of some uncertain event. It can be created by such an event (and may be fee simple), it can be enlarged (again perhaps fee simple), or it can be terminated. The condition must be valid and must not violate good morals or public policy. Many states have put time limits on conditions which cause forfeiture because the law abhors forfeitures, for they too tend to make land inalienable.

Many estates upon condition are created by wills. An example of such an estate is provided by the provision which a man makes in his will to provide for his widow by leaving her certain lands "during the space of her widowhood." If she should remarry, her estate in that land would terminate and title would revert to the estate from which it came, that of the deceased husband (unless such a provision is ruled to be against public policy).

An ESTATE FOR YEARS usually exists by virtue of a lease. It exists by contract for a definite and specified time period, the length of which is not significant. Such an estate usually exists and continues by virtue of the payment of an interest or rent, but not always.

Closely related to an estate for years is an ESTATE FROM YEAR TO YEAR. It extends for an unspecified period upon the *mutual agreement* of the parties. It is sometimes referred to as an ESTATE AT WILL and is very common. The period may be less than a year—even from week to week or from month to month, depending on how rent is reserved.

All of the above types of estates are less than fee simple, except as stated, and can affect the records which are kept. Let's look now at some of the record types that have arisen out of private land ownership.

II. TYPES OF LAND RECORDS

Some of the records listed here will not be new to you, or even new to our discussion; many were introduced when we discussed probate records. However, as mentioned at that time, land and probate records are generally recorded in different places. I have duplicated to clarify and not to confuse, so don't be confused.

The records are as follows:

ABSTRACT OF TITLE: A condensed history of the title to a parcel of real estate. It should include a summary of every conveyance of title to the property, all restrictions and express easements, and a statement of all liens or charges against it. It will often include maps, plats, and other aids. In most localities abstract offices have been set up by individuals or corporations who will, for a fee, furnish an abstract of the title to any real estate in the jurisdiction. In some places the accuracy of the abstracts is guaranteed; in other places it is not. Though the abstract is not a complete record, it can serve as an (expensive) index to the original records. The description of the land (by subdivision, section, township, and range) is essential in locating a title at the various title and abstract offices because tract indexing is used. (See the discussion on indexes at the end of this chapter.)

ACKNOWLEDGEMENT: A formal statement at the end of an instrument, especially a deed, after the signature of the person(s) who executed the instrument—the grantor(s)—where an authorized official, such as a notary public, certifies that the person(s) who executed the instrument declared to him that he (they) signed the instrument and that it was his (their) own free act and deed. Sometimes called *certificate.*

AFFIDAVIT: A written statement of facts, which is made voluntarily and affirmed by the oath of the party making it. The oath is made before some party legally authorized to administer it. It can be used as evidence. See also DEPOSITION.

AGREEMENT: There are various things upon which two (or more) parties can agree which might be recorded in land records. The term simply implies that the parties have given mutual assent to a particular matter which might change some of their rights or obligations. A typical example might be the agreement made between George Litzinger and his wife Elizabeth (of the first part) and John Boardley and Isaac Perryman (second part) in Baltimore County, Maryland, on March 31, 1802. They signed an agreement which would:

> keep and leave open an alley on the west side of the brick house now occupied by the said Boardley of the width of three feet and running back of the depth of thirty six feet from King Tamany street which alley shall be for the use and benefit of the said parties their heirs or assigns provided always and . . . that the said George Litzinger and Elizabeth his wife their heirs or assigns shall have the privilege and benefit of building over the said alley against the west wall of the said brick house at least thirteen feet from the surface of the earth without the least trouble or interruption of the said Perryman and Boardley their heirs or assigns.

An agreement is similar to a contract (q.v.) yet the term has broader application.

ANTENUPTIAL CONTRACT: This is a contract which a man and his bride-to-be execute wherein the property rights of one or the other or both are delineated. Such agreements are usually made prior to a second marriage and are often for the purpose of securing certain properties for the children of the former union(s), though this is not always the case. So far as I know, these settlements are found in the records of most states but are especially prevalent in states with community property laws and were also common among the Dutch in New Netherland. The following antenuptial contract provides for the inheritance rights of the bride-to-be and her daughter by a former marriage:

> This indenture made this thirteenth day of June . . . one thousand eight hundred and one between Patrick Bennet of . . . Baltimore . . . Maryland of the one part Elizabeth McCay of the same place . . . of the second part and James Bennet of the same place . . . of the third part WHEREAS a marriage is agreed upon . . . to be shortly . . . solemnised between . . . Patrick Bennet and Elizabeth McCay Now

this indenture WITNESSETH that . . . Patrick Bennet in consideration of the . . . intended marriage and of the personal estate which . . . Elizabeth McCay stands possessed of and which . . . Patrick Bennet will be entitled to and also for . . . the sum of five shillings . . . to him . . . paid by James Bennet . . . before the sealing . . . of these presents the receipt whereof is hereby acknowledged hath . . . transferred and set over . . . unto . . . James Bennet . . . all that . . . parcel of ground . . . on Fells Point . . . plat . . . number two . . . TO HAVE AND TO HOLD the said . . . parcel of ground . . . unto James Bennet . . . until said marriage shall take effect . . . and immediately after the solomnization thereof to the use of Patrick Bennet . . . during his natural life and from immediately after the decease of . . . Patrick Bennet in case . . . Elizabeth McCay shall survive him to the use of . . . Elizabeth . . . in the name of a Jointure[1] . . . and will . . . pay . . . unto Ann Alley the daughter of . . . Elizabeth McCay by a former marriage . . . five hundred dollars . . . at . . . the age of twenty one years or day of marriage . . . and the said Elizabeth McCay doth . . . agree . . . to accept . . . the provision before made for her . . . for her Jointure in lieu . . . of all such dower . . . at common law which she . . . might . . . be entitled to out of . . . any freehold lands whereof . . . Patrick Benet . . . shall be seized . . . in case . . . Patrick shall . . . die intestate.

These are also called antenuptial agreements, antenuptial settlements, and marriage settlements. (Chapter 15 has further discussion.)

ASSIGNMENT: In most cases the assignments you will find recorded in land-record books have to do with the assignment of certain property rights such as the unexpired term of a lease or a life estate, but also include the assignment of all types of property rights. It is not uncommon to see trusts, trust deeds, and mortgages involved in assignments.

BILL OF SALE: A bill of sale is a statement indicating a transfer of ownership by sale, and it is not ordinarily a land record. However, bills of sale, especially those involving the buying and selling of slaves, were frequently recorded in the land-record books.

CERTIFICATE: See ACKNOWLEDGEMENT.

CONTRACT: A contract is a reciprocal agreement made between two or more persons to do something for their mutual benefit. The law recognizes a duty therein and it is enforceable under the law. A contract for the sale of land is made prior to the making of the deed and is com-

[1] *Jointure* is an estate provided for the wife on the death of her husband in lieu of dower. In establishing it the husband secures for his wife a freehold estate to take effect upon his decease and to continue at least during her life (again, a life estate but not limited to one-third of the real property as is dower).

pletely fulfilled with the delivery of the deed on the one hand and the payment of the consideration on the other. In such a contract the seller is called the vendor and the buyer is called the vendee. These documents are seldom recorded.

CONVEYANCE: See DEED.

DEED: The deed (or conveyance) is the document of our main consideration in a study of local land records. It is the document by which title in real property is transferred from one party to another. There are different types of deeds but the most common type is the warranty deed (q.v.), which is ordinarily a *deed in fee* because it conveys a fee simple title. It is usually referred to simply as a *deed* and that is how I shall refer to it. Various types of deeds are discussed separately under their various titles. (Note especially WARRANTY DEED and QUITCLAIM DEED.)

DEED IN TRUST: See TRUST DEED.

DEED OF DIVISION: See PARTITION.

DEED OF GIFT: See GIFT DEED.

DEED OF PARTITION: See PARTITION.

DEED OF RELEASE: This is a document which is executed by a lien holder once the lien, mortgage (deed of trust in many states), or other encumbrances have been paid. It returns the complete title to its owner. This is sometimes called a release (q.v.), but it is usually quite different from the document ordinarily referred to as a release.

DEED OF TRUST: See TRUST DEED.

DEPOSITION: I mentioned depositions under probate records, but let me define the term again. A deposition is the written testimony or declaration of a witness to a certain matter. Such a testimony is not taken in open court but may be used there as evidence (under certain conditions) and must be under oath and properly authenticated by the court official (usually the attorney) in charge of taking it. Depositions were often taken to verify land titles and to help settle matters of land dispute because boundary markers were often removed or destroyed and surveys were sometimes inaccurate or based on incorrect reference points. The following document, purporting to be a deposition, but which could more properly be called an affidavit (q.v.), was one of several relating to the same matter. It is typical of those you might find recorded with the local land records:

> A deposition of Nicholas Frost aged about Sixty yeares, or thereabouts, This deponent Sayth that about sixteen or seaventeen yeares since, Thomas Crockett had possession of a necke of Land in Spruse Cricke, lying on the North Side of the cricke, against the field, he now hath. His possession was had by falling tymber & clearing ground, and made preparation to build an house upon the Sd Land,

& further Saith not, Taken upon oath before me Nicholas Shapleigh this 30th of the 4th 1658.

DIVISION: See PARTITION.

DOWER RELEASE: See RELEASE OF DOWER.

GIFT DEED: This is a deed whereby real property is transferred without normal consideration. Usually such deeds transfer real estate from a parent to his offspring, but there is no rule about that. The consideration is often stated as: "for the natural love and affection which I bear towards my son ________ and for other valuable consideration." An example follows:

Know all men by these presents, that I Richard Kirle of Kittery in the County of Yorke, as well for my natural affection & parentall Love wch I bear to my well beloved Son in law, Samuell Knight of Sd Towne & County, as allso for diverse others good Causes & Considerations, me at present especially moving, have freely given & granted, & by these presents do give & grant to sd Samuell Knight Six Acres of Land being part of a Town Grant of fiveteen Acres of Land, lying & being in Kittery, sd Knight Part shall begin at the Great Cove, & so run sixty eight Pole next to the Land, which is now Remonicks Land, and such breadth, as makes up the forementioned Summ of Acres - To have & to hold all & singular the sd six Acres of Land to sd Knight, his Heires, Executors, Administrators, & Assignes forever to their own proper Use & Behoof, freely and Quietly without any matter of Challenge or claim, or demand, of me the sd Kirle, or of any other person or persons wtsoever for me, in my name, by my cause, meanes, or procurement, and without any money or other thing to be yeilded and paid, unto me sd Kirle, my Heires, Executors or Assignes, And I the said Kirle all the sd Land to the sd Knight his Heires, Executors, Administrators, & Assignes, to the use aforesaid against all People doth Warrant & defend by these presents, And farther Know that the sd Kirle, hath put sd Knight in peaceable and Quiet Possession of the sd Land, at the delivering & Sealing of the presents, as wittnesse my hand Seale this twenty seventh day of July one thousand, six hund, & seventy six.

Signed Sealed & delivered in
the presence of us

his
John [mark] Green (signed) Richard Kirle
marke
Thomas Spinney,

LEASE: An agreement which creates a landlord-tenant relationship is called a lease. Because it transfers an estate in real property it is very much like a deed, and all rights of each party are defined within it.

Though the document itself is much like a deed in its format, the title transferred is less than fee simple and its duration is usually specified. The estate which one holds under such an instrument is referred to as a *leasehold estate* or as an *estate for years.*

LETTER OF ATTORNEY: See POWER OF ATTORNEY.

LIEN: A lien is not a land record but should be mentioned because it does relate thereto. It is a claim by one party upon the property of another for security in the payment of a debt. In some (most) states mortgages (q.v.) do not create legal title but are merely liens against the property.

MARRIAGE SETTLEMENT: This can be either an antenuptial contract (q.v.) or a similar postnuptial contract.

MEASUREMENTS OF LAND: As you read old land records you may come across land measurements which are not familiar to you. Let's look at a few of the most common units of measurement which you will encounter:

ACRE: 43,560 square feet, 160 square rods.

CHAIN: Sixty-six feet or twenty-two yards (100 links).

FURLONG: 660 feet or 220 yards (ten chains).

LINK: 7.92 inches. There are twenty-five links in a rod and 100 links (or four rods) in a chain.

MILE: 5,280 feet (eighty chains, 320 rods, or eight furlongs).

PERCH: 5½ yards or 16½ feet; also called *rod* or *pole.*

POLE: 5½ yards or 16½ feet; also called *perch* or *rod.*

ROD: 5½ yards or 16½ feet; also called *pole* or *perch.*

ROOD: As a measurement of length this varies from 5½ yards (rod) to eight yards, depending on locality. It was also used sometimes to describe an area equal to one-quarter acre.

MORTGAGE: A mortgage is a conditional transfer of legal title to real property as security for payment of a debt. It is much like a deed in its form, but if the conditions prescribed therein are met (i.e., the debt is paid) the conveyance becomes void. Under common law actual legal title is transferred by this deed to the mortgagee and he has the right to possess the land. In many states, especially in more recent times, the common law rule of mortgages has been altered and no title is transferred; it is regarded rather as a lien (q.v.) on the property.

PARTITION: When two or more persons hold real estate as cotenants (such as the undivided property left them in a probate settlement) and they wish to divide that property among them, a partition or *deed of partition* is made and recorded. It shows the separate parts taken by each. No additional title is taken or conveyed by any party to such an instrument, but a joint title is divided into separate titles.

PETITION: I discussed petitions along with probate records, but they are also very common in land records. A petition is a request made to a court for action in a matter not the subject of a suit. A good example is provided in the petition recorded in Land Book No. 1 in Kossuth County, Iowa, and made by the administrators of the estate of Thomas Gallion in 1882:

The petition of E. S. Streeter & J. H. Grover administrators of the Estate of Thomas Gallion of Kossuth County – Iowa respectfully shows to this court That the said Thomas Gallion died on or about the 19th day of August 1881 in said county, leaving an estate to be administered upon. Your petitioners were duly qualified administrators of his estate and letters of administration were issued to them on the 30th day of Sept. 1881 which has never been revoked.

Your petitioners duly made and returned a true inventory of all the personal property, book accounts &c of the said deceased on the 14th day of October 1881.

They also published due notice of their appointment as administrators and notified all parties who were indebted to the estate by such publication to pay the debts due the estate, and all creditors to present their claims duly verified for allowance and payment—all of which will more fully appear by a reference to the papers on file in the clerks office.

The amount of property which has come into the administrators hand is valued at	$414.66
The amount which has been paid out for debts and expenses of administration	$ 69.00
The amount set aside to the widow as exempt from execution as provided by Law	$381.16
The amount debts due from the estate	$300.00
The necessary expenses of administration in the future	$ 50.00
Total amount due when the estate will be settled	$419.00

The above said decedent died possessed in fee of a certain tract of land containing eighty acres situated in Kossuth County Iowa described as follows to wit the South half of South west quarter of sec thirty-six (36) in Township # Ninety seven (97) North of range # twenty Eight (28) west of 5th P. M. Iowa.

The whole of which estate was acquired by him since his marriage. Also the following are the names and ages of the devisees of the deceased to wit:

—Jane Gallion widow of Deceased	age 64
Thomas S. Gallion son of Deceased	" 40
John Gallion " " "	" 38
Maggie Stahl daughter of Deceased	" 35

James Gallion son " " " 33
W. J. Gallion " " " " 30
Robert Gallion " " " " 25

Your petitioners therefore allege that the personal estate in the hands of the petitioners is insufficient to pay the debts and the allowance to the family and expenses of administration and that it is necessary to sell the whole or some of the real estate for that purpose.

Wherefore your petitioners pray that an order be made by said court directing all persons interested in said real estate to appear before said Court at such time as it may appoint to show cause why an order should not be granted to your petitioners to sell so much real estate as shall be necessary.

And that after a full hearing of this petition and examinations of the proofs and allegations of the parties interested due proof of the publication of a copy of said order to show cause &c an order of sale be made authorizing your petitioners to sell so much, and such parts of the real estate as said Court shall Judge necessary or beneficial or that such or further order May be necessary in the premises.

(signed) E. S. Streater
(signed) J. H. Grover.

POWER OF ATTORNEY: When a person is unable to act for himself in a certain matter and appoints another to act for him, the document by which he does so is called a power of attorney or *letter of attorney*. The person thus appointed becomes an *attorney in fact* in the performance of specified acts. If a man who lives in Iowa inherits property from his grandfather who died in North Carolina and he wishes to sell that property, he may make a power of attorney authorizing his brother who lives much closer (or anyone else he chooses) to act as his agent in selling the property. As long as he is acting within the limits specified in the power of attorney the closer brother (or other person) can do all things as if he were actually the Iowa brother. John Cox made such a document in 1810:

Know all men by these presents that I John Cox, of Knox County and state of Kentucky have made ordained Constituted & appointed, and by these presents do make ordain Constitute & appoint Samuel Cox Junr my true & Lawful attorney, for me & in my name, but For my use to do perform & Transact all my Business In the State of Virginia To make a deed of Conveyance To a Certain tract of Land Lying in Grayson County in the State of Virginia it being the Same Which Robert still Sold as agent for me To a Certain William Byers, To Collect all money or Moneys which may be due me and to Transact any other Business Which may be Necessary for my wellfare and Well Standing in the Said State of Virginia and what ever Lawful act my said attorney may do or Cause to be done for me and in My

Name I do by these presents ratify and Confirm, in witness where of I have here unto set my hand and affixed my seal this 28th day of August 1810.

Teste his
Nathan Cox John X Cox
Richard Cox mark

QUITCLAIM DEED: A quitclaim deed is an instrument by which a person releases all title, interest, or claim which he may possess in certain real properties without making any warrants thereto. (He merely conveys all he has.) The title or claim released is *not necessarily* a valid one, but on many occasions it is the instrument of a valid conveyance of land. One example of a situation which might produce a quitclaim deed would be an error in a land survey. When the error is corrected the party affected by it often makes a quitclaim deed releasing all claim to the erroneous paper title which he held before the correction. A primary use is to remove clouds, or potential clouds, from real estate titles.

RELEASE: A release is a document by which a person gives up, to another, his right to something in which he has a just claim. Such a conveyance must be, under common law, to a person who has either possession or an interest in the property. It does not constitute a unilateral cancellation of rights but must be supported by lawful consideration. A cotenant of undivided lands can transfer his rights to another cotenant by a release. (There is an example of a release in chapter 15.)

Releases are sometimes, erroneously, confused with assignments (q.v.). They are also quite different from deeds of release (q.v.) in most jurisdictions.

RELEASE OF DOWER: The nature of dower was discussed briefly under probates, but it might be worthwhile to review a couple of essential points here just to show why such documents exist. Dower, of course, is the right (to a life estate) which the widow has in the real estate of her deceased husband under the common law. But the significant thing is that any property which he has procured in fee simple during their marriage is subject to his widow's dower claim. This means that even though a man sells property, his widow can come back after his death, even if it has been fifty years since the sale, and legally claim dower rights in it. Consequently, when a person bought a piece of land he was usually careful to see that the wife of the grantor signed the deed or executed a release of her dower rights. Through such she relinquished all claims. Though genealogically it may tell no more than her name, the release of dower, by giving that name, provides evidence which may sometimes be found in no other place.

Releases of dower will ordinarily not be found in public domain states, but there are exceptions. It was more common in these states for the wife to sign the deed.

RELEASE OF MORTGAGE: See DEED OF RELEASE.

SURRENDER: A surrender as a land record is much like a deed in its form and involves the yielding or giving up of a lease (an estate for years) before its term has expired. It is not a unilateral abandonment of the lease but is made with the mutual consent of both parties.

TAX RECORDS: Through the years tax records have been widely recognized as an important source of genealogical evidence. When many of the early census schedules were lost they were replaced (reasonably well) by contemporaneous tax lists. Others have been published separately; and many others have been microfilmed. In some places, during the early periods, you can follow your ancestors through the tax lists as if they (the lists) were a yearly census. We will look later at how these records may provide data to help solve pedigree problems.

TRUST DEED: In most states where you find trust deeds recorded in the land records you will find that they are instruments of real property financing similar to mortgages. They operate by placing the title to real property in one or more trustees to secure the payment of a debt. For example, the State of Maryland passed early legislation allowing the legal title to the property of certain insolvent debtors to be transferred to trustees in behalf of the creditors. The instrument of such a transfer was referred to as a *deed of trust* or trust deed. Though the approach may be slightly different, these records are not unlike those which may be found in several other states and in the District of Columbia. The arrangement under which such a trust is established allows the property to be sold in case of default and for the application of the proceeds to pay the debts, turning all surplus back to the debtor. A trust deed has *nothing* to do with trustees of an organization conveying their title to property.

WARRANTY DEED: A warranty deed is perhaps the most important and common type of deed. By it the grantor warrants (by covenant) the title of the property he sells; and should the title become faulty because of paramount claims against it, or for any other reason, the grantor (or his heirs) may be sued on the warranty. See also DEED.

You will also find other kinds of documents, including various court orders (decrees) and miscellaneous probate instruments, recorded in land-record books in various localities. Some states, as mentioned in chapter 14, even require the filing of certain final papers of probate with the custodian of local land records to be recorded as proof of title. The important thing is for you not to be too fussy about what you find in land records; just use what you find there. In all states the recording acts provide that most any document may be recorded upon payment of the proper fee. And most documents affecting land titles are recorded to make those titles secure.

III. USING LAND RECORDS

I have used up a great deal of space in defining and describing but have said little about the value of land records. And knowing all about them is not very helpful if they contain nothing of value.

My earlier observation about land records being among the best sources for American genealogical research is true. Land and probate records are, in fact, the American researcher's "bread and butter," and what was said about the general value of land records in chapter 16 is especially true of those land records which arise from private ownership. When you consider that a large percentage of your American ancestors were probably land owners, that good land records exist right from the beginning of most of the early permanent settlements in America, and that the older records uniquely contain much more genealogical data than their modern counterparts, then you can begin to comprehend the significance of this much-overlooked genealogical source.

A. Relationships

You already know that local land records contain the names of men's wives, a very useful tool in their (the men's) identification, but did you know that these records also contain many other statements of relationship? Someone has suggested that statements of relationship (other than husband and wife) are found in about 10 per cent of the early American deeds—and the earlier the better. My own experience suggests that this figure is probably about right, but in some localities the percentage is somewhat higher—much depended upon local custom. But regardless of what the percentage might have been, the important thing is that if *any* reasonable possibility at all exists of your finding in a deed a relationship which will help solve a genealogical problem, you ought to be ready and willing to search for that deed. There are *many* such possibilities.

This brings me back to an old theme—one which I hope is indelibly stamped on your memory by now—that you must search the records for *everyone* of your surname (including spelling variations). Remember that in this business of finding relationships in records, you cannot determine beforehand what you are going to find. You cannot afford to pick and choose if you want to be successful in research.

To illustrate some of the possibilities let's look at a few representative samples from deeds of Baltimore County, Maryland. One of the most helpful of deeds is the one where joint heirs in an estate combine as cotenant grantors to sell their property. Consider the following example:

> This Indenture made this twenty fifth day of April in . . . Eighteen hundred and one between Ignatius Diggs and Charlotte his wife formerly Charlotte Weaver and Lewis Weaver of Baltimore County of the one part and Joshua Jones of the Same County of the other part WHEREAS Daniel Weaver by his last Will and Testament bearing date the 22^{d} March 1797 did devise and bequeath as follows. . . .
>
> [The deed then goes on to quote part of the will in which Daniel Weaver named his son Daniel Weaver, daughter Elizabeth Hesson and daughter Charlotte Weaver.] . . . WHEREAS the said Daniel Weaver [the son] after having Complied with the Conditions aforesaid departed this life intestate leaving the aforesaid Charlotte and Lewis TOGETHER with Elizabeth Hesson now the Wife of Benjamin Morrison and John Weaver now under age his heirs and legal representatives. Now this Indenture WITNESSETH that the said Ignatius Diggs and Charlotte his wife and Lewis Weaver for . . . three hundred and eighty five Dollars. . . .

This is as far as we need to go. There is a lot of good relationship information in that deed even though the relationships between all persons are not completely clear. Relationship data like these are *often* found in deeds where there are co-grantors. Now let's look at another deed:

> This indenture made this twenty second day of September in the year of our Lord one thousand eight hundred and one by and between Andrew Boyd the Elder of the City of Baltimore of the one part and Elizabeth Boyd and Mary Boyd of said City and daughters of the Said Andrew Boyd of the other part. [James P. Boyd signed as a witness.]

The foregoing is a deed of gift, and a quite unusual one at that—it has co-grantees. Here's another interesting deed:

> This indenture made the thirtieth day of May in the year of our Lord eighteen hundred and one between John Hollins of the city of Baltimore in Baltimore County and state of Maryland Merchant Samuel Smith of the same County and State Esquire and Margaret his wife William Patterson of the same County and State Esquire and Dorcas his wife William Lee Forman of the same City County and

> State Merchant and Jane his wife and Joseph Spear of the same City County and State Merchant and Barbara his wife which said Margaret Smith Dorcas Patterson Jane Forman and Barbara Spear are the daughters of William Spear deceased late of Baltimore County and State aforesaid Merchant of the one part and Martin Eichelberger of the same City County and State Merchant of the other part WHEREAS by a decree of . . . chancellor of the said State of Maryland made in a cause depending in the High Court of Chancery of the said State between Ephraim Robinson and other Plaintiffs and Mary deceased and their respective husbands have agreed to join with the Spears heir of John Spear deceased defendant bearing date the first day of July in the year seventeen hundred and ninety-nine it was by the said Chancellor . . . adjudged ordered and decreed that the before named John Hollins be and he was thereby appointed trustee for making sale of the real estate late of the said deceased or so much thereof as would be necessary for the payment of his just debts. . . . by public auction . . . and whereas the said Children of the said William Spear deceased and Sisters of the said John Spear also deceased and their respective husbands have agreed to join with the said John Hollins as trustee . . . In the conveyance.

A document with genealogical evidence better than this one might be hard to find.

Also, well buried in land records are relationships of persons who are neither grantor nor grantee. These, of course, are much harder (in fact often impossible) to find, but their value cannot be denied. Consider the following:

> THIS INDENTURE made this Sixteenth day of June in . . . one thousand eight hundred and one Between John Tolley Worthington of Baltimore County and State of Maryland of the one part and Caleb Merryman of the said County and State of the other part WHEREAS William Ridgley of John by his deed of indenture bearing date the thirteenth day of April in . . . One thousand Seven hundred and Ninety five and recorded among the Land records of Baltimore County Court in Liber WGN° TT folio 73 for the Considerations therein mentioned did Convey unto the said John Tolley Worthington . . . all that part of a tract called Well's mannor . . . in the County aforesaid which was devised to the said William by the last Will and Testament of his father John Ridgley late of Baltimore County deceased.

This deed provides collateral evidence of the relationship between William and John Ridgley but, as good as it is, would be virtually impossible for the Ridgley researcher to find since it would not be indexed under either name. However, the deed is referring to a will where that same relationship is probably stated and which is likely quite findable.

B. Places

In addition to giving relationships, deeds and their cousins are also useful because of the places of residence they state for both grantors and grantees. In all of the instruments just quoted you will note that this was true; and that information is of value. However, it is usually of even greater value if the party you seek is stated to be from a place other than where the deed was recorded. If, for example, the grantee buys property before he moves into the county, the deed tells his immediate origin and can facilitate an extension of research. And if the grantor sells his land after moving away, the deed will tell where he has gone and facilitate your search for him and his family in later records.

C. Proving Connections Through Land Descriptions

Very often the genealogist will trace a pedigree back to a situation where an ancestor has one or more contemporaries with his same name and it is impossible, on the face of it, to distinguish one from the other in existing records so that the pedigree can be accurately extended. In circumstances like this, land descriptions *can* sometimes provide evidence to help solve the problem. The technique is quite simple if the approach fits the situation. Let's look at the approach.

You tackle the problem in conventional fashion—i.e., you work from the known to the unknown gathering data from the land records on all persons of the surname. If you can do this, the process will not be complicated and will not involve any special kind of research, but can be easily handled during the evaluation and tabulation of your research findings.

Not every genealogical problem can be solved by using land descriptions. In fact this approach can work only when two specific conditions are present:

1. There is a *positive identification* of *your* ancestor at the time he disposes of a specific tract or parcel of land.
2. There is a direct statement of relationship—preferably a lineal relationship—between your ancestor and someone else in the instrument by which that same ancestor acquired title to that same property.

You must know that your ancestor owned the land and that he disposed of it by a deed (or will) in which you positively identify him as grantor. (There must be *no* possibility of this person being his like-named counterpart.) You may identify him by the name of his wife—this is very common —or by his signature or mark, or by some other means. Regardless of method, that identification is essential.

The more deeds of this nature you find the better will be your chances for success. You must carefully note the description of the lands being sold. (This is quite easy where the Rectangular Survey system was used but more difficult where land was described by metes and bounds unless the tracts were given specific names.)

Next you must find the instrument by which title to this tract of land was acquired by your ancestor. If the land was acquired from a relative and a statement of relationship between your ancestor and that relative is given, you are in luck. Any relationship thus stated increases your chances for solving the problem—but of course lineal connections are preferable. You may find the land in question devised to your ancestor in his father's (or other relative's) will, and a will serves our purposes here as well as a deed.

It all boils down to this: If you find your ancestor, John X, selling 100 acres of land of the same description as William X sold to his son John sixteen years earlier, you have a pretty good case. This can be tricky, though, because sometimes tracts are divided or combined with other tracts when they are sold.

D. Other Tricks for Hard Cases

When clues to identity are hard to find and family connections are scarce, it is worthwhile to go into the land records in greater depth to mine the hidden value so often overlooked. Consider the following approaches. Though they are often time-consuming, they are worth the time they take:

1. Look for companion documents. When you have identified a land record of interest to you, look at all of the deeds for a few pages before and a few pages after it. In your search identify any records where the parties are the same (or obviously connected) and where the land is in the same general area. Study these, abstract them (see next chapter), and identify what useful data they may contain which are pertinent to your problem.

2. Check for deeds on adjoining properties. Tract books, land surveys, plat maps, and property descriptions in deeds to or from your ancestor will give names of those whose property is adjacent to his. Deeds pertaining to those adjacent tracts may contain valuable data on the subject property. The two owners may be related, they may have come together from the same place of origin, or the properties may have been parts of the same original patent or grant. Clues of great worth (and even specific details) relative to these and other matters may be found in these documents which are not in your ancestor's deeds.

3. Locate and plat out the property description of your ancestor's land on a county map. This can be helpful in many ways, but most importantly it shows you the location of the property in relation to such things as cemeteries and churches. This information may prove invaluable. When the land is in a public land state you can prepare township-range model sheets using the diagram in Figure 2 of chapter 16. Using a blank model sheet locate the subject property. Next, look up the section in the tract book and list all real property within a two-mile radius and check it out. Records relating to these adjacent tracts just might have pertinent data or useful clues, as already stated. The names of the owners of the adjacent property can also be used in connection with the census records to identify whether your ancestor is the land owner in question if there is more than one person with the same name.

4. Account for both the acquisition and disposition of every tract of your ancestor's land. Elizabeth Shown Mills suggested in her presentation to the National Genealogical Society's 1985 conference in Columbus, Ohio, that you make an "in" and "out" table with five columns.[2] Column one contains that land's legal description, two and three tell the date and means of acquisition, and four and five tell the date and means of its disposal. Those who fail to account for both the "ins" and the "outs" risk missing some important clues and/or genealogical evidence. I suggest checking tract books (or land-entry books), where applicable, to determine whether your ancestor got his land in the public domain from the federal government, and then seeking the details of the grant or purchase in appropriate records.

IV. USING TAX RECORDS

There are various kinds of tax records—in fact you will seldom find two exactly the same—but they can generally be divided into three main types:

1. Real property tax records.
2. Personal property tax records (primarily livestock and slaves).
3. A combination of the other two.

All of these are good, but those which show records of persons taxed for personal property often have an advantage because they pick up persons established in the community but who owned no land. Persons who owned little of anything may not be found on any of these lists.

Depending on locality and time period, tax records on real property usually show the amount of land; its location (including on what water-

[2] From personal notes taken by the author at the conference.

FIGURE 1—KENTUCKY TAX LISTS

Name	Land (acres)	County	Water course	In whose name entered	In whose name surveyed	In whose name patented	White males over 21	Blacks over 16	Total Blacks	Horses and mares	Value of land per acre	Total valuation	chn. 4-14	chn. 7-17
1819:														
Cobb, William							1			1		$40		
Elisha							1			2		$90		
Asa							1			1		$40		
John	100	Owen	Eagle	Phillips & Young	same	same	1			3		$500		
Daniel							1			1		$40		
1820:														
Cobb, Thomas	100	Owen	Eagle	H. Marshall	same	same	1	1	1	4		$1,000		
William							1			1		$50		
John	100	Owen	Eagle	Phillips & Young	same	same	1			2		$500		
Elisha							1			2		$80		
Asa							1			1		$50		
Daniel							1			1		$40		
1821:														
Cobb, Asa							1			1		$30		
William							1			1		$30		
Elisha							1			1		$60		
Daniel							1			1		$40		
John	100	Owen	Eagle	Phillips	same	same	1			2	4	$500		
Thomas	100	Owen	Eagle	Marshall	same	same	1	1	1	4	5	$1,050		

FIGURE 1—(continued)

Name	Land (acres)	County	Water course	In whose name entered	In whose name surveyed	In whose name patented	White males over 21	Blacks over 16	Total Blacks	Horses and mares	Value of land per acre	Total valuation	chn. 4-14	chn. 7-17
1822:														
Cobb, William							1			2		$70	3	
Asa							1			1		$30		
Elisha							1			1		$65	1	
Thomas	100	Owen	Eagle	Marshall	same	same	1	1	1	4	2	$1,050	4	
Daniel							1			1		$40	3	
1823:														
Cobb, Asa							1			2		$60		
Elisha							1			1		$50		
Daniel							1			1		$50		
William							1			1		$100		
Thomas	100	Owen	Eagle	Marshall	do	do	1			4		$1,250		
John							1							
1824:														
Cobb, Thomas	100	Owen	Eagle	Marshall	do	do	1			4		$1,200		
William							1			1		$80		
Elisha							1			1		$50		
Asa							1			1		$75		
Daniel							1			2		$80		
1825:														
Cobb, William	100	Owen	Eagle	Weaver	same	same	1			1	3	$540		
Daniel							1			2		$150		
Asa							1			1		$100		
Elisha							1			3		$150		

FIGURE 1—(continued)

Name	Land (acres)	County	Water course	In whose name entered	In whose name surveyed	In whose name patented	White males over 21	Blacks over 16	Total Blacks	Horses and mares	Value of land per acre	Total valuation	chn. 4-14	chn. 7-17
1825 (cont'd):														
Cobb, Thomas	100	Owen	Eagle	Marshall	same	same								
same	300	Owen	Stevens	May & Co.	same	same	1			5	3	$1,450		
1826:														
Cobb, Thomas	100	Owen	Eagle	Weaver	same	same	1			5		$950		
Elisha							1			2		$100		
William	100	Owen	Eagle	Weaver	same	same	1			2		$325		
Asa							1			1		$65		
Daniel							1			1		$40		
1827:														
Cobb, William	100	Owen	Eagle	Weaver	do	do	1			2		$330		
Thomas	100	"	"	Marshall	do	do	1			4		$750		
Elisha	100	"	"	Weaver	do	do	1			1		$200		
Daniel	100	"	"	"	do	do	1			2		$280		
John	50	"	"	Asburn	do	do	1			2				
same	27	"	"	May & Co.	do	do						$350		
Asa	97½	"	"	Weaver	do	do	1			2		$200		
1828:														
Cobb, John	102	Owen	Eagle	May & Co.	do	do	1			2	3	$356		
Elisha	100	"	"	Weaver & c	do	do	1			1	2	$250		
Thomas	100	"	"	Marshall	do	do	1			4	6	$750		
Daniel	100	"	"	Weaver	do	do	1			1	2.50	$280		
Asa	107	"	"	"	do	do	1			2	2	$239		

FIGURE 1—(continued)

Name	Land (acres)	County	Water course	In whose name entered	In whose name surveyed	In whose name patented	White males over 21	Blacks over 16	Total Blacks	Horses and mares	Value of land per acre	Total valuation	chn. 4-14	chn. 7-17
1829:														
Cobb, Asa	97½	Owen	Eagle	Weaver	do	do	1			2	2	$750	3	
Elisha	100	"	"	"	do	do	1			2	2	$250	3	
Daniel	60	"	"	"	do	do	1			2	5	$350	4	
Thomas	100	"	"	Marshall	do	do	1			4	5	$660	3	
William	100	"	"	Weaver	do	do	1			4	3	$460	4	
1830:														
Cobb, Elisha	100	Owen	Eagle	Weaver	do	do	1			2	2.50	$300		
Daniel	60	"	"	"	do	do	1			2	5	$350		
Asa	106	"	"	"	do	do	1			1	2.50	$310		
William	100	"	"	"	do	do	1			3	5	$625		
1831:														
Cobb, Elisha	100	Owen	Eagle	T. Weaver	do	do	1			3	2.50	$350		
Daniel	60	"	"	"	do	do	1			2	5	$360		
Asa	106½	"	"	"	do	do	1			1	2.50	$300		
William	100	"	"	"	do	do	1			3	5	$600		
1832:														
Tax list is missing														
1833:														
Tax list is missing														
1834:														
Cobb, Asa	106	Owen	Eagle	Weaver	do	do	1			2	2.50	$325		
Elizabeth	40	"	"	"	do	do				1	3	$150		

FIGURE 1—(continued)

Name	Land (acres)	County	Water course	In whose name entered	In whose name surveyed	In whose name patented	White males over 21	Blacks over 16	Total Blacks	Horses and mares	Value of land per acre	Total valuation	chn. 4-14	chn. 7-17
1834 (cont'd):														
Cobb, Elisha Jr							1			1		$10		
Daniel	100	Owen	Eagle	Weaver	do	do	1			2	5	$560		
Elisha	100	”	”	”	do	do	1			3	3	$410		
1835:														
Cobb, Asa	106	Owen	Eagle	Weaver	do	do	1			2	3	$390		
Daniel	100	”	”	”	do	do	1			3	5	$600		
Elisha	100	”	”	”	do	do	1			4	3.50	$500		
Elizabeth	95	”	”	”	do	do				1	2	$270		
Elisha Jr							1			2		$30		
1836:														
Cobb, Elisha	100	Owen	Eagle	Weaver	do	do	1			3	5	$700		
Daniel	100	”	”	”	do	do	1			3	6	$730		
Elizabeth	40	”	”	”	do	do				1	25	$1,050		
Asa	106	”	”	”	do	do	1			2	3	$458		
Elisha Jr	100	”	Richland	Weaver	do	do	1			1	3	$330		
1837:														
Cobb, William	100	Owen					under age			1	2	$260		
Elisha Sr	950	”					1			5	5	$1,493		
Daniel	50	”					1			5	19	$1,200		
Elizabeth	100	”								1	8	$850		
Asa	156	”					1			1	6	$1,061		
Elisha Jr	100	”					1			1	2	$260		

FIGURE 1—(continued)

Name	Land (acres)	County	Water course	In whose name entered	In whose name surveyed	In whose name patented	White males over 21	Blacks over 16	Total Blacks	Horses and mares	Value of land per acre	Total valuation	chn. 4-14	chn. 7-17
1838:														
Tax list is missing														
1839:														
Cobb, Asa	206										5	$1,030		
Danl	157										6	$942		
Elisha Sr	168										6	$1,008		
Danl F.	100										3	$300		
Wm	100										3	$300		
Elisha Jr	140										2.50	$350		
1840:														
Cobb, Elisha Sr	100	Owen	Eagle				1			3		$753		2
Asa	205	"	"				1			2		$940		3
Daniel F.	100	"	Elk				1			2		$275		
Daniel	155	"	Eagle				1			2		$1,670		1
Elisha Jr	140	"	"				1			2		$323		
William	100	"	Elk				1			2		$375		
1841:														
Cobb, Elisha Sr	110	Owen	Eagle				1			4		$744		3
Asa	207	"	"				1			3		$990		5
William	100	"	Elk				1			2		$350		
Daniel	155	"	Eagle				1			2		$1,076		1
Daniel F.	100	"	"				1			2		$275		
Elijah							1			1		$50		
Elisha Jr							1			1		$40		1

course); the persons in whose name it was originally entered, surveyed, and patented; and its appraised valuation.

All states did not keep good early tax records so this will not be a source you will use on every problem, but you need to keep it in mind. Let's look at Kentucky where some of the best tax lists were kept in early periods. Figure 1 illustrates the value of these records. For the illustration I have chosen the surname Cobb and followed it through twenty-three years of tax schedules in Owen County. Note carefully the nature of the information and the knowledge which can be gained when you consider everyone of the surname, every year, over a long period of time. (In this example I actually stopped before I would have ordinarily.) There is no reason to stop if the family is still there.

I know that these records leave many questions unanswered, but when other records—such as deeds, probates, marriage records, etc.— are used in conjunction with this tax information, you can tell quite a lot about the persons involved.

Tax lists are usually kept in columnar form, as you can observe. For this example I cheated a little and put everything on one standardized form, but the forms of the actual schedules vary somewhat from year to year as witnessed by some of the blank spaces left on my form. Also, you should know that some of these lists have other minor columns which I omitted. As you study the example you will observe that there is nothing spectacular about tax lists. They just contain good basic data which might somewhere, sometime, provide clues you need to help solve a genealogical problem.

V. LAND-OWNERSHIP MAPS

Another useful source for some time periods and some localities is the old county land-ownership map. In 1967 the Geography and Map Division of the Library of Congress in Washington, D.C., had some 1,449 pre-twentieth century land-ownership maps from 1,041 different U.S. counties. Most of these are counties in the northeastern states, north central states, California, Texas, and Virginia. They comprise in total nearly one-third of all American counties. About 7 per cent of these maps are of pre-1840 vintage and about 24 per cent were published between 1840 and 1860. About 38 per cent were published between 1860 and 1880 and approximately 30 per cent between 1880 and 1900.[3]

---

[3] Richard W. Stephenson (comp.), *Land Ownership Maps* (Washington, DC: Library of Congress, 1967), pp. vii-viii.

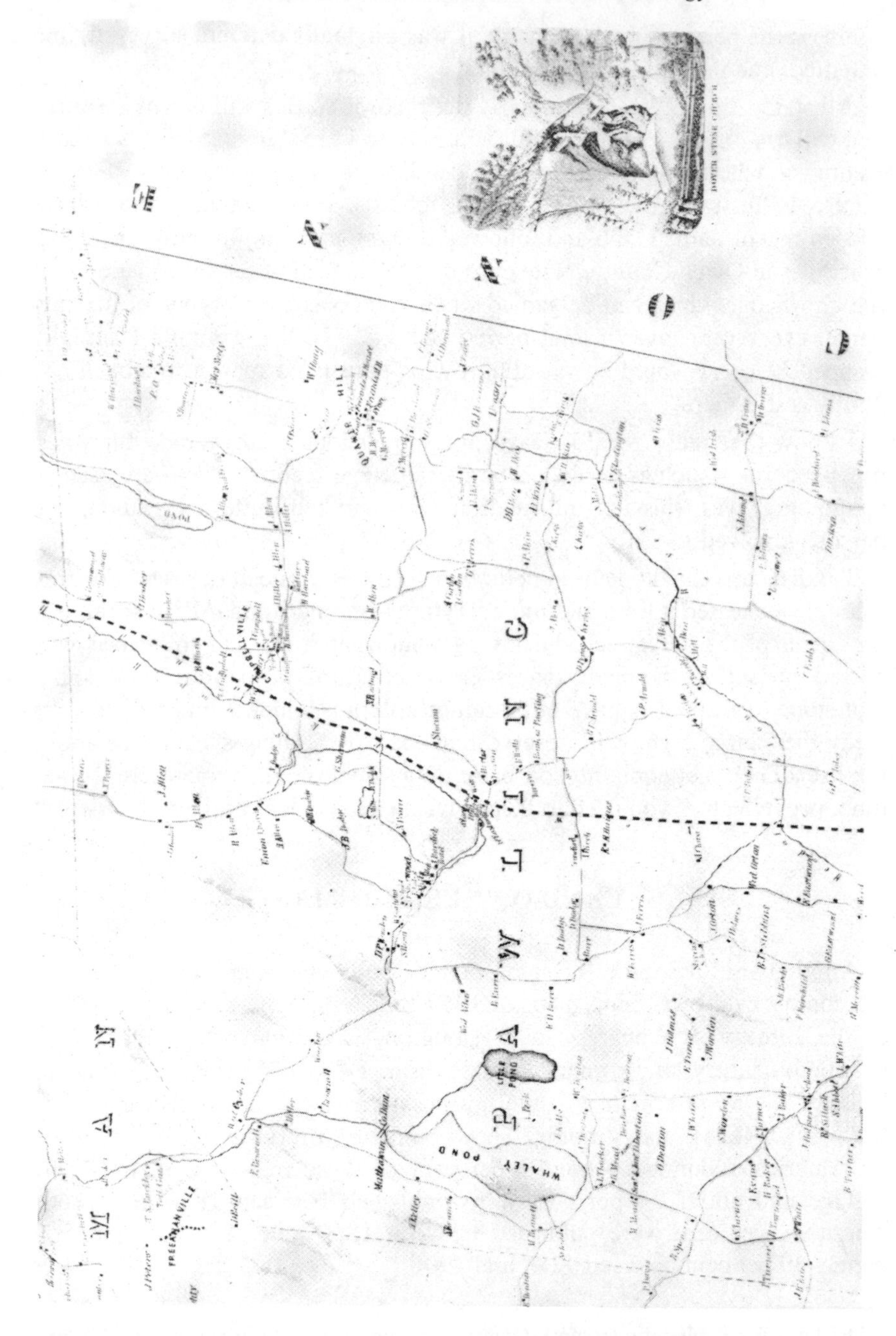

FIGURE 2—LAND OWNERSHIP MAP FOR PART OF DUTCHESS COUNTY, NEW YORK (1:42, 240—1850—J. C. SIDNEY)

These maps antedate county platbooks and topographical surveys of the U.S. Geological Survey, and scales vary from 1:3,960 to 1:600,000. Seventy-six per cent have scales larger than 1:100,000.[4] In most cases the names of land holders at the time the map was made are recorded directly on the map. Thus their genealogical and historical value is quite obvious (see Figure 2).

Reproductions of most of these maps (usually photostats) are available from the Photoduplication Service, Library of Congress, Washington, DC 20540, for a small reproduction and mailing fee. Rates lists and cost estimates are furnished upon request. Payment must be made in advance on all orders for photoduplicates.

As a guide to the land-ownership map holdings of the Library of Congress, Richard W. Stephenson of the Geography and Map Division has compiled a checklist of the library's nineteenth-century county maps in the small booklet identified in footnote number three of this chapter. The booklet is available from the Superintendent of Documents, U.S. Government Printing Office, Washington, DC 20402, for a reasonable price.

Useful maps in the National Archives are described in chapter 20 of *Guide to Genealogical Research in the National Archives*. (See 20.3, "General Land Office Records," pages 255 and 257.) These include approximately 42,000 survey plats used by the General Land Office and the local land offices. These plats are for several of the states.

VI. AVAILABILITY OF LAND RECORDS

Now that you are more familiar with the value and use of local land records, let's look quickly at their availability.

A. Location

In most states land records are under county jurisdiction, but there are too many exceptions for me to give that as a standing rule. Following is a list of the custodians of these land records in the several states. The record of every land transaction (if it has been recorded) is made in the jurisdiction where the land in question happens to lie:

ALABAMA:	Probate Judge of county.
ALASKA:	Recorder of judicial district.

[4] *Ibid.*, pp. vii-viii.

ARIZONA:	County Recorder.
ARKANSAS:	Circuit Clerk of county.
CALIFORNIA:	County Recorder.
COLORADO:	County Clerk and Recorder.
CONNECTICUT:	Town Clerk.
DELAWARE:	County Recorder of Deeds. (Use is restricted to attorneys at law, but the LDS Family History Library has all deed books up to 1850 on microfilm.)
D.C.:	Recorder of Deeds (515 D Street, N.W., Washington, DC 20001).
FLORIDA:	Clerk of County Circuit Court.
GEORGIA:	County Superior Court.
HAWAII:	Register of Conveyances, Honolulu.
IDAHO:	County Recorder.
ILLINOIS:	County Recorder of Deeds. (In counties under 60,000 population the County Clerk is the Recorder.)
INDIANA:	County Recorder.
IOWA:	County Recorder of Deeds.
KANSAS:	County Clerk has transfer books recording all transfers before deeds can be recorded by the County Register of Deeds.
KENTUCKY:	County Clerk (also called Clerk of County Court).
LOUISIANA:	Recorder of Mortgages and Register of Conveyances in the parish.
MAINE:	Register of Deeds for county. (In Aroostook and Oxford counties there are two registries each. In Aroostook County there is a Northern Registry at Fort Kent and a Southern Registry at Houlton. In Oxford County there is a Western Registry at Fryeburg and an Eastern Registry at South Paris.)
MARYLAND:	Clerk of the Circuit Court for the county. (In Baltimore City it is the Clerk of the Circuit Court for the city.) All land records for Maryland before the federal Constitution was ratified in 1788 are in the Hall of Records, Annapolis. There are also many records right up to the twentieth century housed at

the Hall of Records, but this is purely at the discretion of county officials and not because of law. Some of these records were housed in the State Land Office at Annapolis but that office was recently abolished and the records transferred to the Hall of Records.

MASSACHUSETTS: The Registry of Deeds in the county, except for five counties with more than one registry office each. (Berkshire County has a Northern District at North Adams, a Middle District at Pittsfield, and a Southern District at Great Barrington. Bristol County has a Northern District at Taunton and a Southern District at New Bedford. Essex County has a Northern District at Lawrence and a Southern District at Salem. Middlesex County has a Northern District at Lowell and a Southern District at Cambridge. Worcester County has a Northern District at Fitchburg and a Worcester District at Worcester.) You need to be acutely aware of dates of creation of various counties and districts.

MICHIGAN: County Register of Deeds.

MINNESOTA: County Recorder.

MISSISSIPPI: Clerk of the Chancery Court in the county. (In the district if the county is divided.)

MISSOURI: Recorder of Deeds in the county.

MONTANA: County Clerk and Recorder.

NEBRASKA: Register of Deeds in the county. (In counties of less than 16,000 the County Clerk is ex-officio Register.)

NEVADA: County Recorder.

NEW HAMPSHIRE: County Registry of Deeds. (Formerly the Town Clerk had jurisdiction.)

NEW JERSEY: County Register in counties that have them (Camden, Essex, Hudson, Passaic, Union). County Clerk in other counties. All land records prior to 1800 are in the State Library, Bureau of Archives and History, Trenton. A few later ones are also there.

NEW MEXICO: County Clerk. (He is ex-officio Recorder.)

NEW YORK:	County Clerk (except in New York, Kings, Queens, and Bronx counties where they are in custody of the Register of the City of New York).
NORTH CAROLINA:	County Register of Deeds.
NORTH DAKOTA:	County Register of Deeds.
OHIO:	County Recorder.
OKLAHOMA:	County Register of Deeds. (County Clerk is ex-officio Register.)
OREGON:	County Clerk (except in Home Rule counties: Benton, Records and Elections; Hood River, Records and Assessment; Lane, Director of Records and Elections; Multnomah, Recording Department of Assessments and Records; and Washington, Recording Division of Records and Elections).
PENNSYLVANIA:	County Recorder of Deeds.
RHODE ISLAND:	Town and City Clerks (except City of Providence has a Recorder of Deeds).
SOUTH CAROLINA:	Register of Mesne (pronounced *mean*) Conveyances or, if none, the Clerk of the County Court. (All prior to 1785 were recorded at Charleston.)
SOUTH DAKOTA:	County Register of Deeds.
TENNESSEE:	County Register.
TEXAS:	County Clerk.
UTAH:	County Recorder.
VERMONT:	Town and City Clerks.
VIRGINIA:	Clerk of County or City. (See chapter 19 for further information on courts and jurisdictions in Virginia.)
WASHINGTON:	County Auditor.
WEST VIRGINIA:	Clerk of County Commission.
WISCONSIN:	County Register of Deeds.
WYOMING:	County Clerk.[5]

In those New England states of Connecticut, Rhode Island, and Vermont where land records are kept in the town it is important in tracing a family

---

[5] *Martindale-Hubbell Law Directory,* 120th ed. (Summit, NJ: Martindale-Hubbell, Inc., 1988), Vol. VIII (by permission) and correspondence with various court officials.

to search the records of all towns of interest *including* "parent" towns in the period before the newer town was divided off—also in New Hampshire, where all but the most recent records are in the towns. This is essentially the same principle you follow when you search the records of parent counties in other states.

The LDS Family History Library has quite extensive collections of local land records on microfilm. These records are a "must" source whenever county records are filmed. So if you have access to that library's collections, check the catalog for holdings in the localities of your problems.

There are a few situations where restrictions have been imposed on the use of land records and the public cannot have direct access to them. The Delaware State Legislature passed a bill a few years ago which restricted the direct use of land records to attorneys at law. Laws like this one are a direct affront to the right of public access to public records. I believe that such laws, if tested, would be found unconstitutional. Often the careful researcher can still gain access to these records if he makes application to the resident judge before visiting the county courthouse.

B. Indexes

Most local land records are well indexed, both by names of grantors and by names of grantees. (These are usually separate indexes but they are sometimes combined.) Thus you can generally put your hand on most of the records pertaining to your ancestors without a great deal of difficulty. There are a few limitations in these indexes but you can learn to live with them if you are aware of them. Some of the main limitations are:

1. If there is more than one grantor (or grantee) the index often refers only to the one named first in the instrument. The fact that there are other parties involved is sometimes indicated by merely putting *et al.* (and others) in the index after the name of the first party.

2. If a trustee, a guardian, an attorney, an executor, an administrator, a commissioner, or any other legal agent (including the sheriff or other court representative who sells land for tax purposes) acts as the grantor in a deed in behalf of your ancestor, you will not usually find your ancestor's name in the index but will more likely find the name of the legal representative (if only you knew who he was, or even that such a sale had taken place!). Suggestions given under "Other Tricks for Hard Cases," earlier in this chapter, can be very helpful here.

3. Most indexes are not strictly alphabetical but are usually alphabetical only by the first letter or two of the surname, then alphabetical by the first

letter of the given name, then chronological. In any case it will generally be necessary for you to go through the entire index of the initial letter of your ancestor's surname to find all entries relating to that surname.

4. In most localities record custodians have developed master indexes to land records. These master indexes are especially easy to use because they eliminate the need for checking multiple volumes to find a few entries, but they often lull us into a false sense of security. You should be aware that these master indexes are often incomplete. Therefore, if you have access to the individual volumes and if they are indexed, it is a good idea to check those indexes. Many master indexes were compiled from the indexes to individual volumes, and it is easy for an indexer to inadvertently skip entries.

5. A few states in the public domain (Iowa is a good example) have no direct indexes to the parties to land transactions, but rather all land records are indexed according to tract. Under this type of index a line or column is assigned to conveniently sized tracts (maybe a section, quarter-section, platted block, or lot). In such cases it is necessary to know the subdivision, section, township, and range (or block number) in order to find the records. These indexes are an asset to those who examine land titles and can be valuable to the genealogist once he has located his ancestor's land, but they are not good finding tools. They usually pose problems for the genealogist.

Sometimes survey descriptions of a man's land are given in a biographical sketch as found in a county history. The petition by the administrators of Thomas Gallion's estate in Kossuth County, Iowa, used as an example earlier in this chapter, was located in this way.

In many states there are several other indexes in addition to those for grantors and grantees. In Idaho, for example, twenty-seven separate indexes are required by statute. You may find some of these useful.

You *must* use the indexes. In spite of their shortcomings they are good and they provide easy access to most land records. If you do not have personal access to the records, do not be afraid to write to a record custodian and ask him to check specific names in an index for you; but be sure your requests are reasonable and that you are willing to compensate him for the time spent in your behalf.

In its microfilming program the LDS Family History Library always films indexes when it films the land records. If you have access to these films you will find them easy to use—just as easy as reading the same indexes at the courthouse. And again I remind you that when you use indexes you must consider every possible spelling of the name you seek.

314 GENERAL INDEX TO DEEDS

Ba to Bl GRANTOR

Given Name	Baa to Bal Page	Bam to Baz Page	Bea to Bel Page
A....B	1	73	157
C....D	10	80	162
E....F	18	88	167
G....HI	24	95	171
I....Jo	32	103	176
KL....M	48	130	187
NO....PQ	54	138	190
R....S	57	141	193
T....UV	64	148	198
W....XYZ	67	151	200

To find Name by this Table—Find FIRST TWO or FIRST THREE Letters of Surname which are printed in alphabetical order at top of Column Divisions in black faced type. In same Column, underneath, opposite Initial Letter of First Given Name find Page on which the Name is written.

GRANTORS			GRANTEES	WHERE RECORDED Book	Vol.	Page	DATE OF DEED Month	Day	Year	DATE OF RECORD Month	Day	Year	LOCATION
Black	et ux James		Caroline F May	K	10	440	Dec	17	1873	D	17	1873	Conestoga St City
Bleacher by Shf		John	John Hildebrand	P	10	224	Nov	17	1873	Feb	3	1875	Providence
Black	et ux James		George Varnan	U	10	598	Apr	16	1868	Sep	13	1876	W James St
Blackburn		John A	Joseph C Taylor	D	Mis	367	Feb	11	1863	May	26	1877	L Britain
Black		John	Henry Stoltzfus Gdn	E	Mis	127	Apr	1	1879	May	21	1879	Release
Black	James		Abraham A Myers	E	Mis	81	Dec	28	1872	Jun	24	1879	S Water St
Blaul	Jacob		Louis Blaul	L	11	299	Mar	29	1880	Mar	29	1880	E Lemon St Lanc
Black	et ux James		James Warren et al	M	11	432	Oct	27	1873	Jul	22	1880	S Water St
Black		John	Elizabeth S Dickey	F	11	289	Feb	18	1881	Feb	21	1881	E Orange St Lanc
Black	et ux James		Anna Martha Miller	F	11	436	Mar	31	1881	Mar	31	1881	133-135 E King StLanc
Black	et ux James		John R Diffenbach	T	11	222	Mar	30	1882	Mar	30	1882	N Duke St Lanc
Blank	Jacob		John B Barbour	W	11	77	Jan	9	1882	Jun	23	1882	E Earl R of W
Blank		John S	John B Barbour	X	11	269	Jan	2	1883	Jan	5	1883	Right of Way
Black	James		Sarah A Musselman	Z	11	394	Apr	2	1883	Apr	2	1883	N Duke St
Black	James R		William Black	Z	11	593	Mar	29	1883	Apr	9	1883	Release
Black	et ux	John R	Eliza E Haldeman	B	12	23	Feb	20	1882	Apr	19	1883	Salisbury
Black		Joseph H	John W Brubaker	D	12	86	Apr	1	1884	Apr	2	1884	Columbia
Black	et ux James		James Moore	E	12	413	May	19	1884	May	24	1884	S Water St
Blair	et ux James		Fanny A Blair	G	12	381	Mar	1	1884	Jan	2	1885	Fulton Twp

FIGURE 3—A GRANTOR INDEX TO LOCAL LAND RECORDS

C. Other Cautions

We sometimes encounter situations where an ancestor is not listed in the land record indexes, even though he appears as a land owner in local tax lists. This could mean a couple of things. It could mean that he didn't record his deed(s), that you are not looking in the right place in the indexes, or that the indexes are incomplete. Do not be afraid in such cases to read deed books, deed by deed, for the appropriate time periods. This doesn't mean reading entire deeds—only identifying the parties.

Deeds are not always recorded. The law does not require that they be recorded. Recording provides protection for the property owner, but it is up to him to take advantage of that protection.

18

Abstracting Wills and Deeds

Considerable time has already been spent discussing the importance of taking adequate research notes and getting all available information on everyone of the surname. Let's now discuss how best to accomplish this feat—how to get the required information from the records into your notes in a meaningful and readily usable form without omitting anything of significance.

It sounds quite simple, but when you get down to bare facts there are some obstacles—it is often difficult to tell what is important and what is not. Your experience will teach you best, but perhaps some carefully thought-out suggestions can be of assistance while you are gaining experience.

I. ABSTRACT VS. EXTRACT

Chapter 7 introduced abstracts and extracts but didn't really say much about relative values, so let's look at them now in a little more depth. First let's define our terms: ABSTRACT means to summarize or abridge or to take essential thoughts only. Chapter 17 mentioned abstracts of title, and from the above definition it should be clear why they are so called. Contrast this term with EXTRACT, which means to take out of another source or to copy, usually signifying that the material or item being copied is copied in its entirety from a larger work, as one will is taken from a book of wills or one biographical sketch from a book of such sketches. TRANSCRIBE also means to copy, but *any* copy or reproduction is referred to as a transcript or transcription.

Most records need to be extracted. Census schedules, vital certificates, church register entries, tax lists, immigration records, passages from books, etc., all fall into this category. With these records an exact extract is essential to proper analysis. But wills, deeds, most other court records, and early military pension and bounty land warrant application papers can and should be abstracted.

This chapter deals with the abstracting of land and probate records. It is especially important that the genealogist learn how to abstract them because there are often hundreds of documents in one locality relating to the surnames of interest. There is so much in these records that is nothing more than legal gobbledygook that it is folly to waste time and money copying it; and to do so can even cause problems. It adds unnecessary bulk to your research notes and increases the amount of time needed for evaluation since you must sift through this redundant verbiage to ferret out essential facts.

Some say it is best to make a verbatim extract of every pertinent record you find or, still better, get a photocopy of every record. They argue that such copies ensure that you have all the information you need and that it is correct. The argument is valid; however, if you are careful and precise in your abstracting you can have the same assurance without the added time, effort, or expense. Most genealogists who argue for the complete copy are searching for specific individuals only and not for everyone of the surname —definitely the wrong approach.

The only universal rule about abstracting that I can offer is this: GET ALL THE ESSENTIAL FACTS. Don't try to be too brief, and when you are not sure if something is important, copy it. It is better to get too much information than not enough. As you gain experience your ability to discern will become more acute.

One measure you can take to help assure that the information you put into your abstract will not be misinterpreted is to keep everything in the first person, just as it is in the document. If a man says in his will: "I leave to my son John such and such property . . .," you should *use the same pronouns he used*—and be consistent in this throughout.

Some genealogists like to make abbreviated abstracts, copying only dates, names, and relationships from wills; and names, dates, considerations (price), and relationships from deeds. These brief abstracts may be all right on rare occasions, but they cannot ordinarily be classified as good research notes. In addition to overlooking significant genealogical data, it is much easier to make errors when you are looking only for those limited items of information. A good case in point is the abstract of George Blackburn's will in chapter 14 where the abstracter who went through picking out the names of George's children listed two unrelated persons—Negro slaves—as children in the family, and then missed some of the actual children.

As you do your research—if you intend to do good, reliable work—you must make fairly detailed abstracts (depending on the records). The only requirement is that you follow the rule: Get all the essential facts!

II. THE NATURE OF THE ABSTRACT

Every abstract you make must fit naturally into your note-keeping system, and there must be a notation on your research calendar of every record you search. Every abstract must include a complete reference to its source by locality, volume (or book or liber, etc.), and page (or folio)—and also serial numbers of microfilms where appropriate. It must also clearly state the type of record and include all dates important to the document—the date made and the date recorded for a deed, and the date made and the date probated (sometimes date recorded) for a will.

Some persons use prepared forms for abstracting different types of records. These are fine, especially for the beginner who may wonder what is significant and what is not; however, you must be careful of these because valuable information in the records may not fit the form.

I prefer not to use these forms for abstracting wills and deeds, not because they are bad, but mainly because they require more space and add bulk to the note file. (Usually only one deed or one will is abstracted on one page of notes when forms are used, while you are not limited to this extent otherwise.) If this bulk doesn't bother you, you may want to develop and use some type of form.

A. Abstracting Deeds

Whether or not you use a form there are certain basic data which must be abstracted. In addition to the complete locality, relevant dates, and source information, you should consider the following eight items as being essential to a deed abstract:

1. The parties of the deed—the grantor(s) and the grantee(s).
2. The places of residence of those parties.
3. The consideration involved—the price paid and any stated terms.
4. A description of the land—including size (acreage) and location. (If metes and bounds were used this might include a relationship to a watercourse or other body of water, or a road and/or connection to the

lands of other persons, and/or a brief history of the title of that land, and of the beginning of the metes and bounds—such as "Beginning at a sweet gum tree on the shore of William's Bay at the corner of the land belonging to Matthew Quick"—and the name of the tract, if it has one—as in Maryland.) In the public domain states the description will usually be in terms of subdivision, section, township, range, directions (compass bearings), and distances.

5. Relationship information. These are relationships of type and between any persons—not just the grantor and grantee.

6. Miscellaneous information. (This category is the most difficult to define because you never know what you are going to find in a land record. A deed may also include special terms, restrictions, or privileges that are significant. A man may have sold land and preserved a right of way through the land he sold. Or he may have reserved a small corner where the family burial plot was located. Anything else of value you must determine from the record itself.)

7. The names of witnesses—exactly as they appear. (Today's deeds do not usually have witnesses but rather acknowledgements by notaries.)

8. The signature(s) of the grantor(s). (Though you do not find actual signatures in the land-record books in the days before photocopy recording, it is often helpful to know whether a man signed his own name or whether he used a mark, and this *is* indicated in the deed books.)

9. Any release of dower rights by the wife of the grantor. (Such releases are often recorded immediately following the deeds to which they pertain—but not always.)

B. Abstracting Probate Records

As you abstract probate records there are nine items to consider in addition to the type of document, the source, locality references, and the essential dates. They are:

1. The name of the testator—the person who made the will.

2. Any additional description of the testator—such as place of residence, occupation, inferences of age or state of health, etc.

3. All persons named in the will should be listed in the order named, in direct connection with . . .

4. Any relationships stated for those persons to either the testator or to each other, and . . .

5. The essentials of the bequests and devises made to these persons. (This should include any land descriptions, names of Negro slaves, amounts of money, and all other property of consequence.)

6. Miscellaneous information. (Again, this is a difficult category to define because wills are just as unpredictable as deeds. But usually any special explanations, restrictions, or privileges might fall into this classification.)

7. The name(s) of the executor(s) and any relationships or connections which are stated between him (them) and the testator.

8. The names of witnesses—exactly as they appear.

9. The signature of the testator. (As with deeds it is often useful to know whether a man signed his name or made his mark. This evidence may help support a connection sometime. And though the wills in the registers are not the originals and do not show original signatures, they do indicate if a mark was used, and marks were usually duplicated from the original documents.)

Now that we have discussed the essentials of abstracting deeds and wills, let's look at some actual documents and the abstracts of them. The deeds abstracted here were recorded in Washington County, Virginia, and the wills in Guilford County, North Carolina.

III. ABSTRACTS OF DEEDS

A. Example No. 1

DEEDS OF WASHINGTON COUNTY, VIRGINIA—BOOK 11 (1831-1834), PAGE 6.

This Indenture made this first day of November in the year of our Lord one thousand eight hundred and thirty one Between Jacob Lynch commissioner appointed for the purpose by the County Court of Washington of the one part and Andrew Shannon of the County of Washington and State of Virginia of the other part: Whereas in a suit in chancery depending in the County Court of Washington aforesaid wherein Andrew Shannon is Complt and Hannah Warsham, David S, Joseph, Jonathan M. Warsham and Jesse Lee & Edith his wife, widow and heirs of William Warsham deceased, John & Joseph Warsham, Eliza and Robert Warsham children & sole heirs of Robert Warsham Jr dec^{d}, Thomas Warsham, Jeremiah Warsham, The children and heirs of Beary Warsham, decd, the children & heirs of Jefferson W. Warsham, dec, John, Maria, Polly, George, and the other five children of Patsey Smith dec^{d} & Tobias Smith her husband, William Mackey & Ruth his wife, being all heirs of Robert Warsham the elder deceased are defendants, it was on the 18th day of May 1831 adjudged ordered and decreed that Jacob Lynch who is hereby appointed Commissioner for the purpose do convey to the Complt all the lands in the bill mentioned, except the portion of Lee & wife and the interest therein of Polly Rockholds heirs according to the partition between the Complainant and Lee and wife which is hereby affirmed, with covenants of special warranty against himself and his heirs: and the Complt be forever quieted in the possession and enjoyment of the lands hereby decreed to be conveyed: Now therefore This Indenture Witnesseth: That the said Jacob Lynch for and in consideration of the promises Doth hereby grant, bargain & sell unto the said Andrew Shannon and his heirs, the tract of land above mentioned which according to the plot filed among the papers in said suit in Chancery contains one hundred and fifty three acres 135¾ poles, and is bounded as followeth to wit Beginning at two Spanish oaks and poplar N 43° W 78 poles to a black oak, N. 53° W 140 poles to two white oaks & a black oak N. 53° E 160 poles to a double Socerwood & a white oak S. 39° E 88 poles to a Spanish oak and Sugartree 39° 23′ E. 144.2 poles to a stake on the patent line S 63° 40′ W 54 poles to the Beginning excepting such interest az the heirs of Polly Rockhold dec[d] may have therein with all its appurtenances. To Have and To Hold the above described tract of land with all its appurtenances unto the said Andrew Shannon and his heirs forever. And the said Jacob Lynch for himself and his heirs doth covenant with the said Andrew Shannon and his heirs that he the said Jacob Lynch and his heirs, the said tract or parcel of land, except az before excepted, unto the said Andrew Shannon and his heirs against all claim which said Lynch or his heirs, hath acquired thereto under the decree aforesaid will warrant and forever defend In Witness whereof the said Jacob Lynch hath hereunto subscribed his name and affixed his seal the day & year first written.

(signed) Jacob Lynch

[No witnesses signed.]

This Indenture of bargain and seal was acknowledged in the clerks office of Washington County on the 11th day of November 1831 before David Campbell clerk of the said County by the said Jacob Lynch as his act and deed and admitted to record.

Not only does the above deed challenge the ability of the abstracter, it also suggests that court records in Chancery will hold some valuable information on the Warsham family. The sad part about a record like this one is that the researcher looking for records of the Warsham family may never find it because it is indexed with Jacob Lynch, the court-appointed commissioner, as grantor. (This is one of the problems with indexes to land records discussed in the last chapter.)

Now let's see if we can make an abstract:

DEEDS OF WASHINGTON CO, VA—BK 11 (1831-4) P. 6.

Deed from JACOB LYNCH, Commissioner, to ANDREW SHANNON of Wash. Co.—result of suit in Chancery 18 May 1831 in which sd. SHANNON was complt. and the defend's were: "HANNAH WARSHAM, DAVID S., JOSEPH, JONATHAN M. WARSHAM & JESSE LEE & EDITH HIS WIFE, WIDOW & HEIRS OF WILLIAM WARSHAM DECD, JOHN & JOSEPH WARSHAM, ELIZA & ROBERT WARSHAM CHN & SOLE HEIRS OF ROBERT WARSHAM JR DECD, THOMAS WARSHAM, JEREMIAH WARSHAM, THE CHN & HEIRS OF BEARY WARSHAM, DECD, THE CHN & HEIRS OF JEFFERSON W. WARSHAM, DECD, JOHN, MARIA, POLLY, GEORGE, & OTHER 5 CHN OF PATSEY SMITH DECD & TOBIAS SMITH HER HUSBAND, WILLIAM MACKEY & RUTH HIS WIFE, BEING ALL HEIRS OF ROBERT WARSHAM THE ELDER DECD."—By court order LYNCH to transfer all lands mentioned in bill except portion of LEE & wife & interest of POLY ROCKHOLD'S HEIRS according to partition btw SHANNON & LEE—plot of tract filed with papers in suit—53 acres, 135¾ poles—Beginning at 2 Spanish oaks and poplar . . .—(adj. land holders and identifying topographic features not named)—no witnesses signed—(signed) Jacob Lynch—1 Nov 1831—Ack. & recd: 11 Nov 1831.

You will note that I used several abbreviations in this abstract, but names are not abbreviated unless they are abbreviated in the record being abstracted. They are always copied *exactly as they are found.* Note also that I have done a lot of capitalizing. This makes the abstract much easier to use and the data therein easier to tabulate. You can underline with similar effect. Without additional evidence some of the relationship information in this deed could be very easily misinterpreted. In cases like this you should do as I have done and copy the information verbatim rather than try to interpret it. (Anything copied verbatim is put in quotation marks.) By following these procedures you can save yourself a lot of headaches and questions later when you begin to analyze your notes.

B. Example No. 2

DEEDS OF WASHINGTON COUNTY, VIRGINIA—BOOK 11 (1831-1834), PAGE 289.

This Indenture made this 23d day of July 1833, Between James Mobley of the one part and Peter Mayo of the other part, both of Washington County, Virginia: Witnesseth that the said James Mobley for and in consideration of one dollar to him in hand paid, doth bargain and sell unto the said Peter Mayo and his heirs the following property To wit, two negro boys, one named William about 13 years old, and one named Mark about ten years old, being slaves left him Mobley by his father John Mobley dec[d] To Have and To Hold said property unto said Peter Mayo and his heirs against the claims of all persons whomsoever. In Trust: Nevertheless, that if the said James Mobley or his heirs, shall on or before the 23[d] day of July 1834 will and truly pay or cause to be paid unto James C. Hayter the just and full sum of three hundred dollars with interest from this day which is justly due him, together with the expense of drawing and recording this Indenture, then this Indenture to be void. And in further Trust that if said James Mobley or his heirs shall fail to pay the said sum of three hundred dollars with interest on or before the 23[d] day of July 1833 [sic] then it shall be lawful for the said Peter Mayo or his heirs, executors or administrators to proceed to sell the above described property at public sale, to the highest bidder for ready money, having advertised the time and place of sale twenty days by putting up an advertisement for that purpose for that space of time at the front door of the Courthouse in Washington County, and out of the proceeds of said sale to pay said Hayter whatever may be due him of the debt aforesaid the expense of drawing and recording this Indenture, the expense of sale and six per cent to said trustee for his trouble, and the overplus if any to said James Mobley or his heirs, and if the property should not pay the debt, he promises to pay the balance and binds his heirs thereto In Witness whereof said parties have hereunto set their hands and seals this day and year first above written.

(signed) James Mobley
(signed) Peter Mayo

[No witnesses signed.]

At a court continued and held for Washington County the 23[d] day of July 1833.

This Indenture in trust between James Mobley of the one part and Peter Mayo of the other part, was acknowledged in court by the said Mobley and Mayo as their act and deed and ordered to be recorded.

As you may have noted from reading it, the above instrument is a trust indenture and was made to ensure the payment of a debt. (It is not a trust deed because it does not deal with real estate, but it is nevertheless recorded in the deed registers.) If, and when, that debt is paid the indenture becomes void. Let's abstract it:

DEEDS OF WASHINGTON CO. VA.—BK 11 (1831-4) P. 289.

Indenture in trust from JAMES MOBLEY to PETER MAYO, both of Wash. Co.—for $1—2 negro boys, William, age 13, & Mark, age 10—slaves left to MOBLEY by HIS FATHER JOHN MOBLEY, DECD—to secure payment of $300 debt owed by MOBLEY to

JAMES C. HAYTER, due 23 July 1834—if debt not pd property to be sold at public sale by MAYO to pay debt—no witnesses signed —(signed) James Mobley, Peter Mayo—23 July 1833—Ack. & Recd: same day.

C. Example No. 3

DEEDS OF WASHINGTON COUNTY, VIRGINIA—BOOK 12 (1834-1837), PAGE 45.

This Indenture made this 30th day of January in the year of our Lord one thousand eight hundred and thirty between Joseph Warsham and Nancy his wife of the County of Washington and State of Virginia of the one part and John Hacket of the said County and State of the other part Witnesseth that the said Joseph Warsham & Nancy his wife for and in consideration of the sum of ________ current money of the United States to them in hand paid, the receipt whereof is hereby acknowledged do grant bargain and sell unto the said John Hacket a certain piece or parcel of land, lying and being in the County of Washington on the waters of the North fork of Holstein and in the rich Valley being part of two surveys one of 190 acres patented to John McHenry & one of 50 acres patented to Job Crabtree, and bounded as follows, to wit, Beginning at a Sugar tree and Buckeye Sapling on the South line of the said 50 acre survey thence for a division line between said Hackett and Warsham N 9½° W. 61 poles to two Buckeye saplings and a Stake in a rich hollow N 45° W 38 poles to a white oak dogwood and Maple Sapling N 66° 27 poles to a white oak and Dogwood N 3° E 17 poles crossing the creek to a white oak at the mouth of a cave near where a beech stood a corner of the 190 acre survey and with a line thereof S 75° W 90 poles to a white oak and maple N. 84° W 7 poles to a white oak thence leaving said lines S 17° E 39 poles to a Locust bush on the top of a hill S 28½° E 110 poles to a dogwood and small buckeye bush N 55° E 52 poles to the Beginning containing fifty four acres be the same more or less with all its appurtenances. To Have and To Holde, the said piece or parcel of land with all its appurtenances unto the said John Hacket and his heirs to the sole use and behoof of him the said John Hacket and his heirs forever. And the said Joseph Warsham and Nancy his wife for themselves and their heirs do covenant with the said John Hacket and his heirs that they the said Warsham & wife and their heirs, the said piece or parcel of land with all its appurtenances unto the said John Hacket and his heirs against the claims of all persons whomsoever, shall Warrant and will forever defend. In Witness whereof the said Joseph Warsham & Nancy his wife have hereunto subscribed their names and affixed their seals, the day and year first above written.

signed sealed and delivered (signed) Joseph Warsham
in presence of [No witnesses (signed) Nancy Warsham
named.]

Washington County, to wit,

We Joseph C. Trigg and Tobias Smith justice of the peace of the county aforesaid in the state of Virginia do hereby certify that Nancy Warsham the wife of Joseph Warsham parties to a certain deed bearing date on this 30th January 1830 and hereunto annexed personally appeared before us in our County aforesaid and being examined by us prively and apart from her husband and having the deed aforesaid fully explained to her she the said Nancy Warsham acknowledged the same to be her act and deed and declared that she had willingly signed sealed and delivered the same and she wished not to retract it given under our hands & seals this 30th January 1830.

(signed) Joseph C. Trigg
(signed) Tobias Smith

At a Court held in Washington County the 27th day of October 1834 This Indenture of bargain & sale between Joseph Warsham & Nancy his wife of the one part and John Hacket of the other part was acknowledged in Court by the said Warsham as his act and deed and together with the certificate of the acknowledgment of the said Nancy made thereto ordered to be recorded.

There is nothing unusual about this deed. It is probably very much like most deeds you will find for your ancestors and presents very few problems for the abstracter. Your abstract might look something like this:

DEEDS OF WASHINGTON CO, VA—BK 12 (1834-7) P. 45.

Deed from JOSEPH WARSHAM AND WIFE NANCY of Wash. Co. to JOHN HACKET of Wash. Co.—for (price not stated)—tract in Wash. Co. on N. fork of Holstein [sic] in the rich Valley, part of 2 surveys (one of 190 acres patented to JOHN McHENRY & one of 50 acres patented to JOB CRABTREE), "Beginning at a Sugartree and Buckeye sapling on S. line of said 50 acre survey . . ." —54 acres—no witnesses signed—(signed) Joseph Warsham, Nancy Warsham—Certif. of acknowledgement made by Nancy—30 Jan 1830—Recd: 27 Oct 1834.

D. Example No. 4

DEEDS OF WASHINGTON COUNTY, VIRGINIA—BOOK 12 (1834-1837), PAGE 40.

This Indenture made this tenth day of October in the year of our Lord one thousand eight hundred and thirty one Between Isaiah

Austin heir at Law of James Austin deceased of the county of Washington of the one part and John Austin of Atkens Tennessee of the other part Witnesses that the said Isaiah Austin the father and heir at law of James Austin deceased for and in consideration of the sum of two thousand dollars current money of the United States to him in hand paid, the receipt whereof is hereby acknowledged doth grant bargain and sell unto the said John Austin two several tracts of land adjoining each other lying and being in the County of Washington on the waters of the middle fork of holston river, One which was conveyed to the said James by deed bearing date the 4th of October 1823 executed to him by James Edmondson and William Buchanan executors of William E. Buchanan deceased bounded as follows to wit, Beginning on two white oaks and dogwood N. 16½° West 88 poles to a white oak and hickory North 1° East 54 poles to a white oak & Black oak on the side of the knob, South 54½° West 136 poles North 62½° West 36 poles South 29½° West 58 poles South 66° West 146 poles to a black oak on the great road South 57° East 120 poles to a white oak, South 12½° East 36 poles to a hickory and dogwood North 62° East 114 poles to the Beginning containing two hundred acres be the same more or less. Also one other tract conveyed to the said Isaiah Austin by James Edmondson bounded az follows to wit Beginning at three chestnut oaks on a ridge on said Edmondsons line thence with the same S 27° E 70 poles to two white oaks corner to same S 5° E. 16 poles to a white oak and black oak corner to James Austins land, thence with Austins line S 57° W 136 poles to two hickories and white oaks N 70° W 36 poles to a maple on the side of a Knob S 32° W 58 poles to a white oak S 65° W 76 poles to a stake on said James Austins line thence with Benjamin Sharps line N 37° W 14 poles to a white oak and two hickories Thence N 50° E 122 poles to two white oaks & ash by a swamp thence N 45° E 180 poles to the Beginning. containing ninety five acres with all its appurtenances: To Have and To Hold the said tracts or parcels of land with all their appurtenances unto the said John Auston and his heirs to the sole use and behoof of him the said John Austin and his heirs forever. And the said Isaiah Auston for himself and his heirs doth covenant with the said John Austin and his heirs that he the said Isaiah Auston and his heirs the said tract or parcels of land with all appurtenances unto the said John Auston and his heirs against the claims of all persons whomsoever, shall and will forever defend. In witness whereof the said Isaiah Auston hath hereto subscribed his name and affixed his seal the day and year first above written.

Signed sealed & delivered
in presence of — Isaiah X (his mark) Austin

John H. Fulton — Bev R. Johnston
John C. Cummings — Charles S. Bekem

At a Court held for Washington County the 27th day of October 1834 This Indenture of bargain & sale between Isaiah Austin of the one part and John Austin of the other part was proved in court by the oath of John H. Fulton, Beverly R. Johnston and Charles S. Bekem three of the subscribing witnesses thereto to be the act and deed of said Isaiah and ordered to be recorded:

There is the deed; here is my abstract of it:

DEEDS OF WASHINGTON CO, VA—BK 12 (1834-7) P. 40.

Deed from ISAIAH AUSTIN, FATHER & HEIR AT LAW OF JAMES AUSTIN, DECD of Wash. Co. to JOHN AUSTIN OF ATKENS, TENN. (both names sometimes spelled AUSTON in the deed)—for $2,000—2 tracts adj. each other on middle fork of Holston River—1 conveyed to sd JAMES AUSTIN by JAMES EDMONDSON & WILLIAM BUCHANAN, EXORS OF WILLIAM E. BUCHANAN, "Beginning on two white oaks and dogwood . . ." on the great road (200 acres)—other conveyed to ISAIAH by JAMES EDMONDSON, "Beginning at 3 chestnut oaks on a ridge on sd EDMONDSON's line . . ." adj. JAMES AUSTIN'S land & sd EDMONDSON AND BENJAMIN SHARP (95 acres)—witnesses: JOHN H. FULTON, JOHN C. CUMMINGS, BEV(ERLY) R. JOHNSTON, CHARLES S. BEKEM—(signed) Isaiah X (his mark) Austin—10 Oct 1831—Recd: 27 Oct 1834.

E. Example No. 5

DEEDS OF WASHINGTON COUNTY, VIRGINIA—BOOK 12 (1834-1837), PAGE 366.

This Indenture made this first day of December 1835 between Amelia Conn Senr and Amelia Conn Jr. both of Washington County Virginia. Witnesseth that the said Amelia Conn Sr for & in consideration of the natural love and affection which she bears unto her daughter the said Amelia Conn Jr. & for the further consideration of one dollar to her in hand paid hath granted given bargained & sold to the said Amelia Junnor thirty two acres of the tract of land on which she the said Amelia Conn Sr at the present resides to include the dwelling house & spring and to be laid off in convenient form, To Have and To Hold the same unto the said Amelia Conn Jr. & her heirs forever. But the said Amelia Sr reserves to herself the right to the possession and exclusive enjoyment of the said land and premises during her natural Life at the termination of which the said Amelia Conn Junr or her heirs shall be entitled to enter upon the same In witness whereof the said Amelia Conn Senr hath set her hand & seal the day and year first above written.

Attest
David Parks — Amelia IE (her mark) Conn
John Melton
John Parks

This Indenture of bargain & sale between Amelia Conn Sr of the one part and Amelia Conn Jr of the other part was proved in the Clerk's office of Washington County on the 2nd day of March 1836 before David Campbell Clerk of the said County by the oath of David Parks one of the subscribing witnesses thereto to be the act & deed of said Amelia Senr. At a court held for Washington County the 22[d] day of August 1836—

It was proved in Court by the oath of John Parks another witness thereto to be the act & deed of said Amelia Senr—And at a Court continued and held for said county the 23[d] day of August 1836—It was further proved in Court by the oath of John Melton another witness thereto to be the act & deed of said Amelia Senr and ordered to be recorded.

And the abstract:

DEEDS OF WASHINGTON CO, VA—BK 12 (1834-7) P. 366.

Gift deed from AMELIA CONN SR TO HER DAU AMELIA CONN JR, both of Wash. Co.—for love and affection & $1—32 acres of tract where AMELIA SR. now resides, including dwelling house & spring, to be laid off—AMELIA SR reserves right to possession during natural life—witnesses: DAVID PARKS, JOHN MELTON, JOHN PARKS—(signed) Amelia IE (her mark) Conn —1 Dec 1835—Recd: 23 Aug 1836.

Let's look now at the mechanics involved in abstracting wills.

IV. ABSTRACTS OF WILLS

A. Example No. 1

WILLS OF GUILFORD COUNTY, NORTH CAROLINA, BOOK A (1771-1813), PAGE 37.

Whereas Thomas Cox of Richland Creek in Guilford County and North Carolina yeoman being but weak in body but in perfect mind and memory and taking into consideration the certainty of death and ye uncertainty of life hath thought good to make order and appoint this my last will and Testament in manner and form following revoking and disr—tling all manner of will or wills before by me made this only to be my last will and Testament.

Imprimis [first]—I commit my soul to Almighty God who gave it me and my body to be decently buried by my brother Solomon Cox and William Wierman who I appoint my Executors to see the accomplishment of this my last Will and Testament and make full satisfaction for all funeral charges and other Worldly debts every where to be paid. —

I leave and give to my beloved wife a fether bed & bed cloaths a side sadle and bridle and the third part of all the remainder part of my personal estate excepting only such particular artickels as are herein hereafter mentioned and given to particular persons.

I leave and give to my son Thomas one hundred acres of land including the improvements whereon I live to him his heirs and assigns forever—I leave and give my son Joshua one hundred acres of land to be laid of for him on the South side of the aforesaid tract and joining Solomon Cox's land to him his heirs and assigns forever. I leave and give my son Daniel one hundred acres of land to be laid of for him on the west side of my son Thomas' land to him his heirs and assigns forever.— I leave and give my son John one hundred acres of land to be laid of for him on the North side of my son Thomas' land to him his heirs and assigns forever.— I leave and give to my son Abner all the remainder part of my lands to be laid of for him where it should be most suitable to be valuable.— I leave and give my daughter Sarah a fether bed.— I leave and give my daughter Martha a fether bed to be made of the benefits of my improvements, and it is my will and desire that my wife shall live with my son Thomas on his place if she so wishes so long as she lives single—and I leave and give to my son Thomas ten pounds prock money—and it is my will and desire that my children have larning at least to read and write.— I leave and give to my son Abner fifteen pounds prock money—and I leave the remainder part of my personal estate to be equally divided among all my children—and it is my will that my sons shall possess every one his part of my estate at the age of twenty one years and that my daughters shall everyone possess her part at the age of eighteen years—and it is my will that if any of my sons do not live to the age of twenty one years that then his or their lands shall be sold to the highest bider of his brethren and the price thereof be equally divided amongst his brethren—and it is my will that if any of my children do not live to the years above ordered to possess their estates at that then his heirs or their personal estate shall be equally divided amongst the living ones.

Signed and sealed in the
presence of (signed) Thomas Cox

Wm Garner
Stephen Hussey (jurat)
John Kenworthy

North Carolina, Guilford County, November Court 1771. Then the within last will & Testament of

Thomas Cox was proved in open court by the oath of Stephen Hussey one of the subscribing witnesses thereto and motion ordered to be recorded. Then Solomon Cox and William Wierman (who by the Testator were left Executors of the within will) came into court and qualified as such &c.

An abstract of Thomas Cox's will might look something like this:

WILLS OF GUILFORD CO, N.C.— BK A (1771-1813) P. 37.
WILL OF THOMAS COX, Richland Creek, Guilf. Co, Yeoman —weak in body—Exors: MY BROTHER SOLOMON COX & WILLIAM WIERMAN.

To my BELOVED WIFE (NOT NAMED)—certain personal property.
To my SON THOMAS—100 acres including improvements whereon I now live.
To my SON JOSHUA—100 acres on S. side of aforsd tract—adj. SOLOMON COX.
To my SON DANIEL—100 acres on W. side of SON THOMAS.
To my SON JOHN—100 acres on N. side of SON THOMAS.
To my SON ABNER—all the remainder part of my lands.
To my DAU SARAH—fether bed.
To my DAU MARTHA—fether bed.
MY WIFE to live with my SON THOMAS as long as she is single (if she desires).
To my SON THOMAS—10 pounds prock[lamation] money.
To my SON ABNER—10 pounds prock money.
ALL MY CHN shall learn to read and write.
Remainder of personal estate divided equally among chn.
SONS to possess their part of estate AT AGE 21, and DAUS AT AGE 18.
If son dies before 21 land to sell to highest bidding brother, price equally divided amongst his brethren.
If any child die before of age, personal estate divided equally to other children.

Witness: WM GARNER, STEPHEN HUSSEY, JOHN KENWORTHY.

(signed) THOMAS COX.

Not dated—Proved: Nov Crt 1771.

The way I have abstracted this will takes a little more space than it would have if I had just listed one item right after the other with only dashes between, as I did with the deeds. You can do it the other way, but this format makes for easier tabulation.

B. Example No. 2

WILLS OF GUILFORD COUNTY, NORTH CAROLINA—BOOK A (1771-1813), PAGE 224.

This first day of February in the year of our Lord one thousand eight hundred and fourteen I Robert Lamb of the State of North Carolina and County of Guilford: being sound in health of bodday minde and memmory do make this my last will and testament at the same time revoking all former wills made by me, declaring this to be my last will & Testament.

Firstly—I give and bequeath unto my three sons namely Samuel, Simeon and John Lam all the lands that I have previously put them in possession of together with there stock and every spicice of property that I have heretofore given them.

I also give and bequeath unto my four daughters and my grand daughter namely Elizabeth White Deborah Hoggatt Ester Hodson Ann Reynolds Margate Balilen each and every of them the whole property which I have heretofour given them.

I allso give and bequeath unto my beloved wife all my household furniture together with all the live stock which I am now in possession of the same to be subject to hir use and benefit during hir natureal life and at hir death the same to be devided eaqually between my three sons my four daughters and my grand daughter as above named—and lastly after my just debts are paid I give and bequeath all the rezidue of all my estate what eaver and whearever to my eight children as above named equally devided between them and at the same time. I appoint my friend Zino Worth and do impower him to act as the Executor of this my last will and Testament to which I have hereunto set my hand and affixed my seal the day and date above mentioned.

Daniel Worth (Jurat)
Benjamin Hall — Robert X (his mark) Lamb

For probate &c. of the foregoing Will—see min. Doc. No. 4 page 409.

There is the will; now let's abstract it:

WILLS OF GUILFORD CO, N.C.—BK A (1771-1813) P. 224.
WILL OF ROBERT LAMB of Guilf. Co—in good health.

To my 3 SONS SAMUEL, SIMEON & JOHN LAM—all lands and property I have previously given them.

To my 4 DAUS AND MY G DAU ELIZABETH WHITE, DEBORAH HOGGATT, ESTER HODSON, ANN REYNOLDS, MARGATE BALILEN—property I have heretofore given them.

To my BELOVED WIFE (NOT NAMED)—all household furniture and livestock now in my possession, during her natural life—

at her death to be divided among my 3 SONS, 4 DAUS AND G DAU.
All residue to my 8 CHN, above named, equally.
Exor: My FRIEND ZINO WORTH.
Witness: DANIEL WORTH, BENJAMIN HALL.
(signed) ROBERT X (his mark) LAMB.
Dated: 1 Feb 1814—No date of probate given ("FOR PROBATE, ETC., SEE MINUTE DOCKET #4, P. 409.")

Notice that the above will suggests the use of another record. You would make a serious mistake if you failed to look up the court record (minute docket) where the information about the probate of this will is recorded. I also inserted commas between some names in this abstract, but *only when their placement was obvious.*

C. Example No. 3

Some other types of probate records contain very few specific genealogical data yet are significant in other ways. Consider, for example, the account of the administrator of his activities in probating an estate. Names and dates are significant, but often little else. Here is an example:

SETTLEMENTS OF ESTATES, GUILFORD COUNTY, NORTH CAROLINA, 1844-1853, PAGE 104.
MAY Term 1846

May 15th 1846—We the undersigned Justices of the Peace in aforesaid County having met at the house of James S. Watson Admr of Eleanor Watson Decd in pursuance of an order of Court to us directed proceeding to settle with said Admr and find as follows:

Dr. to amount of Sales $198.57
Vouchers

[Immediately following is a long list of accounts, the names of which are probably, but may not be, without significance. Because of this factor, it is usually desirable at least to make an abstract of the foregoing and then list the names. In this account the names were:]

M.D. Smith, Washington Donnett, Walter McConnel, Saml Nelson, Francis Obriant, Catharine Clark, L. W. Doakes, Rev. John A. Gritter, DR. L. W. WATSON, James R. McLean, Sarah Mathews, Mrs. Dick.

[These names may provide some clues to connections with other persons when considered with other evidence.]

(signed) F. Shaw J.P.
(signed) E. Denny J.P.

All information in this chapter is given only as a suggestion. I am not trying to dictate the specific form or content of your abstracts, but merely suggesting that your abstracts, though brief, must be complete enough to meet the demands of thorough scientific research. I hope my suggestions and examples will be helpful and will expedite your research. But, above all, your notes must be both complete and correct, because these records (land and probate records) are the "bread and butter" sources of American genealogical research. Relevant evidence found in land and probate records is usually limited so you are going to need all the information that is there—in just the way it is there.

19

Court Records

To some it may seem strange to include an entire chapter on court records since many of the records already discussed have been court records of one type or another—notably land, probate, and guardianship records. However, other types of court records may also be valuable genealogically and deserve our attention.

The story is told of a man who was going down the highway and stopped to help a lady motorist whose car had stalled. When he asked what the trouble was, she replied that she thought something was wrong with the clutch. The man went around and lifted the hood and, after looking inside, went back to report that the motor had fallen from its mounts and was lying on the ground beneath the vehicle. Her reply (in all seriousness): "Thank goodness it wasn't the clutch."

Somehow this woman got the idea that there were only certain things that could go wrong with her car, and if the problem was not one of those then it was of little consequence. The beginning genealogist often falls into the same trap as he tells himself that only certain records are of value and that others are not worthy of serious consideration. However, when he happens to need those other records—when they fit his problem—they are of great importance.

It has been my experience that court records, as a category, though not among the most important records in existence, are in some cases extremely valuable. When court records exist for your ancestor, or when you find a situation which suggests their probable existence, you should take heed.

I. BACKGROUND AND DEFINITION

Court records, as discussed in this chapter, are the records of actions on civil matters. Roughly, court records are divided into two categories—criminal (public)[1] and civil (private). This work will not discuss criminal court records except to define them and to state that there is considerable overlap in records of criminal and civil actions in most courts. Criminal actions deal with the bringing of public offenders to justice. Crimes are defined and punishments are established by statute. Civil actions deal primarily with the protection of individual rights, and most civil actions have two parties (plaintiff and defendant) opposed to each other for the recovery of a right or the redress of a wrong which the plaintiff claims to have suffered because of the acts of the defendant. It should be noted, however, that non-adversary proceedings, such as name changes, naturalizations, adoptions, and the like, may also have significant genealogical importance.

Extensive records are maintained by the courts. Every writ, affidavit, complaint, answer, summons, subpoena, judgment, injunction, petition, motion, deposition, pleading, sentence, order, decree, and all proceedings and testimony of every case are detailed in the courts' records and filed in systematic order. The extent and volume of these records is almost unbelievable to the layman.

II. A MISCONCEPTION

The LDS Family History Library and other organizations have filmed some court records besides those already discussed in previous chapters—mainly court minutes, dockets,[2] and court orders—but only on rare occasions do they film the court files themselves (and in some localities where minutes, dockets, etc., have been filmed, not all of these). Many researchers have received the impression that these films represent all court records available in the localities from which they come—a serious error to make. These films generally represent only a minute portion of the available court records.

---

[1] Public law is that branch of law which involves the state in its sovereign capacity. Other forms of public law, of little concern to us here, include Constitutional, administrative, and international law.

[2] Dockets are brief chronological abstracts of court actions and judgments prepared by the court clerk. In many states the law requires that these be indexed also.

I am not saying that these filmed court records have no value, because some are extremely useful. Court dockets and minutes are especially good,[3] and usually contain things such as judgments, decrees, commissioners' reports and resolutions, and various other court actions. Entries vary all the way from the simple notation that the action has been continued (carried over) until a later date, to the detailed account of activities of an administrator in a probate matter. Some of these minutes and dockets are also indexed, which makes them quite easy to use. Those who have done microfilming in these records have been more inclined to film some types of court records than they have others. The minutes, dockets, and court orders are bound and easily accessible, while loose files are much more difficult to work with (besides their prodigious volume).

In a few cases, as with judgments of the Maryland Court of Appeals, some quite extensive court records have been filmed but, generally speaking, those records designated as "court record books" and "court orders" have only limited value.

You must never hesitate to write to the court where you have indication of the existence of valuable court records pertaining to your ancestors; in a given case this may be the most intelligent move you could make.

III. THE AMERICAN COURT SYSTEM

It is impossible, in the limited space available here, to explain the intricacies of the American court system, but I will try to give you an idea of the essential nature of the system. In addition to the distinctions between civil and criminal matters, already alluded to, there are some basic distinctions, the discussion of which may benefit your understanding of U.S. court records. These include:

1. State courts vs. federal courts.
2. Law vs. equity.
3. Trial courts vs. appellate courts.

1. State courts vs. federal courts: There are two sources of court control —the individual states and the federal government. The federal government,

[3] If you have ancestry in North Carolina never overlook the old minutes of the County Superior Courts, a few of which are on film, and of the old Courts of Pleas and Quarter Sessions, which are almost completely microfilmed. In some states lists of pending equity cases—called *lis pendens*—have also been filmed and have some genealogical value.

in addition to the U.S. Supreme Court, controls the U.S. Courts of Appeals set up in the circuits and the U.S. District Courts (and some others which I will not discuss here). The federal District Courts, which often include whole states as districts, have jurisdiction over all admiralty and maritime causes, most criminal cases indictable under federal laws, and many civil matters.

The courts set up under state statute differ from one state to another and, of course, are subject to structural change at the will of the several state legislatures. One thing that may be confusing to those trying to distinguish between state and federal courts is that many of the courts have the same names. Several of the states have District Courts and several others have Circuit Courts. They usually include several counties in each district or circuit, but in New England some states have several districts in each county.

Every state has a Supreme Court, but every Supreme Court is not the same. In most states the Supreme Court is a court of final appeal, but in New York it is a court of general original jurisdiction which possesses limited appellate jurisdiction. Some states have County Courts with ordinary civil jurisdiction, limited criminal jurisdiction, appellate jurisdiction of justices of the peace or magistrates, as well as jurisdiction over probate and guardianship matters. In other states, courts of various other names perform these functions. In many states you will find Circuit Courts; others have Courts of Common Pleas, and still others have Superior Courts. Some states may have several of these. Some states have Justice-of-the-Peace Courts and others have Magistrate Courts; others have both. Both of these courts usually have limited original jurisdiction and may not be courts where records are kept. Some have Family Courts and some have Small Claims Courts, etc., etc., etc. Each state has its own system, and you have to get used to the idea that what is called by one name in one state is called by another name some place else.

As you use court records—or seek to use them—you should understand that federal court records usually have limited value to the genealogist. Most of the court records in which you will probably be interested are in the state court system. For many reasons, mostly jurisdictional, only a small percentage of actions are brought in the federal courts.

2. Law vs. equity: At common law the terms *equity* and *chancery* (which are synonymous) are used to describe one type of court proceeding and the term *law* is used to describe another. Equity means "justice" and relates to impartial justice between two parties whose claims (or rights) conflict. Except where bound by common law (i.e., legal precedent), judicial discretion may be exercised and traditionally there is no right to jury trial.

In an action at law one seeks to recover monetary damages for injuries to himself, his property, his pocketbook, or his reputation; while in a suit in equity he seeks to compel someone to do something (specific performance decree) or to stop doing or refrain from doing something (injunction). Equity courts handle divorces, foreclosures of liens, receiverships, partitions, trusts, *real property controversies* (with *lis pendens*), etc.

Two of the most important types of actions at law are founded in *contract* and *tort*. A tort is a wrong or injury arising out of the law, not associated with a contract but involving a legal duty, a breach of that duty, and injury as a result of the breach. It involves injury to one's person (including his reputation and feelings) or his property. Assault, battery, trespass, misrepresentation, defamation, and negligence are common torts.

Equity came into existence in England as the result of lengthy power struggles between Parliament and the Crown. When Parliament said no more legal writs could be created by the King's courts as a source of relief, except those which already existed, the Crown named chancellors (and created chancery courts) with authority to give equitable relief in situations where the law provided no relief to those wronged.

Concerning the early history of American civil actions (equity actions especially) one legal writer, during the first part of this century, wrote:

> The American colonies were settled during the most influential period of the chancery court in England, and it, along with other serviceable institutions of the mother country, became engrafted on the judicial system of the various colonies. In most of them the equity powers were exercised by the royal governor in conjunction with his council, while in Rhode Island, during the colonial period, the assembly acted as a court of chancery. In all of the colonies, except Pennsylvania, the chancery existed as a distinct tribunal from the common law courts. In Pennsylvania equity was administered by the law courts and, according to the procedure of the common law, until the middle of . . . [the nineteenth century]. When the colonies became states, they either established separate courts of equity, presided over by chancellors, or conferred the equity powers upon the ordinary law courts with a provision for its exercise according to the forms and procedure of chancery. . . .
>
> . . . The American states and territories may be divided into three groups as regards the method followed of administering equity jurisprudence. These are:—
>
> First. Those states in which separate courts of chancery are maintained, and law and equity are administered by distinct tribunals under different modes of procedure. In this group the chancery court is copied after the Court of Chancery in England, and is similar as to powers and jurisdiction. This group . . . [has historically included] Alabama, Delaware, Mississippi, New Jersey and Tennessee.

> Second. Those states in which law and equity are still administered in their distinct and appropriate forms, but by the same court. The boundaries between the two as to jurisdiction being jealously guarded, and the chancery jurisdiction not ceasing because the statutes confer the same powers on law courts. The most important member of this group . . . [has been] the federal government of the United States, comprising the various federal courts, which follow[ed] the system uniformly and are not influenced by state legislation. The states . . . [which have historically belonged] to this group are Arkansas, Florida, Georgia, Illinois, Maine, Maryland, Massachusetts, Michigan, New Hampshire, New Mexico, Pennsylvania, Rhode Island, Vermont, Virginia and West Virginia.
>
> Third. This group includes the states and territories which have adopted the Civil Code. In these the distinction between actions at law and suits in equity is abolished, and all relief is said to be administered through the uniform procedure of civil action. The effect of this is not, however, to abolish entirely the distinction between law and equity, though affording a common method of administration. The fundamental principles of equity are regarded, and it is even quite common to refer to actions involving equity principles as equitable actions, as distinguished from law actions. The abolition of the distinction between suits in equity and law as made by the Codes does not allow of the bringing an action not previously cognizable either in law or equity.[4]

The states of most interest to us here are those which maintained separate courts for dealing with actions in law and equity, Mr. Chadman's first group: Alabama, Delaware, Mississippi, New Jersey, and Tennessee. Of these, Alabama and New Jersey no longer maintain separate courts. New Jersey maintains separation of law and equity, but does so in two separate divisions of the same court. Delaware, Mississippi, and Tennessee have been joined by Arkansas in maintaining separate courts.

These states (both the ones with present-day separation, and also the ones which have changed) are significant because of your need to be aware of the existence of two sets of records, either one of which might be important. And I might state that the records of equity courts often have special value because of the nature of the subject matter. For example, the law was often deemed incapable of giving adequate relief whenever the subject matter of

---

[4] Charles E. Chadman (ed.), *Chadman's Cyclopedia of Law* (Chicago: American Correspondence School of Law, 1912), Vol. 8, pp. 185-187. (The reason I have used a source so old is to capture the true historical background and significance of the American legal system. Obviously much information in such sources is now out of date but the history does not change.)

the dispute was unique, thus sending the matter into equitable jurisdiction. Thus, suits relating to possession of and title to land often were tried in equity. One of the most popular types of equitable actions involving land has been an action for ejectment. An ejectment action provides for the recovery of possession. Its significance to the genealogist is that the record of the court contains information on the history of the land and its title, especially important when the title to the land in question stayed in the same family for several generations—not an uncommon occurrence in earlier times. Under such a circumstance the record might provide information on several generations of the family. The dispute may be over the title to an entire tract or it may involve the placement of a boundary which became obscure or was unobserved when relatives owned both tracts.

Today most states make no distinction between law and equity causes to the extent that the intent is to do justice in each case without concern for cumbersome traditional distinctions. When traditional legal remedies are considered appropriate, they are applied; and when equitable remedies are called for, they are applied. Though there are differences from state to state, most have abolished distinctions between pleadings, parties, sittings, and dockets; but principles, causes, rights, remedies, and defenses are generally still intact and are available as appropriate. You should be aware, however, that many of the states have only recently adopted this approach.

In the old law courts a person could not bring a simple action to set aside a contract, to force compliance with it, or to recover damages because of its breach. He would instead bring an action in *covenant* (to recover monetary damages), or *debt* (to recover a specific sum for a contract breach), or *assumpsit* (to recover damages if the agreement was not under seal), or *detinue* (to recover specific chattels rightfully taken but wrongfully retained), or *replevin* (to recover specific chattels unlawfully taken). A damage suit (tort action) would be either in *trespass* (for monetary damages), *trover* (for damages to property or goods by interference or improper detention), or *deceit* (damages due to any injury committed deceitfully).

3. Trial court vs. appellate court: The trial court is the court of original jurisdiction where the case is tried. The appellate court is the court where a case goes on appeal from the decision of the trial court. To understand the significance of this you should know that most cases filed are never tried (they are settled—or otherwise dismissed—first); and most cases tried are never appealed.

The record of every case filed, whether it comes to trial or not, is in the trial court. This is a significant indicator of which records—those of the trial court or those of the appellate court—are most valuable to the researcher. Another important indicator is the fact that no new evidence may be introduced during an appeal. Thus, even if you find a record in the appellate court, you will find no more information there than you would in the trial court record.

Trial court records certainly have the most potential value for us, but if a case has been appealed that fact also can help you locate the trial court record. The reported opinion of the case in the appellate court will tell you the court of original jurisdiction where the trial took place. That information permits you to go back to the trial court record.

IV. RECORDS AND ACCESS

There are various indexes, minutes, court order books, and dockets available which can facilitate your access to the records. Dockets deserve special mention here because of their value in helping you find the records. A civil docket entry is a short statement giving an abbreviated account of an important act of the court in the conduct of a case. Each important act of the court and of the parties in each case is docketed this way, and all docket entries for a single case are entered on the same page. The law usually requires these dockets to be indexed. Though the dockets themselves often contain bits of valuable information, their chief function, insofar as the genealogist is concerned, is to provide access to the actual court case files.

In addition to the regular civil docket (or "register of actions," as it is sometimes called) the researcher will also encounter various other types of dockets, including trial dockets, execution dockets, and judgment dockets. These are different from civil dockets, but may all prove useful in helping you locate various court records. The trial docket (or trial list) is a list or calendar of cases set to be tried during a specified term of the court. An execution docket is a list of executions against defendants' property made by the sheriff to satisfy the various courts' judgments. A judgment docket is a list of the court's judgments kept in connection with the book in which all judgments of the court are recorded. The judgment docket and judgment book are kept very carefully because they provide official notice to all the world of judgments and liens. They are always readily available and are easy to use. Entries in the judgment docket are usually made in alphabetical sequence by the names of the defendants against whom the judgments were granted.

A court order book is also different from a civil docket. It contains only the mandates and directions of the court and does not list all papers filed with the court as the docket does. These orders are made and entered by the court in response to the motions of the parties concerned. Order books are ordinarily kept in a chronological sequence as the orders are issued by the court, and there may be several entries, over a period of time, relative to a specific case.

Each case filed with the court is kept in its own separate file (or dossier), and each file has a number to identify it. Once you learn the case file number (from the docket, court order book, or elsewhere) you may secure the file for examination and thus have access to the entire record of the action.

A. Divorce Records

Divorce records were discussed briefly in chapter 10 but, because they are essentially court records, it is appropriate to discuss them further here. Many wonder about the genealogical value of divorce records because they do not understand them, but if the couple who sought the divorce had children, the names and ages of those children are usually given in the court records (though not on the certificate). Dates of birth (or ages) of both parties, state or country of birth of both parties, the date and place of the marriage, plus the date and grounds for the divorce itself are also given.

In most states the court having authority to grant divorces is the court which has control over other equity matters. There are only a few exceptions to this. Following is a list of the courts having jurisdiction in divorce cases in the several states. The records are ordinarily kept in these courts and, in many cases, are open to public use:

ALABAMA:	Circuit Court in county.
ALASKA:	Superior Court in district (there are four judicial districts).
ARIZONA:	Superior Court in county.
ARKANSAS:	Chancery Court in county.
CALIFORNIA:	Superior Court in county.
COLORADO:	District Court in county.
CONNECTICUT:	Superior Court in county.
DELAWARE:	Family Court (after 1975) and Prothonotary (to 1975) in county.
D.C.:	Family Division, Superior Court (from September 1956) and U.S. District Court for District of Columbia (for earlier records).
FLORIDA:	Circuit Court in county.
GEORGIA:	Superior Court in county.
HAWAII:	Family Court Division, Circuit Court (there are four judicial circuits).

IDAHO:	District Court in county (County Recorder).
ILLINOIS:	Circuit Court in county.
INDIANA:	Circuit and Superior Courts in county (County Clerk).
IOWA:	District Court in county.
KANSAS:	District Court in county.
KENTUCKY:	Circuit Court in county.
LOUISIANA:	District Court in parish (Parish Clerk).
MAINE:	District Court in county.
MARYLAND:	Equity Court in county.
MASSACHUSETTS:	Probate Court in county.
MICHIGAN:	Circuit Court in county (County Clerk).
MINNESOTA:	District and County Courts in county (concurrent jurisdiction).
MISSISSIPPI:	Chancery Court in county (Chancery Clerk).
MISSOURI:	Circuit Court in county.
MONTANA:	District Court in county.
NEBRASKA:	District Court in county.
NEVADA:	District Court in county (County Clerk).
NEW HAMPSHIRE:	Superior Court in county.
NEW JERSEY:	Superior Court (Chancery Division, Family Part) in county.
NEW MEXICO:	District Court in county.
NEW YORK:	Supreme Court in county (County Clerk).
NORTH CAROLINA:	District Court in county.
NORTH DAKOTA:	District Court in county (in Family Court Division in counties over 10,000).
OHIO:	Court of Common Pleas in county.
OKLAHOMA:	District Court in county (Clerk of Court).
OREGON:	Circuit Court in county (County Clerk).
PENNSYLVANIA:	Court of Common Pleas in county (Prothonotary).
RHODE ISLAND:	Family Court in county. (In Superior Court prior to 1961.)
SOUTH CAROLINA:	County Court (Clerk of Court). (Divorce was not legal in state until April 1949.)
SOUTH DAKOTA:	Circuit Court in county (Clerk of Court).
TENNESSEE:	Circuit Court and Chancery Court in county (concurrent jurisdiction) (Clerk of Court).

TEXAS:	District Court in county.
UTAH:	District Court in county (County Clerk).
VERMONT:	Superior Court in county.
VIRGINIA:	Chancery side, Circuit Court in county or city. (See section on Virginia later on in this chapter.)
WASHINGTON:	Family Court (a department of Superior Court) in county.
WEST VIRGINIA:	Circuit Court, Chancery side, in county.
WISCONSIN:	Circuit Court in county.
WYOMING:	District Court in county.[5]

In addition to the records of divorce kept in these courts, many states have legislation which requires that a copy of the divorce certificate also be filed with the state department of vital statistics. And in some states that department is a source of divorce records. It is a good general rule that these records are quite recent, but there are a few exceptions. Records are available from the state vital statistics offices from the dates indicated below. (This list may be amended at any time, and you should refer to the most current issue of the booklet published by the U.S. Department of Health and Human Services, from which the list was compiled, for current data and more detailed instructions):

ALABAMA:	Since January 1950.
ALASKA:	Since 1950.
ARKANSAS:	Since 1923. (No certified copies, coupons only.)
D.C.:	Since January 1, 1982. Records before September 16, 1956, are in U.S. District Court for District of Columbia; records since that date are in Superior Court for District of Columbia, Family Division.
FLORIDA:	Since June 6, 1927.
HAWAII:	Since July 1951.
IDAHO:	Since January 1947.
KANSAS:	Since July 1951.
KENTUCKY:	Since June 1958.

[5] *Where to Write for Vital Records* (Hyattsville, MD: United States Department of Health and Human Services, 1987); *Martindale-Hubbell Law Directory,* 120th ed. (Summit, NJ: Martindale-Hubbell, Inc., 1988), Vol. VIII (by permission).

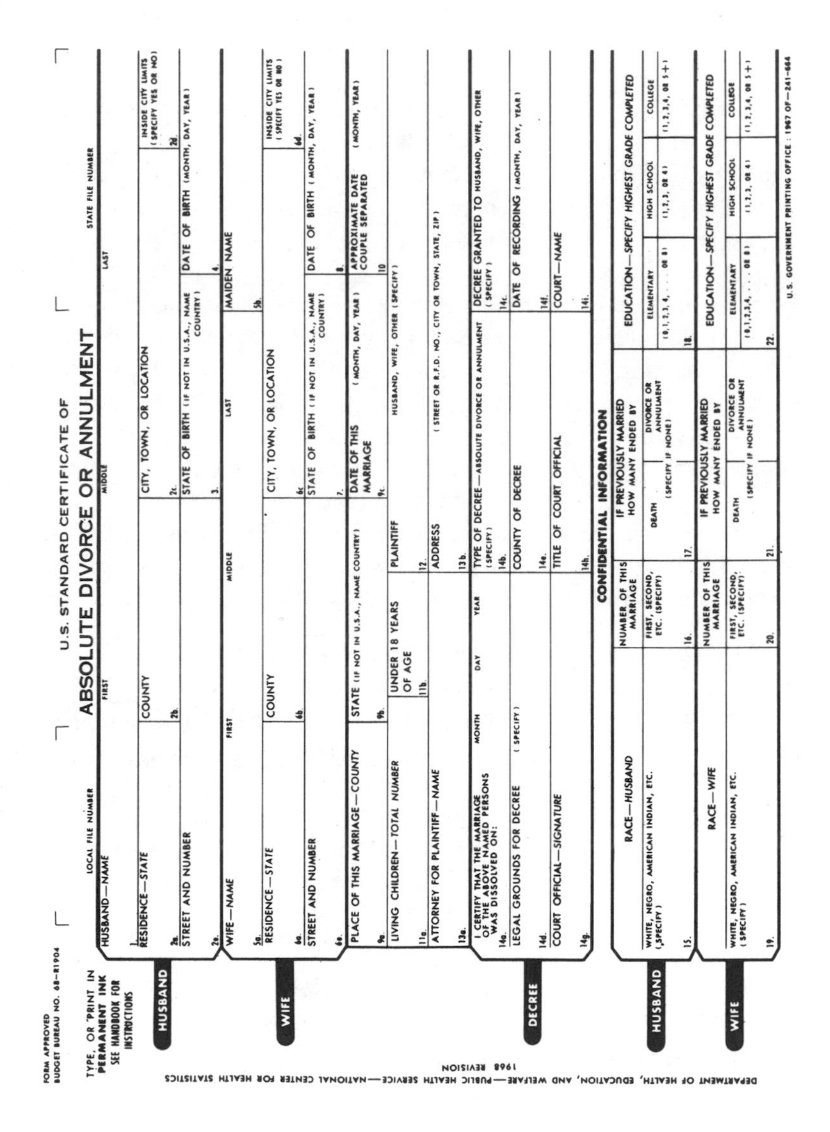

FORM APPROVED
BUDGET BUREAU NO. 68-R1904

TYPE, OR PRINT IN PERMANENT INK
SEE HANDBOOK FOR INSTRUCTIONS

LOCAL FILE NUMBER

U.S. STANDARD CERTIFICATE OF
ABSOLUTE DIVORCE OR ANNULMENT

STATE FILE NUMBER

HUSBAND

1. HUSBAND—NAME — FIRST — MIDDLE — LAST
2a. RESIDENCE—STATE | 2b. COUNTY | 2c. CITY, TOWN, OR LOCATION | 2d. INSIDE CITY LIMITS (SPECIFY YES OR NO)
2e. STREET AND NUMBER | 3. STATE OF BIRTH (IF NOT IN U.S.A., NAME COUNTRY) | 4. DATE OF BIRTH (MONTH, DAY, YEAR)

WIFE

5a. WIFE—NAME — FIRST — MIDDLE — LAST | 5b. MAIDEN NAME
6a. RESIDENCE—STATE | 6b. COUNTY | 6c. CITY, TOWN, OR LOCATION | 6d. INSIDE CITY LIMITS (SPECIFY YES OR NO)
6e. STREET AND NUMBER | 7. STATE OF BIRTH (IF NOT IN U.S.A., NAME COUNTRY) | 8. DATE OF BIRTH (MONTH, DAY, YEAR)

9a. PLACE OF THIS MARRIAGE—COUNTY | 9b. STATE (IF NOT IN U.S.A., NAME COUNTRY) | 9c. DATE OF THIS MARRIAGE (MONTH, DAY, YEAR) | 10. APPROXIMATE DATE COUPLE SEPARATED (MONTH, YEAR)
11a. LIVING CHILDREN—TOTAL NUMBER | 11b. UNDER 18 YEARS OF AGE | 12. PLAINTIFF — HUSBAND, WIFE, OTHER (SPECIFY)
13a. ATTORNEY FOR PLAINTIFF—NAME | 13b. ADDRESS (STREET OR R.F.D. NO., CITY OR TOWN, STATE, ZIP)

DECREE

14a. I CERTIFY THAT THE MARRIAGE OF THE ABOVE NAMED PERSONS WAS DISSOLVED ON: MONTH DAY YEAR | 14b. TYPE OF DECREE—ABSOLUTE DIVORCE OR ANNULMENT (SPECIFY) | 14c. DECREE GRANTED TO HUSBAND, WIFE, OTHER (SPECIFY)
14d. LEGAL GROUNDS FOR DECREE (SPECIFY) | 14e. COUNTY OF DECREE | 14f. DATE OF RECORDING (MONTH, DAY, YEAR)
14g. COURT OFFICIAL—SIGNATURE | 14h. TITLE OF COURT OFFICIAL | 14i. COURT—NAME

CONFIDENTIAL INFORMATION

HUSBAND

15. RACE—HUSBAND — WHITE, NEGRO, AMERICAN INDIAN, ETC. (SPECIFY) | 16. NUMBER OF THIS MARRIAGE — FIRST, SECOND, ETC. (SPECIFY) | 17. IF PREVIOUSLY MARRIED HOW MANY ENDED BY — DEATH — DIVORCE OR ANNULMENT (SPECIFY IF NONE) | 18. EDUCATION—SPECIFY HIGHEST GRADE COMPLETED — ELEMENTARY (0,1,2,3,4, ... OR 8) — HIGH SCHOOL (1,2,3, OR 4) — COLLEGE (1,2,3,4, OR 5+)

WIFE

19. RACE—WIFE — WHITE, NEGRO, AMERICAN INDIAN, ETC. (SPECIFY) | 20. NUMBER OF THIS MARRIAGE — FIRST, SECOND, ETC. (SPECIFY) | 21. IF PREVIOUSLY MARRIED HOW MANY ENDED BY — DEATH — DIVORCE OR ANNULMENT (SPECIFY IF NONE) | 22. EDUCATION—SPECIFY HIGHEST GRADE COMPLETED — ELEMENTARY (0,1,2,3,4, ... OR 8) — HIGH SCHOOL (1,2,3, OR 4) — COLLEGE (1,2,3,4, OR 5+)

1968 REVISION
DEPARTMENT OF HEALTH, EDUCATION, AND WELFARE—PUBLIC HEALTH SERVICE—NATIONAL CENTER FOR HEALTH STATISTICS

U.S. GOVERNMENT PRINTING OFFICE : 1967 OF—241-664

FIGURE 1—STANDARD CERTIFICATE OF DIVORCE OR ANNULMENT
(Certificates with this format are in current use in many states.)

LOUISIANA:	From Orleans Parish only.
MAINE:	Since January 1892.
MICHIGAN:	Since 1897.
NEBRASKA:	Since January 1909.
NEW HAMPSHIRE:	Since 1808.
NEW JERSEY:	From beginning (Superior Court, Chancery Division, State House Annex, Rm. 320, CN971, Trenton, NJ 08625).
NEW YORK:	Since January 1963.
NORTH CAROLINA:	Since January 1958.
OREGON:	Since 1925.
RHODE ISLAND:	Beginning unknown (Clerk of Family Court, 1 Dorrance Plaza, Providence, RI 02903).
SOUTH CAROLINA:	Since July 1962.
SOUTH DAKOTA:	Since July 1905.
TENNESSEE:	Since July 1945.
UTAH:	Since 1978. (Only short form of certified copies available from state office.)
VERMONT:	Since January 1860.
VIRGINIA:	Since January 1918.
WASHINGTON:	Since January 1968.
WISCONSIN:	Since 1907.
WYOMING:	Since May 1941.[6]

Some other states have state-wide filing of divorce records but do not issue certified copies of the decrees. Most of these offices will verify information for you and will forward inquiries and requests to the appropriate courts. These states include:

CALIFORNIA:	Since January 1, 1962.
COLORADO:	Index, except for records of 1940-67.
CONNECTICUT:	Index since 1947.
DELAWARE:	Since 1935.
GEORGIA:	Since June 9, 1952.
ILLINOIS:	Since January 1962.
IOWA:	Brief statistical record since 1906.
MARYLAND:	Since January 1961.
MASSACHUSETTS:	Index since 1952.

[6] *Ibid.*

MINNESOTA:	Index since January 1970.
MISSISSIPPI:	Since 1926.
MISSOURI:	Index from July 1948.
MONTANA:	Since July 1943.
NEVADA:	Since January 1968.
NORTH DAKOTA:	Index since 1949.
OHIO:	Since September 1949.
PENNSYLVANIA:	Since January 1946.
TEXAS:	Since July 1968.
WEST VIRGINIA:	Index since 1968.[7]

Divorce records are ordinarily indexed and, as indicated earlier, they are public records in many states so they are usually quite easy to procure and use. However, there are some states, such as New York, where divorce records are open only to the parties of the action. Because of the current privacy concerns these states are becoming increasingly numerous. Where the records are available, all that is usually necessary to secure copies is to write to the proper court giving the names of the parties and the approximate year of the divorce action. You should also state your relationship and the purpose for which the copy of the record will be used. There will be a fee—likely somewhere around $3 to $5—but the amount can vary considerably, even within the same state.

B. Citizenship and Naturalization Matters

1. Background. Naturalization is the granting of citizenship rights to aliens as if they were native-born. Article 1, Section 8, Clause 4, of the U.S. Constitution authorized the formulation, by Congress, of a "uniform Rule of Naturalization," and beginning in 1790 Congress began to enact legislation to control the naturalization of aliens.

During the colonial period there were few naturalizations of citizens. Only Europeans (from the continent) were not already considered as citizens because of the British control of the colonies. Since that time, however, naturalization of aliens in America has generally been handled in the courts, and much of our present naturalization policy is based on some of the earliest Congressional acts. There have been many modifications, but the policy has generally been consistent.

Prior to the enactment of the Fourteenth Amendment in 1868, all citizenship was said to be in the state and not in the nation. In some places the

[7] *Ibid.*

process of becoming a citizen (during the early periods) was quite simple. The immigrant merely signed a statement of allegiance as he came off the ship. Because of this some of the early books of citizenship lists are given in chapter 21 as immigration lists. In reality that is all they were. A good example of this is Montague S. Giuseppi, *Naturalizations of Foreign Protestants in the American and West Indian Colonies . . .* , 1921 (Baltimore: Genealogical Publishing Co., 1964 reprint). Another is William H. Egle, *Names of Foreigners Who Took the Oath of Allegiance to the Province and State of Pennsylvania, 1727-1775, with the Foreign Arrivals, 1786-1808,* 1892 (Baltimore: Genealogical Publishing Co., 1967 reprint).

The Fourteenth Amendment guaranteed national citizenship and extended it to all persons born or naturalized in the U.S. and subject to its jurisdiction. (This still excluded tribal Indians, natives of unincorporated territories, and children of foreign ambassadors.)

There was no comprehensive regulation of naturalization until 1906, when Congress established the Bureau of Immigration and Naturalization[8] and formulated a specific procedure to be followed concurrently by this new bureau and the courts with naturalization jurisdiction. Before 1906 naturalization matters were entirely within the jurisdiction of the courts.

The process of naturalization is quite cumbersome and the records have suffered somewhat because of the overlapping jurisdictions. Some groups have been working to bring about a modernization of the system with only one agency being responsible. The present process of naturalization requires the alien first to file a petition for naturalization with the Immigration and Naturalization Service. (These records go back to the creation of the Bureau in 1906 and those created within the last seventy-five years are confidential.) Until recently a declaration of intention, often called "first papers," has also been required. Following an investigation by the Immigration and Naturalization Service (which can be waived) the applicant files a petition for naturalization with the clerk of the court where he resides. Next he is examined by someone from the office of the Immigration and Naturalization Service, following which he must appear before the judge of the court for a final hearing. At the hearing he must be recommended by an Immigration and Naturalization Service representative. An oath of allegiance is taken and a certificate of naturalization is issued.

The main difference between this procedure and the procedure followed prior to 1906 is that the court took care of the whole process in the earlier period.

---

[8] The name was changed in 1933 to the Immigration and Naturalization Service, in the Department of Labor, and it was transferred to the Justice Department in 1940.

Naturalization proceedings can take place in any U.S. District Court, in any court of record of the several states, and (historically) in the district or supreme courts of the territories. *All proceedings are required to be recorded* by the clerk of the court.

Children under sixteen acquire citizenship through the naturalization of their parents and, between 1855 and the Cable Act of 1922, a woman automatically became a citizen either by marrying a citizen or by the naturalization of her husband.

In instances where territories are annexed by the United States, all residents of those territories can become citizens by collective naturalization through legislative enactment (as with Hawaii, Texas, Puerto Rico) or by treaty (as with Louisiana, Florida, Alaska, the U.S. Virgin Islands).

2. Location of the records. Many documents relating to naturalizations in U.S. federal courts, especially the records created after September 26, 1906, are in the National Archives Field Branches. A detailed list of the holdings in the various field branches, by state, is found in the *Guide to Genealogical Research in the National Archives,* pages 63-68. After September 26, 1906, records of naturalization can be found both in the courts and at the Immigration and Naturalization Service (INS). Prior to 1906 only the courts were involved. If your ancestor was naturalized in a state court, the record will almost certainly still be found there.[9]

In the past there has been a prohibition against the copying of naturalization records. However, the present policy is not so restrictive, and some uncertified copies are now permitted, and searches are allowed for genealogical purposes. In February 1973 the INS sent a letter to the courts with custody of such records, which letter included the following instructions:

> Until now, clerks of court have been restricted to furnishing such information orally only. This restriction has been removed and the clerks of court may now furnish uncertified copies or information in writing, by printing, by photocopy or by any other reproductive process, as well as orally, in accordance with the rules of the court. Clerks of court do not require the consent or approval of this Service for the making and issuance of such uncertified copies or information.[10]

---

[9] About two-thirds of naturalizations take place in 200 federal courts with the other one-third taking place in about 1,800 state courts.

[10] From a letter of instruction to a federal court clerk, from the Omaha, Nebraska, office of INS, as quoted in James C. and Lila Lee Neagles, *Locating Your Immigrant Ancestor* (Logan, UT: The Everton Publishers, Inc., 1975), p. 59. In 1986 and 1987 the commissioner of INS declined to respond to two requests from the author for further clarification of current official policy.

OMB No. 1115-0088
Expires 3-31-85

UNITED STATES DEPARTMENT OF JUSTICE
Immigration and Naturalization Service

Fee Stamp

APPLICATION FOR VERIFICATION OF INFORMATION FROM IMMIGRATION AND NATURALIZATION SERVICE RECORDS

TYPE OR PRINT THE NAME AND MAILING ADDRESS OF THE PERSONS TO WHOM INFORMATION OR COPIES OF RECORD SHOULD BE RETURNED IN THE BOX BELOW:

NAME	
STREET ADDRESS	
CITY, STATE ZIP CODE	

PERSON CONSENTING
NAME AND ADDRESS

SIGNATURE OF PERSON CONSENTING

1. CHECK TYPE OF VERIFICATION REQUESTED:
   - ☐ LAWFUL ADMISSION FOR PERMANENT RESIDENCE
   - ☐ AGE OR DATE OF BIRTH
   - ☐ NATURALIZATION OR CITIZENSHIP
   - ☐ GENEALOGICAL INFORMATION *(See instructions 6 and 7.)*
   - ☐ OTHER (CERTIFICATE OF BIRTH DATA, ETC.)

2. STATE PURPOSE FOR WHICH DESIRED

2A. NAMES OF BENEFICIARIES

3. NUMBER OF COPIES DESIRED, IF ANY:

4. IF INFORMATION IS FOR SOCIAL SECURITY BENEFITS, SHOW SOCIAL SECURITY NUMBER:

DATA FOR IDENTIFICATION OF THE RECORD TO BE VERIFIED

5. FAMILY NAME GIVEN NAME MIDDLE NAME
6. ALIEN REGISTRATION NUMBER
7. OTHER NAMES USED, IF ANY
8. NAME USED AT TIME OF ENTRY INTO UNITED STATES
9. PLACE OF BIRTH
10. DATE OF BIRTH
11. PORT ABROAD FROM WHICH LEFT FOR UNITED STATES
12. PORT OF ENTRY INTO UNITED STATES
13. DATE OF ENTRY
14. NAME OF VESSEL OR OTHER MEANS OF ENTRY

GIVE THE FOLLOWING FORMATION FOR VERIFICATION OF NATURALIZATION OR CERTIFICATE OF CITIZENSHIP

15. NAME ON CERTIFICATE
16. CERTIFICATE NUMBER
17. DATE ISSUED
18. ADDRESS WHEN CERTIFICATE WAS ISSUED
19. NAME AND LOCATION OF NATURALIZATION COURT OR IMMIGRATION OFFICE ISSUING CERTIFICATE OF CITIZENSHIP
20. SIGNATURE OF APPLICANT

DATE:

DO NOT COMPLETE THIS BLOCK — RESERVED FOR GOVERNMENT USE ONLY

THE RECORDS OF THE IMMIGRATION AND NATURALIZATION SERVICE REFLECT THE FOLLOWING; VERIFICATION OF INFORMATION REQUESTED WAS MADE ON THIS DATE SHOWN AT RIGHT

- ☐ LAWFUL ADMISSION FOR PERMANENT RESIDENCE ON ______ AT ______
- ☐ NATURALIZATION INFORMATION AS SHOWN ABOVE IS CORRECT.
- ☐ NATURALIZATION IN (COURT) ______ ON (DATE) ______
- ☐ AT (LOCATION) ______
- ☐ DATE OF BIRTH ______
- ☐ ARRIVAL RECORD DATED ______ SHOWED SUBJECT'S AGE AT TIME TO BE ______
- ☐ UNABLE TO IDENTIFY ANY RECORD
- ☐ COPIES ATTACHED AS REQUESTED
- ☐ CERTIFICATE OF CITIZENSHIP IN (OFFICE) ______

ON (DATE) ______

SIGNATURE ______

TITLE ______

PRIVACY ACT IDENTIFICATION (WHEN REQUIRED)	☐ IDENTITY ESTABLISHED IN PERSON	Approved By:	DATE
	DOCUMENTS ATTACHED ☐ G-652 Affidavit ☐ OTHER (List)		

FORM G-641 (REV. 5-5-83)N

FIGURE 2—THE FORM USED TO SECURE INFORMATION FROM RECORDS OF THE IMMIGRATION AND NATURALIZATION SERVICE (FORM G-641)

Those seeking information from the files of the INS should use form G-641, Application for Verification of Information from Immigration and Naturalization Service Records. Instructions are included with the form.

The Works Projects Administration (WPA) undertook a project in the 1930s to make photocopies of pre-1906 naturalization records and to index them, but the project managed to cover only the courts in four New England states—Maine, Massachusetts, New Hampshire, and Rhode Island—before it was terminated. These 5″ x 8″ photocopies, covering the period 1787 to 1906, are in the National Archives together with a card index (Soundex system, as described in chapter 11). The forms in these files (as in the naturalization files of any court) usually contain information on:

> place and date of birth and of arrival in the United States, place of residence at the time of applying for citizenship, and sometimes the name of the ship on which the immigrant arrived and his occupation.[11]

If your ancestor lived in New Jersey you will find naturalization records from 1749 through 1810 in the State Library, Archives and History Division, at Trenton. Also in New Jersey, the WPA made a "Guide to Naturalization Records" in the courts of that state (December 1941) as part of their program to inventory vital statistics records. In Massachusetts naturalizations from 1885 to 1931 are on file in the Archives Division at the State House in Boston.

A very useful book on immigration and naturalization records is Neagles' *Locating Your Immigrant Ancestor,* cited in footnote number ten.

3. Nature of the records. Before you begin research to find the records of naturalization for an ancestor, you should know when that ancestor became a U.S. citizen. Records of naturalization usually include declarations of intention, naturalization petitions, depositions, and records of naturalization.

Declarations of intention are used by applicants to renounce allegiance to foreign governments and to declare their intention to become U.S. citizens. They normally preceded other documents by at least two years and were sometimes not required if the applicant had served in the military (with an honorable discharge) or entered the country as a minor. As to their specific content, those prior to 1906:

---

[11] Meredith B. Colket, Jr., and Frank E. Bridgers, *Guide to Genealogical Records in the National Archives* (Washington, DC: The National Archives, 1964), p. 141.

> usually show, for each applicant name, country of birth or allegiance, date of the application, and signature. Some show date and port of arrival in the United States.[12]

The records after 1906 contain more detail, including:

> such information as applicant's name, age, occupation, and personal description; date and place of birth; citizenship; present address and last foreign address; vessel and port of embarkation for the United States; U.S. port and date of arrival in the United States; and date of application and signature.[13]

Naturalization petitions were used to make formal application for citizenship by those who had met the residency requirements and who had declared their intention to become citizens. Information on these petitions for each petitioner includes:

> name, residence, occupation, date and place of birth, citizenship, and personal description . . . ; date of emigration; ports of embarkation and arrival; marital status; names, dates, places of birth, and residence of applicant's children; date at which U.S. residence commenced; time of residence in state; name changes; and signature. Copies of declarations of intention, certificates of arrival, and certificates of completion of citizenship classes are often interfiled with petitions. Petitions after 1930 often include photographs of the applicants.[14]

Naturalization depositions are formal statements by other persons in support of the applicant's petition for naturalization.

> The records indicate the period of applicant's residence in a certain locale, and other information, including . . . appraisal of the applicant's character.[15]

The papers which document the granting of citizenship are *records of naturalization* and *oaths of allegiance*. Later records are in the form of certificates. These records are typically found in the court of naturalization in chronological arrangement, often in bound volumes which include surname indexes. Many of these records relating to early naturalizations are

---

[12] *Guide to Genealogical Research in the National Archives,* rev. ed. (Washington, DC: The National Archives, 1983), p. 63.

[13] *Ibid.,* p. 63.

[14] *Ibid.,* p. 63.

[15] *Ibid.,* p. 63.

difficult to locate because of lack of uniform policy requirements. Court minutes are the only source for many of the earlier naturalization records and the court orders relating thereto.

> In some cases, all records for one person have been gathered together in a **petition and record,** which usually included the petition for naturalization, affidavits of the petitioner and witnesses, the oath of allegiance, and the order of the court admitting the petitioner to citizenship.[16]

4. Special helps and other sources of naturalization information. In a case where the citizen who had been naturalized, or the alien who was seeking naturalization, filed a homestead claim or applied for a passport, these applications (homestead and passport) are normally in the National Archives. (Passport records are among the General Records of the Department of State, Record Group 59; and homestead records, already discussed in chapter 16, are in the Records of the Bureau of Land Management, Record Group 49.) They give the name of the court where the naturalization took place, and they may prove to be valuable if you do not know the location of that event. Often copies of the naturalization records are included in those files.

You might also receive assistance from the 1870 federal census. It indicated whether or not males over twenty-one were U.S. citizens. If an immigrant is reported as a citizen you know that there must be naturalization papers somewhere.

Anytime you know that your ancestor was a naturalized citizen it is worthwhile to spend whatever time is necessary to locate the record of that naturalization. This record can bridge the gap to the ancestral home in the Old World. Remember, however, that persons born in the U.S. are citizens even though their immigrant parents may never have sought naturalization. If your immigrant ancestor did not seek American citizenship there will be no such record.

V. LEGISLATIVE RECORDS

In some jurisdictions during some time periods, some legal issues were handled and resolved by legislative action rather than by the courts. This was true in virtually every state to some extent. Types of actions which

---

[16] *Ibid.*, p. 63.

might be included vary from state to state, but typical of such matters are legal name changes and divorces.

Records of these legislative actions are found in the sessions laws of the states involved. These are in legislative libraries within the states as well as in many of the larger law libraries.

VI. ADOPTION RECORDS

Adoption records are almost exclusively closed to the public. They are sealed by the court to protect the privacy of those involved—both the natural parents, the adopting parents, and the child. They can be opened only by court order for "good cause shown." Genealogical curiosity has not normally satisfied this requirement. Even the LDS Church, with its great emphasis on genealogy, supports this approach. It is contrary to Church policy for an adopted person to seek the identity of his natural parents. In the case of health problems where heredity may play an important role in diagnosis and treatment, the Church suggests that the parents' medical history may be obtained but not their identities.[17]

In recent years, however, some jurisdictions have become more sympathetic to the "rights" of the adopted to know their parentage. The records in these states can be quite easily accessed. There are also other things that can be done to trace natural parentage. For the benefit of those adopted individuals who desire to pursue the identity of their natural parents, I recommend the following books:

Askin, Jayne and Bob Askam. *Search: A Handbook for Adoptees and Birthparents*. New York: Harper and Row, 1982.

Rillera, Mary Jo. *Adoption Searchbook*. 2nd ed. Westminster, CA: Triadoption Publications, 1985.

VII. SPECIAL NOTE ON VIRGINIA

Many genealogists have difficulty in Virginia research because they fail to allow for the idiosyncrasies of her court system. They try to treat her like any other Southern state, never looking for records anywhere except in the county. This may work fine most of the time, but if you will carefully note

---

[17] *General Handbook of Instructions* (Salt Lake City: The Church of Jesus Christ of Latter-day Saints, 1989), section 6, p. 7.

some of the lists of various courts given in this chapter and in the chapters on wills and land records, you will see that there are some significant exceptions in Virginia, and some date back a long way. This means that some very important records are not found in the county courthouses but rather in the cities. A city in Virginia is a municipality which is independent of the county in its total operation.

Once incorporated as a city, a Virginia municipality establishes its own courts and government separate and distinct from the county in which it is geographically situated. The following table shows Virginia's independent cities, as they are called, the counties within whose boundaries they are located, and the dates of their incorporation. The dates in parentheses are the dates they were incorporated as towns.

City	*County where geographically located*	*Incorporation date*
Alexandria	Fairfax and Arlington counties	(1779) 1852
Big Lick	(see Roanoke)	
Bristol	Washington County	(1856) 1890 (from town of Goodson) (added additional territory from Washington County in 1970)
Buena Vista	Rockbridge County	(1890) 1892
Charlottesville	Albemarle County	(1801) 1888
Chesapeake	formerly Norfolk County (now extinct)	1963 (by merger of Norfolk County and City of South Norfolk)
Clifton Forge	Alleghany County	(1884) 1906
Colonial Heights	Chesterfield County	(1926) 1948
Covington	Alleghany County	(1833) 1954
Danville	Pittsylvania County	(1830) 1890 (North Danville added in 1869)
Emporia	Greensville County	1967
Fairfax	Fairfax County	(1874) 1961 (formerly called Providence)
Falls Church	Fairfax County	(1875) 1948
Franklin	Southampton County	(1876) 1961
Fredericksburg	Spotsylvania County	(1782) 1879
Fredericktown	(see Winchester)	
Galax	Carroll and Grayson counties	(1906) 1954 (formerly called Bonepart)

Hampton	formerly Elizabeth City County (now extinct)	(1849) 1908 (Elizabeth City Co. and town of Phoebus added in 1952)
Harrisonburg	Rockingham County	(1849) 1916
Hopewell	Prince George County	1916 (City Point added in 1923)
Lexington	Rockbridge County	1966
Lynchburg	Campbell County	(1805) 1852 (added additional territory from Campbell County in 1970)
Manassas	Prince William County	1975
Manassas Park	Prince William County	1975
Martinsville	Henry County	(1873) 1928
Nansemond (merged into Suffolk in 1974)	formerly Nansemond County (now extinct)	
Newport News	formerly Warwick County (now extinct)	1896 (city of Warwick added in 1958)
Norfolk	formerly Norfolk County (now extinct)	(1737) 1845 (Berkeley added in 1906)
Norton	Wise County	(1894) 1954 (formerly called Prince's Flat)
Petersburg	Dinwiddie and Prince George counties	(1784) 1850 (Blandford, Pocahontas and Ravensworth added in 1784) (added additional territory from Dinwiddie and Prince George counties in 1970)
Poquoson	York County	1975
Portsmouth (now in Chesapeake)	formerly Norfolk County (now extinct)	(1836) 1858
Radford	Montgomery County	(1887) 1892 (formerly called Central City)
Richmond	Henrico and Chesterfield counties	(1782) 1842 (added Manchester—or South Richmond—in 1910 and Barton Heights, Fairmount and Highland Park in 1914)
Roanoke	Roanoke County	(1874) 1902 (formerly called Big Lick) (added additional territory from Roanoke County in 1970)
Salem	Roanoke County	1968
South Boston	Halifax County	(1884) 1960

South Norfolk	(see Chesapeake)	
Staunton	Augusta County	(1801) 1871
Suffolk	Nansemond County (now extinct)	(1808) 1910 (absorbed Nansemond in 1974)
Virginia Beach	formerly Princess Anne County (now extinct)	(1906) 1952 (Princess Anne County added in 1963)
Warwick	(see Newport News)	
Waynesboro	Augusta County	(1834) 1948 (Basic City added in 1923)
Williamsburg	James City and York counties	(1722) 1884
Winchester	Frederick County	(1779) 1784 (formerly called Fredericktown) (added additional territory from Frederick County in 1970)

In several of the above cities the records date back to their incorporation as cities and in many instances to their incorporation as towns. If your ancestors lived within the area of any of these cities after their incorporation that fact is probably important to your research.

Though these independent cities are legally separated from county jurisdiction I have listed the counties in which they are situated to facilitate your locating them. Many of them, in fact, are the seats of county government in those counties. These include Charlottesville (Albemarle County), Covington (Alleghany County), Emporia (Greensville County), Fairfax (Fairfax County), Manassas (Prince William County), Martinsville (Henry County), Richmond (Henrico County), Salem (Roanoke County), Staunton (Augusta County), Williamsburg (James City County), and Winchester (Frederick County).

As the above list attests, many of these independent cities have only recently achieved such status and, at present, have negligible genealogical significance. There will, no doubt, be others created in the future.

Some of the old Virginia counties no longer exist because they have been absorbed by the independent cities. In such cases the records of these counties are in the custody of the city courts. These extinct counties include:

Alexandria County	Became Arlington County in 1920. Much of the area is now in the city of Alexandria.
Elizabeth City County	Now in the city of Hampshire (since 1952).

Nansemond County	Now in the city of Suffolk. (Part was originally in the city of Nansemond, which was absorbed by Suffolk in 1974.)
Norfolk County	Now in the city of Chesapeake (since 1963). (Chesapeake also has records of the former independent cities of Portsmouth and South Norfolk.)
Princess Anne County	Now in the city of Virginia Beach (since 1963).
Warwick County	Now in the city of Newport News (since 1958).

All court records, including land and probate records, are in the jurisdiction of the courts of these cities and are not in the county courts. Formerly these were Corporation Courts but are now called Circuit Courts.

A useful book for understanding Virginia and her history is *A Hornbook of Virginia History,* 3rd ed. (Richmond: The Virginia State Library, 1983). I recommend it to anyone who has Virginia ancestry.

VIII. CASE REPORTS, REPORTERS, AND DIGESTS

Reports of the various courts of appeal in the states also provide a way to locate some trial court records. These reports are composed of the published opinions of the judges in the appellate courts to which the cases have been brought. They are accessible through the use of court digests which provide a table of cases (by both plaintiffs and defendants—by surname only) as well as a subject (or point-of-law) index to the reports. The reports are no substitute for the case files of the trial courts, but they do provide a way to get at the case files. They give the name of the court of original jurisdiction and the date of the court's decision. This will help you locate briefs and case files.

In addition to the state reports, since the 1880s the comprehensive reporters and digests of the seven regions of the National Reporter Series, the four federal court series, and the supplemental reports for New York State and (more recently) California are also important. The regional reporters include some cases from the state appellate courts which are not in the state reports, as they contain reports of cases from all courts of appellate jurisdiction. The state reports (with but few exceptions) are limited to cases in the state Supreme Court.

What may be a useful tool is the table of cases in the *American Digest* (St. Paul, MN: West Publishing Co.). Of special note are volumes twenty-one through twenty-five of the 1911 edition of this publication wherein is printed "A Complete Table of American Cases from 1658 to 1906." Subsequent editions (published every ten years) update this table. The tables of cases are virtually unusable if the surname you seek is common.

All of the various court reports and digests can usually be found in law libraries (at the local courthouse), and occasionally in other libraries.

An aid to finding the proper digests is Appendix 3 of Frederick Charles Hicks, *Materials and Methods of Legal Research,* 3rd rev. ed. (Rochester: The Lawyers Co-operative Publishing Co., 1942). This appendix contains a list of the various volumes of court reports, arranged by state.

IX. CONCLUSION

In most states, court records of one type or another go back to the very beginning, thus providing a useful source of genealogical evidence. However, many of the most valuable court records—the older records and case files—are stored in out-of-the-way places because they are not in current use and space is scarce. Often the present records custodian is unaware of the location (and frequently the existence) of such records. In some cases the WPA inventories of the various county courthouses are useful, but often the information therein, which was current in the early 1940s, is somewhat antiquated. In searching for these records the genealogist will do well to employ diligence and imagination.

The records and files of some court actions are voluminous. You may find hundreds of pages of various kinds of papers in the file of just one case. In such situations it is certainly impractical for you to copy all of this material into your notes; however, you will find it worthwhile to go through the papers and abstract everything of significance. It has been my experience that the *complaint* of the plaintiff (the portion at the beginning of the case where the cause is explained, also sometimes called the petition, declaration, or statement of claim), the *answer* of the defendant to the complaint, and the *decree* (the *final judgment)* are usually of the most genealogical significance. (This, however, is not to discount the value of other information which may be in the file.) The complaint and the answer, which are the formal allegations and defenses of the parties, are called *pleadings*.

Court records, with some justifiable exceptions, are open to the public use. If they are not on film for the locality you need (and they usually are not) you should contact the court or pay a personal visit to the courthouse. And, as you have observed from some of the examples used in earlier chapters, other records often tell of the existence of important court records.

20

Church Records

The story is told of the old cowboy who visited the Grand Canyon for the first time. He is reported tying his horse to a tree then sauntering out to the ledge to look down into the canyon. "Ah took one look," he said, "and then ah wished ah'd tied m'self to the tree and let the horse look down into the canyon."

This is about the way American church records affect many researchers. These records constitute a vast, relatively-unexplored and little-known source of genealogical evidence, and they can be awesome to the average genealogist. However, they are different from the Grand Canyon in that they are usually not as easy to locate—and that is our biggest problem.

I am not saying that no one has ever made good use of American church records (that would certainly be an error), but rather that these church records quite generally present some unique problems which significantly limit their use. In New England and the northern colonial states, however, church records present few problems and have much wider use than is typical elsewhere in the country.

I. TYPES OF RECORDS

In many respects the records of most churches are not unlike vital records. They deal with the same essential identifying data—births, marriages, deaths—only in a slightly different way. Rather than the actual birth, the church ordinarily reports the baptism or christening—usually a few days later. Instead of a marriage license or bond, the church keeps a record of the actual marriage and of the banns. And instead of the death, the church is more likely to record the burial. But because of the near proximity of these dates—timewise—they serve the same purpose, and they were generally kept in a much earlier time period than were civil vital records. These three—christenings, marriages, and burials—are usually the most important, and certainly the most widely used, church records in genealogical research. They are ordinarily kept in books called *registers.*

Another kind of church record that has special genealogical value is the record which indicates removal to or arrival from another congregation. Most churches kept records of this type so that faithful members would be welcomed into the church when they moved to a new location, but each church had a different name for them. The Society of Friends (Quakers) called them *certificates of removal,* the Protestant Episcopal Church (Church of England) called them *letters of transfer,* the Baptists called them *letters of admission,* the Congregationalists called them *dismissions,* and the Latter-day Saints (Mormons) called them *certificates of membership.*

These records are useful because they allow a family to be traced with relative ease from one locality to another, sometimes a very difficult matter without such assistance. The problem with them is that they are usually incomplete.

Other types of church records include confirmations, lists of communicants, membership lists, excommunications—all of which are frequently recorded in the registers—plus vestry minutes and proceedings (Protestant Episcopal Church), sessions minutes (Presbyterian Church) and other minutes which include financial reports, disciplinary actions and fines toward backsliders, and (for the Friends) disownments and manumissions. These records often contain information of significant family history value.

It might be well to mention now, though it will be discussed more thoroughly later, that the nature of church records is greatly affected by the position (and by this I do *not* mean geographical location) of the church in the community. In places where there is a *state church* (one which is recognized by law as the official church and is supported by the government) the church records are usually much better and are more often complete. This emphasizes one of the chief problems of American church records as a source of genealogical evidence: The U.S. has a complete separation of church and state. Politically this is wonderful, but genealogically it has disadvantages.

During the colonial period our nation did experience the existence of state churches in some of the colonies. For example, many of the New England colonies adhered to the Congregational Church; in Virginia the English (Protestant Episcopal) Church was the official church. Other colonies—notably Georgia, Maryland, and South Carolina—also held the P.E. Church as a state church at various times. In New Netherland the Dutch Reformed Church was the state church.

America was truly unique in her religious development. During settlement she combined persons from many European nations who brought with them the religions of their homelands and tried to make those religions dominant. The English tried hard—the colonies were mostly English so there was an extra advantage. However, any advantage proved small, especially after the passing of the Toleration Act by William III in 1689. State churches did exist but they did not stand unchallenged, and the only remedy left to the framers of the Constitution, in light of the multiplicity of churches and of national origins, was to separate completely the powers of church and federal government. Thus there was never a national church in the United States though some state establishments persisted long after the Revolution (especially in New England). It was not until after the Fourteenth Amendment was adopted that the provisions of the Constitution were applied to the states also.

II. THE NATURE OF THE RECORDS

Perhaps the best way to explain the true nature of church records is to show examples of them. The examples which follow are from the Congregational Church in New England (Maine), from the Protestant Episcopal (P.E.) Church in the South (Virginia), from the Lutheran Church in the central-Atlantic states (Pennsylvania), from the Baptist Church, and from the Society of Friends. Remember that these are only examples and that church records often vary considerably even within the same denomination. There is frequently extensive variance in records of the same congregation when a new minister or a new clerk took over the record-keeping duties.

A. Congregational Church

Let's begin with a Congregational Church—the Second Church of Kittery (Maine). This church, like most Congregational Churches, kept a record of baptisms, but note that these are not always baptisms of infants and that some important information was not included in the record:

1. Baptisms.

1725—Ap—David Libby Junr
Ester his wife
Mary Smal Jos: wife
Eban^{r} Libby
Sept^{r}—Joseph son of Joseph Harn^{d} Junr—
Decem^{r}—Catharine my Daughter [the minister]
Feb.—Saml & Hep^{h} child^{n} of Saml Hanscom in Private

1726—July.—Two Children of Nathan Spinney—
Edward Chapman son Simon
31—Jno Libby & Ephra^{m} Libby, adult—
Elisha son of John Libby
Mary Daughter of Richd King

1727—May—Eleanor Daughter of Deacon Tetherly
June 25—Nathl son of Peter Staple—
July 3d Sab—Tho: Knight—
Sept 3—David Libby & Son David
Saml Son of Samuel Winget on her acc^{t}—

A few years later the information was a little more detailed, but not much:

1764

Aug 29 Gabriel son of William Tetherly
Eunice dau of John Spinney J^{r}

Sep 24 Jotham, son of Samuel Emery

Oct 1 Nathan Bartlett, Jr, son of Nathan

1765

Apr 21 J. Gowen, wife of William Gowen

May 12 John Kennard owned the covenant & had his child baptized named John

June 9 Mary child of Mr. Tho Hammend & wife who renewed their baptismal covenant

July 14 Joshua son of Jonathan More. 3d Sabbath in Oct Joseph son of William Stacy

Oct 10 Joel & David sons of Ephraim Libby, Jr.

Nov 23 Samuel son of Tobias Shapleigh

2. Communicants.

The following is from an undated list (sometime between 1727 and 1746) of "Males Belonging to the Communion." Such lists were also made of female communicants, but they did not often state the given names of married women—only "Mrs.":

Joseph Hamond	Edward Chapman mov'd
Nic° Shapleigh	Christopher Sargent mov'd
Sam¹ Hill	Robert Staple
Daniel Fogg	James Staple jun^r
John Staple	Phylip Cooms mov'd
Stephen Tobley	Josiah Paul
William Tetherly	Jeremiah Paul mov'd

3. Dismissions.

Also recorded among sundry notes which the minister kept of the church's (and his own) activities are records of persons moving in and out. These are called dismissions:

June 1749—Had Deacon Simon Emerys Dissmission from the Church of Berwick Read to the Brethren, and then voted for receiving him into communion with us—

July 30, 1778—Jerusha Hanscom was dismissed from this chh & recommended to the 2nd chh of Berwick.

July 7, 1817—Sarah Thimison was dismissed from this chh and recommended to the chh of X^t in Temple.

4. Notes.

As mentioned earlier, the ministers in this particular church kept notes in journal form of some of the church's activities. There is not a lot of information in these of value to the genealogist, but they should be considered for their historical value. The following notes are typical:

Novembr^r 6—1721—

The chh met at the House of Brother James Staple, in order to make choice of Two Suitable Persons for Deacons: And after Prayer to the Great Head of the chh, for Direction in this Important affair—the Members by written votes, chose William Tetherly, & James Staples for this offices.

Octob^r 6, 1727

Being ye Lords Day: After the Public Exercises were over I Stay'd ye Brethren of ye chh, & Laid before them ye Error which I apprehended those of o^r Brethren, viz. Ham^d, Tobey, Rogers, Hanscom, Tob: Leighton, in withdrawing communion from this chh & in Continuing in their Separation from it: observed to them y^t they had broken their Covenant with us which was to Submit to ye watch & Discipline of this chh, & walk orderly & in Comunion with us: and Laid before them our Duty; which was to call them to an acc^t & proceed with them in a way of admonition in the first place, Publickly before the chh to bring them to a sense of y^r disorderly doings.

In addition to these notes and to the lists of communicants given earlier, this church also kept a list of persons admitted to full communion with the church, as follows:

> 1746, May 18, Admitted Abigail Wittum wife of Eben[r]—
>
> 1747, Aug[t] 30. Admitted Cumbo, a Negro woman of Capt Bartletts.—
>
> 1748, Ap[l] 10. Admitted Wid[o] Judith Gowen—
>
> 1751, Aug[t] 4. Jane Remick, wife of Nath Remick—
>
> 1754. July. Samuel Fernald—
>
> 1754. Decem[r] 1: John Heard Bartlett: who had a Liberal Education at Harvard Colledge.—
>
> 1756 June, Joanna Preble the wife of Edward Preble.

5. Burials and marriages.

In this particular church there are no records of burials or marriages preserved, though this is not the case in all Congregational churches.

B. The Protestant Episcopal Church (Church of England)

The Protestant Episcopal Church has generally kept quite good records in America, but many of those records have not been preserved. The examples used are from two separate churches—the Augusta Parish in Augusta County, Virginia, where we will take a comprehensive look at vestry minutes,[1] and the Immanuel Church in Hanover County, Virginia, where we will also peek at the vestry minutes, but shall be chiefly concerned with church registers.

1. Vestry minutes.

The P.E. Church in colonial times had a very close connection with the civil government of Virginia, as already discussed, and many things you will find in the records of the vestry you might more typically find in civil court records if you were in some other part of the country or in a later time period. One example which will not be illustrated but will only be mentioned is the record involved with the processioning of land. This involves the formality of determining the limits and boundaries (metes and bounds) of the several private estates within the parish. The processions tell the amount of land (number of acres) that each person owns. Another good example is the record kept of orphans and illegitimate children.

---

[1] The vestry is a group of church members who oversee and manage the temporal affairs of the church.

a. *The poor, orphans, and illegitimate children.* The church, through the vestry, was responsible for the material sustenance and physical well-being of the parish members and kept careful records of the manner in which this obligation was discharged. In addition to the widows, the physically incapable, the habitually poor, and children who were unable to provide for themselves were objects of special concern. A large portion of vestry minute space was often devoted to them. Bastardy bonds, such as the following, are quite common and can be of great genealogical value:

> 1748/9 Feby 14th KNOW all men by These Presence that we Christopher Finney and William Armstrong are held and firmly bound unto James Lockhart and John Madison Churchwardens for the Parish of Augusta in the just and full sum of Fifty Pounds Currt money of Virginia to which Payment will and truly to be made and done we bind us and Each of our Heirs and Assigns firmly by these Presents as witness our Hands and Seals this 14th day of February 1748/9.
>
> THE CONDITION of this obligation is such that whereas Sarah Simmons Single Woman hath this day before me Charged Christopher Finney Taylor for getting Her with Child which Child when Born will be a Bastard and may be Burdensome To our Sd Parish of Augusta if the said Finney shall be and appear at our next Court to be held for sd County then & there to do what may be by the sd Child then this obligation to be void or Else to Remain in force and Virtue in Law & c.
>
> Taken before me Robt Cunningham (signed) Christopher Finney
> (signed) Wm Armstrong

Also, as the result of efforts to remove the care of children from the church, it was common to find apprenticeship records wherein an orphan or an illegitimate child (the record usually indicated which) was bound as an apprentice to some responsible party. (Some illegitimate children were apprenticed to their reputed fathers.) Following is an apprenticeship document for Peter Smith, a child who was deserted:

> THIS INDENTURE Witnesseth that we James Lockhart and John Archer Churchwardens of Augusta County at the November Court In the Year of our Lord MDCCL it was agreed that the Churchwardens bind out an orphan Child belonging to Nicholas Smith named Peter Smith and as he is now Run away it appearing to the Court that all his Children is like to become Burdonsome to the Parish of Augusta there being no Persons to care of ye sd Children it is ordered yt ye Churchwardens bind out the sd Peter Smith to Elijah

McClenachan who appeared in Court & agreed to take the sd Peter Smith According to Law Pursuent To which they bind him unto ye s^d^ Elijah McClenachan to serve him his Heirs or assigns untill he shall be full Twenty one years of Age he being now Four years of Age during all which Term ye sd Peter Smith his sd master and mistress shall Faithfully serve their Secrets keep their Lawful commands everywhere gladly obey he shall do no Damage to his master or Mistress he shall not Waste his S^d^ master or mistresses Goods nor lend them unlawfully to any He shall not commit Fornication nor Contract matrimony during ye sd Term he shall not Play at Cards Dice or any unlawful Game he shall not absent himself Day nor night from his said Master or mistresses service unlawfully nor haunt Ale Houses Taverns or Play Houses but in all things behave himself as a Faithful servant out to do & ye sd Elijah McClenachan shall Teach or cause him to be Taught to Read write and Cast up Acct^s^ & shall Provide for & Procure to him meat Drink Washing & apparel & all other necessaries fitting for such an apprentice the sd Term and for the true Performance of every the said Covenants & agreements either of the Parties bind themselves to the others firmly by these Presents In witness whereof this XXIJ Day of November 1752 & the sd Elijah McClenachan shall give sd Peter Smith when free such freedom dues as the Law directs likewise to Learn him or cause him to be instructed in the Cooper Trade or some other & c.

Signed Sealed and delivered	(signed) James Lockhart
In Presence of—	(signed) John Archer
Wm Preston	(signed) Elijah McClenachan

b. *Money*. The vestry minutes are also concerned with the incoming of money from various sources:

1753	Dr To the Parish of Augusta	
	To Cash paid . . . by Mr John Madison	£30 – 0 – 0
	To Ditto by William Henderson a fine	2 – 10 – 0
	To Ditto by Widow Smily a fine	2 – 10 – 0
	To Ditto by James Greenlee his servants fine	2 – 10 – 0
	To Ditto by Andrew Beard for swearing	0 – 10 – 0
	To Ditto by Robert Gwin his Daughters fine	0 – 10 – 0
	To Ditto collected by James Greenlee Constable for swearing	1 – 0 – 0
	To Ditto by John Mason Constable for swearing	0 – 10 – 0
	To Ditto by Henry Gay his Daughters fine	2 – 10 – 0
	To Jean Campbells Fine	2 – 10 – 0
	To a Deposit in his Hands the 6th Augt 1750	52 – 14 – 5
	To Interest on the same 2 years	5 – 4 – 0

To Viter Mauck's part of the Quitrent money	4 – 18 – 3
To Cash of John Graham for swearing	1 – 0 – 0
To Cash pd.. by David Stuart late Sheriff	1 – 12 – 3

They were also concerned with the outgoing of that same money:

2 Nov 1752

David Stuart Sheriff Produced an Acc[t] against this Parish out of which he is allowed the sum of £1"15"2 and ordered that he be Paid the same.

Ordered that Margaret Frame be allowed the sum of £6"0"0 for the maintainance of one of Her Children this insuing year it appearing To this Vestry that it is an Object of Charity.

It appears to this Vestry that Hewan Mathers is an object of Charity it is therefore ordered that he be allowed £4 for this Present Year to be laid out at the Discretion of the Church-wardens for Cloaths only

Ordered that the Rev[d] John Jones be allowed at the rate of £50 p[r] annum to commince from the first Day of Sep[r] 1752 It appearing to this Vestry that the Glebe Buildings are not yet Finished and the said Jones having acquainted this Vestry that John Lewis Gen[t] (the undertaker of the same) Agrees to allow him at the Rate of £20" p[r] annum until the same be Finished, for which he declares himself Satisfied and acquits this Vestry and Parish of any further charge for the same.

Ordered that a Reader of this Parish be allowed the sum of £6"5 yearly and that the Rev[d] M[r] Jones have a Liberty to Choose the same to officiate at y[e] Court House.

Ordered that W[m] Preston be allowed the Sum of £5" p[r] Annum to serve as a Clerk for this Vestry and that, to Commence from the first Sep[r] 1752.

Ordered that a Register Book be Procured for the use of this Parish and Delivered to the Rev[d] M[r] Jones.

And . . .

			s	*d*
1753	To Cash pd the Revd John Jones as Hd Rect	£50"	0"	0
	To Cash to CoLo James Patton (Asst) Rect	9"	19"	7
	To Hewan Mathers one of the Poor of this Parish	4"	0"	0
	To 2¾ Gallons of Wine for the Sacrament	1"	7"	6
	To Diging a Cellar in the Glebe House	2"	5"	0
	To Robert McClenachan H[d] order of Vestry	2"	13"	4

To David Stuart & Wm Hinds for carriage of the vestry books	1"10" 0
To Julian Mauck for keep a Blind Woman	1" 4" 3
To Patrick Porterfield for Nursing an Orphan Child	9" 4" 0
To Widow Thing for Burying John Lowdon	4"10" 0
To the Quitrents of the Glebe Land for the Years 1747:48:49:50"51 & 52	1"9"11½
To Cash to Thomas Moffit at Sundrys one of the Poor	4"13" 4
To Peter Mauck on Account of a Blind Woman	9" 6" 9
To Lambert Booper an Object of Charity	2"12"10

c. *Other matters.* Various other types of notes are also found in vestry minutes. The following is particularly reminiscent of documents arising out of the "poor laws" of England which required that the parish of origin (called "parish of settlement") be responsible for their poor regardless of where they may have removed themselves:

> August 6th 1750
>
> On the information of CoL^{O} John Buckanan that one ——— [sic] Morrice is lately come into this Parish with a numerous Family who is likely to become chargeable to this Parish Its ordered that the Churchwardens move the said Morrice to the place from whence he came——According to Law and bring in their Charge for the same at the laying of the next Parish Levy unless he give Security for indemnifying the said Parish.

Even biographical material can be found in vestry minutes upon occasion. In the minutes of the Immanuel Church, Hanover County, Virginia, on October 21, 1878, there was recorded an obituary for one of the churchwardens or vestrymen. It was copied from the *Southern Churchman*:

> BASSETT—Departed this life on the 25th of August, 1878, at his residence, Clover Lia in the county of Hanover, George Washington Bassett, Esqr, in the seventy ninth year of his age. By the death of Mr. Bassett, a prominent and valient member of the old fashioned Virginia gentry has been taken away from the few who still survive and the church has been deprived of a wise and devoted member.
>
> Mr Bassett was descended from the ancient and honorable family of the Bassetts of Eltham in the county of New Kent, which for two centuries exercised so prominent an influence in their native county and was so active in the civil and, ecclesiastical affairs of Virginia. The sister of Mrs. Washington, Miss Anna Maria Dandridge, married Mr. Bassett's grandfather and between the families of Mount Vernon and Eltham there was always maintained the most intimate and

cordial relations. Early in life Mr. Bassett became a communicant of the Episcopal Church and at once manifested the most active zeal for its prosperity in the neighborhood in which he resided. He sat in many of the conventions of the diocese and was always found in hearty cooperation with those ——— and, devoted, men to whom so much of the prosperity and advancement of the church in Virginia is firstly due.

In the year of 1843, soon after his removal, to his estate in Hanover, Mr. Bassett became much concerned at the prostrate condition of the Church in his neighborhood, and the adjoining counties of King William and New Kent. The parishes had died out and been without rectors or church services for more than half a century. With extraordinary patience and self denial Mr. Bassett awakened the interest and aid of the few Churchmen scattered over the large extent of the country and, the church was reorganized and a clergyman appointed, to labor in the lower part of Hanover County, two parishes in King William and one in New Kent.

Mr. Bassett's money, his time and, personal influence were issued unsparingly bestowed, and, his faithful services were much abundantly rewarded.

He saw the Church of his fathers happily restablished and with slight interruptions it has continued to prosper to this day. So far as ——— judgment may venture it seems certain that but for Mr. Bassett's exertions the Church would, have died out utterly or remained ——— and, useless as he found it in this part of Virginia.

Like so large and sorrowful a number of the prominent families in old, Virginia, Mr. Bassett sustained severe damage to his temporal prosperity from the effects of the late war and, other causes beyond his control. Estates held from a long line of honored ancestry were almost wholly ——— but his patient submission to his Master's dispensations and his unmurmuring acquiescence in what had befallen him without any hope of amelioration were most touching and edifying to witness.

No complaints ever fell from his lips and he seemed heartily thankful for the comforts yet left to him in his declining years.

For heaven his last days were his best days, and it is a most precious memory to his many friends, that the religion of his early manhood was so full of steadfastness and afforded, so many precious consolations when he was wasted and feeble and slowly passing away to his rest in heaven.

The community of which Mr. Bassett was so conspicuous a member for so many years will long remember his as a ——— friend, a hospitable, sympathising neighbor, and though not a perfect, yet an humbel minded, earnest and devoted, Christian.

2. Registers of the P.E. Church.

The registers of the Immanuel Protestant Episcopal Church are quite typical of those kept in other churches of the same denomination, though, as mentioned earlier, there is no set pattern—they vary even with the minister. Let's look at some register entries:

a. *Baptisms.*

Name of infant	*Name of parents*	*Name of sponsors*	*Date and age*
William Braxton	Carter & Ellen Roy	Parents	1857 April 1 yr
Carter			1857 April 3 yr
William Roy	Thomas H. & Susan Carter	W^m H Roy & Sally V B Tabb	1857 June 5 yrs
James Bernard	Thos & Sally Q. Gardiner	E. P. Meridith	1857 July 10 2 yrs
Blanch Bell	Mrs McGehee	Mother & uncles	1857 Sep 8 yrs
Note this Baptism was at Wht Sulphur Springs. The parties of Bolvin County, Miss. (Post Office Victoria)			
Charles Pinkney	Thos & Sally Q Gardiner	E. P. Meredith	1858 May 29 3 mo
Edmon Fitzhugh	Rob^o W. & H. V. B. Tomlin	Parents	1858 July 9 yrs
Thomas Nelson Carter	Thomas H. & Susan Carter	Mrs. Ann Wickham Mrs Ann Carter	1858 Nov

These baptisms contain quite complete information, but records of baptisms just a few years later are somewhat more informative:

At Hempstead July 5th 1873—
Ellen Douglas, daughter of W.W. & Fanny Gordon Born Aug 11th 1873 [sic]

1874: Nov 16. At the house of James S. & Delia Kelley their child Mary Egbert born May 6th last
Sponsors, Mrs B. B. Bassett & Mrs Annette L. Ingle
Rev J. E. Ingle of the Diocese of Maryland officiating

1876: Apr 28th—At Mrs Blake's. King William Co.
Rush Aldridge Hunt
Son of Jones Rush Lincoln (and Elizabeth Aldridge Blake his wife deceased)
born Ap 8 1866
Sponsors Rev E. A. Dalrymple STD, Miss Sophia L. Lincoln—by proxy.

Oct 14th at Hampstead, New Kent.
Laura Robinson daughter of W. W. & Fanny Gordon
born July 10th 1876.

1877
Oct 5th at the Rectory.
Lydia Bock, daughter of Francis E. & Emma Keene Habersham
born Sept 20th
Sponsors: Mrs Emma Keene, Miss Ella Habersham, Newton Keene, by proxy.

b. *Confirmations.*

Confirmations tell us very little—just names and dates:

Name of candidates	*By whom administered*	*Date*
Ella Moore Bassett	Rt Rev Wm Meade D.D.	1857 Nov.
Augusta Lewis	"	"
Sarah Ann Baker	"	"
Thos. H. Carter	"	1860 Nov. 4th
Mary M. L. Newton	"	" "
Henry Franklin Baker	"	" "
Mary Louisa "	"	" "
Maria Carter Wormly	"	" "
Bettie A. Polaka	Confirmed in Lexington, Ky	
May Dabney	" Charlottesville, Va	
O. T. Baker	Rt Rev J. Johns D.D.	1866 Nov.
Robt H. "	"	"
Margt E. "	"	"
Susan C. L. "	"	"
Anna J. "	"	"
Maria Dabney	"	"
Sallie C. Darricotte	"	"

c. *Communicants.*

1.	Geo W. Bassett sen	
2.	Betty Barnett Bassett	
3.	Geo W. Bassett Jr.	
—	Judith F. F. Bassett	Removed
4.	Carter Warner Wormley	
5.	Ellen Bankhead Wormley	
6.	Sallie Lightfoot Wormley	
—	Turner	Removed to Frederick, Md
7.	Mary Sheet	
8.	Susan E. Carter	Withdrawn
—	Robert W. Tomlin	Died July 22d 1862
9.	Wm A. R. Brockenborough	

—	William Sayre	Removed
—	Elizabeth Sayre	Died Dec 8th 1860
—	Mildred Ruffin	Removed to Frankfort, Ky
—	Margaret Tyler	Transferred to St Peters Parish
—	Betty Tyler	Transferred to St Peters Parish
10.	Wm A Baker	Died June 24, 1873
11.	Sarah A. Baker	
12.	Judith O. Johnson	
—	Sally A. Gardiner	Removed to Kanawha 1860
—	Virginia T. Carroway	Removed and dead
—	Ella M. Bassett	Removed to Jefferson C. Nov 1860
13.	Annette L. Bassett	
14.	Sarah A. E. Baker	Removed to California
15.	Sarah Eliza Blake	Withdrawn

d. *Marriages.*

Name of parties	*Where married*	*Date*
Wm A. Tignor & Ann E. Clifton	Immanuel Church	1857 Oct 13th
John Peris Points & Elizth Garlick Tyler	Turwood Hannvill	1858 April 18th 11: AM
Henry J. C. Vass & Lavinia Via	Black Creek Church	1858 April 18th 3 PM
Wm Robt Boyd & Margt Farley Smith	Immanuel Church	1859 Sept 28 10: AM.
Barnett Bassett Sayre & Mildred Campbell Ruffin	Marlbourne	1859 October 4 12 AM

e. *Deaths and funerals.*

Wm Roy infant son of Dr Thos & Susan Carter died Sunday May 2^{d} and buried at Pampatake on Monday May 3^{d} [1857]

James Tyler died July — 1857 and buried by Mr Points

Mrs. ——— White aged about 100 buried Oct 2/58

Mrs Bently Waker Apr 12/59

Miss Polly White June "

Elisha White 69 Nov 23^{d} "

C. W. Robt Wate abt 60 Aug 11 1860

Mrs Eliz. Sayre died on 8th Decr buried Decr 10th at Marlbourne

This infant son of Mrs Sayre 19 "

Susan Cath^{n} daughter of Mrs Blake died 25th & buried 27th Aug 61

Later funeral and death records are typically more informative than the earlier ones:

1876 March 25th

Mrs Harriet Clopton, aged 78, was buried at the cemetery near the dwelling house of her son

March 31—In New Kent County from his residence at The White House. William A. Cooke—aged about 30.

April 25th—At Hampstead, New Kent, Virginia—Jane Farland eldest daughter of Wm W. Gorton Esq.—aged seventeen years. One who belonged to be with Christ!

1877—March 1st. Mrs Maria D. Woodee a recent Communicant of this Church, aged 27 or 28 years was buried at Shinmer [?] Hill this day.

1878—Feb 13: Mr James Tucker a citizen of Hanover Co., aged 62, died, It is said of the disease of the heart suddenly

Apr. 24. Mrs. Judith Johnson—aged 71

August 27th—George W. Bassett Sr.

Born Aug 23, 1800—Died Aug 25, 1878. A Communicant from early life and Warden of Immanuel Church from its organization. When he moved to the County, he found the Colonial Church extinct, and by his efforts, and liberal aid, was Immanuel Church built subsequently—

He lies in its cemetery, — May his rest be peace.

Nov 7—Ramaliel Philips, son of William and Caroline Philips, died Nov 6th 1878, aged 19 years, buried in the cemetery of Immanuel

C. The Lutheran Church

The Lutheran Church was the dominant religion in many areas during the early history of this country, and also had a large following in other areas. Lutheran records are generally quite complete but, as with the records of other churches, much depends on the minister or clerk. Also, Lutheran Church records are not unlike the records of some other churches, notably some of the branches of the Reformed Church. The following examples are from the records of the Goshenhoppen Lutheran Church, Montgomery County, Pennsylvania.

1. Register of families.

The register of families contains detailed information on all members of the congregation and their families. It is arranged by family and looks like this:

The names of the Members of the Congregation their wives and Children, began in the year 1751.

1. John Michael Reiher, age 62 years, born 1689 father John Michael Reiher, Mother Annie Catherine, from Rohrbach near Zinze in Courtebarg. Anno 1732 he came to America. He married

   (1) In the year 1708, Anna Maria, daughter of Dietrich Seeland and Amelia, of Nurnberg, died 1742.

   (2) In the year 1743, Maria Catherine, Reformed, born 1713, died 1750, daughter of Henrich Schneider of Asohpissen in the Palatinate and of Catharine daughter of Abraham Schneider.

   (3) In 1751, Sept 12, Maria Christine, born 1718, Nov 18 at Borna in Electoral Saxony, daughter of George Gerlach and Susanna, who is now with her daughter. Married (1) John Christopher Hoepler, died Aug 18, 1750 at sea, where he was buried.

   The children of this marriage are as follows:

   1. John Christian, born 1739, Jan 18, bapt 29 ditto
   2. John George, born 1743, Nov 17. Bapt Nov 18
   3. John Gottleib, born 1748, Jan 23, bapt Jan 25
   4. John Henry, born 1750, Dec 11, bapt Dec 20

   In the year 1750, she with her mother and parents in law came to America and married (2) Michael Reiher. Michael Reiher has the following children of the first and second marriage.

   1. Anna Maria, died
   2. John Carl, born 1711, Dec 15, bapt. Dec 17
   3. Anna Maria, born 1712, Dec 5, bapt Dec 8
   4. John Martin, born 1716, Jan 9, bapt Jan 11
   5. Anna Sarah, born 1718, March 24
   6. Anna Catharine, born 1729, Dec 6
   7. Anna Barbara, born 1745
   8. George Philip, born 1750

2. Lists of communicants.

This is a periodic list of persons who received communion, made approximately every two or three months. In this case the names were arranged more or less alphabetically:

Nov 4 1751

1. Bausberger, Laurence
2. Bauersax, John Nicholas
3. Bausmann, Conrad
4. ——— Anna Eva, his wife

5. Berckheimer, Leonhard
6. ——— Catharine, his wife
7. Berckheimer, Valentine
8. Bering, Adam
9. Bittner, Henry
10. ——— Christinea, his wife

3. Confirmations.

The following list is dated June 24, 1752:

1. Elias Schneider, age 18 years, son of Conrad Schneider, see p. ——
2. John Martin Schmidt, age 17 years, son of Henry Schmidt.
3. Peter Gabel, 14 years, son of Philip Gabel, see p. ——
4. Christian Hoepler, 13 years, son of John Christopher Hoepler, see p. ——
5. George Philip Gabel, 12 years, son of Philip Gabel, see p. ——
6. Michael Schneider, 16 years, son of Conrad Schneider, see p. ——
7. Anna Margaret Klein, 23 years, wife of John Klein.
8. Elizabeth Schmid, 17 years, da. of Martin Schmid
9. Maria Agatha Klingele, 17 years, da. of Georg Frederick Klingel and wife Maria Agnes, of Conestoga, living at Samuel Schuler's
10. Evan Margaret, 15 years, da. of Philip Kresler; her mother Barbara is dead.

4. Marriages.

(1751)

1. John George Goerkes, single, Lutheran, admitted to the Lord's Supper with his father William Goerkes living in New York, married Anna Zipperle, single, Lutheran, da. of the late Frederick Zipperle and Catharine of Rhinesbeck, who lived at George Weigele, bro. of her mother, Banns published (1) in Old Goshenhoppen, June 30, (2) at same place July 14, (3) at Falkner Swamp July 21. Married at Old Goshenhoppen, July 23, in the church with a wedding sermon. The text was taken from Tobit 4:1-7, 13-16.

Later marriage records have much *less* detail:

(1780)

Jan 11. George Schwenck	and	Susanna Weis
Febr 8, George Lemle	and	Barbara Haas
May 11. Henry Graf	and	Charlotte Schwarz
July 18 Jacob Gros	and	Susanna Klein

5. Baptisms.

There was not much change in the information or format in the baptism records over the years. They are all about like these:

(1751)

Children	*Parents*	*Sponsors*
Elisabeth b. July 7, 1751 bapt Aug 4	Jacob Grotz and Elizabeth at Shippack	Henry Bittner and Christina fr Shippack
Anna Margaret b. July 24, 1751 bapt Aug 4	Henry Bittner and Christine	Jacob Grotz and wf Elizabeth

There was also a special record kept of the baptisms of illegitimate children:

Names of the baptized children, who were born out of wedlock.

George Philip, born Febr 16, 1753, bapt Febr 25 1753 in the schoolhouse. His father is said to be Henry Lips, a servant accross the river. The mother is single, named Elizabeth, living at John Fischer's, Godparents: Philip Wenzel and wife Christine, both newcomers.

Anna Elizabeth, born Dec 27, 1754, bapt. March 9, 1755. Parents: His father is said to be John Peter Kabel His Mother Anna Barbara Kircher, da of the late John George Kircher, single.
Godparents: John Frederick Kircher, single and Elizabeth Schwenck, single, da of the late Peter Schwenck.

Barbara, born July 21, 1763.
Parents: John Daub, died and Catharina
Sponsors: John Kantz and wife Barbara

Manli, born 1767, parents: Michael Gaugler and Catharine Gaugler.
Sponsors: Kilian Fischer and Elizabeth Nuagesser.

6. Dead who were buried publicly.

1. Eva Margaret, born 1751, March—died Jan 31, 1752, buried Febr 2nd, in cemetery in front of the Old Goshenhoppen Church, on Sunday before the morning service. Parents: John Jacob Kayser and Anna Maria, Ref.
2. Jacob Eckmann, age 65 years, born 1687, from Switzerland, the Canton of H. Gall, born in Runnelshorse, Reformed. Father Librich Eckman, who left only one son, Jacob, and his widow

Anna Maria. Anno 1752, July 3 he died and was buried in our Church yard at Old Goshenhoppen on July 4, 1752.

The same is true of the burials as was true of the marriages—the later ones have less detail:

1776

On April 5, was buried Catharina, da of Henry Hemsinger schoolmaster here, her age 2 years, 8 months.

On May 31, was buried Catharine, da of the late Herman Waische, her age 5 years, 10 months.

On June 6, was buried Catharine, da of George Boyer, her age 3 years less 5 weeks.

D. The Baptist Church

The Baptist Church records which I have chosen to examine with you (briefly) are those of the Woodbury Baptist Church in Cannon County, Tennessee. The records are called "minutes" and the entries are diverse. They include financial accounts, lists of converts (name only), notations of letters of admission, annual membership lists (also name only), and accounts of church business meetings. Following are the minutes of a business meeting:

Saturday Jan. 26, 1889

Baptist Church of Christ met in Conference at Woodbury. Minutes of last meeting called for and Read and approved. No unfinished business refured to. Bro. J. R. Rushing anonce the minutes of last association. Are on the table, and all can get them that want to. Bro. D. B. Vance give notice of the death of Sister Juda A. Ferrell. A notice from the Clerk of North Fork, Missionary Baptist Church notify the church of this place that Bro. Wm. St. John and wife was Received into that church Oct. 1888 by letter granted them by this church. By motion and 2nd Bro. J. G. Moore, Bro. J. C. New, Bro. D. B. Vance appointed as a commity to examine the windows of the church, come upon some plan of Repairing the same. Investigate the cost of Repairs and Report to the church next meeting. A motion was made to appoint a commitee to see Sister Sue Talley about Dancing. Bro. Moderator appoint the Deakons of the church as the commity. By motion church vote to cloth the committy with the authority to interview all other disorderly members. Bro. J. D. New made a financial report to the church moved and 2nd.

E. The Society of Friends (Quakers)

The last denomination from whose records we will draw specific examples is the Quakers. Regardless of where you go you will find consistency in the nature of the Friends' records. They do not vary extensively either with the passage of time or from one locality to another. The records are based on a "Meeting" system. The local congregation meets weekly and is called a *Weekly Meeting.* Each Weekly Meeting group has a *Preparative Meeting* wherein the business of the congregation belongs. A *Monthly Meeting* comprises several Weekly Meetings and is the meeting wherein most of the business of the church is transacted and recorded. There are both men's and women's Monthly Meetings. It is the Monthly Meeting records that are generally considered to be of the most genealogical value, though other records do have some value.

Several Monthly Meetings make up a *Quarterly Meeting* and several Quarterly Meetings come together to make up a *Yearly Meeting,* and some branches of the organization have *Three-Year Meetings.* These latter three are mainly administrative divisions and their records are not so useful to the family researcher.

Thomas W. Marshall, writing in the introduction to Hinshaw's *Encyclopedia of American Quaker Genealogy* (Vol. I), made the following observations about Quaker records. I recommend your careful study of this material if your ancestors have Quaker connections:

> The records kept by Friends Monthly Meetings during the eighteenth and nineteenth centuries usually consisted of a record of births and deaths, a record of marriage certificates, and minutes covering all proceedings and discussions coming before the monthly sessions of the meeting. As the men and women met separately, two sets of minutes were kept. In some meetings the marriage records were kept in the same book with the birth and death records; in others they were kept in a separate book. The birth and death records are never complete. In some cases whole families are omitted; sometimes the older children of a family are recorded and the younger ones omitted. The percentage of births recorded appears to be considerably higher than that of deaths. In only a few meetings was it the practice to record the birth dates and parentage of the father and mother of a family. Place of birth was not usually recorded, for either parents or children.
>
> None of the earlier meeting records contains a list of the membership. When a monthly meeting was divided to establish a new one, all members of the old meeting who lived within the verge of the new automatically became members of the new meeting without any list of their names being entered in the records of either meeting. A person who became a member in this way, unless he took some active part in the affairs of the meeting, was married, or was complained of for some breach of discipline, might continue in membership until the end of his life without his name ever appearing in the records.

The records of marriage certificates are much more complete than birth and death records. In a few meetings every marriage accomplished in the meeting is fully recorded. Others are nearly complete, —with only a few marriages missing. Since the regular procedure in the marriage involved two appearances of the couple before both men's and women's meetings prior to marriage and subsequent reports of the committees appointed to attend the marriage ceremony, there is ample record of each marriage in the minutes even though recording of the marriage certificate may have been overlooked. The record in the minutes, however, does not give the names of the parents of the persons married nor the exact date of the marriage. The report of the committee that the marriage had been accomplished was made in the next succeeding meeting, thus fixing the date within a month.

The minutes of sessions of the monthly meetings cover many subjects . . . During the periods of migration the minutes relating to certificates of membership received and issued are the most numerous and have the greatest interest. Records of disciplinary action against members for violation of the rules of the Society occupy much space. Members were "dealt with" on a great variety of complaints, including fiddling and dancing, drinking intoxicating liquor to excess, serving in the militia or other armed forces, using profane language, fighting, failure to meet financial obligations, marrying contrary to the order used by Friends, deviation from plainness in apparel or speech, joining another religious society, etc. Unless the offending member expressed sorrow for his misconduct and brought a signed paper condemning the same, he was usually disowned. The number so disowned runs into thousands. Many of them, after a shorter or longer time, produced the necessary paper of condemnation and were reinstated in membership. A minute showing that a person presented a satisfactory paper condemning his misconduct, implies that he was retained or reinstated in membership, as the case might be, whether the fact is specifically stated or not. Often, following the disownment of a member (perhaps many years later) the minutes may record a request for membership coming from a person of the same name, but with no reference to previous membership or disownment. In such cases it is usually impossible to tell whether the two minutes refer to the same person or to two individuals with the same name. A great many of those who were disowned never asked to be reinstated but remained outside the Society for the rest of their lives. The names of these persons never appear in the records again.

When individual members of families removed from one monthly meeting to another they were furnished removal certificates setting forth the fact of their membership in good standing and recommending them to the fellowship of the monthly meeting to which they were removing. In the earlier days these certificates were usually prepared and signed in advance and carried by the members to their new place of abode. Later, it appears to have become more the custom to wait until the new home had been established and then send back a request that the certificate be forwarded. A condition to the granting of a certificate was that the member's "outward affairs" be satisfactorily settled. The certificate usually stated that this had been done. When a certificate was issued to a family the fact was generally recorded in the men's minutes so far as it applied to the husband and sons, and in the women's minutes as it applied to the mother and daughters. The names of children were frequently omitted in the minutes of the issuing meeting but were usually recorded by the receiving meeting. The fact that John Jones and family (men's minutes) and Mary Jones and daughters (women's minutes) were granted certificates to the same meeting on the same day does not guarantee that John and Mary were husband and wife. Such an assumption would be correct in the majority of cases but would sometimes be erroneous. Confirmatory evidence should always be sought.

If a man and woman contemplating marriage were members of different monthly meetings they made their declarations of intention in the meeting of which the woman was a member. The man was required to bring a certificate from his meeting stating that he was a member in good standing and free from marriage engagements with others. This certificate did not transfer his membership to the woman's meeting, but only made it possible for him to marry there. After marriage, the wife usually obtained a certificate, issued in her married name, transferring her membership to her husband's meeting.

Marriage contrary to the Friends' order, variously referred to in the minutes as "marriage by a priest," "outgoing in marriage," "marriage contrary to good order," "marriage out of unity," "marriage contrary to discipline," etc., and spoken of in every day speech as "marriage out of the meeting," was the cause of more complaints and disownments than any other single offense . . . Unfortunately the minutes rarely give the name of the person to whom the offending member was married. The record relating to a woman usually refers to her as Mary Jones, formerly Brown, thus giving a clue which is not available in the case of a man. In a large percentage of cases of marriage contrary to Friends' order, only one of the parties was a member. When both parties to a marriage engagement were members in good standing, there was usually no reason why they might not apply to the meeting, and receive permission to marry under its authority, but there were some exceptions. Marriage between first cousins or others of close relationship was forbidden by the rules of the Society. Parental objection may have been a bar to a marriage in meeting in some cases. In other cases the couple married out of meeting for no other reason than to accomplish their purpose more quickly and without the formality which was necessary to a marriage in meeting.[2]

The examples of Friends' records used here come from the Monthly Men's Meeting of Smithfield, Rhode Island, and from the same meeting of Hampton, New Hampshire. The following are typical entries taken at random from the minutes:

(SMITHFIELD)

—28th of 1st Mo 1802

This meeting Recd a Certificate of Removal from Swanzy Monthly Meeting in favor of Job Chace his wife Sibel and their Children whose names are Earl, Cromwell, Pillena Joanna and Lamira Chase which being read Excepted and ordered Recorded.

—29th of the 4th Month, 1802

This Meeting Recieved a Certificate of Removal from Southkingstown Monthly Meeting in favor of Alice Rathborn which being Read is Excepted

—Monthly meeting 30th of the 9th Mo 1802

The women inform that they have come to a conclusion to Disown Rhoda Smith with which this Meeting unites.

Smithfield preparitive Meeting informed this that Reuben Shearman Desires a Marriage Certificate to Uxbridge Monthly Meeting. Chad Smith and William Buffam are appointed to take the necessary care theirin and if nothing appear to hender prepare a Certificate and bring to next Monthly Meeting

—Monthly Meeting 25th of the 11th Mo, 1802

Smithfield Preparatives Meeting inform this that Daniel Inman Proposed Laying his Intention of Marriage with Abigail Mowry before this Meeting he producing a Certificate from Uxbridge Monthly Meeting. And they appeared in this Meeting and Declaired their Intentions accordingly and were Directed to next Monthly Meeting for an answer.

—Monthly Meeting 30th of the 12th Mo, 1802

Smithfield preparitive Meetg informed this Meetg that Elisha Shearman was in the practice of Keeping Company with one not a Member of our Society in order for Marriage Whereupon Row-

[2] Thomas W. Marshall, Introduction to *Encyclopedia of American Quaker Genealogy,* Vol. I, ed. by William Wade Hinshaw, 1936 (Baltimore: Genealogical Publishing Co., 1969 reprint), pp. ix-xi.

land Rathborn Joseph Bartlet Seth Kelly and Stephen Aldrich Are appointed with such others as the womens Meetg may appoint to make a visit to the family endeavoring to feel after the mind of Truth theirin and Report their Sence thereon to next Monthly Meetg

Daniel Inman and Abigail Mowry appeared in this Meetg and Continued their intentions of Marriage and Recvd and Answer accordingly and Zaccheus Southwick and Daniel Smith are Appointed to have the Necessary Care theirof according to Discipline and Report to next Monthly Meeting.

This Meetg is informed that James Clemence a member theirof is gone to live a few monthes in the verge of Bolton Monthly Meetg and Desires a few lines to Certify his right of Membership, the Clerk is Directed to furnish him with a Coppy of this Minute

—M M at 27th on 1st Mo 1803

The Committee on the Case of Elisha Shearman inform that they have had an opportunity with him and that he is married out of the good order of friends and Does not appear to them to be in Sutable Disposition of mind to Make friends Satisfaction. This Meetg after Solidly Considering the same Do with the unity of the womens Meetg Disown unity with him as a Member and Elisha Kelly and Rowland Rathborn Are appointed to inform him their of his right to appeal Draft a Testimony of his Denial and report to next Monthly Meetg.

The Committee on the Case of Philip Walden request for his Children report that some care has been taken in sd Matter but not being ready to make full report at this time Sd Case is referd under the same friends Care and Directed to Report to next Monthly Meetg.

The Committee to have Care of Daniel Inman and Abigail Mowry Marriage report that according to their observation it was Conducted in an orderly Manner and that the Certificate is Delivered to the Regester

—M M on 28th of 4th Mo, 1803

The Committy appointed to Prepare a Certificate for Joseph Bartlette to uxbridge Mo Meeting in order for marriage presented one wich Being Read with Some alteration is agreed to and Sined by the Clark.

—6th Mo, 30th, 1803

This Meeting appoints Caleb Pain to read the Testamony of Denial aginst Elisha Shearman at a publick Meeting in this Place and lodge the same with the Regester to be recorded and report to our next Monthly Meeting.

—11 Mo, 24th, 1803

The Women presented a Testimony of Denial against Waty

Bartlett formerly Buffum which was read and agreed to in this Meeting.

—4th Mo, 26th, 1804

The Committee appointed to prepare a Removal Certificate for Elisha Thornton Jur to Newbedford Monthly Meeting presented one which being read with some Alterations is approved and signed by the Clerk.

—6th Mo, 28th, 1804

Our Beloved Friend Jonathan Wright attended this Meeting with a Certificate from hopewell Monthly Meeting in Virginia dated 6d of 2th Mo, 1804—Expressive of their Unity with him as a Minister, whose Company and Gospel Labors have been exceptable to us.

(HAMPTON)

Joseph Dow deceaced this Life ye 4th of ye 2thMonth 1703

Eastor Green Dcsesed Ye 24th of Ye 7th Month 1703

Abraham Green Juner dyed ye 11th of Ye 3th month 1703

Thomas Lankster & Ye widow Musey Kiled ye 19th of Ye 6th mon 1703

Jeams Pearintun Lost at sea Ye 12 day of the same. 1718: in his 55 year

Hannah Pearintun: daughter of James Pearingtun and Lydia his wife Born the 14th day of Ye 2 mo: 1708

Lydia Mussey Pearintun Born ye 10th day of ye 9th mo 1671

1737: The: 3 day of the 10th mo Lydia Pearintun dyed in her: 66 year.

A Record of the Births of the Children of Jonathan Hoag and Comfort his Wife as Followeth (viz)—

Peter Hoag: Son of the afore Said Jonathan Hoag and Comfort his wife Born the: 21 Day of ye: 12th month Called February 1738/9

Hephsabe born the: 25th of ye 9th mo Called November 1741

Hussa born the 10th day of the seccond month April 1744

Anna born the 1st day of the Sixth month Called August 1745

Mary born the 10th day of the Sixth month Called August 1747

Abraham born the 25th day of ye 7th mo Called September 1748

Isaac Born ye: 7th day of the 7th mo; Old Stile Called September 1752

1742

Whereas Jonathan Hardy son of John Hardy of Hampton in the Province of New Hampshier in New-England and Lydia his wife And Bathshabe Stanyan daughter of James Stanyan of Hampton in the province afore said And Ann his wife haveing publickly decleared their Intentions of takeing Each other in Marrage before severall monthly meeting of the people Calld Quakers in hampton and Almsburg according to the good order useed amongst them: Whose proseedings there in after deliborate Considiration Thereof: they apearing Clear of all others Relateing to marrage And haveing consent of parents and Relations Conserned were approved by the said Meetings—

Now these are to Certify all Whom it may Consern that for the full Accomplishing of their sd Intentions this fourteenth day of the seventh month called September Anno Domini one Thousand Seven hundred and forty two: They the Said Jonathan Hardy and Bathshaby Stanyan appeared in a Publick assembley of the aforesd People (and others) Meet to gather for that purpose at our meeting house at hampton afor'sd And sd Hardy takeing sd Stanyan by the hand openly Decleared that he took Bathshabe Stanyan to be his Wife Promiseing through the Lords assistance to be unto her a Kind and Loveing husband untill it Shall please God by Death to seperate us: (or to that Effect) and then and their in sd assembly sd Stanyan publickly decleared that she took Jonathan Hardey to be her Husband promiseing through the Lords assistance to be unto him a true and faithfull Wife untill it shall please God by Death to seperate us or words to ye same Import. And the Said Jonathan Hardy and Bathsaby Stanyan as a farther Confirmation thereof did hereunto Set their hands (she according to the Custom of Marrage assumeing the name of her husband) And wee whose names are hereunto Subscribed being present at their Solomnizeing of Said Marrage and Subscription as afore sd have here unto set our hands as witneses the day and year above written—

Jonathan Hardy
Bathshaby Hardy

Phebe dow	Philip Rowell	James Stanyan
Elizabeth dow	Jonathan Hoag	Joseph Stanyan
	Winthrop Dow	Merry Newbegin
	Abraham Dow	Rebeckah Hunt
	Nathan Hoag	Jonathan hoag jr
		Comfort Hoag
		Elizabeth Hunt

F. The Roman Catholic Church

The Roman Catholic Church probably has as good records as any other denomination. The sacramental records (registers) of the church are exceptional in the completeness of the information they contain. By church law the records were carefully kept and well preserved—and these laws were strict.

There is, however, some difficulty in doing research in the records of the Roman Catholic Church. Reasons for these difficulties include:

1. Historically the records have been kept in Latin.
2. There are few indexes (not so different from most other churches).
3. Most records are still in the parishes and little effort has been made to centralize them.
4. Church law stipulates that the records may be searched only by the priest and that the priest will issue a certificate (not a copy of the original record).

Though some dioceses are bringing in the records from the parishes for microfilming, this has not essentially changed the policy of restricted usage. The filming is only for preservation purposes and not for research. It is a hopeful sign, however, that this is the beginning of some centralization activity. And some day there may be a change in the research and access policy relating to at least the older records.

G. Other Churches

I have not pretended to cover the entire spectrum of church records in this discussion. That would be an impossible task within the limits of this work. You are, no doubt, acutely aware of many of my omissions and probably feel that many other religions and sects might be profitably discussed. I have passed over the records of the Eastern Orthodox Church, the Presbyterian Church, the Methodists (including the Methodist Episcopal Church which became so strong after the Revolutionary War), and the Anabaptists and their offspring (including the Mennonites, the Amish Mennonites, and the Hutterites). I have also neglected the Reformed Church groups (Calvinistic) which came out of Holland (the Reformed Church in America and the Christian Reformed Church), the German Palatinate (the Reformed Church in the United States, which later became the Evangelical and Reformed Church), Hungary (the Free Magyar Reformed Church in America), and France (the Huguenots). And no attention has been paid to the various splinters from the Lutheran Church which came to America

FIGURE 1—PRESBYTERIAN BAPTISM RECORDS

from central Europe. These include the Brethren Churches (also known as Dunkers, Tunkers, and Dunkards) and the Pietist groups (especially the Unity of the Brethren, better known as Moravians). I have also ignored Jewish records and Latter-day Saints (Mormon) records. And on and on . . .

While I regret that further coverage cannot be given, I feel that my examples represent an appropriate cross-section of typical American church records and should give you a "feel" for almost any church records you might encounter. I think it is more important to talk about how these records can be located than what they look like. If you find them, you can discover the nature of their contents quickly enough.

III. LOCATING CHURCH RECORDS

A. Problems and Solutions

Church records are of no value if you cannot find the ones that fit your specific problems. In America, where church and state are separate and where people with ancestry from all over Europe lived side by side and intermarried, there are two main problems:

1. Determining the church with which your ancestor had affiliation.
2. Locating the records of that church in the locality where your ancestor lived.

Clues to solve the first problem might come from many sources. Perhaps the family's present affiliation can help you, or the national origin of the family, or family tradition. You might find your answer in a will or a deed or on a tombstone. It may be in an obituary. Or there may be a clue in the locality where your ancestor resided—it may have been the settlement of a particular religious denomination—but you must know the locality's history to determine this. (A person may have belonged to several churches during his lifetime. This was quite common on the frontier, because if a town had only one church, that was usually where the town's residents [especially the Protestants] went to worship, regardless of former affiliation.) In later years obituaries, death certificates, hospital records, etc., contain statements of religious preference.

The second problem may be the more difficult of the two. There are some helps and reference tools to assist in locating church records, but even these are quite incomplete and may be misleading if we are not aware of their limitations. There is, in fact, no complete guide to American church records. This is an area which lies wide open to further study. The personnel at the

LDS Family History Library have done some studies on the location of church records, but they have a long way to go before the true objective is attained.[3]

Some useful studies were made in the 1930s and early 1940s as part of the Historical Records Survey under the auspices of the Works Projects Administration (WPA) of the "New Deal." The "Inventories of Church Archives" which resulted from these studies were excellent for the geographic areas and the churches they covered at the time they were made, but much of the information in them is now outdated. Many of the records have since been moved and many which were in private hands are now completely untraceable.[4]

We must not assume that church records do not exist just because we have been unable to find them; on the other hand, it would be foolish to say that no church records have ever been lost or destroyed, because many of these records are no longer in existence. The vestry minutes of the Immanuel Church in Hanover County, Virginia, of which I gave an example earlier, show this quite clearly. The biographical sketch (obituary) of George Washington Bassett tells some of the history of the Immanuel Church:

> In the year 1843, soon after his removal, to his estate in Hanover, Mr. Bassett became much concerned at the prostrate condition of the Church in his neighborhood, and the adjoining counties of King William and New Kent. *The parishes had died out and been without rectors or church services for more than half a century.* [Emphasis added.]

Was this common? What of records during this "more than half a century"? What about records of the earlier period before the church "died out"? All of these questions should be considered in a study of American church records. The same thing may have happened in hundreds of other churches. What does happen to the records when a church becomes defunct? It has been suggested by some that many records of the English Church met their doom during the Revolutionary War as part of an action of reprisal against the British, but I am unaware of any specific situations of this nature.

---

[3] See Jimmy B. Parker and Wayne T. Morris, "A Definitive Study of Major U.S. Genealogical Records: Ecclesiastical and Secular" (Area I, no. 36), World Conference on Records and Genealogical Seminar (Salt Lake City: The Genealogical Society of The Church of Jesus Christ of Latter-day Saints, 1969).

[4] See chapter 10 for a list of the guides to the WPA inventories of church records in the several states.

B. Finding the Records

If you can find early American church records they are peerless as a source of genealogical evidence, so let's consider some steps you might take:

1. First consider that the records are still in the custody of the church where they were kept, if that church still exists.
2. An advertisement in a local newspaper will often lead to the whereabouts of available records, especially those in private hands.
3. Don't be afraid to ask questions—of ministers, chambers of commerce, old-timers; anyone who might know.
4. The records of many churches have been published, especially in genealogical and historical periodicals, and are thus available. These are generally not too accessible either from the standpoint of finding the proper magazine or of knowing that an article of value is within it. One of the best approaches is to use the various periodical indexes listed in chapter 6.

A few church records are also published in book form (both alone and in conjunction with other records) and you should be aware of this possibility. Look under the locality of interest in your library catalog. I mentioned Hinshaw's work on the Quakers earlier in this chapter.[5] These seven volumes (in eight) contain abstracts of Monthly Meeting records, are indexed, and are quite useful as far as they go; but they certainly do not cover all Quaker records. They are, however, a representative example of published American church records.

In using published church records, as with all published sources, remember that they present secondary evidence and frequently contain copying errors.

5. Many church records are now being microfilmed by the churches themselves and by other agencies. Historical societies often preserve microfilm copies as well as originals, and copies are frequently available for sale or for reading. The LDS Family History Library has microfilmed the records of many churches throughout the U.S. and you may find it worthwhile to check its holdings before making a lot of other searches.
6. Libraries and historical societies have collected many church records (especially in their local areas) and these are readily available for searching. One of the big problems is to determine just who has the records. The *National Union Catalog of Manuscript Collections* can be useful in that effort.[6]

---

[5] William Wade Hinshaw, *Encyclopedia of American Quaker Genealogy,* 7 vols. (in 8), 1936——. (Vols. 1-6 have been reprinted by Genealogical Publishing Co., Baltimore. Vol. 7 is available from the Indiana Historical Society.)

[6] See bibliographic references under "bibliographies" in chapter 6 and footnote number 5 in chapter 9, and the textual discussion relating thereto.

C. Some Record Locations

With no indication of specific congregations or of the actual extent of the records, I offer the following as a *partial* list of church record depositories in states east of the Mississippi. Further information on the exact nature of the various collections and the addresses of these depositories must be determined from other sources.

ALABAMA:
1. Samford University, Birmingham—Baptist (Georgia and Alabama).
2. Department of Archives and History, Montgomery—Methodist, Baptist, P.E., Presbyterian, Roman Catholic.

ARKANSAS:
1. Hendrix College, Conway—Methodist.

CONNECTICUT:
1. Bristol Public Library, Bristol—Congregational (local).
2. Farmington Museum, Farmington—Congregational (local).
3. Archives of the Episcopal Diocese of Connecticut, Hartford—P.E.
4. Connecticut State Library, Hartford—various (more than 700 churches).
5. The Missionary Society of Connecticut, Hartford—Congregational.
6. Peck Memorial Library, Kensington—Congregational (local).
7. Wesleyan University Library, Middletown—Methodist.

DELAWARE:
1. Delaware Public Archives Commission, Dover—various.
2. University of Delaware Library, Newark—Presbyterian, Baptist.
3. Historical Society of Delaware, Wilmington—various.

D.C.:
1. American Catholic Historical Association, Catholic University of America—Roman Catholic.

GEORGIA:
1. Emory University Library, Atlanta—Methodist.

ILLINOIS:
1. McCormick Theological Seminary Library, Chicago—Presbyterian (including records formerly at Lane Theological Seminary in Cincinnati, Ohio).
2. Garrett Biblical Institute Library, Evanston—Methodist.
3. Knox College Library, Galesburg—Presbyterian, Congregational.
4. Church of the Brethren Historical Library, Elgin—Brethren (Dunkers).
5. Bethany Theological Seminary, Oak Brook—Brethren (Dunkers).
6. Lutheran Church in America, Chicago—Lutheran.
7. Chicago Theological Seminary, Chicago—Congregational.

INDIANA:

1. Franklin College Library, Franklin—Baptist.
2. Archives of the Mennonite Church, Goshen—Mennonite and Amish Mennonite.
3. Archives of DePauw University and Indiana Methodism, Greencastle—Methodist.
4. Henry County Historical Society Museum, New Castle—Quaker (local).
5. New Harmony Workingmen's Institute Library, New Harmony—Methodist (local).
6. Earlham College Library, Richmond—Quaker.
7. Old Catholic Library, Vincennes—Roman Catholic.

KENTUCKY:

1. College of the Bible Library, Lexington—Disciples of Christ.
2. Margaret I. King Library, U. of Kentucky, Lexington—mainly Baptist and Presbyterian, but also Disciples of Christ and Shaker.
3. Filson Club, Louisville—Shaker (Mercer County).
4. Louisville Presbyterian Theological Seminary Library, Louisville—Presbyterian.

MAINE:

1. Parson Memorial Library, Alfred—Baptist, Congregational, Methodist (all local).
2. Androscoggin Historical Society, Auburn—Baptist (Lewiston).
3. Bangor Public Library, Bangor—various (limited).
4. Hubbard Free Library, Hallowell—Congregational, Unitarian.
5. Louis T. Graves Memorial Library, Kennebunkport— ? (local).
6. University of Maine Library, Orono—Baptist (in Polermo).
7. Maine Historical Society, Portland—various (scattered).
8. Colby College Library, Waterville—local country churches.

MARYLAND:

1. Hall of Records, Annapolis—various (more than 400 volumes).
2. Archives of the Archdiocese of Baltimore, Baltimore—Roman Catholic.
3. Baltimore Yearly Meeting of Friends (Hicksite), Baltimore—Quaker.
4. Baltimore Yearly Meeting of Friends (Orthodox), Baltimore—Quaker (extensive).
5. Maryland Diocesan Library, Baltimore—P.E. (extensive).
6. Maryland Historical Society, Baltimore—P.E. (local).
7. Methodist Historical Society, Baltimore—Methodist.

MASSACHUSETTS:

1. Amesbury Public Library, Amesbury—Congregational (local).
2. Amherst College Library, Amherst— ? (local).

3. Barre Town Library, Barre— ? (local).
4. Beverly Historical Society, Beverly—Congregational (local).
5. Congregational Library, Boston—Congregational (extensive).
6. Massachusetts Diocesan Library, Boston—P.E.
7. New England Methodist Historical Library, Boston—Methodist (very few registers).
8. Dedham Historical Society, Dedham—Congregational, P.E. (local).
9. Haverhill Public Library, Haverhill—various (nearly 200 volumes).
10. Ipswich Town Hall, Ipswich— ? (local).
11. Marlborough Public Library, Marlborough— ? (local).
12. Universalist Historical Library, Crane Theological School, Tufts University, Medford—Universalist.
13. Nantucket Historical Association, Nantucket—Quaker (local).
14. Friends Meeting House, New Bedford—Quaker.
15. Andover Newton Theological School Library, Newton Center—Baptist. (Has collections formerly in New England Baptist Library.)
16. Forbes Library, Northampton—Congregational.
17. Northborough Historical Society, Northborough— ? (local).
18. Peabody Historical Society, Peabody—Congregational, Unitarian, Baptist (all local).
19. Petersham Historical Society, Petersham—Church of Christ (local).
20. Berkshire Athenaeum, Pittsfield—Shaker and (mainly) Quaker.
21. Essex Institute, Salem—various.
22. Shrewsbury Historical Society, Shrewsbury— ? (local).
23. Goodnow Public Library, South Sudbury— ? (local).
24. Historical Room, Stockbridge Library, Stockbridge—Congregational (local).
25. Old Colony Historical Society, Taunton—Congregational, Baptist.
26. Narragansett Historical Society of Templeton, Templeton— ? (local).
27. Westborough Historical Society, Westborough— ? (local).
28. J. V. Fletcher Library, Westford— ? (local).
29. Winthrop Public Library, Winthrop—Methodist (local).
30. Worcester Historical Society, Worcester—Congregational, Baptist, Universalist (local).
31. Woburn Public Library, Woburn—Congregational (Woburn and Burlington).

MICHIGAN:

1. Michigan Historical Collections, U. of Michigan, Ann Arbor—Presbyterian, Baptist, Congregational, Methodist *et al.*
2. Archdiocese of Detroit Chancery, Detroit—Roman Catholic.

3. Burton Historical Collection, Detroit Public Library, Detroit—Roman Catholic and various Protestant (extensive).
4. Flushing Township Public Library, Flushing— ? (local).
5. Thompson Home Library, Ithaca—Congregational (local).
6. Jackson City Library, Jackson— ? (Jackson County).
7. Kalamazoo College Library, Kalamazoo—Baptist *et al.*
8. Port Huron Public Library, Port Huron— ? (local).
9. Hope College, Van Zoeren Library, Holland—Dutch Reformed.

MINNESOTA:

1. Pope County Historical Society, Glenwood— ? (local).
2. Blue Earth County Historical Society, Mankato— ? (local).
3. Hennepin County Historical Society, Minneapolis—various.
4. Historical Society of the Minnesota Conference of the Methodist Church, Minnesota Methodist Headquarters, Minneapolis—Methodist (extensive).
5. Evangelical Lutheran Church Archives. Luther Theological Seminary, St. Paul—Evangelical Lutheran.
6. Historical Committee of the Baptist General Conference, Bethel Theological Seminary, St. Paul—Baptist (extensive).
7. Minnesota Historical Society, St. Paul—P.E. (extensive for state).
8. Weyerhauser Library, Macalester College, St. Paul—Presbyterian.
9. Gustavus Adolphus College Library, St. Peter—Evangelical Lutheran.

MISSISSIPPI:

1. Mississippi Conference Methodist Historical Society, Millsaps College Library, Jackson—Methodist.
2. Mississippi Department of Archives and History, Jackson—Southern Presbyterian.

NEW HAMPSHIRE:

1. New Hampshire State Library, Concord—various.
2. Dover Public Library, Dover—Baptist (local).
3. University of New Hampshire Library, Durham— ? (local).
4. Dartmouth College Library, Hanover—Congregational.
5. New Hampshire Antiquarian Society, Hopkinton—various.

NEW JERSEY:

1. Blair Academy Museum, Blairstown—Presbyterian, Methodist.
2. Cape May County Historical Association, Cape May—Quaker.
3. Monmouth County Historical Association, Freehold—various.
4. Drew University Library, Madison—Methodist (including papers formerly held by the Methodist Historical Society of New Jersey).
5. Morris County Historical Society, Morristown—various (local).
6. New Brunswick Theological Seminary Library, New Brunswick—Reformed Church (extensive).

7. Rutgers University Library, New Brunswick—various (on film).
8. Sussex County Historical Society, Newton—various.
9. Passaic County Historical Society, Paterson—various.
10. Seventh Day Baptist Historical Society, Plainfield—Seventh Day Baptist.
11. Princeton Theological Seminary, Princeton—Presbyterian (N.J. Synod).
12. Salem County Historical Society, Salem—Quaker.
13. Atlantic County Historical Society, Somers Point—Quaker *et al.*
14. Somerset County Historical Society, Somerville—various (local).
15. State Library, Archives and History Bureau, Trenton—various.

NEW YORK:

1. New York State Library, Albany—various (extensive).
2. Cayuga County Historical Society, Auburn—Congregational.
3. Buffalo Historical Society, Buffalo—Baptist, Presbyterian.
4. Ontario County Historical Society, Canandaigua—various (local).
5. Cobleskill Public Library, Cobleskill—various (local).
6. New York State Historical Association and Farmers' Museum, Cooperstown—various (Otsego County).
7. Cortland County Historical Society, Cortland—various (local).
8. Green County Historical Society, Coxsackie—various (transcripts).
9. Department of History and Archives, Fonda—Dutch Reformed *et al.*
10. Pember Library and Museum, Granville—Presbyterian (local).
11. Colgate University Archives, Hamilton—Baptist.
12. Hempstead Public Library, Hempstead—various (local).
13. Huntington Historical Society, Huntington—Presbyterian, P.E. *et al.*
14. Dewitt Historical Society of Tomkins County, Ithaca—Methodist, Presbyterian *et al.*
15. Columbia County Historical Society, Kinderhook—various.
16. Senate House Museum, Kingston—Dutch Reformed *et al.*
17. Daughters of the American Revolution Library, LeRoy—various.
18. Wayne County Division of Archives and History, Lyons—various (local).
19. Huguenot Historical Society, New Paltz—Huguenot.
20. Jean Hasbrouck Memorial House, New Paltz—Dutch Reformed, Methodist.
21. Holland Society of New York Library, New York City—Dutch Reformed, Lutheran, French Reformed, German Reformed.
22. New York Genealogical and Biographical Society, New York City —various (extensive).
23. New York Historical Society, New York City—P.E. and various.
24. Queens Borough Public Library, New York City—various.

25. Society of Friends Records Committee, New York City—Quaker.
26. Union Theological Seminary Library, New York City—Presbyterian (defunct parishes in Manhattan).
27. Yivo Institute of Jewish Research, New York City—Jewish.
28. Historical Society of Newburgh Bay and the Highland, Newburgh—various (local).
29. Shaker Museum Foundation, Inc., Old Chatham—Shaker.
30. Oswego County Historical Society, Oswego—Presbyterian (local).
31. Portville Free Public Library, Portville—Presbyterian (local).
32. Suffolk County Historical Society, Riverhead—various (local).
33. American Baptist Historical Society, Rochester—Baptist (extensive, including Samuel Colgate Baptist Historical Collection formerly at Colgate University).
34. Colgate Rochester Divinity School Library, Rochester—Baptist plus some Dutch Reformed and German Evangelical.
35. Saratoga County Historian's Office, Saratoga Springs—various (local).
36. Schenectady County Historical Society, Schenectady—Presbyterian, Dutch Reformed.
37. Schoharie County Historical Society, Schoharie—Dutch Reformed, Lutheran, Methodist, Presbyterian.
38. Staten Island Historical Society, Staten Island—Dutch Reformed, Methodist.
39. Onondago Historical Association, Syracuse—various (local).
40. Syracuse Public Library, Syracuse—various (transcripts).
41. Syracuse University Library, Syracuse—Methodist (central and western New York).
42. Hancock House, Ticonderoga—Quaker, Presbyterian, Methodist Episcopal *et al.*
43. Troy Conference Historical Society, Ticonderoga—Methodist.
44. Utica Public Library, Utica—United Presbyterian, Congregational *et al.* (of Paris, NY).
45. Waterloo Library and Historical Society, Waterloo—various (local).
46. Westchester County Historical Society, White Plains—Baptist, Congregational, Methodist, Presbyterian.
47. New York Yearly Meeting Archives, New York City—Quaker.
48. American Baptist Historical Society, Rochester—Baptist.

NORTH CAROLINA:

1. Duke University, Durham—Methodist Episcopal (extensive).
2. Guilford College Library, Greensboro—Quaker (extensive).
3. High Point College Library, High Point—Methodist.
4. Historical Foundation of the Presbyterian and Reformed Churches, Montreat—Presbyterian, Reformed (very extensive).
5. Catawba College Library, Salisbury—German Reformed.

6. Moravian Archives, Winston-Salem—Moravian.
7. Smith Reynolds Library, Winston-Salem—Baptist.

OHIO:

1. Great Cleveland Methodist Historical Society, Berea—Methodist (especially German Methodist).
2. Mennonite Historical Library, Bluffton College, Bluffton—Mennonite, Anabaptist.
3. American Jewish Archives, Cincinnati—Jewish.
4. Historical and Philosophical Society of Ohio, Cincinnati—various.
5. Western Reserve Historical Society, Cleveland—Shakers *et al.*
6. Ohio Historical Society, Columbus—Quaker, Freewill Baptist, Methodist, Presbyterian, Shaker.
7. Historical Society of the Evangelical United Brethren Church, Memorial Library, United Theological Seminary, Dayton—Evangelical United Brethren and predecessors, Methodist.
8. Ohio Wesleyan University Library, Delaware—Methodist, Methodist Episcopal.
9. Rutherford B. Hayes Library, Fremont—P.E. (local).
10. Oberlin College Library, Oberlin—Congregational (formerly belonged to Ohio Church History Society).
11. Toledo Public Library, Toledo—Presbyterian (local).
12. Otterbein College Library, Westerville—Evangelical United Brethren.
13. Public Library of Youngstown and Mahoning County, Youngstown—various (typescript).
14. Ashland Theological Seminary, Ashland—Brethren (Dunkers).

PENNSYLVANIA:

1. Lehigh County Historical Society, Allentown— ? (local).
2. Old Economy, Pennsylvania Historical and Museum Commission, Ambridge—Harmony Society.
3. Tioga Point Museum and Historical Society, Athens— ? (local).
4. Archives of the Moravian Church, Bethlehem—Moravian.
5. Bethlehem Public Library, Bethlehem—various (typescript).
6. Delaware County Historical Society, Chester—various.
7. Presbyterian Historical Society of Coatesville—Presbyterian (local).
8. Bucks County Historical Society, Doylestown—various (extensive).
9. Easton Public Library, Easton—various.
10. Lutheran Historical Society, Gettysburg—Lutheran.
11. Lutheran Theological Seminary Library, Gettysburg—Lutheran.
12. Historical Society of the Evangelical and Reformed Church, Lancaster—Reformed.
13. Lancaster County Historical Society, Lancaster—various.

14. Vail Memorial Library, Lincoln University—various.
15. Fulton County Historical Society, McConnellsburg—Presbyterian, Reformed (local).
16. Susquehanna County Historical Society, Montrose—various.
17. Moravian Historical Society, Bethlehem—Moravian.
18. Historical Society of Montgomery County, Norristown—various.
19. Schwenkfelder Library, Pennsburg—Schwenkfelder.
20. American Swedish Historical Museum, Philadelphia—various (mostly Lutheran).
21. Christ Church Library, Philadelphia—P.E.
22. Department of Records, Society of Friends of Philadelphia—Quaker.
23. Genealogical Society of Philadelphia—various.
24. Historical Society of Pennsylvania, Philadelphia—Universalist *et al.*
25. Historical Society of Philadelphia Annual Conference of Methodist Episcopal Church, Philadelphia—Methodist, Methodist Episcopal (extensive).
26. Lutheran Theological Seminary Library, Philadelphia—Lutheran (extensive).
27. Presbyterian Historical Society, Philadelphia—Presbyterian (extensive, including church records from Lyman C. Draper Collection in State Historical Society of Wisconsin).
28. Historical Society of Western Pennsylvania, Pittsburgh—Presbyterian, Reformed.
29. Pittsburgh Theological Seminary Library, Pittsburgh—Presbyterian, Reformed.
30. Historical Society of Berks County, Reading—various (local).
31. Lackawanna Historical Society, Scranton—various.
32. Scranton Public Library, Scranton—Baptist.
33. Monroe County Historical Society, Stroudsburg—various (local).
34. Northumberland County Historical Society, Sunbury—various (local).
35. Friends Historical Library, Swarthmore College, Swarthmore—Quaker.
36. Uniontown Public Library, Uniontown—various (local).
37. Washington and Jefferson College Historical Collections, Washington—various.
38. Greene County Historical Society, Waynesburg—various.
39. Wyoming Historical and Geological Society, Westtown—various.
40. Friends Historical Association, Haverford College Library, Haverford—Quaker.
41. Landis Library, Lancaster Mennonite Conference Historical Society, Lancaster—Mennonite.
42. Ephrata Cloister, Ephrata—Seventh-day Baptists.

43. Philip Schaff Library, Lancaster Reformed Seminary, Lancaster—Reformed
44. American Catholic Historical Society of Philadelphia, Philadelphia—Roman Catholic.

RHODE ISLAND:

1. Newport Historical Society, Newport—Quaker, Congregational, Baptist.
2. Moses Brown School, Providence—Quaker.
3. Rhode Island Historical Society, Providence—Baptist, Unitarian, Congregational, Quaker.

SOUTH CAROLINA:

1. South Carolina Historical Society, Charleston—Congregational, P.E.
2. South Carolina Department of Archives and History, Columbia—P.E.
3. South Caroliniana Library, U. of South Carolina, Columbia—various.
4. Wofford College Library, Spartanburg—Methodist.

TENNESSEE:

1. McClung Historical Collection, Lawson McGhee Library, Knoxville—Baptist, Methodist, Presbyterian.
2. Burrow Library, Memphis—Presbyterian.
3. Joint University Libraries, Nashville—various.
4. Methodist Publishing House Library, Nashville—Methodist.
5. Tennessee Historical Society, Nashville—various.
6. Tennessee State Library and Archives, Nashville—various.
7. Disciples of Christ Historical Society, Nashville—Disciples of Christ.

VERMONT:

1. Vermont Historical Society, Montpelier—Congregational *et al.*

VIRGINIA:

1. Randolph-Macon College Library, Ashland—Methodist.
2. University of Virginia Library, Charlottesville—Baptist, Lutheran, Methodist, Presbyterian.
3. Hampden-Sydney College Library, Hampden-Sydney—various (local).
4. Union Theological Seminary Library, Richmond—Presbyterian (extensive).
5. Valentine Museum, Richmond—Quaker (typescript).
6. Virginia Baptist Historical Society, University of Richmond, Richmond—Baptist.
7. Virginia Diocesan Library, Richmond—P.E.
8. Virginia Historical Society, Richmond—various.

9. Virginia State Library, Richmond—various, including Baptist, Methodist, Quaker, Lutheran, German Reformed, Presbyterian (extensive).[7]

WEST VIRGINIA:

1. West Virginia Department of Archives and History, Charleston—Baptist, Methodist.
2. West Virginia Collection, West Virginia University Library, Morgantown—various.

WISCONSIN:

1. State Historical Society of Wisconsin, Madison—various.
2. Joyce Kilmer Memorial Library, Campion Jesuit High School, Prarie Du Chien—Roman Catholic (local).
3. Racine County Historical Room, Racine—various (local).
4. Waukesha County Historical Society, Waukesha—various (local).

These depositories are few but significant, and you should do all you can to locate the church records you need. After all, if they can be found, church records provide the best genealogical information available before the start of civil vital records. The examples in this chapter provide ample evidence of that fact. The effort expended in search of church records is well used.

The researcher should become familiar with Peter G. Mode, *Source Book and Bibliographical Guide for American Church History,* 1921 (Boston: J. S. Canner & Co., 1964 reprint). This scholarly work is a peerless reference for the genealogist and historian who seek a better understanding of church history and religious development in America. Another important reference work is E. Kay Kirkham, *A Survey of American Church Records,* 4th ed. (Logan, UT: Everton Publishers, 1978).

---

[7] A very useful aid for the researcher who will use these records is Jewell T. Clark and Elizabeth Terry Long (comps.), *A Guide to Church Records in the Archives Branch of the Virginia State Library* (Richmond: Virginia State Library, 1981).

21

American Aids to Finding the Home of the Immigrant Ancestor

Normally one of the most difficult problems which the American family researcher must face is tracing his ancestors across the ocean to a specific place in the Old World. It does no good, generally, to know they came from England or Germany or Denmark unless you know exactly where they lived in England or Germany or Denmark. This is usually essential for continued research. The purpose of this chapter is to help you solve this origin problem and to provide assistance in solving other genealogical identification problems by the use of American-generated records. I do not have all the answers for either, but I think I can help.

This chapter is primarily concerned with immigration records or ships' passenger lists—those lists which were made when our ancestors (none of whom was native to this country unless he was an American Indian) came here. The sad thing about this is that there is no complete collection of passenger lists and some of the ones that are available are either quite difficult to use or have serious information gaps. And though this is true, much is happening to add to our understanding. The National Archives has an ambitious microfilming program aimed at making these records more accessible. Also many people are working with the records to produce indexes and specialized compilations for the benefit of researchers. Because of these factors, and the rapid pace at which important materials are appearing, it is impossible for any book (including this one) to be completely up to date on the subject. Even the *Guide to Genealogical Research in the National Archives,* upon which I have relied heavily, is now somewhat dated. The most comprehensive and up-to-date book on the subject is Michael Tepper's *American Passenger Arrival Records* (Baltimore: Genealogical Publishing

Co., 1988). And though time may quickly date some of the details, it is, and will no doubt continue to be, the definitive work on American ships' passenger lists.

Fortunately, passenger lists are not the only possible source of information about the ancestral home. Court records of various kinds, especially those relating to naturalization and citizenship, are very significant. Land entry records in the public domain, certificates of vital events, obituaries, probate records, military records, church records, and others (including old letters and family records) may contain the needed information. If so, your problem is a much simpler one. Hence you should keep your eyes open for this information right from the inception of your research. Some of these possibilities were discussed in earlier chapters, so let's look now at the passenger lists and see just what they are and how they can help us.

I. IMMIGRATION RECORDS: THEIR NATURE AND VALUE

There are three types of ships' passenger arrival lists that are of general interest to us:

A. Customs Passenger Lists.
B. Immigration Passenger Lists.
C. Customs Lists of Aliens.

The National Archives in Washington, D.C., has most of the American passenger lists which are in existence. These date mostly from 1820 to 1945.

A. Customs Passenger Lists

The category of Customs Passenger Lists can also be subdivided as there are (1) original lists, (2) copies and abstracts, and (3) transcripts from the U.S. State Department.

1. Original lists.

There are original lists for the years between 1820 and 1902 available for only the following sixteen ports (listed in alphabetical order by state):

Mobile, Alabama—1820-79 (with gaps)
Middletown, Connecticut—1822-33
Savannah, Georgia—1820-26
New Orleans, Louisiana—1820-1903

Bath, Maine—April 1806[1]
Baltimore, Maryland—1820-91 (with gaps)
Boston, Massachusetts—1 January 1883-29 July 1891, 1891-99, 1912
Fall River, Massachusetts—June, August, September 1865
Gloucester, Massachusetts—December 1905
New Bedford, Massachusetts—1823-99
Provincetown, Massachusetts—1887-89, 1893, 1895-96
Perth Amboy, New Jersey—1801-37 (with gaps)[1]
New York City, New York—1820-17 June 1897, 1840-74, 1875-97 (with gaps)
Philadelphia, Pennsylvania—1 January 1800-December 1882, 1820-54, 1883-99[1]
Newport, Rhode Island—1820-75 (with gaps)
Providence, Rhode Island—1820, 1822-31

Some of these original lists have been filmed. These include the lists for Mobile (M575); Savannah (M575); New Orleans (M259); Baltimore (M255); Boston, 1883-91 (M277); New York, 1820-97 (M237); and Philadelphia, 1800-82 (M425).

These records were prepared by the ships' masters and generally tell the:

> name of vessel, name of master, name of port of embarkation, date of arrival, name of port of arrival, and for each passenger, name, age, sex, occupation, name of country of origin and country of intended settlement, and date and circumstances of death en route, if applicable.[2]

2. Copies and abstracts.

The copies and abstracts cover a period between 1820 and 1905. Some of these are just the same as the originals, and in many cases they can be used to fill gaps in the original lists. They were prepared by the customs collectors and were forwarded (usually every quarter) to the State Department in accordance with statute. Many collectors made abbreviated abstracts of the original lists to forward to Washington. The National Archives has some copies and abstracts of the Customs Passenger Lists for seventy-one Atlantic Coast and Gulf of Mexico ports, but for no port are the records complete for the entire eighty-five-year period.

---

[1] Some Cargo Manifests for 1800-19—and a few later—with names of passengers not on Customs Passenger Lists comprise the pre-1820 portion.

[2] *Guide to Genealogical Research in the National Archives,* rev. ed. (Washington, DC: The National Archives, 1983), p. 43.

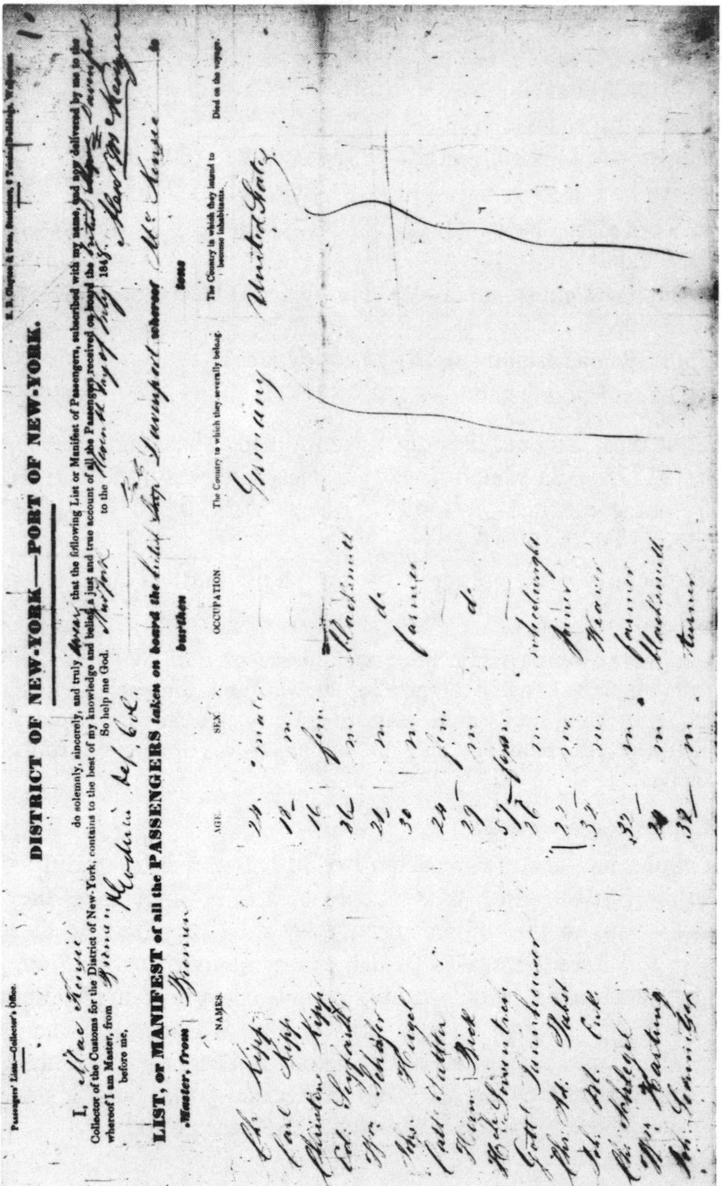

FIGURE 1—CUSTOMS PASSENGER LISTS MANIFEST FOR THE PORT OF NEW YORK

3. Transcripts from the U.S. State Department.

The transcripts of lists in the State Department typically give the:

> name of the vessel, quarter year of arrival, name of master, name of district or port of arrival, and, for each passenger, name, age, sex, occupation, name of country of emigration, and country of intended settlement, and information about death en route, if applicable.[3]

In the National Archives there are eight manuscript volumes of these transcripts covering only December 31, 1819, to December 31, 1832 (thirteen years), with one volume (No. 2) between September 30, 1820, and September 1821 missing. The volumes are arranged by quarter-year of arrival, then by district or port, then by name of vessel, then by name of passenger. The National Archives also has a printed manuscript volume entitled *Letter from the Secretary of State, with a Transcript of the List of Passengers Who Arrived in the United States from the 1st October, 1819, to the 30th September, 1820* (16th Cong., 2d Sess., S. Doc. 118, Serial 45, Vol. 4).[4] There is also a typescript index. You will note that this latter work begins the records three months earlier than the others. The National Archives has State Department transcripts for forty-seven ports. The records were apparently prepared by the State Department from the abstracts they received from the customs officials at the ports.[5]

One very useful tool is a book entitled *Passengers Who Arrived in the United States, September, 1821-December, 1823* (Baltimore: Magna Carta Book Co., 1969). This book was compiled from the State Department transcripts and contains more than 15,000 names of passengers on about 2,000 ships into forty ports of entry. The book is indexed.

In addition to these Customs Passenger Lists, several ports, including Perth Amboy, New Jersey (1801-19); Alexandria, Virginia (1798-1819); and Philadelphia (1800-19), have Cargo Manifests available in the National Archives which extend their passenger lists to a slightly earlier period than those of other ports.

You may be disappointed in the Customs Passenger Lists. Their contents, as you will have noted, do not include information on specific places of

---

[3] *Ibid.*, p. 43.

[4] Reprinted in 1967 by Genealogical Publishing Company as *Passenger Arrivals, 1819-1820,* with an index.

[5] For a table showing all ports with dates of all available passenger lists, see *Guide to Genealogical Research in the National Archives,* pp. 48-57.

origin—only country. Though they may be useful for other purposes, they do not solve the problem we set out to solve initially. And even though some of these lists are indexed—and they are the earliest official passenger lists available, and the easiest of the available passenger lists to use—they are not the most informational.

For the benefit of those who have access to the LDS Family History Library, I might also mention that it is these original Customs Passenger Lists (for New York, Philadelphia, Baltimore, New Orleans, Boston, and "miscellaneous ports"— including Baltimore, Mobile, New Bedford, New Orleans, and Philadelphia)—and their indexes (Soundex)—which the library has on microfilm.

B. Immigration Passenger Lists

The earliest Immigration Passenger Lists are for the port of Philadelphia and begin in 1883. Most other ports have records beginning somewhat later than this, several starting in 1891. There is also, as you can probably guess, some restriction on the use of these records. Both the records and their indexes are considered confidential and are restricted for a fifty-year period. The indexes are even more restricted because several years are indexed together and they cannot be used unless *all* entries on the roll of microfilm are over fifty years old. An additional problem is that certain indexes are arranged chronologically and thus are only alphabetized (by initial letters of surnames only) day-by-day after first being arranged by shipping line. (You have to know quite a bit about the arrival of the person you seek to even use the indexes.) There are indexes available for the ports of Boston; New York; Philadelphia; Portland, Maine; and Providence, Rhode Island (among others).

The thirty-six ports which have Immigration Passenger Lists in the National Archives are (listed in alphabetical order by state):

Mobile, Ala.	Apr. 3, 1904 - Dec. 24, 1945
Hartford, Conn.	Feb. 1929 - Dec. 1943
Apalachicola, Fla.	Sept. 4, 1918
Boca Grande, Fla.	Oct. 28, 1912 - Aug. 16, 1935
Carrabelle, Fla.	Nov. 7, 1915
Fernandina, Fla.	Aug. 29, 1904 - Aug. 7, 1932
Jacksonville, Fla.	Jan. 18, 1904 - Dec. 17, 1945
Key West, Fla.	Nov. 1898 - Dec. 1945
Knights Key, Fla.	Feb. 7, 1908 - Jan. 20, 1912
Mayport, Fla.	Nov. 16, 1907 - Apr. 13, 1916
Miami, Fla.	Oct. 5, 1899 - Dec. 29, 1945
Millville, Fla.	July 4, 1916

Panama City, Fla.	Nov. 10, 1927 - Dec. 12, 1939
Pensacola, Fla.	May 12, 1900 - July 16, 1945
Port Everglades, Fla.	Feb. 15, 1932 - Dec. 10, 1945
Port Inglis, Fla.	Mar. 29, 1912 - Jan. 2, 1913
Port St. Joe, Fla.	Jan. 12, 1923 - Oct. 13, 1939
St. Andrews, Fla.	Jan. 2, 1916 - May 13, 1926
St. Petersburg, Fla.	Dec. 15, 1926 - Mar. 1, 1941
Tampa, Fla.	Nov. 2, 1898 - Dec. 30, 1945
West Palm Beach, Fla.	Sept. 8, 1920 - Nov. 21, 1945
Brunswick, Ga.	Nov. 22, 1904 - Nov. 27, 1939
Savannah, Ga.	June 5, 1906 - Dec. 6, 1945
New Orleans, La.	Jan. 1903 - Dec. 1945
Portland and Falmouth, Me.	Nov. 29, 1893 - Mar. 1943
Baltimore, Md.	Dec. 12, 1891 - Nov. 30, 1909
Boston and Charlestown, Mass.	Aug. 1, 1891 - Dec. 1943
Gloucester, Mass.	Oct. 1906 - June 1923, Feb. 1, 1930 - Dec. 1943
New Bedford, Mass.	July 1, 1902 - July 1942
Gulfport, Miss.	Aug. 27, 1904 - Aug. 28, 1954
Pascagoula, Miss.	July 15, 1903 - May 21, 1935
New York, N.Y.	June 16, 1897 - Dec. 31, 1943
Philadelphia, Pa.	Jan. 1883 - Oct. 22, 1945
Providence, R.I.	June 17, 1911 - June 1943
Charleston, S.C.	Apr. 9, 1906 - 1945
Georgetown, S.C.	June 17, 1923 - Oct. 24, 1939[6]

The information in these Immigration Passenger Lists (or *Manifests,* as they are frequently called) varies somewhat with time period and with state statute. Those for Philadelphia (the earliest port to have them) contain the:

> name of master, name of vessel, names of ports of arrival and embarkation, date of arrival, and, for each passenger, name, place of birth, last legal residence, age, occupation, sex, and remarks.[7]

Federal law began to prescribe the form in 1893 and, beginning that year, the form required the following information for each passenger:

> [F]ull name; age; sex; marital status; occupation; nationality; last residence; final destination; whether in the United States before, and, if so, when, and where; and whether going to join a relative and if so, the relative's name, address, and relationship to the passenger. The format of the immigration passenger lists was revised in 1903 to include race, in 1906 to include a personal description and birth-

[6] *Ibid.*, pp. 48-57.

[7] *Ibid.*, p. 47.

> place, and in 1907 to include the name and address of the nearest relative in the immigrant's home country.[8]

As you can see, under certain circumstances these can be very useful records.

Some of the Immigration Passenger Lists are indexed. One index which is arranged alphabetically by the passengers' names is called *Index to Passenger Lists of Vessels Arriving at Miscellaneous Ports in Alabama, Florida, Georgia, and South Carolina, 1890-1924*. This index is on twenty-six rolls of microfilm (T517). All other indexes are by port. Microfilmed indexes are available for Boston (T790, T521, T617), New York (T519, T612, T621), Philadelphia (T526, T791), Portland and Falmouth (ME) (T524, T793), and Providence (RI) (T518, T792). These can be used when only the port and the approximate date of arrival are known. When the exact date and port are known, go directly to the passenger lists.

There is a microfilmed card index (1900-52) for New Orleans (T618), as well as a brief unmicrofilmed card index (1900-January 1903). Baltimore has indexes from 1897 to July 1952 (T520). New Bedford, Massachusetts, has indexes covering July 1, 1902, to November 18, 1954 (T522).

With regard to Baltimore, it should also be noted that an 1833 Maryland state law required ships' masters to submit to the mayor lists of passengers arriving in the port of Baltimore. These "city lists" were microfilmed by the National Archives with the Customs Passenger Lists (M255—fifty rolls) and are useful in filling gaps. There are, however, two separate indexes to these borrowed "city lists" (M326—twenty-two rolls) and the Customs Passenger Lists (M327—171 rolls). Both are Soundex indexes.

C. Customs Lists of Aliens

Customs Lists of Aliens are perhaps the least significant shipping or passenger lists in the National Archives, not because their information is lacking, but mainly because they relate to only Beverly and Salem, Massachusetts, 1798 and 1800. These records (about ten ships) were made in compliance with an act of Congress, but the existence of any such records from other ports is currently unknown. There are no indexes because the records are so brief. These records include some or all of the following information:

> [N]ame of vessel, name of master, date of arrival, names of ports of embarkation and arrival, and, for each alien, name, age, birth-

---

[8] *Ibid.*, p. 47.

place, name of country of emigration, name of country of allegiance, occupation, and personal description.[9]

These brief lists were published in the *New England Historical and Genealogical Register* in July 1952 (Vol. 106, pp. 203-209.)

D. Other Immigration Records

In addition to the records described above, there are other records relating to immigration located in various depositories around the U.S. Some of these include:

Massachusetts Archives Division at the State House, Boston—has some immigration records, 1848-1891. (There is an index on 282 rolls of microfilm—M265—available at the National Archives.)

College of the Holy Cross Library at Worcester, Massachusetts—has a collection on Irish immigrants and their descendants in Worcester, 1840-1900.

Burton Historical Collection, Detroit Public Library, Detroit, Michigan—has records of the Michigan immigration agency from 1848 to 1880 and papers relating to the Detroit and Mackinac customs offices, 1789-1876.

Museum of the Netherlands Pioneer and Historical Foundation, Holland, Michigan—has extensive manuscripts relating to the settlement of western Michigan by Dutch immigrants.

Hendrick Hudson Chapter Library, Hudson, New York—has Cargo Manifests, 1739-44.

Yivo Institute for Jewish Research, New York City—has about 300 autobiographies of Jewish immigrants who came from Eastern Europe to the United States in the 1880s and 1890s, plus some 10,000 letters from European relatives to Jewish immigrants.

Historical Society of Pennsylvania, Philadelphia—has the Gilbert Cope Collection which includes some ships' registers among other historical and genealogical materials, 1682-1924.

University of Texas Library, Austin—has papers relating to German, French, and English immigration to Texas.

The Church of Jesus Christ of Latter-day Saints, Historical Department, Salt Lake City, Utah—has records of LDS Church members immigrating to "Zion" from Europe between 1849 and 1932. There are shipping lists from the British Mission (1849-55, 1899-1925), the Scandinavian Mission (1854-96, 1901-20), the Netherlands Mission

---

[9] *Ibid.*, p. 56.

(1904-14), and the Swedish Mission (1905-32). There is also a card index to these records, and both the records and the index are on microfilm at the LDS Family History Library.[10]

Some of the records in the above lists you will find to be very good sources while others will have little genealogical value. And you will, no doubt, find other useful original immigration records in other depositories.

Many researchers will be interested to learn that during the summer of 1984 archivists at the Washington National Records Center in Suitland, Maryland, fortuitously opened some storage crates to discover extensive passenger lists (at least 10,000 volumes for various ports, mostly on the West Coast). The collection includes records for the ports of Honolulu, Portland, San Diego, San Francisco, San Pedro, Seattle, El Paso, Galveston, Miami, Newport News, Port Huron, and Oswego. I understand that microfilming has begun.

Also of interest to many with ancestral roots in Germany and Eastern Europe are the Hamburg Passenger Lists which cover emigration from Hamburg, Germany, to America between 1850 and 1934. The 274 rolls of film in this collection are housed currently in the Historic Emigration Office of the City of Hamburg at the Museum of Hamburg History. The records are partially indexed and searches will be made by competent staff researchers for the year you designate for $30. The fee for searching each additional year is $10.

> Usually the list contains the name of each person aboard a ship. It gives the husband's name, plus that of the wife, children and other family members traveling with them. Also given are the ages, occupations or professions and the last place of residence before emigration.[11]

The museum address is Museum für Hamburgische Geschichte, Holstenwall 24, 2000 Hamburg 36, West Germany.

The other German city from which many American immigrants came was Bremen. Bremen also kept passenger lists, beginning in 1832, which told the same type of information about emigrants, including their places of origin. However, these records were systematically destroyed by German archivists because of lack of storage space and a variety of other reasons. A

---

[10] For further details see "LDS Records and Research Aids" (Series F, no. 1), Research Papers of The Genealogical Society of The Church of Jesus Christ of Latter-day Saints.

[11] From the *North Central N. D. Genealogical Record,* as quoted in *Federation of Genealogical Societies Newsletter* (Vol. 9, No. 1), January/February 1985, p. 6.

partial reconstruction of these Bremen passenger lists—for the port of New York only—is found in a three-volume work (with additional volumes promised) called *German Immigrants: Lists of Passengers Bound from Bremen to New York, 1847-1867,* compiled by Gary J. Zimmerman and Marion Wolfert (Baltimore: Genealogical Publishing Co., 1985-88). Zimmerman and Wolfert have extracted records from the Customs Passenger Lists for the port of New York in the National Archives (film M237) where the port of embarkation was identified as Bremen whenever a specific place of origin was stated (not just Germany). This amounted to approximately 21 per cent of the Bremen-tied passengers coming to New York during this time period.

Another significant project, which is putting ships' passenger lists onto a computer data base and publishing them, is going forward at the Temple University–Balch Institute Center for Immigration Research in Philadelphia under the direction of Dr. Ira A. Glazier. Project workers hope to index, by name, the original passenger lists, according to the countries from which the immigrants came, for all U.S. ports between 1820 and 1897.

The Irish and German manifests include information on "place of origin" which many of the other records do not. Unfortunately, most of the places given are not specific but are only the country. Thus far the project has produced fourteen published volumes of indexes:

Glazier, Ira A. and Michael Tepper (eds.). *The Famine Immigrants: Lists of Irish Immigrants Arriving at the Port of New York, 1846-1851.* 7 vols. Baltimore: Genealogical Publishing Co., 1983-86.

———— and P. William Filby (eds.). *Germans to America: Lists of Passengers Arriving at U.S. Ports, 1850-55.* Wilmington, DE: Scholarly Resources, Inc., 1988. (There are seven volumes so far but the work is continuing.)

Later projects, which will include Italian, Eastern European, and English emigrants, are promised.

Perhaps this is the proper place to also note the possible existence of additional passenger lists for the port of New York beyond those kept under federal statutes and housed in the National Archives. In 1824 the New York Legislature adopted "An Act Concerning Passenger Vessels Arriving in the Port of New York." This act required the master of every vessel arriving in port to make a writing within twenty-four hours containing the *name, place of birth, last legal settlement, age, and occupation* of every person who should have been on board.[12]

[12] *City of New York v. Miln* [36 U.S. (Pet.) 102].

The location of these reports is unknown and the Municipal Archives and Records Center of New York reports knowing nothing of their existence.[13]

E. Books

There have been numerous books published which contain records and lists of immigrants to America. Many of these are very early and though they certainly do not cover all early immigrations, they can be quite useful. Following is a list of some of these books:

Banks, Charles Edward. *The English Ancestry and Homes of the Pilgrim Fathers.* (1929). Baltimore: Genealogical Publishing Co., 1962 (reprint).

———. *The Planters of the Commonwealth.* (1930). Baltimore: Genealogical Publishing Co., 1961 (reprint).

———. *Topographical Dictionary of 2,885 English Emigrants to New England, 1620-1650.* Ed. by . . . Elijah E. Brownell. (1937). Baltimore: Genealogical Publishing Co., 1957 (reprint).

———. *The Winthrop Fleet of 1630.* (1930). Baltimore: Genealogical Publishing Co., 1961 (reprint).

Bevier, Louis. *Genealogy of the First Settlers of New Paltz.* (1909). Baltimore: Genealogical Publishing Co., 1965 (reprint).

Bolton, Ethel. *Immigrants to New England, 1700-1775.* (1931). Baltimore: Genealogical Publishing Co., 1966 (reprint).

Boyer, Carl, III (comp. and ed.). *Ship Passenger Lists: National and New England (1600-1825).* Newhall, CA: the compiler, 1977.

———. *Ship Passenger Lists: New York and New Jersey (1600-1825).* Newhall, CA: the compiler, 1978.

———. *Ship Passenger Lists: Pennsylvania and Delaware (1641-1825).* Newhall, CA: the compiler, 1980.

———. *Ship Passenger Lists: The South (1538-1900).* Newhall, CA: the compiler, 1979.

Brandow, James C. *Omitted Chapters from Hotten's Original Lists of Persons of Quality.* Baltimore: Genealogical Publishing Co., 1982.

Bristol and America. A Record of the First Settlers in the Colonies of North America, 1654-1685. . . . (1929 and 1931). Baltimore: Genealogical Publishing Co., 1967 (reprint).

Brock, Robert A. *Documents, Chiefly Unpublished, Relating to the Huguenot Emigration to Virginia and to the Settlement at Manakin-Town.* (1886). Baltimore: Genealogical Publishing Co., 1962 (reprint).

---

[13] Letter from Elizabeth M. Eilerman, Assistant Director, dated January 10, 1973.

Browning, Charles H. *Welsh Settlement of Pennsylvania.* (1912). Baltimore: Genealogical Publishing Co., 1967 (reprint).

Cameron, Viola Root. *Emigrants from Scotland to America, 1774-1775.* (1930). Baltimore: Genealogical Publishing Co., 1959 (reprint).

Coldham, Peter Wilson. *The Complete Book of Emigrants, 1607-1660.* Baltimore: Genealogical Publishing Co., 1987.

———. *The Complete Book of Emigrants in Bondage, 1614-1775.* Baltimore: Genealogical Publishing Co., 1988.

———. *The Bristol Registers of Servants Sent to Foreign Plantations, 1654-1686.* Baltimore: Genealogical Publishing Co., 1988.

Colket, Meredith B., Jr. *Founders of Early American Families: Emigrants from Europe 1607-1657.* Cleveland: Howard Allen, 1975.

DeVille, Winston. *Louisiana Colonials: Soldiers and Vagabonds.* Mobile, AL, 1963. Distributed by Genealogical Publishing Co., Baltimore.

Dickson, Robert J. *Ulster Emigration to Colonial America, 1718-1775.* London: Routledge and Kegan Paul, 1966.

Dobson, David. *Directory of Scots Banished to the American Plantations, 1650-1775.* Baltimore: Genealogical Publishing Co., 1983.

———. *The Original Scots Colonists of Early America, 1612-1783.* Baltimore: Genealogical Publishing Co., 1989.

Drake, Samuel Gardiner. *Result of Some Researches Among the British Archives for Information Relative to the Founders of New England.* (1860). Baltimore: Genealogical Publishing Co., 1963 (reprint).

Egle, William Henry. *Names of Foreigners Who Took the Oath of Allegiance to the Province and State of Pennsylvania, 1727-1775, with the Foreign Arrivals, 1786-1808.* (1892). Baltimore: Genealogical Publishing Co., 1967 (reprint).

Faust, Albert Bernhardt and Gaius M. Brumbaugh. *Lists of Swiss Emigrants in the Eighteenth Century to the American Colonies.* 2 vols. (1920-25). Baltimore: Genealogical Publishing Co., 1968 (reprint in one volume).

Filby, P. William (ed.). *Philadelphia Naturalization Records: An Index to Records of Aliens' Declarations of Intention and/or Oaths of Allegiance, 1789-1880, in United States Circuit Court, United States District Court, Supreme Court of Pennsylvania, Quarter Sessions Court, Court of Common Pleas, Philadelphia.* Detroit: Gale Research Co., 1982.

———. *Philadelphia Naturalization Records Found in Various Order Books of 92 Local Courts Prior to 1907: An Index to Records of Aliens' Declarations of Intention and/or Oaths of Allegiance, 1789-1880.* Detroit: Gale Research Co., 1982.

Fothergill, Gerald. *Emigrants from England 1773-1776.* (1898-1901). Baltimore: Genealogical Publishing Co., 1964 (reprint).

————. *A List of Emigrant Ministers to America, 1690-1811.* (1904). Baltimore: Genealogical Publishing Co., 1964 (reprint).

French, Elizabeth. *List of Emigrants to America from Liverpool, 1697-1707.* (1913). Baltimore: Genealogical Publishing Co., 1962 (reprint).

Giuseppi, Montague Spencer. *Naturalizations of Foreign Protestants in the American and West Indian Colonies Pursuant to Statute 13, George II, C. 7.* (1921). Baltimore: Genealogical Publishing Co., 1964 (reprint).

Greer, George Cabell. *Early Virginia Immigrants, 1623-1666.* (1912). Baltimore: Genealogical Publishing Co., 1960 (reprint).

Hackett, J. Dominick and Charles M. Early. *Passenger Lists from Ireland* (reprinted from the *Journal of the American Irish Historical Society,* vols. 28-29). (1929-31). Baltimore: Genealogical Publishing Co., 1965.

Hartmann, Edward George. *Americans from Wales.* Boston: The Christopher Publishing House, 1967.

Hinman, Royal R. *A Catalogue of the Names of the First Puritan Settlers of the Colony of Connecticut; with the Time of Their Arrival in the Colony, and Their Standing in Society, Together with Their Place of Residence, as Far as Can be Discovered by the Records.* (1846). Baltimore: Genealogical Publishing Co., 1968 (reprint).

Hotten, John Camden. *The Original Lists of Persons of Quality: Emigrants, etc., Who Went from Great Britain to the American Plantations, 1600-1700.* (1874). Baltimore: Genealogical Publishing Co., 1974 (reprint).

Jewson, Charles Boardman. *Transcript of Three Registers of Passengers from Great Yarmouth to Holland and New England, 1637-1639.* (1954). Baltimore: Genealogical Publishing Co., 1964 (reprint).

Joseph, Samuel. *Jewish Immigration to the United States from 1881 to 1910.* New York: Arno Press, 1969.

Kaminkow, Jack and Marion J. Kaminkow. *A List of Emigrants from England to America, 1718-1759. Transcribed from . . . Original Records at the Guildhall, London.* Baltimore: Magna Carta Book Co., 1964.

Kaminkow, Marion J. and Jack Kaminkow. *Original Lists of Emigrants in Bondage from London to the American Colonies, 1719-1744.* Baltimore: Magna Carta Book Co., 1967.

Knittle, Walter Allen. *Early Eighteenth Century Palatine Emigration.* (1937). Baltimore: Genealogical Publishing Co., 1965 (reprint).

Krebbs, Friedrich. *Emigrants from the Palatinate to the American Colonies in the Eighteenth Century.* Norristown, PA: Pennsylvania German Society, 1953.

Langguth, Otto. "Pennsylvania German Pioneers from the County of Wertheim." (Tr. and ed. by Donald H. Yoder in the *Pennsylvania German Folklore Society Yearbook,* Vol. XII). Allentown, PA, 1947.

Munroe, J. B. *A List of Alien Passengers Bonded from January 1, 1847, to January 1851.* (1851). Baltimore: Genealogical Publishing Co., 1971 (reprint).

Myers, Albert Cook. *Immigration of the Irish Quakers into Pennsylvania, 1682-1750.* (1902). Baltimore: Genealogical Publishing Co., 1969 (reprint).

Newsome, Albert R. *Records of Emigrants from England and Scotland to North Carolina, 1774-1775.* (1934). Raleigh: Department of Archives and History, 1962 (reprint).

Olsson, Nils William. *Swedish Passenger Arrivals in New York, 1820-1850.* Chicago: Swedish Pioneer Historical Society, 1967.

————. *Swedish Passenger Arrivals in U.S. Ports 1820-1850 (Except New York).* Saint Paul, MN: North Central Publishing Co., 1979.

Persons Naturalized in the Province of Pennsylvania (1740-1773). (Reprinted from *Pennsylvania Archives,* Ser. 2, Vol. II). (1876). Baltimore: Genealogical Publishing Co., 1967.

Putnam, Eben. *Two Early Passenger Lists, 1635-1637.* Baltimore: Genealogical Publishing Co., 1964 (reprint).

Rasmussen, Louis J. *San Francisco Ship Passenger Lists.* 4 vols. Colma, CA: San Francisco Historic Records (1965-70). (Part of the *Ship 'n Rail* series, San Francisco Historic Records.)
Vol. 1 — 1850
Vol. 2 — April 1850-November 1851
Vol. 3 — November 1851-June 1852
Vol. 4 — June 1852-January 1853
(This series was anticipated to extend through records of 1875.)

Revill, Janie. *A Compilation of the Original Lists of Protestant Immi-Grants to South Carolina, 1763-1773.* (1939). Baltimore: Genealogical Publishing Co., 1968 (reprint).

Rupp, Israel Daniel. *A Collection of Upwards of Thirty Thousand Names of German, Swiss, Dutch, French and Other Immigrants in Pennsylvania from 1727 to 1776.* 2nd rev. and enl. ed. (1876). Baltimore: Genealogical Publishing Co., 1965 (reprint).

————. *Index to the Names of Thirty Thousand Immigrants . . .* by M. V. Koger, n.p., 1935.

Schenk, Trudy, Ruth Froelke, and Inga Bork. *Wuerttemberg Emigration Index*. 4 vols. (of six proposed volumes). Salt Lake City: Ancestry, 1986-.

Schlegel, Donald M. *Passengers from Ireland: Lists of Passengers Arriving at American Ports Between 1811 and 1817*. Baltimore: Genealogical Publishing Co., 1980.

Scott, Kenneth R. (comp.). *British Aliens in the United States During the War of 1812*. Baltimore: Genealogical Publishing Co., 1978.

————. *Early New York Naturalizations: Abstracts of Naturalization Records from Federal, State, and Local Courts, 1792-1840*. Baltimore: Genealogical Publishing Co., 1981.

———— and Kenn Stryker-Rodda (comps.). *Denizations, Naturalizations, and Oaths of Allegiance in Colonial New York*. Baltimore: Genealogical Publishing Co., 1975.

Sheppard, Walter Lee, Jr. (ed.). *Passengers and Ships Prior to 1684*. Publications of the Welcome Society of Pennsylvania, Vol. 1. Baltimore: Genealogical Publishing Co., 1970.

Sherwood, George. *American Colonists in English Records*. 2 vols. (1932-33). Baltimore: Genealogical Publishing Co., 1961 (reprint in one volume).

Simmendinger, Ulrich. *True and Authentic Register of Persons Who in the Year 1709 Journeyed from Germany to America*. (Tr. by Herman F. Vesper). (1934). Baltimore: Genealogical Publishing Co., 1963 (reprint).

Skordas, Gust. *The Early Settlers of Maryland*. Baltimore: Genealogical Publishing Co., 1968.

Stanard, William G. *Some Emigrants to Virginia*. 2nd ed. enl. (1915). Baltimore: Genealogical Publishing Co., 1953 (reprint).

Stapleton, Ammon. *Memorials of the Huguenots in America, with Special Reference to Their Emigration to Pennsylvania*. (1901). Baltimore: Genealogical Publishing Co., 1964 (reprint).

Strassburger, Ralph Beaver and William J. Hinke. *Pennsylvania German Pioneers*. 3 vols. (1934). Baltimore: Genealogical Publishing Co., 1966 (reprint of volumes one and three).

Swierenga, Robert P. *Dutch Immigrants in U.S. Ship Passenger Manifests, 1820-1880*. 2 vols. Wilmington, DE: Scholarly Resources, Inc., 1983.

Tepper, Michael (ed.). *Emigrants to Pennsylvania, 1641-1819: A Consolidation of Ship Passenger Lists from the "Pennsylvania Magazine of History and Biography."* Baltimore: Genealogical Publishing Co., 1975.

————. *Immigrants to the Middle Colonies: A Consolidation of Ship Passenger Lists and Associated Data from the "New York Genealogical and Biographical Record."* Baltimore: Genealogical Publishing Co., 1978.

————. *New World Immigrants: A Consolidation of Ship Passenger Lists and Associated Data from Periodical Literature.* 2 vols. Baltimore: Genealogical Publishing Co., 1979.

————. *Passengers to America: A Consolidation of Ship Passenger Lists from the "New England Historical and Genealogical Register."* Baltimore: Genealogical Publishing Co., 1977.

————. *Passenger Arrivals at the Port of Baltimore 1820-1834.* Baltimore: Genealogical Publishing Co., 1982.

————. *Passenger Arrivals at the Port of Philadelphia 1800-1819: The Philadelphia "Baggage Lists."* Baltimore: Genealogical Publishing Co., 1986.

Virkus, Frederick A. (ed.). *Immigrant Ancestors. A List of 2,500 Immigrants to America Before 1750.* (Excerpted from the *Compendium of American Genealogy,* Vol. VII). (1942). Baltimore: Genealogical Publishing Co., 1963.

Yoder, Donald H. (ed. and trans.). *Emigrants from Wuerttemberg; the Adolf Gerber Lists.* (Reprinted in the *Pennsylvania German Folklore Society Yearbook,* Vol. X). Allentown, PA, 1945.

The above is only a partial list and should be considered as such; there are many more immigration sources. Note also that information found in many such books is of questionable accuracy (because of its origin) and should be verified before it is accepted.

Of special note to the genealogist is *A Bibliography of Ship Passenger Lists, 1538-1825,* originally prepared by Harold Lancour and revised by R. J. Wolfe, 3rd ed. (New York: New York Public Library, 1963). Updating the work of Lancour and Wolfe is the 1981 work of P. William Filby entitled *Passenger and Immigration Lists Bibliography 1538-1900.*[14] This work is a companion to the three-volume work *Passenger and Immigration Lists Index* and its annual supplementary volumes published by Gale Research Co.[15]

---

[14] P. William Filby, *Passenger and Immigration Lists Bibliography 1538-1900* (Detroit: Gale Research Co., 1981), with 1984 supplement and a 2nd (cumulative) edition in 1988.

[15] P. William Filby and Mary K. Meyer (eds.), *Passenger and Immigration Lists Index: A Guide to Published Arrival Records of About 500,000 Passengers Who Came to the United States and Canada in the Seventeenth, Eighteenth and Nineteenth Centuries.* 3 vols. (Detroit: Gale Research Co., 1981), with annual supplements.

II. LOCATING AND USING IMMIGRATION RECORDS

With some genealogical problems there is untold value in immigration records. With this in mind let me review some of the information already given and provide more detailed information on locating and using these records.

If your ancestor was an early immigrant you would certainly not want to overlook the possibility of finding information about him and his origin in one of the available books. If he was a more recent immigrant the ships' passenger lists may be a worthwhile source for you to consider, especially the Immigration Passenger Lists where they apply, because of the information they contain about Old World origins. And though there are informational limitations in the Customs Passenger Lists, they too can be helpful.

Considering that the Customs Passenger Lists gave the name, age, sex and occupation of each immigrant and tell the date of his arrival in America, plus the port from which he sailed, they can be useful tools for identifying your ancestor and separating him from all other persons of the same name.

I have already mentioned that the main difficulty in locating people in the Immigration Passenger Lists is the chronological arrangement of the indexes. These indexes are arranged first by year; then under each year they are arranged by ship; under each ship or shipping line they are arranged, in part, by class of passenger, and then alphabetically by the first letter of the passenger's surname. There are slight variations from one port to another, but all are difficult to use.

There are alphabetical indexes to the Boston port from 1902 to June 30, 1906, and the New York port from June 16, 1897, to June 30, 1902; and the alphabetical card index to the Customs Passenger Lists in the Philadelphia port also serves as a partial index to its Immigration Passenger Lists until 1906. These indexes are located in the National Archives and make the lists a little easier to use.

The Immigration Passenger Lists are difficult to use. What it all boils down to is this: It is almost essential to have specific information about an immigration before you can find the record of it. You *must* know the name of the port, and the more specific the date you have the better off you are. The name of the ship is also very helpful. When you consider that thousands of persons entered the U.S. through some of the larger ports each year you can appreciate the value of specific information. It is possible to make a general search of passenger lists for a given port, but I do not recommend it if there is some other way.

There are also records in the National Archives of the names and dates of arrival of the vessels in the several ports. These tell the ports from which each ship sailed and may help you find the name of the ship on which your ancestor arrived, if you know the approximate time. This information on ports of embarkation can save a lot of searching if it is properly used.

Other aids in finding passenger lists are naturalization records, land entry records (especially homestead entries), and passport applications. Naturalization records tell the name of the port and date of arrival of the alien into the United States.[16] Homestead entry papers include a copy of the naturalization proceedings and, of course, show the date and port of arrival also, plus the place of birth of the entryman. If a naturalized citizen applied for a passport to travel abroad, perhaps to return to his homeland for a visit, the application papers show the original date and port of his arrival into this country.

One of the more useful books published on the subject of locating immigrant ancestors is Neagles' *Locating Your Immigrant Ancestor*.[17] The book thoroughly discusses the subject and makes many helpful suggestions about locating and using records pertaining to those who emigrated to the United States from other lands. The authors make useful suggestions for those who would utilize these important records. Also of interest is a little book on naturalization procedures by John J. Newman, recently published by the Indiana Historical Society.[18]

III. PASSPORT APPLICATIONS

All passport applications filed with the U.S. State Department from 1791 to 1905 are in the National Archives, but at no time during that period were passports required by law, except during part of the Civil War. Many persons, however, did secure passports for the protection which they afforded.

The applications from 1810 through 1905 are bound, and there are various card and book indexes covering the period from 1834 to 1905.

The earliest applications were merely letters of request, but other papers often accompanied them and were filed with them. Those other papers included expired passports, birth certificates, certificates of citizenship, etc. Regarding record content, the *Guide to Genealogical Research* says:

---

[16] See chapter 19 for more detailed information on naturalization records.

[17] James C. and Lila Lee Neagles, *Locating Your Immigrant Ancestor: A Guide to Naturalization Records* (Logan, UT: Everton Publishers, 1975).

[18] John J. Newman, *American Naturalization Processes and Procedures* (Indianapolis: Indiana Historical Society, 1985).

> A passport application varies in content, the information being ordinarily less detailed before the Civil War period than afterward. It usually contains the name, signature, place of residence, age, and personal description of the applicant; names or number of persons in the family intending to travel; the date; and, where appropriate, the date and court of naturalization. It sometimes contains the exact date and place of birth of the applicant and of spouse and minor children, if any, accompanying the applicant; and, if the applicant was a naturalized citizen, the date and port of his arrival in the United States, name of vessel on which applicant arrived, and the date and court of naturalization.[19]

Passports, of course, are a source with limited value. They are of use only if your ancestor traveled abroad and happened to secure one. But it was common for immigrants to secure passports when they traveled to their homelands to visit (even when not required to do so by law) because they were in danger of being drafted into military service if they went without them.

IV. CONCLUSION

Properly used, immigration records, passport records, etc., can lead to invaluable information about specific places of European origin which you may not find in other records. They may also lead to information about your ancestor after his American arrival. In case his name is common, specific dates and places from these records can help you separate him from his contemporaries of the same name.

Be aware of the value of these records and, when the occasion calls for it, use them wisely. But don't expect them to solve all of your problems.

---

[19] *Guide to Genealogical Research in the National Archives,* rev. ed. (Washington, DC: The National Archives, 1983), p. 246.

22

Military Records: Colonial Wars and the American Revolution

Much of modern history can be told in wars. Nearly every generation of Americans has known war. Genealogically war is a two-sided coin—it is destructive on the one hand (to human lives and property as well as to records) and it is creative on the other hand (fostering great medical and technical advances, etc., to help people live longer, and also creating many useful records of its own). Thus, in restrospect, we look on past wars with mixed emotions; but as genealogists we must be familiar with various effects of war. Especially must we be familiar with military records; complete research depends upon it.

I. BACKGROUND AND HISTORY

Even the early colonists in America knew war's sting. From King Philip's War in 1675 down to the time of the Revolutionary War with Great Britain there were few periods of peace. The Indians and the French were the main adversaries of the British colonists.

The Revolutionary War, 1775-83, pitted brother against brother and father against son as thirteen of the twenty-two British-American colonies chose to declare their collective independence from Mother England.

Following the Revolution, British opposition to the Embargo Act and a number of other factors, not excluding the greediness of the United States for more territory, led to another war with Britain, 1812-14. This proved to be a very sad conflict for the Americans because their national capital, Washington, D.C., was seized by British troops and burned.

Though the War of 1812 was the last war with Britain, the Indians still remained a threat on much of the American frontier, and throughout the nineteenth century various and sundry Indian wars were waged.

In 1846, again mostly as a result of some greedy tendencies, the U.S. was drawn into war with Mexico. Texas had already been annexed and we had our collective eyes on a great deal more Mexican territory. This war ended in 1848.

In 1861, as a culmination of many pressures brought to bear by the slavery issue and the secession of certain Southern states from the Union, war was declared and the most costly war, in terms of human lives and suffering, that our country has ever known, began. The war did not end until 1865, after 364,511 had died and 281,881 more had been wounded. This too was a "family affair," as siblings fought under opposing flags.

The year 1898 brought war with Spain as a result of the Cuban insurrection of 1895, and then came the twentieth century with two great world wars and other major military involvements in Korea and Vietnam. These are the highlights in the story of American military activity and, for the genealogist, each war has produced its own records, though many military records created in this century are not yet available for public searching.

II. THE RECORDS

As the term "military records" is used in the next two chapters it refers to any and all records of all branches of armed service—army, navy, coast guard, marine, etc. These records can normally be divided into two classes:

A. Service records.
B. Records of veterans' benefits.

Both types are considered here as both are significant.

As you already know, there is little conformity in American genealogical sources. Many sources are undefinable in terms of specific content, and though we have general ideas about what they contain (or at least ought to contain), we are never really sure what any specific document is going to say until we read it. This phenomenon is just as true of military records as it is of other records—especially those military records relating to the early wars.

My only advice is for you to seek out those which are pertinent and read them—I think you will be pleasantly surprised. As far as service records go, you are in a better position to locate information if your soldier ancestor had an officer's commission, but the enlisted man was, in his later years, more often in a position to receive assistance through veterans' benefits. An excellent guide to those military records located in the National Archives is *Guide to Genealogical Research in the National Archives* (1983), to which frequent references have already been made in other chapters and which I will lean upon heavily in the next two chapters (even beyond what footnotes might indicate). I also rely heavily on Colket and Bridgers, *Guide to Genealogical Records in the National Archives* (1964).

III. COLONIAL WARS

There are no official national records of wars before the Revolution since the United States of America did not exist. The only records which have survived are a few colonial and local militia records—mainly rolls and rosters. These lists are not extensive (nor is the information they contain), but many of those located have been published. Most of these lists contain only the names of the soldiers and the military organizations in which they served. The chief value of these records is that they give names, dates, and places allowing us to put the person thus found in a specific place at a specific time—often an important genealogical necessity. In most cases there were no particular benefits provided for veterans of colonial service, though there were exceptions to this. For example, Governor Dinwiddie and the Council of Virginia offered 200,000 acres of bounty land in the Ohio River Valley to Virginia troops who served in the French and Indian War. Some other colonies did the same, but there are no general records. Records which exist are in the individual states.

A short bibliography of a few published works arising out of the colonial wars follows:

Andrews, Frank DeWitte. *Connecticut Soldiers in the French and Indian War*. Vineland, NJ: The compiler, 1923.

Bockstruck, Lloyd D. *Virginia's Colonial Soldiers*. Baltimore: Genealogical Publishing Co., 1988.

Bodge, George M. *Soldiers in King Philip's War, Being a Critical Account of that War, with a Concise History of the Indian Wars of New England from 1620-1677, Official Lists of the Soldiers of Massachusetts Colony Serving in Philip's War. . . .* 3rd ed. (1906). Baltimore: Genealogical Publishing Co., 1967 (reprint).

Buckingham, Thomas. *Roll and Journal of Connecticut Service in Queen Anne's War, 1710-1711*. New Haven: Acorn Club of Connecticut, 1916.

Chapin, Howard Millar. *Rhode Island in the Colonial Wars. A List of Rhode Island Soldiers and Sailors in King George's War, 1740-1748.* Providence: Rhode Island Historical Society, 1920.

———. *Rhode Island in the Colonial Wars. A List of Rhode Island Soldiers and Sailors in the Old French and Indian Wars, 1755-1762.* Providence: Rhode Island Historical Society, 1918.

———. *Rhode Island Privateers in King George's War, 1739-1748.* Providence: Rhode Island Historical Society, 1926.

Clark, Murtie J. *Colonial Soldiers of the South, 1732-1774.* Baltimore: Genealogical Publishing Co., 1983.

Connecticut Historical Society. *Rolls of Connecticut Men in the French and Indian Wars, 1755-1762.* 2 vols. Hartford, CT: The Society, 1903-05.

Lewis, Virgil A. *Soldiery of West Virginia in the French and Indian Wars; Lord Dunmore's War; the Revolution; the Later Indian Wars. . . .* (3rd Biennial Report of Department of Archives and History, 1911.) Baltimore: Genealogical Publishing Co., 1967 (reprint).

New York Historical Society. *Muster Rolls of New York Provincial Troops, 1755-1764.* New York: The Society, 1892.

Pennsylvania Archives. "Officers and Soldiers in the Service of the Province of Pennsylvania, 1744-1764." *Pennsylvania Archives,* Series 5, Vol. 3, pp. 419-528. Harrisburg, 1906.

Pomeroy, Seth. *Journals and Papers.* Society of Colonial Wars, 1926. (Published by the Society of Colonial Wars in the State of New York at the request of its Committee on Historical Documents; edited by Louis Effingham DeForest—Publ. No. 38.)

Rhode Island. Society of Colonial Wars. *Nine Muster Rolls of Rhode Island Troops Enlisted During the Old French War.* Providence: The Society, 1915.

Robinson, George Frederick and Albert Harrison Hall. *Watertown Soldiers in the Colonial Wars and the American Revolution.* Watertown, MA: Historical Society of Watertown, 1939.

Taylor, Philip F. *A Calendar of the Warrants for Land in Kentucky. Granted for Service in the French and Indian Wars.* (Excerpted from the *Year Book of the Society of Colonial Wars in Kentucky,* 1917.) Baltimore: Genealogical Publishing Co., 1967 (reprint).

IV. THE REVOLUTIONARY WAR

A. Service Records

When the War for Independence began there was no official United States government and hence very few records were made of the troops who fought

—rosters and rolls mainly, as in the colonial confrontations. However, this war was the beginning of U.S. military records, and machinery was set up to make a record of those who served. Though some of these already scant early records have been destroyed by fire, those that remain are still very important.

At the National Archives there are records which have been abstracted onto 3½" x 8" cards by the Adjutant General's Office, containing all information from muster rolls (lists of men in a particular military unit), pay rolls, etc., for each individual soldier. Each soldier's cards have been placed in a separate jacket-envelope which is filed according to whether he served in the Continental Army, in a state organization, or in another branch of the service. These compiled military service records are indexed in three indexes—a master name index, a name index for the Continental Army troops, and an index for each state.

Though there is some variation, these records show such information as:

> the name, rank, and military organization of the soldier; if available, the name of the State from which he served; the date that his name appears on one or more of the rolls; sometimes the date or dates and period of his enlistment or the date of his appointment; and rarely the date of his separation from the service.[1]

There are also some other service-record documents at the National Archives which have been card-indexed by the names of the individual soldiers. These include many different kinds of records—orderly books, rosters, oaths of allegiance, receipts, enlistment papers, correspondence, etc. —and usually contain information on the soldier's military unit. However, the records are varied and there is no set information formula.

All of these records are in Record Group 93, War Department Collection of Revolutionary War Records, at the National Archives.

B. Veterans' Benefits

Records relating to veterans' benefits for Revolutionary service have more to offer the genealogist than do service records, mainly because most of the legislation bestowing or making possible such benefits was not passed until

---

[1] Meredith B. Colket, Jr., and Frank E. Bridgers, *Guide to Genealogical Records in the National Archives* (Washington, DC: The National Archives, 1964), pp. 49-50. The reader is also referred to *Guide to Genealogical Research in the National Archives* (1983), pp. 88-89, for greater detail.

many years after the war's termination. There were basically two kinds of benefits available:

1. Pensions.
2. Bounty land.

1. Pensions.

Pension benefits and the nature of pension records are ably described by Colket and Bridgers:

> Pensions were granted by Congress to invalid or disabled veterans; to widows and orphans of men who were killed or died in service; to veterans who served a minimum period of time if they were living at an advanced age; to widows of veterans who served a minimum period of time if the widows were living at an advanced age; and, in some instances, to other heirs. Pensions granted on the basis of death or disability incurred in service are known as death or disability pensions. Pensions granted on the basis of service for a minimum period of time are called service pensions.[2]

There were some very early pensions granted by the individual states to those who were disabled in the Revolutionary War. Many of these were assumed by the federal government for payment beginning in September 1789. In 1792 it became possible for a disabled serviceman to apply directly to the federal government for a pension through the U.S. Circuit and District Courts, but the applications for these pensions were all destroyed by a fire in the War Department in November 1800. This is the reason that you find few Revolutionary pension applications dated prior to 1800. There was also a fire in August of 1814 (War of 1812), but it was not quite so thorough in its destruction.

About the only records from the old Invalid (death and disability) Series which seem to be extant are:

a. *Reports submitted to Congress.* There were eight reports from the War Department of pensions during 1792, 1794, and 1795 submitted to Congress, all of which were transcribed and indexed in "Class 9" of U.S. Congress, *American State Papers,* pages 58-67, 85-122, 125-128, 135-145, 150-172 (Washington, DC: Gales and Seaton, 1834). The information pertaining to the individual pensioners has been transcribed and interfiled in separate envelopes with the Revolutionary service pension papers.

---

[2] *Ibid.*, p. 77.

> Each entry in the 1792 report contains the name of the invalid pensioner, his rank, his regiment, the nature of his disability, and the date of the commencement of the pension. Each entry in the 1794 and 1795 reports contains the name of the invalid applicant; his rank; his regiment, company, or ship; the date and place of his becoming disabled; the place of his residence at the date of the report; and, as a rule, evidence of action on the claim.[3]

The original reports are at the National Archives in Records of the U.S. House of Representatives, Record Group 233, and Records of the U.S. Senate, Record Group 46. The 1792 report is in the second volume of a House publication called "Reports War Department 1st Cong. 3rd Sess., to 2nd Cong. 2nd Sess." The seven reports for 1794 and 1795 are in a Senate volume entitled "War Office Returns of Claims to Invalid Pensioners."[4]

b. *Reports retained by the War Department.* Some records, containing essentially the same types of information (with some duplication) as do the reports submitted to Congress, were retained by the War Department for the years 1794-96 and are in the National Archives in a bound manuscript entitled "War Office Letter Book 1791-97" (pages 526-612). In 1958 the National Genealogical Society published the 1796 reports in its quarterly magazine.[5]

c. *A book entitled Revolutionary Pensioners of 1818*, based on a report dated March 28, 1818, made by the Secretary of War and listing all U.S. pensioners (including invalid veterans, widows and orphans), was published by the Genealogical Publishing Co., Baltimore, in 1959. Some 5,495 pensioners are listed.

Notwithstanding the loss of the early pension files, much of the information therein being forever lost, there are extensive records of pensions which were applied for after 1800 under the various acts of Congress. The first *service* pensions (remember Colket and Bridgers' distinction between invalid and service pensions) were granted under an act dated March 18, 1818, and the latest ones were granted by an act of February 3, 1853. There was much liberalization in the qualifications of a pensioner in those thirty-five years. Perhaps the most liberal act (as compared to its predecessors) was the one passed on June 7, 1832, which made pensions available to all who

---

[3] *Ibid.*, p. 79.

[4] See *Guide to Genealogical Research in the National Archives*, rev. ed. (Washington, DC: The National Archives, 1983), p. 125.

[5] "Recently Discovered Records Relating to Revolutionary War Veterans Who Applied for Pensions Under the Act of 1792," *National Genealogical Society Quarterly*, XLVI, nos. 1-2 (March 1958), pp. 8-13, and (June 1958), pp. 73-78.

GENERAL SERVICES ADMINISTRATION
NATIONAL ARCHIVES AND RECORDS SERVICE

ORDER FOR PHOTOCOPIES CONCERNING VETERAN

(See reverse for explanation)

DO NOT WRITE IN THIS SPACE

RECEIPT NO.	DATE
62612	6-15-64

SEARCHER

FILE DESIGNATION: David Hurlbut S 45401

State of New York }
Broome County }

On this 9th day of September 1820 personally appeared before Jon^a Lewis one of the Judges of Broome Common Pleas David Hurlbut aged 63 years resident in the Town of Lisle in said County who being first duly sworn according to law doth on his oath declare that he served in the revolutionary War as follows – that he enlisted in the Company Commanded by Captain Albert Chapman in Col Heman Swifts Regiment in the month of August in the year 1777 – and served three years – Discharged at Peeks Kill. That he made declaration to obtain a pension on the 25th day of April in the year 1818 Number of pension Certificate

And I do solemnly swear that I was a resident Citizen of the United States on the 18th day of March 1818 and that I have not since that time by gift sale or in any manner disposed of my property or any part thereof with intent thereby so to diminish it as to bring my self within the provisions of an act of Congress Entitled "an act to provide for certain persons engaged in the land and naval service in the Revolutionary War" passed on the 18th day of March 1818 And I have not nor has any person in trust for me any property or securities contracts or debts due to me nor have I any income other than what is contained in the schedule hereunto annexed and by me subscribed

Schedule

One Cow – Two Hogs – one pot – 2 old Kettles – Tea Kettle – old pair of Tongs and Shovel – one Crane and Hooks – two Spinning wheels – one Reel five old Chairs – old Chest with drawers – one Table – one old Chest – two wash tubs, 2 pails – three Tubs, 1 Keg – one Spider – four old meal bags – one old Churn three wooden bowls – one brown Earthen pan. 6 Earthen plates four bowls – one Sugar bowl – four Tea Cups and Saucers – Tea pot a Cream pot two bottles pair old Sad Irons one Pitcher one pair old Steelyards – one old meat barrel Eight drag teeth one pair old plow Irons – one Chain two old axes two old Hoes two Shares, 1 Crooked do 1 saw – one old Candlestick one Sythe

Jon^a Lewis

David Hurlbut

This deponent further declares that he is by occupation a farmer but is wholly unable to pursue it or any other business being only able to walk the house and Considered by Physicians to be in a consumption has a Wife and 5 Children – the name of his wife Lois, her health not very good, yet able the greatest part of the time to do her work in the house aged 44 years. Henry oldest Child living at home aged 14 years Albert aged 13 years Maria aged 8 years Gideon aged 6 years Louisa aged 3 years – The Children as may be perceived are not able to do but very little towards their support

Jon^a Lewis

David Hurlbut

FIGURE 1—VETERAN'S DECLARATION AS PART OF A REVOLUTIONARY WAR PENSION APPLICATION

had served at least six months, regardless of their need. All acts after 1832 applied to widows of servicemen as well as to servicemen themselves.

At the National Archives the original pension application papers are in linen-lined envelopes arranged alphabetically by the names of the servicemen and are completely indexed. The index was published by the National Genealogical Society in its quarterly magazine during the period between 1946 and 1963 (volumes 20, 40, 44, 50). It is now available in book form[6] and has also been microfilmed. Many libraries have copies of it.

2. Bounty land.

As an added inducement to get men to serve in the American forces, free land was promised. There was not money to pay the troops so this was the logical answer. Some soldiers or, if the soldiers were killed, their heirs, took up the land soon after the war (based on an act of 1788) on special reservations set aside for that purpose by Congress. Special warrants (bounty land warrants) were issued by the Secretary of War. Many others took up land under later acts. The last major bounty land act was passed in 1855. It provided a bounty of 160 acres to anyone who fought in a battle or served at least fourteen days. It applied to all men who had served in any war up to that time and not just to those with Revolutionary service.

Beginning in 1830 it became possible for holders of warrants which had not been used to patent land in the designated reservations to surrender or exchange them for scrip certificates (sometimes merely called *scrip*) which would allow the land to be taken up anywhere in the public domain. The warrants capable of surrender were of three types:

a. Federal warrants to the U.S. Military District of Ohio.

b. Virginia warrants (for service in the Virginia State Line) for land in Kentucky.

c. Virginia warrants (for service in the Virginia Continental Line) for land in either Kentucky or the Virginia Military District of Ohio.

The records of these surrendered warrants generally provide (in addition to the warrantee's name) the names of any heirs filing the claim and their relationships to the warrantees, their places of residence, and the date the warrant was surrendered. They are in the National Archives and are all indexed.

---

[6] *Index of Revolutionary War Pension Applications in the National Archives,* rev. ed., NGS Special Publ. No. 40, comp. by Frank Johnson Metcalf, Max Ellsworth Hoyt, Agatha Bouson Hoyt, Sadye Giller, William H. Dumont, and Louise Dumont (Washington, DC: National Genealogical Society, 1966).

You will note from the foregoing that Virginia, as a state, issued bounty land warrants to her veterans. The records of these Virginia warrants, as well as the federal warrants, are in the National Archives.

Many bounty land warrant applications filed prior to 1800 are also believed to have been destroyed by that same War Department fire which took the early pension applications, but records identifying the 14,757 applicants whose papers were destroyed (by name) still exist at the National Archives.

All remaining bounty land warrant applications for those who claimed land based on Revolutionary War service have been interfiled with the Revolutionary War pension application papers at the National Archives and are indexed with them in the National Genealogical Society's Index mentioned in footnote 6 on the preceding page.

If both a veteran and his widow applied for a pension, or if one claimed bounty land in addition to a pension, all papers for all claims have been filed together in the same jacket-envelope.

One group of records not in the National Archives in which many researchers have special interest are the records of Virginia military grants in Ohio, which are found in the Richard Clough Anderson papers at the Virginia State Library, Richmond.

C. Information in the Files

It is difficult to tell exactly what kind of information you will find in a particular pension or bounty land file. A file can be composed of anything from a single summary card (because of the loss of early records) to an envelope containing several pages. In a typical file you will usually find:

> the name, rank, military or naval unit, and period of service of the veteran. If he applied for a pension, it shows his age or date of birth, place of birth, and place of residence. If the widow applied, it shows the date and place of his death, her age and the place of her residence, the place and date of her marriage to the veteran, and her maiden name.[7]

Though all of this information may not be found in every file, there might be other, additional information such as a page from a family Bible to establish proof of age or of a marriage. There may even be a marriage certificate. Often affidavits of relatives, in-laws, and neighbors are included in the file and relationships are stated. Frequently the veteran traced all his

[7] Colket and Bridgers, pp. 80-81.

movements and told of all the places he lived between the time of his service and the filing of his application. And so on. There are many possibilities.

Sometimes the heirs of the veteran would file for benefits. The following is a declaration and power of attorney filed for that purpose.

> State of New Hampshire
> County of Coos
>
> On this Second Day of August AD 1851 Be it known that before me James Washburne Justice of the Peace in and for the County of Coos aforesaid Personally appeared Miles Hurlburt aged 51 years and Betsey Young aged 57 years and Maid oath in due form of Law that they are the Children of Daniel Hurlburt and that there is No widow Living of Daniel Hurlburt who was a Soldier in the revolutionary war and that the Said Daniel Hurlburt Died at Clarksville in the State of New Hampshire on or about the 14 Day of January AD 1829 and that their said Mother Died at Stewartstown New Hampshire on or about the 12 Day of october AD 1849 and that they make this Declaration for the Purpose of receive from the united States any and all money or moneys Back Pay or survey bounties or land or pension that May be Lawfully due them as Children afforesaid and onely Surviving heirs and That Furthermore they hereby Constitute and appoint F E Hassler Washington City D C their tru and Lawful attorney for and in their name to transact and receipt for any Money or Moneys they may be entitled to hereby rectifying and conforming whatsoever their Said attorney legally do in the Premises.
>
> (signed)
>
> Acknowledged Sworn to & Subscribed before me the Day and Year afore Said. } Miles Hubbert Betsey Yonge
>
> (signed) James Washburn Justice of the Peace

A bounty land application file is much like a pension application file in its contents. The reason for this is that the same things had to be proven—that service was rendered and that the applicant was entitled to benefits. Generally, a bounty land file contains:

> the name, age, residence, military or naval unit, and period of service of the veteran; and the name, age, and place of residence of the widow or other claimant. If the application was approved, the file shows also the warrant number, the number of acres granted, the date issued, and, where appropriate, the name of the assignee.
>
> If the file was destroyed, the card used as a substitute shows the name of the veteran, his grade, his military or naval unit, the warrant number, the number of acres granted, the date issued, and, where appropriate, the name of the assignee.[8]

---

[8] *Ibid.*, p. 92.

INDEX OF REVOLUTIONARY WAR PENSION APPLICATIONS 843

O'DONAGHY (or O DONAGHEY), Patrick, N. Y., Agness, W20997
O'DONOHY, Patrick, N. Y., BLWt. 7574. Issued 9/28/1790 to Alexander Robertson, assignee. No papers
O'DORNER (or O DORNEN), Murty, Pa., S40215
ODUM, Seybert, Ga. Agcy., Dis. No papers
O'FERRELL (or O'FARRELL), Dennis, Va., S25072
OFFICER, James, Pa., S31280
OFFUTT
Jessee, S. C., Obedience, R7769
Nathaniel, S. C., S31887
O'FLAHERTY, John, N. J., BLWt. 8618. Issued 4/20/1792. No papers
O'FLYING (or O FLING, FLING), Patrick, Cont., N. H., War of 1812, S35542, Rejected Bounty Land Claim of 1812. For family history, etc., consult Wid. Ctf. 16785 of Edmund O'Flying, Pvt. U. S. Inf. War of 1812. Also see Claim for bounty land allowed on account of services of Lt. Patrick O'Flying, War of 1812, 23 W. S. Inf. who died Nov. 1, 1815. Wt. 3 for 480 A., Act of 4/14/1816. (No original papers in this claim)
OGDEN
Aaron, N. J., S19013; BLWt. 1610-300-Capt. Issued 6/11/1789. No papers
Barne (or Barney), N. J., S38279, BLWt. 773-200
Benjamin, N. J., S31281
Daniel, N. Y., BLWt. 7563. Issued 7/30/1792. No papers
David, Conn., Sally, W17414
David, N. Y., BLWt. 7581. Issued 7/13/1792. No papers
David, N. Y., Susannah, W24364
Edmond, Conn., Navy, Sebal, R7777
Eliakim, N. J., BLWt. 8607. Issued 6/20/1789. No papers
Gilbert, N. Y., R7770
James, N. J., Ruth, R7772
Jedediah, N. J., S32419
John, Mass., Naomi Burnap, former wid., W15618
John, N. Y., BLWt. 7559. Issued 8/26/1790 to Elijah Rose, assignee. No papers
Jonathan, N. Y., S11154
Joseph, Conn., S38277
Joseph, N. J., S11155
OGDEN (continued)
Ludlow, N. J., Comfort, W187
Matthias, N. J., BLWt. 1609-500-Col. Issued 6/11/1789. No papers
Nathaniel, Cont., N. J., BLWt. 1281-100
Nathaniel, N. J., S34454
Noah, N. J., BLWt. 8610. Issued 6/11/1789 to Matthias Denman, assignee. No papers
Obadiah, N. Y., Martha, R7771, BLWt. 45715-160-55
Samuel, N. J., S38273
Stephen, N. Y., Va., S7775
Stephen D., N. J., R7776
Sturges (or Sturgess), Conn., S14049
OGEN, Thomas, Va., BLWt. 12444. Issued 3/1/1794. No papers
OGG, James, R. I., BLWt. 3369. Issued 5/16/1791 to Deborah May, Admx. No papers
OGILBY, George, Pa., BLWt. 10185. Issued 6/25/1794 to Gideon Merkle, assignee. No papers
OGILVIE, Kimbrough, N. C., S14050
OGLE, Benjamin, Va., R7778
OGLESBY
Elisha, Va., S1866
Jesse, Va., Celia, W1987; BLWt. 28525-160-55
Richard, Va. res. of wid. in 1812, Susan, R7779
O'GULLION (see GULLION), John B.
OHARA
(or O HARRO), Francis, Pa., Nancy, BLWt. 233-100
George, N. J., Elizabeth, W5442
John, Va., S25340
John, Md., Susan, W9215
(or OHARRA), Joseph, Pa., Mary, BLWt. 224-100
Patrick, Pa., BLWt. 10184. Issued 4/3/1794 to John Phillips, assignee. No papers
OHL
Henry, Pa., S2030
(or OHE), John, Pa., S22428
OHLEN
Henry G., N. Y., Cathrina, S43100, W19935
Henry G., N. Y., BLWt. 7570. Issued 8/26/1790 to William Carr, assignee. No papers
OHMET, John, Pa., S40218
O'KAIN (or CANE), James, Pa., BLWt. 319-100

FIGURE 2—A PAGE FROM *INDEX OF REVOLUTIONARY WAR PENSION APPLICATIONS,* PREPARED BY THE NATIONAL GENEALOGICAL SOCIETY

D. The Index

The *Index of Revolutionary War Pension Applications in the National Archives* as prepared by the National Genealogical Society is very simple to use. It is arranged alphabetically (with cross-references for variant spellings of surnames). It gives the name of the serviceman, generally the state from which he served, the name of any other claimant (such as a widow), where appropriate, and the number of the pension or bounty land file. The file number may be prefixed with an "S" (indicating that the applicant was a *Survivor* and a pension was granted), an "R" (which means the application was *Rejected*), a "W" (indicating a *Widow's* pension), a "BLWt" (meaning it was a *Bounty Land Warrant* application), or a "BL Reg" (showing that the *Bounty Land* claim was *Rejected*).

There are asterisks (*) by some of the names in the index to indicate that the papers relating to those soldiers' applications have been published in the *National Genealogical Society Quarterly*. The date and page of publication are always given.

It is appropriate also to mention that rejection of an application did not mean that the applicant was a liar fraudulently seeking a pension for service he did not render. Many applications were rejected because the veteran was unable to establish sufficient proof of his service—usually either a discharge or the affidavit of a fellow soldier was required. If you have served in the armed services yourself, think how difficult it might be to prove you served if no records of your service were kept. Other claims were rejected because of insufficient service, remarriage (in the case of a widow), service of a non-military nature, etc.

In several instances the words "no papers" appear after an applicant's name in the index. This means that the pension application papers of this veteran have been destroyed, probably by fire as indicated earlier.

E. Obtaining the Records

It is not necessary to go personally to the National Archives to check these pension and bounty land files. A service has been established which allows you to request papers from these files through the mail. For a nominal fee you can secure photocopies of records from the file of any veteran you choose. There is a form—NATF Form 80—which you should use to request these records—one file per request form. Copies of the form can be obtained free from the National Archives, Washington, DC 20408. You send no money with your request for copies; you are billed for the copies when they are sent to you. If copies of the complete file are not sent to you because of the size of the file, you can order copies of all documents by making a specific request. You will be notified of the cost of the copies. If you want a microfilm copy you will find it is less costly (and just as readable) if you request a *negative* copy.

It usually takes about one month to get an answer to most requests to the National Archives, so it will pay you to develop a little patience and perhaps work on another project while you wait.

Beginning in January 1969 a program to microfilm the Revolutionary War pension and bounty land applications was initiated by the General Services Administration. That filming produced two microfilm publications. One includes the complete contents of every file (M804—2,670 rolls), and the second includes up to ten pages (picking the most significant documents) from each file (M805—898 rolls). Both publications are available for purchase, and many genealogical libraries have them available. The LDS Family History Library and National Archives Field Branches have the larger publication.

For those without direct access to a library with the pension films, a rental program has been established so they can order individual microfilm rolls for searching at their local libraries. Microfilm publication M804 is described as to its roll-by-roll contents in a pamphlet available free of charge from the National Archives. Microfilm can also be ordered by individuals direct from the National Archives through the Microfilm Rental Program. Other related Revolutionary War files available through the rental program include a "General Index to Compiled Service Records of American Revolutionary War Soldiers" (M860—58 rolls) and "Compiled Service Records of Revolutionary War Soldiers" (M881—1,097 rolls).

As the name of the program implies, census microfilms are also available. See chapter 11 for further details.

Also of interest is a three-volume work giving the library call numbers at the LDS Family History Library for the U.S. military records:

Deputy, Marilyn *et al.* (comps). *Register of Federal United States Military Records: A Guide to Manuscript Sources Available at the Genealogical Library in Salt Lake City and the National Archives in Washington, D.C.* 3 vols. Salt Lake City: Corporation of the President, The Church of Jesus Christ of Latter-day Saints, 1985.

Vol. 1— 1775-1860

Vol. 2 — The Civil War

Vol. 3 — 1866-World War II, and records of various branches of the military.

F. Pension Payment Records

Other possible sources of information about a person who secured a pension for his service during the Revolution are in the records of the Pension Office and of the Treasury Department, which are in the National Archives. There are several possibilities:

1. A printed manuscript entitled "Revolutionary War and Acts of Military Establishment, Invalid Pensioners' Payments, March 1801 through September 1815" is arranged alphabetically under the states in which the pensioners were living when they received their pensions. An entry in this manuscript:

> shows the name and rank of the pensioner, the name of the State in which payment was made, and amount paid in March and September of each year. If the pensioner died or moved to another State during the period of the records, the fact is indicated, and in some cases the date of death is shown.[9]

2. There are fourteen unnumbered manuscript volumes relating to the payment of Revolutionary pensioners in Alabama, Arkansas, California, Connecticut, Delaware, District of Columbia, Florida, Georgia, Illinois, Indiana, Iowa, Kentucky, Louisiana, Maine, Maryland, Massachusetts, Michigan, Minnesota, Mississippi, Missouri, Nebraska, New Hampshire, New Jersey, New York, North Carolina, Ohio, Oregon, Pennsylvania, Rhode Island, South Carolina, Tennessee, Texas, Vermont, Virginia, and Wisconsin. These are for payments made under the various acts from 1818 to 1853, and under each state they are arranged in alphabetical groupings (first letter of surname) according to the act under which the pension was granted. There is *not* a lot of useful information in these volumes. An entry in them shows:

> name and rank of pensioner, state in which payment was made, and amount paid in March and September of each year. If the pensioner died or moved to another state during the period of the records, the fact is indicated, and in some cases the date of death is shown.[10]

3. There are twenty-three pension-payment volumes from the records of the Treasury Department which cover 1819 through 1871. These records have been microfilmed as *Ledgers of Payments, 1818-1872, to U.S. Pensioners Under Acts of 1818 Through 1858, From Records of the Office of*

---

[9] *Ibid.*, p. 86.

[10] *Guide to Genealogical Research in the National Archives*, p. 128.

ORDER FOR COPIES OF VETERANS RECORDS
Please see Page 1 of this form for instructions.

Date Received (NNMS)

1. FILE TO BE SEARCHED *(Check one box ONLY)* ▶ ☐ PENSION ☐ BOUNTY-LAND WARRANT APPLICATION *(Service before 1856 only)* ☐ MILITARY

REQUIRED MINIMUM IDENTIFICATION OF VETERAN
Items 2, 3, 4, 5 (and 6 when applicable) MUST be completed or your order cannot be serviced.

2. VETERAN *(Give last, first, and middle names)*
3. BRANCH OF SERVICE IN WHICH HE SERVED ☐ Army ☐ Navy ☐ Marine Corps
4. STATE FROM WHICH HE SERVED
5. WAR IN WHICH, OR DATES BETWEEN WHICH, HE SERVED
6. IF SERVICE WAS CIVIL WAR ☐ Union ☐ Confederate

PLEASE PROVIDE THE FOLLOWING INFORMATION, IF KNOWN

7. UNIT IN WHICH HE SERVED *(Name of regiment or number, company, etc., name of ship)*
8. IF SERVICE WAS ARMY, ARM IN WHICH HE SERVED ☐ Infantry ☐ Cavalry ☐ Artillery *If other, specify:*
9. KIND OF SERVICE ☐ Volunteers ☐ Regulars
10. PENSION/BOUNTY-LAND FILE NO.
11. IF VETERAN LIVED IN A HOME FOR SOLDIERS, GIVE LOCATION *(City & State)*
12. PLACE(S) VETERAN LIVED AFTER SERVICE
13. DATE OF BIRTH
14. PLACE OF BIRTH *(City, County, State, etc.)*
15. DATE OF DEATH
16. PLACE OF DEATH *(City, County, State, etc.)*
17. NAME OF WIDOW OR OTHER CLAIMANT

Do NOT write below — Space is for our reply to you

☐ YES We have located the file you requested above. The cost is $5.00 for the record.

We have copied all or part of the file for you. Make your check or money order for $5.00, payable to **NATIONAL ARCHIVES TRUST FUND (NNMS).** Do NOT send cash. **Return your payment AND this invoice in the enclosed envelope. If the return envelope is missing,** send your payment AND this invoice to: National Archives Trust Fund Board, P.O. Box 100221, Atlanta, GA 30384. We must have this invoice to match your payment with your copies. WE WILL HOLD THESE COPIES AWAITING RECEIPT OF PAYMENT FOR 30 DAYS ONLY, FROM DATE STAMPED BELOW.

☐ NO We were unable to locate the file you requested above.

☐ **REQUIRED MINIMUM IDENTIFICATION OF VETERAN WAS NOT PROVIDED.** Please complete items 2 (give full name), 3, 4, 5, and 6, and resubmit your order.

☐ **A SEARCH WAS MADE BUT THE FILE YOU REQUESTED ABOVE WAS NOT FOUND.** When we do not find a record for a veteran, this does not mean that he did not serve. You may be able to obtain information about him from the archives of the State from which he served.

☐ See attached forms, leaflets, or information sheets.

NNMS USE ONLY
SEARCHER
DATE
FILE DESIGNATION

949684

▶ *THIS IS YOUR MAILING LABEL. Print your name (Last, First MI) and address within the block below. PRESS FIRMLY - the information MUST appear on all copies.*

A

NAME *(Last, first, middle)*
STREET
CITY, STATE
(Zip Code)

INVOICE/REPLY

NATIONAL ARCHIVES TRUST FUND BOARD
NATF Form 80 (11-87)

FIGURE 3—NATF FORM 80 CAN BE USED TO ORDER COPIES OF MILITARY RECORDS FROM THE NATIONAL ARCHIVES

ORDER FOR COPIES OF VETERANS RECORDS

INSTRUCTIONS FOR COMPLETING THIS FORM

Submit a separate set of forms for each file you request (see Item 1) **WE WILL SEARCH ONLY ONE FILE PER FORM.** Remove this instruction sheet. Do NOT remove any of the remaining three pages of this form. Items 2-6 MUST be completed or we cannot search for the file. Print your name (last first middle) and address in the box provided. This is your mailing label; the information MUST appear on all copies. Mail the completed form to:

Military Service Branch (NNMS)
National Archives and Records Administration
7th and Pennsylvania Avenue, NW
Washington, DC 20408

DO NOT FORWARD PAYMENT WHEN SUBMITTING THIS FORM FOR SEARCH. When we search your order, photocopies will be made of records that relate to your request. At that time we will invoice you for the cost of these copies. **WE WILL HOLD THESE COPIES AWAITING RECEIPT OF PAYMENT FOR 30 DAYS ONLY.** After that time, you must submit another form to obtain photocopies of the file.

USE ONLY NATF FORM 80 TO OBTAIN COPIES OF VETERANS RECORDS. We cannot process requests submitted on reproductions of this form. Write to the address below to obtain additional copies of this form.

DUE TO THE HEAVY VOLUME OF REQUESTS, PLEASE ALLOW A MINIMUM OF 8-10 WEEKS FOR PROCESSING OF YOUR ORDER.

Do NOT use this form to request photocopies of records relating to service in World War I or II, or subsequent service. Write to: National Personnel Records Center (Military Records), NARA, 9700 Page Boulevard, St. Louis, MO 63132

IMPORTANT INFORMATION ABOUT YOUR ORDER

We can only search for a record based on the information you provide in Blocks 2-17. The success and accuracy of our search is determined by the completeness and accuracy of the information you provide. When you send more than one form at a time, each form is handled separately. Therefore, you may not receive all of your replies at the same time.

Military service records rarely contain family information. Pension application files generally are most useful to those who are doing genealogical research and contain the most complete information regarding a man's military career. We suggest that you first request copies of a man's pension file. You should request copies of a bounty-land warrant file or a military record only when no pension file exists. **If the veteran's service was during the Revolutionary War, bounty-land warrant applications have been consolidated with pension application papers. You can obtain both files by requesting the pension file only.**

Often there are many files for veterans of the same or nearly the same name. If there are **five or fewer files** for men with the same name as the individual in whom you are interested, we will examine all the relevant files and compare their contents with the information that you have provided us. If the veteran's identity seems obvious, we will furnish you a copy of the file we think is the correct one.

If there are more than five files, we will not make a file-by-file check to see if the information in the numerous files matches that provided for the veteran in whom you are interested. In such cases, we suggest that you visit the National Archives and examine the various files, or hire a professional researcher to examine the files for you. We do not maintain a list of persons who do research for a fee; however, many researchers advertise their services in genealogical periodicals, usually available in libraries.

When we are unable to provide copies of all documents, because of the size of a pension or bounty-land warrant application file, we will send copies of the documents we think will be most useful to you. You may order copies of all documents in a file by making a specific request. We will notify you of the cost of the copies.

Additional copies of this form and more information about the availability of records pertaining to military service or family histories may be found in our free genealogical information leaflets and forms. These may be requested by writing to:

Reference Services Branch (NNIR)
National Archives and Records Administration
7th and Pennsylvania Avenue, NW
Washington, DC 20408

PLEASE SEE THE REVERSE OF THIS PAGE FOR THE TYPES OF RECORDS THAT CAN BE ORDERED WITH THIS FORM.

NATIONAL ARCHIVES TRUST FUND BOARD NATF Form 80 (11-87)

INSTRUCTIONS

FIGURE 4—INSTRUCTIONS CONCERNING NATF FORM 80

the Third Auditor of the Treasury (T713—twenty-three rolls). The entries are arranged according to the act of Congress under which they were obtained and the pension agency involved. The information necessary to locate an entry in these volumes can be found in the pension application file (i.e., the name of the veteran, the name of the pensioner, act of Congress under which latest payment was made, and the amount of payment if there was more than one pensioner with the same name). There is a typed "Key to the Pension Payment Volumes Relating to Revolutionary War Pensioners" in the National Archives building which will help guide you to the entry you seek.

The information in these pension-payment books includes:

> name of the pensioner, name of the veteran (if different), name of the pension agency through which payment was made, the quarter and year of last payment to the pensioner. When an heir or legal representative claimed an unpaid balance due the pensioner at the time of death, the date of death of the pensioner is given and the date final payment was made to the family or heirs.[11]

4. After you consult the pension-application file and the pension-payment volumes (No. 3) you will have sufficient information to enable you to locate a Final Payment Voucher. The vouchers cover 1819 through 1864 and are filed under the states of the pensioners' residences, by the pension agency, quarter year of final payment, and act under which the pension was granted, and then alphabetically by the first letter of the pensioner's surname. A few of these have been filed with the papers in the pension-application files. Final Payment Vouchers show:

> the date and place of death of the pensioner and the names of heirs. These vouchers will usually exist only if the date of death of the pensioner appears in one of the pension-payment volumes described above.[12]

Items 1 and 2 above are in the National Archives in Record Group 15, Records of the Veterans' Administration (as are the pension and bounty land applications), and items 3 and 4 are in Record Group 217, Records of the U.S. General Accounting Office.

G. Books on Revolutionary War Soldiers

Another important source of information on persons who served in the War for Independence is books. Hundreds of books have been written

---

[11] *Ibid.*, p. 130.

[12] *Ibid.*, p. 130.

(especially relating to the several states and even counties and towns) giving information about these servicemen. There are rosters, lists of soldiers buried in this or that place, histories, lineages, etc., any of which may prove helpful in determining if your ancestor served in the Revolutionary War.

Do not overlook these possibilities. Most libraries, especially genealogical libraries and libraries in the localities concerned, have many such books. And these books are essential when you consider that so many of the original records have been either lost or destroyed.

A number of books with lists of American (and allied) participants in the Revolutionary War are listed here:

(Alabama) Mell, Annie R. W. *Revolutionary Soldiers Buried in Alabama.* Montgomery, 1904.

(Alabama) Owen, Thomas M. *Revolutionary Soldiers in Alabama.* (Alabama State Archives Bulletin 5, 1911.) Baltimore: Genealogical Publishing Co., 1967 (reprint).

(Alabama) Thomas, Elizabeth W. *Revolutionary Soldiers in Alabama.* 2 vols. Tuscalloosa, AL: Willo Publishing Co., 1960-61.

Callahan, Edward W. *List of Officers of the Navy of the United States and of the Marine Corps, from 1775 to 1900. . . .* New York, 1901.

(Connecticut) *Lists and Returns of Connecticut Men in the Revolution, 1775-1783.* (Connecticut Historical Society Collections, Vol. 12.) Hartford: The Society, 1909.

(Connecticut) Middlebrook, Louis F. *History of Maritime Connecticut During the American Revolution, 1775-1783.* 2 vols. Salem, MA, 1925.

(Connecticut) *Pension Records of the Revolutionary Soldiers from Connecticut.* (21st Report of the National Society, D.A.R., 1919.) Baltimore: Genealogical Publishing Co., 1982 (reprint).

(Connecticut) *Record of Service of Connecticut Men in the I, War of the Revolution; II, War of 1812; III, Mexican War.* Hartford: Adjutant General's Office, 1889.

(Connecticut) Richards, J. E. *Honor Roll of Litchfield County Revolutionary Soldiers.* Litchfield, CT: D.A.R., 1912.

(Connecticut) *Rolls and Lists of Connecticut Men in the Revolution, 1775-1783.* (Connecticut Historical Society Collections, Vol. 8.) Hartford: The Society, 1901.

Dandridge, Danske. *American Prisoners of the Revolution.* (Copied from the papers of the British War Dept., 1911.) Baltimore: Genealogical Publishing Co., 1967 (reprint).

Delaware Archives. 5 vols. Dover: Public Archives Commission of Delaware, 1911-19. Vols. 2 and 3 are in print.

Dickore, Marie (trans.). *Hessian Soldiers in the American Revolution: Records of Their Marriages and Baptisms of Their Children in America . . . 1776-1783.* Cincinnati: D. J. Krehbiel Co., 1959.

(District of Columbia) Ely, Selden M. *The District of Columbia in the American Revolution, and Patriots of the Revolutionary Period Who are Interred in the District or in Arlington.* (Records of the Columbia Historical Society, 21.) Washington: The Society, 1918.

Eelking, Max von. *The German Allied Troops in the North American War of Independence, 1776-1783.* (Trans. and abridged from German by J. G. Rosengarten, 1893.) Baltimore: Genealogical Publishing Co., 1969 (reprint).

Ellet, Elizabeth F. *The Women of the American Revolution.* 3 vols. New York, 1848-50.

(France) Ministère des Affaires Etrangères. *Les Combattants Francais de la Guerre Americaine, 1778-1783.* (Senate doc. 77, 58th Cong., 2d sess., 1905.) Baltimore: Genealogical Publishing Co., 1969 (reprint).

(Georgia) Blair, Ruth. *Revolutionary Soldiers' Receipts for Georgia Bounty Grants.* Atlanta: Department of Archives and History, 1928.

(Georgia) Hitz, Alex M. *Authentic List of All Land Lottery Grants Made to Veterans of the Revolutionary War by the State of Georgia.* 2nd ed. Atlanta: Department of Archives and History, 1966.

(Georgia) Houston, Martha L. *Six Hundred Revolutionary Soldiers and Widows of Revolutionary Soldiers Living in Georgia, 1827-1828.* Athens, GA, 1965 (reprint). Available from Heritage Press, Danielsville, GA.

(Georgia) Knight, Lucian L. *Georgia's Roster of the Revolution. . . .* (1920). Baltimore: Genealogical Publishing Co., 1967 (reprint).

(Georgia) McCall, Mrs. Ettie S. *Roster of Revolutionary Soldiers in Georgia and Other States.* 3 vols. (Vol. I, 1941 is a reprint). Baltimore: Genealogical Publishing Co., 1968-69.

Hamersly, Thomas H. S. *Complete Army and Navy Register of the United States of America, from 1776 to 1887.* New York, 1888.

————. *Complete General Navy Register of the United States of America, from 1776-1887. . . .* New York, 1888.

Hayward, Elizabeth McCoy. *Soldiers and Patriots of the American Revolution.* Ridgewood, NJ: The author, 1947.

Heitman, Francis Bernard. *Historical Register of Officers of the Continental Army During the War of the Revolution, April, 1775, to December, 1783.* New rev. enl. ed. (1914). Baltimore: Genealogical Publishing Co., 1967 (reprint).

(Illinois) Clift, Garrett Glenn. *List of Officers of the Illinois Regiment, and of Crockett's Regiment Who Have Received Land for Their Services.* Frankfort, IL: S.A.R., 1962.

(Illinois) Meyer, Virginia M. *Roster of Revolutionary War Soldiers and Widows Who Lived in Illinois Counties.* Chicago: Illinois D.A.R., 1962.

(Illinois) Walker, Harriet J. *Revolutionary Soldiers Buried in Illinois.* (1917). Baltimore: Genealogical Publishing Co., 1967 (reprint).

(Illinois) Walker, Homer A. *Illinois Pensioners Lists of the Revolution, 1812, and Indian Wars.* Washington, DC, c. 1955.

(Indiana) O'Byrne, Mrs. Estella. *Roster of Soldiers and Patriots of the American Revolution Buried in Indiana.* 2 vols. Brockville, IN: Indiana D.A.R., 1938, 1966. Volume I was reprinted by Genealogical Publishing Co., Baltimore, in 1968.

(Indiana) Waters, Margaret R. *Revolutionary Soldiers Buried in Indiana. Three Hundred Names Not Listed in the Roster by Mrs. O'Byrne.* 2 vols. (1949, 1954). Baltimore: Genealogical Publishing Co., 1970 (reprint in one volume).

Kaminkow, Marion J. and Jack Kaminkow. *Mariners of the American Revolution.* Baltimore: Magna Carta Book Co., 1967.

(Kentucky) Burns, Annie W. *Abstracts of Pension Papers of Soldiers of the Revolutionary War, War of 1812, and Indian Wars, Who Settled . . . in Kentucky.* At least 21 vols. Washington, 1935— .

(Kentucky) Quisenberry, Anderson C. *Revolutionary Soldiers in Kentucky.* (Excerpted from *Year Book, Kentucky Society, S.A.R.*, 1896.) Baltimore: Genealogical Publishing Co., 1959 (reprint).

(Kentucky) Wilson, Samuel M. *Catalogue of Revolutionary Soldiers and Sailors of the Commonwealth of Virginia to Whom Land Bounty Warrants Were Granted by Virginia for Military Services in the War of Independence.* (Excerpted from *Year Book, Kentucky Society, S.A.R.*, 1913.) Baltimore: Genealogical Publishing Co., 1953 (reprint).

(Maine) Flagg, Charles Alcott. *An Alphabetical Index of Revolutionary Pensioners Living in Maine.* (1920). Baltimore: Genealogical Publishing Co., 1967 (reprint).

(Maine) House, Charles J. *Names of Soldiers of the American Revolution (from Maine), Who Applied for State Bounty Under Resolves of March 17, 1835, March 24, 1836, and March 20, 1836, as Appears of Record in Land Office.* (1893). Baltimore: Genealogical Publishing Co., 1967 (reprint).

(Maine) Houston, Ethel Rollins. *Maine Revolutionary Soldiers' Graves.* Maine D.A.R., 1940.

(Maine) Miller, Frank Burton. *Soldiers and Sailors of the Plantation of Lower St. Georges Who Served in the War for American Independence.* Rockland, ME: A. J. Huston, 1931.

(Maryland) Brumbaugh, Gaius Marcus and Margaret R. Hodges. *Revolutionary Records of Maryland, Part I.* (1924). Baltimore: Genealogical Publishing Co., 1967 (reprint).

(Maryland) McGhee, Lucy K. *Pension Abstracts of Maryland Soldiers of the Revolution, War of 1812, and Indian Wars Who Settled in Kentucky.* Washington, DC, n.d.

(Maryland) *Muster Rolls and Other Records of Service of Maryland Troops in the American Revolution, 1775-1783.* (Archives of Maryland, Vol. 18, 1900.) Baltimore: Genealogical Publishing Co., 1972 (reprint).

(Maryland) Newman, Harry Wright. *Maryland Revolutionary Records.* (1938). Baltimore: Genealogical Publishing Co., 1967 (reprint).

Massachusetts Soldiers and Sailors of the Revolutionary War. 17 vols. Boston: Massachusetts Secretary of State, 1896-1908.

(Massachusetts) Smith, Elizur Yale. *Vital Records of Saudisfield, Massachusetts . . . Saudisfield Revolutionary Soldiers.* Rutland, VT: Charles E. Tuttle Co., 1936.

(Massachusetts) Wolkins, George G. *Beverly Men in the War of Independence.* Beverly, MA: Beverly Historical Society, 1932.

(Michigan) Silliman, Sue I. *Michigan Military Records.* (Michigan Historical Commission Bulletin 12, 1920.) Baltimore: Genealogical Publishing Co., 1969 (reprint).

(Mississippi) Welch, Alice T. *Family Records, Mississippi Revolutionary Soldiers.* Mississippi D.A.R., 1956.

(Missouri) Burns, Annie W. *Missouri Pension Records of Soldiers of the Revolutionary War, War of 1812, and Indian Wars.* Washington, DC, 1937.

(Missouri) Houts, Alice K. *Revolutionary Soldiers Buried in Missouri.* Kansas City: The author, 1966.

(Missouri) McGhee, Lucy K. *Missouri Revolutionary Soldiers, War of 1812 and Indian Wars Pension List.* Washington, DC, 1955.

(Missouri) Pompey, Sherman L. *A Partial Listing of Veterans of the American Revolution, the Civil War, and the Spanish War, That are Buried in Certain Missouri Cemeteries.* Warrensburg, MO: Johnson County Historical Society, 1962.

Neagles, James C. *Summer Soldiers: A Survey & Index for Revolutionary War Courts-Martial.* Salt Lake City: Ancestry Publishing Co., 1986.

(New Hampshire) *Miscellaneous Revolutionary Documents of New Hampshire, Including the Association Test, the Pension Rolls, and Other Important Papers.* (New Hampshire State and Provincial Papers, 30.) Manchester, NH, 1910.

(New Hampshire) *Rolls of the Soldiers of the Revolutionary War, 1775-1782.* 4 vols. (New Hampshire State and Provincial Papers, 14-17.) Concord and Manchester, NH, 1885-89.

(New Jersey) Stryker, William S. *Official Register of the Officers and Men of New Jersey in the Revolutionary War.* (1872). Baltimore: Genealogical Publishing Co., 1967 (reprint).[13]

(New York) Beauchamp, William Martin. *Revolutionary Soldiers Resident or Dying in Onondaga County, N.Y.* Syracuse: Onondaga Historical Society, 1913.

(New York) Daughters of the American Revolution, Chautauqua County Chapters. *Soldiers of the American Revolution.* Jamestown, NY: Mrs. L. N. Shankland, 1925.

(New York) Fernow, Berthold. *New York in the Revolution.* (Vol. 1 of *New York State Archives* and Vol. 15 of *Documents Relating to the Colonial History of the State of New York.*) Albany, 1887.

(New York) Mather, Frederic Gregory. *The Refugees of 1776 from Long Island to Connecticut.* (1913). Baltimore: Genealogical Publishing Co., 1972 (reprint).

(New York) *Muster and Pay Rolls of the War of the Revolution, 1775-1783.* 2 vols. New York: The New York Historical Society, 1916.

New York [State]. Comptroller's Office. *New York in the Revolution as Colony and State.* . . . 2nd ed. Albany, 1904.

——— ———. *Supplement* by Erastus C. Knight. . . . Albany, 1901.

(New York) Tallmadge, Samuel *et al. Orderly Books of the Fourth New York Regiment, 1778-1783.* 2 vols. New York: The New York Historical Society, 1916.

(North Carolina) Daughters of the American Revolution, North Carolina. *Roster of Soldiers from North Carolina in the American Revolution.* (1932). Baltimore: Genealogical Publishing Co., 1967 (reprint).

(Ohio) Daughters of the American Revolution, Ohio. *Official Roster of the Soldiers of the American Revolution Buried in the State of Ohio.* Columbus, 1929.

(Ohio) ———. *Soldiers of the American Revolution Who Lived in the State of Ohio.* (Official Roster II and III.) 1938, 1959.

(Pennsylvania) Cowan, Lucy Marie Davis. *Revolutionary Soldiers of Warren County, Pennsylvania.* New York: Frederick H. Hitchcock, 1926.

---

[13] The index to this volume, *Index of the Official Register of the Officers and Men of New Jersey in the Revolutionary War,* as prepared by the Historical Records Survey of the WPA in 1941, was reprinted by Genealogical Publishing Co., Baltimore, in 1965.

(Pennsylvania) Egle, William H. *Pennsylvania in the War of the Revolution: Associated Battalions and Militia, 1775-1783. (Pennsylvania Archives,* Ser. 2, Vols. 13-14.) Harrisburg, 1890-92.

(Pennsylvania) Fendrick, Virginia Shannon. *Revolutionary Soldiers of Franklin County, Pennsylvania.* Waynesboro, PA: B. Rohrer, n.d.

(Pennsylvania) "List of Officers and Men of the Pennsylvania Navy, 1775-1781." (*Pennsylvania Archives,* Ser. 2, Vol. 1, pp. 243-434.) Harrisburg, 1896.

Peterson, Clarence S. *Known Military Dead During the American Revolutionary War, 1775-1783.* (1959). Baltimore: Genealogical Publishing Co., 1967 (reprint).

Pierce, John. "Register of the Certificates Issued by John Pierce, Esquire, Paymaster General and Commissioner of Army Accounts for the United States. To Officers and Soldiers of the Continental Army Under Act of July 4, 1783. First Published 1786 in Numerical Order." (*17th Report of the National Society, Daughters of the American Revolution,* 1915, pp. 147-712. Baltimore: Genealogical Publishing Co., 1973 (reprint).

(Rhode Island) Cowell, Benjamin. *Spirit of '76 in Rhode Island.* (1850). Baltimore: Genealogical Publishing Co., 1973 (reprint).

Saffell, William T. R. *Records of the Revolutionary War: Containing the Military and Financial Correspondence of Distinguished Officers, Names of the Officers and Privates of Regiments, Companies, and Corps, with Dates of Their Commissions and Enlistments. . . .* 3rd ed. (1894). Baltimore: Genealogical Publishing Co., 1968 (reprint).

(South Carolina) Boddie, William Willis. *Marion's Men; a List of Twenty-five Hundred.* Charleston: The author, 1938.

(South Carolina) Burns, Annie W. *South Carolina Pension Abstracts of the Revolutionary War, War of 1812, and Indian Wars.* 12 vols. Washington, DC, c. 193?.

(South Carolina) Ervin, Sara Sullivan. *South Carolinians in the Revolution.* (1949). Baltimore: Genealogical Publishing Co., 1965 (reprint).

(South Carolina) Moss, Bobby G. *Roster of South Carolina Patriots in the American Revolution.* Baltimore: Genealogical Publishing Co., 1983.

(South Carolina) Pruitt, Jayne C. C. *Revolutionary War Pension Applicants Who Served from South Carolina.* Fairfax, VA: Charlton Hall, 1946.

(South Carolina) Revill, Janie. *Copy of the Original Book Showing the Revolutionary Claims Filed in South Carolina Between August 20, 1783, and August 31, 1786.* (1941). Baltimore: Genealogical Publishing Co., 1969 (reprint).

(South Carolina) Salley, Alexander S. *Accounts Audited of Revolutionary Claims Against South Carolina.* 3 vols. Columbia: The State Co., 1935-43.

(South Carolina) *Stub Entries of Indents Issued in Payment of Claims Against South Carolina Growing Out of the Revolution.* 12 vols. Columbia: Department of Archives and History, 1910-57.

(Tennessee) Allen, Penelope Johnson. *Tennessee Soldiers in the Revolution.* (1935). Baltimore: Genealogical Publishing Co., 1975 (reprint).

(Tennessee) Armstrong, Zella. *Some Tennessee Heroes of the Revolution.* 5 vols. (1935). Baltimore: Genealogical Publishing Co., 1975 (reprint).

(Tennessee) ———. *Twenty-four Hundred Tennessee Pensioners; Revolution, War of 1812.* (1937). Baltimore: Genealogical Publishing Co., 1975 (reprint).

United States. Bureau of the Census. *A Census of Pensioners for Revolutionary or Military Services: With Their Names, Ages, and Places of Residence Taken in 1840.* (1841). Baltimore: Genealogical Publishing Co., 1967 (reprint).

———. *Census of Pensioners, A General Index for Revolutionary or Military Service (1840).* (Prepared by The Genealogical Society [now the Family History Department] of The Church of Jesus Christ of Latter-day Saints, Salt Lake City.) Baltimore: Genealogical Publishing Co., 1965.

———. House of Representatives. *Digested Summary and Alphabetical List of Private Claims Which Have Been Presented to the House of Representatives from the First to the 31st Congress, Exhibiting the Action of Congress on Each Claim. . . .* 3 vols. (1853). Baltimore: Genealogical Publishing Co., 1970 (reprint).

———. *Revolutionary Pensioners of 1818. Message from the President of the United States, Transmitting a Report of the Secretary of War. . . .* (1818). Baltimore: Genealogical Publishing Co., 1959 (reprint).

———. Secretary of War. *Pension Roll of 1835.* (Senate doc. 514, 23d Cong., 1st sess., ser. 249-51, 3 vols., 1835.) Baltimore: Genealogical Publishing Co., 1968 (reprint in 4 vols.).

———. Secretary of War. *Revolutionary Pensioners. A Transcript of the Pension List of the United States for 1813. . . .* (1813). Baltimore: Genealogical Publishing Co., 1959 (reprint).

———. Senate. *Pension List of 1818.* (Senate doc. 55, 16th Cong., 1st sess., ser. 34, vol. 4, 1820.) Baltimore: Genealogical Publishing Co., 1955 (reprint).

————. Senate. *Rejected or Suspended Applications for Revolutionary War Pensions, Report of the Secretary of the Interior, 1852.* (1852). Baltimore: Genealogical Publishing Co., 1969 (reprint).

(Vermont) Crockett, Walter H. *Revolutionary Soldiers Buried in Vermont.* (1903-07). Baltimore: Genealogical Publishing Co., 1973 (reprint).

(Vermont) Goodrich, John E. *Rolls of Soldiers in the Revolutionary War, 1775-1783.* Rutland, VT: Charles E. Tuttle Co., 1904.

(Virginia) Brumbaugh, Gaius Marcus. *Revolutionary War Records. . . .* Vol. I, all published. (1936). Baltimore: Genealogical Publishing Co., 1967 (reprint).

(Virginia) Burgess, Louis Alexander. *Virginia Soldiers of 1776.* 3 vols. (1927-29). Baltimore: Genealogical Publishing Co., 1973 (reprint).

(Virginia) Dorman, John F. *Virginia Revolutionary Pension Applications.* (Continuing series, vol. 1—). Washington, DC: The author, 1958—.

(Virginia) Eckenrode, Hamilton J. *List of Revolutionary Soldiers of Virginia.* (Special Report of Dept. of Archives and History, 1911.) Richmond: Virginia State Library, 1912.

(Virginia) ————. *Supplement.* (Special Report of Dept. of Archives and History, 1912.) Richmond: Virginia State Library, 1913.

(Virginia) Gwathmey, John H. *Historical Register of Virginians in the Revolution: Soldiers, Sailors, Marines, 1775-1783.* (1938). Baltimore: Genealogical Publishing Co., 1973 (reprint).

(Virginia) McAllister, Joseph T. *Virginia Militia in the Revolutionary War.* Hot Springs, VA, c. 1913.

(Virginia) Saffell, William. *Records of the Revolutionary War. List of Virginia Soldiers. . . .* 3rd ed. (1894). Baltimore: Genealogical Publishing Co., 1969 (reprint). The reprint edition includes an index by Joseph T. McAllister originally published in 1913.

(Virginia) Stewart, Robert A. *The History of Virginia's Navy of the Revolution.* Richmond, 1933.

(Virginia) Wilson, Samuel M. *Catalogue of Revolutionary Soldiers and Sailors of the Commonwealth of Virginia to Whom Bounty Land Warrants Were Granted by Virginia for Military Service in the War for Independence.* (1913). Baltimore: Genealogical Publishing Co., 1953 (reprint).

(West Virginia) Johnston, Ross B. *West Virginians in the American Revolution.* (1959). Baltimore: Genealogical Publishing Co., 1977 (reprint).

(West Virginia) Lewis, Virgil A. *Soldiery of West Virginia in the French and Indian War; Lord Dunmore's War; the Revolution; the Later Indian Wars. . . .* (1911). Baltimore: Genealogical Publishing Co., 1967 (reprint).

(West Virginia) Reddy, Anne W. *West Virginia Revolutionary Ancestors Whose Services Were Non-military and Whose Names, Therefore, Do Not Appear in Revolutionary Indexes of Soldiers and Sailors.* (1930). Baltimore: Genealogical Publishing Co., 1963 (reprint).

V. USING REVOLUTIONARY RECORDS

Many beginning genealogists overlook Revolutionary War records as a research source, mainly because they do not recognize valid clues. Many do not even think about the possibility that their ancestor may have served unless they read somewhere that he actually did. However, there are several clues which might indicate the need for considering these records:

1. Any time the line on which you are working was in America prior to the time of the war, you must consider these records. Even if a lineal ancestor did not serve, perhaps a relative (maybe a brother) of the same surname did, and records of his service or his pension application would also provide useful data about your ancestors of the same name—names, dates, and places especially.

2. If a known male ancestor was in America at the time of the Revolution and was of age to serve, the possibility of service must certainly be considered.

3. If a known ancestor was born in America anytime within the period beginning just before the war and ending two decades after it, you must consider the possibility that his (or her) father served, even though you may not know the father's name. The index to pensioners provides a ready list of servicemen (at least those who applied for pensions) of the surname you seek who served from the state or the general region from which your ancestors came. Books about Revolutionary War veterans in the state(s) where your ancestors lived might also help suggest some possibilities to you.

If your ancestral line is not traced back to this period there is seldom good reason to spend time searching records of soldiers or of the war. You have too little to go on. There will be plenty of time to use these records when your research and analysis indicate the need for them.

VI. LOYALISTS AND THE REVOLUTIONARY WAR

Perhaps your people were in America before the Revolution but you can find no evidence of service by them. There may be a number of reasons for this, including the possibility that they belonged to a pacifist church such as the Society of Friends (Quakers). But, on the other hand, there is also the possibility that they were sympathetic to the cause of the Crown rather than to that of the revolutionaries.

If you do not know where your ancestors were during the Revolution because you have not traced them that far, but you find them coming out of Canada (or even Florida or the West Indies) in later years, the same possibility exists. It is estimated that as many as one-third of the colonial population were Loyalists. Among the Loyalists were British government officials and their friends, English Church ministers, and others whose positions or wealth depended upon British sovereignty. Technically speaking, however, all of these persons were not Loyalists though often called such—pro-British or Tories, yes—but not Loyalists. A true Loyalist was one who actively participated in the war to aid the cause of the Crown, usually in British uniform. The Tories did suffer, especially if they refused to take an oath of allegiance, but their property was not usually confiscated and they were not generally charged with treason as were their Loyalist cousins.

Many of these Tories have been called Loyalists—in fact all of those who went to Canada were so called—but many Tories went other directions too (and they were free to do so). However, there is generally no record of loyalism or of confiscation of property in the former American homes of the Tories who emigrated to Canada. Also, these Tories were not eligible for land grants there.

In addition to Canada and Florida, many Loyalists and Tories went to the West Indies (especially Jamaica) and some returned to Britain. Canada, however, seemed to be the favorite place; in Upper Canada (now Ontario) four-fifths of the settlers came from the American colonies.

A. Printed Loyalist Sources

Some of the printed sources on Loyalists (and Tories) in the American Revolution are:

Bradley, Arthur Granville. *Colonial Americans in Exile; Founders of British Canada.* Toronto: E. B. Dutton and Co., 1932.

Brown, Wallace. *The King's Friends. The Composition and Motives of the American Loyalist Claimants.* Providence: Brown University Press, 1966.

———. *The Good Americans. The Loyalists in the American Revolution.* New York: William Morrow and Co., 1969.

Bruce, R. M. *Loyalist Trail.* Kingston, Ont.: Jackson Press, 1965.

Campbell, Wilfrid. *Report on Manuscript Lists in the Archives Relating to the United Empire Loyalists, with Reference to Other Sources.* Ottawa: printed for use of the Archives Branch, 1909.

Canniff, William. *The Settlement of Upper Canada.* Toronto: Dudley and Burns, Printers, 1869.

Clark, Murtie J. *Loyalists in the Southern Campaign of the Revolutionary War.* 3 vols. Baltimore: Genealogical Publishing Co., 1981.

Coldham, Peter Wilson (comp.). *American Loyalist Claims, Volume 1.* Washington, DC: National Genealogical Society, 1980. *Note:* See footnote 14, this chapter, for more details.

Craig, Gerald M. *Upper Canada. The Formative Years, 1784-1841.* Toronto: McClelland and Stewart, Ltd., 1966.

Cruikshank, Ernest Alexander (ed.). *Settlement of the United Empire Loyalists on the Upper St. Lawrence and Bay of Quinte in 1784.* Toronto: The Ontario Historical Society, 1934.

DeMond, Robert O. *Loyalists in North Carolina During the Revolution.* (1940). Baltimore: Genealogical Publishing Co., 1979 (reprint).

Evans, G. N. D. *Allegiance in America: The Case of the Loyalists.* Reading, MA: Addison-Wesley Publishing Co., 1969.

Flick, Alexander Clarence. *Loyalism in New York During the American Revolution.* New York: Columbia University Press, 1901.

Fraser, Alexander. *Second Report of the Bureau of the Archives for the Province of Ontario.* Ottawa, 1904.

Gilroy, Marion (comp.). *Loyalists and Land Settlement in Nova Scotia.* Halifax: Public Archives of Nova Scotia, 1937.

Hancock, Harold Bell. *Delaware Loyalists.* Wilmington: Historical Society of Delaware, 1940.

Harrell, Isaac Samuel. *Loyalism in Virginia.* Durham: Duke University Press, 1926.

Jones, Edward Alfred. *Loyalists in Massachusetts, Their Memorials, Petitions and Claims.* (1930). Baltimore: Genealogical Publishing Co., 1969 (reprint).

———. *Loyalists of New Jersey.* Newark: New Jersey Historical Society, 1927.

Kelby, William. *Orderly Book of the Three Battalions of Loyalists Commanded by Brigadier-General Oliver de Lancey, 1776-1778.* (1917). Baltimore: Genealogical Publishing Co., 1972 (reprint).

New York [State]. *Minutes of the Commissioners for Detecting and Defeating Conspiracies in the State of New York. Albany County Sessions, 1778-1781.* 2 vols. Albany: The State of New York, 1909.

The Old United Empire Loyalist List (reprint of *The Centennial of the Settlement of Upper Canada by the United Empire Loyalists, 1784-1884*). (1885). Baltimore: Genealogical Publishing Co., 1969 (reprint).

Peck, Epaphroditus. *Loyalists of Connecticut.* New Haven: Yale University Press, 1934.

Pringle, J. F. *Lunenburgh or the Old Eastern District.* Cornwall, Ont.: Standard Printing House, 1890.

Raymond, W. O. *Loyalist Transport Ships, 1783.* Saint Johns: New Brunswick Historical Society, 1904.

Reid, William O. *The Loyalists of Ontario: The Sons and Daughters of the American Loyalists of Upper Canada.* Lambertsville, NJ: Hunterdon House, 1973.

Ryerson, Adolphus E. *The Loyalists of America and Their Times: 1620 to 1816.* 2 vols. Toronto: William Briggs, 1880.

Sabine, Lorenzo. *Biographical Sketches of Loyalists of the American Revolution.* 2 vols. (1864). Baltimore: Genealogical Publishing Co., 1979 (reprint).

Siebert, Wilbur Henry. *The American Loyalists in the Eastern Seigniories and Townships of the Province of Quebec.* (Transactions of the Royal Society of Canada.) Ottawa: The Society, 1913.

————. *The Colony of Massachusetts Loyalists at Bristol, England.* Boston: Massachusetts Historical Society, 1912.

————. *The Flight of American Loyalists to the British Isles.* Columbus, OH: F. J. Heer Co., 1911.

————. *The Legacy of the American Revolution to the British West Indies and Bahamas.* Columbus: Ohio State University, 1914.

————. *The Loyalists and Six Nation Indians in the Niagara Peninsula.* (Transactions of the Royal Society of Canada.) Ottawa: The Society, 1916.

————. *Loyalists of East Florida, 1774 to 1785.* 2 vols. DeLand, FL: Florida State Historical Society, 1929.

————. *The Refugee Loyalists of Connecticut.* (Transactions of the Royal Society of Canada.) Ottawa: The Society, 1916.

————. *The Temporary Settlement of Loyalists at Machiche, P.Q.* (Transactions of the Royal Society of Canada.) Ottawa: The Society, 1916.

Singer, Charles G. *South Carolina in the Confederation.* Philadelphia: University of Pennsylvania Press, 1941.

Smith, Paul H. *Loyalists and Redcoats.* Chapel Hill: University of North Carolina Press, 1964.

Starke, James H. *The Loyalists of Massachusetts, and the Other Side of the American Revolution.* Boston: The author, 1910.

————. *The United Empire Loyalists.* (United Empire Loyalist Transactions.) Toronto: The United Empire Loyalists of Canada, 1917.

Stewart, E. Rae. *Jessup's Rangers as a Factor in Loyalist Settlement.* (Three history theses.) Toronto: The Ontario Archives, 1961.

Tyler, John W. *Connecticut Loyalists: An Analysis of Loyalist Land Confiscation in Greenwich, Stamford and Norwalk.* New Orleans: Polyanthos, 1977.

United Empire Loyalists' Association of Canada, Toronto Branch. *Loyalist Lineages of Canada, 1783-1983.* Toronto: Generation Press, 1984.

United Empire Loyalists: Enquiry into the Losses and Services in Consequence of Their Loyalty; Evidence in the Canadian Claim. 2 vols. Toronto: Ontario Archives, 1904-05.

Upton, L. F. S. *The United Empire Loyalists: Men and Myths.* Toronto: Copp Clark Publishing Co., 1967.

Van Tyne, Claude Halstead. *Loyalists in the American Revolution.* New York: Peter Smith, 1929.

Wallace, W. Stewart. *The United Empire Loyalists. A Chronicle of the Great Migration.* (Vol. 13 of *Chronicles of Canada.*) (1914). Toronto: Glasgow, Brook and Co., 1972 (reprint).

Walton, Jesse M. *Quaker Loyalist Settlement, Pennfield, New Brunswick, 1783.* Aurora, Ont.: The author, 1940.

Waugh, John Thomas. *United Empire Loyalists.* Buffalo: University of Buffalo Press, 1925.

Wright, Esther Clark. *Loyalists of New Brunswick.* Fredericton, N.B.: The author, 1955.

Yoshpe, Harry Beller. *Disposition of Loyalist Estates in the Southern District of the State of New York.* New York: Columbia University Press, 1939.

The New York Public Library also has a collection of American Loyalist claims papers. And the New Jersey State Library, Archives and History Department, has records of Loyalists in that state whose estates were confiscated. There is also information on Loyalists from Sussex County, New Jersey, in an article by Thomas B. Wilson entitled "Notes on Some Loyalists of Sussex County, New Jersey," in *The Ontario Register,* Vol. 2, No. 1, 1969, pages 31-47.

A helpful periodical for the use of those interested in Loyalists and their records is the *Loyalist Gazette,* published by the United Empire Loyalists of Canada, 23 Prince Arthur Avenue, Toronto, Ontario. It is a semi-annual publication.

B. Canadian Loyalist Sources

Concerning official Loyalist sources in Canada, I quote from a genealogical booklet prepared by the Public Archives of Canada and published by the Queen's Printer and Controller of Stationery in Ottawa:

> A list of Loyalists in Upper Canada, compiled in the Office of the Commissioner of Crown Lands, and presently kept in the Crown Lands Department in Toronto, records names, contemporary residence and descendants; we [the Public Archives of Canada in Ottawa] have a transcript of this list. A similar list also in our holdings was retained in the Executive Council Office. Comparable lists were not compiled in other colonies.
>
> The Audit Office Series (A.O. 12 and A.O. 13) is perhaps the most rewarding source for the genealogist. The first of these contains evidence in support of Loyalist claims for losses sustained during the American Revolution together with the proceedings of the investigating commission, and the second records the evidence of claimants only. It should be emphasized that by no means all of the Loyalists who suffered losses as a result of adherence to the Crown submitted claims, often because of the considerable expense entailed. These records give location of former residence in the various American colonies, size of families, often the dependents' names, details of military service and residence at the time of the claim . . . These records are on microfilm [at the Public Archives]. The originals are in the Public Record Office, London, England. The Series is completely indexed.
>
> A further source, though one generally listing heads of families with the number of dependents, are the nominal lists and returns of Loyalists in the Haldimand Papers [which list the settlers by township], the originals of which are in the British Museum, in London. We [the Public Archives] have transcript copies of these lists, completely indexed.[14]

---

[14] The Public Archives of Canada, "Tracing Your Ancestors in Canada" (Ottawa: The Queen's Printer and Controller of Stationery, 1967), pp. 17-18. Note that claim records in the Audit Office Series (A.O. 13) are being abstracted in a series being published by the National Genealogical Society, called *American Loyalist Claims*. The first volume (NGS publication no. 45) was compiled by Peter Wilson Coldham and was published in 1980. The work is provided with an index which greatly facilitates its use.

The LDS Family History Library in Salt Lake City also has a microfilm copy of these two Audit Office Series (A.O. 12 and A.O. 13) plus their indexes.

23

Military Records: After the Revolution

I. BETWEEN THE REVOLUTION AND FORT SUMTER

The records arising out of the American Revolution, though they contain less information than some which followed, set a pattern for the records of later wars. And as we look at these other wars we see that there are still essentially just two kinds of records:

A. Service records.
B. Records of veterans' benefits.

For our discussion of the records of wars between the Revolution and the American Civil War let's again divide the records according to these categories rather than by war.

A. Service Records

1. Compiled military service records (similar to those made on 3½″ x 8″ cards for Revolutionary soldiers) exist for those who served during this period. They include the following:

a. *Records for the period between the Revolution and the War of 1812 (called the post-Revolutionary War period).* These records (M905—thirty-two rolls) ordinarily show the soldier's:

> name, rank, and military organization; the dates he was mustered in and out; and where available, the State from which he served.[1]

[1]Meredith B. Colket, Jr., and Frank E. Bridgers, *Guide to Genealogical Records in the National Archives* (Washington, DC: The National Archives, 1964), pp. 53-54.

b. *Records for the War of 1812*. These are compiled military service records dated 1812-15. Most are arranged by state or territory and then by unit. The information is basically the same as in the compiled service records of the post-Revolutionary War period.

c. *Records of Indian and related wars*. These are dated between 1817 and 1857 and, in addition to the Indian wars, include (among others) records of the troops who, under Colonel Albert Sidney Johnston, were sent to Utah in 1857 and 1858 to put down a chimerical rebellion—the so-called "Utah War" or the "Utah Expedition." The information is about the same as in the service records already mentioned except that the state from which the soldier served is not always indicated.

A table showing the microfilmed indexes to the combined service records of volunteers during the various Indian Wars is on page 95 of the *Guide to Genealogical Research in the National Archives*, rev. ed. (Washington, DC: The National Archives, 1983).

d. *Records of the Mexican War, 1846-48*. The records contain all the information included in those of previously-mentioned wars, plus the soldier's age is sometimes given. A name index to these service records is called *Index to Compiled Service Records of Volunteer Soldiers Who Served During the Mexican War* (M616—forty-one rolls).

All of these compiled service records are indexed in their separate series. Each one has a master name index, and each set of records except those of the Mexican War also has indexes to the various states and the non-state organizations from which the men served. This means that it is usually easier to locate a soldier's service record if you know the state from which he served or the organization with which he served. (This information is found in pension-application records if a pension was claimed.)

These compiled service records are all located in Record Group 94, Records of the Adjutant General's Office, in the National Archives.

2. Miscellaneous military records, 1784-1815, are also in this group. These records consist of:

a. *Post-Revolutionary War manuscripts.*
b. *Miscellaneous records of the War of 1812.*
c. *Prisoner-of-war records of the War of 1812.*

The first two groups of records here have master card indexes to all names therein, but the prisoner-of-war records are only partially indexed, and then in separate indexes. There are not a lot of genealogical data in any of these records, and most of the information of value can also be found in other service records. These miscellaneous military records are also in Record Group 94 along with the compiled service records.

3. Naval service records are varied, but are not unlike the army service records, though a little more complete during this early period. The records in the National Archives include:

a. *Records relating to commissioned officers.* In Record Group 45 there are several series of these, among which are:

1) *Register of Officers, May 1815-June 1821.* This listing, which is alphabetical by first letter of surname, gives each officer's name, rank, date of appointment to that rank, age, and the remarks of his superior concerning his promotion potential.

2) *Statements of the Place of Birth of Officers, 1816.* This one manuscript volume includes name, age or date of birth, and place of birth for each officer and is almost exclusively for officers whose surnames begin with the letters "C" and "D."

3) *Statements of the Place of Birth and Residence of Officers, 1826.* Entries are alphabetical in two manuscript volumes (excluding chaplains and pursers) and show the name, state or territory of birth, state or territory from which appointed, and state or territory of which each officer was a citizen.

4) *Records of Officers Serving in 1829.* This is one indexed manuscript volume which outlines the service record of every officer then serving in the Navy.

5) *Statements of Service Written by Officers, 1842-43.* These are two bound manuscripts, largely filled out from memory in response to a questionnaire, outlining the service record of each officer then serving, to the end of 1842. There are two additional manuscript volumes with letters of transmittal and supplemental biographical statements of some officers.

6) *Abstracts of Service of Officers (in Lettered Volumes).* These include all officers who served between 1798 and 1893 (including noncommissioned officers). There are fifteen separate manuscript volumes, A-O, with two of the volumes (J and O) being bound in two separate parts. Each bound manuscript covers a specific period of time. Some are indexed; others are alphabetical. They show for each officer the name, date of appointment, dates of changes in rank and nature of the termination of service (M330—nineteen rolls).

7) *Records of Officers in Numbered Volumes.* These thirty-eight manuscript volumes relate mainly to officers appointed between 1846 and 1902, though there are some later entries. There is a master index and an entry for an individual officer usually gives his name, birth date, birthplace, date of entering duty, ranks held, duty stations, place of residence, death date and place.

8) *Register of Engineer Officers.* This one manuscript volume relates to officers of the Engineer Corps of the Navy from 1843 to

1899. Each entry shows name, date of birth, place of birth, date of appointment, date of death or retirement, place of death, and a detailed service record.

b. *Registers of admissions of midshipmen or cadets.* These registers (also in Record Group 45) relate to those admitted to the U.S. Naval Academy at Annapolis, 1849-1930, and are arranged chronologically by date of appointment. An entry for an appointee gives name, birth date (early registers give age instead), signature, name of parent or guardian, place of residence.

c. *Records of enlisted men.* These records cover enlisted men between 1798 and 1956. The records are extensive.

1) *Muster rolls and pay rolls of vessels.* These cover the period between 1798 and 1844 and are in bound manuscript volumes. They are not indexed, but one volume ordinarily relates to only one vessel for a specific period of time. Some vessels have several volumes. They are arranged alphabetically by the names of the vessels, and each volume is arranged chronologically. Volumes relating to the Frigate *Constitution,* 1798-1815, are indexed. Once you find the person you seek these records often enable you to follow him throughout his naval career, as some entries show the name of the vessel from which a man came or to which he went upon reassignment. If you find your ancestor on the Frigate *Constitution,* or find from other sources such as pension records that he served on a certain vessel, you might trace him through his entire naval service in these rolls. Muster and pay rolls through 1859 are in Record Group 45. Those for 1860-1900 are in Record Group 24. Some are microfilmed.

2) *Muster rolls and pay rolls of shore establishments.* These mainly cover 1805-49 and 1859-69. They are also in bound manuscript volumes. The arrangement is the same as for vessels in number one above and the information and use are also basically the same.

3) *Registers of enlistments.* These are three manuscript volumes covering 1845-54, and the arrangement is alphabetical by the first letter of the surname. Volumes one and two are continuous for 1845 to 1853, and volume three is for 1854 only. These registers are indexed and the index, on microfilm, is incorporated into the *Index to Rendezvous Reports, Before and After the Civil War, 1846-61 and 1865-84* (T1098—thirty-two rolls). Each entry in the register shows name, date of enlistment, place of enlistment, birthplace, and age. There is also a "remarks" column, often containing information on the names of ships and duty stations to which assigned and date of discharge.

4) *Weekly returns of enlistments at naval rendezvous.* These returns cover the period 1855-91 and are bound in volumes chronologically. The entry for each enlistee shows his name, date and term of enlist-

ment, rating, birthplace, age, occupation, personal description, and (sometimes) residence. Reference to any previous naval service is also included. The non-Civil War returns are indexed with the registers in number three above (T1098).

5) *Jackets for enlisted men.* The jackets are alphabetically arranged for the period 1842-55 and normally show name, full service record, and place of residence after service.

6) *Certificates of consent.* This one manuscript volume covers 1838 to 1840 and contains certificates signed by parents or guardians allowing youths between thirteen and eighteen to become naval apprentices and to serve until they were twenty-one. A certificate gives the boy's name, his birth date, and the name of his parent or guardian. There is no index.

4. Marine Corps service records may also have some significance for you. They include:

a. *Records of commissioned officers.*

1) *Letters of acceptance.* These consist of three manuscript volumes dated 1808-62. Volume one is alphabetical by surname and covers 1808-16. The other two volumes cover 1812 to 1862 and are arranged chronologically. Each letter shows name, date commission was accepted, and (after 1830) state or territory of birth, and state or territory from which appointed. Some give place of residence.

2) *Card list of officers.* These alphabetically-arranged cards, covering 1798 to 1941, show name, year of appointment, and rank.

b. *Records of enlisted men.*

1) *Service records.* These records, in individual jackets, cover 1798-1895. They are arranged by year of enlistment, then by first letter of the surname, and then by date of enlistment. There is a group of cards showing name and the date and place of enlistment which serve as an index to these records. The jackets themselves usually contain information relating to name, date of enlistment, place, term of enlistment, age, personal description, occupation, and sometimes date and circumstances of separation from the Marine Corps.

2) *Card list of enlisted men.* These records cover 1798 to 1941 and are the cards mentioned in number one which serve as an index thereto.[2]

5. There are also books available which contain rolls and rosters and biographical information of servicemen during this period between the

[2] All preceding information on service records between the Revolution and the Civil War is from Colket and Bridgers, pp. 65-76, and from *Guide to Genealogical Research in the National Archives,* pp. 89-95 and 111-119.

Revolution and the Civil War. Many libraries have good collections. I refer you to the bibliography at the end of this chapter. You should also refer to the bibliography in chapter 22. Some of the books listed there relate to this period of military history as well as to the Revolution.

B. Veterans' Benefits

1. There are four series of pension records which deal with those who served between the Revolution and the Civil War and, depending on the time or war of your ancestor's service, you may be interested in one or more of them.

a. *The "Old Wars" (or "Old War") Series* relates to death and disability claims for service during this entire period under various Congressional acts (the first in 1790). The claims concern service in the regular army, navy, or Marine Corps during the War of 1812, Mexican War, Indian wars, and in some cases the Civil War. The files have been arranged alphabetically, and there is also an index on microfilm to the entire series, 1815-1926 (T316—seven rolls). The pension files contain information on:

> name, rank, military or naval unit, and period of service of the veteran. If he applied for a pension, it shows his age or date of birth, place of residence, and sometimes place of birth. If the widow applied, it shows her age and the place of her marriage to the veteran; and her maiden name. If the veteran left orphans, it shows their names, ages, and the places of their residence.[3]

b. *The War of 1812 Series* contains papers for claims based on service between 1812 and 1815, primarily granted under acts passed in 1871 and 1878.[4] The files are arranged alphabetically.

Interfiled with these pension papers at the National Archives is a sub-series relating to death and disability claims which was previously a part of the "Old Wars" Series, plus some War of 1812 bounty-land warrant applications from the post-Revolutionary War series. These additions increase the value of the files tremendously because the records of many more soldiers are thus included, and the added records originated soon after the war.

Regarding the information in these War of 1812 pension files, Colket and Bridgers tell us:

---

[3] Colket and Bridgers, p. 82.

[4] The fact that service pension acts were not passed until so long after the war is one of the chief shortcomings of these records. Relatively few servicemen, and even few widows, lived that long.

A veteran's declaration shows the name, age, and place of residence of the veteran; if married, the maiden name of his wife; the place and date of their marriage; his rank; his military or naval unit; the date and place of his entering the service; and date and place of his discharge. A widow's declaration shows the name, age, and place of residence of the widow; the date and place of their marriage, with the name of the official who performed the ceremony, the date and place of the veteran's death; his rank; his military or naval unit; the date and place of his entering the service; and the date and place of his discharge.[5]

c. *The Mexican War Series* is the result of an act of Congress in 1887 and is based on service performed between 1846 and 1848. Pensions were available to veterans who served sixty days and to their widows who were not remarried. A few of the death and disability files from the "Old Wars" Series are now included among the files of this series. Several different documents are included in the files, though each pensioner's file will not contain all of them. The files are now arranged alphabetically and there is also a master index on microfilm, *Index to Mexican War Pension Files, 1887-1926* (T317—fourteen rolls). Information in these files is as follows:

A veteran's declaration shows the name of the veteran; the dates and places of his birth, his enlistment, and his discharge; and the places of his residence since service. The declaration of a widow seeking a pension shows the same information about the service of the veteran; her name, age, and place of residence; the date and place of her marriage to the veteran, with the name of the person performing the ceremony; and the date and place of the death of the veteran. A filled-out questionnaire shows the maiden name of the wife; the date and place of the marriage of the couple and name of the person performing the ceremony; the name of a former wife, if any, and the date and place of her death or divorce; and the names and dates of birth of living children.[6]

d. *The Indian Wars Series* resulted from an act of Congress passed in 1892 and other, later acts. The first act provided service pensions to veterans of wars between 1832 and 1834 and their widows, if not remarried. Later acts extended the benefits to all who served in Indian wars between 1817 and 1898. There are also some files in this series which were formerly filed with the "Old Wars" Series. The files are arranged alphabetically, but there is also a microfilm index to this series

---

[5] *Ibid*, pp. 82-83.

[6] *Ibid.*, p. 83.

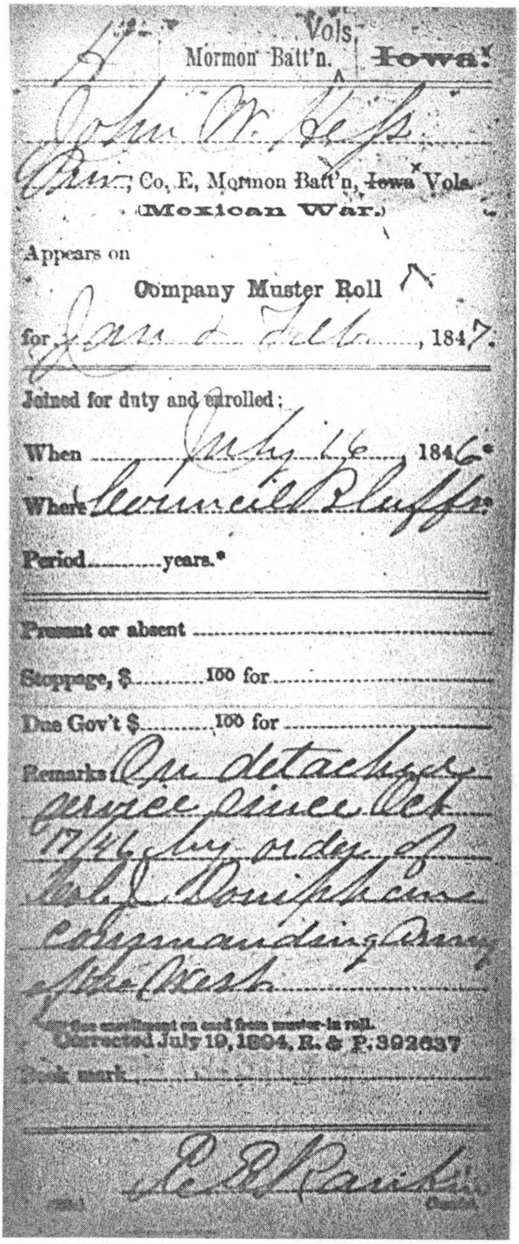

H | Mormon Batt'n. | ~~Iowa~~ Vols.

John W. Hess

Priv., Co. E, Mormon Batt'n, ~~Iowa~~ Vols.

(Mexican War.)

Appears on

Company Muster Roll

for Jan & Feb, 1847.

Joined for duty and enrolled:

When July 16, 1846.

Where Council Bluffs.

Period .... years.*

Present or absent ....

Stoppage, $........100 for ....

Due Gov't $........100 for ....

Remarks On detached service since Oct 17/46 by order of Col. Doniphan commanding Army of the West

Corrected July 19, 1894, R. & P. 392637

Book mark ....

FIGURE 1—MUSTER ROLL NOTATION FROM THE COMPILED SERVICE RECORDS OF THE MEXICAN WAR

at the National Archives, *Index to Indian Wars Pension Files, 1892-1926* (T318—twelve rolls).

> The information in the files varies depending upon the act under which the pension was applied for, the number of years of the veteran's survival after the war, and whether or not he was survived by a widow. A file contains some or all of the following information: the name, Army unit, and place of residence of the veteran; a summary of his Army record; his age or the date of his birth; the place of his birth; date and place of his marriage; the date and place of his death; and the names of their surviving children, with the date and place of birth of each.[7]

Access to *some* files in all four of these pension series can be obtained through the use of the first part of the *Remarried Widows Index*. This index is in two parts, one part relating to non-Revolutionary War claims prior to the Civil War and the other part relating to the Civil War and all later military service up to World War I. The index is alphabetical by the names of the remarried widows. The name of the former husband is indicated plus his service unit and the file or certificate number.

As with Revolutionary War pension application files, copies of these pension application files can also be ordered by mail. NATF Form 80 is used for this purpose. (See the illustration of this form [Figure 3] in chapter 22.)

2. Bounty-land warrant applications for service after the Revolutionary War are all filed together in one series, except that the War of 1812 applications were interfiled with the pension claims relating to that same war as noted earlier. The files are much like the bounty-land application files for the Revolutionary War—many in fact were granted as a result of the same legislation. They are merely filed in separate series. All files in this series are arranged alphabetically by the names of the veterans and there is no index.

The information in a bounty-land application file usually includes:

> name, age, residence, rank, military or naval unit, and period of service of the veteran, and sometimes his personal description. If the applicant was an heir it shows such information as the date and place of death of the veteran, the name of the heir or heirs, and the degree of relationship. If the application was approved it also shows the number of the warrant, the number of acres granted, and the year of the act under which the warrant was granted.[8]

---

[7] *Ibid.*, p. 85.

[8] *Ibid.*, p. 93.

Both the pension application files and the bounty-land application files are in Record Group 15, Records of the Veterans Administration, at the National Archives. Copies of these records and the compiled service records can be secured by the process which we described earlier in connection with records of Revolutionary service. You can use NATF Form 80 to acquire a copy of the file, if you desire, after requesting a price quotation. You should also note that much of the information given in pension and bounty-land applications is the very information you will need to locate a copy of a soldier's service record. The last bounty land act passed by Congress in 1855 authorized issuance of warrants for 160 acres to those who had served for at least fourteen days or in a battle.

II. THE CIVIL WAR, 1861-65

You have probably already noticed that military records are quite typical of most genealogical sources in that the later ones are better than the earlier ones. This fact holding true, records of the Civil War are better than those of any of the wars we have thus far discussed. Still, they are appropriately divided into the same two types:

A. Service records.
B. Records of veterans' benefits.

A. Service Records

Colket and Bridgers describe the Union Army service records:

> The compiled military service records of the Union forces of the Civil War . . . consist of card abstracts and documents relating to individual soldiers, such as voluntary enlistment papers, prisoner-of-war papers, hospital bed cards, and death reports. The cards and sometimes the documents relating to one soldier are filed in a jacket-envelope. The jacket-envelopes for men in State organizations are arranged by name of State; thereunder by arm of service such as cavalry, artillery, infantry; thereunder numerically by regiment; thereunder alphabetically by name of soldier. The jacket-envelopes for men in other organizations such as the U.S. Sharp Shooters are arranged similarly. Many of the documents relating to individual soldiers in State organizations are not filed in the jacket-envelopes with the related card abstracts but are filed separately in alphabetical order at the end of the file for the State. Some jacket-envelopes include cross-references to the names on the regimental papers that are filed with the muster rolls.

> In addition to these basic files there is a separate file of card abstracts pertaining to both volunteer and Regular Army staff officers, which is arranged alphabetically by name of officer.[9]

There is no master index to these Civil War service records, but rather a separate name index for each state and for each organization not connected with a specific state. This means that in order to locate the service record of your Union Army ancestor you must know the state or the organization with which he served. A table giving the microfilm publication numbers for both the indexes and the compiled service records—state-by-state—is on page 97 of the *Guide to Genealogical Research in the National Archives*. The records of many states have not yet been filmed.

These service records contain the same information on each soldier as do the compiled service records of the earlier wars, plus

> the date of a change in his rank, and the date, place, and nature of his discharge. For some soldiers there is a voluntary enlistment paper or an abstract that shows his age, the town or county of his birth, his occupation, and a personal description. If the soldier was hospitalized, a bed card shows his age, nativity, evidence of whether or not he was married, his place of residence, and the date and occasion of his being wounded. If he died in service, a casualty sheet shows the date and place of his death.[10]

Other records relating to Union Army service are as follows:

1. Service histories of volunteer units. At the same time that service records for the individual Union Army soldiers were compiled, the War Department compiled service histories of volunteer units. These have been microfilmed as *Compiled Records Showing Service of Military Units in Volunteer Union Organizations* (M594—225 rolls).

2. Civil War draft records. There were three classes of CONSOLIDATED LISTS made as a result of an act passed by Congress in March 1863. These three included:

a. Persons subject to military duty between the ages of 20 and 35 years and unmarried persons above the age of 35 years and under the age of 45 subject to military duty.

b. Married men aged above 35 and under 45.

c. Volunteers.

---

[9] *Ibid.*, p. 55.

[10] *Ibid.*, p. 56.

Entries in each class are arranged in alphabetical order by the first letter of the surname within the various states and Congressional districts. Information relating to each man listed on these records includes:

> name; place of residence; age on 1 July 1863; occupation; marital status; state, territory, or country of birth; and, if a volunteer, in what military organizations he served.[11]

There are also some DESCRIPTIVE ROLLS of varying formats and arrangements for each of the enrollment districts. They contain much good information but, as with the consolidated lists, you must know the Congressional district in which a man lived in order to find him. The descriptive rolls contain the same information as the consolidated lists, plus:

> physical description, place of birth, and whether accepted or rejected for military service. The entries in many volumes, however, are not complete.[12]

If you know the county in which he lived, you can determine the Congressional district by checking the *Congressional Directory for the Second Session of the Thirty-Eighth Congress of the United States of America* (Washington, DC, 1865). A photocopy of this directory is in the National Archives central search room. The National Archives also has available a list of Civil War districts which gives, for each state, the names of the counties in each district. National Archives personnel, Military Archives Division, will determine the Congressional district and search the draft records for you if you know the county where the person was living, or the ward of the city if he was living in a large city.

3. Burial records of soldiers. Most of the burials in these records (in fact almost all of them) relate to soldiers buried at U.S. military installations. There are four volumes relating to burials in the U.S. Soldiers' Home in Washington, D.C., 1861-68, and they are indexed. There is a checklist of installations included, and most of the registers are arranged alphabetically by the name of the installation.

> The arrangement, inclusive dates, and contents of the burial registers vary considerably. As a minimum they show for each soldier his name, his military organization, and the date and place of his burial. The registers for the U.S. Soldiers' Home also show the soldier's rank; the town, county, and State of residence before enlistment; the

---

[11] *Guide to Genealogical Research in the National Archives,* p. 99.

[12] *Ibid.*, p. 99.

name and residence of his widow, relative, or friend; his age; his nativity; the cause, date, and place of death; the date of his burial; and, sometimes, the place of his burial.[13]

Some compiled lists of Union Soldiers buried at the U.S. Soldiers' Home, 1861-1918, give the name, military organization, date of death, and place of burial of each soldier. There is a separate set of lists for each state from which the soldiers originated.

There are also some lists of soldiers buried in national cemeteries, mainly between 1861 and 1865 (some as late as 1886). These lists give the same information as the lists of soldiers buried at the U.S. Soldiers' Home mentioned above.

4. Headstone applications. Between the years 1879 and 1925 the federal government, by an act of Congress, erected headstones on the graves of Union servicemen, regardless of place of burial. (Other acts provided for headstones on the graves of those who served in the Revolutionary and other wars.) The applications for these markers are arranged chronologically by state and county of burial, and there is a card index to applications filed between 1879 and 1903. Each application tells name, rank, military organization, date of death, cemetery of interment and its location, and name and address of applicant.

At the National Archives Field Branch in Alexandria, Virginia, there are some later applications, including those for headstones for Confederate soldiers, as per act of 1929.

5. Naval service records.

a. *Age certificates of officers (both naval and marine).* These records were made as a result of an act approved by Congress in December 1861 relating to retirement. They are for 1862 and 1863, are arranged alphabetically and are also indexed. Each certificate shows name, rank, and birth date, and is signed by the officer.

b. *Biographies of officers.* There are three indexed manuscript volumes of these. They were prepared about 1865 and contain much good, detailed information (though actual detail and content vary considerably). Their chief shortcoming is that they are very incomplete in their coverage.

c. *Records of appointees, 1862-1910, to the U.S. Naval Academy.* These records are filed numerically in individual jacket-envelopes. They also include the applications of those who applied but were not accepted.

---

[13] Colket and Bridgers, pp. 61-62. See also *ibid.*, pp. 144-145.

Though these records are in the National Archives, an index is located at the Bureau of Naval Personnel in Washington. A jacket normally contains information on the applicant's:

> name, his place of residence, the name of his father and, where appropriate, the date of his appointment and the date of his commission as ensign.[14]

d. *Weekly returns of enlistments at naval rendezvous.* These are as they were described under naval service records of the pre-Civil War period. However, there is a separate microfilm index relating to Civil War service (T1098).

In addition to the records listed here, there are also many records relating to service during the pre-Civil War period which overlap into the Civil War era and even later. They were discussed earlier in the chapter.

B. Veterans' Benefits

Veterans' benefits for those who served in the Civil War are almost exclusively pensions. As mentioned in chapter 16 in the discussion of land entry records in the public domain, there were no bounty land warrants issued for service in the Civil War. Insofar as land is concerned, Civil War veterans (both Union and Confederate) were given special consideration in Homestead legislation.

All pension applications relating to service between 1861 and 1934 are filed in one series, excluding World War I and certain Indian wars already discussed.[15] This series of pension applications is called the "Civil War and Later" Series and, in addition to Union Army Civil War pensioners, it includes pension applications relating to service in the Spanish-American War, the Philippine Insurrection, the Boxer Rebellion, and the Regular Army. Both death/disability pensions and service pensions are included in this one series. As mentioned earlier, a few naval death and disability pensions from the first part of the Civil War are also included in the "Old Wars" Series.

The information and the documents in the files vary tremendously, depending upon the act of Congress under which the applicant sought relief, as well as other factors. An applicant's file will contain some or all of the following information:

---

[14] *Ibid.*, p. 70.

[15] Note that if the "Indian Wars" Series fails to disclose a pension application for a veteran of one of the later Indian wars, a search of the "Civil War and Later" Series is recommended.

> [The applicant's] name, military or naval unit, and place of residence . . . ; a summary of his military or naval record; his age or the date of his birth; place of his birth; date and place of his marriage; date and place of his death; the maiden name of his wife; the date of her death; and the names of their surviving children with the date and place of birth of each.[16]

There are two indexes to these files—an alphabetical name index (name of veteran), and an organization index for use if you know the state and the organization in which the soldier served.[17] There are definite advantages in the latter if you have the necessary information to use it. The "Veterans' Schedules" of the 1890 census can be of considerable assistance here. (See chapter 11.) Also remember that access to *some* of these files can be had through use of the second part of the *Remarried Widows Index* discussed earlier in this chapter.

Copies of Union Army service and pension files can be obtained from the National Archives through use of NATF Form 80, as discussed in chapter 22. (For a price quotation write to the Archivist, Civil War Branch, National Archives.)

C. The Other Side of the War: The Confederacy

As the Confederate troops evacuated Richmond in 1865, the Confederate military records were taken to Charlotte, North Carolina, by the adjutant and inspector general, who transferred them to a Union officer. The records were taken from there to Washington, D.C., along with various records that had been captured from the Confederates during the war. In 1903, the Secretary of War, who had custody of the records, persuaded the governors of most of the Southern states to lend the War Department their military personnel records for copying. All of these records now comprise a goodly portion of the War Department Collection of Confederate Records, Record Group 109.[18]

Records for Confederate forces are not as good as the records of Union Army troops, but there are some records and you should be aware of them. There are three series in the National Archives of COMPILED MILITARY SERVICE RECORDS of Confederate troops. (All of these have also been micro-

[16] Colket and Bridgers, p. 85.

[17] The alphabetical index is called *General Index to Pension Files, 1861-1934* (T288—544 rolls). The organization index is called *Organization Index to Pension Files of Veterans Who Served Between 1861 and 1900* (T259—765 rolls).

[18] *Guide to Genealogical Research in the National Archives*, pp. 100-101.

filmed.) These records were compiled on cards by the War Department from various records, including prison and parole records, muster rolls, returns, rosters, pay rolls, appointment books, and hospital registers. All cards relating to the same individual soldier are generally in the same jacket-envelope. The three series are:

1. Those filed by state. (This is the largest series—by far.)
2. Those for troops who served in non-state organizations.
3. Those for officers and enlisted personnel doing their jobs.

There is a consolidated alphabetical name index (M253—535 rolls) as well as an index for each of the states. All have been microfilmed. The information in these records is not extensive. Table 14 on page 102 of the *Guide to Genealogical Research in the National Archives* gives the microfilm publication numbers for both the indexes and the compiled service records. Colket and Bridgers describe the records as follows:

> A jacket-envelope shows the name of the soldier, the name of the State from which he served, the name of the company and regiment, and his rank. The cards and papers in the envelope show other information, such as the dates of changes in the soldier's rank, the date and place of his enlistment and discharge, his occupation, and his personal description. If the soldier was captured, they may show the date of his death, if it occurred in camp, or the date of his release and parole. References to the original records are included on the cards.[19]

There are also various *minor* records in the National Archives, including some "Citizens Files" and some "Amnesty and Pardon Records" which mainly give information on places of residence.

These Confederate records in the National Archives are likewise available through the use of NATF Form 80, and you should also be aware that the individual Southern states provided pensions for veterans who served under the "Stars and Bars" and that records of these are available from those states. Inquiries regarding such pensions should be addressed to the appropriate state depositories and custodians. These include the following:

ALABAMA: The Alabama Department of Archives and History, Montgomery.

ARKANSAS: Arkansas History Commission, Old State House, Little Rock.

---

[19] Colket and Bridgers, p. 99.

FLORIDA:	State Board of Pensions Office, Tallahassee. (These are also on film at the LDS Family History Library.)
GEORGIA:	Confederate Pension and Record Department, State Capitol, Atlanta.
LOUISIANA:	Office of Supervisor of Confederate Pensions, State Department of Public Welfare, Baton Rouge.
MISSISSIPPI:	The Mississippi Department of Archives and History, Jackson.
NORTH CAROLINA:	The North Carolina Department of Archives and History, Raleigh.
SOUTH CAROLINA:	The South Carolina Department of Archives and History, World War Memorial Building, Columbia.
TENNESSEE:	Tennessee State Library and Archives, Nashville.
TEXAS:	Comptroller Public Accounts, Austin.
VIRGINIA:	Pension Clerk, Department of Accounts and Purchases, Richmond.

III. AFTER APPOMATTOX

The Civil War ended with General Lee's surrender at Appomattox Courthouse in April 1865, but this did not end the United States' involvement in war. However, most of the wars have been in quite recent times so not too many records are readily available. In fact, there are restrictions on modern service records. But let's take a quick peek at some of the records which are available (and a few which are not) that you ought to know about.

Not including the skirmishes with the Indians already discussed, perhaps the major military and naval confrontations during the period prior to World War I had to do with America's encounters with Spain—the Spanish-American War (1898-99) and the Philippine Insurrection (1899-1901). The Puerto Rico Regiment of U.S. Volunteers (1899-1901) is included. There are compiled service records (separate) for those who served in these wars and in the Puerto Rico Regiment which contain:

> such information as the name, rank, and military organization of each soldier; the dates and places that he was mustered in and out; his place of residence; his occupation; and, if single, the name and address of a parent or guardian.[20]

[20] *Ibid.*, p. 58.

There is a master name index to the service records of the Spanish-American War (and the Puerto Rico Regiment) as well as an index for each state's volunteer organizations and federal volunteer organizations. There is a master index, but no state or organizational index, to service records of the Philippine Insurrection.

As already mentioned, pension records for these wars are included in the "Civil War and Later" Series. All of these records are in the National Archives, Record Group 94, Records of the Adjutant General's Office.

The Boxer Rebellion in China in 1900 brought out 5,000 American troops, but no special or separate service records have been compiled for these men. Records of this service are included among the records of the regular army discussed later in this chapter.

Many of the various records which relate to service in earlier periods overlap into this post-Civil War period, as you may have already noted; but there are a few other records in the National Archives coming exclusively out of this period which deserve mention:

1. *Quarterly Returns of Naval Enlistment on Vessels, 1866-91,* are bound in a chronological arrangement in the National Archives. There are forty-three volumes. Those between 1866 and 1884 are indexed with the Weekly Returns of Enlistments at Naval Rendezvous mentioned earlier.

> Most entries show, under the name of the vessel, the name of the enlisted man, date and term of enlistment, rating, a reference to any previous naval service, place of birth, age, occupation, and personal description. Some entries show place of residence.[21]

2. *Naval Apprenticeship Papers, 1864-1889,* are alphabetically arranged (first two letters of surname) as part of Record Group 24, Records of the Bureau of Naval Personnel, at the National Archives. These are forms filled out by the parents of thirteen- to eighteen-year-old youths being placed in naval apprenticeship. Each paper shows name; place of service; date entering service; name of parent or guardian; residence of parent or guardian; apprentice's birth date and birthplace; and name, residence and relationship of parent or guardian. Between 1864 and 1869 there are also testimonials of character.[22]

3. *A Register of Naval Apprentices, 1864-1875,* is indexed and has to do with apprentices who served on the training ships *Sabine, Portsmouth,* and *Saratoga.* An entry in the register gives name, birth date, birthplace, date

[21] *Guide to Genealogical Research in the National Archives,* p. 114.

[22] *Ibid.,* p. 115.

and place of enlistment, name of parent or guardian, and date of leaving the service. This single register is also a part of Record Group 24, Records of the Bureau of Naval Personnel. It is indexed by the first letter of the surname.[23]

4. *A Register of Living and Retired Marine Corps Officers, 1899-1904,* relates chiefly to those who served in the Spanish-American War. It is indexed and gives name, birth date and place, state from which appointed, and service records from 1899 to 1904. This register is in Record Group 127.[24]

If a soldier happened to spend time in a home for soldiers there is another possibility of finding information about him. There are branches of the National Home for Disabled Volunteer Soldiers in Togus (near Augusta), Maine; Dayton, Ohio; Wood (near Milwaukee), Wisconsin; Kecoughtan (near Hampton), Virginia; Leavenworth, Kansas; Sawtelle (near Los Angeles), California; Roseburg, Oregon; Marion, Indiana; Danville, Illinois; Mountain Home (near Johnson City), Tennessee; Hot Springs, South Dakota; and Bath, New York, with records at the National Archives for some of these beginning in the last half of the 1860s and going as late as 1934. There is a historical register for each branch, and all are indexed. One page in a register is devoted to each patient. The *Guide to Genealogical Research in the National Archives* describes that page and its contents:

> Each page of the register is divided into four sections: *military history, domestic history, home history, and general remarks.* The veteran's *military history* gives the time and place of each enlistment, rank, company and regiment, time and place of discharge, reason for discharge, and nature of disabilities when admitted to the home. The *domestic history* gives birthplace, age, height, various physical features, religion, occupation, residence, marital status, and name and address of nearest relative. The *home history* gives the rate of the pension, date of admission, conditions of readmission, date of discharge, cause of discharge, date and cause of death, and place of burial. Under *general remarks* is information about papers relating to the veteran, such as admission paper, army discharge certificate, and pension certificate; information also was entered about money and personal effects if the member died while in residence at the branch. [Emphasis added.] [25]

---

[23] *Ibid.*, p. 115.

[24] *Ibid.*, p. 116.

[25] *Ibid.*, p. 143.

These are part of the Records of the Veterans Administration, Record Group 15. Records of the homes in Biloxi, Mississippi; St. Petersburg, Florida; and Tuskegee, Alabama, are not available at the National Archives.

Among other significant records, there are also records in the National Archives relating to inmates of the United States Soldiers' and Airmen's Home from 1851. The home is located in Washington, D.C.

> Records of greatest genealogical value in Records of the U.S. Soldiers' Home, Record Group 231, consist of general and monthly registers of members, hospital records, and death records. To use the records, the researcher must know which home the subject of research lived in [Note that in addition to the home in Washington three temporary homes were established by Congress in East Pascagoula (also called Greenwood Island), Mississippi; New Orleans, Louisiana; and Harrodsburg, Kentucky (Western Military Asylum). The National Home in Washington was also originally called the Washington Asylum before 1859.] and the approximate date of admission, hospital treatment, or death.[26]

Records for the U.S. Soldiers' Home include hospital records, 1872-1943; death records, including registers (1852-1942) and certificates (1876-89 and 1913-29); and case files for deceased members, 1880-1942.

IV. THE REGULAR ARMY OR REGULAR ESTABLISHMENT

The military records discussed thus far have dealt mainly with those who enlisted or were drafted into service in the various wars. However, throughout U.S. history there have been men who have enlisted in the service without regard to whether there was a war. Many of these men were professional soldiers. Early records of the regular army are fragmentary but they do exist. There are muster rolls covering the period between 1791 and 1912 and registers of enlistments, 1784-1914, in addition to special records for those who had officers' commissions. Of all these papers, the enlistment papers and registers of enlistments contain the most genealogical data. The enlistment papers are in jacket-envelopes and are filed alphabetically, for the most part, in three separate series (1784-1815; 1798-1894; 1894-1912) at the National Archives.

These enlistment papers are similar to what the military now calls the soldier's "personnel file," and they usually give:

---

[26] *Ibid.*, pp. 143-144.

> the soldier's name, place of enlistment, date, by whom enlisted, age, occupation, personal description, regimental assignment, and certification of examining surgeon and recruiting officer. The papers relating to enlistments after 15 July 1894 include description and assignment cards, prior service cards, certificates of disability, final statements, inventories of effects, and records of death and interment, if appropriate.[27]

Enlistment registers are also at the National Archives for the period between 1798 and 1913. They are arranged more or less alphabetically. Each entry relates to a single enlistment, but the entries vary in their detail, some prior to 1815 being quite abbreviated.

> The register entries for the period 1798–30 June 1821 contain soldier's name, military organization, physical description, date and place of birth, enlistment information, and remarks. Entries in the remarks column contain cryptic references to the source record from which the information was obtained. A partial key to the references, generally a two-initial abbreviation of the title of the original record, appears in volume one of the enlistment registers. The source documents cannot now be identified in all cases. Complete service information is not given for every soldier; in particular, the date or reason for termination of service may not be supplied.
>
> The registers for the period 1 July 1821–1913 are uniform in content. A two-page entry contains the same information that appears on the enlistment paper, as well as information relating to the termination of service. The left-hand page gives the enlisted man's name; date and place of enlistment; by whom enlisted; period of enlistment; place of birth; age; civilian occupation at the time of enlistment; and personal description.
>
> The right-hand page gives the number and arm of service, company, and information relating to separation from service. If the individual was discharged, the date, place, and reason for discharge are given, as well as rank. Varying additional information, such as on courts-martial or desertions, appears in the remarks column. For the period 1821-1913, the remarks column does not show the source of the information. The enlistment information was copied from the enlistment papers; the termination information came from muster rolls and other records.[28]

Pension files for soldiers in the Regular Establishment are filed in the National Archives with the pensions of the other series.

---

[27] *Ibid.*, p. 80.

[28] *Ibid.*, pp. 80-81.

V. WORLD WAR I

The release of information from service records and pension records for those who served in World War I and later wars is governed by the Freedom of Information Act of 1967 (as amended in 1974) and the Privacy Act of 1974. At present, you can obtain access to information in the World War I Selective Service (draft) records if you know the address at which your ancestor lived at the time he registered. This address is essential for determining the Selective Service board. This is mainly a problem in larger towns where there might have been more than one draft board, and city directories can frequently help you find the solution. These draft records are located in the National Archives Field Branch, 1557 St. Joseph Avenue, East Point, Georgia 30044. They are part of Records of the Selective Service System (World War I), Record Group 163. These include mainly draft registration cards, docket books, and classification lists. Draft registration records contain:

> information supplied by each registrant, including name, address, date of birth, age, race, citizenship status, birthplace, occupation and employer, dependent relative, marital status, father's birthplace, and name and address of nearest relative. They are arranged alphabetically by state, thereunder by local board, and thereunder by individual registrant.[29]

If you need additional information on men in the Armed Forces during periods later than the dates of the records in the National Archives, take note of the following address:

National Personnel Record Center (Military Records)
NARA
9700 Page Boulevard
St. Louis, Missouri 63132

Most information of a personal nature may be furnished only with the written consent of the veteran or, if the veteran is deceased, his next of kin. Further details about the release of information from these records is given on Standard Form 180 or may be obtained from the St. Louis Center.

VI. MILITARY RECORDS IN THE STATES

In addition to the military records already discussed, many states have collections of records of soldiers who served from them. Very often state

---

[29] *Ibid.*, p. 106.

militia and other state-troop records are useful genealogical tools, and the state's Adjutant General or other record custodian can be a great benefactor to your genealogical cause. You should use these records as well as any books which might be published about the military men and military history of the states. Many of these records have been published in genealogical periodicals and many others have been microfilmed. If you have access to the LDS Family History Library's collections, check its holdings very carefully for the states of your interest.

You should also be aware of the existence of records relating to civilians during wartime. A summary of such records found in the National Archives is in chapter 10 of *Guide to Genealogical Research in the National Archives,* pages 149-156.

VII. PRINTED MILITARY SOURCES

There are several books relating to those who have served in the armed forces of this country since the Revolution. It would be impossible to name all such sources here, especially since most of them relate to servicemen from specific geographic areas. However, a brief bibliography follows:

Blakeney, Jane V. *Heroes, U.S. Marine Corps, 1861-1955; Armed Forces Awards, Flags.* 1st ed. Washington, DC: Blakeney Publishers, 1957.

Boatner, Mark Mayo. *The Civil War Dictionary.* New York: David McKay Co., 1959.

Cullum, George Washington. *Biographical Register of the Officers and Graduates of the U.S. Military Academy at West Point, NY, From Its Establishment, in 1802, to 1890; With the Early History of the United States Military Academy.* 3 vols. 3rd ed. Boston: Houghton, Mifflin Co., 1891.

Hamersly, Lewis Randolph. *The Records of Living Officers of the U.S. Navy and Marine Corps.* 7th ed. rev. New York: L. R. Hamersly, 1902.

Moore, Frank (ed.). *The Portrait Gallery of the War, Civil, Military, and Naval; A Biographical Record.* New York: G. P. Putnam for Derby and Miller, 1864.

Officers of the Army and Navy (Regular and Volunteer) Who Served in the Civil War. Philadelphia: L. R. Hamersly, 1894.

Powell, William Henry. *List of Officers of the Army of the United States from 1779-1900, Embracing a Register of All Appointments in the Volunteer Service During the Civil War and of Volunteer Officers in the Service of the United States, June 1, 1900. Compiled from the Official Records.* (1900). Detroit: Gale Research Co., 1967 (reprint).

————. *Records of Living Officers of the United States Army.* Philadelphia: L. R. Hamersly, 1890.

————. *Officers of the Army and Navy (Volunteer) Who Served in the Civil War.* Philadelphia: L. R. Hamersly, 1893.

———— and Edward Shippin (eds.). *Officers of the Army and Navy (Regular) Who Served in the Civil War.* Philadelphia: L. R. Hamersly, 1892.

Schuon, Karl. *U.S. Marine Corps Biographical Dictionary; the Corps' Fighting Men, What They Did, Where They Served.* New York: Franklin Watts, Inc., 1963.

————. *U. S. Navy Biographical Dictionary.* New York: Franklin Watts, Inc., 1965.

Simmons, Henry Eugene. *A Concise Encyclopedia of the Civil War.* New York: A. S. Barnes and Co., 1965.

United States. Adjutant General's Office. *Official Army Register.* Washington: U.S. Government Printing Office, 1802—. The title varies somewhat over the years: *Register of the Army of the United States; The Army Register of the United States; Army Register; Official Army and Air Force Register.*

United States, Bureau of Naval Personnel. *Register of Commissioned and Warrant Officers of the United States Navy and Marine Corps.* Washington: U.S. Government Printing Office, 1814—.

United States Naval Academy, Annapolis. Alumni Association. *Register of Alumni, Graduates and Former Naval Cadets and Midshipmen.* Annapolis: United States Naval Academy, 1886—. The title varies somewhat over the years: *Annual Reunion; Annual Reunion and Register of Graduates; Register of Graduates.*

Refer also to the bibliographies in chapter 22. Some of the works listed there relate to post-Revolutionary servicemen and military history as well as to those of the earlier periods.

VIII. WHEN TO USE MILITARY RECORDS

Chapter 22 discussed some circumstances to which you need to be sensitive in relation to the use of Revolutionary War records. The same basic principles apply to the use of all American military records. If your ancestor lived at a time when he could have served in a war or if any close relatives of his (or hers) could have served in a war, you must consider a search of military records as a simple research necessity. Do not wait until you find a clue that your ancestor had military experience; just go ahead and make your search in the records of the appropriate war.

However, any clues you have can be helpful because they can help you zero-in on your target with greater accuracy. I have mentioned many times the increased usability of military records when you have specific data on the organization to which your ancestor belonged, or at least the state from which he served. Such clues can be found in various places—family records, old letters, Bibles, tombstones, obituaries, local histories, church records, vital records (especially death certificates), etc., are all likely sources. You *must* know the state to use Civil War service records.

There is no specific time during a search when military records should be used—this varies from problem to problem—but usually they are one of the first sources to consider once you begin research on an individual who may have had military service or may have been closely related to someone else who did. This is because the information found in military records is often of such a nature that it facilitates the use of other sources and suggests new possibilities.

IX. CONCLUSION

In concluding this discussion of military records, let me restate the basic fact which makes the use of these records so important: Wars have been an integral part of American history and, as such, have produced indispensable genealogical records of literally millions of persons. These are records which not only hold the key to successfully extending many pedigrees, but also contain valuable family history information that helps you see your ancestors as the real persons they were and not just as names on a pedigree chart.

Study carefully the *Guide to Genealogical Research in the National Archives* in addition to what you have read in these last two chapters. Section B (chapters 4-9) of that book holds a vast store of information about military records as a genealogical and family history source. The National Archives has also published a little pamphlet entitled *Military Service Records in the National Archives of the United States* (General Information Leaflet F, rev. ed., 1985) that you may find helpful.

24

Cemetery and Burial Records

I. BACKGROUND

Many inexperienced genealogists get the idea that if they have found a death certificate or an obituary or a church register entry of a burial they have found all the important information arising out of a death. They are sometimes right, but there are occasions when it is a serious mistake to overlook the tombstone or other cemetery record.

This situation reminds me of a cartoon I saw showing a junior executive standing before his boss's desk receiving the following bit of wisdom: "We've never doubted your ambition and drive and self-discipline, Higgins. It's your lack of ability that concerns us." [1] Perhaps it would be appropriate to say that cemetery and burial records are to death certificates, obituaries, and church burial registers what ability is to ambition, drive, and self-discipline. Without them something significant is missing and you just might not get the job done. Also, you will frequently find that these other sources (i.e., death certificates, obituaries, and burial registers) do not exist and hence cannot be used.

There are two kinds of cemetery records with which family researchers are concerned:

A. Gravestone and monument inscriptions.

B. Records kept by cemetery management and caretakers (sextons' records).

---

[1] Used with permission of *The New Yorker*. All rights reserved.

There is a great deal of variation in both the completeness and the accuracy of these records, as you will see from the examples which follow, but because of the very nature of the information they deal with, they must be considered important and should be consulted early in your research.

There are five different kinds of cemeteries in America. They include:

1. The churchyard, where members of a church are buried right on the church grounds. This custom was brought to America from the Old World and was especially prevalent in the colonial states.
2. The church-owned cemetery, not connected with nor adjacent to the church building, but owned and operated by the church.
3. The government-owned cemetery—either town, county, state, or national—owned collectively by the people and supported and maintained by tax monies.
4. The privately-owned, non-church, cemetery—usually owned by a corporation and operated as a business enterprise. The U.S. has many of these, and they are especially common in more recent years.
5. The family cemetery. This is often just a small corner of the family farm or estate, perhaps in a grove of trees in an out-of-the-way location, set aside for the burial of family members and relatives.

All of these types of cemeteries are common in America and each presents its own problems for the genealogist—the cemetery may be difficult to locate, there may be no sextons' records, or it may be something else.

One of the most difficult problems is to determine the place of burial. If your ancestor lived in a large community there are usually several possible places of burial. Two of the best sources to help you solve this problem are obituaries and death certificates, but both have limitations if the death was early.

Once you find the name of the cemetery it is usually not too difficult to determine its location. Local government officials, church officials, funeral directors, and old-timers can frequently provide the answers.

I will talk later about how to find the records, but let's look first at some typical tombstone inscriptions to see how they might help us.

II. TOMBSTONE INSCRIPTIONS

A. From the Rexburg Cemetery, Madison County, Idaho:

Charlotte Helena
Dau. of

Peter & Charlotte Flamm
Died Apr. 5, 1891
aged 3 Ys, 8 Ms, 7 Ds.

Melissa Henry Smith
Born July 11, 1827
Wood Co., Virginia
Died June 15, 1896

In memory of
Mary A. Roberts
& infant son
Wife of Alfred Ricks
Born Oct. 7, 1870
Died Jun. 30, 1892
We trust our loss will be their gain,
And that with Christ, they've gone to reign.

James Eckersell
Aug. 5, 1839 — Mar. 6, 1917

FARNSWORTH
Albert S.
1891 — 1895
Blanche
1906 — 1909
Ralph
1913 — 1914

Jacob Spori
Born Mar. 26, 1847
Died Sept. 27, 1903

Magdalena R. Spori
Born Feb. 6, 1851
Died Sept. 14, 1900

John Plain Smith
May 14, 1843
- - - - - - -
His Wife
Elizabeth Andrews
Feb. 6, 1846
Dec. 6, 1915
Sons
Mickle A.

Aug. 8, 1883
Jan. 19, 1905
Joseph A.
Dec. 1, 1881
July 19, 1908

B. From the Long Cemetery, between Spencer and McMinnville, Tennessee:

Harriet Grissom
April 5, 1852 — October 27, 1883
Daughter of Elisha and Elizabeth Boulding
Wife of S. B. Grissom

S. B. Grissom
November 14, 1847 — November 1, 1908

William Grissom
March 7, 1797 — December 23, 1869

Evey Grissom
May 1, 1797 — Jan 25, 1816
Wife of William Grissom

C. From Spencer Cemetery No. 1, Spencer, Tennessee:

BURDIN WHEELER
TENNESSEE — 1 LT. ELLIOTT'S CO.
LAUDERDALE'S TENN. MTD. INF.
CHEROKEE WAR 1887

D. From Sycamore Cemetery at Gasaway (near Woodbury), Cannon County, Tennessee:

Mollie E., Dau of
G. G. & Martha Melton
Wife of Geo. Hancock
Born May 22, 1862
Died February 11, 1894
"Blessed are they which do
hunger and thirst after
righteousness for they
shall be filled."

Selmar, Son of
G. E. and M. E. Hancock
Born May 10, 1883

Died February 6, 1900
Aged 16 y's, 8 m's, & 25 d's

Polly, Wife of Bartlet Marcum
Mother of Arch Marcum
Born January 24, 1807
Died May 7, 1855

Jacob K. King
Born March 5, 1844
Died August 2, 1897
Aged 53 Y's, 4 M's, 27 D's
"Think of me as you pass by.
As you are now, so once was I.
As I am now so you must be.
Prepare for death and follow me."

Mathie D. Keaton
June 15, 1897 — Dec. 11, 1918
Enlisted Oct. 29, 1918 at
Woodbury, Tennessee
Died at Camp Wadsworth, S. C.
Buried at Sycamore Church
December 15, 1918.
"Dearest brother thou hast left us.
Here thy loss we deeply feel
But tis God that has bereft us.
He can all our sorrows heal."

A. H. Markum
Born September 29, 1846
Died March 23, 1903
Aged 56 yrs. 5 m. 24 days
A. Markum & A. H. Owen
Married May 6, 1864
Joined the M. E. Church S. 1892

Pvt. John E. Hancock
Co. F. 57, Pis. Inf.
June 7, 1896
Died Oct. 10, 1918 in France.

E. From Highland Cemetery, Carter County, Tennessee:

Laura Etta Singleton
Feb. 4, 1853
Age 77 yrs. 1 mo. 2 days

Died March 6, 1930
"Member United Daughters of Confederacy"
She done all she could.

James Calvin Singleton
Nov. 12, 1843
Sept. 25, 1928
Served his country
In Co. A, 5th
Bat., N. C. Calvery [sic]
Southern Confederacy
Blessed are the dead which die in the Lord.

F. From the Dorsey graveyard, on a farm at Monongalia, West Virginia:

[All on one stone]

Mary E. Dorsey, born June 28, 1828, died Feb. 14, 1863
Emma L. Dorsey, born Sept. 10, 1860, died Apr. 10, 1863
Delia T. Dorsey, born Mar 10, 1831, died Aug 7, 1910
Warren C. Dorsey, born Oct 2, 1911, died Dec 16, 1911
Marion Hough Dorsey, born May 17, 1875, died Dec 16, 1900

It is plain, even from these few examples, that the information found on tombstones is fairly unpredictable. You never know what might be on a gravestone until you see it. Usually you can count on finding at least a name and a death date (which do not help particularly unless you cannot obtain the information from other sources), but often, especially on those tombstones which are not too recent, you can find a wealth of genealogical data. Dates of birth, places of birth, places of marriage, names of parents, names of spouses, names of children, religious affiliation, military service (even specific organization and war)—they *can* all be found on gravestones. The foregoing examples have illustrated this.

There is also an advantage when you go personally to a cemetery to view, as a whole, all of the graves on the same cemetery lot. People are usually related in some way or they would not be buried on the same lot. Perhaps herein lies another clue that will facilitate your research. It is best to go to the cemetery personally, if you can, because you will be aware of all aspects of the genealogical problem and will be in an excellent position to capitalize on clues that others might overlook. However, it is certainly permissible to send an agent, working in your behalf, to read tombstones. Also, if the tombstone inscriptions have been transcribed or published, you will find value in these. A publication is a poor substitute for a personal visit, but this is true of practically every source the genealogist uses.

There are two reasons why printed and transcribed tombstone inscriptions are inferior to the personal visit:

1. There is always the possibility of transcription errors.
2. The arrangement of these sources often causes confusion about who is buried in which lot, hence who is related to whom.

These shortcomings, however, may not be too serious and, in fact, may be outweighed by virtues. For example, the ravages of time and nature may have since rendered your ancestral tombstones unreadable. Or "progress" may have destroyed or moved the cemetery. Or vandals may have damaged or destroyed valuable monuments. Where these things have happened the transcripts are the only alternative.

Various local chapters of the Daughters of the American Revolution (DAR) have undertaken extensive projects of copying gravestone inscriptions and have copied inscriptions from many thousands of cemeteries. The Works Projects Administration (WPA) undertook similar projects during the Great Depression of the 1930s, but not so extensively. The Daughters of the Utah Pioneers (DUP) and the Idaho Genealogical Society have likewise engaged in these projects, as have many others. Also, tombstone inscriptions have been frequently published in genealogical and historical periodicals.

When you venture to the cemetery on your own, be prepared and equipped to handle any contingency. I do not want to discourage you, but you will find that many cemeteries have been abandoned and thus have become overgrown with weeds, briars, and brambles. So be prepared to deal with the problem. You may find that some tombstones have sunk into the ground or have tipped over. You will also find that many inscriptions have become eroded beyond legibility. (Often those which have sunken and are overgrown with brush have withstood the erosive forces a little better because they have been protected.)

When you visit old cemeteries, don't wear your best clothing. You might also find it helpful to take along tools to cut through the thicket and to dig out buried gravestones. A good stiff-bristled (not wire) brush will also be useful for cleaning off the dirt. An eroded inscription can often be made legible by rubbing chalk or soapstone over it. (Use the side of the chalk stick for this.) There are a number of techniques that different persons use, but I do not recommend anything that would mar or deface a gravestone in any way. Some persons clean the inscription sufficiently and then take a photograph. This way the copy is always accurate. Most tombstone hunters seem to favor this method, but you should not rely too much on the photographic processes unless you have high quality equipment and are proficient in its use. If your pictures don't turn out you may have a serious problem.

Be careful of the information on tombstones. Most of it is probably accurate, but remember that an engraver can make errors as easily as can a printer. Also, many a tombstone is not put on the grave until many years after the death, and the dates are often supplied from someone's memory. Be especially watchful for errors in dates of one day, one month, or one year—these are the most easily-made errors and are thus the most common.

III. SEXTONS' RECORDS

Sextons' records vary in content and nature even more than do tombstone inscriptions. For a family cemetery there will be no sextons' records at all. In fact, you are fortunate if most graves have tombstones on them. Church cemeteries seldom have any record of burials aside from what is kept in the church's registers (and with some churches a book telling which church member owns which cemetery lot). Most other cemeteries—those owned by the government and those which are owned privately—usually maintain some type of record. Sometimes these are merely books or plats showing lot ownership, but even these can save you a lot of wandering and wondering when you are looking for the graves of your forebears in a large cemetery. Other cemeteries have extensive records on everyone buried therein—sometimes quite a bit more complete than the information engraved on the tombstones, but you never know this until the tombstones have been checked. (In more recent years the nature of these records has been the subject of legislation in most states.)

Let's look at two typical examples of sextons' records (of the not-too-recent variety).

A. From the town of Skowhegan, Somerset County, Maine:

Lot No. 24 Timothy Snow

Date of decease	*Name of person interred*	*Age*
1867—Aug 7	Raymond Snow Child removed from Snow's tomb	Aged 22 years
1880—Sept 23	Timothy Snow	Aged 77 years 6 mos
Sept 18, 1881	Lilliam M. Brageton	" 3 month 10 days
Aug 19, 1897	Lirluri [?] G. Tracy, Dau of T. Snow	" 36 years

These records are indexed and are arranged numerically by lot number, which has nothing to do with the dates the lots were purchased. There are many relationships stated (though none are asked for), and if the ownership of the lot changed hands (after the death of the original purchaser) the old owner's name was crossed out and the new name entered. Both names are readable and both are indexed. If a person's remains are moved to another lot or another cemetery the record usually gives the details. Also, the date of purchase for some of the lots is given.

B. From Spanish Fork City Cemetery, Utah County, Utah:

Name in full	Johnson, William
Father	John Peterson
Mother	Vilborg Thordurson
Husb. or wife	single
When born	27 April 1868
Where born	Westmania Island, Iceland
When died	7 March 1882
Cemetery where buried	Spanish Fork, Utah

These cards are filed alphabetically, but here the married women are listed under their maiden surnames (quite unusual), so some of them may be difficult to find. Also, I notice that the spouse's name is seldom given. The card usually just says "married" in the "Husb. or wife" blank and, in many other instances, the cards have blanks which have not been filled in. Few give the specific place of birth as does the sample card, but usually only the state or country.

These are examples of quite typical sextons' records and are not unlike those you might find for your ancestors in numerous localities. These records are generally in the custody of the present sexton or in the office of the county or town clerk. If not, these people can tell you where they are kept. The information found therein is basic genealogical data and, unless you already have it, it is information you will need for your genealogical record. Remember, however, that the evidence is mostly secondary (especially for older persons), and no more reliable than the informant who provided it (and you seldom know who that was). Also, as with most other records, the more recent ones are better in many respects than those of older vintage.

IV. HELPS IN FINDING THE RECORDS

We have already discussed how difficult it might be to determine a place of burial, and I might add that even knowing the name of the cemetery doesn't solve all of your problems. Large cemeteries are usually easy enough to find (they are probably listed in the telephone directory), but the smaller ones, especially family cemeteries, are more difficult.

It is not impossible to solve location problems, however. One writer suggests three possible sources of help:

1. Ask—chambers of commerce, city hall, anyone who might know or who would know whom to ask.
2. U.S. Government Geological Survey maps of the locality have sufficient detail that even the tiny graveyards are pinpointed.
3. Know the laws of the state which govern cemetery and burial policy.[2]

V. RECORDS OF FUNERAL DIRECTORS

Another record, closely related to those already discussed in this chapter, deserves mention. This is the record kept by the funeral director (or undertaker) who performed the pre-burial duties for the dead ancestor. Today the funeral director is usually responsible for initiating and filing the death certificate, and frequently the obituary notice. Most funeral directors also maintain private records equally as good as the official records which are kept. Some of these records contain useful information not included on the death certificate. (For example, they often give the name of the insurance companies with whom the deceased had his life covered, and, in case you are not aware, insurance companies also have extensive genealogical data in some of their records. However, insurance records are private and, like the funeral director's records, are available only at the discretion of company officials.)

It has been my experience that most funeral directors are very cooperative and more than willing to help you find information in their records. Remember, however, that their records are private, and when they open them to you it is a favor and not a legal obligation.

---

[2] Richard H. Hale, "Cemetery Records as Aids to Genealogical Research" (Area I, no. 15), World Conference on Records and Genealogical Seminar (Salt Lake City: Genealogical Society of The Church of Jesus Christ of Latter-day Saints, 1969).

Since the beginning of vital records in America, death certificates have given the name and address (usually only the city) of the funeral director who took care of the body. Your local funeral director has a directory, the *American Blue Book of Funeral Directors* (New York: National Funeral Directors' Association, biennially), which can help you locate names and addresses, or you can find those names and addresses in local telephone directories.

When a person dies in a place where he did not reside, the body is often handled by a funeral director at the place of death. It is embalmed there and prepared for the return home. This is good to remember when you are looking for the funeral director's records and cannot locate them in the home town. When the problem is a recent one, the obituary notice may provide a clue to this kind of situation, and the death certificate (filed in the state of death) will give specific information.

Some funeral directors' records go back more than 100 years,[8] but they certainly do not have to be that old to be valuable. As with death certificates, if they deal with persons who died in their old age, these records can bridge two or three generations of time. They can provide names, dates, places, etc., invaluable to continued research.

VI. CONCLUSION

In American genealogical research there are many sources to consider, and we often have no inkling of the specific content of many of them. This uncertainty and the necessity of possessing a knowledge of myriad sources make American research the most difficult genealogical research in the Western world (and also the most interesting and challenging). And though this uncertainty is characteristic of records relating to burials, you may take comfort in the knowledge that these records are a basic kind of source. You always know that the information you discover will be solid genealogical data—names, dates, places, relationships.

---

[8] Norman E. Wright and David H. Pratt (*Genealogical Research Essentials* [Salt Lake City: Bookcraft, 1967], p. 282) report finding records as early as 1841.

PART 3

Some New Ideas

25

Computers in Genealogy

Computers are becoming more and more important in the world of genealogy—not just because of the indexes they now make available, but because of the assistance they can give to the genealogist in working with his own records and because there can be access through computer networks to the records of others. Computers, of course, won't do your research, prepare your research notes, or link the generations together for you, but they can provide convenient storage and retrieval of genealogical data. And with the technological advances made in the 1980s, small desktop computers—personal computers (or PCs) as they are called, but which are more accurately microcomputers—have become available, affordable, and very functional. And there are many available software programs—programs to meet almost any demand and satisfy any fancy.

Having said this much, however, we are left in a quandary—the quandary of making a decision on what computer (hardware) and computer programs (software) to buy. In light of all that is available it would certainly be unwise to just rush out and buy a computer and a software package without first analyzing your needs and expectations and then carefully considering the options available to satisfy them. Too often we learn after the fact that we did not make the best choice and that it would have been wiser to invest our money elsewhere. There are just too many possibilities—as well as too great a divergence of personal preferences—for us to shoot from the hip in choosing our computer software and the computer to operate it.

The hardware and the software are both important—like the chicken and the egg—but contrary to what many believe, the software decision should be made first. Once you know what you want your program to do, you can select a software program to do it—then, if you don't already have a computer, you can buy one that can handle the program. To buy the computer first—if you have a choice—is not wise because it can lock you into software choices that may prove frustrating. My purpose in this chapter is not to tell you what choices to make or to even tell you what the choices are, but to give you an overview of the basic types of options and then discuss some criteria to guide you in making the best choice.

I. TYPES OF PROGRAMS

There are three types of programs available that can handle genealogical data. Each is different, though some programs may have features of more than one category. The three program types are:

A. Word-processing programs.

B. Data base programs.

C. Genealogy programs (which are actually specialized data base programs).

Let's look just quickly at each type.

A. Word-Processing Programs

Word-processing programs are designed to store data for you, put it in the format you desire, and then print it out on demand. Such programs provide for easy corrections, deletions, and additions. You can put in any kind of information you desire in the format of your choice, and you can store and retrieve that information, or any part of it, as you may choose, even modifying the format if you wish. Most programs also permit you to search for any word or phrase you desire. A word-processing program is ideal for the person compiling a family history. Some such programs, of course, are more versatile and easier to use than others, but deluxe features usually have their price. However, all things considered, a program that is difficult to operate will be a source of constant frustration and will not be a bargain at any price.

B. Data Base Programs

Data base programs are designed primarily to store data for easy retrieval. The variety of retrieval options is what usually makes data base programs popular. You can search for and quickly retrieve very specific data. For example, you can search for and print out everyone named William or everyone born in February or just about anything else that might appeal to you for whatever reason. You can also get alphabetical or chronological printouts. It should be said, however, that most data base programs are not for the novice. Most require that the operator know basic computer principles, as the operator must design the format, screens, and report layouts.

C. Genealogy Programs

Genealogy programs are much more sophisticated in dealing with genealogical data. They are designed to keep track of specific data of interest to genealogists. They can deal with pedigree links, they can make various indexes (the nature and extent of which depend on the specific program), and some (but not all) are able to produce reports. Some also have limited word-processing capability so that text can be added to the basic forms and charts.

Of course some genealogy programs are more sophisticated than others. Essentially there are three types of genealogy programs available:

1. Basic programs.
2. Sophisticated programs.
3. Special-application programs.

Their natures are much as the above designations would suggest. The typical *basic program* stores minimal data—usually pedigree charts and family group records. Some are menu driven and some are not. In addition to the basic fields, the *sophisticated programs* have some powerful search programs, room for text, and often the capability for the user to create some of his own fields. *Special-application programs* relate primarily to special indexing features and thus provide the versatility of accomplishing very specialized functions that strike the buyer's fancy. Some functions are almost gimmicks, but if the user wants a particular gimmick and is willing to pay the price requested, that is his business. These special applications are in addition to basic, and often some sophisticated, applications.

II. BUYING A COMPUTER PROGRAM (AND A COMPUTER)

My first word of advice is that you look at the actual software program yourself and see how it works—don't just read the manufacturer's description of the product. Talk to dealers and to someone who has the program and uses it. Dealers can give you lists of names. It is also recommended that, when you are narrowing down your selection, you get the user manuals and study them. Compare the features and the operation as they relate to your own expectations.

Do not rush out to buy a program on the spur of the moment just because someone has given you a glowing testimonial of how wonderful computers are for genealogy. This decision deserves your very best shot. Look around. See several different programs function. Have them demonstrated and try some of the operations. This will give you a basis to help you make your choice. Make notes about those features you like and those you dislike. And don't be afraid to ask questions or to discuss specific features with dealers.

To assist in your search you may find helpful a book entitled *Directory of Genealogical Software,* edited by Karen B. Cavenaugh (Fort Wayne, IN: Genealogy/Computer Consultants). This book is updated annually and is available from the publisher at 2238 Cimerron Pass, Fort Wayne, IN 46815. It gives system requirements, capabilities, review citations, price, vendor support data, and sources for more than fifty manufacturers.

Once you begin to feel comfortable and have enough knowledge about programs to act intelligently, you are ready to begin a specific process to help you make your choice. When you have reached this point you have probably already seen enough of the programs to know that you do not like some of them because of what they will not do. Your next step is to make a list of eight to ten features that are important to you. Because it is not likely that you will find all of these features on any one program, you should now number those features in the order of their importance. These may include print features, such as whether the system can print what you want it to—e.g., family group records, pedigree charts, reports, indexes, maps. Search capabilities may be important to you. How many fields or information categories can be searched on by the program? Is that significant to you? Are there any specific fields that you feel *must* be searched on to meet your personal needs?

You may have certain expectations concerning indexes and indexing capability. If so, make that clear on your list. If the speed of the program is important, put that on your list too. There may be other features you like from what you have observed; you must decide. Put these on your list too. Then don't trim your list too much.

As you compare your list of desired features with available programs, talk to dealers and to owners again and ask lots of questions. Don't be afraid to read. Learn all you can about each program on your list. Read reviews in preference to sales literature (though I admit it is sometimes difficult to tell the difference because some promotional materials are often printed in the form of reviews and/or some reviews are written by people with vested interests).

In the selection process you must give high priority to ease of operation and ease of learning. When all is said and done these are the most important criteria for most computer users. Some beginners choose to buy software that is very basic with the idea that they will purchase a more sophisticated software program later—and with a little luck both programs can be run on the same computer. (But it will be important to be able to easily convert the data from your first program to the program you choose to succeed it.) It is a fact, however, that most of us really don't know what we want—what works best for us and which features we will never use—until we have used a system for a while. If you choose to follow this route, this chapter on software selection may be much more meaningful to you the second time around.

As you complete your final selection there are six essential steps:

1. Eliminate all programs that do not meet your needs. If you already have a personal computer then your options are limited to programs your computer can run.

2. Select those programs acceptable to you that are within your price range.

(It is a fact that price is usually an important factor. And this is the main reason you should usually choose your software program before you buy your computer. Where would it leave you if you had a computer for which you could buy no program that you find satisfactory?

I have made much of this point—selecting program before hardware—but it would also be unrealistic to pretend that you have no other use in mind for your computer aside from genealogy. It is unwise to choose a genealogy program that can be run only on a computer that will not run programs to satisfy your other needs. Think about that too as you make your decision.)

3. Get copies of user manuals and study them. Carefully compare the features and the operation as they relate to your expectations.

4. Learn about warranties and dealer support. Ask users how well the dealer and the manufacturer stand behind their goods.

5. Find out about upgrades in the programs and the policy of the various manufacturers with regard to these.

6. Make a decision. (If you have done your homework, you can be assured that your decision will be a good one and that you will be happy with it.)

For further discussion and helpful insights into the role of computers in genealogy you will enjoy reading Paul A. Andereck and Richard A. Pence's *Computer Genealogy: A Guide to Research Through High Technology* (Salt Lake City: Ancestry, 1985). This is an excellent survey of the current situation and an intuitive look at the future of computers in genealogy.

26

Family History: Going Beyond Genealogy

I. WHY FAMILY HISTORY?

After all that has been said about genealogy and the significance of making correct connections and putting together complete families, there are still other important possibilities. In recent years many genealogists have caught a new vision and have had opened to them whole new vistas, as they have become not just genealogists but also family historians. That probably sounds strange, but I have the feeling that many who have thought they were involved in family history in the past now have a whole new concept of what family history really is.

Family history is essentially a new field of history—the result of a "marriage" of sorts between history and genealogy. Only a few years ago this seemed like a most unlikely union. However, even to cite such a marriage is overly simplistic. Family history also includes other fields of study, such as demography, geography, psychology, sociology, and literature.

While the goal of the genealogist has traditionally been to identify and link together past generations of ancestors into pedigrees, the goal of today's family historian is to do that as well as to understand something of the lives and times of specific persons, couples, or families over one or more generations.

Members of The Church of Jesus Christ of Latter-day Saints often quote a scripture in connection with their interest in ancestors. I won't quote it here, but it is found in Malachi 4:5-6 and speaks of turning "the hearts of the children" to "their fathers." That is an interesting concept—and an interesting process. To really complete this heart-turning process we must know more than just names, dates, places, and relationships. We must know *them* (the people involved) and what they experienced. We must know something of the things that mattered to them most. We must feel something of the things which they felt. For example, I can turn my heart much more readily to the grandmother who bore twelve children if I can relate to what she must have felt of tragedy in her life as she buried eight of those children before they reached the age of five. It also gives me greater appreciation for her as I gradually comprehend the difficulty of her pioneer existence in a two-room log cabin on the frontier.

One thing that has happened to the field of history in this unlikely marriage is that the historian has discovered that he can enrich his understanding of the past by seeing it from the perspective of those most affected by its events. He has also discovered that the family and the individual had a greater impact on historical events than was previously thought possible, and that the effect of an event on individuals, families, and communities may be more important than the event itself.

> They saw that they could enrich our understanding of history by recounting how most people lived and worked, by analyzing the options that were open to them, and by finding out what values and expectations they shared. Historians also took a fresh approach to historical change, portraying human events as moving from the bottom up rather than from the top down. No longer were the common folk seen only as those who endured the deeds and misdeeds of history's movers and shakers. In the words of Gertrude Himmelfarb, "The victims of history have become its principle agents and actors."[1]

Recall how Alex Haley captured the fancy of the entire nation in the late 1970s with his story of *Roots*. Though there has been some disagreement about the quality of Mr. Haley's research and the accuracy of his conclusions, you cannot ignore his impact. Mr. Haley has done more to generate more interest in more people in their families' pasts than all of the world's great genealogists combined.

I'm not sure we understand all of the reasons for the success of *Roots* but, regardless of that, its message struck America very close to home, perhaps pricking our collective consciences because of how little we know of our own ancestors.

Allan J. Lichtman quoted the anthropologist David Schneider as saying the following at a symposium on kin and communities:

---

[1] Allan J. Lichtman, *Your Family History* (New York: Vintage Books, 1978), p. 5.

> The most rootless yearn for roots; the most mobile bemoan their placeless fate; the most isolated yearn for kin and community, for these represent the basic things that make life worth living for many people.[2]

Our understanding of our ancestral roots enhances our understanding of ourselves. Says Professor Lichtman:

> Psychologists in clinical practice have suggested that the person who understands the patterns of thinking and feeling that emerge over generations of family history is likely to function better as a secure, responsible, self-directed person.

He cited a case in point:

> As a part of their psychiatric training at Georgetown University Medical School, many students of Dr. Murray Bowen, a pioneer in family therapy and himself a family historian, have explored their own family histories. After many years of working with families, Dr. Bowen observed that "it became increasingly impossible to see a single person without seeing his total family sitting like phantoms alongside him." Although Thomas Wolfe may have correctly noted that you can't go home again, each of us takes a large chunk of home along with us wherever we go.[3]

The challenge I give you as a genealogist is to reach beyond the vital statistics to a new world of understanding, both of your ancestors and of yourself. Preserve those details of your family in written form that will bring understanding to many others and truly enable their hearts—along with your own—to turn to their fathers. Someone has said that there is little point in digging up an ancestor if you aren't going to make him live. If that is true—and I believe it is—your job is not finished until you feel a bit of what he felt, have shared vicariously in his joys and heartaches—perhaps shed a tear with him in his sorrow, laughed at the humor in his life, and felt pride in his accomplishments.

II. SOURCES

The sources of family history information are mainly those that are found in the home. They include various family documents, material objects or

---

[2] *Ibid.*, p. 11.

[3] *Ibid.*, pp. 11-12.

artifacts, photographs, and the evidence derived from oral interviews. In addition, however, much family history data is also found, but is often overlooked, in the traditional sources of genealogical evidence, especially original records.

A. In the Home

The homes of relatives, and even your own home, may contain documents and material objects of great importance to your family's history. Professor Lichtman gives the following lists: [4]

HOME SOURCES

Family documents	*Material objects*
The family Bible	Books and magazines
Letters	Toys and games
Telegrams	Athletic equipment
Post cards	Records
Diaries	Tape recordings
Journals	Guns
Appointment calendars	Knives
Ledgers	Souvenirs
Account books	Maps
Bills	Ornaments
Canceled checks	Trophies
Bankbooks	Medals
Bank statements	Posters
Credit cards	Buttons
Employment records	Jewelry
Tax records	Clocks and watches
Social security card	Coins and stamps
Identification cards	Bottles and cans
Driver's licenses	Boxes and containers
Hunting and fishing licenses	Bottle tops
Wills	Instruments
Deeds	Appliances
Bills of sale	Machinery
Insurance policies	Locks
Stocks and bonds	Metalwork
School records	Tools
School assignments	Furniture
Military records	Clothing
Medical records	Needlework

[4] *Ibid.*, pp. 86-87.

Prescriptions
Church records
Citizenship papers
Passports
Marriage licenses
Birth certificates
Baptismal certificates
Confirmation certificates
Court records
Yearbooks
Scrapbooks
Clippings
Awards and citations
Calling cards
Greeting cards and invitations
Recipe files
Baby books
Family histories and genealogies
Memoirs
Poetry
Quilts
China
Silverware
Plates
Mugs
Glassware
Bowls and pitchers
Mirrors
Knick-knacks
Candlesticks
Rugs
Painting
Sculpture
Plaques
Religious objects
Photographs
Albums
Home movies
Houses and apartments
Factories, offices, and stores
Cemeteries

With regard to the use of material objects in family history, Lichtman says:

> Material objects . . . are more difficult to use than written documents. Nevertheless, when thoughtfully approached, many seemingly commonplace objects can add to your knowledge of family history. Items like quilts and samplers may actually record such events as births and marriages. More than just supplying information, the things people owned and used often remind us of skills, habits, and styles of life that have now disappeared. A set of surveyor's tools or a roll-top desk might evoke the life of an ancestor, lending us a little of his physical presence that otherwise might seem so remote. When shown to a relative, objects might trigger a flood of reminiscences about an earlier time. If you locate your great uncle's tools and place them before him, he will probably respond with stories from his working days. If you show your grandfather the chalice that he brought with him from Russia, he may better recall his life in the old country. . . . Not all objects have a story behind them, but attics, basements, and closets are filled with objects stored for sentimental or other reasons, and often they can reveal much about the people who owned and used them.[5]

[5] *Ibid.*, pp. 95-96.

Once found, precious documents and artifacts should be properly preserved. If you have questions on proper methods for preserving documents and heirlooms check with a qualified expert, such as curators of museums and historical societies. Lichtman gives some basic guidelines:

> Check all storage places for fire hazards, possible water leaks, and excessive vibrations. Try to retain moderate and stable temperature and humidity. A temperature between 60 and 70 degrees Fahrenheit and a humidity between 40 and 60 percent are appropriate for most items. Keep strong light off your possessions, and try to protect them from dust, dirt, and pollution. Watch for signs of insects and other pests; if necessary, call on the services of a professional exterminator. Don't pile up fragile documents or stuff them in drawers. Don't put Scotch tape on items, mount them on ordinary paper or wood, lean them against one another, or clean them with common household products. In some cases you may even want to purchase transparencies for covering documents or acquire cabinets, shelving, racks, boxes, and containers especially designed for specific types of items. If you don't use such storage facilities, make sure to properly line drawers, shelves, and boxes. If you must transport them, pack them with great care. Always remember, when unsure what to do, seek the aid of qualified experts.[6]

B. The Use of Photographs

In her presentation at the World Conference on Records in 1980, May Davis Hill suggested that "photographs are more than mere illustrations of what some person looked like. . . . Photographs," she said, "provide expanded information seldom available from other sources."[7] She suggests that we train ourselves to examine every detail of a picture and not just that which is observable by superficial observation. This practice will enable us to actually enter people's homes and glimpse details of their lives. Each photograph should be considered as an original document of family history with potentially valuable information about the subjects. One major advantage of these, especially of snapshots, is that most families have so many of them, often spanning relatively long periods of time and many significant family transitions. They chronicle change and are primarily remembrances of "events" more than of daily life in the family. They show us what our ancestors looked like, but they also tell us much more.

---

[6] *Ibid.*, pp. 102-103.

[7] May Davis Hill, "The Story Behind Your Photographs," Paper No. 353, *World Conference on Records.* Vol. 2 (Salt Lake City, 1980), p. 36.

Mrs. Hill says there are two things that can help sharpen our observations of photographs in order to extract other details. The first is to train the eye to see every detail. The second is to cultivate the habit of curiosity about historical facts. Concerning the first she says:

> The eye becomes lazy when not often used for exploratory purposes. If family photographs have been in one place for a long time, one ceases to see them. Changing them about can bring out features and relationships never before perceived. If you wish to see more in a familiar image, put it in a place where you write or are otherwise mentally active. Leave it there while you work, but not long enough for the images to settle in your mind as they would in a permanent arrangement. The eye unconsciously examines the image before it while the mind is active. Facts which have lain hidden can pop into consciousness under such circumstances.[8]

Concerning the habit of curiosity, she points out that this can help us with photographs that are not dated. She suggests careful observation of such details as clothing styles and hair styles:

> If there is a tennis court, for example, take into account the fact that tennis was introduced in this country on Long Island in 1874. It would take a few years to spread elsewhere. Obviously a knowledge of costume is useful, and a certain amount of knowledge of history of photography helps with dating as well. Like tintypes and Herbert Hoover's round collar, some things persist beyond the time of their greatest prevalence, however, particularly among the aged. For instance, many women who were widowed in the Civil War continued to wear the styles of that time—the center-parted hair and the full skirt bordered with braid—until the 1890s. The tendency continued well into the twentieth century.[9]

Put your old photograph collections in the order you want to ultimately keep them, then number the photographs. This will allow you to put them in different arrangements for study and for comparison with one another and then to return them easily to the preferred arrangement. Consider not only photograph collections which may have come into your hands, but also those in possession of other—especially older—relatives. Get copies of those that are significant to you.

There are always lessons in old photographs. As we sort through the unidentified and undated pictures of our forebears we learn the value of

---

[8] *Ibid.*, p. 13.

[9] *Ibid.*, p. 136.

carefully identifying and dating our own photographs for the benefit of posterity.

> Generally the more you know about a photograph, the more valuable it becomes as source material for family history. Where was the picture taken? What was going on at the time? Was someone present who isn't in the picture? Why was the picture taken? Was it taken by an amateur or a professional? Was the picture posed or spontaneous? Be careful to distinguish between the posed, formal photograph and the spontaneous snapshot. The photographer often controls the pose of a formal photograph and may even select the objects that appear in the picture. Yet formal photographs posed by the family itself may reveal much more about the family life than a snapshot would. Whereas much information can be teased from the analysis of a formal photograph, the effect of snapshots is cumulative.[10]

When all is said and done, photographs tell us more about their subjects than do any other historical documents.

C. Conventional Genealogical Sources

The thing that is significant here is that the family historian can take the same sources which he used as a genealogist and look a little deeper than he has looked before. He can go beyond the names, dates, places, and relationships to mine that priceless information that tells of people's lives and circumstances. There are many clues and insights to the realities with which our ancestors lived.

The property bequeathed and devised by one's will tells us much about that person. We learn whether he was rich or poor, and even the nature of his personal goods and treasures. His will can provide information about all aspects of family life. It can disclose his occupation and the tools he used in plying his trade. It can tell us of his religious affiliation, much of his lifestyle and personal tastes, his political preferences, his favorite charities, and his feelings about family members. In addition to wills, other documents relating to the administration of the estate may also have significant value. Consider, for example, what you could learn of an ancestor's way of life from a detailed inventory of his personal estate. In days gone by, inventories were not as general (or unspecific) as they are today. An inventory today might merely list "household furnishings," while the same document a century or two ago listed household items in minute detail, even to counting the knives, forks, spoons, and pewter mugs.

---

[10] Lichtman, pp. 113-114.

The census schedules have much valuable personal information on the individuals enumerated. Note the headings of the various columns and you will see that we are told much about education and literacy; about wealth, property, and consequent social status; health matters; and even whether the person was gainfully employed and the nature of his employment. Birth places of family members also tell much about the family's mobility.

Passenger lists in more recent years give "personal descriptions" of the immigrants. Military records and some land entry records often do the same. How valuable that is!

Details of military service can be found in service and pension records. Pension applications can also give details of family wanderings. Church records—if one is willing to leave behind the registers of christenings, marriages, and burials—will tell of financial contributions, special services rendered, and even of disciplinary actions.

Even local histories, though they may not specifically mention your ancestors, can provide insights into their lives and the events and circumstances that affected and even molded those lives. All of this is now a part of you.

III. HISTORICAL CONSIDERATIONS

As you look at the lives of your ancestors, try to understand the "causes" of what you perceive. Ask why these people did what they did. The answers to these questions are priceless. For example, you might consider (but do not limit yourself to) the following list of inquiries. They are designed to trigger your curiosity and facilitate your investigation:

1. Why was the family living where it was? What factors caused them to choose that particular area in preference to another? Was it a matter of matching job skills with available employment? Or was some other factor involved?

2. What was the Americanization process like for your immigrant ancestor? This is an especially important inquiry if your ancestor spoke no English (or little English) or was part of a racial minority. What struggles did the family members have because of language/racial barriers? How did they deal with these obstacles? How did their standard of living suffer (if it did) because of these problems so common to immigrants? Did the family change the family name (or its spelling)? Why? Did the American dream go sour? Why did they come to America at all?

3. What was the home like where the ancestral family lived? How different was their home from your own? What "modern conveniences" did the

home have to offer? Central heating? Modern plumbing and bathroom facilities? Ample kitchen cupboard space? Closet and storage space? Was there a basement? An attic?

4. Who lived in the home? Were there other persons living there besides members of the immediate family? Who were they? Perhaps grandparents or cousins, or maybe employees or apprentices—or even boarders? How long were they there? What influence did the presence of these persons have on the family?

5. What were the circumstances of daily family life? Consider such things as sleeping accommodations or even seating arrangements at the dinner table. Our children, who today feel deprived if they don't have their own private bedrooms, would be greatly surprised at some of the arrangements in the homes of their ancestors where large families shared restricted quarters. What were the household furnishings like? What about the household tasks and the tools used to perform those tasks? What chores were assigned to the children? What fuel was used for heating and/or cooking? How was it obtained? How stored? What about food preservation methods and insect control methods before the days of refrigeration and modern insecticides? What about varmint control?

6. What was your ancestors' courtship like? What did they do on dates? How did they meet? How long did the courtship last? How similar or dissimilar was their courtship from courtships of today? Why?

7. Are there any unique sayings or expressions that were used by the family or family members? Some of these are priceless. I remember fondly an expression my own father used as I was growing up to describe someone of small stature: "He'd have to stand on a brick to kick a duck!"

8. What were the traditions that became part of the family? Were family members independent and self sufficient? Did scrupulous honesty prevail in all things? Was the family raised on a tradition of hard work? What was the sexual morality? How important was service to others? Did the family have and read good literature? What books were part of the family "library"? Were there any traditions of going to certain places or doing certain things on certain holidays?

9. What was the size of the family? What benefits and/or problems did the family size carry with it?

10. What were the nature and quality of intra-family relationships? Did the brothers and sisters get along well together? Were any of them best friends? Were there any, and what was the nature of, rivalries among the children? What was the nature of family discipline? Did father rule with an iron hand, or did he "spare the rod and spoil the child"?

11. What was the family social status and/or financial condition? Were they considered well-to-do? What did that mean? How would their circumstances compare with your own? Were they (or were they not) considered "important" people in the community? Why? How did they get along with their neighbors? How were they perceived by others?

12. What was the extent of the family's involvement in civic affairs? What difference did this involvement (or lack of it) make? Were there any special interests involved?

13. Did the family have any pets? What were they? How important were they to the family members? How did they feel about having animals in the house? Did everyone feel the same way about these things? How were any differences resolved?

14. What circumstances surrounded deaths in the family? How did the family members deal with death and its realities? How intimate was the family with death? Did they bury any young children? Teenagers? Was the breadwinner snatched away in his prime leaving a destitute widow and young family? How did they cope? Or were family deaths confined to aged grandparents whose lives had essentially been fulfilled? What were the causes of death that the family dealt with? The circumstances associated with death (and often the illness preceding death) can give significant insight.

15. How was medical care handled? Were folk remedies used freely and extensively? Did they have access to good medical practitioners? Did any family members have serious health problems? Allergies? Problems relating to hearing and/or vision? How did these affect their lives?

16. What did the family do about religion? Were there any significant family religious observances? Were there any special traditions or practices associated with religious holidays? Did they study the scriptures as a family? Did they attend church regularly? Together? What church? What effect did this have on their lives? Were they called on to sacrifice for their religious beliefs? What do you know of their personal feelings about, and their relationships with, Deity? Did they pray regularly—as individuals and/or as a family?

17. What foods did they eat? How was their diet different from your own? What were their favorite foods? How was their food prepared? What methods did they use for food preservation?

18. How did the scientific events of the day affect the family? What, for example, was the effect of the electric light, the telephone, the automobile, the radio, the telegraph, etc., on the family? Did they read a newspaper regularly—daily or weekly? Did they have a modern bathroom? Was the

family able to afford these advantages? Were they quick to accept the "new fangled"? Or were some of these things troubling to them?

19. How did your ancestors travel, and how mobile were they? If they moved, what was the distance involved and how long did it take? What was the reason for the move and who else moved with them? What were conditions like along the way? How did they make the move? What did they do at night along the way? Was security or safety a problem?

20. What educational opportunities were available? What was the highest level of education achieved? What were the schools like? How large were the student bodies? How many students in the classes? How many grades in each class?

21. What did they do for entertainment? Was most entertainment family-centered, church-centered, school-centered, community-centered? How important was so-called "entertainment"?

22. How did the major historical events of the day affect the family? Such things as wars and economic depressions are of special interest. There is great potential for a major effect. Did any family member serve in the military? In actual combat? Was there an injury and, if so, was it serious and/or permanent? Was any family member reported as missing in action, killed in action? Was any family member a prisoner of war? Where? How long? Did the "family fortune" survive bad economic times? Was there any loss of social status with the loss of economic status?

23. Did your ancestor or any family member have any special talent? What was the talent? How widely was it recognized? Did this prove to be valuable or important for the family? If so, how?

24. What was the family's political affiliation? How extensive was family or individual involvement in political matters? What effect did this have on the family?

The whole idea behind the foregoing inquiries is to give you a fresh approach to understanding your ancestors by viewing them in the context of the events of their daily lives, examining why they did what they did. You can appreciate them much more—turn your heart to them, if you will—if you can understand how they were like you and how they were different. Such a view is made possible only by inquiry into the intricacies and intimate details of their lives.

IV. WRITING FAMILY HISTORY

As you gain new insights into your family history it will be important to preserve what you learn. But having said this, I must back up and put your gathering of data into a proper perspective. There are certain steps that must be followed, as with any research. One ought not to just jump in without preparation.

A. Choose Your Focus

If you are going to write meaningful family history, decide beforehand just what type of work you wish to do. There are a variety of possibilities and you must decide what your focus will be before you embark. You may, for example, decide to write a life sketch of a specific ancestor, or perhaps a historical "portrait" of a couple. Another possibility is to compile the history of a specific nuclear family. Such may not be significantly different in content from the historical portrait of the husband and wife. The approach, however, may be very different. In the portrait you would zero-in on the couple—keeping the focus on them—with the children coming and going.

A more ambitious focus is the history of an extended family. You might consider doing a history of one of your two sets of grandparents and their descendants. However, you might like to get a little experience with a less demanding project first.

Another interesting possibility is to write your own autobiography.

B. Decide on the Questions You Will Ask

I have already talked about possible inquiries. The questions you choose will depend on your subject and the specific focus you choose. Your questions should be designed to help you to not only discover events but to learn the causes of events—to try to find out why people did what they did. In dealing with living relatives you may ask questions either in person or in a mail questionnaire, depending on the accessibility of your source. If the source is also the subject, your approach will be somewhat different than if your source is another member of the family—such as a surviving spouse, sibling, or child. And even if your subject is still living, you will also want to ask questions of some—perhaps several—other "witnesses."

I suggest that you make a preliminary list of questions ahead of time. You can add to the list later as you think of other things and as new avenues of inquiry are opened up. In fact, if you are doing an oral interview, you will add questions during the course of the interview. The same is true as you work with records and documents. One unexpected bit of information can open up whole new vistas for exploration.

The oral interviewer will, of course, make use of a good portable tape recorder during the interview. He will also conduct himself so as to help the interviewee forget about the recorder's presence. He will just start the machine and let it run without worrying about pauses or gaps. He will put the microphone down and "leave it be." He will interact with the machine only as necessary to turn over or change the tape.

A good list of sample questions for a mail questionnaire is found in the appendix to *Your Family History* by Allan J. Lichtman (beginning on page 192). The questions listed there may not all fit your subject, but they can serve as a launching pad to give you some ideas.

If you are dealing with a subject who is dead, some of the questions you pose will have to be answered—if they can be answered at all—by information found in records and documents, or photographs, or perhaps family artifacts. But even in this case it is important to decide on the questions to be asked. This gives direction and cohesiveness to your research.

C. Collect Your Data and Materials (Do Your Research)

Oral sources, where available, are possibly the most important, but as already shown, your research must certainly not be limited to such, even if your subject is living.

Nothing of much importance will happen unless you do your research. But remember that research could go on "forever" and you still would not have the answer to every question. At some point you must stop collecting data and start organizing it.

D. Correlate Your Findings with the Historical Context

It is important, for a complete understanding of your subject(s), to take the information you have gathered and relate that information to events going on outside the family (both locally and in the larger society). National and world events might have considerable impact. You will understand your subject much more completely if you can see the events of his life in the larger context. Many local histories have been written. They are invaluable as a means of enhancing your understanding of ancestors and their lives. Note that insights and perspectives gained from such histories may also open up new avenues of investigation.

E. Create—Write Your Story

Do not be intimidated by the task of writing. Don't feel the pressure of creating a great classic or a work of great proportions. It is much better to plan something modest and simple and to complete it than to plan something grand and glorious and never get it off the ground.

Be selective in what you write. You cannot write everything. One Pulitzer Prize-winning author said that the secret of his success was in knowing what to leave out. Be fair to your subjects by presenting their lives objectively and truthfully without trying to say too much. In writing whatever it is you decide to write, consider your audience and what their interests are.

You don't have to write a book, nor do you have to "publish," in the traditional sense, what you produce. It may just be a sensitive, specialized little history that you wish to share only with your closest relatives.

V. OBJECTIVITY IN FAMILY HISTORY

Before concluding this discussion I want to offer a few thoughts on the subject of objectivity. This is a quality of extreme significance both to the genealogist and to the family historian. Sometimes we are so determined to be objective and unbiased that our very determination carries biases with it. The cool, detached presentation of facts may itself be biased because of its failure to be sensitive to important realities. James B. Allen made an excellent statement that illustrates the point:

> [G]enuine objectivity recognizes that truth can be distorted by a mere presentation of a multitude of facts. The documents you have, for example, may well reveal an embarrassing incident in an individual's life—but does objectivity demand that you tell it? Was the incident such a minor variation in the person's total life that merely telling it gives undue emphasis to it, and leaves a misleading impression of his character? Will it really make any difference if some such stories are left out? Or, if your integrity demands that you deal with it, are you capable of putting it into words that will not distort the reader's view of your subject's over-all personality, or otherwise leave a wrong impression? If not, should you be writing this person's history at all? . . .
>
> The biographer's task, then, is complicated—especially when it comes to keeping problems in proper perspective as he deals with them.[11]

May your pursuit of family history be rewarding. May your heart, as a result of that pursuit, be truly turned to your fathers. And may you understand both yourself and your forebears better.

---

[11] James B. Allen, "Writing Mormon Biographies," Paper No. 16, *World Conference on Records*. Vol. 2 (Salt Lake City, 1980), p. 3.

Index